How to Market Training & Information

**Everything You Need to Know to Sell
Seminars, Workshops, Conferences,
Tapes, Videos, Books, Software
and Other Self-Improvement
or Continuing Education
Products & Services.**

By

Don M. Schrello, Ph.D.

4th Edition, completely revised and updated.

SD┃┃ **SCHRELLO DIRECT MARKETING**

P.O. Box 1610 • Long Beach, CA 90801 • (800) ENROLL-X • FAX (310) 493-0962

How to Market Training & Information

Everything You Need to Know to Sell Seminars, Workshops, Conferences, Tapes, Videos, Books, Software and Other Self-Improvement or Continuing Education Products & Services.

By

Don M. Schrello, Ph.D.

ISBN 0-935823-10-7

This publication is a greatly expanded and completely revised fourth edition of a third edition work entitled *How to Market Training Programs, Seminars & Instructional Materials*, copyright © 1984, 1985 and 1988 by Schrello Direct Marketing, Inc. The current work also incorporates and updates the relevant contents of *The Seminar Market*, copyright © 1980 by D. M. Schrello.

Printed in the United States of America.

10 9 8 7 6 5 4 3 2 1

To Georgia, who's *still* always on my mind.

DMS

TABLE OF CONTENTS

PREFACE

This manual is for everyone who wants to do a better job marketing training, education, self-improvement or information products and services. This includes training programs, seminars, workshops, conferences, courses, tapes, videos, books, software, multi-media or computer-based instructional materials and a huge array of other Human Resource Development (HRD) products and services.

This publication is a greatly expanded and completely revised fourth edition of our popular *How To Market Training Programs, Seminars & Instructional Materials* handbook. It needed to be re-titled to reflect the much broader and more comprehensive scope of this latest edition.

How To Market Training was originally stimulated by numerous requests from those who read my 1980 research report *The Seminar Market*, and asked for a "How-To-Do-It" manual on the subject.

A little background may be in order:

When I researched *The Seminar Market* it described the then-known universe of training in North America, with emphasis on open enrollment programs. At the time, I foolishly thought I knew everything there was to know about the business and was convinced that what the industry needed most in order to grow was just a more complete picture of itself.

Today, more than a decade later, I realize how little I knew then. Thanks to the thousands of people who've called and written, I understand better how vast, complex -- and nearly invisible -- the training industry *really*

is. And I see more clearly than ever that the industry's biggest need *isn't* for more information about the marketplace (which will help), but rather, how to control the astronomical costs of sales and marketing.

How many other industries do you know that spend one-third to one-half of every dollar on sales and marketing? That's why everyone said, "Tell us how to sell more for less cost. Tell us how to avoid those costly sales and marketing mistakes that others have already made." These were reasonable questions that deserved thoughtful answers. And fortunately, I had several excellent sources of data from which to draw these answers.

To start with, I had the original source for the first edition of this manual: my personal files, data, and experience -- assembled over more than 15 years of building a successful multi-million dollar business marketing training products and services. Since then I've been able to expand my perspective with data drawn from industry surveys, client programs and elsewhere.

In addition, my product/marketing and planning processes -- presented for many years in the highly successful *PRODUCT EVALUATION and PLANNING Seminar* and the *PLANNING and CONTROL workshop* -- have been adapted for the training and information industry and are included in Chapter 2, on selecting products and markets, and Chapter 5, on planning. These methods have wide application outside training as well.

Once the writing was underway, it was evident that even a comprehensive manual such as this could only serve as a starting point for each individual's application. Frequently, adaptations, modifications -- or just plain answers to questions -- are needed to put these methods to practical use. Hence, the 2-day *How To Market Training Programs Seminar* was created to meet this need. This manual serves as the seminar reference text as well.

When we first published *How To Market Training*, there were fewer training resources, and we tried to compile the most necessary ones in *References and Resources*, a separately bound publication included as an Appendix. Today, there are lots of good references and directories of the training and information industry, and more are appearing all the time. We've tried to include the most important references and resources right in the text, where they're easy to find when you need them. More are in Appendix A, References and Resources, for those who want to dig deeper, but we're focussing on those pertaining to marketing training and information, rather than training in general.

Our goal for this handbook is simple: If you need it to market or sell your training, continuing education, self-improvement or information product or service, you'll learn about it here. Where there's already expert help available (for example, to hone your selling skills, find a sponsor or get your book published) you'll learn how to access that help here. It's a simple test -- one that you the reader will decide if we've passed.

Don M. Schrello, Ph.D.
Long Beach, California

ACKNOWLEDGMENTS

This work reflects the contribution of literally thousands of owners and managers of training and information businesses. These are the good people who have bought my books, attended my seminars -- and who wouldn't settle for a general answer to their specific questions. Questions like when, how much, how many and why. I'm especially grateful to those who didn't even stop there but instead asked the tough follow-on questions they needed answered in order to market and sell their services and products. There's no doubt these experiences helped lead to the practical orientation of this book.

I want to particularly thank the many loyal employees and friends I've been privileged to work with over the past 25 years. This honest, dedicated and hard-working family -- for that's what they are -- experienced good times and bad: Runaway successes and explosive growth, double-digit inflation and recessions, hiring so many great people (and a few bad apples). And all the while they skillfully and (usually) quietly corrected for any bad decisions and mistakes I made, so the business could succeed in spite of me. It was really they who taught me what it takes to succeed in the training and information business.

My clients deserve special gratitude for their continued support and confidence. They provided the opportunity for the principles in this handbook to be tested and proven in a wider range of conditions than any individual business could ever provide. Their experiences, problems, successes and anecdotes are scattered throughout, but hopefully in a way that only they will recognize.

While the vast majority of what's presented is based on my personal experience, other sources and references have also been used. It is my desire to give full and complete credit for any and all such sources used and individuals quoted. Any errors or omissions in this regard are completely unintentional, and I want to apologize for them in advance. Your cooperation in notifying me of such defects will ensure that they are corrected in future editions of this manual.

And I could not overlook my heartfelt thanks to three contributors without whom this book would not exist. First, Verna R. Cook, our Director of Client Services and my assistant for this 4th Edition, personally did most of the research, particularly the surveys for Chapters 6 and 7. I noticed her wearing her glasses more during that period.

Next, Mary Kitzmiller's knowledgeable and crisp editing brought professionalism to this edition that was clearly lacking in earlier ones. I still marvel at her ability to spot errors I've looked at but not seen for seven years.

Finally, Georgia H. Schrello typed every one of my drafts (she calls it "bashing") and all of my hard-to-decipher changes (always with good grace). She got the computer manuscript close enough to final form for me to make some of the easy changes myself and, in the process, to look like I knew what I was doing. Georgia also added her special attention to many of the details I overlooked.

DMS

WHAT'S NEW ABOUT THIS EDITION

The mid-1990s are the Customer Service and Value years. And we're working hard to give you *more value* for less money in this all-new edition. It has:

At Least four times More Information than the 3rd Edition -- and 20% more pages.

Every Word and Idea Examined For Relevance and Updated for Today's Marketplace. If it's been retained from the previous edition, it's because it's *still* the best information available.

Five All-New Topics not presented in the 3rd Edition:

1. Face-to-face selling (whole new chapter)
2. Showcases (whole new chapter)
3. Forecasting event attendance (major new section)
4. Selecting marketing database software (major new section)
5. Typical sales and marketing programs (new section)

Proven, Proprietary Methods to Do at Least Six Critical Tasks:

1. Decide what products/markets represent your best opportunities (Chapter 2)
2. Figure out the right way to market your training or information products/services (Chapter 3)
3. Plan your whole marketing campaign (strategy *and* tactics) (Chapter 5)
4. Select mailing lists (Chapter 7)
5. Estimate direct mail response rates (Chapter 5)
6. Forecast attendance at seminars and workshops (Chapter 6)

And -- Best of All -- We've Been Able to Cut the Price significantly by switching from the costly looseleaf binder format to a less expensive perfect-bound, softcover edition.

Apart from that, here's what's completely new: Chapter 3, How to Pick The Best Sales and Marketing Strategy, is totally new. It contains typical sales and marketing programs broken down both by type of organization *and* by the type of product/service being marketed.

Chapter 6, The Challenge of Seminars and Other Open Registration Events, is greatly expanded and completely rewritten to include all the planning steps you need for seminars, understanding how seminars make money and a brand-new never-before-published section on how to forecast final event attendance based on early registrations.

Chapter 13, Creating and Maintaining Your Marketing Database, is entirely rewritten and brought up-to-date. It provides what you need to know to pick the best marketing database software and hardware for your business and use it to the greatest advantage.

Chapter 10, Showcases and Other Events Designed Primarily for Selling, is new and xiv How to Market Training & Information

covers today's hottest means to support your face-to-face selling of big-ticket services and products.

Chapter 4, on face-to-face selling, is also new. It shows how to do a better selling job and where to turn for help in developing your sales capability and honing your sales skills.

Chapter 1, the training industry overview, contains all new statistics and a fresh perspective on the size and composition of both the demand *and* the supply sides of the training industry.

Chapter 2, Selecting Marketable Products

and Services, still has our proven "Is It Real?", "Can We Win?" and "Is It Worth It?" model, plus new information on pricing.

Chapter 9, Smarter Printing and Mailing, has latest printing prices, current lists of printers, and up-to-date information about what the USPS drive for automation means to you.

Chapter 12, dealing with other sales and marketing methods, is greatly expanded and includes new sections on newsletters, user conferences, writing and publishing a book, infomercials and much more.

HOW TO USE THIS MANUAL

This manual is organized by chapter, each covering an important topic for marketing and selling training, continuing education or information. For the most part, each chapter is basically independent of the others, so you may start anywhere. Wherever possible, cross-references to other related chapters and sections of the book are included.

But for maximum utility, start with Chapter 1. It sets the stage with an overview of the training industry, its size and scope, and some of the key players. There's a lot of new information included that's never before been published, so even experienced marketers of training and information will find this interesting.

What to read next depends on where your business is. If -- like most readers -- you already have in mind a training, education or information product (in this manual, product includes services, such as consulting) and you've targeted a market (group of customers), then skip Chapter 2 and read Chapter 3. There you'll learn how to find the best way to market your product to your targeted customers. Following Chapter 3, you need only read the chapters pertaining to your chosen marketing approach.

On the other hand, if you're thinking of entering a new business, launching a new product or entering a new market, you should next read Chapter 2. It applies our famous "Is It Real?", "Can We Win?" and "Is It Worth

It?" methods to select and refine the most balanced product/market combination possible. Then go on to Chapter 3 and any others you need to execute your strategy.

Most remaining chapters begin with a step-by-step process for accomplishing an important task. The process may be followed by helpful worksheets that generally have their own step-by-step instructions, and a sample showing the completed worksheet.

Most chapters also contain "tips" or brief summaries, recommendations, conclusions -- or occasionally opinions -- based on my experience with the subject. Wherever possible, these tips are grouped by subject within the chapter.

Finally, chapters may also contain reprints of selected charts or articles that have appeared elsewhere. These articles provide additional background or useful examples to further illustrate the subject.

Unlike many books, this manual tries to present the key "How-to-Do-It" steps for marketing and selling training and information with an absolute minimum of background or development. It does not present the basics in areas where there is already a large body of literature or practice. For example, there is no attempt to include the basics of writing advertising copy. But the manual *does* include the dos and don'ts peculiar to writing advertising for training and information products and services.

To access these other resources, please turn to Appendix A, References and Resources. It's an annotated guide to virtually all the supporting products and services you'll need to successfully market your training, education or information products or services, ranging from books, directories and periodicals, through associations, courses, consultants, services and computer software.

The second publication included as Appendix B is A Vocabulary of Common Terms for Marketing Training and Information. This contains definitions of the most often used words and phrases in this field. Although intended primarily for the newcomer, even the "experienced hands" who wrote it agreed they learned a great deal.

The thoughtful marketer will find this manual a source of ideas rather than a cookbook or "formula" for success. To be sure, those just starting will find here most everything they need to begin marketing their products and services. But as they gain experience, they will need to re-read, adapt, modify and build upon what's in this manual in order to achieve the greatest insight and success. This is not a static field: So, while the principles may remain unchanged over time, you can be sure the specific applications will need constant attention and revision.

ABOUT THE AUTHOR

Don M. Schrello, Ph.D. is Chairman and Chief Executive of Schrello Direct Marketing, Inc. of Long Beach, California. He's been in the training and information industry for the last 25 years, during which time he's:

- Started and sold three multi-million dollar training businesses,

- Helped found the Instructional Systems Association (ISA),

- Served as a consultant to, or director of, many of the top training, publishing and information companies and associations in the world.

- Authored 50 books, seminars and other publications, including:

  -*The Complete Marketing Handbook for Consultants*

  -*How to Market Training Programs, Seminars & Instructional Materials*

  -*The Seminar Market*

  -*Marketing In-House Training Programs.*

  -*Improving Your Competitive Position*

  -*The Product Evaluation and Planning Seminar*

  -*The Strategy Development Workshop*

He understands the special needs and problems of large organizations and their management, too. For nearly a decade, before starting his first business, he held senior management positions in marketing and new products with one of the country's largest high-technology companies.

ABOUT SCHRELLO DIRECT MARKETING, INC.

Schrello Direct Marketing (SDM) assists any organization, individual or institution who sells or markets training programs, seminars, instructional materials or other information products and services.

Specializing in all facets of this unique and demanding type of sales and marketing, SDM offers training seminars, team-building workshop sessions, books, software and a complete range of consulting services, including strategic sales and marketing audits, evaluating and selecting products and markets, conducting market research and surveys, developing marketing plans, reviewing promotional campaigns, database marketing advise and more.

NOTES

AN INTRODUCTION TO THE $200 BILLION (AND GROWING) U.S. TRAINING MARKET

This manual contains the information you need to successfully market your training programs, seminars, conferences, human resource development services, videos, books, audiovisuals and virtually any other information or skill-building products or services.

This chapter "sets the stage" with an overview of:

1. The process for marketing training -- a process that provides the structure for the rest of this handbook.

2. The U.S. training marketplace -- who buys training, who provides training -- and in both cases, how much.

3. Today's training products and services -- what types of training are offered, what media are employed, and how training is delivered in various size organizations.

4. Where the training industry is going (at least one person's opinion).

5. Some of the hot international markets for training.

Remember, we've tried to keep the text to the minimum needed to communicate the essentials. Otherwise this manual would be two or three times its present size. The result is a format of brief, self-contained paragraphs, each on a different -- but usually related -- topic.

To Start, Here's What We Mean by "Marketing":

Marketing is the job of identifying the needs/wants of selected customer groups, arranging for the appropriate goods/services to fulfill those needs/wants, and providing timely, relevant information on which those customers can make enlightened, voluntary buying decisions.

And Here's What We Mean by "Training":

Training is any product or service that develops human skills/abilities, conveys information/knowledge or changes an individual's attitudes/perceptions and is not part of an elementary, secondary or degree program.

The Marketing Process

The *process* of marketing training programs, seminars, instructional materials, consulting and related products and services consists of the five distinct steps shown on the next page.

The Marketing Process

1. Identifying Your Customers
- Need/Want
- Size
- Price Range
- Geographic Location
- Distribution
- Competition
- Differentiation

2. Defining Your Product
- Hardware
- Software
- Services

3. Selecting Your Sales Method
- Face-to-Face
- Telemarketing
- Direct Mail
- Events
- Other
- Combinations

4. Evaluating Your Opportunity
- Is It REAL?
- Can We WIN?
- Is It WORTH It?

5. Planning Your Implementation
- Set Objectives
- Program Tasks
- Identify Responsibilities
- Schedule Tasks
- Budget Resources
- Set Standards and Specifications
- Analyze Risks
- Establish Controls
- Monitor Results
- Take Corrective Action

We'll expand on these steps in three of the following chapters: Chapter 2, Selecting Marketable Training Products and Services, covers Steps 1, 2 and 4. Chapter 3, How to Pick the Best Sales and Marketing Strategy, is devoted entirely to Step 3. And Chapter 5, How the Pros Plan a World-Class Marketing Campaign, will show you how to execute Step 5.

And of course the entire handbook is devoted to helping you skillfully execute every step of the marketing plan you create.

Think of the first three steps in the process as completely intertwined and interdependent, like the following diagram:

How Market, Product and Sales Method Are Related

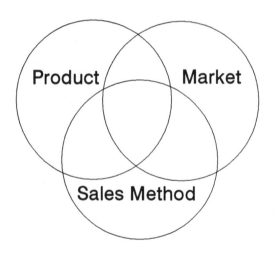

THE HALF-TRILLION DOLLAR U.S. "LEARNING ENTERPRISE"

The size of the U. S. "Learning Enterprise" boggles the mind. (Incidentally, the term *The Learning Enterprise* was coined by Anthony P. Carnevale and Leila J. Gainer as the title for their summary report of a landmark 2-year project in the late 1980s, conducted by the American Society for Training and Development (ASTD) for the U.S. Department of Labor.) With a budget of almost one-half trillion dollars a year, learning employs one of every six workers, and touches more than one-half the population as learners on and off the job. The U.S. spends more per capita on learning than any other nation on earth.

In the middle of this page is the estimated annual budget breakdown, in billions of dollars. I'll warn you in advance, even these huge numbers probably *under*estimate the true size of the enterprise, because reliable information is so hard to come by.

These figures include both *education* (elementary and secondary schools and the degree-granting portion of colleges and universities) and *training* (everything else).

We're only interested in the $204 billion for training and skill development. For comparison, this is about twice as big as the personal-computer business and only a little smaller than the entire U.S. defense establishment.

And the growth rate for training is incredible: Many of the top firms that supply the field are growing 20%-40% annually. What's more, the prospects are for this growth to continue -- and even accelerate -- for the foreseeable future!

The U.S. "Learning Enterprise"

$ 157.0	Elementary and Secondary Schools
$ 80.0	Universities and Four-Year Colleges (Degree Programs)
$ 237.0	**Education Subtotal**
$ 37.5	Postsecondary Occupational Education/Training
	$ 17.6 Formal Military Training (Appropriation)
	$ 11.5 Junior Colleges, Vocational and Technical Institutes
	$ 8.4 Community, Government and Other Schools
$ 30.7	Training Industry
	$ 11.8 Private Training Companies and Consultants
	$ 11.2 College and University Non-Degree/Extension Programs
	$ 7.7 Associations, Professional and Trade Organizations
$ 135.8	Employer-Conducted Training and Development
	$ 35.8 Internal Training Departments (Salaries & Facilities)
	$100.0 Informal, On-The-Job Training, Apprenticeships
$ 204.0	**Training Subtotal**
$ 441.0	**Grand Total (Billions)**

THE DEMAND SIDE: WHO CONSUMES TRAINING -- AND HOW MUCH

Five Population Groups Who Consume Training

To understand the scope and complexities of this huge industry, let's look at the five groups that are the main "consumers" of training.

Their numbers are shown in the bar graph at the top of the next page.

Here's who's included in each group:

Government and Quasi-Government Employees are those employed in Federal,

State and local governments, active and reserve military, the Post Office, national transportation agencies, etc.   This group also includes police and fire departments as well as public school teachers and administrators. All in all, more than one of every six workers is in government (which may help explain why the average family pays over $16,000 in taxes every year out of a median family income of $37,783).

Populations of 5 Groups Who Consume Training

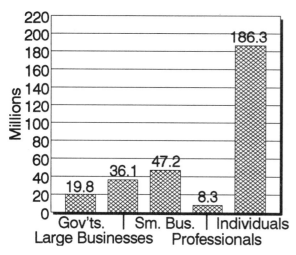

Employees in Large Businesses are those in firms with 100 or more employees. These businesses train managers, salespeople, production workers, new hires -- in fact, just about everyone. Some of the training is done by or through formal training departments. The rest -- some would say the majority -- is done by other parts of the business, without training department involvement.

Employees in Small Businesses are those in firms with *less* than 100 employees. Dun and Bradstreet reports 7.9 million such businesses, 5.7 million of them with nine or fewer employees. With as many as one million new business start-ups a year, this group has also become the jobs "engine" of the U.S. economy and a major, widely-dispersed -- but easily accessible -- consumer of training.

Professionals and Practices include doctors, dentists, nurses and other health professionals, attorneys, accountants, architects, engineers, brokers -- even consultants. Continuing Education requirements for licensing

and certification makes this group consume training out of all proportion to their numbers. And the office/support staffs of these practices is also included in this group.

Adult Individuals. The first four population groups have their training paid by their employer or business. This fifth group buys training with their *own* money and receive the training on their *own* time, usually outside normal working hours. Such individually paid training ranges from golf, tennis, skiing and flying lessons on the one hand, through art, music, dance and language training, to fitness, diet and substance abuse programs on the other.

Here's How Much Each Group Spends

The following bar graph shows our estimate of how much each of the above five groups spends annually on training. From the $204 billion training total shown on Page 1-3, we've removed the $17.6 billion for formal military training, and the $100 billion estimated for informal, on-the-job training and apprenticeships (a slice of the training pie that's getting larger and more formal all the time). We estimate that the remaining $86.4 billion is divided this way:

How Much They Spend

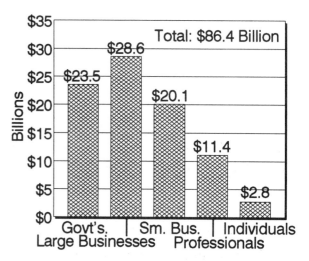

These expenditures do *not* include travel costs, per diems, salaries of those being trained or any allowance for productivity lost while workers are being trained. It's all training materials and training services!

Where Do These Figures Come From?

We start with *Training* magazine's October issue, their annual overview of the Training Industry. It contains the results of a survey taken by Lakewood Research every year since 1981 and is probably the most authoritative annual data available. Recently, their estimate of the Industry's size has been about $45 billion, about half our projection.

Why the Difference?

There's nothing wrong with the quality of *Training's* data -- as far as it goes. It's just that it leaves out these four very important pieces of the training marketplace:

1. Training in large organizations that doesn't involve the training department, like most technical training, product training, and training paid for out of management or project budgets. Some argue that this category dwarfs the training that *does* go through the training department. Many successful training salespeople agree, since they've learned how to tap those budgets.

2. Training done by small businesses, those with less than 100 employees. The old notions that these businesses don't do much

training is demonstrably wrong for the 1990s. Besides, with about 8 million small businesses -- and over 3,000 new ones starting every day -- *whatever* training they do has a huge multiplier attached.

3. Training and continuing education by professionals and their practices. Professional firms *are* formally included in the Lakewood survey, as are professionals employed in large organizations. It's just that most professional practices are less than 100 employees. Furthermore, this group budgets far more for education and training than any other population.

For example, *Medical Meetings* magazine estimates $6.7 billion in annual expenditures by three million healthcare professionals alone. Multiply even a fraction of that by all the other professions, and you can see what a huge slice of the training pie this represents.

4. Training taken by adult individuals on their own time and paid for personally.

We estimated the annual budgets for these missing pieces using three sources: (1.) Projecting the Lakewood results for how training budgets vary as a function of organization size to smaller organizations, (2.) using published, per-person training expenditures referenced in the ASTD/Department of Labor study previously mentioned and (3.) making some conservative assumptions about the fraction of large organization training that doesn't involve the Training Department.

THE SUPPLY SIDE: WHO PROVIDES TRAINING -- AND HOW MUCH?

Who supplies this huge appetite for training products and services? The answer is a network of resources every bit as vast and complex as the demand for training itself. Reduced to its simplest, these are the five major sources for training in the U.S.:

Internal Practitioners, including HRD/training departments, as well as line management involved in training both the company's *customers* and their *employees*.

Schools/Institutions, such as public and

private schools, non-degree programs at colleges and universities (including community colleges), vocational schools, technical institutes, hospitals, libraries and museums, churches and government-operated or government-supported training centers.

Private Training Companies, including film/video producers, seminar sponsors, packaged training program suppliers, correspondence schools and external consultants/practitioners.

Associations, including professional associations and societies (e.g.: AICPA, AMA, APA, SME, etc.), local business organizations, (e.g.: YPO, Chambers of Commerce, Executive clubs, etc.), national business associations (e.g.: AMA, Conference Board, etc.), trade groups (e.g.: FTD, AIHAC, etc.) and labor unions.

Retail Stores, such as book sellers, audio/video stores, computer shops and an increasing number of similar establishments.

How Much Does Each Type Of Supplier Get?

The way our estimated $86.4 billion of annual training expenditures is divided among the five supplier groups is shown in the following chart:

Suppliers Annual Income

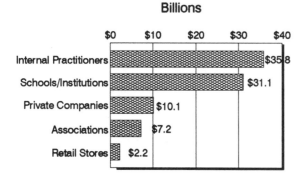

Putting together the "Demand" and "Supply" sides of the U.S. Training Industry, the following picture results (the numbers shown are billions of dollars annually).

Demand-Supply Matrix

	Govern-ments	Large Bus.	Small Bus.	Profess'ls & Practices	Adult Individuals	
Internal Trainers	$13.9	$17.2	$4.7	--	--	$35.8
Schools/ Instit'ns	$5.1	$6.6	$10.3	$7.3	$1.8	$31.1
Private Tr. Co's	$3.1	$2.7	$2.2	$2.0	$0.1	$10.1
Assoc-iations	$1.4	$1.8	$2.2	$1.2	$0.6	$7.2
Retail Stores	--	$0.3	$0.7	$0.9	$0.3	$2.2
	$23.5	$28.6	$20.1	$11.4	$2.8	$86.4

Training Is a Truly "Cottage Industry"

Training is a wide-open market. No single organization or institution -- or even a group of them -- dominates this field. It's so highly fragmented that there's room for hundreds ... even thousands ... of new suppliers. Here's a breakdown of 6,000 of the organizations listed as training suppliers on the Schrello Direct Marketing Training Industry Database, grouped according to their estimated sizes:

Sizes Of Training Suppliers

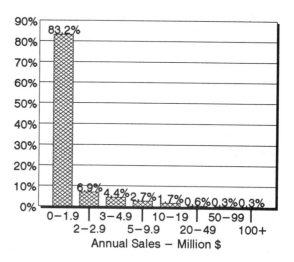

This listing includes both profit-making and nonprofit organizations in the middle three supplier groups above: schools/ institutions, private training companies and associations.

Many U.S. training firms obtain a significant fraction of their revenues from foreign purchases. Thus, the industry's total annual sales based on an analysis of the *suppliers* ought to exceed the total based on an analysis of the domestic U.S. *customers'* training budgets by -- say -- 10%-15%. The reason it doesn't in the table above is because there are substantially *more* than 6,000 suppliers in the U.S. -- nearly 11,000 by our latest count.

Some of the Largest Training Providers

On page 1-8 is a short, selected list of some of the largest U.S. training providers. Because most of these firms are privately held, it's difficult to obtain reliable sales statistics. But a number of published directories -- and the Schrello Direct Marketing Database -- do provide some consistent information, on which this listing is based.

Training Firms Average Nearly $137,000 Sales per Employee

Using this same published data, it's possible to gauge annual sales productivity per employee, as shown in the graph at the bottom of this page.

Financial Performance of a Representative Training Supplier

The Income Statement for one year's operations of a hypothetical -- but typical -- mid-size organization supplying training programs or instructional materials might look like this (in thousands of dollars):

Revenue	$20,000	100.0%
Cost of Goods Sold	6,300	31.5%
Gross Margin	$13,700	68.5%
Marketing & Sales Costs	6,680	33.4%
General & Administrative Expenses	5,160	25.8%
Interest Expenses	340	1.7%
Net Income Before Taxes	$ 1,520	7.6%

These financial figures will change depending on the product(s) being sold. For example, packaged program suppliers are usually more profitable than custom course developers and consultants. Public seminar firms are often less profitable than those who work exclusively with large company customers.

And on-site technical training that requires the trainers to bring their own hardware can be *very* expensive, reducing or even eliminating the otherwise attractive profits such programs can produce.

The profitability shown above compares favorably with other industries as reported by Robert Morris Associates in their *Annual Statement Studies*:

Computer software	0.4% - 6.2%
Publishing	3.5% - 6.7%
Advertising	0.9% - 1.9%

Annual Sales per Employees for Training Providers
(Based on published information)

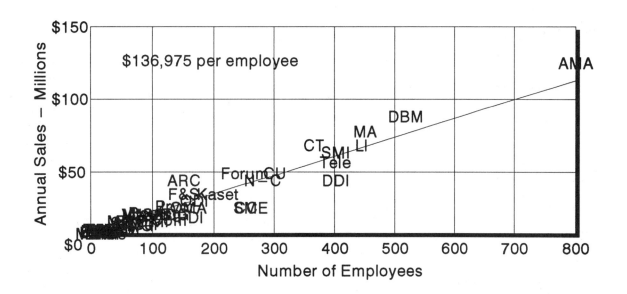

Some Major Providers of Training

1. Business/ Management

Assoc. for Quality & Partici-
  pation (AQP)
Amer. Management Assoc.
Blanchard Training & Dev't.
Blessing/White
Brookings Institution
Bryant College
CareerTrack
Ctr. for Creative Leadership
Ctr. for Professional Ad-
  vancement
Communispond
Covey Leadership
Development Dimensions,
  Int'l. (DDI)
Walt Disney Training & Dev't.
Dun & Bradstreet Bus. Edu-
  cation Services
Inc. Seminars
Karrass Negotiation
Kaset Int'l.
Kepner-Tregoe Assoc.
Menninger Management In-
  stitute.
National Seminars
Nightingale-Conant
Northwestern Univ.
NTL Institute
ODI
Padgett-Thompson
Personnel Decisions, Inc.
Philip Crosby Assoc.
Practical Management Inc.
Pryor Resources
SkillPath
The Conference Board
The Executive Committee
Univ. of Michigan
Young Presidents Assoc.
Zenger-Miller

2. Sales & Sales Manage-
  ment

Dale Carnegie
B.J. Chakiris
The Forum Corp.
Learning Int'l.
Max Sacks Int'l.
SMI Int'l.
Tack Training
Wilson Learning
Zig Ziglar

3. Computer/Technical

Amer. Soc. of Mechanical en-
  gineers (ASME)
AT&T
Brown & Caldwell Consulting
  Engineers
Deltak
Digital Equipment Corp.
Drake Training & Technolo-
  gies
ECC Int'l.
George Washington Univ.
IBM
Inst. of Electrical & Electronic
  Engineers (IEEE)
Instrument Soc. of Amer.
Learning Tree Int'l.
NCR Corp.
Novell
Science Research Assoc.
Soc. of Manufacturing Engi-
  neers (SME)
Technology Transfer Inst.
Telemedia
Ziff Inst.

4. Accounting/Finance

Amer. Inst. of Certified Public
  Accountants (AICPA)
Amer. Management Assoc.
Arthur Andersen/Andersen
  Consulting
California CPA Foundation
Deloitte & Touche
Ernst & Young
KPMG Peat Marwick
McKinsey & Co.
National Assoc. of Accoun-
  tants
Price Waterhouse

5. Medical/Dental

Amer. Educational Inst.
Amer. Dental Assoc. (ADA)
Amer. Hospital Assoc. (AHA)
Amer. Medical Assoc. (AMA)
Amer. Seminar Inst.
CME, Inc.
Current Concept Seminars
Harvard Medical School
UCLA Medical School
University Learning Systems

6. Other Professional

Amer. Bankers Assoc. (ABA)
Amer. Bar Assoc. (ABA)
Amer. Inst. of Architects (AIA)
Amer. Inst. Of Chartered Life
  Underwriters (AICLU)
Credit Union Nat'l Assoc.
  (CUNA)
Insurance Inst. of Amer.
Life Office Management As-
  soc. (LOMA)
Nat'l Assoc. of Realtors
Portland Cement Assoc.
Practicing Law Inst.

7. Personal/Individual Skills

Alcoholics Anonymous
ARC Int'l
Berlitz
Drake Beam Morin
Elder Hostels
ELS Learning Centers
EST/Forum
Evelyn Wood Reading Dy-
  namics
Franklin Quest
Inlingua
Int'l Correspondence Schools
Learning Annex
Marriage Encounter
National Univ.
New Beginnings
Outward Bound
Pecos River Ranch & Learn-
  ing Center
Sybervision Systems
Toastmasters, Int'l.
YMCA/YWCA

8. Investment

Geneva Corp.
Public Storage
Resort TimeShares

9. Other

Amway
Chamber of Commerce of the
  U.S.
Nat'l Education Corp.
Nat'l University
NuSkin
U.S. State Department

Sales And Marketing Costs Dominate

Before leaving this brief review of training supplier financial performance, take a moment to notice that marketing and sales costs consume one-third of every revenue dollar. And even this large percentage understates the true amount, because in small companies such as these, top management spends lots of time selling -- time that's rarely charged as such. And this is not a recent phenomena: The percentage consumed by sales and marketing has been steadily increasing, as the following graph at the bottom of the page shows.

The reason for the high marketing and sales costs are simple: Training and related fields stand or fall on sales and distribution. There is no doubt that this is *THE* most important consideration. Without a means of sales and distribution, the best training product or service will surely fail.

Put another way:

> *Good training products are abundant and cheap. It's good sales and marketing that's scarce and expensive.*

Sources of Information on Training Programs and Providers

Because the training picture changes constantly, it's sometimes hard to take a "snapshot" or make apples-to-apples comparisons, check the competition -- or even find a course you might want to take.

The best present sources -- and there aren't a lot of them -- are summarized in Chapter 12 in the section on using directories, on-line databases and locator services. There are other sources in Appendix A, References and Resources. But don't get excited; there's *still* no one source of all (or even most) of the information on training programs. Anyone want to start a new business supplying this information?

Sales and Marketing Costs Versus Time

Average percentage of total revenue

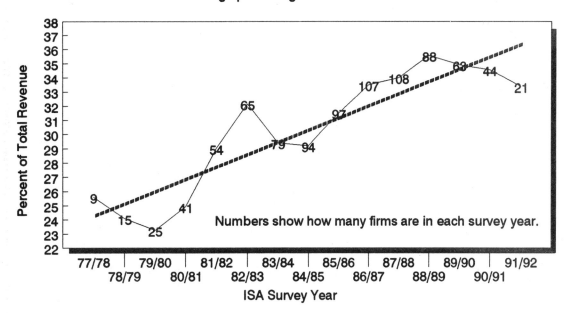

AN OVERVIEW OF TODAY'S TRAINING PRODUCTS AND SERVICES

Here's a short list of the various ways today's training is being delivered:

- Live Seminars, Workshops, Conferences
  - Off-the-Shelf, Tailored, Custom-Developed. Etc.
- Consulting
- Video Tapes or Films
  - With or Without Supplemental Materials
- Audio Tape Cassettes
  - With or Without Printed Materials
- Books and/or Other Printed Self-Study Materials
  - No Electronic Media
- Live Training At-a-Distance
  - Via Teleconferencing, Satellite, Radio, Telephone, etc.
- Games or Simulations
- Other Media-Based Formats
  - Computer-Based Training (CBT)
  - Interactive Video (IV, CD-I)
  - Laser Disk (CD/ROM)

A poll of training suppliers has shown the following breakdown of the types of products and services from which their sales revenues were derived:

Type of Product/Service	% of Sales	Gross Margin
Seminars & workshops	46%	60%-80%
Off-the-shelf programs	25%	75%-90%
Custom-designed programs	23%	50%-90%
Consulting services & other	6%	30%-60%
	100%	

"Off-the-shelf" usually refers to media-based packaged training programs. However, some firms do not distinguish between those programs which are media-based and those which are instructed live. To that extent, there may be some overlap between the top two categories above.

Every Public Seminar Is an In-House Program Too

A representative revenue "mix," obtainable with minimum sales effort, would be 50% public and 50% in-house programs. But the in-house programs would usually be far more profitable, having much lower selling costs and perhaps twice the gross margin as the public programs.

The four main variables used in describing a training program are:

1. Open-to-the-public vs. in-house programs
2. Individual vs. group instruction
3. Media-based vs. a live trainer
4. Off-the-shelf vs. custom-developed programs

These variables can occur in various combinations and can be represented in various shades and shadows. For example, a training program could employ self-paced, media-based segments interspersed with group sessions as well as custom-developed modules.

There Is No One "Best" Way to Deliver Training

Under different circumstances, each of the combinations described above can be superior to the rest -- while still other conditions could make any one inferior to others. Why is this important? Because good marketing starts with the proper match between the customer's needs/wants and the product/service being offered. If a particular type of training is inappropriate, no amount of marketing can change that. Conversely, the marketer's job is made easier and more effective when the type of training matches the customer's needs/wants. (More on this in Chapter 2, Selecting Marketable Products and Services.)

Major Types of Training Programs & Media

METHOD OF INSTRUCTION	OPEN TO THE PUBLIC		IN-HOUSE PROGRAMS		
	Individual/Self-Instruction	Group Instruction	Individual/Self-Instruction	Group Instruction	
				Off the Shelf	Custom Developed
Media Based:					
• Books	✓ **$13 B**		✓	**$9 B**	
• Audio/Video/Film	✓		✓	✓	✓
• Computer Based/Interactive	✓	(few examples)	✓	✓	✓
Live Instruction (May Include Use of Media):				**$22 B**	
• Outside Instruction	**$42 B** ✓			✓	(Infrequently)
• Inside/Employee Instructor			(Administrative only)	✓	✓

The diagram on the following page, Types of Training Programs Used by Businesses of Various Sizes, illustrates how organizations of different sizes divide their training between open-to-the-public sessions, in-house presentations by outside resources and in-house presentation by the organization's own personnel. The figure, adapted from the author's book, *The Seminar Market*, is intended to show relative amounts of training, not absolute numbers.

Open Enrollment/Public Programs

Open-to-the-public courses represent a huge and growing segment of training, with a scope and complexity that almost defies description. There are two principal ways this training is delivered:

1. Open group instructional programs -- almost exclusively conducted by live instructors -- are divided among schools, colleges and universities on one hand; associations, professional groups and other nonprofit organizations on another; and profit-making training organizations on still a third hand.

2. Individual/self-instructional materials and programs is the second major component of open-to-the-public training and is almost always media-based. These range from self-help books, audiovisual courses and periodicals, individually purchased or available at local libraries, through correspondence courses, to video tape, video disk and computer-based training, the latter increasingly available through book stores, computer stores and directly from the creator by mail or phone.

Open-to-the-public training (either live-instructed group training or media-based individual programs) is frequently the approach of choice for an organization when one or more of the following circumstances exist:

■ There are comparatively few people from

the organization to train at any one time

- Those to be trained are geographically dispersed
- A suitable open-to-the-public course is already offered
- It's desirable for trainees to meet other participants and exchange ideas with them
- An existing program is to be previewed or "tried on" for eventual customizing or

licensing in the organization.

The large number and rich variety of open-to-the-public courses, their ready accessibility, their comparatively low cost and the modest commitment of resources needed to get started using them, all combine to make these courses -- individual/self-instructional or live groups -- the cornerstone of training for all but the very largest customers' organizations.

Types of Training Programs Used by Businesses of Various Sizes

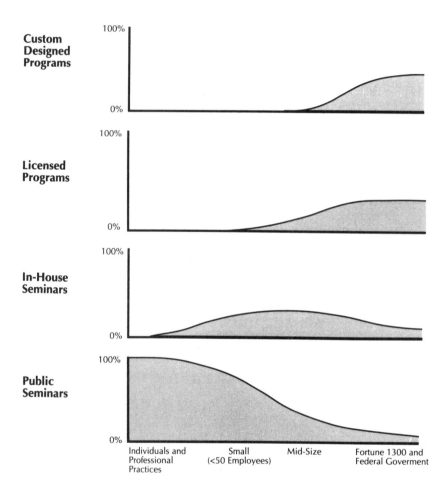

Primary Outside Providers of Business Educational Products and Services

Type of Providing Organization		Skills Training	Knowledge Acquisition	
			Current and Evolving	Established and Accepted
Specialized Training Organizations and Individuals		High	High	Low
Business, Trade, and Professional Associations		Medium	High	Low
Schools, Colleges, and Universities	Nondegree Programs	Low	Medium	Medium
	Degree Programs	Low	Medium	High

Legend: ▓ = Public Seminars

In-House/On-Site Programs

In-House Presentations by Outside Resources is the choice for training in an organization when:

- The training is best presented by an "outside expert"
- It saves money and/or time over sending the participants away to open-to-the-public sessions of the same course
- There are team-building and/or proprietary application objectives requiring "at-home" participation
- There are (generally) 10-12 or more persons to be trained at one time
- It's desired to "pilot" test a new or customized program which will later be presented by in-house personnel.

In-House Presentations by In-House Resources can be best for an organization when:

- There are large numbers of people to be trained
- Greater flexibility in scheduling/timing is desired than can be accommodated by outside resources
- An adapted, tailored or otherwise special course is needed to meet the organization's needs.

SOME OBSERVATIONS ON CURRENT TRENDS AND THE FUTURE OF TRAINING

Today's Hottest Training Medium Is The Lowly Audio Tape

A large installed base of players/equipment is needed for any mass training market to emerge, and audio tape cassettes are the latest example. Last year more audio tape players were sold than any previous year -- and it's 30-year-old technology! Sales of batteries are exploding, as are audio cassette-based training and information programs. As much as 40% of the growing number of books-on-tape are self-improvement/training titles.

One audio tape producer recently learned what we discovered 20 years ago. Their greatest marketing success was by direct mail to audio tape buyers lists, even buyers of audio tapes on unrelated topics. Seems that audio tape buyers will buy *anything* on audio!

Video Tape Has Come to Have a Limited Role in Training

A recent Lakewood Research survey found that in big companies -- where video tape is the most frequently used training medium -- it makes up only 12.4% of the total training time. That's about one hour in an eight-hour session. Many instructional design experts also believe that about seven minutes of video per hour of instruction is maximum.

Of course, video tape *can* be useful in training for:

- Record/playback for practice/coaching and live feedback
- For demonstrating/modelling behavior
- For showing what can't conveniently be brought into the classroom, like big-name experts, equipment, site visits.

Although widely used, video tape has *not* turned out to be the major factor for self-instruction that everyone expected. The reason seems to be that it's all-consuming and linear; people can't jump around or do something else while they're watching a video tape.

All this has confounded the early champi-ons who thought video tape would replace all other training media.

Interactive, Multi-Media Training May be Big -- Tomorrow

That same Lakewood Research survey also found that the use of computer interactive video for training in large organizations hasn't grown in three years. Clearly, this technology also hasn't lived up to the pundit's explosive growth predictions.

This medium is ideal for individual instruction of large numbers of differently qualified learners. Looking more like something you'd find in a video arcade than in a classroom, users often describe these courses as "exciting," "easy" and "fun" and actually ask to take them. Trainers report improved learning effectiveness, greater flexibility and shorter learning times.

From the supplier's view, production cost for interactive video training is currently about $100,000 for two hours and dropping. With greater access to multi-media computers or specialized players (CD-I), use of this format should increase and costs should fall.

These courses are inherently reusable, encouraging customers to train *more* people with *fewer* units. To counter this, suppliers must design courses so each participant receives or consumes something, or requires periodic updating.

Developing multi-media training is highly interdisciplinary, involving computer programmers, video technicians and instructional designers. Training as a craft has become training as a technical discipline, requiring better management skills, more planning and a much greater "up-front" investment in each course. These courses also require frequent updating, both to adapt to constantly changing hardware/software *and* to meet competition.

Right now this type of training is used only by the largest organizations and government. But don't yet conclude there isn't a mass market. Once these programs are in all digital format (including video segments) they can be easily edited, reformatted, combined -- and transmitted anywhere instantly. This could prove to be *the* most important factor in determining the successful training providers of the 21st Century.

Technology is Redefining Jobs *and* Job Training

Two trends could completely change how we think about training, and how we get it. These are: (1.) Installation of high-capacity (fiber optic or microwave) voice/video/data interactive communications (the so-called "Electronic Superhighway") that can make teleconferencing an everyday event, even from the home (actually, home catalog shopping may be the biggest driving force for this) and (2.) smart, adaptive software that can provide context-sensitive, "just-in-time" help/training for any task even remotely involving a computer.

No one knows where this will all lead, but plenty of major corporations are interested. So stay tuned for further developments.

By the way, as perspective, remember that easel pads, overhead transparencies, slides, etc., have been around for years, yet they are not used universally in training -- and are often used poorly.

Watch Out for Technology "Cults"

Every new technology develops an appeal and a following independently of its ultimate value. This occurs in both customer *and* supplier organizations (including the latter's sales force). Look beyond this group of enthusiastic believers to assess the true potential of the technology.

Buying Training, *Using* the Training and *Going* to Training Are *Not* All the Same

To understand a mass market, look at yourself or those around you. You buy books you haven't read -- tapes you haven't listened to or watched. This "library mentality" applies to training as well.

Today's training technology permits more individual, self-paced training and less group training. But don't bet on this eliminating live training seminars and conferences. These meetings will likely continue (as they have for thousands of years) because the motivation for them goes beyond just satisfying skill or information needs. Travel, companionship and forming new relationships all play a role in driving meeting attendance.

That's why I'm personally cautious about a recent A.D. Little study for the Boston Port Authority that predicted up to 25% less travel by the year 2010 because of improved communications technology. Don't bet on it!

Cost-Justification of Training Is Still in the Future

There's lots of *talk* about justifying training on a cost/benefit basis. But there's no evidence that customer demand for this is any greater than it's ever been -- and that's pretty low. We used to offer to conduct before-and-after measurements to prove the bottom-line results of our training, but few organizations ever accepted. Most didn't want to objectively measure training.

SOME BUSINESS STATISTICS AND TRENDS OF INTEREST FOR MARKETING TRAINING

More than Ten Million U.S. Businesses

That's how many exist today, and there are between 600,000 and one million new business start-ups each year -- maybe more!

According to Dun & Bradstreet (D&B), less than one-sixth of these businesses -- 1.3 million -- have 10 or more employees, and only about 2% have 100 or more employees.

These percentages hold within plus or minus 2% for every state. In terms of sales, only 3% of all U.S. businesses are over $5 million, and only 10% are over $1 million. And 25% have annual sales of less than $100,000.

D&B also reports that 80% of all businesses are "single-location" firms, 11% are "branch locations" of other businesses, and 9% are "headquarters" (having one or more branch locations).

Here's what these D&B statistics look like in tabular form. There's not fully 10 million business here because the larger number comes from the IRS which "sees" more businesses than D&B because of businesses in the home and because of new business start-ups D&B hasn't yet caught up to.

No. Employees	No. Businesses
0- 4	4,568,044
5- 9	1,227,259
10- 14	406,350
15- 19	193,211
20- 49	415,824
50- 99	152,172
100-499	107,035
500-999	12,846
1,000 and over	14,865
Not available	1,016,518
Branches	911,974
Total	9,028,098

Change, Change, Change

D&B reports that during an average month they add 45,000 businesses, delete 37,000 businesses and record 500,000 changes to their files. These numbers are all increasing.

This translates into a highly mobile population. Here are some representative figures on the rate of annual moves/changes in title, address, organization name, job, etc. as a function of level:

Top Executives	15%
Vice Presidents	20%
Middle Managers	30%
Supervisors, Clerical Workers	40%

Small Businesses Drive the U.S. Economy

Nearly 70% of the work force is employed in organizations with fewer than 250 employees. And firms with less than 99 employees create 76% of all new jobs.

In the same time that the Fortune 500 companies reduced their total employment by 4.4 million, the economy produced 20 million new jobs because of employment growth at smaller firms.

Peter Drucker observed that new-job creation since 1980 is mainly in "low-tech" or "no-tech" businesses, such as apparel makers, restaurant chains, and the like. Eighty of *Inc. Magazine's* list of the 100 fastest-growing publicly-held companies between five and fifteen years old were low-tech or no-tech.

What About People in the Work Force?

We've concentrated a lot on business statistics, but training is, first and foremost, about people. Here are some U.S. Government statistics that help describe this side of the work force:

- America's population is 255 million, with ethnic and racial minorities making up 25%.

- One in seven U.S. residents speaks a foreign language at home, and more than half of the U.S.'s 32 million foreign-language speakers speak Spanish.

- Civilian work force is 118 million and growing. Unemployment is about 6.5% and shrinking.

- Women represent about 47% of today's work force and are not projected to reach 50% until the year 2005.

- America has 2.1 million janitors, 1.8 million engineers, 1.4 million waiters and waitresses, 870,000 police and detectives, 744,000 lawyers, 575,000 doctors and 77,000 pro athletes.

- 7.2 million people have more than one job.

- One out of eight people is 65 or older, with the median age at 33.1 years, up from 30.2 in 1950.

- 64 % of Americans own their homes.

THE INTERNATIONAL TRAINING MARKET

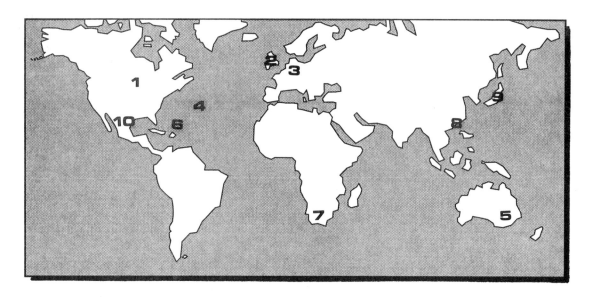

All the Same Marketing Rules Work -- Only Better

Europe, United Kingdom, Canada and English-speaking Pacific Rim all follow the same marketing rules as U.S., including having well-developed direct mail capability.

Direct mail abroad is two to three times more costly than in the U.S. However, response rates for training are often three to four times as high, for two simple reasons: (1.) Training is more highly valued, and (2.) people get less mail. Chapter 7 has a section on international list and mailing resources.

Pricing, Exchange Rates and Getting Your Money Out Are Three More Variables

With pricing and currency differences, international programs can be much more profitable than the same program sold in the U.S.

Distributors Can Make the Process Easy

Smaller U.S. training companies can arrange distributors and/or licensees abroad that will sell in their country or region. Some international distributors have a long track record and excellent relations with the firms they represent. A starter list is included at the end of this section.

Five Good Reasons to Go Global

There are at least five reasons for the U.S. training supplier to consider going international:

1. Export your successful U.S. product/service
2. Grow your business by expanding into new markets
3. Stabilize your business since different countries experience economic fluctuations at different times.
4. Provide travel opportunities for you and your colleagues
5. Tap fresh ideas you can bring back home

Language Isn't a Big Problem

Don't automatically think you need to translate your English language program to start marketing globally. Here's a three-step approach that can get you started:

1. U.S. attendees traveling abroad
2. Foreign nationals attending an English-language program

3. Foreign nationals attending a program in their native language

The Top Ten International Training Markets

Here are the top foreign markets for U.S. training organizations, in roughly descending order of importance.

1. Canada. About the size of the United States, with about 10% of its population, two aspects of Canada are particularly noteworthy:

First, 85% of its population is within 100 miles of Toronto. Although there are important cities in West Canada (including rapidly growing Vancouver), most of today's Canada is on the Toronto/Montreal axis.

Second, Canada has two distinct cultures, with 73% of the population speaking English and the remaining 27%, mostly in Quebec, speaking French. Although about 20% of Quebec speaks fluent English, the high degree of nationalism and affection for the French culture and language make it very unlikely that a program can be successful in French-speaking Canada unless it is translated, promoted and delivered in Canadian French.

Canadian postal rates are up to 50% higher than in the U.S. But the average Canadian businessperson receives 50% fewer pieces than in the U.S., so response rates are higher, as much as double the U.S. response. And Canada has fewer bad debts and last-minute event cancellations than the U.S.

There used to be difficulties shipping training materials across the border and arranging temporary work permits for instructors. These problems are diminishing. Hopefully, the North American Free Trade Agreement (NAFTA) will eliminate them. Also, be aware that the Canadian Post Office has been known to have crippling strikes: 150,000 of our seminar brochures were once "trapped" in the Canadian mails during a four-week strike.

All major U.S. training firms also have major operations in Canada.

2. United Kingdom/England. U.K. represents roughly one quarter of the U.S. population on a land area smaller than Oregon. It's a very sophisticated market for all training products/services and has a well-developed marketing infrastructure, mostly based in London. Many U.S. training firms have successfully expanded into the U.K., notably Forum Corporation, Development Dimensions International, Communispond, CareerTrack, Kepner-Tregoe, Padgett-Thompson and others in the area of managerial, supervisory and sales training. Deltak, The Center for Professional Advancement and Learning Group International are representative of the large group of U.S. technical training organizations operating in the U.K.

Spoken U.S. English comes across well, but printed materials need to be "translated" into U.K. English.

3. Europe. Europe has double the U.S. population on about half the land area. Think of Europe in two parts: Northern European, primarily Germanic origin, highly industrialized, literate and very sophisticated. Thirty-eight percent (38%) of the population speak English, although in many cases, they prefer their native tongue. The rest of Europe is of Latin origin and includes France, Italy, Spain, Portugal, etc.

France has about the same population as the UK in the area roughly the size of Texas. Its an excellent market for training promoted and delivered in French. The other big market is the newly united Germany, which now totals 78 million people in an area smaller than California. Many training companies that have been successful elsewhere have found a slow, rocky road to success in Germany, where promotion and delivery is expected to be in German.

The rest of northern Europe -- the Scandinavian countries -- are far more bilingual and ready to accept English-language courses. Moreover, there are successful agents/distributors that will help American firms evaluate the market and decide if the domestic U.S. product will work.

Management training firms like the American Management Association, Kepner-Tregoe, DDI and The Center for Professional Advancement have all had successful European operations for many years. Technical organizations like Learning Group International, Deltak and State of the Art Seminars have delivered technical training successfully.

4. Bermuda and the Caribbean. Although Bermuda is in the mid-Atlantic, not the Caribbean, these are lumped together. With few locals, think of these as additional locations for domestic U.S. or Canadian seminars, rather than truly "International." Most have a British, French or Dutch origin but derive their major income from North American travelers. Success here depends on whether your particular population will find this location attractive. Small business executives and professionals often use these resorts to "get away." Individuals and middle managers in large organizations, on the other hand, often view such meeting sites as a "boondoggle," producing lower attendance.

5. Australia and New Zealand. Australia has the population of New York City on a land mass roughly the size of the 48 contiguous states; New Zealand, the population of Washington, DC, on a land area the size of Colorado. Both countries together (we in the U.S. think of them together -- even though they are separated by a thousand miles of ocean) do have a surprising amount in common and share much in training and seminars.

Australia and New Zealand have a well-developed, sophisticated, domestic meetings business and direct mail infrastructure to promote them. Most Australians in the training business travel to the U.S. (and to the U.K.) searching for good subjects, products and promotional techniques. And a number of American firms have had success in Australia and New Zealand.

6. Meetings and Seminars Aboard Cruise Ships. This as another variant of the Caribbean story. If you "scratch the surface" you'll find a lot going on aboard cruise ships. For example, a recent Queen Elizabeth II crossing I made found C. Everett Koop, Edwin Newman and other lesser known seminar presenters offering a series of meetings for the enlightenment of passengers.

But watch the tax consequences!! Some years back, the IRS singled out seminars aboard cruise ships for disallowance. (The exception was U.S. flag carriers -- of which there is only one: America Hawaii Steamship Line, serving the Hawaiian island.)

If you're interested in knowing more, contact:

THE WORKING VACATION, INC.
4277 Lake Santa Clara Dr.
Santa Clara, CA 95054
Phone: (407) 727-9665
Contact: Lauretta Blake

7. South Africa. South Africa's 39 million people makes it a bit smaller than France and the U.K., and a bit larger than Canada. But this population occupies some 471,000 square miles or an area about 3/4 the size of Alaska.

South Africa has been a fertile source for U.S. training, and English is the accepted business language. DDI, McLagan and others have successful training businesses in South Africa. The country's long history of pirating, and recent unrest, make many U.S. firms reluctant to admit their presence there.

8. The Far East. Although the region includes more than 60% of the world's population, we're only interested in the "hot spots": Singapore, Hong Kong, Malaysia and the Philippines. These have well-developed training businesses and an infrastructure to promote them. Most have management associations similar to AMA, that sponsor business conferences and seminars. And English is a good business language for these countries, so there's usually no need to translate.

9. Japan. About one-fourth of Japan's 123 million people are concentrated in the greater Tokyo/Yokohoma area. Its land mass of 145,000 square miles makes it smaller than California! Surprisingly, Japan has had some very successful experiences by U.S. training firms, including Wilson Learning, ARC International and more recently Learning Group International. A number of rules for success have evolved, including allowing plenty of time, three to five years being about as fast as anyone has succeeded. You also need to be there, in the country, with primarily Japanese management. A fair amount of trust is required, but it is really the only effective way to payoff.

While Japan has a very sophisticated direct mail system, all postage was first class until about 1987, so the arrival of bulk third-class mail is fairly recent. Obviously your promotion and training needs to be translated into Japanese in order to succeed.

10. Mexico. Mexico has about one-third the of U.S. population on a land area about one-fifth its size. The 17 million people in Mexico City make it roughly the same as the New York metropolitan area. While the technological sophistication in the rest of the country is still growing, Mexico City is a very advanced society. Furthermore, there are a growing number of Americans in Mexico City.

The North American Free Trade Agreement (NAFTA) is expected to open Mexico for U.S. training programs and meetings. Right now it's primarily a destination resort for U.S. participants.

11. Everywhere Else. The previous 10 areas represent less than 25% of the world's population. The other 75% is in Asia with 3 billion people, Africa with 650 million people, South America and the former USSR with 300 million people each, and Central America with about 150 million people.

Right now, these areas are not promising training targets. That could change at any time. For example, the former USSR and Communist Block countries desperately need the kind of help U.S. training programs could provide. But they lack the infrastructure needed to promote and conduct them. Similarly, China's huge population makes meetings an ideal means of communication, but again without infrastructure.

International Distributors

The following list of some selected international distributors is presented without endorsement or recommendation as a starting point for those considering such a relationship. Their names have been drawn from our database of long-time members of U.S. professional and/or trade associations, or those who already represent a U.S. training supplier.

GILMORE & ASSOCIATES
130 Bloor St. West - Suite 700
Toronto, ON M5S 1N5 CANADA
Phone: (416) 926-1944; Fax: (416) 926-1351
Contact: Mr. Blake N. Gilmore, Chief Executive
Officer

M. R. COMMUNICATIONS CONSULTANTS
221 Dufferin Street
Toronto, ON M6K 1Y9 CANADA
Phone: (416) 539-9520; Fax: (416) 539-9604
Contact: Mr. Mervyn Rosenzveig, Chief Executive Officer

PERFORMANCE LEARNING & MANAGEMENT
SYSTEMS INC.
420 Mc Gill Street - Suite 100
Montreal, PQ H2Y 2G1 CANADA
Phone: (514) 861-7000; Fax: (514) 861-1616
Contact: Mr. Pierre Dorais, Chief Executive Officer

MENTOR HUMAN RESOURCE GROUP
P. O. Box 224
Pymble, NSW 2073 AUSTRALIA
Phone: 2-498-7411; Fax: 2-498-8122
Contact: Mr. Kenneth J. Simper, Chief Executive Officer and Managing Director

TRAINING DYNAMICS
68 Pitt Street
Sydney, NSW 2000 AUSTRALIA

THE TRAINING RESOURCE COMPANY
191 Clarence Street
Sydney, NSW 2000 AUSTRALIA

AVDIEV PERFORMANCE TRAINING
390 St. Kilda Road
Melbourne 3004 AUSTRALIA
Phone: 03-267-6666; Fax: 03-267-7496
Contact: Ms. Julie Macphee, MA, Management Consultant

AUSTRALIAN INSTITUTE OF MANAGEMENT
New South Wales Division - P. O. Box 328
North Sydney, NSW 2060 AUSTRALIA
Phone: 92-0791
Contact: Mr. Peter Peterson, Chief Executive Officer

ORGANIZATION EFFECTIVENESS GROUP
10 Domain St. - P. O. Box 32 096
Devonport, Auckland 9, NEW ZEALAND
Phone: 09-453 305; Fax: 09-453-305
Contact: Mr. Hugh C. Oakley-Browne, Founding Director

NEW ZEALAND ASSOCIATION FOR TRAINING
AND DEVELOPMENT
P. O. Box 2279
Wellington NEW ZEALAND
Phone: 64-4-721-179
Contact: Mr. Leone Black, Officer

TACTICS PRIVATE LIMITED
1703 Horizon Tower East
15 Leonie Hill Road, 0923, SINGAPORE
Phone: 65-732-4796
Contact: Ms. Rissa Seigneur, President

DECISION PROCESSES INTERNATIONAL
Far East Shopping Ctr., 545 Orchard Road
0604, SINGAPORE
Contact: Mr. Andrew Sng, Partner

THE HONG KONG MANAGEMENT ASSOCIA-
TION
26 Canal Road West - 2nd Floor
HONG KONG
Phone: 547-9346; Fax: 572-1660
Contact: Mr. Rick S. K. Tam, Senior Manager

ASIAN TRAINING & DEVELOPMENT
Suite 2039 W. - E. S. D. A. - Greenhills
San Juan, Manila, PHILLIPINES
Phone: 63-2-9217-319

INTERNATIONAL PUBLICATIONS LTD.
538 Kinston Road - Raynes Park
London SW20 8DT ENGLAND
Phone: 81-543-9919; Fax: 81-543-9782
Contact: Mr. William J. Reddin, Chief Executive
Officer

DECISION PROCESSES INTERNATIONAL
P. O. Box 518 Haversham Milton
Keynes MK19 7DH ENGLAND
Contact: Mr. Jim Collingham

SUGRUE & ASSOCIATES TRAINING
15 Clonturk Park
Drumcondra, Dublin 9 IRELAND
Contact: Ms. Brenda M. Sugrue, Ph.D., Director

KASANEN TRAINING GROUP
Heikkilantie 6 - Place 100
Helsinki 00211 FINLAND

OY RASTOR AB
Wavulinitie 3
Helsinki 00210 FINLAND
Phone: 358-0-692-5101; Fax: 358-0-692-2663
Contact: Mr. Ilpo Linko, Chief Executive Officer

SMG SERVICE TRAINING LTD.
Topeliuksenkatu 3BA4
Helsinki 00260 FINLAND
Phone: 358-0-441-922
Contact: Mr. Erkki Lakkakorpi, Executive Vice
President

BRATT INTERNATIONAL AB
Box 141
Lund S221 00 SWEDEN
Phone: 46-46-312-000; Fax: 46-46-305-338;
Contact: Mr. Bertil Bratt, Chief Executive Officer

INVESTKONTAKT AB
Roslagsgatan 56
Stockholm 113 54 SWEDEN

BOERTIEN & PARTNERS
Strawindkylaan 551
Amsterdam 1077 XX NETHERLANDS

AKTI-KURSUS
Gi Lundtoftevej 7 - D. K-2800
Lyngby, DENMARK
Phone:45-42-88-8000;Fax:45-42-88-8200
Contact: Mr. Lars Kristensen, Managing Direc-
tor

EUROFORM S. R. L.
Via Montebello 30
Milano 20121 ITALY

SIAMAR LTDA
Rue Tabapua 1244
Sao Paolo, SP 04533 BRAZIL

CATHO PROGRESSO PROFISSIONAL
A1 Joaquim Eugenio De Lima 56
Sao Paolo, CEP 01403 BRAZIL

BANCO MERCANTIL/TORRE MERCANTL
Piso 33 Avenida Andres Bello 1
Caracas 1010-A VENEZUELA

PELICULAS MEL S. A.
Uruapan 17 Col Roma
D. F. 06700, MEXICO

DECISION PROCESSES INTERNATIONAL
Jose Ma Rico 121-401 A1 403
Co. Del Valle, MEXICO
Contact: Mr. Mario Borghino

NOTES

2

SELECTING MARKETABLE PRODUCTS AND SERVICES

Selecting the correct product and targeting the correct market are important choices for any business -- but vital for training and information, where sales and marketing is the most difficult part. All of the remaining choices, such as the sales method, timing, advertising, media, etc., are based upon careful and considered identification of the key market variables and on the characteristics of the product or service which will best satisfy the customer's needs and wants.

The methods presented in this chapter are based on those developed by the author many years ago for making sound product and marketing decisions. These methods were the foundation for the author's well-known PRODUCT EVALUATION and PLANNING Seminar, which has been attended by over 100,000 managers and executives from organizations of all types and sizes for more than 20 years. Moreover, these methods have been adopted as the way product and market decisions are made in hundreds of the best managed, most successful companies in the country.

These proven methods have a number of important benefits for any product/market decision-making:

1. They offer a consistent, systematic and repeatable approach.

2. They help ensure that no significant consideration is overlooked.

3. They make it possible to compare widely different product/market opportunities to each other on a common basis.

4. They provide a means to choose among various alternative approaches for a single product/market opportunity.

5. They help develop documented product/marketing criteria that reflect the organization's strategy, its past successes/failures *and* the vision, values and style of the top managers.

6. They furnish a means for everyone on cross-functional teams to participate in the decision-making process in a balanced, harmonious way.

In this chapter, the terminology and approach of these proven methods has been specifically adapted for training programs, seminars, instructional materials and information products and services of all kinds. Numerous specific tips and recommendations are also presented, as well as additional information related to the product/market selection process in general.

STEPS IN THE PRODUCT/MARKET SELECTION PROCESS

Business decisions involving PRODUCTS and MARKETS are generally made in seven distinct steps:

1. Define Your Product/Market Opportunities.

2. Establish the Considerations on Which Your Selection Will Be Based.

3. Establish Your Selection Criteria.

4. Collect Information on Every Consideration for Each Product/ Market Opportunity.

5. Evaluate Each Product/market Opportunity Against the Criteria.

6. Select Your Best Product/market Opportunity.

7. Plan the Implementation of Your Selection.

The first part of this chapter provides handy worksheets and guidelines for accomplishing the first six of these steps. The seventh step is addressed in Chapter 5, on planning.

To get started, below is a list of product possibilities for those involved in training and information. The list can be helpful in stimulating your thinking or in suggesting additional opportunities you may wish to consider.

First look through the list and mark the items most relevant to your kind of business. Now look through this smaller list and indicate those you do not now offer -- but could. Be sure to add any that you feel are missing, and change the terminology to better fit your business.

Training and Information Product Possibilities

Publications	Events	Services	Recorders
			Monitors
Books	Showcases/Previews	Consulting	Computers
Booklets	Seminars	Research/Surveys	Binders
Magazines	Workshops	Custom Course	Games/Puzzles
Newsletters	Conferences	Development	
Directories	Institutes	Discount Buying	**Supplies**
Job Aids	Short Courses	Referral Services	
Case Studies	Film Fairs	Finder Services	Pens
Tests	Festivals	Editing	Blank Tapes
Forms	Demonstrations	Clipping Services	Easel Pads
Worksheets	Briefings/Overviews	Tape/Film	Computer Disks
Posters	Trade Shows/Expos	Duplication	Paper
		Slides	Certificates
Media-Based		Printing	
Programs	**Courses**	Trainer Training	**Other**
		Sales Represent-	
Audio Cassettes	Correspondence	ation	Association
Films	Courses		Memberships
Film Strips	Self-Paced	**Hardware**	Authoring Systems
Video Tapes	Instruction		Computer Software
Video Disks	Tutorials	Projectors	Simulations
Compact Disks	Workbooks	Screens	Gifts
Computer		Easels	Mail Lists
Diskettes		Players	
Computer On-Line		Cameras	
Records			

PRODUCT/MARKET OPPORTUNITIES WORKSHEET

This worksheet will help you (1.) define your product, (2.) identify the market or market segments for that product, and (3.) select one or more of these product/market combinations for further study.

1. First Describe Your PRODUCT in terms of its *hardware, software* and *services.* Remember that the product of interest is the one your customer obtains (or will obtain), so think of it from the customer's viewpoint.

2. Next Describe Your MARKET for that product. Start by describing the *need/want* that it satisfies. Then identify the major variables that describe your best customers for the product. Generally these include the customers' *type of business* and *organization size,* the *price range* they're interested in, their *geographic locations.* and the *means of distribution* used to reach them. But your description might use other factors that are more important to you; for example, the buyer's position in the organization, the kind of equipment they now have, prior buying history, etc. Add these on the lines provided and fill in the pertinent customer information.

3. Now Note ALTERNATIVES with a check mark if there are any in any of the areas describing your PRODUCT or MARKET, such as several versions or models of the product, or several different and distinct customer groupings. Examples of different customer groupings might include finding several distinct types of businesses, widely different-sized organizations or separate means of distribution, all represented in your description of the market. Experience shows that it's best to treat each of these alternatives separately.

4. Use the PRODUCT/MARKET MATRIX at the bottom of the worksheet to help relate these separate product and market alternatives more sharply. It provides room for one or more major product alternatives across the top and two major market segments down the side and for two further subalternatives within each -- up to 16 combinations in all. Use the information at the top of the sheet to help you select the most important alternatives -- or those with the highest priority for further study. Put check marks -- or numbers -- in the cells of the matrix having the combinations of greatest interest. Chances are that only a few of the many possible combinations will emerge.

5. Finally, Select the Single Version of the Product and Single Segment of the Market which are best matched and can serve as the basis for the rest of your work on SUCCESSFUL DIRECT MARKETING.

Below is a sample of how this worksheet might be used:

FOR (OPPORTUNITY NAME) ___SDM___

		Describe	Alternatives
PRODUCT:	Hardware	*Notebook, dividers, etc.; Handbook*	✔ Seminar vs Handbook
	Software	*Data, methods, procedures*	
	Services	*Instruction, credit, hotel arrangements*	✔ Duration
MARKET:	Need/Want	*How to market training products/services*	
	Cust. Business	*consultants, publishers, associations, co. trng. departments, universities*	
	Cust. Org. Size	*All sizes*	
	Price Range	*TBD*	
	Geographic Location	*U.S. (west vs. nat'l?); Canada*	✔
	Distribution	*Direct marketing; Joint w/ assoc.*	✔
	Competition	*Few others*	
	Differentiation	*TBD*	
	Sales Method (s)	*Direct mail & telemarketing*	
	Other		

PRODUCT/MARKET MATRIX

		PRODUCT			
		Seminar			Handbook
MARKET		*1 day*	*2 days*	*3 days*	
Direct Mktg. Alone	Western U.S. only	✔	✔	✔	
	National U.S.		#1	Test	#2
	U.S. and Canada		Test		✔
	Joint with other Organizations	✔	✔	✔	

Opportunities Worksheet

FOR (OPPORTUNITY NAME) _____

	Describe	**Alternatives**
PRODUCT: Hardware	_____	_____
Software	_____	_____
Services	_____	_____
MARKET: Need/Want	_____	_____
Cust. Business	_____	_____
Cust. Org. Size	_____	_____
Price Range	_____	_____
Geographic Location	_____	_____
Distribution	_____	_____
Competition	_____	_____
Differentiation	_____	_____
Sales Method	_____	_____
Other	_____	_____

PRODUCT/MARKET MATRIX

PRODUCT

MARKET

PRODUCT/MARKET SELECTION CONSIDERATIONS

The key to the entire selection process was the author's discovery more than 20 years ago that every *product* decision, every *market* decision -- indeed every *business* decision -- ultimately involves a very small set of considerations. What's more, these considerations are the *same* for every type of product, from lipstick and spacecraft to books and seminars, and the *same* for every kind of market, from corporations and professionals to schools and individuals.

What are these considerations? They are the areas, topics or subjects on which the decision-makers want/need information in order to make their decisions. Depending on the particulars of the product, the market and the individuals involved, the type and amount of information needed/wanted may vary considerably, as can its method of presentations and other details. But the basic categories into which that information divides -- the CONSIDERATIONS themselves -- remain surprisingly constant, especially at the most fundamental levels.

Since the basic function of the CONSIDERATIONS is to obtain and organize information to be used for making a decision, it's most convenient to think of these CONSIDERATIONS as questions: the critical questions that must be asked -- and satisfactorily answered -- before a decision can be made.

The author has found that most unsuccessful product/market decisions result from failure to ask the right questions in advance -- especially the one question that would have revealed the fatal flaw early when it could have been easily corrected or else the project dropped.

Fundamentally every decision involves CONSIDERATIONS stemming from three questions:

> ## Is It Real?
> ## Can We Win?
> ## Is It Worth It?

"Is It Real?" deals with all those considerations pertaining to the marketplace you are trying to serve. These considerations immediately divide into two questions of fundamentally equal importance: "What Is the Market?" and "What Is the Product That Market Demands?." These two questions -- and all the more detailed questions they suggest -- can *only* be answered by looking at the world outside your organization: the customers you're trying to reach and the products that are now being offered to satisfy those customers' needs/wants.

"Can We Win?" is different. It deals with all those considerations pertaining to your competitive position: How do you stack up against the others who are trying to serve the same market, offering the same (or similar) products? These considerations immediately divide into the subordinate questions that address the two fundamental competitive issues: "How Does Our Product Compare to Others?" and, "How Does Our Company, Institution, etc., Compare to Others?" These two questions -- and all the more detailed questions they suggest -- can *only* be answered from the customer's perspective: What do your customers consider in order to decide which product to buy and/or whom to buy it from?

"Is It Worth It?" is again totally different. It deals with all those considerations internal to your organization. These considerations immediately divide into two questions of fundamentally equal importance: "What Is the Financial Performance?" and "What Other Contribution Does It Make?" These two questions -- and all the more detailed questions they suggest -- can *only* be answered by a careful and realistic plan and by a hard look at your organization's strategy, objectives, etc.

The best product/market decisions are those that give balanced consideration to these three separate questions.

What follows are PRODUCT/MARKET SELECTION CONSIDERATIONS tailored for making decisions on training programs and information. It shows the basic questions discussed above developed to the next level of detail: 24 questions in all. And four of these questions are further detailed as an example of how the process could be continued.

Experience shows that the 24 questions at the third level are on excellent balance: They are sufficiently detailed to draw out the wide variety of information needed to make product/marketing decisions, yet global enough to remain the same across a wide range of diverse types of training and information products/services and markets. We'll call these our 24 PRODUCT/MARKET SELECTION CONSIDERATIONS.

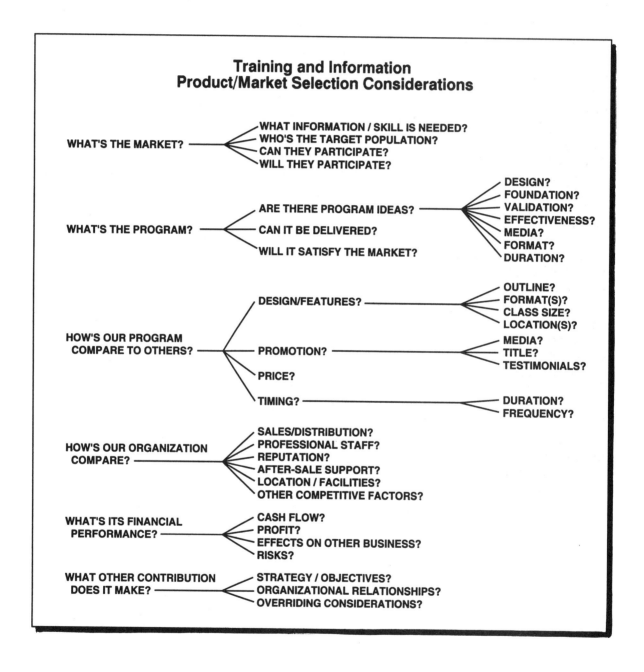

**Training and Information
Product/Market Selection Considerations**

WHAT'S THE MARKET?
- WHAT INFORMATION / SKILL IS NEEDED?
- WHO'S THE TARGET POPULATION?
- CAN THEY PARTICIPATE?
- WILL THEY PARTICIPATE?

WHAT'S THE PROGRAM?
- ARE THERE PROGRAM IDEAS?
  - DESIGN?
  - FOUNDATION?
  - VALIDATION?
  - EFFECTIVENESS?
  - MEDIA?
  - FORMAT?
  - DURATION?
- CAN IT BE DELIVERED?
- WILL IT SATISFY THE MARKET?

HOW'S OUR PROGRAM COMPARE TO OTHERS?
- DESIGN/FEATURES?
  - OUTLINE?
  - FORMAT(S)?
  - CLASS SIZE?
  - LOCATION(S)?
- PROMOTION?
  - MEDIA?
  - TITLE?
  - TESTIMONIALS?
- PRICE?
- TIMING?
  - DURATION?
  - FREQUENCY?

HOW'S OUR ORGANIZATION COMPARE?
- SALES/DISTRIBUTION?
- PROFESSIONAL STAFF?
- REPUTATION?
- AFTER-SALE SUPPORT?
- LOCATION / FACILITIES?
- OTHER COMPETITIVE FACTORS?

WHAT'S ITS FINANCIAL PERFORMANCE?
- CASH FLOW?
- PROFIT?
- EFFECTS ON OTHER BUSINESS?
- RISKS?

WHAT OTHER CONTRIBUTION DOES IT MAKE?
- STRATEGY / OBJECTIVES?
- ORGANIZATIONAL RELATIONSHIPS?
- OVERRIDING CONSIDERATIONS?

EVALUATING PRODUCTS AND MARKETS

There are many ways of evaluating or rating things. Movies and restaurants are rated with various numbers of stars or checkmarks. Bonds are rated with letters. And people often use the 1 - 10 scale for rating friends and other informal purposes.

All of these schemes serve a common purpose. *They are a shorthand way to reflect the application of human judgment to the information* available about whatever it is that's being evaluated.

For business decisions, especially those involving products and markets, there's a simple, proven, effective evaluating approach that's "felt comfortable" to seasoned executives for more than 15 years. This approach is particularly powerful when the information on which the decision will be based has been carefully separated into clear and independent areas -- such as the 24 PRODUCT/MARKET SELECTION CONSIDERATIONS previously described.

The recommended evaluation approach is based on "+'s" and "-'s." A "+" is assigned to any consideration in which the information elicits reactions such as: Wow! Super! Great! Superior! Way Above Expectations! A "-" is given to any consideration where the information elicits reactions such as: Terrible! No Way! Poor! Unacceptable!

Experience shows that the "+'s" and "-'s" are the exception rather than the rule. Together, these two extremes add up to no more than about 1/4 to 1/3 of all the considerations. The information collected for the vast majority of considerations -- 2/3 to 3/4 of them -- doesn't generate any extreme reactions at all. Use the symbol "0" to show that these are O.K. -- neither "+" nor "-."

Of course, any time you spot a "-," it's a flag that you've found something unacceptable. In those cases, you'll want to do three things: (1.) see what's needed to remove the "-" (change it to a "0" or even a "+"); (2.) revise your plans accordingly; and then (3.) reevaluate the opportunity as altered.

For example, a "-" may have shown up because of a marketing shortcoming that you determine could be overcome by hiring several people. Evaluation of the revised opportunity needs to reflect the time and costs connected with that hiring -- and possibly the risks if you're not able to hire the right people.

Obviously, your evaluation of "+'s" and "-'s" could be done "from scratch" by just examining the available information and applying your best judgment to it. But using even a few criteria -- documented standards for assigning the "+'s" and "-'s" -- will improve your evaluation consistency, as well as aid in communicating your standards throughout the organization.

That's why developing these PRODUCT/MARKET SELECTION CRITERIA is the next subject.

PRODUCT/MARKET SELECTION CRITERIA WORKSHEET

This worksheet allows you to summarize on one page the CRITERIA used to select your PRODUCT/MARKET OPPORTUNITIES. Your final list of criteria will require the detailed examination of your currently successful products and markets and any recently past failures. However, the following process will enable you to compile a "starter" list of criteria in just a few minutes.

1. First, Think Through the List of Areas for Criteria, organized in the six (6) SELECTION CONSIDERATIONS. These are the subjects most frequently used for training and information Product/Market selection criteria. Cross out, edit or revise what's there to make it better fit *your* business, and use the blank lines to add any other areas unique to your business. Stimulate your thinking by reference to your organization's strategy (company, division or business unit), your annual operating plan or your current goals and

objectives, if you have them with you.

2. Now Formulate the Criteria for "+'s" and/or "-'s" in each area and record them on the two right-hand columns. A single area may give rise to several CRITERIA, and criteria need not be stated for *both* "+'s" and "-'s." Note that you can have both *quan*titative examples ("Market growth -- 18% annually" ("+") and "7%" ("-")) and *quali*tative examples ("Broad and lasting market" ("+"); "Unique contribution" ("+"); "Customer sees it as everyone else's" ("-")).

3. Finally, Test Your Criteria by thinking through their application to your known successes and recent failures. Also test your criteria to be sure they're capable of being repeatedly and consistently applied to all opportunities in your business or business unit.

Here's a sample of a completed worksheet:

CONSIDERATION	AREA	CRITERIA −	CRITERIA +
	Type of information/skill needed		Marketing/planning
	Target population		Training industry
	Demand cycle	Not stable or growing.	
What is the MARKET?	Market size/growth/stability		>20% growth/year
	Life-cycle position		
	Distribution possible	Doesn't use D/M.	
	market location		Largely Western U.S.
	_____		
	_____		Seminar format.
	Technology/media employed		
...AL	Process(es) know-how required		
...rmance?	...vation/... ...ssible		
	_____		
	_____		
	Direction/objectives		Serves training indust.
What OTHER	Relation to current programs/customers		
CONTRIBUTION	Use of human resources or materials		Uses existing capab.
does the program	Organization/individual relations		
make?	Special considerations		
	_____	Conflicts with	
	_____	commitments.	

Selection Criteria Worksheet

CONSIDERATION	AREA	CRITERIA	
		-	**+**
What is the MARKET?	Type of information/skill needed Target population Demand cycle Market size/growth/stability Life-cycle position Distribution possible ----------- -----------		
What is the PROGRAM?	Technology/media employed Process(es) know-how required Innovation/uniqueness possible Learning curve/cost savings ----------- -----------		
How does our PROGRAM compare with others?	Features/benefits/uniqueness Differentiation versus commodity Price range Market "niche" possibilities Lead versus follow competition ----------- -----------		
How does our ORGANIZATION compare?	Capabilities fit (all areas) Production process used Sales method used Distribution employed Market share/position ----------- -----------		
What is the program's FINANCIAL performance?	Investment required and timing Demanded returns and timing Risk levels Risk-return relationship ----------- -----------		
What OTHER CONTRIBUTION does the program make?	Direction/objectives Relation to current programs/customers Use of human resources or materials Organization/individual relations Special considerations ----------- -----------		

PRODUCT/MARKET SELECTION INFORMATION WORKSHEET

This worksheet provides a means to summarize and evaluate the information you have in each of the 24 SELECTION CONSIDERATIONS for a given PRODUCT/MARKET OPPORTUNITY. It is not a substitute for more detailed information gathering, merely a summary.

1. Start with the First SELECTION CONSIDERATION under WHAT'S THE MARKET?; namely, INFO/SKILL NEEDED? Summarize concisely what information you have about this aspect of the market for the particular product you're examining. Refer to any documentation you have, or discuss the matter with other informed and/or responsible persons in your organization. Proceed in the same manner through all 24 SELECTION CONSIDERATIONS.

2. Next, Check Your Information. First, be sure you've collected both kinds of information: *Facts* and *Opinions*. Often the opinion of your responsible, informed associates is a good substitute for facts in cases where the facts either aren't available or are too expensive/time consuming to obtain.

Let your thinking go! It will frequently happen that as you are working on one consideration, you'll think of a piece of information that belongs somewhere else. Take a moment to jot that information down in its proper place and continue.

When you've completed your summary of the INFORMATION on all 24 SELECTION CONSIDERATIONS, take a moment to look it over and be sure something isn't left out.

3. Now EVALUATE Your Information. Look at the information for the first consideration compared to your PRODUCT/MARKET SELECTION CRITERIA (see separate worksheet). If you don't have applicable criteria, apply good judgment -- your own or that of your responsible, informed associates -- to the summarized information. Either way, determine if the information shows that your opportunity *exceeds your standards* for that consideration (a "+"), or if it's *unacceptable* (a "-"). Everything else is acceptable and need not be noted; *it's only the exceptions ("+'s" and "-'s") that you need to flag.*

Proceed this way through the EVALUATION of all 24 SELECTION CONSIDERATIONS. Then go back and do a summary evaluation in each of the six overall selection consideration areas. Continue to apply your own judgment on whether to give an overall "+" when one or more of the constituent considerations is "+" ... but never fail to give an overall "-" when any subordinate consideration is "-." After all, "-" means unacceptable ... and you never want to bury that!

Below is a sample of what a portion of your completed worksheet might look like:

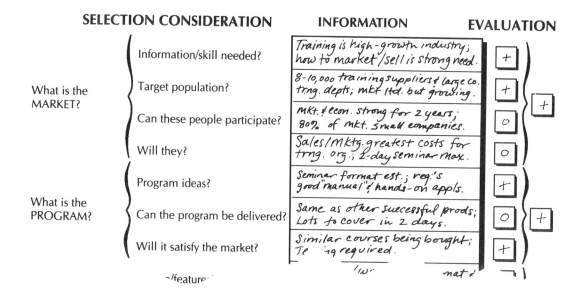

SELECTION CONSIDERATION		INFORMATION	EVALUATION
	Information/skill needed?	Training is high-growth industry; how to market/sell is strong need.	+
What is the MARKET?	Target population?	8-10,000 training suppliers & large co. trng. depts; mkt. ltd. but growing.	+
	Can these people participate?	Mkt. & econ. strong for 2 years; 80% of mkt. small companies.	o
	Will they?	Sales/mktg. greatest costs for trng. org.; 2-day seminar max.	o
	Program ideas?	Seminar format est.; req's good "manual" & hands-on appls.	+
What is the PROGRAM?	Can the program be delivered?	Same as other successful prods; Lots to cover in 2 days.	o
	Will it satisfy the market?	Similar courses being bought; Te...ng required.	+

Selection Information Worksheet

SELECTION CONSIDERATION		INFORMATION	EVALUATION
What is the MARKET?	Information/skill needed?		☐
	Target population?		☐ ☐
	Can these people participate?		☐
	Will they?		☐
What is the PROGRAM?	Program ideas?		☐
	Can the program be delivered?		☐ ☐
	Will it satisfy the market?		☐
How does our PROGRAM COMPARE with others?	Design/features?		☐
	Promotion?		☐ ☐
	Price?		☐
	Timing?		☐
How does our ORGANIZATION compare?	Sales/distribution?		☐
	Professional staff?		☐
	Reputation?		☐ ☐
	After-sale support?		☐
	Location/facilities?		☐
	Other factors?		☐
What is the program's FINANCIAL performance?	Cash flow?		☐
	Profit?		☐ ☐
	Other business impact?		☐
	Risks?		☐
What OTHER CONTRIBUTION does the program make?	Strategy/objectives?		☐
	Organizational relationships?		☐ ☐
	Overriding considerations?		☐

PRODUCT/MARKET SELECTION
TIPS

Be Clear About Your Target Market

Be specific in defining your market (customer groups), and don't mix together markets with differing characteristics. For example, small businesses almost always behave differently than large ones even if your customer has the same position title in each. Treat each separately in the selection process.

People Self-Select the Way *They* Want to Learn

Experience shows that customer buying preferences for various types of training and information products tend to repeat and that there's little crossover from one type to another. For example, self-paced program buyers are excellent prospects for more self-paced programs, tapes or books but may be poor prospects for seminars or conferences.

Small Changes in Product Can Make a Big Difference

Small changes in the product can make a big difference in how it's perceived in the marketplace and how your product compares to competition. An example is adding audio tapes to a self-paced print program. Remember that your product includes three elements: the physical "hardware," the software *and* services.

Cross-Functional Participation Pays Off

Be sure those who are going to be involved in implementing your product/market decision *also* participate in making it. And the earlier in the decision-making they can participate, the better their input. That's part of the magic behind today's emphasis on cross-functional teams and self-directed, empowered work groups.

It Helps to Have a New Product "Champion"

Most new ventures (products and/or markets) require a "champion" with vision and persistence to keep the project moving ahead until it can stand on its own. This is especially important in larger organizations.

"Is It Real?" Key For Brand-New Products/Services

For something that's never been done before, spend your greatest time and effort determining that the market *really* exists and that a product/service really *can* be delivered which satisfies the market. This is the area that trips up most innovative ideas.

Remember the Pioneers: They're the Ones with Arrows in 'Em.

There are proven market-share and learning-curve advantages that can go with being the first one in a new market or with a new technology (see *The Experience Curve* in the next section). But the vast majority of organizations will do much better by shooting to be second -- and not being last. Where advanced technology is involved in training and information, don't push the state-of-the-art too hard. Even if you can be first, pull back a little and let someone else prove that it's real.

"Can We Win?" Is Vital in Competitive Markets

If there's existing or likely competition (same or similar products/services aimed at the same market), then give your greatest time and attention to competitive comparisons: us versus our competitors as seen by the customer. This is particularly important for products sold primarily face-to-face.

Within *"Can We Win?"*, organization versus organization comparisons are most important when selling services and intangibles, and for any product which is ordered now but delivered later. Examples include custom program development, consulting and train-the-trainer.

Use Your In-Basket to Do Low-Cost Market Research

Look at what the high-volume direct marketers of training and information are selling. They're usually in better touch with marketing trends and can afford more market testing. Compare their promotions for two consecutive years and see if they're offering the same products promoted in the same ways or if they've changed.

Use readily available catalogs of national training and information suppliers to get up-to-date competitor prices, course offerings, and the like. This can be a valuable source of marketing information worth thousands of dollars to you -- and it costs absolutely nothing.

Marketing and Sales Is Critical

Training and other information products and services stand or fall on sales and distribution. There is no doubt that this is THE single most important consideration. Without a means of sales and distribution, the best training and information product or service will surely fail.

Guard Against Internal Sales-Method Rivalries

In general, when an organization uses two (or more) sales/distribution methods to reach the same market, conflict or friction will always exist between them because each is viewed as a threat to the other. A common training example is direct marketing and face-to-face sales. No training supplier has yet succeeded in putting these two important selling methods together.

Two Ways to Make Money in Public Seminars

Due to high selling costs, there are basically only two ways to make money on public seminars: (1.) Get the courses, materials and presenters at low/no cost, or (2.) sell enough to the participants at/after the course to offset the cost of the initial sale. In the latter case, it's important to handle the accounting properly; be sure at least some of the initial public seminar costs *are* actually charged against those later sales, or a misleading profitability picture will result and internal, organizational friction will result.

Balance Open Registration and In-House/On-Site Sales

Many large training organizations sell *only* open registration events or *only* in-house/on-site events. But a better approach is to expect about a dollar of in-house/on-site revenue for every dollar derived from public seminars. Any big revenue discrepancy between these two types of programs signals good growth potential -- if you make the right investment to boost sales and marketing for the one that's low.

Training Products Have Long Lives

Training products that make it through the introduction stage have traditionally had a long useful life with only minor updating. Many training suppliers report continued strong sales of products introduced 10-15 years ago or more, some merely transferred to today's media.

Costs Decline with Experience

Expect your business to follow an experience curve whereby costs decline as total volume increases. A realistic expectation is for costs to decline 15%-25% each time total accumulated volume doubles (see *The Experience Curve* on the next page).

Finding Criteria Is Hard Work

Product/market selection criteria reflect the organization's strategy, values, beliefs, -- and much more. They're difficult to develop and almost always controversial. But even a few defined and accepted criteria can work won-ders to improve your product/market decision-making process, particularly criteria for *minuses* that show you when to drop a product.

Strive for Balance

Your best product/market opportunity is one that, on balance across the six major SELECTION CONSIDERATIONS, comes out with one or more pluses and no negatives.

Pay Particular Attention to Areas You Want to Ignore

Many times the desire to "skip over" some CONSIDERATION comes from concern that there's really a problem there. Pay *particular* attention to those.

Don't Spoil a Good Decision by Poor Execution

Your implementation planning is as important as your product/market decision. Many times the correct decision is made but it's botched in the implementation.

Audit Your Entire Product Line Every Year

The process for selecting *new* products and/or markets also works for evaluating your existing ones, or proposed changes to them. Use this method to conduct an annual "audit" of your existing product/market offerings. You'll likely be surprised at the important results obtained.

THE EXPERIENCE CURVE

Many people are familiar with the experience curve concept first popularized by The Boston Consulting Group and others. This concept -- where unit costs can decline by a predictable percentage every time cumulative volume doubles -- has been well-validated for many industries. And in electronics, computers and other high-technology fields, this predictable cost decline has been used strategically to guide product pricing and investment decisions and, in turn, has had a significant impact on market share.

This important concept is equally valid in the training and information field. The curve below shows actual data for a real training company during a 10-year period. It shows that, overall, per-student costs declined 22% every time cumulative volume doubled. Do you know the corresponding curve for your business?

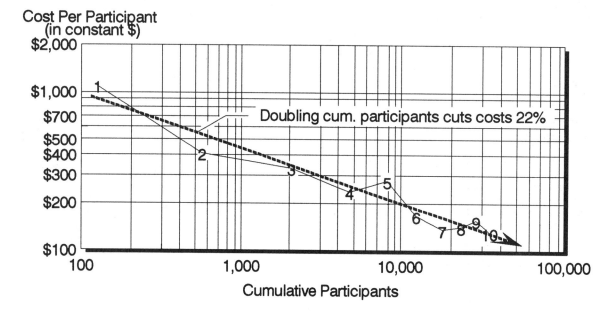

PRICING TIPS

"Is It Real?", "Can We Win?" and "Is It Worth It?" depends heavily on price. Here's a few thoughts on this important subject.

Only the Marketplace Determines Prices

What a willing, informed buyer will pay for your product or service determines its price. Anything else is guess work.

If you're just getting started, there are two pricing steps you *must* take: (1.) Look at all similar products aimed at similar markets and how they're priced, and (2.) be prepared to lower (or raise) your initial price to respond to market rejection (or acceptance) once you do start selling. It's certain that your first price won't be your best price.

Public Seminars

Open-enrollment seminars, workshops and conferences are priced per person and paid in advance. Discounts for multiple enrollments are common, either by a straight discount for the second and subsequent enrollment or by charging an added organizational registration fee for the first enrollment.

Consider offering a larger discount to those committing more participants. This can be done with an annual agreement, advance booking of the participants by name or even selling certificates or tickets. Here's an example for a 3-day management program:

	Price	Discount /Partic.	%
Individual Participant	$895 each	--	--
Multiple Enrollment (Two or more enrolled at one time and billed on one invoice)	$795 each	$100	11%
Group Enrollment (10 or more enrolled at one time and billed on one invoice)	$700 each	$95	12%
Certificates (20 or more pre-paid coupons, billed on one invoice; User(s) must register in advance for sessions)	$650 each	$50	7%

Later in this chapter is representative data on public seminar pricing. The illustrations are presented as a guide to how competitor price data can be displayed to help you see trends and draw conclusions. There's also information in Chapter 5 on how public seminar price effects direct mail response rates.

In-House/On-Site Seminars

These are usually priced per session, or per person with a minimum number in a session. In either case, expenses such as instructor travel costs, away-from-home living expenses, shipping and international duties/customs charges are additional.

Here's a sample in-house pricing structure that's consistent with the open enrollment prices shown above:

	Price	Discount /Partic.	%
Single In-House Workshop - for up to 16 participants ($5,000 retainer required to hold dates)	$9,500 Plus expenses		
Additional Part's over 16	$600 each	$50	8%
Series Rate - Four (4) or more In-House Workshops, for up to 16 participants each, Scheduled at one time and retainer billed on one invoice (Larger of $18,000 or 50% retainer required to hold dates)	$8,800 plus expenses		
Additional Part's over 16 in any workshop	$550 each	$50	8%

The discount is in relation to the "certificate" prices shown in the previous table.

Licensing and Train-The-Trainer

Licensing pricing is usually based on one of three approaches:

1. A Certification Fee Plus Materials. Client trainers are checked-out and certified to teach the course to their employees using student materials bought in volume against a steeply discounted schedule.

2. A Royalty. A royalty is paid by the client for each person they train or each copy of your materials they print (similar to author-publisher royalties).

3.   *Site-License Fee*. This fee gives basically unlimited use of the course for a period of time at one location.

Here's an example of licensing pricing that's consistent with the above in-house prices:

Client Course Leader Training & Certification:
(Note: A minimum of 100 participant materials is required for each Course Leader trained and certified.)

First Course Leader............$14,800 plus expenses

Second Course Leader trained at the same time as the first....................$ 9,700 plus expenses

Third and subsequent Course Leaders trained at the same as the first and second.........................$ 7,600 ea. plus expenses

Participant Materials: (Note: Volume discount schedule applies per order shipped and invoiced at one time; discounts are not cumulative with prior or future orders.)

	Price	Discount /Partic.	%
1 thru 19	$395 each	--	--
20 thru 99	$350 each	$45	11%
100 thru 199	$295 each	$55	16%
200 thru 499	$260 each	$35	12%
500 thru 999	$225 each	$35	13%
1,000 or more	$195 each	$30	13%

Your Prices Must Make Sense Across All Delivery Options and Durations

If you put together the open-enrollment pricing, in-house pricing and licensing pricing shown in the preceding three sections, you get costs per person trained shown in the table at the bottom of this page. Large organization training directors are looking for these kinds of deep discounts in order to train hundreds or even thousands of employees.

The table immediately below shows how the above base pricing for a 3-day program might look for shorter duration events.

Pricing for Various Duration Events

Duration	Public Seminars		In-House Presentations		
	Single Seat	2 Or More Enrolling At Once	Basic Fee (Up To 16)	Per-Part. Charge (Over 16)	Retainer Amount
1/2 Day	$245	$195 each	$2,400	$150 each	$1,200
1 Day	$345	$275 each	$3,600	$225 each	$1,800
1-1/2 Day	--	--	$4,800	$300 each	$2,400
2 Days	$545	$450 each	$6,000	$375 each	$3,000
3 Days	$895	$795 each	$9,600	$600 each	$5,000

Customer's Per-Person Costs - (Before Expenses)

Population Trained	Individ. Publics	Multiple Enroll.	Group Enroll.	Certificates	In-House Sessions	Series Rate	Licensing: No. Leaders 1	2	3	4	5	6
1	$895											
2	$895	$795										
10	$895	$795	$700									
16	$895	$795	$700	$650	$600							
20	$895	$795	$700	$650	$600							
30	$895	$795	$700	$650	$600							
40	$895	$795	$700	$650	$600							
50	$895	$795	$700	$650	$600							
64	$895	$795	$700	$650	$600	$550						
100	$895	$795	$700	$650	$600	$550	$443					
200	$895	$795	$700	$650	$600	$550	$334	$383				
300	$895	$795	$700	$650	$600	$550	$309	$342	$367			
400	$895	$795	$700	$650	$600	$550	$297	$321	$340	$359		
500	$895	$795	$700	$650	$600	$550	$255	$274	$289	$304	$320	
600	$895	$795	$700	$650	$600	$550	$250	$266	$279	$291	$304	$317
700	$895	$795	$700	$650	$600	$550	$246	$260	$271	$282	$293	$303
800	$895	$795	$700	$650	$600	$550	$244	$256	$265	$275	$284	$294
900	$895	$795	$700	$650	$600	$550	$241	$252	$261	$269	$278	$286
1,000	$895	$795	$700	$650	$600	$550	$210	$220	$227	$235	$242	$250
1,100	$895	$795	$700	$650	$600	$550	$208	$217	$224	$231	$238	$245
1,200	$895	$795	$700	$650	$600	$550	$207	$215	$222	$228	$234	$241
1,300	$895	$795	$700	$650	$600	$550	$206	$214	$220	$226	$231	$237
1,400	$895	$795	$700	$650	$600	$550	$206	$213	$218	$223	$229	$234
1,500	$895	$795	$700	$650	$600	$550	$205	$211	$216	$221	$227	$232
1,600	$895	$795	$700	$650	$600	$550	$204	$210	$215	$220	$225	$229
1,700	$895	$795	$700	$650	$600	$550	$204	$209	$214	$218	$223	$227
1,800	$895	$795	$700	$650	$600	$550	$203	$209	$213	$217	$221	$226
1,900	$895	$795	$700	$650	$600	$550	$203	$208	$212	$216	$220	$224
2,000	$895	$795	$700	$650	$600	$550	$202	$207	$211	$215	$219	$222
2,100	$895	$795	$700	$650	$600	$550	$202	$207	$210	$214	$218	$221

Books and Other Printed Materials

These are usually priced per item, with volume discounts available. Since the book business has traditional distribution channels (to universities, schools, libraries, and to the public through "The Book Trade," discounts, payment terms, return privileges, complimentary/review copy practices, etc., are all geared to this tradition. (See Chapter 12 for more on the book business and book pricing.)

Films And Video

These are priced for rental *or* purchase. Noncommercial rentals are priced for a length of time or number of showings. Discounts for volume purchases and/or multiple rentals during a period of time are frequent. Short duration previews are also offered by most producers, although they are costly.

Audio Tape Cassettes and Computer Diskettes

These are sold (not rented), usually with a workbook or other printed materials and a binder, box, case or other package to keep the materials organized for use. Pricing is per unit, with price breaks for volume purchases. Extra workbooks are priced separately.

PUBLIC SEMINAR PRICE TRENDS

The graph below illustrates how U.S. public seminar prices have changed during a 10-year period. It shows the single-seat, undiscounted prices of the most popular seminars offered nationally by the largest public seminar suppliers, as a function of course duration.

The lightly shaded area is defined by the curve of top-priced programs above and the bottom-priced programs below. The heavy line through the center shows average prices. The area with vertical cross-hatching shows the corresponding band from the similar illustration in my book *The Seminar Market*.

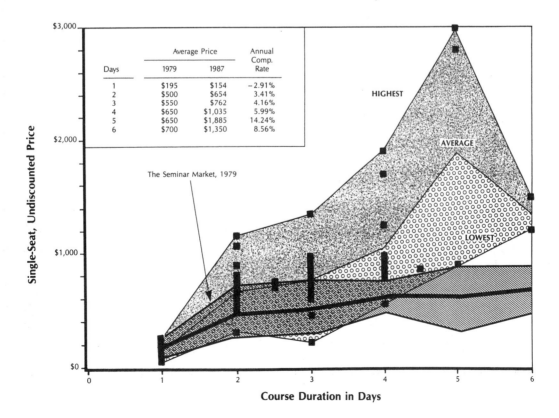

Days	Average Price		Annual Comp. Rate
	1979	1987	
1	$195	$154	−2.91%
2	$500	$654	3.41%
3	$550	$762	4.16%
4	$650	$1,035	5.99%
5	$650	$1,885	14.24%
6	$700	$1,350	8.56%

The chart also shows how prices changed. Although average prices increased 6% annually, there were two important deviations: Large price increases for a few 5-day programs greatly inflated the annual rate, and 1-day seminars greatly increased in number *and* dropped significantly in price.

The graph only shows prices for seminars up to six days duration, although there are many longer courses. But our data shows a strong trend to shorter seminars: Probably a third of all seminars are now 1-day or less, a dramatic shift from the nearly 3-day average when I wrote *The Seminar Market*.

TIPS FOR NEW BUSINESSES

The Start-Up Is Critical

Many new businesses that look easy and profitable once they're going can be difficult to start. For example, consultants typically get 70%-80% of their sales from past clients. What do you do before you have past clients? Seminar companies and publishers rely largely on mailings to past attendees/buyers. What do you do before you have any?

That's why in growth/start-up situations, you *must* figure your costs two ways: what they are now and through the perilous start-up phase, and -- *separately* -- what they'll be after the business is a "going concern."

Businesses Fail Because They Run Out of Money

Lack of sales and undercapitalization are *still* the two biggest reasons new businesses fail. Both amount to the same thing: You run out of money. To avoid this:

1.   Start with at least one year's capital.
2.   Concentrate *all* your efforts on selling.
3.   Don't spend a penny on *anything* that doesn't contribute directly to getting sales or delivering product.

Prompt, Accurate Bookkeeping Shows What's Working

Many entrepreneurs deride bookkeeping as unnecessary "bean counting." Don't make this mistake! Accurate accounting will show whether your business is making or losing money and which marketing and sales efforts are working or not working. Make sure *all* income and expenses are promptly recognized *and* regularly accounted, preferably monthly. An experienced, part-time bookkeeper can do the job reasonably -- and they may furnish you other useful financial advice as well. (There are also some helpful financial analysis worksheets in Chapter 5)

Profitability *and* Cash Both Matter

When evaluating financial performance, always look at *both* profitability and cash flow, starting where you are now and looking ahead up to three (3) years. This is even more critical for a new business, where running out of money can be fatal.

"Getting Customers Isn't Everything; It's the *Only* Thing"

When starting a business, this paraphrase of the familiar saying, often attributed to coach Vince Lombardi (but not originated by him, we're told) couldn't be more relevant. Your *only* goal is to get customers. Devote *all* of your efforts to this and forget about administration or other non-revenue-producing activities (except keeping track of the money).

Don't Cut Sales And Marketing Corners

Don't economize on your marketing and sales efforts at the start. Always give it your very best shot. If that doesn't work, nothing will. Besides, if you market "on the cheap" and the business fails, you'll always wonder whether things would have turned out differently if you had gone first class.

Later you'll have plenty of chance to cut selling costs and improve marketing yields -- but *only* if you're successful finding a marketing and sales approach that works.

Bad Debts Are Usually Not a Problem for Training

Bad debts in the training business have been virtually nonexistent. They are more likely -- but still small -- in mail order sales of books and tapes. Chapter 6 has suggestions to minimize/control bad debts.

The Second Year Is Always Better

It's impossible to overstate the benefits of completing one year in business. After that, you always have "last year" as a comparison. And you've survived the inevitable seasonal fluctuations every business experiences.

Don't Confuse Your Separate Roles as Owner and Employee

When evaluating your business, don't confuse your separate roles as *owner* and as an *employee*. Each separately requires your investment of money and/or time. And each separately gives you a return in money, benefits and/or intangibles.

On your investment as an *owner*, expect returns at least as good as you could get elsewhere. For example, good stock mutual funds currently return about 14% annually. (You *have* figured out how much you've invested in your business, haven't you?)

As an *employee*, expect compensation at least as good as you could get doing the same work for someone else. Remember, the work you do yourself *has* value and would need to be purchased if you weren't there to do it. Ignoring these costs gives you a distorted pic-

ture of the business' financial health.

Make Ownership and Buy/Sell Decisions *Before* You Start

Two (or more) people starting a business together *must* settle all major ownership issues *before* they begin, particularly: (1.) who owns how much of the business and (2.) when and how can each sell out -- or buy out -- the other(s). If not agreed upon in writing at the start, these matters become more difficult to resolve with every passing day.

Dr. Saul Feldman, a very wise and dear friend, once gave me this valuable advice:

> *"Remember, when starting a business, money is dear and paper is cheap. But after the business is successful, the situation is reversed: Then money is cheap and paper is dear."*

It's true.

Sign All Your Own Checks

Comedian Bill Cosby gave this great piece of advice for everyone in business. There is no better -- or simpler -- way to keep your finger on the pulse of your business and protect yourself against unwanted spending.

Warn Creditors *Before* Their Payment is Late

If you run short of cash and see you can't pay bills when they're due, *tell your creditors at once*. Most people dislike doing this and put it off, hoping the problem will fix itself. It rarely does. Once told of your situation, most creditors will work with you through these tight times. But their cooperation is much more difficult to obtain once you've missed their payment.

COPYRIGHT TIPS

NOTE: This is a complex subject on which professional legal advice is needed. The following are presented only for guidance:

Copyright Everything You Print

Make sure everything you print has the copyright you wish printed on it. Only three elements are necessary to secure copyright protection: (1.) the letter "c" in a circle; (2.) the year of printing and (3.) the name of the copyright-holder. Anything else, such as the word "copyright," a statement of prohibited uses, the copyright-holder's address, etc., is optional.

Register Your Copyright

After printing the material with the above three essential elements, register the material with the Copyright Office of the Library of Congress. Get the forms from:

UNITED STATES COPYRIGHT OFFICE
Library of Congress
Washington, DC 20559

Registration proves your copyright intent, dates, etc., and demonstrates the importance you place on the copyright process.

Copyright protects the embodiment of an idea, not the idea itself. If you publish the same idea in different forms, each must be separately copyrighted and registered.

Copyright Violations Are a Serious Problem in Training

The law notwithstanding, a small but significant number of people feel justified in copying and using, without permission, any and all relevant materials they see, regardless of whether or not these materials are copyrighted. If such use deprives the copyright-holder of income they would otherwise be entitled to, then the copier has probably broken the law. This is a serious problem for the entire training industry. The following are a few things you can do to help.

In Big Companies Notify Top Management of Rip-Offs

If you learn of a rip-off in an organization of appreciable size, go to top management and tell your story, asking them to stop all unauthorized use of your materials and to pay you for what use has already been made. Be businesslike, have your evidence and facts straight and be prepared to name names. This works almost 100 percent of the time, because the sums involved are usually insignificant compared to litigation, and the lopsided "big-company-versus-little-vendor" picture makes it likely you'd win any close decision anyway. In a high percentage of cases you'll find that the offending individual has already quit or been fired for some other reason.

Threaten to Sue Smaller Companies and Individuals

For copyright violations by smaller organizations and individuals, you may want to threaten legal action. The likelihood is that such action will only be successful if you can actually prove you've been damaged in some substantial way by the infringement. Nonetheless, the initiation of legal action in those cases where you have a good case (again, you need legal counsel on this) can sometimes lead to a satisfactory conclusion.

Don't Be Passive When You See Copyright Violations

Don't overlook copyright violations of other people's materials. Ask those who distribute copies of articles and other course materials if they received permission to reproduce it. If they claim they have, ask why the copies don't carry that notation. Let authors know about known or suspected copyright violations of their materials. This kind of "neighborhood watch" approach -- or some similar grass roots program for the industry to police itself -- is really the only way this very serious problem can be held in check.

Aggressively pursue any and all deliberately improper uses of your materials, including those by your employees and associates. The costs and inconveniences involved are more than offset by the deterrent value of such actions and their clear demonstration to everyone that you place considerable value on your materials.

HOW TO PICK THE BEST SALES AND MARKETING STRATEGY

This chapter wouldn't exist in a handbook for most businesses. Groceries, clothing, real estate, life insurance, automobiles -- and most other products and services -- are sold through well-established patterns that have evolved over time, often decades or even centuries.

Not so with training and information. Maybe because it's "soft," maybe because it's complicated -- or maybe because whatever training or information you're selling requires the end user to invest still *more* time and effort to get its true value -- selling training is hard work.

Top salespeople and world-class marketers all agree that this is the toughest marketing challenge they've ever faced.

What's more, picking the wrong sales and marketing method is the second most common cause for a new training business to fail. (The first is running out of money. But the two are related, because without the one you can't have the other.)

So the purpose of this chapter is to furnish you the tools to select the correct sales and marketing approach for your products and for the market you're trying to reach. We review the major marketing alternatives available and the circumstances when each is superior or when a "mix" of methods is best.

SALES AND MARKETING METHODS

Look at the table on the next page. It lists the principal sales methods now in use by organizations supplying training programs and instructional materials.

Before we see how to pick the right method(s) from this list, we'll look more closely at the major options.

Direct Marketing

Direct marketing is any communication intended to produce an order, sale, or other action *without* a face-to-face meeting. Direct marketing is distinguished from wholesale and retail sales, and from direct sales made through face-to-face sales calls.

Direct Marketing uses primarily direct mail, telemarketing and media advertising (print or broadcast) in order to make the sale. Direct marketing is usually at its best when there's a product with no established means of distribution, which may be why it's so often used successfully to market training.

Sales and Marketing Methods

1. Face-to-face Selling

- Full-Time Salespersons
  - Home-Office Based
  - Regional Offices
- Part-Time (Sell/Consult or Sell/Teach)
- Representatives/Agents
- Retail Stores

2. Telemarketing

- In-House
  - Full-Time
  - Part-Time
- Outside Services

3. Direct Mail

- Letters (and Other Things) in Envelopes
- Brochure Self-Mailers
- Catalogs
- Postcard Decks
- Everything Else

4. Events

- Seminars/Workshop/Training Programs
- Conferences/Trade Shows/Expos
- Showcases/Previews

5. Other

- Stimulate Referrals
- Write and Publish a Book
- Print Advertising (Classified Ads, Display Ads or Directory Listings)
- Broadcast Advertising (Radio, TV, Cable)
- Publicity
- Everything Else

6. Combinations of Above

- Direct Mail + Telemarketing
- Direct Mail + Face-to-Face Sales
- Telemarketing + Face-to-Face Sales
- Direct Mail + Events + Face-to-Face Sales
- Direct Mail + Telemarketing + Face-to-Face Sales

A recent survey showed the following breakdown of direct marketing expenditures between these various media:

Telemarketing	45.2%
Direct mail	42.1%
Newspapers	9.5%
TV	1.3%
All other media	1.9%
Total:	100.0%

Direct Mail

Although direct mail is second to telemarketing in expenditures, it is *the* most frequently-used direct marketing method for training products and services.

Roughly two-thirds of all direct mail is to households (consumers), and one-third is to non-households (businesses and institutions, including the government). Here's the way the U.S. mail flow breaks down, according to The Direct Marketing Association:

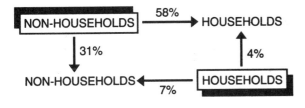

In 1991, direct mail advertising volume was 66,404,601,000 (that's 66 Billion!) pieces. As incredible as that number is, advertising mail (some of which really is "junk") accounts for only 43.2% of all U.S. mail. The accompanying graph shows the explosion in direct mail advertising that's occurred since 1965.

The composition of U.S. direct mail advertising by class of mail is as follows:

First-Class	11.5%
Third-Class	68.0%
Nonprofit	20.4%
International	0.1%
Total:	100.0%

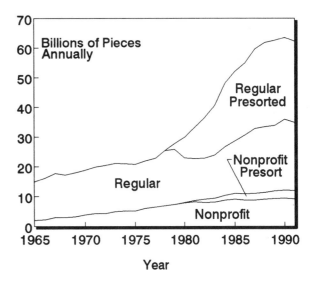

U.S. Third-Class Bulk-Rate Mail Volume

Just about everyone knows that the American Management Association (AMA) is one of the largest direct marketers in the world, sending out tens of millions of pieces of mail every year. And, of course, most major publishers rely heavily on mail and space ads to promote their titles.

But did you know that this is not a new phenomenon? In 1891, International Correspondence Schools (ICS) (acquired by National Education Corp. in 1979) began offering its courses through ads in the *Farmer's Almanac* and similar books. More than 100 years later, the company *still* uses direct marketing and receives an estimated 800,000 inquiries a year for its 38 different training programs.

And the former U.S. School of Music, a direct marketer of correspondence courses, created the well-known ad that began "They laughed when I sat down at the piano."

Direct mail used by trainers is not always described by the hated "J"-word, but rather it is often in the form of personal letters, memos and a variety of other mail-delivered formats. As today's modern computer technology so clearly demonstrates, the line between mail that's personalized by a human and that personalized by a computer is becoming less and less distinct. In fact, it's likely that as you read this, there is within your reach a letter that has been totally computer generated but that appears to have been prepared entirely by a human.

Of course direct mail remains the mainstay of selling seminars, books and many other knowledge-related products and services. It is also the most effective means of getting new sales leads and of inviting prospects to sales events and is the customary means of transmitting proposals and other important documents in the selling process. And direct mail also includes all of the usual brochures, self-mailers, catalogs, postcard decks, and the variety of other formats we all encounter daily.

Chapters 7, 8, 9 and a large part of Chapter 5 are devoted to direct mail.

Telemarketing

Telemarketing is an important and growing branch of direct marketing in which the telephone is used to close the order, rather than either mail or a face-to-face meeting.

Telemarketing expenditures overtook direct mail expenditures in 1982 and have exceeded them ever since.

Telemarketing has two major divisions: (1.) *inbound* telemarketing, where by the customer's call was prompted by some other medium, typically direct mail, print, radio or TV, and (2.) *outbound* telemarketing, where by the call is placed by the salesperson.

The telephone serves primarily as an aid to both direct mail and face-to-face selling. But since the phone is such an essential business tool, much telemarketing know-how already exists. What's been learned by those who sell by telephone for a living needs to be thoroughly understood and incorporated into how you use the phone to sell training products and services.

And for these products and services, telemarketing behaves more like direct mail than like face-to-face selling.

Cold-calling by telephone is *not* usually cost-effective for training. Better to use the telephone along with direct mail, say by calling past customers, attendees or responders who asked for more information. In this role telemarketing can be *very* profitable.

Telemarketing can also support face-to-face selling by setting up appointments for sales calls or by confirming showcase/preview attendees.

Finally, there are many uses of telemarketing, apart from strictly "sales." For example, some of the best market research and client surveys can be conducted by telephone. Such surveys are not only very reliable, they are quick and easy to conduct, returning usable data in a matter of hours or a few days rather than the weeks or months required for other methods.

Telemarketing is covered in greater detail in Chapter 11. Inbound telemarketing, as part of the registrar function, is described in Chapters 6 and 10.

Face-to-Face Selling

As its name suggests, face-to-face selling is conducted in person "... up close and personal," as they say.

For reasons that will become clear in the next section, face-to-face selling is the most frequently used means of selling consulting services. It is typically employed by trainers and consultants just getting started and is used by thousands of sales professionals in the largest training and consulting organizations. Face-to-face selling is used in one-on-one meetings with prospects and clients and also employed during events such as seminars, conferences and other presentations.

Face-to-face selling can be done part-time (such as those who sell their own services -- and then deliver them). It can also be performed by representatives or agents, who obtain a commission for whatever they sell.

Chapter 4 is devoted entirely to face-to-face selling.

Using Events to Sell

Using events to sell has been around a long time. The snake-oil salesperson and carnival pitchman are obvious -- if not appealing -- examples.

Events include seminars, workshops, conferences and tradeshows. They are the most important way to sell seminars and other training events. They can also be an important aid to selling other big-ticket products and services like consulting, train-the-trainer and custom course development. Chapters 6 - 9 have plenty of information on planning and marketing your own events, including events expressly for selling.

One event that's become a powerful sales and marketing aid for face-to-face sales is the free *showcase* or *preview session*. Showcases offer an opportunity for clients and prospective clients to meet under carefully controlled circumstances, which often results in substantial business. Because of their importance, Chapter 10 is devoted entirely to these events.

Training and consulting organizations often find that events arranged and promoted by others are an ideal platform (pun intended) for sales and marketing. You can participate in conferences, trade shows and expositions held by societies or publishers in many ways: as a panelist, speaker or exhibitor, to mention a few. Your organization can even hold a customer or users conference. Making the best use of these events is addressed in Chapter 12.

Other Sales and Marketing Methods -- and Combinations

Trainers and consultants employ a variety of other marketing techniques to stimulate sales. Point 5 of The Process on Page 3-2 lists a number of those used most frequently. Below are even more ideas, including some that may seem "far out."

But of these many other sales and marketing methods, only a few are useful in selling training.

For example, there is no doubt that referrals are the most important source of training business, often amounting to two-thirds to three-quarters of sales. Referrals, of course, do not come in "over the transom" but generally require face-to-face selling or other forms of sales and marketing in order to actually close the business. Referral business can be stimulated by an aggressive program of staying in touch with your current clients and prospects (for example, using a Newsletter) as well as by publicity.

Representative Other Marketing Possibilities

- Matchbooks
- Billboards
- Building signs
- Sound trucks
- Skywriting
- Blimps
- Telephone books
- Taxi, bus ads
- Grocery bags
- Airline ticket envelopes
- Radio
- Broadcast-TV
- Cable TV
- Door-to-door
- Newspapers
  - Display
  - Classified
  - Inserts
- Newsletters

- Magazines
  - Display ads
  - Classified ads
  - Bind-ins/blow-ins
- Bulletin boards
  - Physical
  - Computer
- Posters
- Catalogs
- Directories
- Mail
  - Envelopes
  - Self-mailers
  - Catalogs
  - Postcard decks
  - Statement stuffer
- Telephone
  - Inbound
  - Outbound

- Fax
- Telegram (or equivalent)
- E-Mail
- Distributor
- Retail store
- Trade shows
  - Booth
  - Hospitality suite
  - Work crowd
- Demonstrations/fairs/ festivals
- Point-of-purchase/sale
- Product
  - Package
  - Inserts
  - On the product itself
- Publicity
- Cooperative advertising (with others)

There's plenty of opportunity to use other techniques as well, including classified ads directory listings, display ads, and a wide variety of others. These -- and others -- are described at length in Chapters 11 and 12.

And don't forget about using these methods in combination, because that's how it usually works. Direct mail stimulates a response from someone who then gets a telephone call, followed by a face-to-face meeting. Some of the most frequently used combinations are presented in the marketing programs shown in a few sections.

THREE FACTORS DETERMINE
WHICH SALES METHOD WORKS BEST

Three main variables determine whether direct mail or face-to-face selling is likely to be best for your particular training product/service and for the particular market you're trying to reach. These three variables are: (1.) expected size of the first order (2.) complexity of the sales and (3.) size of the customer's organization. How these three variables influence the choice between direct mail and face-to-face selling is shown in this diagram:

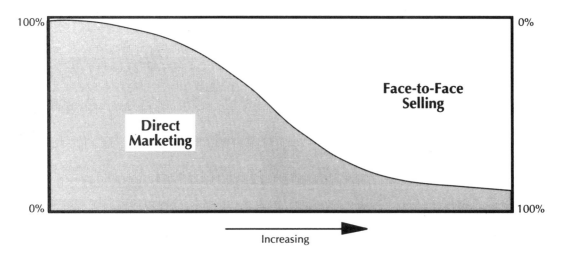

Size of the First Sale

Direct mail has been used to sell some very expensive items like precious metals, collectibles and round-the-world cruises. But for training products and services, direct mail works best for initial sales up to about $3,000 - $3,500. Above this size, face-to-face selling is usually required.

Among the largest sales routinely made by direct mail are long-duration management seminars and executive training programs.

The reason first order size is used, is that once a customer relationship is established, very sizeable *re*orders can often be obtained by mail or telephone.

Complexity of the Sale

Simple sales can be made by direct mail but complex sales usually require one or more face-to-face calls. A simple sale decision would be to buy a book or attend an open-registration seminar. A complex sale would be to schedule an in-house or on-site seminar, train trainers or commission development of a custom course. Direct mail can *support* face-to-face selling of complex sales but cannot *replace* it.

Size of the Customer's Organization

Organization size here actually refers to whether the buying decision is made by one person or by many. Face-to-face selling is absolutely necessary when there are many different individuals (or organizations) involved in the sale, as is usually the case in large organizations. Direct mail can often work when only one person makes the decision, as is frequently the case with individuals and small organizations.

Here's When to Use Each Selling Method

The above general guidelines -- and all our experience -- translate into this brief summary of when each major sales method works best:

1. Direct Mail

- Sells seminars, workshops, conferences, showcases and other events
- Sells books, tapes, videos and packaged training
- Supports face-to-face selling by getting leads

2. Telemarketing

- Supports direct mail for all training product sales
- Supports face-to-face selling by qualifying leads and making appointments
- Sells repeat/follow-on products to existing customers

3. Face-to-Face Selling

- Sells consulting
- Sells in-house/on-site training programs
- Sells custom course development
- Sells train-the-trainer programs

4. Broadcast Advertising / Infomercials

- Sells local events
- Sells packaged training programs with mass appeal

5. Print Advertising

- Sells events (calendar listings and/or classified ads only)
- Supports direct mail for non-event products
- Supports face-to-face selling by increasing name recognition

6. Publicity

- Supports all training products/services

TYPICAL SALES AND MARKETING PROGRAMS

The previous section looked at the various sales and marketing methods and what each does best. This section turns the perspective over two ways.

First, the table on the following page shows the kinds of sales and marketing programs you might select based on *your organization's size* or its geographic focus. These programs are not intended to be rigid recommendations, but rather typical examples of

what many training supplier organizations choose.

Then we look at the most *common training products and services* and show the primary and supporting sales methods that work best for them. Also included are names of some larger firms that exemplify each type of product or service, as well as the key infrastructure skills and capabilities you'll need for success.

Typical Sales And Marketing Programs

	SOLE PRACTITIONER	REGIONAL GROUP	NATIONAL / INTERNATIONAL FIRM	INTERNAL TO A LARGE ORGANIZATION
FACE-TO-FACE SELLING	• Personal time / activity management	• Sales & Delivery specialization • Sales management	• 2–3 levels of sales management • Hiring, training, retention of sales people	• Personal time / activity management • Key managers / staff meetings
DIRECT MAIL	• Standard letters • Small capabilities brochure	• Standard letters • Fancy organiz. brochure • Individual product / service brochures	• Same as Regional Group at left plus … • Sell products • Regular major mailings	• Course catalogs • Brochures / flyers
TELEMARKETING	• Make sales appointments • Stay–in–touch with customers / prospects	• Make sales appointments • Do market research	• Make sales appointments • Do market research • Sell products	• Make sales appointments • Stay–in–touch with customers / prospects
MARKETING DATA-BASE / MAIL LIST	• Manual record keeping or computer word processor / database	• Full capability relational database • Single–user OK	• Full capability relational database • Multi–user / networked	• Any database, word–processor or manual record–keeping system
OPEN SEMINARS	• Thru others	• Conducts few annually	• Regularly scheduled in each sales territory • Many topics	• Regularly scheduled
TRADE SHOWS & CONFERENCES	• Speak at local events only	• Regional shows only (1 – 2/yr)	• Major national / internat'l shows & conferences	• For professional staff recognition only
SHOWCASES	• One annually (local)	• Few annually (in region)	• Regularly scheduled in each sales territory for each product	• Few annually
STAY–IN–TOUCH	• Clippings, article re–prints (3–4 times per year)	• Reprints of articles, speeches • Newsletter	• User conference • Newsletter / magazine • Reprints of articles	• Clipping, articles, reprints (3–4 times per year)
WRITE A BOOK	• Thru a publisher	• Thru a publisher or self–published • Articles / papers	• Self–Published	• Thru a publisher • Internal "white papers"
OTHER	• Publicity • News releases	• Publicity • News releases	• Publicity • News releases • Display / classified ads	• Publicity (in house organ) • Bulletin boards • E – Mail

Sales and Marketing Programs by Product/Service

	Open Enrollment Seminars & Conferences	In–House/ On–Site Programs	Custom Programs & Consulting Services	Books, Tapes Job–Aids, Software	Films, Videos, Multi–Media, Packaged Programs	Marketing Training With In Your Own Organization
Primary Sales Method	Direct Mail	Face–To–Face	Face–To–Face	Direct Mail	Direct Mail	Direct Mail (Internally)
Major Supporting Sales Methods	• Telemarketing • Calendar Listings • Classified Ads	• Showcases • Trade Shows • Open Seminars	• Showcases • Open Seminars • Books • Trade Shows • Print Advertising	• Telemarketing • Open Seminars	• Telemarketing • Film Festivals • Trade Shows • Direct Response Television	• Telemarketing • Face–To–Face • Other Internal Media
Key Infrastructure Skills & Capabilities	• Planning • Forecasting Attendance • The Registrar • Mktg. Database • Low–Cost Printing	• Instructor Scheduling & Relations	• Pricing • Staff Utilization	• Telephone Order Desk • Marketing Database • Product Returns	• Telephone Order Desk • Marketing Database • Previews/ Rentals • Product Returns	• Planning • Forecasting Attendance • The Registrar • Mktg. Database • Low–Cost Printing
Some Examples	• AMA • CareerTrack • CCL • CME • Learning Tree • Pryor • SME	• DDI • Forum • Kaset • Learning Int'l. • ODI • Wilson • Zenger–Miller	• Ctr. Effect. Perf. • Creative Univ. • Golle & Holmes • Sandy • Universal Trng. • Vanguard	• Crisp • Jossey–Bass • Lakewood • Nightingale– Conant • Pfeiffer • Silton– Bookman	• American Media • Blanchard • Calley Curtis • Industrial Trn'g. Systems	• Andersen • AT&T • Coca–Cola • Digital Eqpt. • McDonalds • Motorola • Skill Dynamics

MARKETING TRAINING WITHIN YOUR OWN ORGANIZATION

Follow a Proven Training Process

All trainers have their own favorite process for successful training, but most are similar. Here's the one I like:

1. Establishing needs/objectives
2. Adapting/developing the training program
3. Developing internal marketing/promotion
4. Pre-course participant preparation
5. Conducting the training event
6. Post-training follow-up
7. Ensuring on-the-job application
8. Capturing and reporting training results
9. Keeping the training program current

Those marketing training within their own organization have a big advantage because they can control -- or at least influence -- more of these steps than can external marketers. They, for the most part, can only control Step 5, the training event itself. But it's the steps before and after training that have the most impact on the training's payoff!

Pay Attention to These 11 Marketing Keys

With respect to Step 3 above, here are the "Eleven Keys" to successfully marketing training within your own organization. Also shown are the chapters in this book where you can find more help for each step:

1. Determining Who's the Customer
   (Chapters 1 and 2)

2. Deciding Where It's Held: Training Location and Arrangements
   (Chapter 6)

3. Deciding When It's Held: Scheduling
   (Chapter 5 and 6)

4. Choosing the Program Title
   (Chapter 8)

5. Setting the Price
   (Chapters 2 and 5)

6. Selecting the Sales and Marketing Method
   (Chapters 3, 4, 8, 11 and 12)

7. Preparing Print Media
   (Chapters 8, 9 and 12)

8. Timing Your Marketing/Sales Efforts
   (Chapter 5)

9. Developing Your In-House Prospect List
   (Chapters 7 and 13)

10. Handling Enrollments and Inquiries
    (Chapters 6 and 10)

11. Keeping Attendance Up
    (Chapters 6 and 10)

Our handy booklet *Marketing Training Within Your Own Organization* contains still more help: dozens and dozens of practical tips in these 11 areas, distilled from the best ideas at our workshops for internal training marketers.

Everything's the Same Internally as Externally, with Some Added Benefits:

For one thing, internal mail response rates can run four to six times higher for your own promotions.   Coupled with lower internal mailing costs, this is a BIG advantage.

You also have a larger range of other internal media available than do external marketers -- and again it's free or very low cost.

Examples include posters, bulletin boards, paycheck stuffers, company newspapers, E-mail, lunchroom kiosks, etc. All of this is in addition to the usual external media -- that work even more effectively inside.

Don't Overlook Face-to-Face Selling

Face-to-face selling internally is through participation in staff meetings and in individual meetings with key managers. It's much easier to get the appointments; otherwise, the salesperson's job's much the same as externally.

Many Training Departments Promote Too Little and Too Late

Does your organization distribute only one or two course catalogs a year and expect all your classes to fill? Such infrequent promotion invariably results in a roller-coaster attendance profile with peaks two to three months after the catalogs, followed by valleys. Tests show that distributing three to six catalogs a year is much more cost effective.   If you want increased attendance at your training courses, increasing the number of annual catalogs is your quickest and best way.

And on the subject of timing, all lead times and frequency considerations (see Chapter 5) are unchanged for in-house marketing and are just as important as they are externally.

Sell Training to Suppliers and Customers, Too

Direct mail through the U.S. Postal Service, including renting mailing lists and all the rest, is useful to sell training to your customers and/or your suppliers. All the principles described elsewhere in this book are unchanged.

FACE-TO-FACE: THE *ONLY* WAY TO SELL IN-HOUSE OR CUSTOM TRAINING AND CONSULTING

Face-to-face selling is any situation where a meeting between the salesperson and the customer or prospect is needed to close the sale. It's required for big-ticket training and information sales, generally those that meet one or more of the following:

1. Selling large organizations and institutions

2. Initial order more than $3,000 - $4,000

3. "Complex" sales requiring (say) arrangements for on-site presentations, training of trainers, customizing, identifying population to be trained, etc.

You need face-to-face selling to be successful with:

- In-House/On-Site programs
- Train-the-Trainer/ Licensing programs
- Custom program development
- HRD/OD consulting services

On the day you read this, thousands of face-to-face salespeople will be -- or have been -- busy selling training and information. These salespeople represent thousands of organizations of all sizes, types and locations around the world. The training and information they sell spans all audiences, subjects and methods of delivery.

This chapter draws on that vast experience to present norms and benchmarks for selling training and information face-to-face.

There's information here that will help you personally sell and help you build and manage the face-to-face sales of others.

Face-to-face selling is a complicated, professional business. The best salespeople are so good they can devote an entire career to this form of selling, then make even more money in retirement telling others how they did it. Clearly, no chapter -- or book -- will have everything you need for success. But the resources here, and in the appendix *References and Resources*, should be a good start.

Here's Something Curious:

No training supplier I know has successfully married direct marketing and face-to-face selling. They're either good at one or the other, but not both. For example, American Management Association, the world's largest direct marketer of business seminars, sells over $100 million annually by direct mail, but less than $5 million face-to-face. Other strong direct marketers with few face-to-face sales include CareerTrack, Learning Group, Fred Pryor, SkillPath and The Society of Manufacturing Engineers.

On the other extreme, Learning International, the world's largest sales training organization, sells nearly $100 million annually through their 100-person, worldwide sales marketing. Other strong face-to-face sales organizations with little direct marketing include Development Dimensions International, The Forum Corporation, Wilson Learning, and Zenger-Miller.

Why this polarization? It comes down to people and personalities. When two sales methods coexist, those involved in each see the other as a threat and often work to reduce or eliminate it. There's even evidence for this "immune system reaction": Mergers between one training firm expert in direct marketing and another expert in face-to-face selling have ended up by one method replacing the other in the combined organizations.

EIGHT BENCHMARKS FOR SELLING TRAINING FACE-TO-FACE

This section presents the most important statistics for selling training face-to-face. Use them to gauge your own selling efforts and to evaluate the economics of this sales method for your products/services. The table at the bottom of this page summarizes these eight statistics, which are described in the following sections.

Three of these statistics need to be reduced proportionately for less than full-time selling (a full-time equivalent sales-person or FTESP below). Obviously, a salesperson selling only one day each week will only make one-fifth the calls, handle one-fifth the accounts and produce one-fifth the sales of a full-time salesperson. The remaining five statistics are the same for full-time or part-time selling.

6 - 9 Months or More to Close a New-Customer Sale

It's measured from the first contact until the product is delivered and the bill paid. Today, some salespeople report first sale times as long as 18 - 24 months. This long sales cycle results from the complex nature of the sale and from the need for customers to involve many people in the buying decision. It also has to do with coordinating schedules and other practical considerations.

1. 6 - 9 Months (or Longer) to Close a New-Customer Sale.
2. 5 - 10 Face-to-Face Calls (or More) to Close a New-Customer Sale.
3. Annual Sales Per Full-Time Equivalent Salesperson (FTESP):

1st Year:	$ 50,000 -	$ 125,000
2nd Year:	$300,000 -	$ 600,000
3rd Year:	$500,000 -	$1,000,000

4. 70% - 80% of Sales Are Repeat Business with Current Customers.
5. Proposal Win Ratio:

    First Sale to New Customers: 1:2 to 1:3

    Follow-On Sales to Current Customers: 8:10 to 10:10

6. $5,000-$50,000 First Sale to New Customer (Grows with Experience)
7. 30 - 40 Active Accounts per Full-Time Equivalent Salesperson (FTESP).
8. 8 - 10 Face-to-Face Calls Made Weekly per FTESP.

The long sales cycle dominates everything about selling training face-to-face. It dramatically alters which salespeople will be successful and how they are measured and motivated.

5 - 10 Face-to-Face Calls to Close a New-Customer Sale

Sales and Marketing Management magazine, National Sales Executives Club, Cahners, McGraw-Hill (prior to 1989) and others have compiled statistics on this important sales measure. The number is consistent across capital equipment, consumer goods, material and most services.

Here's how many face-to-face calls are required to close a sale in general:

On the first call 2.0%
On the second call 3.0%
On the third call 4.0%
On the fourth call 10.0%
On the fifth and later call 81.0%

These figures apply to big-ticket training sales as well, requiring an average of between five and ten face-to-face calls to close the first sale with a new customer.

This helps explain why most training sales are made by a local salesperson. It's hard to arrange all those face-to-face meetings if you have to board a plane for each one. In fact, most organizations selling training face-to-face soon learn that they need a local presence to adequately *serve* their clients as well as to sell them.

Training's multi-call selling invalidates almost everything written about one-call selling. Fortunately, there are some good resources listed later in this chapter and in the References and Resources Appendix.

One Full-Time Salesperson Can Sell $1 Million a Year

Surprisingly, this number also turns out to be remarkably consistent across a wide variety of different types of professional and information services and products. Overall, a training salesperson in their third (or later) year, can be expected to produce between one-half million and one million dollars of annual sales. And there are many who sell more: In a recent survey, nearly 20% of more than 1,000 training salespeople were in the "Million-Dollar Club."

Early-years sales are greatly reduced for two reasons: (1.) There's a "learning curve" for this unique kind of selling, and (2.) the long sales cycle rules out "quick" sales early in a new salesperson's career.

Sales people reach full productivity fastest in experienced, face-to-face sales organizations, and more slowly if they're working alone.

70% - 80% of Sales Are Repeat Business with Current Customers

KASET, a leading customer service trainer, finds it's four to six times cheaper to keep a current customer than to get a new one to replace them if they leave. It's even more expensive for training because of the long sales cycle. And, indeed, established training companies regularly report 70% to 80% of their sales from this source, often more.

Of course, reliance on this relatively easier, repeat business can be risky. It can lead to dependence on -- and vulnerability to -- just a few major customers. That's why many experienced training sales organizations insist that a certain fraction of each salesperson's sales must come from new accounts. And they reinforce these policies with quotas, compensation and other incentives.

Win 1 out of Every 2 - 3 New Customer Proposals

Here's another benchmark that's consistent across a wide variety of training, consulting and information products and services. But it's important to distinguish between new business -- a first sale to a new customer -- and repeat or follow-on business with an established customer.

Repeat-business-proposal win ratios as high as 80% to 100% are common. Why? Because working closely with a customer usually leads to written "proposals" only for work that's already been agreed to in advance. The only reason such a proposal would *not* win is some change in the customer's need, organization, budget, etc. I know one training salesperson who has closed her entire annual sales quota in January with a single phone call to her best customer, followed by a one-page letter "proposal" confirming the phone conversation.

The situation is different if the proposal is for the first sale to a new customer. Here it's acceptable to win between one out of two and one out of three proposals you submit. If you win more than one out of two, you're probably being too restrictive and could do better by submitting more proposals. If you win fewer than one out of three proposals to new customers, you probably need to tighten your process for screening opportunities so you submit fewer, but better targeted, proposals.

$5,000 - $50,000 Average First Sale to a New Customer

The size of the first order will vary considerably depending on what's being sold and on salesperson experience. Inexperienced salespeople usually settle for a much smaller order than they will later.

The lower limit is important. It's difficult for face-to-face sales to work at all with average orders much less than about $5,000, be-cause the number of sales calls required (and other costs) makes it difficult for salespeople to earn enough money. This isn't a problem when the first order is small, but you can count on larger amounts for the second and subsequent orders. We've already seen that a high percentage of training sales are repeat orders, so a low initial order that kicks off a new-customer relationship, can have very good long-term payoff.

30 - 40 Active Accounts per Full-Time Salesperson

This benchmark reflects both new and experienced salespersons, as well as new and current accounts. Given the previous salesperson productivity figures, it follows that new salespeople in new territories will usually have more active accounts, while experienced salespeople in established territories will generally have fewer.

8 - 10 Sales Calls per Week

This reflects a full-time salesperson in a metropolitan area and includes the associated correspondence, phone calls, paperwork and travel. In geographically large territories (for example, Los Angeles) this might be reduced to 6 - 8 calls per week.

THE NINE-STEP SALES PIPELINE MODEL

The above benchmarks show that selling training face-to-face is a complex process that takes months or even years. How can you tell where you are during this long time? More importantly, how can you tell what to do next to advance the sale towards its successful conclusion?

Every successful salesperson -- and sales organization -- finds that they need some kind of pattern or "normal" sales process against which they can compare any particular sale to see how it's going. We call that model a *sales pipeline*.

Why Call It a Pipeline?

For me, the word "pipeline" conjures up exactly the right image. There's a reservoir at one end and through the pipe flows a liquid, around bends and corners, past leaky joints and other pipes siphoning it off.

It's just like face-to-face selling. The reservoir is the universe of prospects. At the end of the pipeline are satisfied customers who paid their bills. In between are all of the bends, turns and twists that sales inevitably take.

And like other pipelines, the sales pipeline "leaks." As the relationship progresses toward the sale, there remain fewer and fewer of those that start. Your local water company knows how many houses are connected to its pipeline to make sure there's enough pressure at the start so you get water when you turn on your faucet. And you need to make sure there are enough prospective clients coming in at the start of your sales pipeline so the number remaining at the end are sufficient to meet your sales needs.

Why Use Observable Customer Action?

Take a moment to think about some activities that occur on the way to a successful sale. You might quickly identify the following:

- Send literature
- Call for an appointment
- Request customer information
- Make sales presentations
- Write proposal
- Deliver product (or service)
- Send the bill

These are steps in the sales process all right. But they're all actions *you* take.

Experienced salespeople quickly learn to gauge their progress by what the *customer* does, not by what *they*, the salespeople, do. There are two good reasons for this important shift in focus. First, it gives you the only clear way to tell where you are in the process; what the customer does or doesn't do is, after all, what you're really interested in. Second, it tells you what the *next* step in the process must be and, therefore, what next action you should take to accomplish it.

Examples of customer-initiated actions that might replace the salesperson actions above are:

- Asks you for literature
- Schedules (and keeps) an appointment for your meeting
- Gives you reports, organization charts or other information
- Asks you to submit a proposal
- Sends you a purchase order

- Holds a meeting to kick off your project
- Says your product did more than they expected
- Pays your bill

Each of these actions is easily measured: You can tell *if* it happened and *when*.

Nine Critical Selling Steps.

The following paragraphs describe a Nine-Step Face-to-Face Sales Pipeline based on such customer actions. This pipeline was developed for training but applies to other products and services as well.

The diagram on the next page summarizes the steps. The progression in height of the bars suggests the larger numbers that are required at earlier stages in the process to get one account with a paid bill at the end. Clearly, the exact numbers of prospects required at each stage will vary, depending on what you're selling and to whom you're selling it. Here's what each of the nine steps represents:

1. Suspect. This is the start or "reservoir" for your pipeline. Although, in principle, it could be anyone, in practice your suspects are a much smaller group: those who, you believe, have a need for and can possibly buy your services or products.

You must define the characteristics of this group precisely to focus your prospecting efforts, select mailing lists and get a better "handle" on the market that you serve.

The observable customer characteristics that help identify a suspect includes their position, industry, type of business, organization size and similar variables (see Chapter 2).

2. Inquiry Received. This is the first pipeline step indicating possible interest in *your* services or products -- *any* indication of customer interest, regardless of how it was stimulated. Their action could be triggered by some kind of lead-getting activity, publicity about you, a referral from another customer, receipt of your brochure or a request to correct their mailing address. The observable here is that the prospective customer has done *something* to indicate some interest in you, your products or your services. The prospect "nodded favorably in your direction."

Nine-Step Sales Pipeline Based on Observable Customer Action

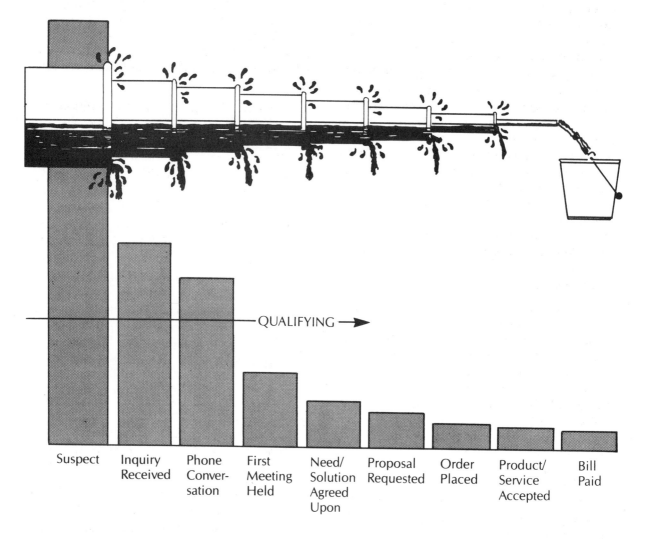

3. Phone Conversation Held. This is the next normal step in the face-to-face selling process. The height of the bar suggests that a high percentage of the inquiries received will be followed up by telephone to explore the prospect's interest and to determine whether further action is warranted. For some sales situations, this step might be skipped entirely, for example, if the evidence of interest was part of a preview or showcase presentation during which the first face-to-face meeting occurred.

If you can't have a phone conversation, then try to set up the first meeting some other way, using mail, Fax, voice mail or E-mail. This might happen if the prospect is too busy to take your call or if your schedule won't allow you call them. But remember, we're try-

ing to focus on observable *customer* behavior. Their willingness to take your phone call and speak to you is an indication of their interest and qualifies them to move to the next step. Your sending them a letter won't accomplish the same purpose until they answer it.

Your telephone conversation will enable you to further "qualify" the inquiry, determining whether a face-to-face meeting is warranted. When in doubt, however, don't try to qualify the prospect on the telephone; merely confirm your receipt of their inquiry and set up a face-to-face meeting to furnish the information that they've requested.

4. First Meeting Held. Some sales situations actually begin at this step, for example, if they result from your participation in a conference or if you've conducted a preview, showcase or seminar. But most face-to-face meetings will take place in the prospect's office, and so you'll need to go through the normal procedures to set a date, confirm it and actually have the meeting.

The first meeting will often show if there's a fit between the prospect's needs and your products or services. Often, the first meeting with one individual will quickly lead during the same visit to a number of other first meetings, culminating finally in a first meeting with somebody whose needs *do* fit your products or services. This is an example of how your relationship with this final party actually *begins* with the first meeting held. This also shows how the first meeting could terminate the selling relationship with the person you originally met if, for example, this were the wrong person.

5. Need/Solution Agreed Upon. At this step in the process you thoroughly understand the prospect's need, and they thoroughly understand what your solution or services can mean to them. In effect they say, "Yes, your services will really help us and we'd like to buy them." By then the prospect knows what your services are going to cost, how long they will take to deliver, etc. In other words, at this stage everything has been agreed upon -- but the order hasn't yet been placed.

This can happen at the first meeting (rarely), or it can happen on the twenty-first meeting (also rarely). This is the most time-consuming part of the sales cycle. The earlier steps can often be handled in a few days or a few weeks. But this step can take months or even years. Because of the long time required to complete this step, changes in the client's situation can have a profound effect. For instance, in large companies, a reorganization can often replace the person you've been cultivating, forcing you to "start over." Or needs that were clear at the start of the process may be different months later. For these reasons, it's important that you *try* to accomplish this step as quickly as possible, recognizing that it is the customer, not you, who will determine how long it will take.

6. Proposal Requested. Don't overlook this step! Occasionally the customer won't formally request the proposal but merely ask you to confirm your discussions in writing. In that case, a simple letter can satisfy the customer's request. Under very informal conditions, this step could be skipped and included with the next step of the client placing the order.

7. Order Placed. Or, what's traditionally called, "the close." In a good training sale, it's merely a confirmation of the details already agreed upon. If there are any surprises remaining for you or the customer at this point, then you've not successfully completed one of the previous steps.

This is a good place to recall a helpful model Larry Wilson used to compare the long-cycle, multi-call training sale to traditional selling:

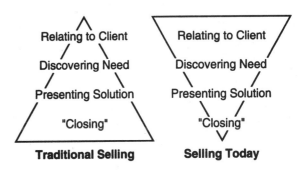

The width of each triangle in the diagram represents the relative amount of time spent in that activity.

8. Product or Service Accepted. Not every order that's placed is actually delivered, and not every product delivered is accepted by the customer. But these occurrences are rare in training -- if you don't promise more than you can deliver.

9. Bill Paid. Finally! If the sale has been structured properly, this will be virtually 100% of the sales situations that make it through the previous step. But not always: Inexperienced salespeople frequently get orders without the customer knowing clearly that they had to pay or how much. Such misunderstandings signal clearly that one or more of the earlier steps in the process was not properly executed.

HOW TO GET GOOD SALES LEADS

The marketing activities that best support face-to-face selling of training programs are, in descending order:

Stay in Touch with Current and Past Customers

Repeat business with current and past customers makes up 70% - 80% of established training suppliers sales. So you're overlooking the biggest piece if you don't stay in touch with your current and past customers. (We recommend at least 6 contacts per year.) Besides, "lovin' 'em and leavin' 'em" is the most common complaint training customers have about their suppliers. There are some great "stay-in-touch" ideas in Chapter 11.

Target Those You Want to Do Business With

When going after new, big company accounts you can easily learn with a few phone calls the exact names and positions of every single person you want to do business with. The challenge is to get them to want to do business with you. That's what takes time and requires all the techniques in this book -- and then some. Targeting this way is often better than some mass-marketing approach.

Hold Showcases/Previews

Free overviews, introductions or "try-me-ons" are good support for face-to-face sales. This is one way to get to meet those you targeted in the previous idea. In fact, it's become so important, Chapter 10 is devoted exclusively to this topic.

Use Open Registration Seminars

Attendees at open registration events are a gold mine of face-to-face sales leads, particularly if the training you're selling is in the same format. But telephone follow-up with attendees MUST occur within the first three (3) working days after the event! If there's interest, you can schedule a meeting for a few days later. (See Chapter 6 for more on open registration events.)

Open registration events also produce face-to-face leads a second way: Your advertising itself will generate inquiries for in-house/on-site presentations of the advertised course. Most such inquiries will NOT convert into sales without active, face-to-face selling, so immediately telephone each such inquirer to qualify them for face-to-face follow-up.

Work Expos, Trade Shows and Conferences

These are a "must" if your competitors are there. At least one show a year will probably pay off in your core market, possibly more. But participation in such events means more than just renting a booth. Chapter 12 has a section devoted to this activity.

Use Direct Mail

Direct mail is a reliable, if not exciting, face-to-face lead getter, producing 1% - 2% response rates after a little tuning. Direct mail responders *must* be screened/qualified *before* they're turned over to the salespeople; otherwise, the poor prospects in the group will cause the salespeople to devalue all such leads. (See Chapters 7, 8 and 9.)

Use Display Advertising for the Right Reasons

In spite of what you've read, this form of advertising has limited impact on training sold face-to-face. If it worked, there'd be a dozen training magazines, each jammed with advertising. Instead we have three magazines, each with a pitiful few ads. But display ads show your salespeople that you love them. And, like trade shows, you can't afford NOT to advertise if your direct competitors do. (For more on advertising, see Chapter 12.)

FACE-TO-FACE SELLING TIPS

Manage Your Activity

It's ACTIVITY that counts -- so spend part of every day/week selling. Track calls, appointments, proposals -- everything -- over a weekly (not monthly or quarterly) basis. For new salespeople, or those just entering selling, the diagram on the next page shows how your time might be divided among the nine pipeline steps during your first three years.

Ask Questions

Spend your time ASKING QUESTIONS to find the customer's critical problem. Doing anything else is a waste of time. Neil Rackham's wonderful book *SPIN Selling*, described in the next section, is a key resource here.

Short Sales Cycles Often Reflect "Cherry Picking"

Training salespeople with consistently short sales cycles may be selling primarily to "hot" leads rather than to accounts they've developed over the long-term. It also may mean there's a lot more sales potential in their territory than they've tapped.

It's as Easy to Sell the Whole Project as It Is to Sell Just Part of It

Once salespeople develop confidence in their ability to sell training, they'll generally find it's as easy to close an *entire* series of on-sites as it is to close a single "pilot" presentation. As a result, the average order size usually grows rapidly. The same applies to train-the-trainer sales.

Be Ready to Meet Large Volume Orders on Short Notice

As average order size -- and customer commitment to large training populations -- increases, customers will inevitably move toward licensing (training of their trainers). It's helpful to keep this in mind as sales grow, so that the ability to train trainers can be activated on short notice. Often Fortune 100 companies will ask for the training of many trainers right away. This train-the-trainer capability will also be important if your capacity to deliver on-sites is to keep pace with the increased ability to sell them.

Don't Fool Yourself that the Telephone Will Do

The telephone has its place in selling, both supporting face-to-face sales and closing publications and product business (see Chapter 3). But it isn't a substitute for face-to-face selling on big-ticket accounts. All our clients who tried found their sales plummet when face-to-face meetings decline.

Develop Standard Products

Most successful firms insist on "standardized" products which have more-or-less "automatic" tailoring to the client. You need to achieve a situation where the clients invariably perceive your program as tailored to their specific needs, whereas your instructional staff routinely perceives the program as delivered the same every time. This sounds impossible, but it actually works out in practice to be the norm rather than the exception.

Sell Training Face-to-Face Within Your Own Organization

If you're selling training within your own organization, face-to-face involves presentations at team meetings and arranging one-on-one sessions with key managers/decision-makers who commit people and/or budgets. Acquiring even a few basic face-to-face skills can really pay off in this setting. And the Pipeline model remains valid too.

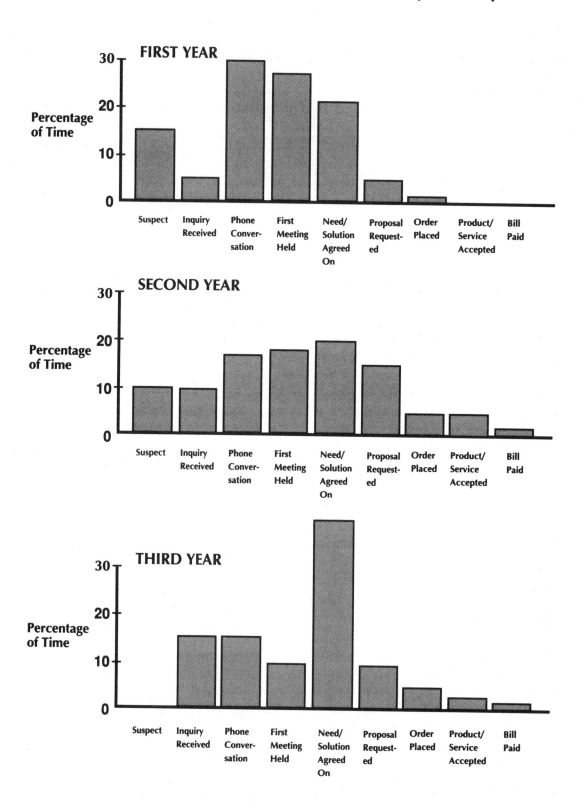

How Sales Time Is Divided Among the Nine Pipeline Steps

PIPELINE STEPS

WHERE TO GET FACE-TO-FACE SELLING HELP

Developing your own face-to-face selling skills is a big job -- and an important one. It's beyond the scope of this book to describe it in detail. Instead, we'll provide some carefully selected resources:

The Best Books

Conventional wisdom is, "You can't learn selling from a book." And it makes sense, since selling is an art form. Nonetheless, here are six great books by the three authors cited most often by the top training salespeople:

1. Conceptual Selling, by Robert B. Miller and Stephen E. Heiman. Miller-Heiman, Inc., 1595 Meadow Wood Lane, Suite 2, Reno, NV 89502. Phone: (702) 827-4411. 1987. $18.50.

2. Strategic Selling: The Unique Sales System Proven Successful by America's Best Companies, by Robert B. Miller, Stephen E. Heiman and Tad Tuleja. William Morrow & Co., New York, NY. 1985. 352 pages. $19.95.

Bob Miller was top sales executive for Kepner-Tregoe Associates, one of the premier training companies, and arguably the first to field a world-wide, face-to-face salesforce. His approach to selling was developed and refined for training products and services. These books contain everything the authors teach in their acclaimed 2-day programs. The Miller-Heiman concept for making complex sales works to remove the element of "luck" from selling and replaces it with proven, visible, repeatable skills.

3. S.P.I.N. Selling, by Neil Rackham. McGraw-Hill, New York, NY. 1988. 197 pages, $22.95.

4. Major Account Sales Strategy, by Neil Rackham. Also McGraw-Hill, $21.50.

5. Managing Major Sales, by Neil Rackham. Harper & Row, New York, NY. 1991. $27.95.

The first Rackham title doesn't refer to managing perceptions. It's an acronym for Situation, Problem, Implication, Need-payoff, a 4-step face-to-face selling model based on Rackham's 12-year research into effective big-ticket selling. It focuses on salesperson behaviors that are best in multi-call situations -- which are quite different from those in traditional, single-call selling. Rackham's other books also reflect his research-based approach to selling.

6. Changing The Game: The New Way to Sell by Larry Wilson. Simon & Schuster, New York, NY. 1987. 286 pages. $8.95.

An insightful perspective on how today's multi-call, relationship selling is fundamentally different from traditional selling, by one of the masters of selling training. Thought-provoking and very helpful.

Sales Training

Take time to learn basic selling skills. They'll help you in many areas of your life, not just in business. Here's a list of some of the most prominent U.S. sales training firms. Obviously, there are many others. Most offer open registration classes during and outside normal working hours, as well as custom-designed courses for organizations.

AMERICAN MANAGEMENT ASSOCIATION
135 West 50th St.
New York, NY 10020-1201
Phone: (212) 586-8100, Fax: (212) 903-8168
Mr. David Fagiano, CEO & President

AMERICAN MARKETING ASSOCIATION
250 So. Wacker Drive, Suite 200
Chicago, IL 60606-5834
Phone: (312) 648-0536
Mr. Elvin J. Schofield, President

DALE CARNEGIE & ASSOCIATES, INC.
1475 Franklin Avenue
Garden City, NY 11530-1613
Phone: (516) 248-5100
Mr. J. Oliver Crom, President & CEO

B. J. CHAKIRIS CORPORATION
900 North Shore Drive, Suite 214
Lake Bluff, IL 60044-2225
Phone: (708) 295-6220, Fax: (708) 295-6386
Ms. Betty June Chakiris, President

THE FORUM CORPORATION
One Exchange Place
Boston, MA 02109
Phone: (617) 523-7300, Fax: (617) 723-5806
Mr. Richard C. Whiteley, Vice Chairman

LEARNING INTERNATIONAL
22 High Ridge Road, Box 10211
Stamford, CT 06904-2211
Phone: (203) 965-8444, Fax: (203) 965-8602
Mr. John J. Franco, President

MILLER-HEIMAN, INC.
1595 Meadow Wood Lane, Suite 2
Reno, NV 89502
Phone: (702) 827-4411
Mr. Stephen Heiman, Chairman

NATIONAL SOCIETY OF SALES TRAINING
EXECUTIVES
1275 Kamus Drive
Fox Island, WA 98333
Mr. Chuck Harper, Administrative Manager

MAX SACKS INTERNATIONAL
1960 E. Grand Avenue, Suite 560
El Segundo, CA 90245-5040
Phone: (310) 640-3380, Fax: (310) 640-2269
Mr. Roy E. Chitwood, President

SALES & MARKETING EXECUTIVES INTER-
NATIONAL
1127 Euclid Avenue, Suite 458
Cleveland, OH 44115
Phone: (216) 771-6652
Mr. Jack Criswell, Executive Director

SALES SKILLS INSTITUTE
705 Mall Germain
St. Cloud, MN 56301
Phone: (612) 253-8390

SYSTEMA CORPORATION
60 Revere Drive - Suite 600
Northbrook, IL 60062-1563
Phone: (312) 498-9530, Fax: (312) 498-9176
Mr. Jack R. Snader, Chief Executive Officer

TBA RESOURCES, INC.
1317 Third Avenue, 9th Floor
New York, NY 10021
Phone: (212) 288-1897, Fax: (212) 288-4376
Mr. Thomas N. Blodgett, Chief Executive Officer

WILSON LEARNING CORPORATION
7500 Flying Cloud Drive
Eden Prairie, MN 55344-3795
Phone: (612) 944-2880, Fax: (612) 828-8835
Mr. David M. Ehlen, Chief Executive Officer

THE ZIG ZIGLAR CORPORATION
3330 Earhart, Suite 204
Carrollton, TX 75006-5026
Phone: (800) 527-0306
Mr. Jim Norman, President & CEO

CHARACTERISTICS OF SUCCESSFUL TRAINING SALES ORGANIZATIONS

Sales Management Skill Is Critical

Successful training sales managers are good at motivating salespeople. The sales manager who is not able to keep his or her new salesperson "up" for months at a time, until their sales start closing, will not be successful. As a consequence, many of the most successful salespeople in this business do *not* make a successful transition into sales management.

Manage Activity, Not Sales

The long sales cycle makes it impossible to gauge the likely success of new salespeople by measuring sales -- or even booked orders. It's necessary to measure salesperson *activity*, against some objective model, like the Nine-Step Pipeline model described earlier. Statistics on how accounts move through the pipeline show new salesperson progress. And the skilled sales manager observes this activity frequently, no less often than weekly.

Commissions Are a Poor Early Motivator

The long sales cycle and many sales calls necessitates a different means of managing, motivating and controlling a sales force than for other businesses. In particular, commissions are a poor early motivator, because a new salesperson may not get their first commission check for nearly a year after hire.

Model Big-Ticket Sales Excellence

Many training organizations model their sales management process after that followed by IBM, Xerox, Hewlett-Packard and other organizations that sell expensive, complex products and services into large organizations.

Have Regional Sales Offices

The large number of sales calls, and the need to make multiple sales calls before closing, means most successful training companies tend to have a regionally based sales force. In concentrated areas like New York, Washington, San Francisco and Chicago, regional offices are staffed with a manager, one or more salespersons and one or more administrative support personnel. In smaller regions, a salesperson might work out of his/her home and have only part-time support.

Hire Proven Sales Ability

The typical training salesperson today is in their late 20's to early 30's, has an MBA, and is very conceptual. In fact, the ability to conceptualize and high personal versatility are two important hallmarks for success for some of the sales organizations. (Personal versatility is the ability to deal with people of greatly different styles and personalities, without causing any of them to feel uncomfortable). Many of the top producers are women.

Some of the best organizations find that two-thirds to three-fourths of their salespeople have already acquired basic sales skills before they're hired and have demonstrated them by above-quota performance against aggressive sales targets in two or more consecutive years. These people can then learn the training business.

The remaining one-third of the salespeople get "turned on" to sales through teaching but are quick enough to learn what they need to know about selling to become successful.

Hire 2 or 3 to Get One Good One

Salesperson attrition in this business is high. About 40% of all salespersons hired do not remain beyond the first year, and one-half to two-thirds are gone by the third year. A rule of thumb is hire two or three to get one that works out. This rather poor track record also exists among those organizations that teach

sales skills and sales management as their principle product lines.

Could this be why so many of the training firms that use face-to-face selling were started by salespeople? Could this be why many training firms started by a charismatic, "natural" salesperson have had repeated failures in hiring a top salesperson?

Choose Employee Salespeople over Commissioned Representatives

Most commissioned sales representatives are unwilling to invest the time and money necessary for deep penetration of large accounts. They tend to work more on "hot leads" and on business they can close on the phone or with minimum travel. Nonetheless, representatives can be a very productive source of business, albeit only a fraction of what an employee salesperson can produce.

Managers instinctively feel that a salaried sales force is much riskier than commissioned representatives. But industry experience suggests exactly the reverse: Sales representatives take almost as much management time as salaried salespeople but produce on average only one-third to one-fifth the sales. That's why organizations that have tried both (Schrello Associates, Forum, Wilson, Blessing/White, etc.) have invariably chosen the salaried sales force. Wilson, Blessing/White and a few others still use representatives, but only in territories where they don't have salaried salespeople.

Incentivize New Accounts

As a salesperson matures in a territory, more and more of their business is repeat orders from established customers, and less and less come from new accounts. This increases the vulnerability of the territory (and the salesperson) to sudden actions by their established accounts. To eliminate this problem, some companies routinely "rotate" accounts among salespersons so that no one person gets "locked in" to an account. Alternatively, continued hiring of new salespersons in a territory can force the redistribution of accounts and thereby encourage new-account development.

Hire Early In The Year

Because of the long sales cycle, it is usually best to hire people early in the fiscal period or budget for no new revenue for at least six to nine months after hiring.

Have Adequate Start-Up Cash

When hiring a new face-to-face salesperson, have at least $100,000 of risk capital. This will cover their base salary, expenses and a training allowance in lieu of commissions. It's roughly double what you'll need if their productivity increases per plan. The diagram at the bottom of the page shows what might happen if -- for example -- the new salesperson's start-up is one quarter late.

Manage for Early Successes

It is very important to have early successes. So the salespersons hired first should be the very best you can find. In this respect, using a "headhunter" is far more efficient. (See Finding Good Sales Candidates in the next section.)

Price Custom Training to Make Money

Avoid excessive sale of customized or truly tailored training products without charging a customizing fee. Most sales people find it easier to promise the customer a highly individualized program in order to close the sale. But if this requires a great deal of professional effort to accomplish, you can lose lots of money in short order.

Salesperson Start-Up Costs

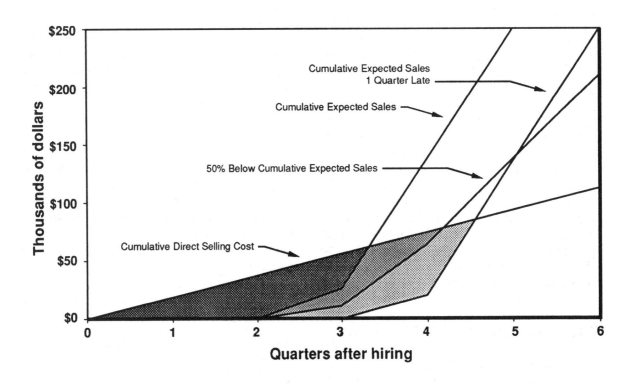

FINDING GOOD SALES CANDIDATES

Look In-House First

Look at current employees who are selling part-time. Is there one whose sales productivity is consistent with the amount of time they've been working? Are they capable of producing more sales if they spend more time selling?

Ask for Referrals

Ask your employees, friends, associates -- even customers -- who might be able to refer someone to you. The best source of employees is usually referral. Don't be disappointed if a good sales candidate doesn't turn up (they're pretty rare). Still, you wouldn't want to overlook a good candidate obtainable this way just in case they *are* there.

Decide Whether to Advertise Yourself or Use a "Headhunter"

Once you've concluded you need to go outside, you have two choices: Use an employment agency (a "headhunter") or obtain candidates yourself. The choice is based upon the amount of time and money you can spend. The headhunter provides pre-screened candidates whom you can then further interview. They'll charge you between 10% - 25% of the hiree's first-year compensation. To do it yourself, you'll need to advertise and then screen the responses. If lots of people are looking for work, you'll have to screen a huge volume of resumes. On the other hand, if few people are looking for work, you may have trouble finding enough good candidates by advertising yourself. Either way, a headhunter usually provides a more reliable route, especially if time is short.

Start with a Good Job Description

Whether you use an agency or do it yourself, the process starts with a good job description that includes a brief description of your firm, the kinds of products/services that will be sold, the market that will be targeted, including managerial level, industry, geographic location and any other important descriptors.

Advertise Where the Best Candidates Will Look

If you decide to advertise yourself, a small ad in a publication read by salespeople (not trainers) works best. Many training firms have had success with ads in the opportunities section of the *Wall Street Journal*, the *New York Times*, the *Los Angeles Times*, and other major regional newspapers. Use a P.O. Box to reduce the volume of acknowledgment paperwork and also to discourage contacts by headhunters trying to sell you their services. An ad like those shown on the next page, placed in the Tuesday, Wednesday or Thursday *Wall Street Journal* will often draw 200 to 400 responses nationwide. A similar ad in the Sunday edition of a major regional paper can easily draw 30 to 50 replies.

In general, you'd like your ad to attract the smallest volume of replies that are likely to contain the best candidates. In this case "best" means most highly motivated to find you. Concentrate your ad on the type of product/service you sell and the market you wish to reach, and don't waste space on your benefits or other puffery.

Pick a Proven Headhunter

If you decide to use a headhunter, demand one who has successfully found salespeople for other training companies. Most agencies develop experience in a few industries and are less successful in others. Besides, screening training salespeople requires a unique set of skills that takes time to learn.

If you're seeking salespeople on a national basis, here are headhunters that training firms tell me they've used successfully:

ABBOTT SMITH ASSOCIATES, INC.
P.O. Box 318
Millbrook, NY 12545
Phone: (914) 677-5300; Fax: (914) 677-3315
Contact: David Brinkerhoff, President

Representative Salesperson "Help Wanted" Ads

SALES/MANAGEMENT

Quarter billion dollar int'l corp. seeks exceptional direct sales professional to spark plug new sales team. Commission/override/residual/car allowance to $86K in 1989, $120K in 1990 for high energy, work-alone producer. Candidates must document $80K earnings history for interview. Send resume and documentation to: **Sales Director, 1111 N. Main, Anytown, NY 10016.**

SALES REPRESENTATIVES

Fast growing, well-established computer company engaged in the vertical market sales of computer systems to distributors throughout the U.S. is seeking sales representatives for selected cities. Applicants must have a driving desire to succeed with substantial experience in the computer marketplace and organizational skills. We offer salary, bonuses and commission of $50,000+ and an excellent benefits package. Send resume to **Director of Sales and Marketing, Fairfield Products, Inc., 19 W. College, College-town, PA 19103.**

Sales Representative

Medical Center has excellent opportunity for a Sales Representative for Industrial Medicine in our Marketing Department.

Major responsibilities will include directing sales to targeted groups, data collection, analysis and reporting, and implementation of a customer service/satisfaction plan. You will also participate in program development and service enhancement activities.

We are seeking a highly motivated self-starter with direct sales experience in a health or medically related service (occupational health services preferred); a Bachelor's degree in business, marketing, or related area; excellent oral/written communication and organizational skills; knowledge of word processing and database management; and the ability to work independently.

Please send resume to **Marketing Department, Medical Center, 1601 Valley Road, Centerville, CA 94561.**

An Equal Opportunity Employer

SALES CONSULTANT

We are a highly respected int'l consulting firm focusing on productivity improvement. Growth requires that we hire a West Coast V.P. Sales who will manage a high-profile sales force as well as participate in direct selling/closing at the presidential level.

You must be able to demonstrate a strong background in executive sales and hopefully be an entrepreneurial individual who prefers a compensation system based on a high commission in addition to base salary. Our sales professionals make substantially more than their counterparts in other productivity consulting firms.

For immediate consideration, please submit resume in strict confidence to:

**Box MN222,
The Journal.**

Equal Opportunity Employer M/F

SALES/MARKETING PROFESSIONAL

Multinational company with growth strategy is in need of a professional sales and marketing executive in one of its technology-driven businesses. Applicants for this management position should have extensive experience in sales of high-priced projects and demonstrated ability to develop effective marketing strategies.

Excellent products await aggressive marketing and excellent technology awaits creative application to customer needs. Location is near an attractive urban center with first-rate recreational assets nearby. Position has high international visibility and potential for promotion. If interested, send resume and salary requirements to
Box MP345, The Times.

Sales Representative

An energetic self-starter who works well with minimal supervision can have an exciting, satisfying, and rewarding career with a company that has a 75-year history of servicing corporate America in a very specialized field. Mature, positive self-image, confidence, and determination are essential characteristics at management levels with which we are involved. Successful sales background, understanding of business organization, creative approach to problem solving and basic PC skills would describe a very attractive candidate. If you are ready to consider a career change that will enable you to run your own show and build a successful repeat business, send your resume to:

**Box BB229
The Tribune.**

CONSULTANTS/TRAINERS

International firm expanding in U.S. needs independent consultants and trainers to represent our company. We offer some of the finest human resource development programs available today. Very high income potential. Extensive training and support. Management, marketing or consulting experience helpful. Send resume or brief history to:

**Research Association,
P. O. Box 981
Yourtown, IL 60622.**

SALES CONSULTANTS
1127 Euclid, Suite 1400
Cleveland, OH 44115
Phone: (800) 875-4000
Contact: Alan Schonberg, President

SALES CONSULTANTS
480 Roland Way, Suite 103
Oakland, CA 94621
Phone: (415) 421-9450
Contact: Tom Thrower, General Manager

This is a fluid business so don't assume there aren't other -- or better -- training salesperson recruiters by the time you read this.

For a comprehensive overview, one of the best sources of recruiter information, is:

The Directory of Executive Recruiters, James H. Kennedy, Editor. Kennedy Publications, Templeton Road, Fitzwilliam, NH 03447. Phone: (800) 531-0007, (605) 585-6544; Fax: (604) 585-9555. 1992. Available in two forms: An 800-page, 5-1/2" x 8-1/2" paperback at $39.95 and a corporate edition, also 800 pages, but 8-1/2" x 11" and hardcover for $79.00.

The smaller version lists contact data on 5,500 search-firm principals in 2,200 firms with 3,600 offices in the U.S., Canada and Mexico. The larger edition, intended for human resource and other executives who retain search firms, includes 30-word descriptions, telephone numbers, staff sizes and revenues, plus 100 pages of text on using executive recruiters.

Look Behind the Slick Resume

Today, you'll likely have quite a few resumes to review. You'll have to read every one personally and try and look beyond today's "high-tech" resume composition and production to see what's really underneath. The time was, when the form of the resume or response letter was at least an indicator. But with so many resume services available, it's likely that all you see will appear highly professional. Screen them against the characteristics described earlier in this chapter. Look for evidence of existing sales ability, for that is the most difficult thing for you to provide. *Remember, you're looking for demonstrated sales ability, not potential.*

Prepare Yourself for Interviewing

There are many effective interviewing workshops, seminars, and media-based training courses, not to mention books. All will better prepare you to conduct a successful recruitment interview. They may also help keep you out of trouble with equal opportunity and discrimination laws. One of the best and most widely available classes is:

The Selection Interview Workshop
DRAKE, BEAM, MORIN, INC.
100 Park Avenue
New York, NY 10017
Phone: (212) 692-7700

This program is regularly offered in 34 U.S. cities and many foreign countries.

There's no doubt that poor interview technique is one of the leading causes of poor hiring. It is further compounded in the sales area because trainers don't hire sales people frequently enough to sharpen and maintain their interviewing skills.

Interview First by Telephone

If you're using a headhunter, move directly to interviews with the best candidates. If you're advertising yourself, the intermediate step before an interview should always be a telephone conversation with the prospect. Work from a script which you prepare prior to placing the phone call. The script should contain at least two main segments: (1.) questions that further test their abilities in selling and (2.) questions pertaining to their resume. If they haven't already said, be sure to ask why they are leaving (or have left) their current employer.

Check References

After you've finished your interviewing, you'll want to check references on the candidates you're considering. Failure to check all references is a real "no-no." The worst hiring mistake I ever made happened because I didn't call the CEO of the previous employer.

NOTES

HOW THE PROS PLAN A WORLD-CLASS MARKETING CAMPAIGN

This chapter has what you need to plan your overall marketing campaign like a professional, even if you've never done it before. It presents three important ingredients: (1.) a step-by-step marketing planning process specially designed for training and information products and services, (2.) hard-to-find planning data on direct mail response rates and on timing, and (3.) handy worksheets to help you plan. Because marketing a training *event* (like a seminar) presents its own unique planning requirements, it's discussed in added detail.

The issue is this: *How do you determine the least costly amount of marketing needed to profitably acquire the attendees, orders or sales leads you need?* If word-of-mouth and referrals pulls in all the business you need without doing *any* marketing, the answer is easy: Don't mess with success! But if this is not your situation -- or if it *is* your situation, but you want to grow -- then this chapter is for you.

Most inexperienced marketers of training and information do their planning backwards. They decide on their marketing budget, or on what kind of marketing they'll do, without regard to the sales they want to produce. They *hope* everything will turn out OK. More often than not it doesn't -- because (as you recall from Chapter 1) sales and marketing is the single most important activity for any training or information organization.

So here's how to do better. Remember, marketing training products and services is fundamentally a numbers game, so good planning begins with a clear process and an equally clear picture of the numbers you want to achieve.

Marketing Training Events Requires the Best Planning of All

Marketing events, like seminars and conferences, demands better planning for at least two reasons. First, they add a critical *time* dimension to your planning. People simply need more time to plan and schedule their attendance at something, particularly during normal business hours. Second, event *economics* is extremely sensitive to the number of attendees: You need enough to cover the event's fixed costs (much more on this in Chapter 6).

If your marketing effort produces more attendees than your event can handle, you've wasted money. But marketing that fails to fill every seat, or that results in cancelled sessions due to under-enrollment, may be even *more* wasteful. The event marketing challenge is to delicately balance three variables for your planning interval (e.g., year, half, quarter, month, ...):

- The volume of marketing/promotion you do.
- The average attendance at each event.
- The number of events you schedule.

The order here *is* important, especially for frequently offered events. When I prepare a marketing plan for an event that's offered repeatedly, the number of sessions is usually the *last* variable I set. That's because when budget, mailing lists or available media limits the amount of promotion I can do (as often happens), then marketing cost becomes essentially fixed. Now the only remaining controllable cost is the cost to hold each session -- and *those* costs are reduced by maximizing average attendance at each session. Under these circumstances, even one session too many during the planning interval can have a devastating effect on profit.

Because of these added complexities of event marketing, we'll devote special attention to events throughout this chapter and return to them again in Chapter 6.

THE PROCESS FOR PLANNING YOUR MARKETING OF TRAINING PROGRAMS AND TRAINING EVENTS

Marketing planning consists of the 14-step process shown below. Notice that five of the steps are unique to marketing events. If you are not planning your marketing for an event, just skip these steps.

Planning Steps For Marketing Training and Information

1. Select Your Product, Target Market, and Planning Interval
2. Set Your Financial Targets
3. Select Your Promotional Possibilities
4. Identify Specific Mailing Lists or Publications
5. Estimate Realistic Response Rates
6. Determine How Much Advertising You Need
7. Calculate Planned Attendees *(Events Only)*
8. Determine Number of Sessions *(Events Only)*
9. Schedule Specific Dates and Locations *(Events Only)*
10. Book Facilities *(Events Only)*
11. Prepare Master Marketing Schedule
12. Produce Marketing Materials
13. Advertise and Promote per the Master Marketing Schedule
14. Forecast Attendance *(Events Only)*

The following sections describe each step.

1. Select Your Product, Target Market, and Planning Interval

Chapter 2 contains specific help for determining your PRODUCT and your MARKET. The TIME PERIOD covered by your plan is usually one year but may be less in start-up situations. Remember, if you're planning an event that will be offered repeatedly during the interval, don't fix the number of sessions yet. That will be done in Step 8.

2. Set Your Financial Targets

The most important financial target is the PRICE, because it determines so much else, especially market response. Chapter 2 has information on prices and pricing.

But price by itself is too narrow. That's why we prefer to talk about your OFFER, which includes the base price, discounts, guarantees, premiums, etc. Also determine your overall REVENUE (desired number of attendees or sales, multiplied by the average price each pays, plus any other income obtained at or from the event or sale) and your acceptable COSTS (for selling, delivery, etc.).

And since this is relationship marketing, the lifetime value of the customer counts more than what you make on any single sale. This is explained in its own section later in this chapter.

3. Select Your Promotional Possibilities

Here's a short list of the most common methods:

- Direct Mail
- Display/Classified Ads
- Telemarketing
- Face-to-Face Selling
- Publicity
- Referrals
- Radio/TV
- Other

Use your prior experience to decide what works best. If you lack experience, use Chapter 3. It shows which methods are most effective for what kinds of training and information products and services.

Next, estimate what fraction of your sales come from each method. Again, use your prior experience or Chapter 3. For example, let's suppose you want to get 30 people to attend a $500 per-person, 2-day seminar. Let's also say you know from experience that ten of these will come from your own face-to-face contacts. That means you need to get 20 additional attendees from new sources. Let's suppose further that experience showed five of these 20 would likely come from calendar announcements placed in trade papers. Now you need only obtain the remaining 15 enrollments from direct mail.

A typical budget for marketing business training and information products and services might be divided as follows:

Direct mail	50-70%
Telemarketing	20-30%
Space ads and trade shows	10-20%
Publicity	5-10%

4. Identify Specific Mailing Lists or Publications

Identify the specific vehicle you'll use *within* each promotional method you selected in Step 3. Again, experience will be your best guide, but Chapters 3, 7 and 12 have plenty of help.

Take direct mail, for example. Here your house list -- those who have already bought from you or responded to your mailings -- can produce four to eight times the response of the best rented list. What's more, they cost only a tiny fraction of what the same quantity of rental names would cost. Here's how that difference translates into financial performance for 200 paid participants in an expensive seminar:

Profit Comparison Between Rental and House Mailing Lists

	Rental Lists	House List
Number of Paid Participants	200	200
Average Price Paid	$975	$975
Total Revenue Obtained	$195,000	$195,000
Direct Mail Response Rate	0.2 /M	0.8 /M
Number Of Pieces Mailed	1,000,000	250,000
Cost Of Mailer Less Label	$250 /M	$250 /M
Cost Of Label	$85 /M	$5 /M
Total Mailer Cost	$335 /M	$255 /M
Total Cost Of Mailing	$335,000	$63,750
Selling Cost Percent	172%	33%
Profit Contribution	($140,000)	$131,250

5. Estimate Realistic Response Rates

This is the most critical step, for mistakes here translate directly into disappointing sales results. Look at the special section later in this chapter for specific help here.

6. Determine How Much Advertising You Need

Start by ranking the specific lists or other promotional sources from Step 4 in declining order of cost-effectiveness. That is, the source likely to produce the most attendees for the least cost would be ranked first, etc.

Next, project the outgoing volume/circulation for each promotional source in the planning interval. For example, if a 5,000 name mailing list would be mailed three times, its total would be 15,000. Reflect list/media limitations, frequency tolerances, budget, etc.

Finally, select from the top-ranked sources as few as possible to get the needed sales or responses.

For example, let's suppose you're using classified ads to get sales leads. To determine the number of ads to run, you need both the total number of leads you want and an estimate of the number you can expect to get from each ad. Here's how our planning steps would look:

- 30 sales leads needed from classified ads. (From Steps 3 and 4)
- 1 Sunday classified ad produces an average of 10 good leads. (From Step 5)
- Therefore, 30 divided by 10 = 3 Sunday classified ads required. (The result of Step 6)

NOTE: The next four steps in the process are unique for marketing EVENTS. If you are not concerned with an event at this time, skip to Step 11.

7. Calculate Planned Attendees (Events Only)

Calculate PLANNED ATTENDEES during the planning interval, from each promotional source as follows: Response Rate x Volume = Total Registrations, which then must be spread over time. If the resulting planned total differs significantly from the desired total in Step 3, repeat and rebalance Steps 3-6.

8. Determine Number of Sessions (Events Only)

Determine number of SESSIONS during the planning interval to profitably handle the planned attendees. Include any limitations, such as maximum participants per session. Here it's easy to see the harmful effects on profit of scheduling even a few too many sessions. Chapter 6 has even more help in figuring this out.

9. Schedule Specific Dates and Locations (Events Only)

See Chapter 6 for help with the best months, days of the week and locations for your training events.

10. Book Facilities (Events Only)

Again, see Chapter 6 for help selecting and negotiating with hotels and meeting facilities.

11. Prepare Master Marketing Schedule

Decide upon and document all the specific actions, dates, budgets and who's responsible for what, so the entire marketing program happens on time and within planned costs. If you're even somewhat planning oriented, you probably already have a favorite way to do this, perhaps with pencil and paper, using your personal/time organizer, or with one of the popular computer planning programs. Either way, you'll find some handy worksheets and checklists further on in this chapter that may make your job even easier.

12. Produce Marketing Materials

Since the promotional sources were selected in Step 6, this step deals with everything else, such as the direct mail package(s), display or classified ad(s) and/or other marketing communication formats to be used. (See

Chapters 7, 9, 11, and 12.) But, above all, see the rest of this chapter for perspective on what's most important.

13. Advertise and Promote per the Master Marketing Schedule

In other words, execute the plan you've just made.

14. Forecast Attendance (Events Only)

Chapter 6 shows how you can use early registration statistics to accurately predict how many will actually attend your event. This is vital planning feedback to enable you to anticipate and handle these inevitable over/under enrollment situations.

WHAT'S MOST IMPORTANT FOR MARKETING SUCCESS

Experience shows that the following 11 factors, listed in descending order of importance, determine the success of your marketing for training programs, seminars, instructional materials and other knowledge/information products and services:

1. List/Media
2. List/Media
3. List/Media
4. Timing (for dated material/events)
5. Location (for events)
6. Duration (for events, media-based and packaged programs)
7. Product name/title/sub-title
8. Offer
9. Price
10. Advertising package/format/design
11. Advertising copy

These are also the highest priority factors to test (See Chapter 8). It's useful to examine briefly each of these items.

1 - 3. List/Media

Everyone knows the old rule about real estate: The three most important factors are location, location and location. Well, the three most important factors in direct marketing are the list, the list and the list.

And where marketing involves other media, like newspapers, magazines, TV, etc., we broaden "list" to include publication, station, etc. Nothing else is as important to the success of your marketing. Over and over again we find that a poor offer to the right list or in the right place succeeds, whereas a polished offer to the wrong list or in the wrong place fails every time.

Especially important is the relative proportion of the mailer's own customer list that's used in relation to external rental lists. Generally a customer list will outperform a good rental list by four to eight times.

4. Timing

This is a major topic for dated materials and for all events. Failure to provide properly timed marketing is one of the common causes of disappointing results, particularly for events. Timing also includes event frequency. There's a section later in this chapter devoted entirely to timing considerations. And there's more in Chapter 6.

5. Location

Location can be one of the critical variables for event promotion. It includes both the geographic location and the facility. Chapter 6 contains additional information on the most popular locations and on working with hotels and meeting facilities.

6. Duration

This is important for events as well as for media-based and packaged training programs, simulations and the like. See the discussion later in this chapter of how event duration effects response rates. Also see Chapters 1, 2 and 6.

7. Product Name/Title

None of us believe you can really judge a book by its cover -- or by its title. Yet tests prove over and over again that title *is* vitally important. For seminars, books and other training and information products, a hard-hitting title that clearly spells out benefits can produce significantly more response than a bland title, devoid of clear benefits. The best way to pick your title is to look at the titles used by high-volume direct marketers for products and services similar to yours.

8. Offer

The offer includes all other product/service elements not specified above. It's a complex mixture of what's being sold, the author/sponsor/speaker, the method of response (e.g., business reply mail versus stamp needed, regular telephone versus toll-free "800" number, Fax, etc.), the guarantee, promotional gifts or bonuses included, etc. It's almost impossible to separate one of these items as more important than all the rest, because the readers form opinions based on their perceptions of the interrelationship between all of them -- and the price. Skilled direct marketing copy writers are able to weave together all these factors, and more, in a very compelling way.

The only way to determine the best offer is through systematic testing.

9. Price

In spite of what you may have heard, training *is* very price sensitive. Those who say otherwise haven't tested it. Occasionally, you'll hear of a situation where a higher price produced greater response than a lower price. But the vast majority of instances are straightforward: Raising the price reduces the number of sales. Whether it reduces the number of sales enough to reduce *total revenue* is al-

ways a question that can only be answered through testing. Don't let anyone tell you otherwise: Price *is* important.

Price also includes discounts, methods of payment, shipping/handling charges, taxes, etc.

Chapter 2 has additional pricing information.

10. Advertising Package/ Format/Design

For marketing in general, the choices are wide-open. But look in your own mail box or magazine rack and you will see a surprisingly small number of accepted formats repeated over and over again for training and information. The reason is that these are the formats that work!

MY strong recommendation is that you not vary significantly from what's being used repeatedly by others to market products/services like yours. This means that the greatest acceptable variety occurs in direct mail, with letters, brochures, catalogs, postcards and more. In the print media, the suitable formats are generally limited to the size of the ad, its placement in the magazine and the number of colors used. There is even less choice for classified ads.

While package/format makes a major difference in the response, it also makes a profound difference in cost. Chapters 8 and 9 address this trade-off in more detail.

11. Advertising Copy

What's written or said is at the bottom of the list, not because it is unimportant, but because the preceding factors are even *more* important. Actually, so much has been written about how to write successful copy that this handbook will only summarize the most important results in Chapter 8.

HOW TO ESTIMATE REALISTIC DIRECT MAIL RESPONSE RATES

In the public seminars I conduct and in speaking engagements before consultants and trainers, the question I'm most frequently asked is, "What sort of response can I expect to my mailings?"

Experienced marketers have their previous history to help them gauge the likely success of any planned mailing. But savvy marketers also know that their experience is at best only a guide, since countless factors affect the actual outcome of any specific campaign. On top of that, the laws of statistics tell us that a single mailing only represents a sample of the results that could be expected from repeating the same mailing many times.

As one who's sold training and information products and services for more than 25 years, and who also has a leaning toward numbers through a background as an engineer and scientist, I decided to tackle this question "head-on." I have been collecting a comprehensive database of information on mailings and their response right from the

time I started in this business. Now, the material fills a dozen file cabinets and boxes stacked high around the walls of a large storeroom. I decided to go through this mountain of data and see if any trends were evident.

The information was mainly of two types: (1.) response data on mailings I was personally involved with, including selling seminars, books, audio tape cassettes, packaged training programs, consulting, and getting leads for sales people; and (2.) articles citing response rates obtained by others, which I'd clipped from various direct marketing magazines and newspapers.

Experience shows that two of the three most important variables affecting direct mail response rates are *what* is offered (e.g., a 1-day seminar, a multi-day conference, a free showcase, etc.), and the *price* at which it's offered. So, the data were grouped for each given type of offer, and response rates were tabulated versus price.

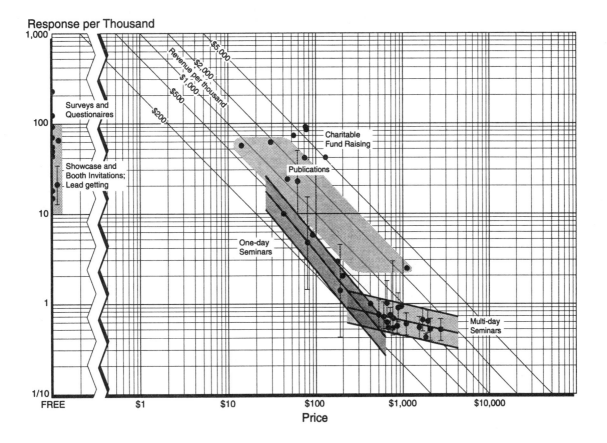

In many cases the data showed a wide range of response rates, reflecting the effects of the third and most important determinant of response, the *mailing lists* used, as well as other variables we'll discuss shortly.

All the data used were for "mature" programs with lists, package design and copy optimized through testing. Lots of data for "one-shot" or introductory programs were available, but these were not used since they would certainly not be comparable to the other information.

Overall, the data from nearly fifty separate programs over a 10-year period were usable. The surprising results are shown in the graph on the previous page.

Here's How to Read the Figure

First of all, notice that this diagram has "logarithmic scales," whereby each successive division represents ten times the previous division. Such a scale is often used to graph results spanning a wide range of values. A well-known example of a logarithmic scale is the Richter Scale for measuring earthquake intensity.

The vertical scale is the fraction of the total mailing that responded as intended, expressed as the number responding per thousands of pieces of mail sent out. For example, 10% response means that 100 replies were received for every thousand pieces of mail sent. Put another way, one response per 1,000 pieces of mail is the equivalent of 0.1% response!

One hundred percent response is nearly impossible. Somewhere between 5% and 15% of the mail won't get delivered due to addressing errors or other problems. And there are some people who wouldn't respond even if you paid them -- literally! The classic proof is that including a $1 bill with a survey questionnaire can boost response only to 40% or 50% from an expected 30%. But that means that five or six of every ten recipients will keep the dollar bill and *still* won't return the survey.

Each data point shown on the figure represents one of the five major types of offers of interest to trainers: *Surveys and questionnaires, lead-getting mailings, publication offers*

(books, tapes, packaged programs, etc.), *1-day seminars*, and *multi-day seminars*. Bars above and below a symbol show the range of response rates found.

The diagonal lines running from the upper left to the lower right of the figure represent lines of constant revenue produced per thousand pieces of mail. They're derived from the response per thousand times the price. For example, one hundred orders for a $10 item, ten orders for a $100 item and one order for a $1,000 item all produce the same $1,000 of revenue. Experienced direct marketers look at revenue per thousand pieces of mail because it represents a quick way to gauge the effectiveness of a mailing, since direct mail costs are usually quoted per thousand pieces of mail. A typical self-mailer sent at non-profit rates may cost $200 to $250 for one thousand pieces (20-25 cents each), whereas a brochure with a letter and reply card in a window envelope mailed by a profit-making firm may cost $400 to $600 per thousand (40-60 cents each).

What do these data mean to you? Here are four conclusions you can draw from this figure.

Increasing Price Always Reduces Responses -- But Doesn't Always Reduce Revenue

The data for multi-day seminars show revenue obtained from a thousand pieces of mail actually increases with increasing price, although the number of registrants obtained goes down.

Seminar sponsors who want to take advantage of this by raising prices need to be sure they also either increase the amount of mail they send or reduce the number of seminars scheduled, or both. Otherwise, they'll end up with sessions being conducted with fewer participants than desired or with sessions that must be cancelled altogether for lack of enrollments. That's why the process outlined earlier in this chapter is so critical.

Events Produce Lower Response than Similarly Priced Non-Events.

One would expect this, given the added requirement that the buyer must also show up at a specified location at a specified time. Put another way, publication offers (books, audio/video tape programs, etc.) generally produce two to ten times the response rates for a given price than do seminar offers.

Multi-Day Seminars Get Lower Response Rates than 1-Day Seminars.

But these longer events are less sensitive to price increases. The data also suggest that at a sufficiently high price, a multi-day seminar might actually outsell a 1-day seminar of the same price, perhaps because of the perception that the longer course would deliver more information than the shorter one of the

same price.

"Free" Offers Don't Always Get Higher Response than Mailings Made to Obtain an Order.

Free offers include preview or showcase announcements, booth or hospitality suite invitations or lead-getting mailings designed to obtain a request for more information. And when these freebies do yield a greater response, it sometimes includes those who take anything that's free but will never buy anything. That's why some direct mail experts suggest that you always test a low-cost *purchase* offer against a request for *free information* as a lead-getter and see which ultimately produces more closed sales.

LEAD TIME, SEASONALITY AND OTHER CRITICAL TIMING ISSUES

Timing is key to event marketing. This section deals with two kinds of timing: *Market timing* factors, such as lead-times, seasonality, response time, multiple mailings and even how many events to promote at once, and *internal timing* matters, like how long it takes to do various tasks.

Event Marketing Lead Times

Lead time is most important for events, particularly training events such as seminars, workshops, conferences, etc. The major determinants of lead time are:

1. The event's duration.
2. Whether away-from-home travel is required.
3. Whether the event is held during normal business hours or on personal time.

Short duration, local events attended on your own time can best be promoted with minimum lead time. Organizations offering one-to three-hour evening programs routinely advertise no more than a week to 10 days before. Many organizations that hold Thursday evening meetings promote them only in the

previous Sunday's newspaper.

On the other hand, events during normal business hours require a minimum of five to six weeks advance notice, even for low-level attendees. Longer duration events, those requiring away-from-home travel or those aimed at upper management require even more lead time. Week-long executive programs for presidents and chairman of the board may need to be promoted as much as five *months* in advance -- and shortening that lead time to only four months visibly and traceably cuts enrollments! Annual conferences are routinely promoted a full year in advance. On the other hand, failure to observe the 5-week lead-time window for 1-day programs can often cut enrollment by one-half or more.

The graph on the next page shows how lead time affects response for 2- and 3-day mid-level management seminars held during normal business hours:

These data were collected over nearly a decade, through more than 50 million pieces of mail for three dozen separate titles held hundreds of times in major North American cities. More than half the attendees traveled

Promotion Lead Time For Events During Business Hours

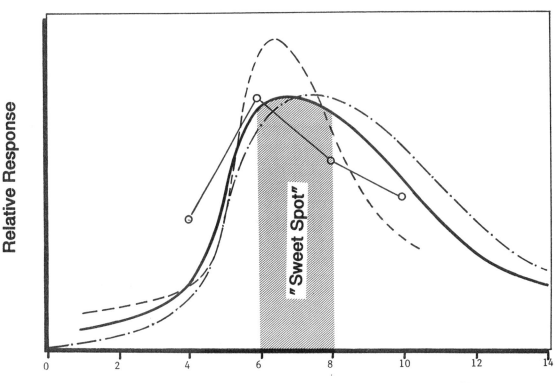

to the seminar. The heavy line represents our data. The various other curves are older estimates of lead time made by others for similar programs.

The most important result is that peak response occurs in a narrow "sweet spot" six to eight weeks before the program begins. This means your announcement must be on the recipient's desk this long prior to the program's start. If your mailing is received earlier or later than this, response is less, falling off much more rapidly as you get closer to the event than it does going the other way. In other words, if you can't be in the "sweet spot," it's better to be too early than too late. Response in the last three weeks is essentially nil, which helps explain why last-minute efforts to rescue an under-enrolled event seldom succeed.

Remember, these lead times are based on when the announcement is *received*. You need to add delivery time to figure when it

should be mailed. For example, Third-Class bulk-rate mail going across the country needs to drop 10 to 11 weeks before the event in order to hit the "sweet spot." First-Class local mail can drop eight to nine weeks ahead.

The message is loud and clear: Get your event advertising delivered on time or suffer significantly reduced attendance.

How Event Duration Affects Lead Time

If your event is a 2-day or 3-day management seminar, your best bet is to use the above data to figure your lead time. But how should you adjust that lead time if your event is longer or shorter?

The chart on the facing page is intended as a rough guide. In the band of data lie all the client data we've worked with, without revealing anyone's proprietary information. All events are during normal business hours.

**How Promotion Lead Time Varies
with Event Duration**

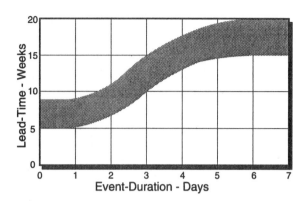

**How Many Dates/Locations to
Promote**

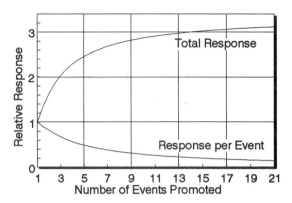

Five Other Factors Affecting Lead Time

Here are several other considerations that will have a bearing on promotional lead time:

1. Type of participant (entrepreneur, manager, non-manager, technical, professional, individual)

2. Who's paying (own business/practice, employer, individually paid)

3. Whether the participant's spouse and/or family is attending

4. Size of participant's business

5. Mailing location in relationship to participant's location

How Many Dates/Locations to Promote?

For regularly recurring events, say those held quarterly or more often, an important planning consideration is how many of those events to promote at once. For example, if you run a particular program four times a year, should your next announcement show only the next date? The next two dates? The next three dates? The whole year?

Here are the two opposing arguments: If you show more dates you get more responders all right. But by showing more dates, you reduce the sense of urgency, and an interested responder may select a later date rather than coming right away. Actually, both arguments are valid, as the following diagram shows:

The left-most point is the situation with a single ad for a single event. We're calling it "one" to keep things simple. Think of the response as one per thousand pieces of mail or one per thousand magazines circulated. And all the responders attend the one and only session advertised.

What happens as you promote more sessions? As the diagram shows, both total response and average attendance per session change.

The upper curve shows what happens to total response as the number of events increases. If you double the number of events (say from one to two), the response goes up by about 60% (from 1.0 to 1.6). Notice that response does not quite double by adding the second date. Doubling the number of events again, (from two to four) again increases response, but this time only by 44% of the response when only two events were shown (from 1.6 to 2.3). This process continues, with the total response increasing as the number of promoted events increases until eventually a point of diminishing returns is reached where the additional, incremental response to one more added date is negligible. This has been tested to literally hundreds of dates and/or locations, producing the following rule:

*"The more events you show the more
people will go."*

The bottom curve in the figure, however, illustrates the "price" you pay. The larger number of responders divide themselves among the larger number of event opportunities. For example, the larger total number of responders associated with showing two dates rather than one now divides the enrollment between the two dates, resulting in a lower *average* attendance at each event. This process continues as additional dates and/or locations are added: Increasing the number of events divides the larger number of total responders among the larger number of events, resulting in a steadily declining *average* attendance per event.

Of course, looking at the *average* enrollment per event is only part of the story. You really need to know *which* of the events they attend, particularly if the events promoted are spread over a period of time. As a rule, the increased enrollments generated by adding additional events comes mostly for dates/locations in another "sweet spot" between six and sixteen weeks from when the promotional piece was received. That means that adding events in the "sweet spot" produces increased enrollments but divides them among the increased number of events in that range. Adding events outside the "sweet spot" -- say beyond 16 weeks -- produces fewer added orders, but they're essentially all orders you wouldn't otherwise have gotten.

What does it all mean? Clearly, if the number of attendees at each event is not critical, your total cost of acquiring those enrollments is reduced when you promote more events. But, if you must achieve a minimum number of enrollments per event, or if the economics of conducting the event is adversely impacted when the enrollment per event declines, then these costs must be balanced against the reduced marketing costs before deciding how many events to promote. Of course, if you are able to increase the volume of your advertising so that the average attendance can be maintained while more dates are promoted, you have achieved the best of both worlds: a lower average selling cost *and* an acceptable cost of delivering the event.

Chapter 6 presents a detailed example of how to make this trade-off.

Seasonality: Is There a Best Time of Year to Market?

Seasonality refers to the effect that time of year has on response rates. It's a complex subject and one that's been given lots of attention by marketers.

Obviously, certain products are very dependent on time of the year. Summer resorts, ski vacations, holiday greeting cards, etc., all must be mailed at the right time of year to be successful.

Kleid's Seasonality Survey of Direct Mail Volume

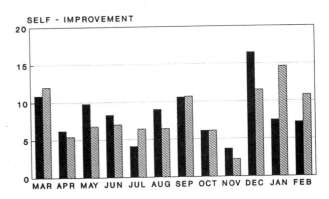

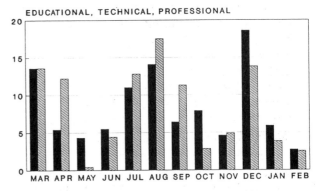

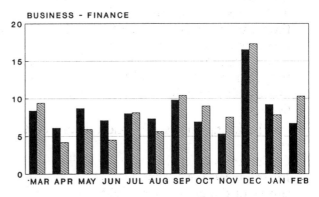

Seasonality Effects on Response

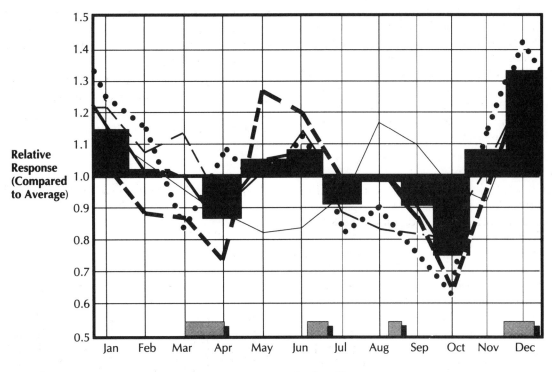

Month of Mailing

But even year-round needs, such as seminars, books, consulting services and other business and professional products, all experience a seasonal effect. Seasonal promotional effects on products expected to have uniform, year-round demand are almost always due to the amount of attention and time the prospect has to read and act on the marketing materials.

The best way to determine whether seasonality is a major factor for your promotion is to read what's available on the subject, look at the seasonal patterns used by others selling the same or similar products and then try and do some careful testing of your own. Admittedly, testing seasonality is a multi-year proposition and is very difficult for the average training or information marketer to undertake.

The facing page shows one example of direct mail seasonality. C. Rose Harper, Chairman and CEO of the Kleid Company, Inc. of New York, annually reports on their survey of direct mail seasonality in a number of categories. We've only shown the three

categories most relevant for us, namely educational, technical and professional, business finance and self-improvement. The graphs show the percentage of mail dropped by survey participants in each month and the five-year average. The implication is that the months when survey participants drop the most mail are the "best" mailing months, while the months in which they dropped the least mail represent the "worst" months.

Another way to look at seasonality is by response. I did such a study some years ago, examining the affect of seasonality for 2- and 3-day middle- and upper-management seminars. We performed a regression analysis on the results of more than eight million pieces of mail over a 4-year period, excluding tests and new product introductions. The objective was to determine whether the month in which the mailings were made had a statistically significant effect on response. The results of that very complex study are shown in the graph at the top of this page.

The heavy bars show the relative response of mailings made in the given month compared to the average. For example, mailings made in January had 15% greater response than the average for the entire year, whereas mailings made in October had 24% poorer response than the average. The various lines on the graph show other expert's estimates of the seasonality effect. The shaded bars at the bottom of the figure represent what Dependable Mailing Lists has called "bad mailing periods" for business products. Notice that there is a rough correlation between these so-called "bad mailing periods" and the results of our study, with the exception of December, where the results are diametrically opposed.

Both figures above confirm that December is the leading month for marketing training products and services, especially using the mail. Why? No one knows for sure, but the best guess is the obvious one: Almost no one ignores mail received during the holiday season. This higher readership -- even of advertising materials -- results in a higher response rate.

When planning tests and other marketing efforts where the absolutely highest response is desired, we like to target the day after Thanksgiving (in the U.S.) as the best mailing time.

One argument that's often made against mailing during the holiday period is that mail is handled by temporary postal workers and therefore may have less chance of being delivered. Actually, the reverse is also likely to be true. Temporary postal workers are more likely to "go by the book" than are the old hands. And what's more, the Third-Class bulk-rate mail is often cleared from bulk-mail handling areas as rapidly as possible in order to make room for the volume of First-Class mail. We have been pleasantly surprised to find our bulk Third-Class mail delivered *more* rapidly during the holiday time period than at other times of the year.

The best explanation for why April is the worst month, apparently has as to do with income tax time in the U.S. -- or perhaps a bit of spring fever.

So the following would seem to be a reasonable rank order (from best to worst) of the months in which to do training and information promotions:

The Best Months to Promote Training and Information

1. December	7.	August
2. January	8.	September
3. June	9.	July
4. May	10.	November
5. February	11.	April
6. March	12.	October

Are Certain Days of the Week Better for Advertising?

The marketing literature contains articles about when your materials should be received for maximum effectiveness. For example, some experts feel that mail received on Tuesday gets greater attention, since mail volume is generally lightest that day. Conversely, since most business mail is received on Mondays and Thursdays, these days are thought to be less effective. And the heavy mail at the beginning of each month, due to government checks and month-end billings, delay bulk Third-Class mail dropped then.

It's difficult to determine whether any of these variables makes much difference on the kinds of marketing trainers do. I've never been able to construct any reliable tests to show it. And given all the other things you must consider, these seem like variables you can safely (?) ignore. Besides, as mail volume has grown, your ability to control delivery date, especially for Third-Class bulk mail has diminished. There's not a lot you can do to control this timing variable even if you wanted to.

For whatever it's worth, here are the heaviest mail volumes received by business and the heaviest volume of newspaper advertising, as a function of the day of the week:

Direct Mail	**Newspaper**
1. Monday	1. Sunday
2. Thursday	2. Thursday
3. Friday	3. Friday
4. Wednesday	4. Wednesday
5. Saturday	5. Tuesday
6. Tuesday	6. Monday
7. Sunday	7. Saturday

How Often Can You Contact Your Prospects?

Regardless of how often you contact your clients and prospects (those who have already responded to your marketing efforts or purchased something from you), you're probably not contacting them often enough. When I was mailing to my own customers four times a year I thought that I would "wear out my welcome." Years later when I was mailing to my client list every five days (yes, that's right over 70 times a year!) I was surprised to learn that each mailing was *still* profitable. The secret of contacting your own clients and responders frequently is package variety and breadth of offers.

But frequency is also important for your *prospecting* activities. Tests have shown that most sales -- especially big-ticket items like seminars -- are closed on or after the fifth sales call. Repetition pays. Prospect lists can be mailed effectively one to three times a year without diminishing response. Display or classified ads should be placed to be seen three to four times minimum, either in the same publication or in related publications with high readership overlap. Telemarketers know that they must devise reasons to call back their prospects again and again, since it's often on the fourth or fifth call that the order will be taken.

Over and over again we've seen that the biggest obstacle to high-frequency direct marketing contact is the direct marketer themselves. It's O.K. if you feel this way, provided you realize that *your* reluctance to do more is costing you money. All of our tests show that you can contact your current clients and prospects far more frequently than you are willing to do so.

Response Effects of Multiple Mailings to the Same List

Multiple mailings can be very effective, particularly when you want maximum sales from a group of fixed size. One type of campaign uses a series of mailings, wherein each asks for action and references previous mailings (subscription renewals and donor solicitations are common examples).

A second mailing of the same piece, within two weeks to one month of the first mailing, will generally produce 60%-70% of the original response. Similar declines occur for subsequent mailings. The following diagram illustrates this.

This diagram can help you decide whether it might be better to mail a second or third time to your house list (or a portion of it) than to rent an outside mailing list.

Response Effects of Multiple Mailings

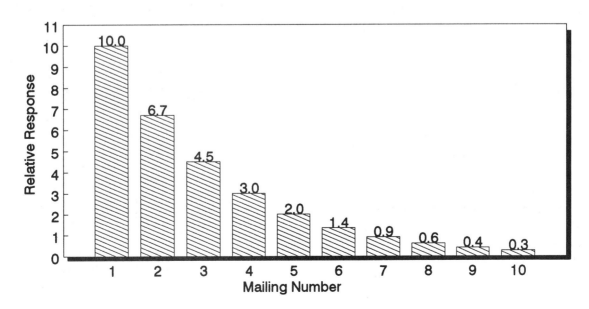

How Far in Advance You'll Need to Start Planning Everything

One final group of timing considerations has to do with your internal timing: allowing enough time to get everything done.

Since much of what you'll need involves outside resources, it's more difficult to control the schedule. Technical problems, shifting priorities, illness and a host of other factors outside your control can and often do conspire to make direct marketing efforts take longer than you anticipated. The only real safeguard against such delays is to START EARLY. And this is even more vital when planning a *new* promotional campaign.

How early is early? It depends on how close you can -- or are willing to -- monitor progress. Starting early is more important if you are alone or have limited personnel to frequently check on your vendors. As a general rule, allow half again as much time for every major event as you think it will take. For example, if ordering mailing lists normally takes three weeks from starting the decision-making until the list is obtained, allow four to five weeks in your plan. And allow six weeks for this same activity when you're doing it for the first time.

To aid in this internal planning, below are some representative times for some of the major marketing activities. Experienced direct marketers can, and often do, accomplish these tasks more quickly. But allow more time until your own experience proves you can do it faster.

Approximate Times for Planning Your Marketing

Selecting mailing lists .... 1 - 2 weeks

Obtaining mailing lists .... 1 - 4 weeks

Typesetting from final copy .... 1 day - 1 week

Preparing camera-ready art .... 1 day - 2 weeks

Newspaper/magazine insertion .... Depends on publication's closing

Printing 1-color, 1 or 2 sides .... 3 - 5 days

Printing 2-4 colors, 1 or 2 sides .... 2 - 4 weeks

Merging/purging mailing lists .... 1 - 3 weeks

Obtaining envelopes from a printer .... 2 days - 1 week

Obtaining envelopes from an envelope manufacturer .... 2 - 4 weeks

Creating personalized letters or envelopes .... 1 - 2 weeks

Affix labels, insert, sort, tie & bag envelopes (mail house) .... 20 M - 50 M pieces per day

Affix labels, sort, tie & bag self-mailer (mail house) .... 50 M pieces per day and up

Insert, label & mail (yourself) .... 300 - 500 pieces per day

WHAT'S A NEW CUSTOMER WORTH?

The answer to this seemingly simple question (Isn't it, "The profit you make on the sale"?) is itself not simple when the customer is obtained through direct marketing. The reason is that direct marketing usually leads to *long-term customer relationships*, and the initial (or "acquisition") transaction is just the beginning.

Of course, if your business is a one-product, "one-shot" operation, you can skip the rest of this subject. But if you just *might* be considering other, future sales of any kind to your customers, then the following is of vital importance to you.

The answer to our initial question, "What's a new customer worth?" depends on the answers to three other questions:

1. How long will the customer relationship last?
2. How much revenue will be derived from it?
3. How much will it cost to get those revenues?

The duration of the customer relationship depends on lots of things, including how satisfied the customer was with what they first bought from you, what else you have to sell them, and the ways you go about maintaining the relationship. Of course, the relationship also depends on factors outside your control, like customer job changes, reorganizations, acquisitions, moving, etc. These relationship changes differ from industry to industry and among organizations within an industry. Fortunately, these relationship changes are fairly predictable and can be described by something called an attrition curve (a term the author first heard used by Mr. Dan Harding of the Center for Direct Marketing).

Here's a range of attrition curves representative of training programs, seminars, instructional materials and other information products/services. For simplicity, they are presented on the basis of 100 customers acquired at time zero:

The fractions shown represent the shape of each curve. The first number refers to the percentage of the initial customers lost in the first year; the second refers to the percentage of those remaining that are lost each year thereafter. The upper curve is representative of business magazines and seminars, while the lower curve is typical for investment advisory subscriptions and the like.

Questions 2 and 3, dealing with revenues and costs, require a detailed look at your products and solicitations. Here's an example to use as a model:

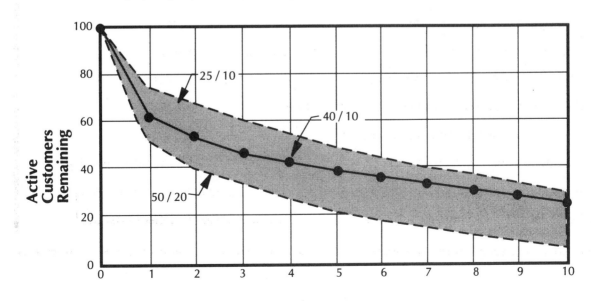

Years After Acquisition

This table assumes that attrition is 40% at the end of the first year and 10% at the end of each year thereafter (the center curve in the previous illustration). Each active customer is solicited with 31 individual mailings and catalogs each year, at a total annual solicitation cost of $8.16 each; cost of goods is 30% for all products, and each active customer yields the following annual revenue:

Net traceable sales from mailings made $24.86
Untraceable sales (33% of traceable) 8.20
Mail list rental income 1.18
 _____
ANNUAL TOTAL $34.24

Notice that in this example, the profit contribution obtained on the "back end" (sales made after the acquisition transaction) significantly exceeds that made on the "front end" (the acquisition transaction itself). Because of high initial selling costs, that's often true in direct marketing.

If you are to be successful in direct marketing, you need to be able to estimate -- even if it's only very roughly -- *both* the attrition curve *and* the cumulative profit contribution that applies to your business. So get out your records and get started -- it's easier than you think!

A Ten-Year History of One Hundred New Direct Mail Customers

Time Period	Number Active	Net Revenue (A)	Cost of Goods (B)	Selling Cost (C)	Profit Contrib. (A-B-C)	Cumulative Contribution
At acquisition	100	$65,000	$19,500	$40,000	$5,500	$5,500
After 1 year	60	2,054	616	490	949	6,449
After 2 years	54	1,849	555	441	854	7,302
After 3 years	49	1,664	499	397	768	8,070
After 4 years	44	1,496	449	357	691	8,761
After 5 years	39	1,346	404	321	621	9,383
After 6 years	35	1,212	364	289	560	9,942
After 7 years	32	1,092	328	260	504	10,446
After 8 years	29	983	295	234	454	10,900
After 9 years	26	883	265	211	408	11,308
After 10 years	23	794	238	189	367	11,675

MARKETING PLANNING TIPS

Training Responder Names Have a Long Life

Training customers have a *long* useful life, perhaps measured in decades. This is because training purchases come in "clumps" as new needs emerge due to life changes, job changes, new technology, etc. Careful tests have shown response rates for previous customers, for the same or new offers, actually *increase* after several years of decline then decline once more to a lower -- but often still acceptable -- level.

The chart at the top of the facing page illustrates this behavior.

Market Differently to Existing Customers than to New Customers

With *existing customers*, your goal is to maintain and build the relationship by (1.) contacting them frequently (one or two times per *month*), (2.) using a variety of media and/or formats and (3.) offering a number of products, services and/or incentives.

Additional sales to your *existing customers* (after their initial response or purchase) is the key to D/M profitability (the so-called "back end"). Many offers are unprofitable on the "front end" but very profitable later.

How Long Should a Name Remain on Your Mailing List?

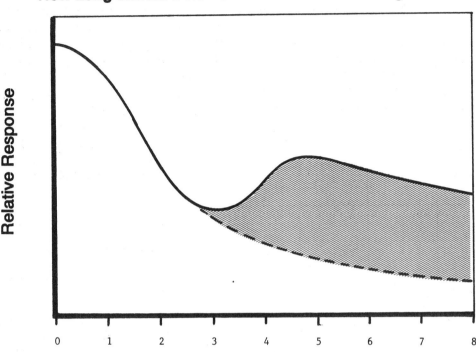

Examples of follow-up products to offer your previous seminar attendees include:

- Same seminar (they'll recruit others)
- Other seminars
- Audio/video tapes and computer diskettes
- Books and booklets
- In-house programs
- Worksheets and job aids
- Consulting services

For prospecting, your goal is to acquire the best *new customers* at the lowest cost. Generally this means a single basic offer (product/service *and* media/format) that testing has proven to be most effective, made one to three times a *year* to each prospect list.

Spend Time Studying Your Current Marketing Results

In planning new programs, all you can do is estimate the *relative* performance of the various lists, packages and media you'll use and test.

In *replanning existing programs*, you have the benefit of absolute numbers. Here are some of the valuable things you already have in an ongoing program that you don't have when planning a new one:

- Customers
- Actual costs
- Response data
- Test results

Allocate time and budget to do thoughtful analysis of your customer/responder list, especially that which will help show you patterns and similarities. For example, which first purchase(s) seems best correlated with substantial later purchases? Which are worst? What are the most frequently appearing position titles for product purchases, etc.?

What to Do Yourself and What to Buy Out

One important planning step is assigning responsibilities: Who is going to do what. This is always an issue because there's never enough time and talent to manage everything that needs to be done.

Nonetheless, there are some parts of your marketing that should almost *never* be delegated, because they are too closely intertwined with your long-term success. The activities that should always be done internally are:

1. Building and maintaining your own client and prospect list.

2. Making list decisions and acquiring and checking rental lists.

3. All contact with responders and customers resulting from your direct marketing, including receiving responses, processing orders, all correspondence and outbound telemarketing.

The common denominator is to maintain control over all aspects of your relationship with your customers and responders.

There are many fine telemarketing and fulfillment organizations, but be cautious using them to communicate with your customers. A possible exception is for the fulfillment of publication orders, whereby you could take and process the orders yourself then send them to a fulfillment house for packaging, shipping and processing product returns. But even this kind of delegation of customer contact should only be attempted after you have thoroughly proven the process entirely within your own office.

What *can* you buy out? The answer is, virtually, everything else! The most common buy-outs will consist of mail house services (don't even think about doing it yourself for more than a few hundred pieces of mail), printing and graphic arts. If you have desktop publishing, it's quite possible even this latter could be done internally -- but you can almost always tell the difference between amateur and professional graphics, so have an artist do the design.

Another activity to consider buying out is writing copy, until or unless you are comfortable with your own ability to do it. This handbook contains plenty of help for you,

and it's quite possible that you really do have the talent to write the copy -- it's only a question of whether you have the experience to do it best. Hiring a professional copy writer may be a useful way to get started, learning from what they do until you can do it yourself.

Distinguish Between Product Economics and the Business as a Whole

For the *business*, you're concerned with the lifetime value of the customer acquisition, assuming you'll sell more of the same product, different products, etc., to that person. For a *product*, what's important is the *profit contribution*: revenues less cost of goods and selling costs. This latter might be planned as a loss for a product, but making whatever value you plan is important! (See the sample financial worksheets later in this Chapter.)

Use Telemarketing when Quick Results Are Needed

Almost every direct marketing program using printed materials or media takes months to plan, execute and get results. Telemarketing is different: It can get you results in a week or less. (See Chapter 11 for more on Telemarketing.)

But remember, when you're marketing seminars or other training events, the lead times presented earlier in this chapter cannot be shortened!

Be Careful when Offering Free Gifts

Offering a sample demonstration record, tape or computer diskette for your product can be very effective, the latter especially with high-tech markets. Usually, charging a nominal amount -- fully applicable to the purchase price -- will best qualify the prospect but reduce the response. If you can stand the expense, try testing a free offer. But remember, it's cost per acquisition of a *full new customer relationship* you're seeking, not just placement of the samples.

Build Experience with Response Times

The time lag (or delay) between when you advertise and when you receive the order, deliver the product, gain customer acceptance (or get a return) and get paid is critical to your planning. This is one place where experience is your best guide, and the graph at the bottom of the page shows how to look at your data.

Each symbol represents a different seminar product or promotional campaign. Overall, the results are based on nearly 2,000 separate seminar enrollments for a variety of 2- and 3-day middle- and upper-management seminars.

There's more information on event lead times in the section on Attendance Forecasting in Chapter 6. And there's information on how to project final direct mail results from early returns in the section on Testing in Chapter 8.

Seven More Requirements for Success in Marketing Training and Information

1. Willingness to Learn lots of new technologies, ways of doing things and how things work. There are so many activities you'll need to understand -- many "behind the scenes" -- that for some, this is the most interesting part.

2. Ability to Manage People, because you can't possibly do it all yourself, so you'll need to work with, and through, others. If you aren't a good people-manager now, you'll need to become one; it's a trainable skill.

3. Good Employee/Suppliers in terms of their professionalism *and* their commitment to excellence. Your job is to find them -- and earn their loyalty.

4. A Systematic Approach that carefully defines what needs to be accomplished and lays out a plan to be sure it gets done on time, within the budget -- and gets done right.

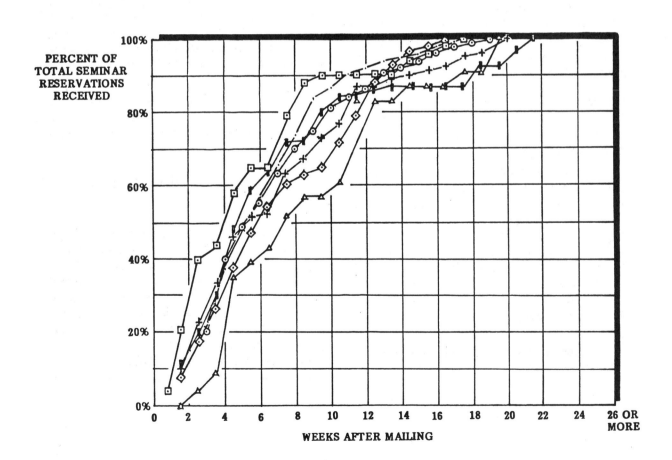

5. *Discipline* to follow your procedures step-by-step every time and resist "shooting from the hip," especially when things go wrong.

6. *Accurate Records* on everything, dated and organized for easy retrieval when needed. This is no business for the disorganized or "back-of-the-envelope" business person.

7. *Luck.*

FOUR HELPFUL TOOLS FOR MARKETING PLANNING

Here are four useful worksheets and other job aids for some of the key steps in the planning process:

1. Setting Marketing Objectives
2. Developing a Master Marketing Plan
3. Analyzing Your Finances
4. Conducting a Risk Analysis.

We lead off this section with a review of the planning process in general.

Steps in the Planning Process

Experience shows there are at least ten distinct steps to planning anything. Obviously, all apply to marketing planning as well.

If we've learned anything over the years, it's this: How well you do each of these steps is less important than that you do each of them. It's the overlooked or omitted step that will get you in trouble every time.

The Planning Process

1. Set Objectives
2. Program Activities
3. Identify Responsibilities
4. Schedule Activities
5. Budget Resources
6. Set Standards and Specifications
7. Analyze Risks
8. Establish Controls
9. Monitor Results
10. Take Corrective Action.

Marketing Program Objectives Worksheet

This worksheet will help you think through and document the objective of your marketing program. It includes identifying both the results you want to achieve *and* the limitations, restrictions or other requirements you must meet as you carry out your plan.

A clear, well-conceived marketing objective will not only give direction and focus to the rest of the steps in your marketing plan, but will also improve your ability to communicate with others whose support you'll need to be successful.

1. Establish the OVERALL OBJECTIVE you're going to achieve with your marketing program. This will be the goal or purpose of your marketing plan. Stated differently, it's the end result or condition you want to exist when the last step in the plan has been satisfactorily completed.

Your OVERALL OBJECTIVE will usually contain specific reference to:

- the PRODUCT(S) being marketed;
- the MARKET, or group of customers, you're trying to reach;
- the RESULT to be achieved.

To help you clarify your OVERALL OBJECTIVE, look at the nearby list of TYPICAL MARKETING PROGRAM OBJECTIVES. These have been written generally, without any reference to a specific PRODUCT or a specific MARKET. Adding that reference to your product and/or market, and rephrasing slightly, can make any of these a good candidate OVERALL OBJECTIVE. For example:

"Increase paid enrollments of new or prospective supervisors in Introduction to Supervision."

"Get sales force leads of qualified trainers interested in designing self-paced instruction."

"*Sell* Corporate Strategy Manual *to executives and planners in mid-size and smaller organizations.*"

2. Identify the SPECIFIC REQUIREMENTS, CONSTRAINTS, LIMITATIONS or RESTRICTIONS that need to be met as you work to achieve the overall goal or purpose you identified in Step 1. These are the "fences" you need to work within: schedules, budgets, relationships to other activities, people availability, etc. Put another way, this section describes the measures of performance you'll use to determine how successfully the OVERALL OBJECTIVE has been achieved.

List what comes to mind quickly, without evaluation or refinement. It's often helpful to review the considerations you used in selecting the product/market you're pursuing (see Chapter 2). Any previous strategic or business decisions should also be reviewed -- the factors considered in those decisions provide a good source of possible specific results to be achieved and/or constraints that have to be met.

When your list is complete, review it to eliminate duplications and rephrase the items so they are as specific as possible. To test whether a statement is specific enough, ask yourself, "How will I know when it is met?" If your answer is not clear, the statement is too general. Specific Standards of Performance are defined in a later planning step. However, at this time you should be specific enough so that these measures and standards can be developed later. As a last step, if any of these constraints are in conflict, it may be necessary to eliminate some items or to make judgments regarding priorities to be placed on meeting them.

3. Designate the One Who Has OVERALL RESPONSIBILITY for this direct marketing program. This is the person who will coordinate all the activities of the marketing plan in order to ensure that the overall objective is actually achieved.

At the right is what the worksheet might look like when completed:

Typical Marketing Program Objectives

- Announce changes in addresses, phone numbers, policies or prices.
- Establish/maintain/increase awareness of an organization.
- Establish/maintain/increase awareness of a product/service (new or existing).
- Conduct market research.
- Distribute samples that get used.
- Test market receptivity to a new product/service.
- Acquire leads/inquiries.
- Qualify leads/inquiries.
- Secure new dealers, distributors or sales representatives.
- Make appointments for live sales calls.
- Generate traffic at/through an office, store or other location.
- Generate trade show traffic.
- Place a product/service for field testing.
- Obtain trial buyers/subscribers.
- Get people to attend a demonstration, fair, festival, etc.
- Close product sales.
- Close service sales.
- Obtain paid participants in a seminar, conference or workshop.

Marketing Objectives Worksheet

A. Overall Objective: Develop & market a 2-day "How to Market Training Programs...." seminar.

B. Specific requirements, constraints, limitations or restrictions to be met while achieving the Overall Objective:

1. Offer monthly beginning early next year.
2. Domestic U.S. only @ start -- Canada & other int'l later next year or early the year after.
3. Avoid conflict -- or even the appearance of conflict -- with our other courses or products.
4. Offer comprehensive "stand alone" course workbook covering all applicable disciplines/skills.
5. Cash flow to stay within bank-approved line-of-credit.
6. Honor all existing client and staff commitments, including vacations.
7. _____
8. _____
9. _____
10. _____

C. Overall Responsibility: Don

Marketing Objectives Worksheet

A. Overall Objective: _____
_____

B. Specific requirements, constraints, limitations or restrictions to be met while achieving the
Overall Objective:

1. _____
_____

2. _____
_____

3. _____
_____

4. _____
_____

5. _____
_____

6. _____
_____

7. _____
_____

8. _____
_____

9. _____
_____

10. _____
_____

C. Overall Responsibility: _____

Marketing Plan Worksheet

The purpose of this worksheet is to help you summarize in one place the major elements in your MARKETING PLAN for a single product/marketing objective. Because detailed work is required in several other areas, additional worksheets are provided elsewhere in this book.

1. Determine the SOURCES OF SALES you'll be relying on to achieve the de-sired sales volume. If necessary, refer to Chapter 3 or to the earlier sections of this chapter. Estimate the volume of sales and/or the percentage of total sales to be derived from each source. And don't forget to consider including "source unknown," which can amount to up to 20% of the sales in some situations.

2. Estimate the DIRECT MAIL VOLUME REQUIRED if direct mail is one of your marketing choices. In addition to the net sales from direct mail (which you identified in Step 1), you'll need to estimate the net sales per M (M = 1,000 pieces of mail). If desired, you can further refine the volume required by breaking down the total into the part you'll obtain from your own *house lists* and the balance that will be required from *rental lists*. The principal difference between the two types of lists is their cost, which can be as much as 20%-30% of the total cost per piece. If necessary, you can also break down the total volume into as many as six separate mailings.

3. Identify the MAJOR TASKS: the main *activity steps* and/or *actions* that need to be accomplished in order to achieve your desired objective. If you are working with a team or feel that you'll have more activities than will fit in the space provided on the worksheet, use a separate sheet to "brainstorm" a list of possible activities. Develop the list of activities quickly, without worrying about their proper sequence. Just be sure that each activity is related to the overall objective.

To stimulate your thinking about the activities that may be needed, use the following three resources: (1.) your MARKETING PROGRAM OBJECTIVES sheet, (2.) the information you collected in Chapter 2 on SELECTING PRODUCTS & SERVICES, and (3.) the SOURCES/MEDIA you identified in Step 1 above. Try to write your Tasks in action-oriented terms: a VERB plus an OBJECT.

4. Select the 10-15 Major Tasks, the ones which represent about the same level of detail. Several techniques will help you do this:

Look at your Tasks from the viewpoint of the person who has overall responsibility. What are the 10-15 major Tasks *this* person will be concerned about in accomplishing the overall objective you defined?

Eliminate those Tasks that are subordinate to, or detailed aspects of, some other Task. These will not be forgotten, but will be considered as part of that Major TASK. To test whether an Activity is too detailed, ask questions such as: "Is this Activity included in another one?" and "Is this a detail of a larger Activity?"

Test your remaining Tasks to see if any are too general and should be separated into greater detail. One way to determine if a statement is too general is to ask whether it could be assigned to *one specific person* or *one specific group* in your organization. If *more* than one person or unit would share responsibility for a Task, it should be separated into several, more detailed Tasks. Each of the 10-15 Major Tasks should be assignable to one individual or one group.

As you consolidate your list down to the 10-15 Major Tasks, it is important that you keep moving and don't allow yourself to become "bogged down." If your final list contains too few Tasks, this will become apparent in later steps of the Planning Process. If too many Tasks are included and the Plan becomes too complicated, you can consolidate some detailed areas later.

5. Sequence the 10-15 Major Tasks so that the results, products or OUTPUTS of each are available for later Tasks that need them. For example, "Write Advertising Copy" would probably come before "Prepare Artwork," which, in turn, would likely precede "Print Brochure." One way to accomplish this sequencing is to determine the INPUTS required to perform each Task. Inputs and outputs are documented information, physical products or other measurable, tangible articles. If a Task's OUTPUT is required as an INPUT to one or more subsequent Tasks, then the Task producing the output must be completed first.

In developing these outputs and inputs, the best procedure usually is to begin with the last Task and list its output(s) first. Then list its input(s). Continue working backwards with the outputs and inputs of other Tasks, until all are sequenced.

When you finish identifying the inputs and outputs for all the Tasks, you can test for completeness by making sure that every required input is generated as an output of some earlier Task. Add Tasks and outputs as necessary until everything matches. Also, check to be sure that each output is used by some task as a required input. Otherwise, unnecessary outputs may be generated (note, however, that some outputs may be used outside the scope of this plan).

6. Copy Your MAJOR TASKS onto the MARKETING PLAN Worksheet, in the sequence in which they must be started. For convenience, you may wish to number each one and to show the organization (or individual) who's responsible for each.

7. Lay Out the MASTER MARKETING SCHEDULE in the form of a bar chart. Start by writing in the date of the last day of the first week to be covered by the schedule above the first column. Continue in the same manner with each week thereafter. Next, add a bar (or other symbol) for fixed *External Events*, such as meetings, holidays, organizational activities, etc., which occur during the period covered by the plan. Try to keep these External Events at the top of the schedule area.

Now sketch in a bar denoting the duration of *each* of the Major Tasks. Stagger or sequence the Tasks so that the outputs and inputs fit together. Use the best estimates of time you (and your teammates) can develop, or use the ranges of times given elsewhere in this notebook.

If -- as often happens -- the total time required exceeds what's available for the whole project, something has to be done. Usually that means somehow cutting down the time to accomplish certain tasks (perhaps accepting higher level of risk as a result), spending greater resources, or rescheduling the completion for later. In any case, such trade-offs invariably balance off five (5) main variables: QUALITY, QUANTITY, COST, TIME and RISK.

When the Task bars are satisfactorily meshed, the Task names can be written in -- or on -- the bars. You can also show significant INPUTS, OUTPUTS or significant MILESTONES that occur in that activity by indexing them with an open triangle under the bar.

As work progresses on each Task, show the degree of completion by filling in the bar on the Master Marketing Schedule. For example, if an activity step were half completed, then the left half of its bar would be filled in. Similarly, fill in the input, output and major milestone triangles as they are accomplished.

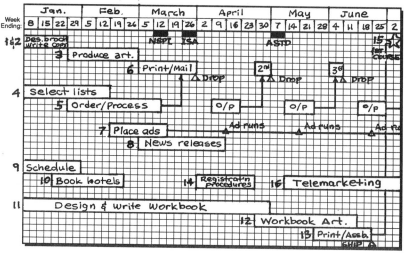

Marketing Plan Worksheet

For (Objective): New Seminar

1. Sources of Sales

Source/Media:	Volume:	%	Resources Budgeted:
Direct mail	180	50%	$63,640
Display ads	18	5%	$8,000
Telemarketing	36	10%	$10,000
Referral & other	72	20%	incl.
Source unknown	54	15%	incl.
Total:	360	100%	$81,640

2. Direct Mail Volume Required

180 Net sales from mail / **1.0** Net sales per M = **180** M needed to mail.

	House Lists:	Renatal Lists:	Total:
Package Cost:	$ 287 /M	$ 287 /M	$ 287 /M
List Cost:	$ 2 /M	$ 85 /M	$ 67 /M Ave.
TOTAL COST:	$ 289 /M	$ 372 /M	$ 354 /M Ave.
x No. to be Mailed:	40 M	140 M	180 M
BUDGET:	$ 11,560	$ 52,080	$ 63,640

Drop No.	House Lists	Rental Lists	Total
1.	6.5	29.5	36.0
2.	7.0	26.0	33.0
3.	5.0	19.0	24.0
4.	8.0	28.0	36.0
5.	7.5	21.5	29.0
6.	6.0	16.0	22.0

Total: 40.0M 140.0M 180.0M

3. – 6. Major Tasks

No:	Activity/Action:	Responsibility:
1	Design Mailer	DS
2	Write copy	DS
3	Produce advertising	RS
4	Select mail lists	DJ
5	Obtain/process lists	GH
6	Print/mail brochures	DJ
7	Place display ads	GH
8	Distrib. news release	CW
9	Schedule seminars	SFC
10	Book hotels	SFC
11	Write Workbook	DS
12	Produce Wkbk. art	CW
13	Print, assemb, ship.	CW
14	Prep. registr. proced.	BF
15	Conduct seminars	DS
16	Conduct telemktg.	BF

7. Master Marketing Schedule

Marketing Plan Worksheet

For (Objective): _____

1. Sources of Sales

Source/Media:	Volume:	%	Resources Budgeted:
Total:		**100%**	

2. Direct Mail Volume Required

_____ Net sales from mail / _____ Net sales per M = _____ M needed to mail.

	House Lists:	Renatal Lists:	Total:
Package Cost:	$ _____ /M	$ _____ /M	$ _____ /M
List Cost:	$ _____ /M	$ _____ /M	$ _____ /M
TOTAL COST:	$ _____ /M	$ _____ /M	$ _____ /M
x No. to be Mailed:	_____ M	_____ M	_____ M
BUDGET:	$ _____	$ _____	$ _____

Drop No.	House Lists	Rental Lists	Total
1.			
2.			
3.			
4.			
5.			
6.			

3. – 6. Major Tasks

No:	Activity/Action:	Responsibility:

7. Master Marketing Schedule

Week Ending:

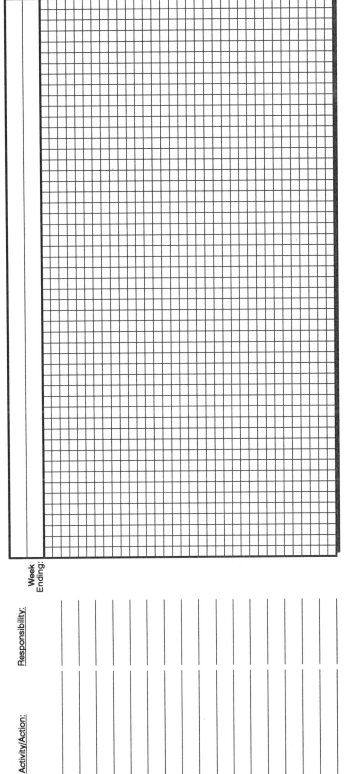

Financial Analysis Worksheets

The worksheets on this page and the next are intended to help you (1.) to define the major income and expense items for a marketing business, and (2.) to calculate the important measures of financial return for the business as a whole and for an individual product.

Many of the financial terms are defined in APPENDIX B, A VOCABULARY OF COMMON TERMS FOR MARKETING TRAINING AND INFORMATION.

Business/Organization Economics
(Typical Operating Statement)

Revenue:	$ _____	Income from all services and products sold
Minus Cost of Goods:	$ _____	Direct and indirect costs of delivering all services and products sold
Gross Margin:	$ _____	
Minus Selling Expenses:	$ _____	Direct and indirect costs for all means of marketing, sales, and distribution
Operating Profit:	$ _____	
Plus Operating Income:	$ _____	For the business of organization as a whole
Minus General and Administrative Expenses:	$ _____	Includes managment, buildings, utilities interest, insurance, etc.
Pretax Income:	$ _____	
Minus Taxes:	$ _____	
NET INCOME:	$ _____	

NOTES:

1. Covers a fixed period of time, usually a month, quarter or year.
2. Reflects all income and expenses for a business or organization.
3. Based on the business/organization as a "going concern" that has been operating -- and will continue to operate -- indefinitely.

Product/Marketing Economics

SALES REVENUE:

_____ units sold x average price each _____ $ _____

Minus refusals, returns and bad debts   _____

Net Sales: $ _____ (A)

MINUS COST OF GOODS:

		$ _____
Direct	Design, development, or acquisition cost	_____
	Production cost	_____
	Cost of services provided	_____
	Cost of premiums	_____
	Shipping costs (net of reimbursements)	_____
Indirect	Publications, artwork, printing	_____
	Warehouse, inventory, carrying costs	_____
	Loss, breakage, shrinkage	_____
	Internal handling of returns	_____

Cost of Goods: $ _____ (B)

Gross Margin (A)-(B): $ _____ (C)

MINUS MARKETING AND SELLING EXPENSES:

Direct	Direct mail (Number mailed x cost per 1000)	_____
	Catalogs	_____
	Newspapers, magazines, and other media	_____
	Sales commissions (including telemarketing)	_____
Indirect	Order processing	_____
	Credit checks and collection fees	_____
	Business reply postage	_____
	Order forms and supplies	_____
	Publicity and news releases	_____
	Sales and telemarketing management	_____
	Sales force travel and entertainment	_____
	Marketing and market research	_____
	Telemarketing telephone expenses	_____
	Cost of money on receivables	_____
	Mail list maintenance	_____

Selling Expenses: _____ (D)

Profit Contribution (C)-(D): $ _____

Risk Analysis Worksheet

Analyzing risk is an important part of any planning process. Although there are many sophisticated ways to do it, a simple risk analysis is both easy to do and valuable, because it helps focus your efforts on the largest risks you take.

This RISK ANALYSIS worksheet provides you with a convenient means to identify, record and evaluate risks. It can be used by one person alone, but it's best used in a group consisting of those individuals who will be participating in the undertaking.

1. WHAT CAN HAPPEN? Use the first column to record all ideas and suggestions of possible events or circumstances which can *prevent* achieving your marketing objectives. For ideas, refer to your PRODUCT/MARKET SELECTION INFORMATION, MARKETING OBJECTIVES and PLANNING worksheets. Almost any item listed on these sheets may be able to suggest a risk event that could happen. Do not attempt to discuss, criticize or evaluate any of these suggestions; merely list all of the items as they come up.

2. HOW LIKELY? Once a range of risks has been identified, go back and evaluate the likelihood that each event will actually happen (probability of occurrence). This evaluation might be done as simply as indi-

cating high, medium and low, or it can be put on a 5-point numerical scale with 5 representing the highest and 1 the lowest.

3. HOW SERIOUS would it be, in terms of the impact on your objectives, if the anticipated event actually did happen? Again, this might be in terms of high, medium and low or on the same 5-point numerical scale.

4. OVERALL RISK. Now put the identified risks in order by combining your estimates of likelihood and seriousness to obtain an estimate of the OVERALL RISK. If you've used a numerical scale for the previous columns, multiply the two numbers together to determine OVERALL RISK. Otherwise, examine your evaluation of likelihood and seriousness and assign high, medium or low descriptors in the OVERALL RISK column.

5. IDENTIFY ACTIONS. Finally, indicate in the last column the ACTIONS you can take for those items representing the greatest overall risk to your objectives. There are two kinds of actions you can take: those which REDUCE OR ELIMINATE the risk (generally taken before the threatened event occurs) and those which LIMIT OR MANAGE the damage done (usually taken during/after the event). Try to think of a way to accomplish each kind of action for each important risk. Here's an example of what a completed worksheet might look like:

FOR (OBJECTIVE): ___SDM Seminar___

(5=High; 1=Low)

WHAT CAN HAPPEN?	HOW LIKELY? A	HOW SERIOUS? B	OVERALL RISK A x B	ACTIONS	
				Reduce or Eliminate	Limit or Manage
Recession.	3	4	12		Buy limited inventory.
					Watch indicators.
Notebook late from production.	3	5	(15)	Start early.	
Can't get adequate rental lists.	4	4	(16)		Build house list.
					Offer booklet.
Low response.	3	5	(15)	Use best adv. Use best lists.	Buy limited inventory.
...ponse.					

Risk Analysis Worksheet

FOR (OBJECTIVE): _____

WHAT CAN HAPPEN?	HOW LIKELY ? A	HOW SERIOUS ? B	OVERALL RISK A x B	ACTIONS	
				Reduce or Eliminate	Limit or Manage

49 Steps to a Successful Conference

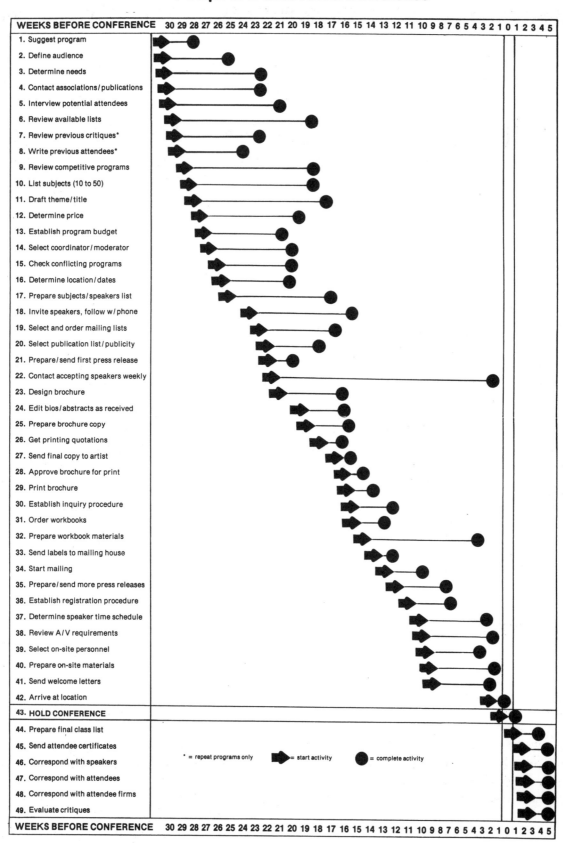

WEEKS BEFORE CONFERENCE	30 29 28 27 26 25 24 23 22 21 20 19 18 17 16 15 14 13 12 11 10 9 8 7 6 5 4 3 2 1 0 1 2 3 4 5
1. Suggest program	
2. Define audience	
3. Determine needs	
4. Contact associations / publications	
5. Interview potential attendees	
6. Review available lists	
7. Review previous critiques*	
8. Write previous attendees*	
9. Review competitive programs	
10. List subjects (10 to 50)	
11. Draft theme / title	
12. Determine price	
13. Establish program budget	
14. Select coordinator / moderator	
15. Check conflicting programs	
16. Determine location / dates	
17. Prepare subjects / speakers list	
18. Invite speakers, follow w/ phone	
19. Select and order mailing lists	
20. Select publication list / publicity	
21. Prepare / send first press release	
22. Contact accepting speakers weekly	
23. Design brochure	
24. Edit bios / abstracts as received	
25. Prepare brochure copy	
26. Get printing quotations	
27. Send final copy to artist	
28. Approve brochure for print	
29. Print brochure	
30. Establish inquiry procedure	
31. Order workbooks	
32. Prepare workbook materials	
33. Send labels to mailing house	
34. Start mailing	
35. Prepare / send more press releases	
36. Establish registration procedure	
37. Determine speaker time schedule	
38. Review A / V requirements	
39. Select on-site personnel	
40. Prepare on-site materials	
41. Send welcome letters	
42. Arrive at location	
43. HOLD CONFERENCE	
44. Prepare final class list	
45. Send attendee certificates	
46. Correspond with speakers	
47. Correspond with attendees	
48. Correspond with attendee firms	
49. Evaluate critiques	
WEEKS BEFORE CONFERENCE	30 29 28 27 26 25 24 23 22 21 20 19 18 17 16 15 14 13 12 11 10 9 8 7 6 5 4 3 2 1 0 1 2 3 4 5

* = repeat programs only   ▶ = start activity   ● = complete activity

THE CHALLENGE OF SEMINARS AND OTHER OPEN REGISTRATION EVENTS

With so many seminars, *someone* must be making money. Right? I mean look, here's just *one* room at the local Holiday Inn: 58 people paid $175 each for a 1-day seminar on Customer Service. Wow! *That's over $10,000!*

What could it cost? A few hundred bucks for the room ... a few hundred more for coffee and soft drinks. Even after the presenter's salary and expenses, there's got to be $7,000 - $8,000 left over. Right?

Wrong! And welcome to the world of seminars.

This chapter will help you understand why that original profit estimate is wrong and how to get a better one. It's divided into several parts. First is the "big picture" of how seminars make money, presented as four rules. Next we look at several planning issues that directly affect meeting marketability and profitability, like where the money comes from, where it goes and when, how many events are scheduled and promoted and when and where the most popular meetings are held. The rest of the chapter covers infrastructure skills vital for meeting success: for example, seminar design, taking enrollments, working with hotels and meeting facilities and forecasting attendance.

THE BIG PICTURE OF THE SEMINAR BUSINESS

Most seminars start with an idea for the event. But successful firms quickly learn four rules:

Seminar Rule No. 1: Good *Product* Is Abundant and Cheap. It's Good *Sales and Marketing* That's Scarce and Expensive.

A good meeting is important. It's just not enough! There are seminar companies with great products that never make it big -- and others with mediocre products where every session is full.

Sales and marketing is clearly the single biggest expense that any seminar organization faces -- and it's the one activity that *must* succeed. Otherwise, no one will ever know if your program is any good or not.

Seminar Rule No. 2: The Number of Participants Is the Key to Profits

Most of the costs for a seminar are fixed long before it ever begins. That's why each extra participant over the break-even point is *very* profitable.

Sure, more participants costs you more for meals, refreshments, materials, etc. It's just that these costs pale next to your sales and marketing costs, development costs, presenter costs, room rental costs, and other costs committed well in advance of the meeting -- and which don't change with the number of the participants.

How do you keep the event full? The most important way is to balance the type and amount of promotion you do and the number of events scheduled. (We introduced this balancing act in Chapter 5. There's more on how to do it in a few pages.)

In seeming (but not real) contradiction to Rule No. 2:

Seminar Rule No. 3: It's a Mistake to Look *Only* at the Event.

Most of what you spend *is* committed before the seminar begins -- but most of what you make comes in after it's over. Surprising as it may seem, some events barely break even or even lose money. But *future* sales to those seminar participants will be easier and less costly in two ways: (1.) It's easier to sell the *same* event through them to others, *plus* (2.)

it's easier to sell *related* products and services to the original attendees, either yourself or by renting their names to others.

An important qualification to the idea that most money comes in *after* the event is back-of-the-room sales *at* the event itself. (Think about popcorn and soft drinks at a movie, for example.) Back-of-the-room sales can make a major financial difference on the event's profitability. And here the presenter and/or design can make a big contribution by positioning those back-of-the-room materials as an important part of what the participant came to the meeting for -- and allowing sufficient time for those sales to take place.

Seminar Rule No. 4: It Takes *Time* to Make Money -- Often Years.

What paces the process is growth of your own house mailing list of past participants. This list dramatically cuts your sales and marketing costs and increases attendance. (See the discussion of these cost differences in Chapter 5.) Time also helps by spreading the original meeting design and development costs over *more* meetings and *more* participants.

A consequence of Rule No. 4 is that a meeting organization that isn't spending 30% to 50% of it's revenue (or more) on sales and marketing, isn't growing as fast as it can. Obviously each business has to balance this "front-end/back-end" profitability equation for themselves. But those who enter the meetings business expecting a quick payoff from their first seminar are often disappointed.

UNDERSTANDING HOW SEMINARS MAKE MONEY

To understand how seminars make money, you need to first understand where the money comes from and where it goes.

Where the Money Comes From

Meetings generate income before, during and after they occur. Here are some sources:

Before the Meeting
- Advance Registration Fees
- Advance Materials Sales
- Sponsorships
- Program Advertisements
- Exposition/Booth Sales
- Contributions/Grants
- Travel Commissions/Allowances

During the Meeting

- At-the-Door Registration Fees
- Back-of-the-Room Sales
  -Tapes/Books/Proceedings
  -Products/Memorabilia
  -Periodical Subscriptions
  -Memberships
- Concurrent Event Sales
  -Pre/Post Conference Workshops
  -Field Trips
  -Lunches/Dinners/Receptions
- Registrations for Future Events

After the Meeting

- Hotel Commissions/"Kickbacks"
- Advance Payments Forfeited
- Cancellation Charges
- Aftermarket Sales of Related...
  -Products (Books, Tapes,...)
  -Services (Seminars, Consulting,...)
- Unrelated Sales
- Mailing List Rentals

There's no hard-and-fast rule about how income *should* be divided among these sources. Some seminars generate no income before or during the meeting, relying entirely on sales made after the meeting. Others require advance payment, and all the money comes in before the meeting ever begins. And obviously, not all of the above income sources apply to every meeting. But the more of these money-makers you *can* include in your seminar, the better.

Where the Money Goes

In the same way as income, meeting expenses are incurred before, during and after the event. Here are some of the reasons for these costs:

Before the Meeting

- Program Design/Development
- Site Selection/Negotiations
- Event Sales/Marketing/Promotion
  -Advertising & Direct Mail
  -Salesperson Compensation
  -Sales Travel & Entertainment
  -Sales & Marketing Communication Costs
  -Proposal Costs
  -Sales & Marketing Management
- Printing/Purchasing Meeting Materials

- Shipping Equipment/Supplies to the Meeting
- Taking/Processing/Confirming Advance Registrations

During the Meeting

- Presenter(s)/Administrator(s)
  -Compensation
  -Travel
  -Away-from-Home Living Expenses
- Meeting-Room(s) Rental
- Computers/Equipment Rental
- Furnished to Participants
  -Books/Materials
  -Refreshments/Breaks
  -Meals/Receptions
- -Entertainment/Events

After the Meeting

- Author/Developer Royalties
- Participant "Money-Back" Refunds
- Return Shipping of Equipment/Supplies
- Accounting & Reporting Meeting Finances
- Profit-Sharing (per Advance Arrangements)
- State/Local Taxes/License Fees Due

Not every meeting will incur every one of these costs. But, (unfortunately) most are present, directly or indirectly, for virtually every meeting.

What Are Fixed and Variable Costs?

If you're in the seminar business, you look at every meeting cost as either "*fixed*" or "*variable*" depending on whether or not it changes with the number of participants. Here are some examples:

Fixed Costs

- Program Design/Development
- Site Selection/Negotiations
- Event Sales/Marketing/Promotion
- Presenter's/Administrator's Compensation and Travel Expenses
- Meeting-Room(s) Rental
- Computer/Equipment Rental

Variable Costs
- Author/Developer Royalties
- Participant Materials/Meals/Refreshments/Breaks
- Sales Commissions
- Profit-Sharing

Program design/development is a good example of a *fixed cost*. This might include the time and expense of researching the seminar, planning and developing the presentations, preparing videos or slides, writing participant materials, training presenters, etc. You incur this cost before the meeting -- sometimes months or even years before. And, once you've spent this money, it's gone regardless of how many people attend -- or don't attend -- your seminar.

Participant meals and refreshments are good examples of *variable costs*, because they are greater with more attendees and less with fewer attendees. Other variable cost examples include the number of assistants or administrators and even -- if you know attendance in time -- meeting-room rental, where you'd get a larger/smaller room to accommodate a larger/smaller audience.

Here are some typical variable costs:

Item	Cost
Instructors	$500/day plus expenses
Administrative Assistant	$150/day plus expenses
Main Meeting-Room Rental	$200/day
Break-Out Room Rental	$100/day each
Projector/Screen Rental	$30/day
Easels/Flipcharts Rental	$20/day
Coffee Breaks	$10/per day per participant
Participant Lunches	$15/per day per participant
Participant Dinners	$20/per day per participant
Cocktail Reception	$10/per day per participant
Notebook, Precourse Materials, Correspondence, Postage & Supplies	$50/participant

How Attendance Affects Profitability

If you conclude from the previous section that fixed meeting costs exceed those that are variable, you're absolutely right. And that's why the number of attendees is so critical: Once there are enough attendees to cover those high fixed costs, additional participants become *very* profitable.

This situation is shown in the series of three charts on the facing page.

All three graphs show dollars plotted against the number of participants. Figure A shows only *expenses*, both the fixed and variable parts. Figure B shows only *income*, increasing in direct proportion to the number of participants, starting with no income for no participants. Figure C shows Figures A and B combined. The point where the income and expense lines cross is called the *break-even point*. There, *income* exactly balances *expenses*. For more participants, income exceeds expenses and the amount of that difference is the *profit*. For fewer participants, expenses exceed income and the difference is the *loss*.

How the Number of Sessions Affects Profitability

The best way to show this is to work through a typical example. Let's take a 1-day business seminar priced at $49 per participant. Let's further assume you can get a mailing list of 10,000 unduplicated names and that direct mail will be your only source of enrollments. The questions is: What is the optimum number of sessions to advertise and hold?

There are actually two answers, one if registration fees represent the only source of income, and a different answer if additional income is expected at or after the seminar. Let's look at the simplest case first.

If Registration Fees Are Your Only Source of Income. The first table on Page 6 - 6 shows the estimated income and expenses connected with holding one through six sessions.

Let's start by looking at the first four columns on the left-hand side of the table.

How Seminar Attendance Affects Profitability

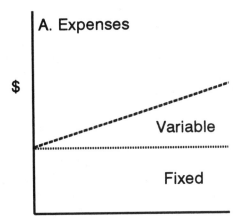

A. Expenses

$

Variable

Fixed

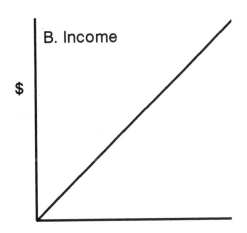

B. Income

$

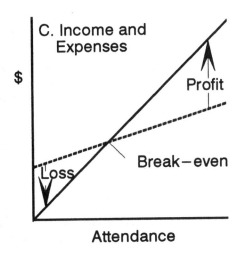

C. Income and Expenses

$

Profit

Break–even

Loss

Attendance

We assume you'll mail all 10,000 brochures at one time, and the response from promoting only a single event would be (from Chapter 5) 7 paid registrants per thousand brochures, or

70 paid registrations total. As you increase the number of events you promote, the second column shows that your response rate increases, more rapidly with the first few added events then less rapidly as still more events are added (again see Chapter 5). The third column in the table shows the total number of paid attendees as the number of events increases. The ninth column shows the income obtained from registration fees paid by these attendees.

Next you need to look at the expenses in columns five through eight. For simplicity, let's consider only three cost elements: The first component is the *selling* cost, assumed to be only the cost of the 10,000 brochures at 25 cents each. Second is the *session fixed* cost, estimated to be $800, including the instructor, meeting-room rental, and the projector and screen. The third component is *session variable* cost, assumed to be $10 per participant, covering refreshments and materials.

Finally, the columns on the right show the profit, obtained by subtracting total expenses in column eight from total income in column nine for each number of sessions. Dividing by the number of paid attendees gives the profit per attendee.

In this example, promoting three events yields the most profit. For a single event and for six events, you actually lose money! The single event is unprofitable because you can't get enough attendees to cover your selling costs. Six events lose money because average attendance at each session is too low to absorb fixed session costs.

Although the numbers change, this same approach reflects the thinking necessary to implement Steps 7 and 8 of Chapter 5's planning process.

How Back-of-the-Room Sales at the Session Changes Things. The previous example shows what happens when registration fees are the *only* source of revenue. What happens if you add revenues from the sale of books and materials at each event?

The second table on page 6-6 shows the answer. The left side of this table is exactly the same as the previous example up to income. Here we assume that each participant spends an average of $12 more at the session for books and other back-of-the-room

Sample Public Seminar Finances

	Increased			Expenses				Income	Profit/(Loss)	
Number Of Events	Response With More Events	Total Paid Attendees	Average Attendees Per Event	Selling	Session Fixed	Session Variable	Total	(All Reg. Fees)	Total	Per Attendee
1	1.00	70	70	$2,500	$800	$700	$4,000	$3,430	($570)	($8.14)
2	1.64	115	58	$2,500	$1,600	$1,150	$5,250	$5,635	$385	$3.35
3	2.03	142	47	$2,500	$2,400	$1,420	$6,320	$6,958	$638	$4.49
4	2.29	160	40	$2,500	$3,200	$1,600	$7,300	$7,840	$540	$3.38
5	2.46	172	34	$2,500	$4,000	$1,720	$8,220	$8,428	$208	$1.21
6	2.59	181	30	$2,500	$4,800	$1,810	$9,110	$8,869	($241)	($1.33)

Sample Public Seminar Finances Including Back-of-the-Room Material Sales

	Increased			Expenses				Income			Profit/(Loss)	
Number Of Events	Response With More Events	Total Paid Attendees	Average Attendees Per Event	Selling	Session Fixed	Session Variable	Total	Reg. Fees	BOTR Mat'Ls	Total	Total	Per Attendee
1	1.00	70	70	$2,500	$800	$700	$4,000	$3,430	$700	$4,130	$130	$1.86
2	1.64	115	58	$2,500	$1,600	$1,150	$5,250	$5,635	$1,150	$6,785	$1,535	$13.35
3	2.03	142	47	$2,500	$2,400	$1,420	$6,320	$6,958	$1,420	$8,378	$2,058	$14.49
4	2.29	160	40	$2,500	$3,200	$1,600	$7,300	$7,840	$1,600	$9,440	$2,140	$13.38
5	2.46	172	34	$2,500	$4,000	$1,720	$8,220	$8,428	$1,720	$10,148	$1,928	$11.21
6	2.59	181	30	$2,500	$4,800	$1,810	$9,110	$8,869	$1,810	$10,679	$1,569	$8.67

materials, with a $2 average cost of goods, leaving a net revenue for these supplemental sales of $10 per participant. The table shows that when registration fees *plus* back-of-the-room (BOTR) materials are considered, profits change dramatically. First and most obviously, none of the sessions now loses money. Second, the number of sessions that maximizes your profit increases from three to four. The table shows that increasing the number of sessions beyond four starts to cut profitability, and at some point adding more events would actually lose money.

Similar reasoning applies if your supplemental sales come from other products or services not delivered at the event, such as consulting, in-house/on-site seminars, books, packaged training courses, software, etc.

SCHEDULING AND TIMING CAN MAKE OR BREAK ANY SEMINAR: PICKING THE BEST TIMES AND LOCATIONS

You've heard it said before: "Timing is everything!" And nowhere is it more important than for seminars. Experience shows THE most common causes of poor attendance are errors in scheduling and timing. For example, promoting a seminar with insufficient lead-time or scheduling a meeting that conflicts with other participant commitments.

Scheduling and timing are intimately related. The words are often used interchangeably for two areas:

1. Event scheduling, including *when* the event is held, (the best season, month, week, day(s), time of day), *where* its held (country, state/province, city, facility, room), *how long* it should be (duration, sessions) and *how many* of the same event can/should be scheduled in a given time interval and location. Although it seems strange to include location considerations, the "*when*" and "*where*" of event scheduling are so intimately connected that nothing else makes sense.

2. Promotion timing, including advertising *lead-time* requirements, *seasonality* effects (best/worst time of year to advertise), promotional *frequencies* (in each medium, to each prospect), *how many* of the same event can/should be promoted at one time and how to balance the "Scheduling-Promotion-Attendance" equation.

All the promotion-related matters were addressed in Chapter 5. Here we'll address the event-specific issues.

The Best Day and Time to Hold Your Seminar

The best time to hold your meeting is when the most attendees can and will come. This sounds obvious, but you'd be surprised how many event planners begin with *their* schedule and commitments, rather than with their attendees'.

The most fundamental timing issue is whether or not your seminar will be held during the target audience's normal business hours. This, in turn, is usually linked to whether the meeting is paid for by the employer, by the attendee or some combination. Most employer-paid meetings are held during normal business hours. A notable exception are meetings for time-billing professionals like doctors, dentists, lawyers, accountants -- and even salespeople. Because these professionals lose income when they're away during normal office hours, medical/professional meetings of almost any duration are usually scheduled on weekends.

Individually-paid meetings are mostly held outside normal business hours. Since these events are often short duration -- say one or two hours -- they are frequently scheduled before or after work or on weekends.

Timing can make a big difference in who attends. For instance, one of our clients offered a series of free, 2-hour sales showcases including both afternoon and evening sessions. Attendees selected which session to attend, and the groups couldn't have contrasted more. Managers and executives from mid-size and large organizations attended the afternoon sessions, while salespeople, professionals, entrepreneurs and individuals attended at night. Needless to say, the resulting sales conversions from the two groups was also quite different.

Here's a summary of our experience with event timing by days of the week. Use this for your planning -- until you get data on your own audience.

For Employer-Paid Events During Normal Business Hours

1. Wednesday
2. Thursday
3. Tuesday
4. Friday
5. Monday
6. Saturday
7. Sunday

For Medical/Professional Events During Normal Office Hours

1. Saturday
2. Sunday
3. Friday
4. Monday
5. Wednesday
6. Thursday
7. Tuesday

For Individually-Paid Events Outside Normal Business Hours

1. Thursday
2. Saturday
3. Wednesday
4. Tuesday
5. Sunday
6. Friday
7. Monday

Schedule all-day (or multi-day) programs in relation to other business or recreation. For example, open-to-the-public, multi-day programs involving away-from-home participant travel seem to work best when they end no later than noon on Friday or begin Monday morning. This apparently provides flexibility for participants to combine their attendance with other business or personal activities. Business programs do best starting and ending mid-week, so that travel is entirely on company time, etc. Your own experience, your best guide.

The Best and Worst Weeks and Months for Seminars

Weekly/monthly differences usually don't impact marketability as much as day of the week or time of day. People attend meetings for a variety of reasons, which tends to "level out" the weekly/monthly effects.

My close associate, the late Bob Janssen, said we made our own seasonality by how we scheduled our seminars. When we were sure August was a bad month, we didn't schedule anything in August. And sure enough, no one came. Later, when we routinely scheduled August seminars, it proved to be a good month after all, although attracting a somewhat different mix of attendees.

In the U.S., the only consistently slow periods for training are Thanksgiving week and the two or three weeks including Christmas and New Year. Even the Monday and Tuesday of Thanksgiving week can draw well for business seminars.

Here's a summary of our experience with event timing by months. Again, use this only as a starting point until you get your own audience data:

For Employer-Paid Events During Normal Business Hours

1. March	7. May
2. February	8. January
3. October	9. December
4. November	10. July
5. April	11. June
6. September	12. August

For Medical/Professional Events During Normal Office Hours

1. September	7. June
2. October	8. February
3. December	9. April
4. March	10. January
5. November	11. May
6. July	12. August

For Individually-Paid Events Outside Normal Business Hours

1. January	4. March
2. September	5. April
3. October	6. February

7. November	10. July
8. June	11. December
9. May	12. August

Don't confuse the above data on when the event is *held* with Chapter 5's seasonality data on when the event is *promoted*. The two are related all right, but in such a complex way that it's better to think about them separately.

The Best Cities and States for Seminars

The question of where to hold your training program has two parts: the city and the facility. The basic rule for both is to schedule your event where your attendees are or will come. We'll consider the geographic part here and the facility part later.

On the facing page is a ranking of states where U.S. business seminars are held, based on an analysis of over 19,000 business seminars from ten leading sponsors, including AMA, CareerTrack, Fred Pryor, SkillPath, D&B and others. The order has changed very little in the last decade.

The second table on the facing page goes one step further, to the most popular U.S. cities for business meetings, found from the same analysis. Each city includes the major metropolitan area it serves; for example, Washington, D.C., includes the adjacent parts of Maryland.

The locations selected for travel in general (including incentive trips, sales meetings and conventions) reflects a somewhat different pattern. Bill Communications' *Successful Meetings* magazine recently surveyed professional meeting planners, and obtained the following Top Ten states and cities used for meetings in general:

Top 10 States	Top 10 Cities
1. California	1. Chicago
2. Florida	2. Orlando
3. Texas	3. Dallas
4. Illinois	4. Atlanta
5. New York	5. Los Angeles
6. Arizona	6. San Diego
7. Georgia	7. New York
8. Washington, DC	8. Boston
9. Nevada	9. New Orleans
10. Pennsylvania	10. Phoenix

These data are helpful when you're just starting out. But it's important for you to understand *your* particular market as soon as possible. For example, my continuing medical-education clients find their most popular locations are indeed resort cities such as Honolulu, New Orleans, Orlando and San Diego. But be careful using resorts if this is *not* the norm for *your* target market.

Resorts can work well for programs aimed at individual professionals, (doctors, lawyers, CPAs, etc.), for CEOs/owners of small businesses or even the top management of mid-size or larger organizations. Resort locations often *reduce* attendance of other groups because of: (1.) higher costs, (2.) difficulty getting there and (3.) perception that the trip is a "boondoggle." Airport and downtown locations in major cities are the best all-around choice.

How Many of the Same Event to Plan

Frequency of course offering is dependent upon the size of the market and frequency and volume you can advertise. For example, several-hour local seminars outside normal business hours can be offered monthly or even more frequently without adverse effects on selling costs. On the other hand, multi-day seminars for top executives can rarely be scheduled more often than quarterly in a given location. Often less frequent scheduling produces better economic return. It's the same scheduling balancing act we've seen before.

And usually a *uniform* schedule of offerings in any one geographic area will be best. For example, if you are going to have four programs in New York each year, schedule them every three months.

Top 40 U.S. States for Public Business Seminars

R/O	State	No.	Percent	Cum.
1	California	2,261	11.7%	11.7%
2	New York	1,388	7.2%	18.8%
3	Texas	1,216	6.3%	25.1%
4	Illinois	1,106	5.7%	30.8%
5	Florida	989	5.1%	35.9%
6	Pennsylvania	837	4.3%	40.3%
7	Georgia	656	3.4%	43.7%
8	Michigan	629	3.2%	46.9%
9	Ohio	622	3.2%	50.1%
10	Massachusetts	518	2.7%	52.8%
11	North Carolina	516	2.7%	55.5%
12	New Jersey	509	2.6%	58.1%
13	Wisconsin	446	2.3%	60.4%
14	Virginia	434	2.2%	62.6%
15	Washington	433	2.2%	64.9%
16	District Of Columbia	416	2.1%	67.0%
17	Minnesota	401	2.1%	69.1%
18	Colorado	388	2.0%	71.1%
19	Missouri	381	2.0%	73.1%
20	Maryland	376	1.9%	75.0%
21	Tennessee	352	1.8%	76.8%
22	Indiana	316	1.6%	78.5%
23	Louisiana	300	1.5%	80.0%
24	Oregon	259	1.3%	81.3%
25	Connecticut	256	1.3%	82.7%
26	Arizona	246	1.3%	83.9%
27	Alabama	231	1.2%	85.1%
28	South Carolina	231	1.2%	86.3%
29	Kansas	188	1.0%	87.3%
30	Iowa	187	1.0%	88.3%
31	Kentucky	178	0.9%	89.2%
32	West Virginia	135	0.7%	89.9%
33	New Mexico	126	0.7%	90.5%
34	Alaska	121	0.6%	91.1%
35	Nebraska	118	0.6%	91.8%
36	Maine	117	0.6%	92.4%
37	Oklahoma	117	0.6%	93.0%
38	Montana	116	0.6%	93.6%
39	Arkansas	114	0.6%	94.2%
40	Utah	109	0.6%	94.7%
	All remaining states	1,023	5.3%	100.0%

Total   19,362

Most Popular U.S. Cities for Public Business Seminars

R/O	City	ST	No.	Percent	Cum.
1	Chicago	IL	1,117	5.8%	5.8%
2	New York	NY	1,107	5.7%	11.5%
3	Washington	DC	677	3.5%	15.0%
4	Atlanta	GA	600	3.1%	18.1%
5	San Francisco	CA	505	2.6%	20.7%
6	Los Angeles	CA	503	2.6%	23.3%
7	Boston	MA	278	1.4%	24.7%
8	Philadelphia	PA	266	1.4%	26.1%
9	Denver	CO	262	1.4%	27.5%
10	Dallas	TX	258	1.3%	28.8%
11	Orange County	CA	243	1.3%	30.0%
12	Miami	FL	237	1.2%	31.3%
13	Newark	NJ	229	1.2%	32.4%
14	Minneapolis	MN	217	1.1%	33.6%
15	Seattle	WA	217	1.1%	34.7%
16	Detroit	MI	209	1.1%	35.8%
17	St. Louis	MO	193	1.0%	36.8%
18	Houston	TX	185	1.0%	37.7%
19	Baltimore	MD	164	0.8%	38.6%
20	San Diego	CA	164	0.8%	39.4%
21	Tampa	FL	164	0.8%	40.3%
22	Phoenix	AZ	140	0.7%	41.0%
23	San Jose	CA	140	0.7%	41.7%
24	Orlando	FL	138	0.7%	42.4%
25	Ft. Worth	TX	136	0.7%	43.1%
26	Jackonsville	FL	126	0.6%	43.8%
27	Pittsburgh	PA	116	0.6%	44.4%
28	Midland/Odessa	TX	110	0.6%	44.9%
29	Milwaukee	WI	110	0.6%	45.5%
30	Providence	RI	110	0.6%	46.1%
31	Spokane	WA	110	0.6%	46.6%
32	Columbus	OH	105	0.5%	47.2%
33	Oakland	CA	103	0.5%	47.7%
34	North Virginia	VA	99	0.5%	48.2%
35	Portland	OR	99	0.5%	48.7%
36	Boise	ID	95	0.5%	49.2%
37	New Brunswick	NJ	95	0.5%	49.7%
38	Cleveland	OH	89	0.5%	50.2%
39	Stamford	CT	89	0.5%	50.6%
40	Cincinnati	OH	85	0.4%	51.1%
41	Sacramento	CA	85	0.4%	51.5%
42	Salt Lake City	UT	85	0.4%	52.0%
	All others combined		9,302	48.0%	100.0%

Total   19,362

HOW TO DESIGN, DEVELOP AND CONDUCT A SUCCESSFUL SEMINAR

Designing a successful seminar is more art than science. It's closer to a successful play, concert, vaudeville show or religious revival than it is to a college class or business meeting. Obviously *who's* coming to the seminar, *where*, *when* and *why* it's being held and *how many* will attend are all important. But successful meetings draw from both the worlds of entertainment and education and involve both analysis and intuition. Perhaps that's why a surprising number of the biggest names in the seminar business were -- or still are -- platform entertainers.

And like most art forms, designing and conducting a successful seminar is best learned by copying the masters. There's no real substitute for seeing what's working well for others -- especially at seminars run by experienced meeting professionals and attended by your target audience. Don't be shy about adapting these ideas for your own program. There'll be plenty of opportunity for originality and creativity *after* you've created a successful program based on what's working for others.

This section consolidates ideas from our more than 25 years in training and from many other sources. It deals primarily with the "front end" of the meeting: it's design, planning and development, especially where those elements have an impact on marketing.

Target Your Attendees

Consulting with those in the meetings business, I see lots of proposed seminars that will never sell. I meet those who have spent years carefully designing a seminar that will never attract enough people to even cover its costs. It's the seminar equivalent of the vanity book: a seminar someone feels strongly must be presented but which will never be attended by more than a handful of people.

The world's best meeting design is worthless if no one attends. So start by paying close attention to the market you're trying to serve. Realistically, how large is this market?

Meetings aimed at every first-level supervisor, every registered nurse or even every individual have vast markets that are easy to identify and easy to reach. There may be lots of competition for your identified market, but at least you won't have the question of whether it's large enough to make the program viable.

One way to determine the probable size of your market is to look at meetings similar to the one you're contemplating that others are holding. How many times are they offered? The catalogs from national associations and seminar providers are a readily available source for this "market research." If there are meetings targeted at those you're trying to reach, you may have confidence that a viable market exists. Be concerned if no one is serving your market. It may be because you're the only one who's thought of it. Or it may be because it isn't real. (See Chapter 2 for tools to help with this "Is It Real?" process.)

Set Your Seminar's Learning and Business Objectives

The successful approach here parallels writing. First start with a clear picture of the meeting results you want. There should be only one overall goal or purpose, but there can be many additional results and/or constraints as well. Some of these will deal with the participants -- some with your organization's financial and other goals.

Next, think clearly about what you want your target participants to know or do after they've attended. This may later suggest the name of the seminar or the major benefits that will make people want to attend.

Finally, be clear about your business objectives for the seminar, especially concerning number of participants, costs, profits, back-of-the-room sales and future implications. Remember, the seminar business pays off over the long run, so don't be surprised if some of your objectives won't be achieved until after the meeting.

Choose Content that Sells

Now that your objectives are clear, make a list of all of the concepts and ideas that could be included in your seminar to achieve the desired outcome(s). Try not to unnecessarily restrict yourself. Use a "mind map," "brainstorming" or other techniques to stimulate your most creative flow of ideas.

Next organize the content into coherent blocks that can be linked together. Think in terms of a mixture of presentation styles and formats as well, seeking topics which can be presented in a variety of ways for more interest, wider participation and better retention value.

Then look at your competitor's programs. Do they suggest additional topics, activities or functions you've overlooked? Especially when you'll have direct competition, you'll need to be able to "win the battle of the program."

Your challenge in this step is to develop the "must have" content without adding unnecessary frills.

Decide how Short Your Seminar Can Be

Always design the shortest meeting possible. Time is money, which is why shorter programs are almost always easier to sell than longer ones. Tests show that reducing course duration can actually be *more* effective in stimulating sales than reducing price. Technical seminars are occasionally an exception, because participants are skeptical they can learn enough in the shorter time.

For a new seminar, look at what's now being offered by competitors or by others to your target market. Is one particular duration the norm? For example, most PC courses are one day while many management courses are three days. Could you offer the same course in less time?

If you are already conducting this seminar, carefully examine your attendees' feedback. Call previous participants and ask them if the program could be shorter and what should be dropped. You'll be amazed at the many good ideas you'll get -- and at the likely consensus on what should be done.

The 1-day (or less) seminar -- which fell into disfavor in the early 1980s -- has returned as the most popular for business seminars. Because direct mail response rates for 1-day seminars are so high, you can conduct more sessions, in more widely-scattered locations, and thereby bring the seminar to an even wider audience. Although promoted heavily by CareerTrack, Fred Pryor, SkillPath and AMA, the 1-day program is rapidly being adopted by others. (For more information on the effect of duration on direct mail response rates, see Chapter 5.)

And what about fractional-day meetings? These are very acceptable for free showcases (see Chapter 10) and other low-cost sales or information meetings. But people will not travel far for fractional-day meetings, so gear your program to the local participant. Multiple-day seminars, on the other hand, can easily be travel-to programs.

Remember, it's easier to expand a program that's proven too short than it is to shorten a program that has too much "fat" in it. When in doubt, err on the side of a shorter program that leaves participants wanting more.

Pick a Winning Title

This extremely important topic is essential whenever seminar design is considered. It's really the key to successful promotion, so it's discussed in depth in Chapter 8.

Is Your Presenter Part of the Product?

If your presenter is part of your product -- someone with high name recognition and appeal to your market -- then this is easy. But be sure the presenter(s) actually *will* produce more sales than the same material presented by an unknown.

Remember that when two or more speakers or session leaders conduct a meeting, the group will invariably favor one of them over the other(s) and will feel one is poorest compared to the other(s). This can be devastating to some course leaders who take it as a personal rejection. Be cautious how your post-meeting surveys are used in these circumstances, and consider using only one leader whenever possible.

Here are some of today's most popular seminar leaders and speakers:

Some Popular Seminar Leaders and Speakers -- and their Topics

- Karl Albrecht.................. Service Quality
- Anthony Alessandra...... Relationship Selling
- Chris Argyris................. The Organization
- Warren G. Bennis.......... Leadership
- Kenneth H. Blanchard... One-Minute Management
- Peter Block .... Consulting
- Lee Boyan .... Sales Selling
- Hyler J. Bracey.............. Inspired Performance
- William C. Byham.......... Employee Empowerment
- Jim Cathcart.................. Relationship Selling
- Daryl R. Conner............. Organizational Change
- Stephen R. Covey .... Personal Effectiveness
- Bert Decker................... Speaking, Communications
- W. Edwards Deming ..... Quality
- Peter F. Drucker .... Management
- Wayne Dyer.................. Motivation
- Ned Herrmann.............. Whole Brain
- Paul Hersey .... Leadership, Management
- Michael J. Kami............ Strategic Planning
- Gary Karrass................ Negotiation
- Beverly L. Kaye .... Careers
- John P. Kotter............... Corporate Culture
- James M. Kouzes.......... Leadership & Innovation
- Barbara Lawton............ The Deming Transformation
- George Labovitz........... Quality
- James W. Newman .... Personal Motivation
- Tom Peters .... Management Innovation
- J. William Pfeiffer.......... Strategic Planning
- Michael E. Porter.......... Competitive Strategy
- F.G. "Buck" Rogers....... Sales
- Geary A. Rummler........ Organizations
- Lester Thurow............... Internat'l. Competitiveness
- Benjamin B. Tregoe ...... Strategic Planning
- Denis Waitley................ Psychology of Winning
- Bob Waterman .... Management, Leadership
- Alan Weiss.................... Management, Consulting
- Richard C. Whiteley ...... Customer-Driven Organiz'n.
- Larry Wilson .... Sales
- Ron Zemke................... Service Quality
- Zig Ziglar..................... Sales, Motivation

Set Minimum and Maximum Group Size

Minimum class size is generally set one of two ways: (1.) on economic considerations or (2.) by the number required for class activities, such as role-plays, case studies, team assignments, etc. Economics usually governs, but it should be lifetime-value economics, not just the break-even considerations on a particular session. (see Chapter 5 for how to figure lifetime value economics).

On the other hand, *maximum* class size is generally set by: (1.) facility limitations, (2.) instructional requirements or (3.) staff limitations. Since meeting rooms are usually reserved far in advance, facility limitations are the most frequent. The solution for this is, of

course, to plan ahead and have an adequate forecasting approach (see later in this chapter).

There's an important point here: Every course developer and instructor wants to limit group size. And they'll find creative reasons why. But the economics say that larger is better. Expect tension on this issue, and *only limit group size when it's absolutely necessary.*

Times and Breaks

This dictates the amount of time your course will occupy during the day. Many first-time seminar planners fail to allocate sufficient time for comfort and refreshment breaks, as well as setting realistic starting and ending times.

For all-day business meetings, start at 8:30 a.m. and quit at 5:00 p.m. A number of sponsors favor the 9:00 a.m. to 4:30 p.m. window, which takes a full hour out of the time available.

Evening sessions typically start at 6:30 p.m. to 7:30 p.m. and rarely last more than 2-1/2 to 3 hours.

All meetings should include 10-15 minute comfort (and possibly refreshment) breaks about every 1-1/2 hours.

Should You Include Food and Beverage Functions?

Opinion is divided on whether or not to include lunches and dinners, with the majority now *not* doing so unless it serves some clear meeting function not achievable any other way (for example, permitting a guest speaker or roundtable discussion). Cocktail functions are useful to stimulate informal contacts and can facilitate follow-on sales if your salespersons are on hand.

Remember that food and beverage functions can be important in negotiating with hotels and meeting facilities, so be sure to read that section later in this chapter before settling this issue. In some cases, facilities will waive meeting-room rental and other charges if you're having a food or beverage function, so the added cost may be less than you think.

Also, be aware that public opinion on the

acceptability of events involving alcohol is changing rapidly and varies from place to place. In California, for example, drinking functions from which most participants must later drive may be viewed very differently than they are in the East or Midwest.

Do Offer Continuing Education Units (CEUs)

Many attendees apply CEUs from training programs and seminars to the continuing education requirements of their profession or employer. The CEU has been designed as a uniform unit of measurement to facilitate the accumulation and exchange of information for individual participation in noncredit continuing education. It will help your marketing to offer CEUs, and for medical and other professional courses it's absolutely essential. The requirements are often not difficult, at least for general CEUs. Professional CEUs usually require approval by a national or state board and can be difficult to obtain.

Get complete information on general CEUs by ordering: *The Continuing Education Unit Criteria and Guidelines* from the Council on the Continuing Education Unit (CCEU), 1101 Connecticut Avenue, N.W., Suite 700, Washington, DC 20036. Phone: (202) 857-1122. ($5.00)

The Critical -- but Often Overlooked -- Marketing Role of Participant Materials

Some seminar designers see participant materials only as a cost, to be reduced or eliminated. This is a mistake. Participant materials can and do stimulate later sales if they're designed properly. Here are some tips:

Notebook/Pass Outs. Include copies of all visual aids you use, supplemental reading material and information about the presenter and his/her organization. These materials, given to each participant, are influenced by four considerations:

1. What participants *need* during the meeting.
2. What participants *expect* will (or should)

be furnished.
3. What will help market the meeting (or aftermarket products/services) to others.
4. How difficult it is to get the materials *to* the meeting (your concern) and *from* the meeting (your participant's concern).

Make the materials useful on an ongoing basis: as an organizer, as a reference source or in some other manner. Make the notebook or other package attractive enough to be kept in full view, even when not in use. This stimulates both repeated use *and* repeated sales. And be sure the outside of the package serves as a good advertisement to a casual observer. (This is easier if the course name contains the benefit statement.)

If you're giving participants too much material to conveniently pack in their luggage to take home, consider furnishing a tote or carry-on bag to hold it all. Just be sure your name, address and telephone number are on the bag!

Job Aids, such as cards, posters, signs, software, toys, checklists, worksheets, calculators, computers and other tools participants can use to apply what they learn. These can be powerful adjuncts to the standard pass outs and can be given to participants or sold at the back of the room. Make sure the course name and your name, address and phone number are on *every* item.

Books, Booklets, Audio and/or Video Tapes and a variety of other print and electronic media that support the seminar. As we've already seen, selling these "back-of-the-room" products greatly improves meeting profitability and provides additional value to participants.

Sales Literature. Furnish each participant a complete set of your sales literature and information on how to order from you. And be sure to show participants where this information is in their package *before* the meeting adjourns.

Course-Completion Certificate. Attractive course-completion certificates or wall plaques can help stimulate referrals. But furnish them *ready-to-hang* (including the nail), not merely *ready-to-frame*.

How to Easily Produce Audio and Video Tapes of Your Meeting for Sale

You can easily and economically acquire sellable audio tapes by having your seminar recorded "live." Most hotels can arrange this through a local sound-recording specialist. A professional or studio-recorded introduction is added to each tape during editing, which may be done by the recording firm or by someone who'll handle the entire project for you. Production includes duplicating and labeling the cassettes, designing and obtaining the packaging and incorporating your printed materials. It's easier than you think. And these "live" recordings are very acceptable to those who are hungry for the information and prefer to learn by listening.

Choose the Best Seating Arrangement

There are six popular seating arrangements for seminars and conferences:

1. Outside an Open "U" with the speaker at the open end. This is great for group interaction but an inefficient use of space; 35-40 people are about the most that can be accommodated this way. Figure a maximum of three people per eight-foot table, and insist that tables be at least two feet wide -- 30 inches is better. Allow at least four to five feet between tables and walls.

2. Amphitheater Style is a "U"-within-a-"U" and is a good way to get more people in a limited space while preserving interaction. Be sure to leave at least three feet between tables.

3. Classroom Style consists of rows of tables, all facing the speaker, with seating on one side. Allow three feet between tables and five-foot aisles. Follow the above table size and seating guidelines. This format is often used for seminars but has the disadvantage that participants look at the back of those in front of them. It's acceptable only when there will *not* be a lot of participant interaction. A variation is to angle the outer tables in a "chevron" pattern facing the front.

4. Banquet (or Island) Seating consists of round tables with six to ten persons per table. Very good for discussion at each table, but about one-third of the spots are poor for prolonged attention to a speaker in one location.

Popular Seating Arrangements

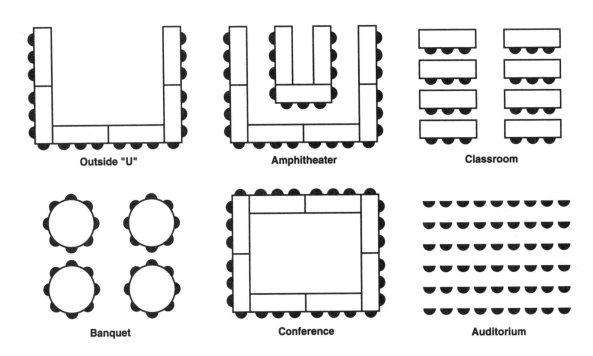

Outside "U"   Amphitheater   Classroom

Banquet   Conference   Auditorium

5. Conference Style guarantees everyone can see (almost) everyone else and avoids having a clear-cut "head table." Use this if there will be no visual aids. Obviously the dimensions can be changed, but if it gets too narrow, then a "head" or power position will emerge.

6. Auditorium Style is row-upon-row of chairs, with no writing provisions, all facing the speaker. This accommodates the most participants in the least space -- with the fewest comforts. Good for short meetings with minimum note-taking or where you specifically want to discourage people from looking through materials. Alternative:

Some facilities have chairs with pull-up writing surfaces.

There are a few other specialized formats you'll encounter. For example, chairs in a circle often facilitates small discussion groups. And break-out clusters are easier with chairs grouped around an easel.

Your seating arrangement will dictate the facilities you'll be able to use and will affect room rental charges. For example, large, round tables are typically available in hotel ballrooms, whereas U-shaped seating is more typically available in smaller meeting rooms. Occasionally your selection of one arrangement over another may even have food and beverage cost implications.

"WIN-WIN" RELATIONSHIPS WITH HOTELS AND MEETING FACILITIES

Use a Meeting Facility that Will Help Your Program Succeed

Here are the main questions you need to answer:

- What type of facility should you use?
- Where should it be located in relation to the population center?
- What kind of meeting room will you choose?
- Should you include food and/or beverage functions.
- How can you negotiate with the facility for the best possible deal?

Today's explosion of public seminars -- not to mention the proportionate growth of hotels geared to support meetings of all sizes -- has given you a wide range of acceptable choices in an area that was once very limited.

Although you can consider virtually any type of meeting facility, including business conference rooms, schools, churches, clubs and even private homes, the best all-around choice is usually a hotel.

Top 39 Hotel Chains for Meetings

Rank	Chain	Locations	Reservations
1.	Marriott	312	1-800-228-9290
2.	Hyatt	168	1-800-233-1234
3.	Hilton	254	1-800-445-8667
4.	Sheraton	416	1-800-325-3535
5.	Holiday Inns	1,656	1-800-465-4329
6.	Westin	77	1-800-228-3000
7.	Radisson	304	1-800-333-3333
8.	Ritz-Carlton	28	1-800-241-3333
9.	Embassy Suites	106	1-800-362-2779
10.	Stouffer	40	1-800-468-3571
11.	Ramada	612	1-800-272-6232
12.	Four Seasons	25	1-800-332-3442
13.	Princess Hotels	7	1-800-223-1818
14.	Omni	46	1-800-843-6664
15.	Doubletree	87	1-800-222-8733
16.	Canadian Pacific Hotels	24	1-800-828-7447
17.	Lowes	14	1-800-235-6397
18.	Inter-Continental	108	1-800-327-0200
19.	Ramada Renaissance	50	1-800-228-9898
20.	Fairmont	5	1-800-527-4727
21.	Meridien	56	1-800-543-4300
22.	Wyndham	31	1-800-822-4200
23.	Adam's Mark	9	1-800-766-6338
24.	Red Lion	53	1-800-547-8010
25.	Registry	14	1-800-247-9810
26.	Days Inn	1,350	1-800-325-2525
27.	Regent	12	1-800-545-4000
28.	Sonesta	3	1-800-766-3782
29.	Howard Johnson	563	1-800-446-4656
30.	Nikko	33	1-800-645-5687
31.	Forte	400	1-800-225-5843
32.	Swissotel	14	1-800-637-9477
33.	Travelodge	520	1-800-578-7878
34.	Mandarin	10	1-800-526-6566
35.	Kempinski	8	1-800-426-3135
36.	Choice Hotels	122	1-800-424-6423
-	Best Western	3,400	1-800-528-1234
-	Residence Inns	180	1-800-331-3131
-	Sofitel	140	1-800-221-4542

Hotels are experienced in handling meetings of all kinds, can set up and rearrange quickly, are convenient for those staying over and generally have the staff and resources to meet unexpected changes and emergencies.

There are plenty of hotels to choose from everywhere. Here's a recent ranking of the top hotel chains considered for meetings, according to a survey taken by *Successful Meetings* magazine.

Tips for Negotiating with Hotels and Meeting Facilities

Everything Is Negotiable. When cutting a deal with a hotel or meeting facility, remember two things: First, *everything* is negotiable. Second, if it's done right, everyone *wins*. Following are some things to ask about before signing on the dotted line and some general tips in this important area.

Start with the Lowest Room Rates. There are usually several types of sleeping-room rates. "Rack Rate" is the posted rate. Others are "Discounted," "Commissionable," "Net," etc. You should generally work on a "Group Rate."

How much you can negotiate depends on time of year, amount of meeting space you need, number of rooms being booked and -- most importantly -- how much total dollar volume you'll bring the property (this includes room service, bar tabs, food functions, green fees, etc.). It's a good idea to document this total revenue and keep it up to date.

Do your homework before calling the property you want. Determine the range of going rates in the city by calling other facilities. Rates are also published in trade journals. Then, when negotiating, you know what kind of deal you are (or are not) getting.

Sample Meeting-Room Arrangement Diagram for Hotels

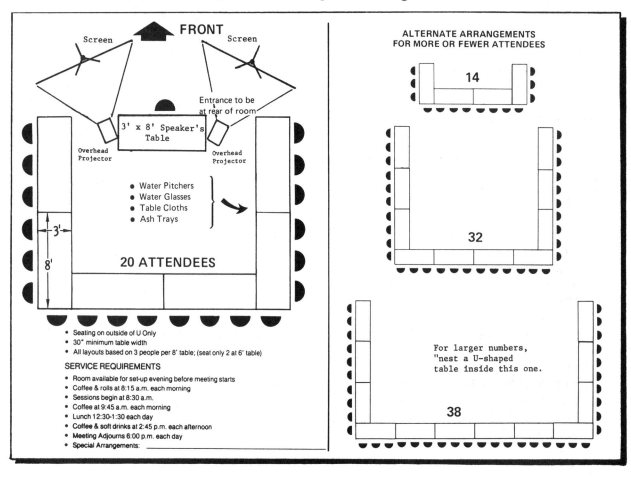

Ask for Complimentary Rooms. If your organization is hosting a major meeting or lots of smaller ones, don't be shy in seeking "comp" rooms. Base your comp room request on the total room-nights booked. A general rule is one comp room for every 50 sleeping rooms and one suite for every 100 sleeping rooms. You may be able to do some trading here, like saying, "Give me your four worst rooms instead of two good rooms."

Expect to pay a meeting-room rental if you are not having a food or beverage function. Try to get a flat room rental rate for the entire year or block of meetings or a sliding scale based on your room pickup, whichever better benefits you.

Be Sure Your Meeting Really Fits Their Room. Don't believe the room capacities in hotel literature. Figure it out yourself using the guidelines in the previous section.

Be on the lookout for posts, corners, inconvenient doors and other obstructions that prevent using the entire room, especially in older properties.

Whatever arrangement you select, be sure to communicate it to the facility in clear, unmistakable terms. Diagrams are less apt to be misunderstood than words, especially since many of those who set up rooms don't speak English. On the left-hand page is a sample of the meeting-room diagram we furnish to facilities.

Save Money on Food and Beverages. Functions involving food or liquor can be very costly if not properly negotiated. Here's some tips:

- Buy coffee and refreshment breaks for your meeting in bulk, not by the person (e.g., order gallons of coffee, dozens of bottles of coke, etc.). It's usually *much* less expensive this way.

- The type of drink plan you use -- by the *drink*, by the *bottle*, or by the *event* -- depends on the consumption habits of your group. Whichever plan you choose, ask what brands will be served. If you're buying by the bottle, ask if the bottles are quarts or fifths and whether you'll get to keep any bottles that are opened but not empty.

- For cocktail parties, ask if dry foods and/or butler service is included. The fees for the bartenders can be negotiated. A good way to bargain on this is to tell the facility, "If I give you 'X' amount of business, then don't charge for the bartender. If I do less, I will pay for the bartender."

- Hors d'oeuvres range in price from the reasonable to exorbitant. There's usually plenty of choices available at the lowest price, and don't be afraid to choose these. Hotels usually want to push their highest priced items.

- The standard policy on meal guarantees is 48-hour notice, with the allowance of a certain percentage over and under. But this is negotiable.

- A light buffet can cost more than a heavy sit-down lunch because of variety, preparation and waste. If you *are* planning a buffet, ask how fast the facility can serve it.

Get Everything in Writing. Send your requirements in writing (see sample FACILITY BOOKING CONFIRMATION on the next page) and incorporate them in any hotel contract you sign. Make any changes directly on the contract so they're less likely to be misplaced. Keep copies of all correspondence with the hotel. Negotiating is a lot easier when you're quoting from something in print.

Other items/services you may need to spell out in the contract include:

- Free receiving and storage services -- and how to get them at the hotel
- Parking fees
- Recreational activity fees (spas, tennis courts, golf courses, etc.)
- Signs and event boards
- Airport pickup and transfers
- Local phone calls/access charges
- The possibility of a free opening cocktail party
- Will your group be named on hotel's liability insurance policy?
- Check-in and check-out procedures
- Billing procedures (including a financial "cushion" for disputed charges)

- Convention service/in-house equipment/audiovisual: How much does it cost and are the charges competitive?

- Cancellation provisions by either party.

FACILITY BOOKING CONFIRMATION

DATE_____ BY:_____
_____Manager, Seminar Arrangements_
FACILITY:_____ PHONE:_____
ADDRESS:_____
MEETING ROOM FOR:_____
MEETING DATES:_____through_____ANTICIPATED ATTENDANCE:___

GUEST ROOM REQUIREMENTS FOR PARTICIPANTS

NO. OF ROOMS:____ARRIVAL DATE:_____DEPARTURE DATE:_____
CUT-OFF DATE FOR ROOMING LIST:____ RATES:Single___Double___
Hotel charges are the responsibility of each individual. Please guarantee each participant for late arrival by his/her own company, as specified on rooming list.

MEETING-ROOM REQUIREMENTS

Date(s)	Times of Day	Meeting-Room Name	Dimensions
_____	_____	_____	_____
_____	_____	_____	_____
_____	_____	_____	_____

Please provide meeting-room diagram, indicating location of windows, doors and any other unusual configurations, such as closets, pillars, etc.

RESPONSIBLE HOTEL CONTACTS

SALES:_____CATERING:_____
NIGHT:_____EMERGENCY:_____

PROGRAM REQUIREMENTS

■ HOTEL ACTIVITIES BOARD: Meeting to begin at 8:30 a.m. (Room set up by 7:00 a.m.)

PLEASE POST AS:_____

■ SEATING ARRANGEMENTS: "U" shaped configuration with seating on the outside only. SEE SEPARATE SHEET FOR DETAILS.

■ VISUAL AIDS: Chalkboard, chalk, eraser; 2 flip charts and easel stands; screen and overhead projector.

■ LINEN: White or pastel colors (not red).

PLEASE SEE ROOM SETUP EXAMPLES ON SEPARATE SHEET

SERVICE REQUIREMENTS:
       8:00 a.m.-Coffee and Danish for_____
       9:45 a.m.-Coffee Refill for_____
       2:45 P.m.-Coffee and Soft Drinks for_____
COCKTAIL RECEPTION:_____
_____
OTHER ARRANGEMENTS:_____
ACCEPTED BY:_____TITLE:_____
DATE:_____DATE:_____
_____Manager, Seminar Arrangements_

PLEASE SIGN ONE COPY AND RETURN FOR OUR RECORDS

Check All Bills Thoroughly, comparing them to your contract and to receipts signed during the meeting. Challenge anything out of line. (Why are the mistakes always in favor of the facility?)

Consider Rooming Lists. This is where you get into the hotel reservation process, between your participants and the hotel. Rooming lists increase your costs and your headaches. The benefit to you is that rooming lists allow you to *prove* the business you're generating for the hotel and thereby negotiate a better deal next time. As surprising as it may seem, most registrants who deal directly with the hotel will *not* identify themselves as attending your program, even if you tell them to do so.

If you use a rooming list, include a Hotel Reservation Request form, like the one shown below, in your confirmation package.

HOTEL RESERVATION REQUEST

If you desire accommodations at the hotel where the seminar is being held, please complete the form below and return it to us in the enclosed envelope. We will make your hotel reservations. While hotel charges are the responsibility of the individual, priority service has been established for Schrello Direct Marketing attendees, assuring you of preferred placement at the lowest rate available to us. PLEASE DO NOT CALL THE HOTEL. As part of our service, we will also handle any changes for you. Simply contact us for assistance.

_____
(hotel)
_____
(address)
_____
(city & state)

NAME:_____TITLE_____
COMPANY:_____
ADDRESS:_____MAIL STOP:_____
CITY:_____STATE:_____ZIP:_____
TELEPHONE:_____EXTENSION:_____
FAX:_____

I would like the following accommodations (check one):

       SINGLE_____at $_____per night
       DOUBLE_____at $_____per night

ARRIVAL DATE:_____DEPARTURE DATE:_____

Please do not write in this box. When your reservation has been made, we will return this completed form to you as your confirmation.
Name:_____Company:_____
Arrival Date:_____Departure Date:_____
Hotel/City:_____Type Room:_____

Your reservation will guaranteed for late arrival by your company.

Confirmed By_____of **Schrello Direct Marketing** on_____

Learn What's Important to the Facility. Overall, listen to the facilities' needs and *hear* them, particularly in the following areas:

- Seasonality: Determine when *they* need *you* the most (and least) and work with them to best schedule your meetings.

- Determine what is most important to the hotel (99% of the time it's the sleeping rooms).

- Point out all advantages to them of having your business.

- Be willing to supply any materials, forms, rooming lists, agenda or other things the hotel might need.

Don't lie. If you're only going to pick up ten rooms, only block ten rooms. Hotel people are constantly on the move, and you'll find them again at another property.

Treat the Facility as People, Not Just an Institution. If the account will be handled by Convention Services or Catering in the future (after being initially booked by Sales), call those contacts and get to know them by name. After all, these people do all the work and ensure the success of your meeting. They're also more honest about the meeting facilities and what their hotel can actually do or not do.

Stay in touch. Follow up on every detail; send relevant clippings, etc. Call to say "hi," attend grand openings, etc. Subscribe to trade magazines and read them.

Also contact the hotel's regional or corporate sales offices -- their salespeople represent an entire chain and see the overall picture better. They'll also do a lot of your work for you.

You may also refer to Chapter 10 on showcases, which includes more on meeting rooms and facility arrangements.

SEMINAR PLANNING REFERENCES

I'd like to think that this handbook is probably your best single reference for success in today's seminar business. It certainly reflects more collective experience than any other source I've seen. And it approaches seminars as a *business*, not just the way an individual picks up a few bucks in speaking fees.

That having been said, seminars involve so many details and have so many places where things can go wrong, that you almost can't have too much help. I also know that different people need different perspectives to fully illuminate a subject.

So here are a few more references that you might look for at your local library:

1. How to Conduct Training Seminars: A Complete Reference Guide for Training Managers & Professionals, by Lawrence S. Munson. McGraw-Hill, 1221 Avenue of the Americas, New York, NY 10020. Phone: (800) 2-MCGRAW or (212) 337-5945. 1992 (2nd Edition). ISBN 0-07-044201-0. (245 pages, $34.95.)

This review of the mechanics of in-house training was first published in 1984. The latest edition includes information on computers, video and teleconferencing, along with the previous edition's material on stand-up training. There are no references and nothing on how to fill the seminars you create. But if you're looking for help setting up or understanding in-house seminars, this is one of the few sources around.

2. How to Organize and Manage a Seminar: What to Do and When to Do It, by Sheila L. Murray. Prentice Hall, 113 Sylvan Avenue, Englewood Cliffs, NJ 07632. Phone: (201) 592-2000. 1983. ISBN 0-13-425199-7. (204 pages, $7.95.)

A practical narrative on many of the key steps to take before, during and after a seminar, conference or other meeting. Sections also contain short interviews with various well-known meeting personalities, as well as plenty of practical suggestions. However, there are few, if any, numbers; if you're seeking costs, times, capacities, percentages, etc., you'll likely need to look elsewhere.

3. The Total Immersion Learning Environment: Its Critical Impact on Meeting Success, by Coleman Finkel. Conference Center Development Corporation, 205 E. 59th Street, Suite 6-F, New York, NY 10128. Phone: (212) 722-6005. 1982. (120 pages, hardcover, $23.95.)

The author is a pioneer in advocating "engineering" of the meeting and learning environment. This book is a wealth of meeting planning detail, touching on practically every conceivable factor that could affect participants. I found the treatment of various seating and room arrangement particularly useful. This book is hard to find, but be persistent: It's worth it!

4. How to Plan Meetings Like a Professional, by Coleman Finkel. Sales and Marketing Management Division of Bill Communications, Inc., 633 Third Avenue, New York, NY 10017. Phone: (212) 986-4800. 1983. ($12.95.)

Solutions to many of the problems that plague meeting planners. Identifies the tasks involved in planning both large and small meetings with suggestions for forms, charts and checklists to use while coordinating the events.

7. *How to Make It Big in the Seminar Business,* by Paul Karasik. McGraw-Hill, 1221 Avenue of the Americas, New York, NY 10020. Phone: (212) 337-5945, (800) 2-MCGRAW. 1992. ISBN 0-07-033185-5. (256 pages.)

Another "How I Got into Seminars" book, aimed primarily at the individual/consultant seeking to add income from this source, rather than those who are already in the business. Despite its basically "mom and pop" orientation, the book is well-written, contains many helpful references and resources and should be read by anyone planning to enter the field.

8. *Money Talks: The Complete Guide to*

Creating a Profitable Workshop or Seminar in Any Field,* by Dr. Jeffrey L. Lant. Jeffrey Lant Associates, Inc., 50 Follen Street, Suite 507, Cambridge, MA 02138. Phone: (617) 547-6372; Fax: (617) 547-0061. 1992 (2nd Edition). (308 pages, 8-1/2" x 11" format, $35.00.)

Recommendations for creating a career offering lectures, seminars and conferences. Discusses promotion techniques and identifying sponsors for your workshops.

9. *How to Create and Market a Successful Seminar or Workshop,* by Howard L. Shenson. Bermont Books, Box 309, Gleneg, MD 21737. 1987 (Revised Edition). (102 pages, $29.00.)

I'm not even sure this is still in print, and it could be hard to find now that Mr. Shenson is deceased. But it was one of the first attempts at a how-to-do-it book, primarily oriented toward 1-day or shorter local seminars promoted by newspaper ads. Includes chapters on how to test-market, getting advance registrations and sponsorships, handling program roll-out and determining the salability of the plan.

TAKING AND PROCESSING ENROLLMENTS

Public seminar registrations are generally received in one of two ways: in written form (by mail, fax, telex, etc.) or orally (by phone or in person). We'll devote this section to considerations applicable to both.

Track Down the Source of *Every* Registrant

The commitment to track down the source of *every* registration or inquiry is the second most important rule of direct marketing. (The first rule is to test every change before you make it. But the two rules work together, because vigorously ferreting out the source of every response shortens the time it takes to complete any test. For example, if the source of only half of your order is known, it takes twice as many orders to reach the same confidence level as it would if you could determine

the sources of every order!)

Help your seminar registrants identify how they learned of you by coding every mail piece, advertisement or publicity release in some distinctive manner (see Chapter 8 for how to do this coding).

Determine the source of referrals -- or orders placed at the direction of another person in the organization -- by finding out the specific name and/or position of this person. Such referral sources, once uncovered, can produce many future participants, referrals, testimonials and more. But they'll rarely let you know that they're out there "selling" your program. You'll have to find out for yourself by insisting on knowing how each responder learned of you.

Recognize that you'll probably never achieve 100% perfection in learning the source of each registration. There will likely always remain a fraction that you simply can't track down, perhaps as high as 20% - 30% for offers that have been around for a while or those which employ many different media.

Designate a Customer-Oriented Registrar

Most organizations settle on one person who serves as "registrar" for public seminar enrollments, even though (depending upon the sponsor's size) many people may be involved. Since this person *is* your company to most enrollees, she or he should be the most customer-service-oriented person on your staff.

The registrar should really know all about the firm's products and services. If they know what they're doing, they'll be self-assured and feel competent. That is important in dealing with customers and handling potentially troublesome situations. Knowledge gives credibility.

Have available the names, organizations, position titles and telephone numbers for satisfied participants in your regularly recurring programs. Try to keep a good cross-section of types of industries, management levels and geographic areas. Give these names out to those asking to check references. But keep a log of how often each name has been given out, and switch to another after two or three uses, unless you know that the person won't object to a greater number.

Be sure your registrar knows all of the options and procedures available. Indecisiveness and being evasive is a real turn-off. It harms credibility, makes the client wary and often makes them wonder if they should speak to someone "higher up."

Have everyone who takes orders by telephone see the good post-meeting surveys originating from your public sessions. This can provide an automatic replenishing of positive impressions and benefits that they can use when talking to other prospects.

Build Your Registration Process Around the Telephone

Today, the majority of advance seminar enrollments are received by telephone, even if these telephone arrangements are later confirmed in writing. So be sure all those serving as "registrar" receive telephone-skills training (see Chapter 11 for more on using the telephone).

Here are some helpful tips.

Prepare Brief "Scripts." If someone calls and doesn't know anything about your organization, be prepared to give a short verbal history, and follow up with printed literature and the offer to provide references. Be similarly prepared to describe each course in a few benefits-oriented sentences. Compile brief, pointed answers to the most often-asked questions.

Accept "Tentative" Registrations. If someone is undecided about a seminar, let them know, in a non-pushy manner, that enrollments are limited, that it would be a good idea to at least get registered. Suggest that later, it's O.K. to transfer to another session or even cancel.

Get Commitment to Attend. It seems almost too simple, but it works. Ask each enrollee in your own words if they're really going to be there. It's amazing how often this question will expose a potential problem, which is always better dealt with earlier rather than later. And the individual's own commitment can be vital in having *that person* uncover and handle objections that arise with his or her decider, payer or influencer or elsewhere in the customer constituencies. (Some organizations take this one step further: They contact the person's boss and get *their* commitment for the participant to attend. This often ensures that last-minute "panics" and other operating matters will have the least possible effect on your participants.)

Use an Order Form designed to help you ask the customer for all the information you need/want. Nothing is more frustrating than to hang up and realize that an important piece of information was not obtained. On the following page is a sample we've used successfully for years.

By the way, we recommend a printed form even *with* an on-line computer database, to provide a written back-up record and to allow registrations even during periods when the computer is "down."

Sample Telephone Order Log

TELEPHONE ORDER LOG

Name _____

Position/Title _____

Company _____

Division _____

Address _____

City _____ ST _____ ZIP _____

Phone (_____) _____ Ext _____

Fax (_____) _____ (800) _____

Type Of Business _____

Nickname (For Placecard) _____

How Customer Learned of SDM _____

_____

Mail Code (On Mailing Label) _____

Action _____

Date _____

Customer # _____

Company Code _____

Product _____

Dates _____

Location _____

Price _____

MC   VISA   AMEX

Expires _____

Purchase Order _____

Invoice To _____

_____

Order Placed By _____

Order Taken By _____

© Copyright SCHRELLO DIRECT MARKETING • Long Beach, CA 90808—4421

Go the Extra Mile with Your Major Clients. Sometimes they demand extra attention and considerations. Even though you may not be obligated to perform special service for them, a little extra attention goes a long way.

Some customers, especially in large organizations, are under considerable pressure to hold or cut costs and to negotiate hard with suppliers of all types for the best possible deal. Be prepared to help them take advantage of your discount policies or to offer a small added concession (*not* involving your basic rate structure) or extra no-cost goods/services as a "deal sweetener" to close the sale.

Use Discounts, Scholarships and "Freebies" Sparingly. Most participants equate *value* and *cost*: "Anything cheap/free can't be worth much." As a result, they tend to cancel and no-show more often, leave early and in other ways demonstrate less interest than full-paying participants.

Here's How to Handle Those Who Want to Attend Free, promising that they're going to give you lots of business later: Tell them to pay for the course they're attending now and you'll give them full credit for it against their first major purchase.

Your Confirming Package Is Part of Your Sales Process

Make sure the confirmation package you send to those enrolling in your programs is complete *and* professional. It's the first thing since your advertising material the person will see from you, and it either increases their desire to attend or starts them thinking they made a mistake. A well-designed confirmation package can stimulate additional enrollments, too, if it shows added benefits for team participation. Here's what to include:

1. Confirming letter from the registrar.
2. Pre-meeting preparation materials (including specific instructions).
3. Invoice or credit-card charge slip.
4. Hotel reservation form.
5. Facility brochure or other literature.

6. Location/facility fact sheet (transportation, restaurants, points of interest, dress code, etc.).

7. Latest copy of your promotional brochure on the program.

8. Reply envelope(s).

Establish Regular Pre-Meeting Communication with Each Registrant

Once a person has responded, your responsibility shifts to establishing a steady, regular pattern of pre-meeting communications aimed at five principal objectives:

1. Closing the Sale, especially for inquiries, but often others aren't really "sold" even though they've signed up.

2. Verifying All Meeting Arrangements and details: times, places, events, etc.

3. Setting Expectations for the course, reaffirming what personal and organizational benefits they'll derive and what they'll have to do in order to get them.

4. Uncovering Potential Obstacles/Objections they now have -- or those that others they depend on may have.

5. Keeping It Sold, which means addressing the obstacles/objections identified in No. 4 above and anticipating (and removing) any other obstacles that arise.

The key to all five of these objectives is a regular pattern of pre-meeting communications by mail and/or telephone no less often than every 10 to 14 days, building up to no less often than weekly for the last four weeks before the program starts.

Interrelate your pre-meeting communication with other enrollment actions to provide a complete picture. For example, if lodging arrangements are to be made by the enrollee, finding out that these arrangements have *not* been made can reveal a possible attendance problem. At the least, you can help save them needless inconvenience if they still do plan to attend. Likewise, failure to receive advance payment of fees can be an early warning of possible attendance problems.

Handling At-the-Door Registrations

If your seminar does not lend itself to advance registrations, such as a several-hour event held outside of normal business hours, then much of the foregoing will be of little value to you. In those cases you need to gear up to handling registrations at the door, often in a very short time frame. For example, a several-hour evening seminar that begins at 7:30 p.m. may have all the people arrive within a 15- or 20-minute period.

You'll need to have extra help for that process, including credit-card forms and a cash box, and help in maintaining some kind of security. Your best advise is to use an individual solely dedicated to this function and not try to have the speaker do it nor to rely on those who are setting up your meeting.

Finally, be alert for the possibility of thievery during this critical stage. Some will take advantage of the confusion attendant to such an event to make off with the cash box when you least expect it. So brief your assistants to be alert for anyone who doesn't seem to belong with the group.

Advance Registration Record Keeping

Most public seminar promoters employ some kind of readily accessible, real-time, up-to-the-minute count of enrollments for each course or session they're promoting. Small organizations can use a manual system, such as a status board, notebook, clipboard, etc., with one section, page or board for each course/session. On the next page is a sample of such a manual enrollment log.

Anyone who takes orders or changes immediately enters the information directly into the proper place, so there's never "a second place to look." Larger organizations, or those with networked computers, may achieve the same real-time status capability with an online computer database. Information on such systems is in Chapter 13.

Sample Manual Seminar Enrollment Log

	Names & Company	Pos.	Tentative	Wait List	Cust. #	Date	How Order Taken (By Whom)	Mail Code	Date Res Recv	$	Date Check Recv	Adv	Date Conf Sent
	CITY Washington, DC						PROGRAM Strategic Planning						
	HOTEL Key Bridge Marriott						DATES March 22-24, 1989						
	ROOM												
	INSTRUCTOR												
1	Kelly J. Kilpatrick / Johnstown Manage.				28146	2/2	Phone — BFA	35 56	2/21	F	2/21		2/3
2	Phil G. Collins / Federal Foods				26882	2/2	Phone — BFA	CC	2/9	F	2/9		2/7
3	Robin Jones / Union Std. Plumbing				28163	2/5	Fax — CAR	F/U	2/5	F	3/21		2/7
4	Toby H. Green / Golden State				28271	2/11	Fax — CAR	REF	2/11	F	2/22		2/13
5	Tracy W. Bowman / Southwest Central				28259	2/17	Mail — CAR	REF	2/17	D	2/17		2/21
6	Ev M. Smith / Statewide Const.				28262	2/17	Mail — BFA	35 66	2/17	F	2/17		2/21
7	Lynn R. Conrad / Rapid Trucking				28601	2/20	Phone — GHS CANCEL 3/15	35 59	2/	F			2/
8	Lee L. Mathys / 1st Nat'l.	✓	?		28240	2/20	Phone — GHS	XB	2/28	F	2/28		2/22
9	Dale Adams / Indep. Telephone				25230	2/21	Phone — BFA	35 55	3/13	F	3/13		2/22
10	Chris K. Mills / Preferred Invest.				13218	2/23	Mail — CAR	X	2/23	D	2/23		2/27
11	Jackie D. Petersen / Computer Specialists				19711	3/24	Fax — CAR TRANSF 3/8	35 57	2/	F			3/4
12	Pat A. Evans / A & M Plastics				28275	2/27	Phone — TBD	35 57	3/7	F	3/7		3/2
	Jay G. Hill				2827		Phone — one	35 55	3/21				3/3

BILLING, CREDIT AND COLLECTION CONSIDERATIONS

Making your mailing starts the really enjoyable part of the process: receiving the registrations, inquiries or other responses. And one important consideration has to do with billing, credit, collections, returns and related matters. Here are some helpful hints in this area, that apply to both product sales (for example, the books and tapes you advertise in your seminar mailer) *and* open registration events:

Use Care Extending Credit

Credit is like any decision on payment terms: It automatically becomes part of your pricing. These matters are inseparable: price, method of payment, payment terms. If you're getting all the business you need or want with cash payment in advance, don't change. But overall, extending credit out-pulls cash-with-the-order almost three to one. So you could possibly increase your sales and profits very substantially by offering some form of credit.

Returns and Bad Debts Are Inevitable

Develop careful records on bad debts and returned orders so you can tell what's "normal" for your products and markets. Be alert for changes from this norm up or down. Also look for correlations or patterns with various offers, prices, mailing lists, geographic areas, etc. In general, higher priced products experience more product returns and refusals than do lower priced ones. Seminars tend to have few or no bad debts.

Aggressively Pursue All Overdue Accounts

Set up an aging system with progressive reminders/letters every 30 days (or less), leading to a telephone collection program after 90 days. Turn any remaining invoices over to a collection service after six months.

Beware of "Phonies"

Train your staff to look out for "phonies" or potentially fraudulent orders, and conduct extra checks to verify their authenticity before filling the order. Such checks include telephoning to verify the order, sending a confirming letter, running a name and address match on credit-card purchases, verifying organization address, comparing with your previous customer or "negatives" files, etc.

"Phonies" are prank responses which will only lead to a loss if you're careless. Usually a phony order will arrive by business reply mail and appear somewhat suspicious in terms of name (for example, we've actually received prank orders from Ima T. Hief and Wind E. Sity), address, size of order, etc. Occasionally, it will be a plausible but totally fictitious person at a nonexistent address, and mail will be returned.

Fraudulent orders are a deliberate attempt to cheat you. Generally, the more widespread your advertising and broader the appeal of your products, the greater potential fraud you can expect. The problem is not great when dealing mainly with businesses, but it can be very serious for consumer products.

Be suspicious whenever one or more of the following elements of a mail order don't match:

- Name and address on outer envelope
- Postmark on outer envelope
- Name and address on order coupon
- Name and address on check

Return all incomplete, incorrect or altered checks to the sender to be corrected, even though in some cases this will lose the sale. On others, consider not shipping the product until the check clears the bank.

Finally, don't just discard the "phonies." Enter them into your database along with all relevant information you've uncovered, and code them to show their exact status. You'll be surprised how these same names come up over and over again. And you'll save lots of time and effort by easily retrieving that earlier information.

"Bill my Company" Requires Added Care

For materials shipped on a "Bill my Company" basis, *never* include the invoice with the order (exception: low-cost items, where the added costs of separate billing can't be tolerated). Send the invoice in a No. 10 window envelope so that it arrives a few days to a week *after* the order does. Invoices included with the shipment frequently (1.) are lost or thrown away with the package and (2.) increase merchandise returns.

How to Handle Price Tests

When *testing* prices in your mailer, always honor the lower price. When *raising* prices, honor the lower price only when a lower-priced order form is used.

HANDLING SESSIONS THAT ARE UNDER-ENROLLED (AND OVER-ENROLLED)

If you apply the forecasting methods presented later in this chapter, you'll almost certainly encounter public seminars you've scheduled which are projected to be over- or under-enrolled. Over-enrollments mean a greater number of expected participants than you can handle either because of room size, limitations due to the nature of the instruction or other reasons.   Under-enrollments mean forecasting that insufficient participants will attend to meet your economic criteria. Both situations require prompt action, but the under-enrolled sessions can be thorny.

How to Boost Attendance at Under-Enrolled Events

Here's a situation you may recognize: A seminar has been under-enrolled for weeks. Everyone hopes for a turnaround, and last-minute surges in enrollments at previous seminars are cited to justify "... waiting a few more weeks." Finally, imminent hotel commitments force someone to take the low enrollment seriously just three weeks before the event. A "cash" program is launched, with the staff calling everyone they can in a last-ditch effort to get more participants. After a frantic -- and frustrating -- three weeks, the event is held with too few participants.

The moral is this: No one can save an under-enrolled event unless they start in time. And for most employer-paid events held during normal business hours, that means a *minimum* of six weeks before the event begins and preferably eight to ten weeks before. Fortunately, it *is* almost always possible to forecast low attendance this far in advance. And while no one can guarantee you'll be able to rescue that low event, at least you'll have time to try.

With sufficient lead-time, your rescue efforts can employ all your customary marketing media.   There's enough time for direct mail (often sent First Class to shorten delivery time) and for telemarketing. I know one seminar firm that offers their telemarketers a special bonus on the *entire* seminar (not just commissions on their sales) if they "save" an event declared to be under-enrolled seven weeks ahead.

Some organizations even maintain a standby list of low-/no-tuition participants who are willing to attend on short notice to keep attendance up. Candidates include employees, church/civic groups -- even students. Instruct them not to discuss fees with other participants or, if pressed, to say they're attending on a scholarship.

But be cautious trying to use free or heavily discounted participants to "fill" sessions at the last minute.   While this technique works well on in-house programs where those desiring the course can be accurately identified well in advance, it's been generally disappointing for open sessions. Most people who call friends and others to attend a free or low-cost session, especially at the last moment, are disappointed to find that in spite of promises and commitments, these "freebies" tend to show up late, leave early and in other ways demonstrate the low value they place on the event.   Unless you do something markedly different, this is *not* the way you'll save your under-enrolled seminar.

Think Hard Before You Cancel a Session

Everyone worries about holding a small seminar, and that's why so many do get cancelled, particularly during a recession. But a seminar can be worth holding with fewer participants than you think!

Felix Gelber, the wise man who helped me start my first seminar business, knew nothing about our meetings but everything about people. He observed that *we* were the ones who were disappointed by low attendance and far too anxious to cancel a session for that reason. He noted that the *participants*, for their part, were usually delighted with the added personal attention they got at the small events -- provided the leaders were enthusiastic and concealed any feelings of disappointment.

And he was right! Our first seminar in New York ended up with only four registrants, each from a separate company. And this despite weeks of frantic sales effort (mostly inept, as we would later learn). We were sure the meeting would be a disaster but went ahead anyway. Well, every one of those four participants showed up and was ecstatic with the course. Each later brought us into their organization to train hundreds of their people. By almost any standard, it was the most profitable seminar we ever held.

When considering whether or not to cancel a seminar or to hold a marginal program, always look at whether those signed up come from a number of separate organizations or represent a group enrollment from a single company. We've sometimes been disappointed when a group enrollment from one company is suddenly cancelled or transferred to another session because of some "panic." Such a move can quickly transform an acceptable session into an unacceptable one. And if it happens close to the seminar date, there's little you can do about it.

Another area of caution when making a decision to hold or cancel a seminar is how many of the registrants have already paid. This is another valuable reason for requiring advance payment. For example, one sponsor, who does not require payment of fees until *after* the course has been completed, routinely has up to 40% of their registrants transfer, cancel or simply not show up. This is an unacceptably high figure and can be cut to 5% -10% by requesting advance payment and threatening the imposition of cancellation fees. But the real purpose in doing this is that those who *do* pay early give you a clear indication of their serious intent to attend. Under these circumstances, look critically at those who haven't yet paid in order to assess the risk you take in deciding to hold a marginal session.

Of course, if you are going to cancel an event, the earlier the better. But certainly not before you've tried to rescue it.

What to Do About Sessions You Must Cancel

Sooner or later every public seminar sponsor needs to cancel a seminar. When this is necessary, call each person enrolled and tell them that the session has been cancelled. Tell them the true reason why (remember, even if you're cancelling because of insufficient enrollments, that's a possible service to the enrollee: For instance, if they wanted to meet and talk with lots of others at the session). If the session has already been rescheduled or if the course is to be offered again in that location, try to re-enroll participants for the

later session. (Note: "Flag" those you've had to move for *your* convenience once, so you can take extra care to *not* do it to them again.)

How to Handle Over-Enrolled Events

Everyone says, "This is the kind of problem we'd like to have," until they have it. And if too many participants really *does* affect program quality, then you need to be extra careful. But from an economic viewpoint, more meeting participants means more profit. So refusing would-be attendees is like throwing money away. If projected attendance based on enrollments exceeds the maximum you've set, your options are:

1. Refuse to take further enrollments for the meeting.
2. Start a waiting list of standbys, who will be accepted as cancellations permit.
3. Get a larger meeting room, more instructors or change whatever it was that set the limit in the first place.

Since last-minute cancellations and no-shows are inevitable, make sure whatever you do is based on projected *attendance*, not *enrollments*.

If you decide to take enrollments on a waiting list, be sure to notify each new enrollee of that fact at once. Make a special phone call for the purpose if the enrollment is received by mail. If they want to have their place confirmed, recommend that they enroll in another session. For those who accept a waiting-list position (which will be most people), follow all your normal confirmation procedures, including a note re-advising them that they're on a waiting list. Avoid giving an actual wait-list number if possible. Keep your waiting list handy, so you can see the situation at a glance. After the program begins, contact the remaining wait-list people to confirm another session.

HELPING THINGS RUN SMOOTHLY ON-SITE
AT THE SEMINAR

No discussion of public seminars would be complete without talking about setting up and running the program at the meeting site. This includes shipping your materials to the site and back again afterward, setting up the room, handling hotel crises and getting and using part-time help.

Who's Who at Hotels

You can't find out if your car repairs are finished by calling the dealer's Sales or Parts Departments. You've got to speak to someone in Service. The same is true at your meeting facility: Knowing which department does what enables you to "speak their language" and get to the right person who can solve your problem. Here's a short tour through a typical hotel:

Sales. Rents all space for conventions and meetings, and books all food/beverage functions, parties ... everything. Once your meeting is booked and you're actually on-site, their main contribution is knowing who to call to get things done.

Convention Services. Coordinates across departments to make sure your meeting works well. Usually only at larger facilities, and/or for larger meetings.

Banquets/Catering are *only* connected with food/beverage functions. They usually have little or nothing to do with meeting rooms other than the ballroom. They can be arrogant and independent, except in smaller properties, where the function is often combined with Sales.

Set-up, Houseman. All refer to those who physically set up (and tear down the tables, chairs, table cloths, water and glasses, etc. It's often part of Banquets/Catering. This is usually the lowest ranking function, often with the poorest language skills.

A/V. Provides screens, projectors, audio-visuals, sound and other meeting-related equipment and supplies, including easels,

pens and chalk. They can be part of Convention Services or Banquets/Catering or a separate department.

Security. Takes care of locking/unlocking meeting rooms, package storage and related matters. This is who you call at 5 a.m. to unlock the meeting room so you can get your notes.

Engineering. Responsible for building heating/cooling and lighting. If your meeting room is boiling, pick up any house phone and ask the operator for "Engineering..."

On-Site Support

One early decision is whether those presenting the session can handle meeting mechanics or whether additional personnel are required. There isn't any "pat" answer to this. I've seen nationally known speakers take their own registrations at the door, collect the money and, when everyone is registered, close the cash box, walk to the platform and present the program. While this wouldn't be my preference, those who follow this technique swear by it.

If you require advance payment and deal mostly with large organizations, don't worry about at-the-door registrations and their added complexity. In these cases the seminar leader can usually handle all the arrangements -- with the help of the hotel or facilities staff -- by arriving the day (or even a few hours) before the meeting.

If you feel some kind of on-site help is required, such as a registrar, consider hiring someone from a local source. The hotel or the local Convention and Visitors Bureau can help you locate personnel of this type. When using temporary personnel for an important event, consider using two different sources as insurance in case one source fails to show up.

If finding local help becomes a problem (it usually is not) or if you see other benefits to having your own coordinator on-site (like schmoozing the hotel or the instructor), then look into the economics. We concluded that having our own coordinator saved us so much money, we couldn't do without them.

Shipping Materials

If your seminars are held in another city, you have to ship participant materials and any other aids you need to conduct the course, so they arrive on time and undamaged. A little advance preparation here can save you lots of money -- *and* lots of headaches.

The first step in planning early is to get sturdy shipping boxes. Flimsy boxes that are easily damaged if dropped or left outdoors in bad weather can ruin your materials, resulting in waste or participant dissatisfaction. I personally favor heavy "telescoping" boxes that surround the materials with a double wall of heavy cardboard. Use plenty of fiberglass strapping tape to be sure the boxes don't accidently split.

Plan early enough to ship your materials via low-cost ground transportation, like Yellow Freight. UPS is a middle ground, but their costs are rising. Overnight service is *very* expensive and should only be employed in true emergencies. Many seminar firms get in the habit of using next-day service and find their costs skyrocket needlessly.

When shipping materials, talk to the hotel and get a specific name and department to send the materials to. Call them and let them know that you've shipped the materials. Then call them a couple weeks later and be sure they've arrived. And -- most importantly -- find out in detail *where* the materials will be stored and *whom to contact* to retrieve them when your people arrive at the hotel. Remember, your faculty or set-up staff will probably be there outside of normal working hours, so be sure they will know how to contact the right person at the hotel.

It's also a good idea to work from a carefully prepared checklist of what will be needed to successfully conduct your meeting. Some of this may be shipped, while other materials may be the instructor's responsibility to provide.

Finally, take steps to get your unused materials returned after the session is concluded.

Failure to do this will quickly reduce everyone's perception of your material's value. Furnish shipping labels for the instructor or administrative staff to use and clear instructions for how to pack and ship the materials.

Handling Crises at the Meeting Site

The key to successful meetings is anticipating that something will go wrong -- then checking vigorously and frequently to make sure it doesn't.

Examples of crises that have happened to us in many years in the business include:

- Having the facility set up the wrong tables in the wrong format for the meeting.
- Showing up at the seminar and learning that the hotel has no record of the event.
- Crippling snow storm that brought the entire city to a halt and closed the airport.
- Learning that there are two hotels on opposite sides of town with the same name, confusing many locals as well as out-of-towners.
- A local government representative who threatens to prohibit the seminar unless the seminar leader can prove they're licensed to conduct seminars in the city (a growing threat in some areas).
- Showing up for the second day of a 3-day meeting only to find the entire meeting room and all materials are gone and in its place is a huge ballroom set up for a Rotary Club breakfast.
- A family crises for an instructor halfway through a multi-day event. (They left in the middle of the night and were seamlessly replaced from 3,000 miles away for the third morning of the session!)

It's impossible to anticipate and prepare for all such emergencies. The key to handling them is to have a flexible, on-site support plan and be able to marshal some on-site resources if and as required. You'll help your overall success by realizing that such crises can and will occur. In fact, in any meeting of long-time seminar sponsors, these are the "war stories" that always get told.

FOLLOWING UP AFTER EVERY SEMINAR

How to Follow Up with Participants

Ask your participants for their comments on the program *after* they've completed their post-course survey but before they leave the seminar. Make accurate notes, or tape record the group's remarks. Then follow up by letter within the next week asking permission to use any good comments in your future advertising. Be sure your letter contains the remark you want their permission to use, and give them the opportunity to edit or amend it.

Ask your participants for the trade publications they read or other media they rely on. If a pattern develops, this could suggest additional mail lists to test or additional advertising possibilities.

After a participant attends, a structured follow-up process will lead to greater customer satisfaction *and* more enrollments. Here's when and how:

1.   Follow Up by Telephone Within 2 - 4 Working Days After the Program Ends, no more -- and no less. The caller should be the registrar or equivalent, *not* a member of the teaching staff.

2.   Say You're Calling to Be Sure the Program Met Their Expectations and they're putting it to work on the job. Probe for specifics.

3.   Solve Any Problems You Uncover. If they had a problem at the session or are having one applying the course back on-the-job or if they have questions about the course, *make resolution of these problems your only agenda.* Arrange professional call-backs, etc., as required to achieve complete customer satisfaction.

4.   Sell Only if the Customer Is Satisfied. Remind them of the next convenient presentation of the program and request the names of others they recommend. Be sure to ask for permission to use their name in your contact. If a third party or superior made the original enrollment decision, get their name

and contact them.

How to Follow Up with No-Shows and Last-Minute Cancellations

Follow up immediately on *every* no-show, by phone or first-class letter. Express concern that they weren't there, and share their disappointment that they couldn't attend. Re-enroll them in another course right then and there, and assure them there will be no penalties or charges. Verify that they still have any advance preparation materials, etc. Send written confirmation of this change at once.

You may need to follow up on no-shows and cancellations many times before they actually attend. Busy people tend to stay busy! But don't give up just because they haven't attended after three or four tries. Try again.

And *do* vigorously re-solicit all cancellations and no-shows with your regular direct mail, even while you pursue the more personalized reminder series outlined above. They will prove to be your most responsive market segment.

Here's How to Handle Those Who Want Their Money Back

Even if you suspect otherwise, start with the belief that the request is genuine and with the policy that they *will* get it back -- and promptly. But your real objective was (and still is) a satisfied customer. Refund their money only after you've explored other remedies that might be better for all concerned. For example, when participant expectations/needs weren't met (the most frequent reason), would everyone be better off if the same person attended a different course tuition-free? How about if someone else from their organization did? If the request stemmed from your inexperienced instructor or a facility problem, try to get the organization to send someone else to another course (again, tuition-free), one that you take special pains to be sure is better.

HOW TO FORECAST FINAL EVENT ATTENDANCE BASED ON EARLY REGISTRATIONS

Everyone in the seminar or conference business is vitally interested in knowing in advance how many will attend their event. Some are almost obsessed with the idea: For example, I know one producer of medical meetings who forecasts attendance at his annual conference twice a day starting months in advance.

This section looks at why and when advance attendance forecasting makes sense. It presents a step-by-step guide to analyze your own enrollment histories and to develop your own forecasting procedure. It even furnishes statistics you can use to forecast attendance *before* you have any data of your own to analyze. And it provides a source where you can send your own enrollment data for analysis and get back a custom forecast model.

Three Reasons to Forecast

There are at least three good reasons to forecast event attendance in advance:

1. So you can take timely action to boost attendance at under-enrolled events.

2. So you can cancel events forecasted to be below acceptable levels, when nothing can be done to save them.

3. So you can make arrangements to accommodate participants at over-enrolled events with the least adverse impact.

These three reasons are also in descending order of how far in advance you need the forecast in order to be effective. Rescuing an under-enrolled seminar means starting at least six weeks before the event begins and preferably eight to ten weeks before. (Fortunately, it's almost always possible to forecast low attendance this far in advance -- and even farther!) Cancellation decisions should be made at least four weeks before the event to inconvenience the fewest participants and preserve hotel relations. Accommodating additional participants usually needs the least lead time of all, often as little as a few days to two weeks.

Why Forecasting Based on Registrations Works

First, we need to understand why we use advance registrations and why we *don't* recommend forecasting based on your marketing and promotion efforts. After all, we went to a lot of trouble to develop these plans and budgets in order to obtain a certain number of attendees. So why can't we simply start there?

Well, in an ideal world, maybe we could. And at first we tried to do it this way. But it didn't take long to see that this approach was woefully inaccurate. For example, promoting four meetings to get an average of 25 attendees at each might result in 50 at one and only seven at another. And imponderables like the economy, politics, news and even the weather can have a large and unpredictable effect on actual attendance at any event, regardless of the marketing or promotion. Finally, after spending more than $100,000 in sophisticated "rocket science" analysis, we've had to conclude that if there is a predictive relationship between promotion and attendance, we sure haven't discovered anyone who's found it.

So what *does* work? The answer is to look instead at the pattern of participant advance registrations. Why? Because experience shows that each type of event seems to have it's own unique enrollment characteristics. This probably occurs because a successful event aimed at a particular audience will end up being promoted the same way time after time, and participant enrollment patterns will be similar. The marketing efforts may be more or less effective, and attendance may be up or down from previous events, but *the pattern of advance registrations will be basically the same.*

To illustrate, let's take an actual example of a particular firm's series of weekend conferences for physicians. For three years and more than three dozen conferences ranging in attendance from 50 to 350, analysis showed that an average of exactly one-half of the final attendees were registered nine weeks before the conference began. Put another way, by merely doubling the number of registrations received nine weeks ahead of a conference, this firm could reliably forecast the actual, final attendance within 10%. That's more than two months in advance, plenty of time to make adjustments to accommodate more or fewer attendees than they anticipated.

The pattern is consistent but different for various types of meetings. For example, enrollments arrive later for 1-day, employer-paid seminars, held locally during normal working hours. Enrollments arrive earlier for multi-day management programs held at resort locations and/or requiring travel, especially if participants need to book hotel rooms in advance. Individually-paid programs held locally and outside of normal working hours fill most slowly of all, often just a few days before the event begins or even at-the-door. Forecasting attendance at these latter events can be difficult or even impossible.

The figure below shows some typical enrollment build-ups for various kinds of meetings. The data span a variety of sources, sponsors, subjects and durations including 1-day to 1-week nationwide management seminars, weekend and midweek medical conferences in both cities and resorts, technical meetings, local meetings and more.

When Forecasting Works Best

Attendance forecasting based on early regis-

trations works best when you have:

1. Consistent Marketing/Promotion. Media mix, early registration requirements/incentives, refund offered and, above all, marketing lead times are the same from meeting to meeting. (See Chapter 5 for more on promotional lead times).

2. Consistent Meeting Scheduling. Meeting duration, locations, time of day, day(s) of week, frequency and the other timing variables discussed earlier in this chapter are unchanged.

3. Consistent Target Audience. Participant's profession/job responsibilities, organization size, level, who pays and similar factors are fixed.

4. Consistent Registration Practices. When a registration is counted (e.g., upon receipt of a call, the registration form, deposit, full payment, etc.), waiting-list procedures, cancellation policies and the like are consistently applied.

Notice that consistency in important factors such as promotional volume, meeting topic, speaker and even price are *not* primary requirements for reliable forecasting. While these factors can and do have a dramatic impact on the *number* of participants, they have a much smaller effect on the *pattern of registrations* and therefore on the accuracy of the resulting forecast. Naturally, the more consistency you have, the more reliable the forecasts will be.

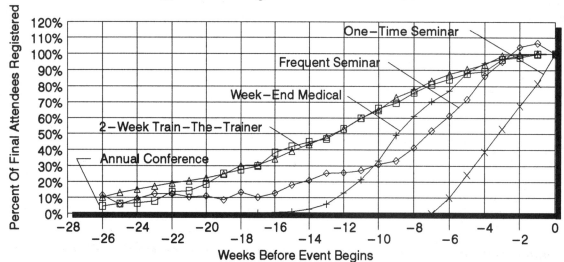

Typical Meeting Enrollment Histories

HOW TO MAKE YOUR OWN ATTENDANCE FORECASTER

We describe here the 5-step process we use to develop for our clients attendance forecasts based on early registrations/enrollments. These forecasts have proven to be reliable, starting as early as four or five months before an event begins, and to improve in accuracy as the event nears.

1. Get Consistent Enrollment Data by Weeks Ahead of Each Event

This first step is critical, for your final result will only be as good as the raw data you use. What you need is a week-by-week history of registrations for each event you want to use in your forecasting analysis. The history should go back as far in advance of the event as possible, hopefully beginning with the very first registration. Ideally, your registration count should be on the same day of each week, the day of the week your event begins.

One seemingly innocent decision is important: When is a registration counted as a registration? In order for the forecasts to be reliable, a consistent definition of when to count a registration is a "must." Is it upon receipt of a phone call? A registration form? An advance deposit? Payment in full? Hotel reservations? You get the idea. Establishing this policy (if it doesn't already exist) is most critical -- and can be controversial.

Your job will be easy if you've kept dated records of each inquiry, registration, payment, confirmation, etc., for each meeting you want to use. If not, you'll have to reconstruct the week-by-week registration history as best you can. The table below shows what your results of this first step might look like.

2. Get Final Attendance at Each Event

What's needed here, for each registration history you've compiled in Step 1, is a single number representing the official, final attendance, by whatever consistent policies you use. In the above table, it's the number at the top of each column, which, in this raw data, is exactly the same number shown in the Week 0 row at the bottom.

Sample Raw Enrollment Data

		337	117	168	234	138	125	147	73	87	114	221	203	163	211	85	407	217	192	156
ACTUAL ATT'S:		337	117	168	234	138	125	147	73	87	114	221	203	163	211	85	407	217	192	156
LOCATION:		S.F	N.Y.C.	L.A.	N.Orl.	Orl.	Chi.	S. D.	Wash.	Sea.	N.Orl.	L.V.	Orl.	L.A.	Chi.	Bos.	Vanc.	Mont.	S.F.	Berm.
START DATE:		9/1	10/27	11/3	12/1	2/9	4/27	6/22	6/29	6/29	8/31	1/15	2/12	4/30	6/18	6/25	7/16	8/20	8/27	9/10
YEAR:		1989	1989	1989	1989	1990	1990	1990	1990	1990	1990	1993	1993	1993	1993	1993	1993	1993	1993	1993
WEEKS	−20	0	0	0	0	0	0	0	0	0	0	0	0	0	0	0	0	1	0	0
BEFORE	−19	0	0	0	0	0	0	0	0	0	0	0	0	0	0	0	1	1	0	0
EVENT	−18	0	0	0	0	0	0	0	0	0	0	0	1	0	0	0	2	1	0	0
BEGINS	−17	0	0	0	0	0	0	0	0	0	0	0	1	0	0	1	3	1	0	0
	−16	2	0	0	0	11	0	0	0	0	0	0	3	0	0	2	4	1	3	7
	−15	16	0	0	0	18	0	0	0	0	0	1	4	0	0	3	4	3	3	7
	−14	39	0	0	0	25	2	0	0	0	0	7	5	1	0	4	18	7	3	7
	−13	69	0	0	0	32	5	0	0	0	6	14	17	3	3	5	31	17	12	7
	−12	122	0	17	0	32	9	17	0	0	14	34	32	12	8	6	61	46	15	47
	−11	156	16	41	10	32	17	31	0	1	24	52	58	36	13	16	91	57	30	63
	−10	190	44	89	17	65	35	43	0	10	37	70	83	61	39	26	134	82	48	84
	−9	224	69	103	53	97	47	64	11	20	56	130	102	77	64	40	191	116	69	116
	−8	258	79	118	96	103	90	84	20	33	70	158	129	92	109	53	275	184	88	130
	−7	307	89	122	150	104	91	105	29	46	80	170	145	108	154	59	365	202	134	163
	−6	315	101	133	204	105	95	121	32	53	84	181	180	124	165	65	376	208	150	162
	−5	319	108	150	214	120	103	130	44	62	85	203	206	140	177	69	388	213	159	164
	−4	322	108	159	220	127	106	139	61	77	92	217	213	155	188	80	399	222	174	162
	−3	328	108	159	227	133	109	147	65	81	98	215	209	157	205	80	407	224	192	159
	−2	331	110	160	238	134	117	150	68	83	99	218	207	159	206	85	403	221	194	158
	−1	331	113	164	248	140	125	152	69	82	111	222	202	161	210	84	401	219	192	157
	0	337	117	168	234	138	125	147	73	87	114	221	203	163	211	85	407	217	192	156

Sample Results of a Simple Enrollment Analysis

	ACTUAL ATT'S:	337	117	168	234	136	125	147	73	87	114	221	203	163	211	85	407	217	192	156	Statistics		
	LOCATION:	S.F	N.Y.C.	L.A.	N.Orl.	Orl.	Chi.	S.D.	Wash.	Sea.	N.Orl.	L.V.	Orl.	L.A.	Chi.	Bos.	Vanc.	Mont.	S.F.	Berm.			
	START DATE:	9/1	10/27	11/3	12/1	2/9	4/27	6/22	6/29	6/29	8/31	1/15	2/12	4/30	6/18	6/25	7/16	8/20	8/27	9/10			
	YEAR:	1989	1989	1989	1989	1990	1990	1990	1990	1990	1990	1993	1993	1993	1993	1993	1993	1993	1993	1993	Low	Avg.	High
WEEKS	−20	0.000	0.000	0.000	0.000	0.000	0.000	0.000	0.000	0.000	0.000	0.000	0.000	0.000	0.000	0.000	0.000	0.005	0.000	0.000	0.000	0.000	0.005
BEFORE	−19	0.000	0.000	0.000	0.000	0.000	0.000	0.000	0.000	0.000	0.000	0.000	0.000	0.000	0.000	0.000	0.002	0.005	0.000	0.000	0.000	0.000	0.012
EVENT	−18	0.000	0.000	0.000	0.000	0.000	0.000	0.000	0.000	0.000	0.000	0.000	0.005	0.000	0.000	0.000	0.005	0.005	0.000	0.000	0.000	0.002	0.031
BEGINS	−17	0.000	0.000	0.000	0.000	0.000	0.000	0.000	0.000	0.000	0.000	0.000	0.005	0.000	0.000	0.012	0.007	0.005	0.000	0.000	0.000	0.002	0.050
	−16	0.006	0.000	0.000	0.000	0.060	0.000	0.000	0.000	0.000	0.000	0.000	0.015	0.000	0.000	0.024	0.010	0.005	0.016	0.045	0.000	0.007	0.080
	−15	0.047	0.000	0.000	0.000	0.130	0.000	0.000	0.000	0.000	0.000	0.005	0.020	0.000	0.000	0.035	0.010	0.014	0.016	0.045	0.000	0.011	0.110
	−14	0.116	0.000	0.000	0.000	0.181	0.016	0.000	0.000	0.000	0.000	0.032	0.025	0.006	0.000	0.047	0.043	0.032	0.016	0.045	0.000	0.027	0.160
	−13	0.205	0.000	0.000	0.000	0.232	0.040	0.000	0.000	0.000	0.000	0.063	0.061	0.018	0.014	0.059	0.076	0.078	0.063	0.045	0.000	0.060	0.240
	−12	0.362	0.000	0.101	0.000	0.232	0.072	0.116	0.000	0.000	0.000	0.154	0.158	0.071	0.038	0.071	0.150	0.212	0.078	0.301	0.000	0.129	0.370
	−11	0.463	0.137	0.244	0.043	0.232	0.136	0.211	0.000	0.011	0.000	0.235	0.263	0.222	0.062	0.188	0.224	0.263	0.156	0.404	0.000	0.213	0.525
	−10	0.564	0.376	0.530	0.073	0.467	0.280	0.293	0.000	0.115	0.000	0.317	0.409	0.374	0.182	0.306	0.329	0.378	0.250	0.535	0.000	0.332	0.672
	−9	0.665	0.590	0.613	0.225	0.703	0.376	0.435	0.151	0.230	0.000	0.566	0.502	0.471	0.303	0.465	0.469	0.535	0.350	0.744	0.000	0.460	0.830
	−8	0.766	0.675	0.702	0.410	0.746	0.720	0.571	0.274	0.379	0.000	0.715	0.637	0.567	0.517	0.624	0.677	0.848	0.456	0.834	0.000	0.611	0.950
	−7	0.911	0.761	0.726	0.641	0.754	0.728	0.714	0.397	0.529	0.000	0.767	0.714	0.664	0.730	0.694	0.897	0.931	0.698	1.045	0.000	0.720	1.040
	−6	0.935	0.863	0.792	0.872	0.761	0.760	0.823	0.438	0.609	0.000	0.819	0.887	0.761	0.782	0.765	0.924	0.959	0.779	1.038	0.000	0.810	1.100
	−5	0.947	0.923	0.893	0.915	0.870	0.824	0.884	0.603	0.713	0.746	0.919	1.015	0.856	0.839	0.812	0.952	0.982	0.828	1.051	0.260	0.865	1.129
	−4	0.955	0.923	0.946	0.940	0.917	0.848	0.946	0.836	0.865	0.807	0.982	1.049	0.951	0.891	0.941	0.980	1.023	0.905	1.038	0.519	0.942	1.150
	−3	0.973	0.923	0.946	0.970	0.964	0.872	1.000	0.890	0.931	0.860	0.973	1.030	0.963	0.972	0.941	1.000	1.032	1.000	1.019	0.730	0.971	1.157
	−2	0.982	0.940	0.952	1.015	0.971	0.936	1.020	0.932	0.954	0.868	0.986	1.020	0.975	0.976	1.000	0.990	1.016	1.010	1.013	0.860	0.989	1.140
	−1	0.982	0.966	0.976	1.060	1.014	1.000	1.034	0.945	0.943	0.974	1.005	0.995	0.988	0.995	0.988	0.985	1.009	1.000	1.006	0.950	1.002	1.100
	0	1.000	1.000	1.000	1.000	1.000	1.000	1.000	1.000	1.000	1.000	1.000	1.000	1.000	1.000	1.000	1.000	1.000	1.000	1.000	1.000	1.000	1.000

Again, this apparently easy step is often harder than it looks. We frequently find discrepancies between "final attendance" counts from different people in an event sponsor's organization. Are freebies counted or not? (We suggest not.) What about those who arrive late or leave early? (We suggest counting all actual attendees who paid, regardless of how long they were there.) Do we reduce the final count for attendees who later become bad debts? (We suggest no.) The matter can be even more complicated if commissions or royalties are involved.

3. Analyze Enrollments Versus Final Attendance

Two methods are presented: a quick, simple analysis, suitable for those with limited data or needing quick results, and a more comprehensive, week-by-week analysis for those with more data or desiring greater accuracy. While the simple analysis can be done with only a pocket calculator, a PC spreadsheet is recommended for both.

A. Simple Analysis. The first step is to create a new table that looks just like the raw-data table on the previous page, but in which the actual enrollment for each week is replaced by the decimal fraction which the enrollment represents of the final attendance at that event. For example, if you have received eight enrollments ten weeks before an event finally attended by 20 participants, then the fraction received is 8 / 20 = 0.40, or forty percent. The left-hand side of the table at the top of this page shows this conversion of the data in the previous table. Notice that the Week "0" row now shows 100% for each event, while the column heading still shows the actual final attendance number.

Once you have converted the raw enrollments to fractions of the final attendance for *each* event, it's a simple matter to determine the average fraction for *all* events by week before the event's start. It's also useful to identify the minimum and maximum fractions received by week before the event. The right-most three columns of the above table shows these three fractions taken from the data at the left in the table. The top of the next page shows a graph of these fractional data.

Obviously, you can do this simple analysis even if you only have data on one event. Of course, in that case, the minimum, maximum and average for each week are exactly the same. But that's when to start developing your forecaster, because your own data -- even for a single event -- is better than anyone else's.

Sample Registrations Build-Up Graph

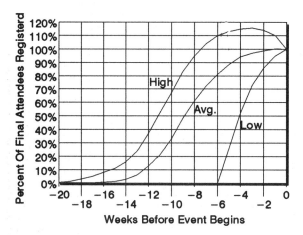

When you get the data from your second event, redo the analysis right away. You'll probably notice some major changes, and that's to be expected. Repeat the process after each additional event you conduct and soon you'll find that the results are not changing very much with the addition of another event. That's when you can stop repeating the analysis after every new event you hold and only do periodic updates.

B. Week-by-Week Analysis. The first step in this somewhat more involved analysis is to plot a graph of enrollments received versus actual, final attendance for each week before the event starts. Since each point on the graph represents only one event, this analysis requires enrollment histories from at least eight to ten events and preferably more. At the right are three such graphs plotted using data for three of the weeks in the prior table.

The lines shown are the results of a statistical analysis of the data. The center line on each graph, labeled "Expected" is the straight line which best fits all the data. The lines labelled "Low" and "High" represent two standard errors on either side of the "Expected" line. This multiple of the standard error is based on experience; some would argue that the Low and High lines should represent three standard errors or even more.

Although statisticians have various methods to do such "curve-fits," we've chosen one of the simplest, based on minimizing the square of the error between each data point and a straight line. If you recall this "least-squares" analysis from a statistics course, you can probably do the job from scratch using just about any PC spreadsheet. If not, don't panic. Recent spreadsheets often have a suitable "regression analysis" already programmed, so even those who know nothing about statistics can do the analysis by merely highlighting the appropriate data and selecting commands from a menu.

Week-by-Week Enrollment Analysis

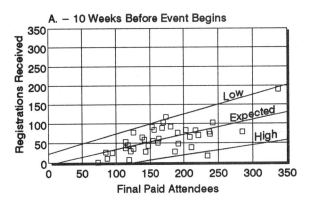

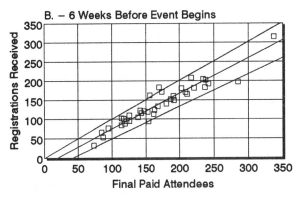

4. Build a Forecasting Model

Your forecasting model is the expected week-by-week build-up of registrations, as a fraction or percentage of the final actual attendance, together with an estimate of how much higher or lower attendance might be.

If you conducted the simple analysis described above, you already have your model in the right-most three columns of the table on Page 6-34, or three numbers for each week before the event.

If you opted for the more complex, week-by-week analysis, your model is the series of weekly graphs and the three lines for each week prior to the event's start. The simplest representation of this model is the two parameters that define each line, namely its zero intercept and its slope, or six numbers in all for each week before the event. These are easy to pick off the graphs manually; but if you've used a PC spreadsheet, there's a good chance these parameters were calculated au-

tomatically. Refer to your spreadsheet documentation for how they're displayed. Below is a sample of these parameters derived from this week-by-week analysis of the earlier data.

Regardless of which method you used, your model now permits you to forecast expected actual attendance -- and a range of uncertainty -- for any future meeting.

But the model itself can tell you some important things about your programs. How early do registrations begin? Can you see your promotion lead times reflected in the pattern of registrations? Does your offer of an early-bird discount or other incentive show up as a "bump" or "dip" in the pattern? On what week are registrations equal to one-half of the final total attendance? One-quarter? Three-quarters? Do registrations exceed attendance in the last few weeks before the event (usually the result of last-minute cancellations, transfers and/or no-shows)? Or does the reverse occur (often because of at-the-door registrants)?

Sample Results of Week-by-Week Enrollment Analysis

Forecast = a + b * (Enrolled)

Expected Forecast Coefficients Weeks			Low Forecast Coefficients: Weeks			High Forecast Coefficients: Weeks		
Before	a=	b=	Before	a=	b=	Before	a=	b=
0	−0.000	1.000	0	−0.000	1.000	0	0.000	1.000
1	1.685	0.985	1	−5.579	0.951	1	9.485	1.022
2	4.514	0.981	2	−2.801	0.947	2	12.366	1.017
3	8.361	0.973	3	−1.262	0.930	3	18.914	1.020
4	9.789	0.993	4	−1.579	0.942	4	22.469	1.050
5	17.076	1.003	5	2.962	0.941	5	33.195	1.074
6	19.627	1.077	6	0.752	0.988	6	42.216	1.183
7	24.456	1.138	7	−0.054	1.019	7	55.446	1.288
8	4.602	1.501	8	−30.841	1.253	8	57.534	1.871
9	−3.820	1.963	9	−49.124	1.531	9	77.020	2.733
10	12.993	2.592	10	−43.028	1.940	10	125.616	3.901
11	36.626	3.372	11	−29.435	2.468	11	178.954	5.318
12	58.081	4.582	12	−19.388	3.258	12	241.693	7.721
13	68.765	8.924	13	−25.328	5.911	13	358.471	18.200
14	73.297	20.662	14	−50.820	11.608	14	1077.567	93.922
15	52.392	64.766	15	−93.032	28.863	15	−1285.484	−265.535
16	−92.144	242.549	16	−178.903	63.908	16	−275.558	−135.105
17	68.458	277.742	17	−104.536	105.156	17	−644.104	−433.136
18	66.487	353.583	18	−110.172	127.616	18	−568.623	−458.793
19	106.495	670.676	19	−65.934	305.220	19	−1813.323	−3398.315
20	66.922	4226.044	20	−144.797	994.364	20	−332.992	−1878.244

Forecasting Actual Seminar Attendance from Early Enrollments

Actual Enrollments In Hand	2 Weeks Before Expected Attends	2 Weeks Before Forecast Range Low	2 Weeks Before Forecast Range High	4 Weeks Before Expected Attends	4 Weeks Before Forecast Range Low	4 Weeks Before Forecast Range High	6 Weeks Before Expected Attends	6 Weeks Before Forecast Range Low	6 Weeks Before Forecast Range High	8 Weeks Before Expected Attends	8 Weeks Before Forecast Range Low	8 Weeks Before Forecast Range High	10 Weeks Before Expected Attends	10 Weeks Before Forecast Range Low	10 Weeks Before Forecast Range High	12 Weeks Before Expected Attends	12 Weeks Before Forecast Range Low	12 Weeks Before Forecast Range High
0	0	0	1	0	0	2	0	0	4	1	0	7	2	0	8	3	0	11
2	1	0	3	1	0	5	2	0	7	3	0	10	5	0	13	7	0	18
4	3	0	5	3	0	7	5	0	10	6	2	14	8	2	19	10	3	25
6	5	2	8	5	2	10	7	2	13	8	3	17	11	4	24	14	5	31
8	6	3	10	7	3	13	9	4	16	11	5	20	14	6	29	18	7	38
10	8	5	12	9	5	15	11	5	19	13	7	23	17	8	35	21	10	45
12	10	6	14	11	6	18	14	7	21	15	8	27	20	11	40	25	12	52
14	12	8	17	13	8	20	16	9	24	18	10	30	23	13	45	29	15	59
16	14	10	19	15	9	23	18	11	27	20	11	33	26	15	51	32	17	65
18	16	11	21	17	11	26	20	13	30	23	13	36	29	17	56	36	19	72
20	18	13	23	19	13	28	23	14	33	25	15	40	32	19	61	40	22	79
22	19	14	26	21	14	31	25	16	36	27	16	43	35	21	67	43	24	86
24	21	16	28	23	16	34	27	18	39	30	18	46	38	24	72	47	26	93
26	23	17	30	25	17	36	30	20	41	32	19	50	41	26	77	51	29	99
28	25	19	32	27	19	39	32	21	44	35	21	53	44	28	83	54	31	106
30	27	21	35	29	21	41	34	23	47	37	23	56	47	30	88	58	34	113
32	29	22	37	31	22	44	36	25	50	39	24	59	50	32	93	62	36	120
34	31	24	39	33	24	47	39	27	53	42	26	63	53	34	99	65	38	127
36	32	25	41	35	25	49	41	29	56	44	27	66	56	37	104	69	41	133
38	34	27	44	37	27	52	43	30	59	47	29	69	59	39	109	73	43	140
40	36	29	46	39	28	55	45	32	61	49	31	72	62	41	115	76	45	147
42	38	30	48	41	30	57	48	34	64	51	32	76	65	43	120	80	48	154
44	40	32	50	43	32	60	50	36	67	54	34	79	68	45	125	84	50	161
46	42	33	53	45	33	63	52	38	70	56	35	82	71	47	131	87	53	167
48	44	35	55	47	35	65	55	39	73	59	37	86	74	50	136	91	55	174
50	45	36	57	49	36	68	57	41	76	61	39	89	77	52	141	95	57	181
52	47	38	59	51	38	70	59	43	79	63	40	92	80	54	147	98	60	188
54	49	40	61	53	39	73	61	45	81	66	42	95	83	56	152	102	62	195
56	51	41	64	55	41	76	64	46	84	68	43	99	86	58	157	106	64	201
58	53	43	66	57	43	78	66	48	87	71	45	102	89	60	163	109	67	208
60	55	44	68	59	44	81	68	50	90	73	47	105	92	62	168	113	69	215
62	56	46	70	61	46	84	70	52	93	75	48	108	95	65	173	117	72	222
64	58	48	73	63	47	86	73	54	96	78	50	112	98	67	179	120	74	229
66	60	49	75	65	49	89	75	55	99	80	51	115	101	69	184	124	76	235
68	62	51	77	67	51	91	77	57	101	83	53	118	104	71	189	128	79	242
70	64	52	79	69	52	94	80	59	104	85	55	122	107	73	195	131	81	249
72	66	54	82	71	54	97	82	61	107	87	56	125	110	76	200	135	83	256
74	68	56	84	73	55	99	84	63	110	90	58	128	113	78	205	139	86	263
76	69	57	86	75	57	102	86	64	113	92	59	131	116	80	211	142	88	269
78	71	58	88	77	58	105	89	66	116	95	61	135	119	82	216	146	91	276
80	73	60	91	79	60	107	91	68	119	97	63	138	122	84	221	150	93	283
82	75	62	93	81	62	110	93	70	121	99	64	141	125	86	227	153	95	290
84	77	63	95	83	63	113	95	71	124	102	66	144	128	89	232	157	98	297
86	79	65	97	85	65	115	98	73	127	104	67	148	131	91	237	161	100	303
88	81	67	100	87	66	118	100	75	130	107	69	151	134	93	243	164	102	310
90	82	68	102	89	68	120	102	77	133	109	71	154	137	95	248	168	105	317
92	84	70	104	91	69	123	105	79	136	111	72	158	140	97	253	172	107	324
94	86	71	106	93	71	126	107	80	139	114	74	161	143	99	259	175	110	331
96	88	73	109	95	73	128	109	82	141	116	75	164	146	102	264	179	112	337
98	90	75	111	97	74	131	111	84	144	119	77	167	149	104	269	183	114	344
100	92	76	113	99	76	134	114	86	147	121	79	171	152	106	275	186	117	351

5. Provide Tools Ordinary People Can Use

Those with an analytical bent, or "techies", will have no trouble using the model in Step 4 directly to forecast future attendance. But in most cases, it makes sense to convert the model into one or more simple tools or job-aids that ordinary people can use. This is especially important to make the organization more robust and less dependent on a single individual.

Three tools are most common:

A. Graphs. Any of the graphs shown in this chapter can serve as a suitable forecasting tool. For example, to use the simple build-up graphs, look at the fraction of final attendance expected on the week ahead of the program you're interested in. Then divide the number of registrations you've actually received on that week by the fraction read from the graph. The result is your forecast.

The graphs produced by the week-by-week analysis are still easier to use. Just pick the graph for the week ahead of the program you're interested in. Look across from the number of registrations you've actually received on that week to the "Expected" line,

then read down to the forecasted actual attendees. Repeat the process to obtain the
"Low" and "High" forecasts.

B. Manual Forecasting Table. You can
use the model to construct a table, similar to
that used for figuring shipping charges, which
will enable just about anyone to do a forecast.
The table is fairly easy to produce with a PC
spreadsheet and almost as easy manually. On
the previous page is a sample of what such a
table looks like. Please note that this table is
not based on the data used elsewhere in this
chapter, but is presented for generic use, before you have your own data. Naturally, your
forecasting table might cover a shorter or
longer period of time or more or fewer attendees.

C. Personal Computer Spreadsheet. The
third useful forecasting tool is to construct a
PC spreadsheet template, that uses the model
to calculate the latest forecast based upon the
current registrations received and today's
date. Once more, a "techie" will immediately
see what's needed and can produce exactly
what the organization can use.

If you do not have the capabilities or other
resources to produce such a spreadsheet, a
later section of this chapter tells how you can
get one developed quickly and at low cost.

What to Use Before You Have Your Own Data

If you're just getting started, you won't have
any data of your own to analyze.

But don't worry, the previous forecasting
table can provide you with a preliminary forecast until you have data on your own program. It's based on hundreds of actual enrollments for 2- and 3-day management programs.

Remember, there are many variables that
may make your results different. For example, longer duration programs will tend to be
at the lower end of the forecast range, while
shorter duration programs are often at the
higher end. And, of course, none of these

forecasting techniques is helpful for programs
obtaining most or all of their registrations "at-
the-door."

So, once you have *any* registration history
of your own -- even for a single session -- use
it in preference to the above "generic" table.
And, of course, data on two of your programs
will be better than one, etc.

Give Us Your Data and We'll Do It For You

For $995 and in only a few weeks, we can
take your raw data, plus your schedule of upcoming events, and return to you a complete,
customized, easy-to-use forecasting kit, including the Lotus 1-2-3 spreadsheet that produces the report shown below.

Specifically, here's what you get:

1. Lotus 1-2-3 Spreadsheet. Ready to
load onto your PC and start forecasting. All
the parameters have been recalculated based
on *your* data.

2. Manual Forecast Table. Similar to the
table above, but customized to reflect *your*
data.

*3. Complete Set of Week-by-Week
Graphs.* Similar to those shown earlier, but
one for each week represented by *your* data.

*4. Summary Enrollment Build-Up
Graph.* Similar to the above, but based on
your data.

5. Raw Data Table. So we (and you) can
verify that the data you sent us has been
properly entered.

6. Floppy Disk. Containing all of the
above, including the graphs in Lotus PIC
files, so they're available for you and your
staff to use and update.

If you're at all interested, call us TOLL
FREE in the U.S. at 1-800-ENROLL-X.
Outside the U.S. call (310) 493-0200, or write
to: SCHRELLO DIRECT MARKETING,
INC., P.O. Box 1610, Long Beach, California
90801-1610.

Sample Output of the FORECASTER Spreadsheet Model

```
**********************************************************
           CONFERENCES ATTENDANCE FORECAST BASED ON SIGN-UPS
**********************************************************

MO DAY  YR THRU WHICH ACTUAL SIGN-UPS ARE USED IS:
 5  18  93
-----------------------------------------------------------------
DATE COURSE                              ENROLLED   FORE-    FORECAST
    BEGINS      COU-             WEEKS     OR      CASTED     RANGE
MO DAY  YR     RSE   LOCATION   BEFORE  ATTENDED  ATTENDS   LO    HI
--- ---  ---   ----  --------   ------  --------  -------   ---   ---
 1  17   93    PEP   LAS VEGAS    0       250       250     250 - 250
 2  10   93    PEP   IRVINE       0       317       317     317 - 317
 2  14   93    F&A   ORLANDO      0       216       216     216 - 216
 4   9   93    PEP   HAWAII       0       172       172     172 - 172
 4  10   93    PEP   NEW YORK     0       135       135     135 - 135
 4  11   93    F&A   ST. LOUIS    0        95        95      95 -  95
 4  24   93    PEP   NEWPORT BEACH 0      107       107     107 - 107
 5  25   93    PEP   LONDON       1        41        42      33 -  51
 6   4   93    F&A   ACAPULCO     2        14        18      10 -  27
 6  19   93    PEP   CHICAGO      5         4        21       7 -  37
 6  25   93    PEP   NEWPORT BEACH 5        0        17       3 -  33
 7  17   93    F&A   VANCOUVER    9         8        12       0 -  99
 8   7   93    PEP   MONTREAL    12         1        63       0 - 249
 9   4   93    PEP   SAN FRANCISCO 16       4       ERR     ERR - ERR
10   2   93    F&A   LA JOLLA    20         3       ERR     ERR - ERR
10   8   93    PEP   WILLIAMSBURG 20        1       ERR     ERR - ERR
10  12   93    PEP   IRVINE      21         6       ERR     ERR - ERR
11  12   93    F&A   CHICAGO     25       158       ERR     ERR - ERR
12   4   93    PEP   NEW ORLEANS 29         2       ERR     ERR - ERR
                                         --------
         TOTAL ENROLLED/ATTENDED ABOVE:   1,534
            PLUS TOTAL PRIOR ATTENDEES:   4,708
         PLUS CANCELLATIONS/NO-SHOWS:       377
                       LESS FREEBIES:       (17)
                                         ========
                TOTAL ORDERS RECEIVED:    6,602

NOTES:  1. "ERR" indicates more than 15 weeks before course begins.
        2. Courses shown as zero weeks before are completed courses.
        3. Enrollments = Orders + Transfers in - Cancels - Transfers
           out - No-Shows.
```

TIPS FOR SEMINARS, CONFERENCES AND OTHER OPEN REGISTRATION EVENTS

Boost Attendance at Each Recurring Event by Pruning the Schedule

If you're unhappy with the average attendance at your regularly scheduled training classes, seminars or other events, there are two actions you can take to improve matters: (1.) increase your volume of promotion, or (2.) reduce the number of times your event is offered. If you can't do the first, you can surely do the second. Here's how it works:

Let's suppose you've been holding a seminar every month and averaging six participants at each, for a total of 72 participants a year. Cut back the schedule to (say) every other month without changing your marketing, and your average attendance will jump to 11 - 12, (that's {72-3}/6=11.5). Cut back to quarterly, and average attendance will jump to 16 (that's {72-8}/4=16).

In each case, your less frequent schedule will result in somewhat fewer total attendees: roughly three fewer per year in the first example and eight fewer per year in the second. But because these slightly fewer attendees divide themselves between a greatly reduced number of sessions, *average* attendance at each session skyrockets.

Help Your Participants Have Lunch "On Their Own"

Look for facilities that have a variety of fast food choices nearby. Many hotel complexes are connected to malls, underground shopping arcades or tourist attractions that provide such convenience. Examples include Crystal City (near Washington National Airport), downtown Minneapolis (and St. Paul), Toronto, Vancouver, Atlanta, San Francisco's Embarcadero, etc.

There's a Big Difference Between Open Registrants and In-House Participants

Public seminar and conference attendees almost always want to attend. In-house participants are sometimes "boxed-and-sent." The result is that public participants are frequently more positive -- and more demanding! Always have your best people conduct your public programs.

Personal Motives Often Lure Attendees

In many public seminars the participants from large organizations are really there to pursue their own personal objectives -- including starting another business or getting a new job.

How Far Will Attendees Travel?

How far away your program will attract participants dictates how you select mailing lists, whether the facility is located near an airport, train station or downtown and how much overnight lodging you'll need. Multi-day regional/national events are easy (people will come from anywhere), as are several-hour local events. (An hour commute is tops.) In-between events usually can't be figured out until you have some experience; for example, my 2-day *How to Market Training Programs Seminar* held recently in Newport Beach, CA, had no one from Newport Beach and only 10% of the participants from Los Angeles. Fully 90% of the participants were from out of state or out of the country.

Contract Instructors Work Well

If you use outside resources (non-employees) to conduct your meetings, be sure they're among your best leaders. Finding them can occasionally be difficult. Often, they'll find you! But once a relationship has been established that's fair to both you and them, there's a good chance the relationship will last a long time.

Be Alert for Laws/Regulations

Some states/cities have attempted to regulate seminars by requiring licensing and/or instructor registration fees. Generally, this is not a problem for small groups, but major sponsors or prominent meetings could trigger action. Make your staff aware of this possibility and have a plan to handle a last-minute attempt to bar people from your meeting, should that happen (it has). Generally, paying the fees -- or agreeing to pay them -- will get the meeting underway.

Since passage of the Americans with Disabilities Act (ADA) in 1992, meeting planners have been fearful. Horror stories have circulated about huge fines for infractions, like not having signing interpreters for the hearing impaired, accommodations for the very obese, etc., when those conditions were not known in advance. This situation is still evolving, so keep a sharp eye out for implications for your events.

Take Major Credit Cards

There is little doubt that using a toll-free (800) telephone number for participants to enroll and accepting the major credit cards for payment improves response, especially for programs aimed at individuals. Whether it improves response enough to justify the added cost can only be determined by testing. Probably, it will. Credit cards are definitely required for at-the-door registrations and for back-of-the-room sales.

Require Advance Registration

Require advance registration (by mail or

phone), advance confirmation and advance payment of fees for virtually all sessions. A possible exception to this rule is a low-cost, local, several-hour session, primarily intended as a step toward a larger sale, and which is promoted through local newspaper or broadcast ads. Be prepared to accept on-site registrations and payments for this type session.

Advance Payment: The Liability That's an Asset

Your accountant will tell you that the money paid to you by participants before they attend (usually called Advance Payments, or Advances for short) is a *liability*. And financially speaking, it is, because you'll need to return the money if they don't attend. But it's a sales and marketing *asset*, because once the money is paid it's much easier to get actual course attendance.

Advertise Cancellation Penalties -- but Don't Impose Them

Prominently advertise a service charge for cancellations close to the meeting's start, that no-shows are subject to the entire fee but that substitutions may be made at any time. While usually unenforceable as a practical matter, the policy does emphasize the importance of notifying you early about cancellations and often will convert a cancellation into a substitution.

If you impose a financial penalty for late cancellations and no-shows, be sure it's well-justified on practical grounds your customers can easily understand. One such justification is limited space in a popular program, where an empty seat at the last minute may have deprived someone else of the chance to attend. Under these circumstances, penalties are more readily accepted.

Distinguish Between Process Problems and Human Errors

When you find an error or problem in your order processing, try to determine if it's a normal *human* error or a deficiency in the *process or procedure* being used. Everyone makes occasional mistakes, and if one individual makes too many you'll need to take ac-

tion. But procedural errors can "institutionalize" or "build in" a problem, causing it to recur every time the same situation exists. Fix these procedural problems at once.

Stick to established administrative processes and don't overlook any small detail, even those that may seem inconsequential. Those small details can come back to haunt you by weakening the company's image and starting the client/company relationship off badly.

Practice Same-Day Response to Calls and Letters

Answer all inquiries, orders and correspondence the same day if possible, and no longer than within two working days. Timeliness is critical in the seminar business.

And if you make a promise to a client, honor it. If you've told them you will check into something and get back to them, do it as quickly as possible. Don't drag your feet and procrastinate -- again, the interest in the customer's needs will be evident and will generate business.

Always Include a New Order Form with Every Confirmation

Be sure it's properly coded so you can trace it back to the type of correspondence it was included with. You'll be surprised how often it will come back with yet another order!

Let Your Packaging Show You Care, Too

Package your material shipments so the contents won't be damaged. The slightly higher costs will be more than offset by increased customer satisfaction and respect for your caring.

Use transparent shrink-wrap on your high-value course materials, audio and video cassettes, computer software and the like. Prominently label them inside the shrink-wrap with a notice that the materials can only be returned for a refund if the seal is not broken. This is difficult to enforce in practical terms, but it does cut down on damaged and questionable returns.

The Personal Touch Goes a Long Way

Sometimes even a 3- to 5-minute phone call that you initiate to a good customer can produce a warm, pleasant, special rapport. The client will know that you are really interested in their training needs and anxious to provide whatever information you can to guide their decisions. Always include a personal note with any literature you send to customers with whom you have established this special relationship. It really is a nice touch and goes a long way to generate more business.

WHERE AND HOW TO GET THE VERY BEST MAILING LISTS

After selecting the product and the market and developing an effective marketing plan, the single most vital element for success is selecting the proper lists. Time and again we see that a poor mailing to a good list will succeed, while the world's best-crafted offer to the wrong list will fail every time.

A recent survey found more than 25,000 lists available in the U.S. today, and approximately 23 billion names are rented or sold annually for marketing purposes. With such a large field to choose from, good lists for any training or information product/service almost certainly exist. This chapter will show you how to find them.

The first few sections are pretty basic, to answer the more common questions of those new to the business. The most advanced material is toward the end of the chapter.

WHAT DO MAILING LISTS LOOK LIKE?

When you buy, rent or exchange a mailing list, you get individual names and mailing addresses to apply to your mailing pieces. This application can be done directly or indirectly, electronically or mechanically. Here are some common formats in which you can receive the list:

4-Up Cheshire

This format is named for the company producing the equipment that cuts the labels, applies adhesive and affixes them to the mail piece. It's merely a computer printout on 11" x 15" fanfolded paper produced to certain specifications. Standard 1" x 3-1/2" labels are printed 4 across and 11 down, for a total of 44 labels per page. Printing is kept within suit-able guidelines so that the Cheshire machine, once adjusted at the start of the run, can affix labels to tens of thousands of pieces with only minor attention. Cheshire labels can be furnished in 1-up, 2-up, 3-up and 5-up formats as well.

Pressure-Sensitive Labels

These familiar 1"-high "peel and stick" labels are common for small offices and hand affixing, and the machine-affixed "piggy-back" format is convenient for responders to put on the reply vehicle. Pressure-sensitive labels are also available in 1-up through 5-up layouts, with 1-up and 4-up "piggyback" being the most popular.

Half-Inch Magnetic Tape

This is the most common format for lists to be processed further before addressing, usually "merging" a number of separate lists into a single list and "purging," or eliminating duplicates. This format is also preferred for personalized mailings where individual letters, and/or envelopes are required.

Floppy Disks

Although the floppy disk (in its various formats) is the personal computer standard, it is only now becoming a serious medium for mailing lists and only for low-volume, specialized applications.

Electronic/On-Line/CD-ROM

A number of national services now permit subscribers to "browse" through their database and select groups or individual names to "download" to a local computer for processing. A variant is the mailing list on CD (Compact Disk)-ROM (Read Only Memory), again processed locally. These are particularly good for short-time campaigns or situations requiring selections of small groups.

What does the label look like? For consumer mailings to home addresses, the standard is the so-called "3-line label."

Mr. John Doe
234 Maple St.
Everytown, IN 45678

For businesses, the standard is a 4- or 5-line label, adding the person's position title and company name:

Ms. Jane J. Jones
President
First Eastern Bank
678 Center Ave.
Chicago, IL 60606

Ms. Jane Jones, Pres.
First Eastern Bank
678 Center Ave.
Chicago, IL 60606

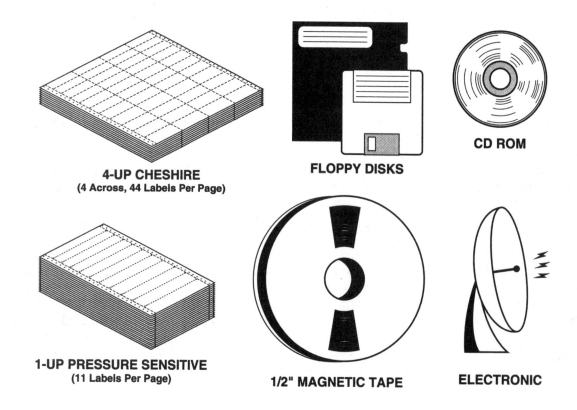

4-UP CHESHIRE
(4 Across, 44 Labels Per Page)

FLOPPY DISKS

CD ROM

1-UP PRESSURE SENSITIVE
(11 Labels Per Page)

1/2" MAGNETIC TAPE

ELECTRONIC

WHAT CONSTITUTES THE "BEST LIST"?

Every direct mail offer has a "universe" of those likely to be interested and, therefore, likely to respond. They range from the most enthusiastic supporters who may actually seek out the product to those who don't care and wouldn't buy under any circumstances. This scale of interest translates into the relative number of sales obtainable from a given vol-ume of mail sent to each group, and this in turn translates into the cost of acquiring each customer.

The following diagram illustrates this for a specific kind of training and information product; namely, a public seminar. Other types of direct marketing offers behave simi-larly, so it's worth discussing this example in detail.

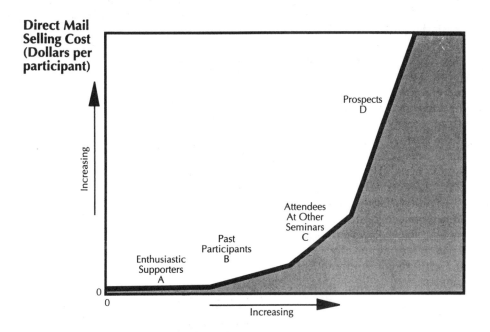

Number of Participants

The diagram shows the relationship between direct mail selling cost, dollars spent per par-ticipant and the number of participants. It shows that selling costs rise ever more steeply with increasing numbers of participants, as the limits of the "universe" are approached.

For simplicity, the curve is broken into four "zones." Zone A consists of those enthu-siastic supporters who seek out the seminar, learn all about it, enroll early and frequently bring colleagues or associates with them. The cost of acquiring these participants is negligi-ble.

Zone B consists of satisfied past partici-pants. While they do not attend the same course again, they are anxious to recommend it, and if they're notified of future presenta-tions they "pass along" the information to others. The cost of acquiring such partici-pants is small. (Zones A and B are represen-tative of your house list and show why this list is so important.)

Zone C consists of attendees at similar seminars, on the same topic or related topics. These lists are usually obtained by rental or exchange. The more recent their attendance, the better prospect they represent. Acquisi-tion costs for this group are higher than for the first two groups, as reflected by the steeper slope of the Zone C curve in the dia-gram. However, these persons respond to di-rect mail advertising at a higher rate than other prospect groups.

Finally, Zone D consists of all other prospective attendees, arranged in order of their most likely interest (see LIST EVAL-UATION later in this chapter). As Daniel E. Harding, of the Center for Direct Marketing, once described it: "Customers line up at your door in the order of their interest in doing business with you."

To summarize, the best targets for public seminar mailings include (in declining order) those who have previously attended the program being advertised, those who have attended similar programs offered by competitors and those who have attended seminars of any kind. After all previous seminar attendees have been exhausted, consider those who have not attended a seminar but who have other characteristics indicating their po-

tential need or desire for seminar participation. Most seminar mailers find that they achieve the best response from those who have already attended a seminar.

The diagram also shows that the practical limit of the "universe" of prospective attendees is really set by economic considerations, specifically the maximum allowable direct mail selling cost. Once this limit is determined, the task is then to find the best mailing lists that allow you to actually reach the desired prospects. The estimated number of such prospects, along with the anticipated response rates, determines the expected attendance at the seminar. For limited attendance seminars, this same approach determines the number of sessions which can be held profitably in a given time period.

Types of Lists

1. Compiled Consumer Lists
- Occupant, telephone directory, motor vehicle licenses, voter registration, etc.

2. Compiled Business Lists
- Businesses (by types of business, sales, number of employees, location, etc.)
- Employees (by function and/or level)
- Government agencies (by location, budget, function, etc.)

3. Occupational and Professional Lists
- National/state licensing bodies (Doctors, lawyers, accountants, teachers)
- Association and society members
- Labor unions
- College/university alumni and/or faculty

4. Life Event Lists
- Moved, changed jobs, promotion, in-the-news, etc.

5. Life Stage Lists
- Senior citizen, parents, homeowner, college student, young married, etc.

6. Customer Lists
- Travel cards (AMEX, Diners, Carte Blanche, etc.)

- Bank credit cards (Visa, MasterCard, Discover)
- Warranty/registration cards
- Retail store customer/charge card

7. Donor Lists
- Colleges, churches, etc.

8. Publication Lists
- Hotline (new or moved subscribers)
- Paid subscribers
- Unpaid/controlled circulation
- Expires, inquiries and trials, only worth testing if subscribers work well

9. Direct Responder Lists
- Mail order buyers/attenders
- Media responded to
- Type of purchase
- Purchase price

10. Event Attenders
- Consumer shows (home, auto, franchising, etc.)
- Trade shows and conferences
- Entertainment events
- Vacation and travel

TYPES OF LISTS AVAILABLE

Mailing lists are available from the widest imaginable range of sources. For example, at the bottom of the facing page are the major types of mailing lists available, in order of their ascending responsiveness to training and information offers.

These lists can be grouped into three broad categories:

1. Compiled Lists

These are taken from published sources, such as telephone books, voter records, directories, membership lists and the like. Compiled lists are often produced in third-world countries, sometimes by those who can't read or write English but who know how to keyboard the characters they see in printed form. Compiled lists are often out of date. More importantly, names on compiled lists have given no indication that they have any interest whatsoever in buying or responding by mail.

Normally, you should avoid compiled lists like the plague for training and information offers. They almost never work.

On the other hand, high-quality compiled lists are sometimes a good way to reach professionals or other groups where societies, state licensing agencies or other means exist to identify them. The best compiled lists for many business purposes are those from Dun & Bradstreet. Their lists of presidents and top executives are a by-product of their credit-reporting services and are usually up-to-date. Other compiled lists are available from Contacts Influential, Market Data Retrieval, National Business Lists and other sources. Interestingly, Dun & Bradstreet has been acquiring other list compilers, so it is possible that some of these organizations may be part of Dun & Bradstreet by the time you read this.

2. Publication Lists

Magazine publishers derive revenue from three sources: (1.) subscription income, (2.) advertising revenues and (3.) mailing list rentals. Magazines that are free (called controlled circulation publications) derive all their income from just advertising and mailing list rentals.

Because mailing list rental income is so important to them, magazine publishers take pains to maintain their lists and use frequent mailings to keep them "fresh." Magazine publishers like to give you as much information about their lists as possible. They normally have more list statistics and more possible selection options, thereby giving you a greater opportunity to refine and pinpoint your selections.

There are several subcategories of magazine lists. The best are the so-called "hot line" lists of new subscribers or those having some other transaction within a specified period. The time interval covered by a "hot line" list is usually dictated by the magazine's total circulation and by the number of address corrections, changes or new subscriptions received. An average "hot line" would cover 30-90 days. When testing magazine lists, always pay the small premium and use the "hot line" (if it exists), since "hot line" names have all of the characteristics of subscriber names, plus the added benefit of being fresh.

Overall, magazine lists represent the best balance for prospecting in Zone D of the Prospecting Costs diagram. In fact, magazine lists are so good for prospecting that some magazines have actually been created to appeal to a group for whom a mailing list was desired. You'll probably use a magazine list sometime in your direct mail efforts.

3. Responder Lists

As their name implies, these consist entirely of those who have already responded by mail. For example, those who attended a seminar, purchased a book, subscribed to a service, etc. Responders correspond to those in Zones B and C of the Prospecting Costs diagram.

How do you know which responder lists to pick? The answer, of course, is those who responded to offers like yours. This includes your closest competitors -- provided they will rent you their list.

The best responder lists are usually event

attenders. They have all of the advantages of other responders, plus the added, demonstrated ability to travel. Event attender lists often work for other offers, including non-events.

THE LIST SELECTION PROCESS

Selecting the best mailing list -- and being sure that you get what you selected -- needs a tight, disciplined process. There are simply too many variables (including forces pushing in directions you don't want to go), to trust that "The System" will produce a favorable result.

Your best bet is to follow a systematic, step-by-step process that experience shows will reduce, if not totally eliminate, many of the most likely problems. Below is the mailing list selection process we've used successfully for many years. In the following sections we'll look at the various people and organizations you'll be dealing with in executing this process and some of the sources you can turn to for the list information you'll need.

List Selection Process

1. Identify your candidate lists.

2. Determine selections available within each list and the corresponding quantities.

3. Determine costs, payment terms and any restrictions on using each list.

4. Develop your list evaluation criteria.

5. Evaluate and rank your candidate lists.

6. Make preliminary selection of a group of lists that meet your mail volume and/or cost requirements.

7. Obtain list-owner rental clearances for your planned offer.

8. Verify the evaluation data you used, and adjust your list selections if/as required.

9. Place your list orders.

10. Inspect each list upon receipt and prior to addressing to be sure you got what you ordered.

11. Keep track of "nixies" (mailing pieces returned as undeliverable) by list and by mailing.

(Alternate Process Beyond Step 9 For Merge/Purge or Other Computer Processing)

10. Inspect sample records dump and tape layout information accompanying each tape, to verify processability and content. If in doubt, get a galley printout of the list to be sure.

11. Conduct merge/purge with other lists and evaluate computer generated duplicate report.

12. Print labels or personalized pieces for the mailing, and inspect prior to affixing or inserting.

13. Keep track of "nixies" by list and by mailing.

WHO'S WHO IN THE WORLD OF LISTS

The world of mailing lists is complex, with many different organizations and individuals participating. You need to know who these people are, or -- more correctly -- the roles they play in the process. Once you have a clear picture of these roles, you'll understand what's going on even when one individual or organization plays several roles.

The diagram on the next page shows the various roles and their interrelationship. The light arrows show the typical communication flow for renting or exchanging a list. The heavy arrows show the movement of the physical mailing list. The broken lines surrounding various roles show the typical combinations that occur.

Here's a short description of each role:

List Owner

The one who assembles the list, owns it, and determines who may or may not rent the list. For responder and publication lists, this is the organization selling a product or service or a publisher. For compiled lists it could be an organization whose sole business is creating and renting mailing lists.

List Manager

The organization, hired by the List Owner, to promote rental of their list. Managers typically receive a 20% commission on list rentals they produce. Most lists are "self-managed" by the List Owner.

List Broker

The "middleman" between the Renter and the Owner, arranging the transaction and collecting/disbursing the money. The better List Brokers also handle all of the communications between and among the other roles involved in the rental process. List Brokers typically get 20% commission on all list orders they place. This is in addition to any List Manager's fees. The Broker's fees are subtracted by them from the list rental payment before paying the balance to the List Owner.

List Maintainer

Today every mailing list is maintained on computer. But that computer may not always be at the List Owner's premises. The Maintainer may be the owner, a computer service bureau working for the Owner or a computer service bureau working for the List Manager and/or List Broker. In fact some lists are available in all three places -- all with varying ages and degrees of currency.

List Renter

The one who needs the list -- probably you. To rent most lists you're going to have to furnish at the very least a sample of the mailing piece you propose to send and an estimated date of when you will mail it. Increasingly, List Owners are demanding a signed list rental agreement which specifies what you may and may not do with the list. Traditionally this has been a very "loose" relationship.

List Processor

Works for the list renter, receiving lists, merging and purging them, producing reports and/or addressing pieces. This role may be played by the mailhouse or by a subcontractor to the mailhouse. But since the List Processor has such a direct and significant effect on the quality of your mailing, you'll want to know them personally.

Mailhouse

The organization that handles the physical assembly of the mailing components and gets them in the mail. Typical operations are addressing, inserting, sealing envelopes, metering, sorting, tying and bagging bulk Third-Class mail, delivering the mail to the Post Office and obtaining all the necessary permits and paper work.

Key Roles for Renting/Exchanging Lists

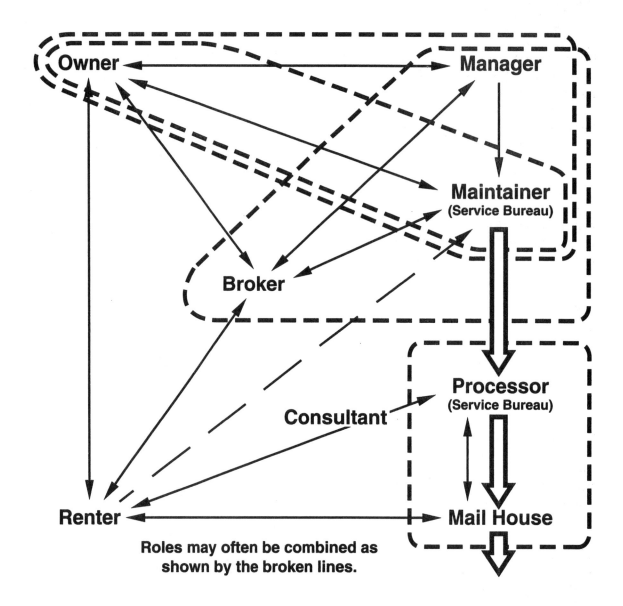

Roles may often be combined as
shown by the broken lines.

WHERE TO GET MAILING LIST INFORMATION

There are three sources of information on mailing lists:

1. Published Directories

The most widely used and most comprehensive is referred to universally as the "SRDS." It's published bi-monthly and contains 10,000 lists:

Direct Mail List Rates and Data
STANDARD RATE & DATA SERVICE (A DIVISION OF OFFICIAL AIRLINE GUIDES, INC.)
3004 Glenview Road
Wilmette, IL 60091
Phone: (800) 323-4601; Fax: (708) 441-2264

Most well-stocked libraries will have at least an older copy of SRDS. And we have more on how to use this valuable resource in a few pages.

SRDS also has a competitor:

The National Directory of Mailing Lists
OXBRIDGE COMMUNICATIONS, INC.
150 Fifth Avenue, Suite 302
New York, NY 10011
Phone: (800) 955-0231; Fax: (212) 633-2938

This annual newcomer claims 20,000 lists, twice as many as SRDS. But our comparisons showed fewer lists of training and information interest than SRDS; for example, the CareerTrack and Fred Pryor lists were missing. Oxbridge also offers their directory on computer diskettes, with quarterly updates.

The biggest problem with directories is that they depend on the list owner's/or manager's initiative to include their lists and to update the information. That's why fewer than half the available mailing lists are in directories. Keep in mind that what you read was written by the list owner/manager, not some neutral third party.

2. List Brokers

In theory, any of the more than 1,000 brokers listed in SRDS could provide the information you need to pick the best mailing lists. But only a handful know enough about marketing training and information to be really helpful. A list of some of them starts on this page. Unless you have a relative in the mailing list business, start with these.

3. Some List Owners

Magazines derive significant income from their mailing lists, and most go out of their way to help prospective renters find and use the best portions of their lists. If you're considering magazine lists, the publisher will furnish you the latest and best information and answer your questions, even if you're going to place your order through a broker.

A CROSS-SECTION OF MAILING LIST BROKERS WHO *MAY* KNOW SOMETHING ABOUT TRAINING

The following mailing list brokers are not all of them (there are thousands) or even the largest ones. It may, however, be a starting point to find a broker who knows (or will learn) your business and who will work hard on your behalf.

AMERICAN LIST COUNSEL, INC.
88 Orchard Road, CN-5219
Princeton, NJ 08543
Phone: (800) 526-3973, (201) 874-4300
Fax: (201) 874-4433
Liza Price, President

ED BURNETT CONSULTANTS, INC.
100 Paragon Drive
Montvale, NJ 07645
Phone: (800) 223-7777, (201) 476-2300
Fax: (201) 476-2411
Ed Burnett, President

DEPENDABLE LISTS, INC.
950 S. 25th Avenue
Bellwood, IL 60104
Phone: (708) 544-1000; Fax: (708) 544-1094
James M. Dolan, President

DIRECT HIT MARKETING, INC.
2575 Stephens Road
Boulder, CO 80303
Phone: (303) 499-0528; Fax: (303) 499-0528
Steve Juedes, CEO

THE DIRECT MEDIA GROUP
200 Pemberwick Road, Box 4565
Greenwich, CT 06830
Phone: (203) 532-1000; Fax: (203) 531-1452
Myles Riely, President, Business List Management Div.

EXECULISTS, INC.
3085 Center Green Drive, MS-27
Boulder, CO 80301-5408
Phone: (303) 442-2233; Fax: (303) 939-8176

GOOD FORTUNE MARKETING, INC.
210 Commerce Blvd.
Round Rock, TX 78664
Phone: (512) 255-6014; Fax: (512) 255-7532
Dennis E. Murphy, President

INFOLISTS, INC.
341 Victory Drive
Herndon, VA 22070
Phone: (703) 834-0100; Fax: (703) 834-0110
Phil Graf, President

INFORMATION MARKETING SERVICES, INC.
8130 Boone Blvd., #310
Vienna, VA 22182
Phone: (703) 821-8130; Fax: (703) 821-8243
Kathryn Shroeder, Vice President

THE KLEID COMPANY, INC.,
530 Fifth Avenue, 17th Floor
New York, NY 10036
Phone: (212) 819-3400
Fax: (212) 719-9727, (212) 719-9788
C. Rose Harper, Chairman/CEO

LAKEWOOD LISTS
50 S. Ninth Street
Minneapolis, MN 55402
Phone: (800) 328-4329, (612) 333-0471
Paul C. Kolars, List Marketing Manager

LIFECYCLE LISTS
1320 Centre Street, Suite 305
Newton, MA 02159
Phone: (617) 964-5057; Fax: (617) 965-5054

THE LIST EMPORIUM, INC.
2000 Shawnee Mission Parkway, Suite 235
Westwood, KS 66205
Phone: (913) 236-6830; Fax: (913) 236-4842
Mark Coulter, President

MARKETRY, INC.
1626 S. Clementine Street
Anaheim, CA 92506
Phone: (714) 239-6700; Fax: (714) 239-6888
Mike Stewart, Vice President

MEC LIST MANAGEMENT
Box 3727
Santa Monica, CA 90408
Phone: (310) 450-0500; Fax: (310) 450-0132
David T. Newman, President

MEGA MARKETING GROUP
18368 Redmond Fall City Road
Redmond, WA 98052
Phone: (206) 885-9796; Fax: (206) 882-1454
Rob Hopping, Vice President

MGI MEDIA SERVICES
1613 Duke Street
Alexandria, VA 22314
Phone: (800) 899-4420, (703) 683-8350
Fax: (703) 549-6057
J. Scott McBride, President

NAMES IN THE NEWS CALIFORNIA, INC.
1 Bush Street, Suite 300
San Francisco, CA 94104
Phone: (415) 989-3350; Fax: (415) 433-7796
Susan Magnusen, CEO

ORGANIZATIONAL TRAINING SERVICES, INC.
3224 Tanager Street
Raleigh, NC 27606
Phone: (919) 859-1121; Fax: (919) 859-4083
John N. Hall, Director

PACIFIC LISTS, INC.
131 Camino Alto, Suite D
Mill Valley, CA 94941
Phone: (415) 381-0553; Fax: (415) 381-9812
Deborah Swackhammer, President

PMM MARKETING, INC.
333 Route 25A
Rocky Point, NY 11778
Phone: (800) 221-0223, (516) 744-4000
Fax: (516) 744-5001

RELIABLE LISTS, INC.
860 Merrimon Avenue, Suite 103
Asheville, NC 28804
Phone: (704) 254-5678; Fax: (704) 254-0160
John Suleiman, President

RESPONSE MARKETING NETWORK
118 Route 9, Suite 179
Wappingers Falls, NY 12590
Phone: (914) 454-6630; Fax: (914) 454-6825
Marsha Walls, President

SEMINAR LIST MANAGEMENT
P. O. Box 9297
Canoga Park, CA 91309
Phone: (818) 882-4714; Fax: (818) 341-0707
Donna Brownell, Vice President

SEMINARS LIST SERVICES
1402 E. Skyline Drive
Madison, WI 53705
Phone: (608) 231-2775; Fax: (608) 231-3070
Howard C. Nelson, Broker & Manager

TAYBI DIRECT, INC.
2500 Ninth Street, Suite 113B
Berkeley, CA 94710
Phone: (510) 548-9181; Fax: (510) 548-1317
Paul Taybi, President

TECHNICAL PUBLICATIONS MAILING LISTS,
INC.
1016 Ascot Drive
Crystal Lake, IL 60014
Phone: (815) 459-0005; Fax: (815) 459-0014
Robert A. McNichols, President

WOODRUFF-STEVENS & ASSOCIATES, INC.
345 Park Avenue South
New York, NY 10010
Phone: (212) 685-4600

Standard Address Abbreviations

U.S. States

Alabama	AL
Alaska	AK
Arizona	AZ
Arkansas	AR
California	CA
Colorado	CO
Connecticut	CT
Delaware	DE
District of Columbia	DC
Florida	FL
Georgia	GA
Hawaii	HI
Idaho	ID
Illinois	IL
Indiana	IN
Iowa	IA
Kansas	KS
Kentucky	KY
Louisiana	LA
Maine	ME
Maryland	MD
Massachusetts	MA
Michigan	MI
Minnesota	MN
Mississippi	MS
Missouri	MO
Montana	MT
Nebraska	NE
Nevada	NV
New Hampshire	NH
New Jersey	NJ
New Mexico	NM
New York	NY
North Carolina	NC
North Dakota	ND
Ohio	OH
Oklahoma	OK
Oregon	OR
Pennsylvania	PA
Rhode Island	RI
South Carolina	SC
South Dakota	SD
Tennessee	TN
Texas	TX
Utah	UT
Vermont	VT
Virginia	VA
Washington	WA
West Virginia	WV
Wisconsin	WI
Wyoming	WY

U.S. Possessions

American Samoa	AS
Federated States of Micronesia	FM
Guam	GU
Marshall Islands	MH
No. Mariana Islands	MP
Palau	PW
Puerto Rico	PR
Virgin Islands	VI

Canadian Provinces

Alberta	AB
British Columbia	BC
Manitoba	MB
New Brunswick	NB
Newfoundland	NF
Northwest Territories	NT
Nova Scotia	NS
Ontario	ON
Prince Edward Island	PE
Quebec	PQ
Saskatchewan	SK
Yukon Territory	YT

Directions

North	N
East	E
South	S
West	W
Northeast	NE
Southeast	SE
Southwest	SW
Northwest	NW

HOW TO USE THE SRDS DIRECT MAIL LIST RATES AND DATA DIRECTORY

Finding a list in SRDS is easy if you know either the name of the list or the list owner; both are indexed near the front of the book.

Browsing for lists of possible interest is more complicated. First, use either the short list of Classifications (reproduced on the next page) or the more detailed Subject/Market Classification Index to identify classifications of interest. Classifications are sequential by number, but not all numbers are used. Within each classification, lists are alphabetical by name: "Big Business Executives" in the B's; "Top Management Executives" in the T's. Since you can't be sure of the list's name, look entirely through each classification of interest.

Don't overlook the two great glossaries on three pages near the front of SRDS: one on lists terms and the other on computer terms.

On the following page is a sample of an SRDS mailing list entry, followed by a data card on the same list from a mailing list broker.

SRDS Classification Numbers & Titles

BUSINESS LISTS

3—Advertising & Marketing
5—Air Conditioning, Plumbing & Heating, Sheet Metal & Ventilating
7—Amusements
9—Appliances
11—Architecture
13—Arts
15—Automatic Data Processing—Computers
17—Automotive, Automobiles, Tires, Batteries, Accessories, Service Stations, Garages
19—Aviation & Aerospace
21—Baking
23—Banking & Financial
25—Barbers
27—Beauty & Hairdressing
29—Boating
31—Books & Book Trade
33—Bottling
35—Brewing, Distilling & Beverages
37—Brick, Tile, Building Materials
39—Brushes
41—Building
43—Building Management & Real Estate
45—Business Executives
46—Business Firms
47—Camps & Camping
49—Cemetery, Monuments & Funeral Suppliers
51—Ceramics
52—Certified Public Accountants and Accountants
53—Chain Stores
55—Chemical & Chemical Process Industries
57—China & Glassware
61—Clothing & Furnishing Goods (Men's)
63—Clothing & Furnishing Goods (Women's)
65—Coal Merchandising
67—Coin-Operated and Vending Machines
69—Confectionery
71—Control & Instrumentation Systems
73—Corsets, Brassieres & Undergarments
75—Cosmetics
77—Dairy Products
79—Dental
81—Department, General Merchandise and Specialty Stores
83—Discount Marketing
85—Display
87—Draperies & Curtains
89—Drugs, Pharmaceutics
91—Educational
93—Electrical
95—Electronic Engineering
97—Engineering & Construction
99—Engineers
101—Farm Implements & Supplies
107—Feed, Grain and Milling
109—Fertilizer and Agricultural Chemicals
113—Fire Protection
115—Fishing Commercial
117—Floor Coverings
119—Florists & Floriculture
121—Food — Processing and Distribution
123—Funeral Directors
125—Fur Trade, Fur Farming, Trapping, Etc.
127—Furniture & Upholstery
129—Gas
133—Giftware, Antiques, Art Goods, Decorative Accessories, Greeting Cards, Etc.
135—Glass
137—Golf
139—Government Administrative Services & Public Works — Municipal, Township, County, State, Federal
141—Grocery
143—Hardware & Housewares
145—Home Economics
147—Home Furnishings

149—Hospitals & Hospital Administration
151—Hotels, Motels, Clubs & Resorts
161—Industrial Distribution
163—Industrial Purchasing
165—Infants', Children's & Teen Age Goods
167—Institutions
169—Insurance
171—Interior Design/Space Planning
173—International Trade
175—Jewelry & Watchmaking
177—Journalism
179—Landscape, Garden Supplies, Seed and Nursery Trade
181—Laundry and Dry Cleaning
183—Leather, Boots & Shoes
185—Legal
187—Lighting & Lighting Fixtures
191—Luggage & Leather Goods
193—Lumber & Forest Industries
195—Maintenance
197—Maritime, Marine, Shipbuilding, Repair & Operating
201—Materials Handling & Distribution
203—Meats & Provisions
205—Medical & Surgical
207—Metal, Metalworking & Machinery
213—Mining (Coal, Metal & Non-metallic)
215—Motion, Talk, Sound, Commercial Pictures, Etc.
217—Motor Trucks & Accessories
219—Motorcycle & Bicycle
221—Moving & Storage
223—Music & Music Trades
225—Notions & Fancy Goods
229—Nursing & Health
233—Ocean Science and Engineering
235—Office Equipment & Stationery
236—Office Equipment Mail Order Buyers
237—Office Methods & Management
241—Optical & Optometric
245—Packaging (Mfrs.) Paperboard
247—Packaging (Users)
249—Paint, Painting & Decorating
251—Paper
253—Parks, Public
255—Petroleum & Oil
257—Pets & Pet Supplies
259—Photographic
261—Plant & Manufacturing Executives
263—Plastics & Composition Products
265—Plumbing
267—Police, Detective & Security
269—Pollution Control, Environment, Ecology, Energy
271—Poultry & Poultry Products
273—Power & Power Plants
275—Printing & Printing Processes
277—Produce (Fruits & Vegetables)
279—Product Design Engineering
281—Public Transportation
283—Radio & Television
285—Railroad
289—Religious
291—Rental and Leasing Equipment
293—Reproduction — Inplant & Commercial
295—Restaurants and Food Service
297—Roads, Streets, Etc.
299—Roofing
301—Rubber
303—Safety, Accident Prevention
305—Sales Management
309—Schools & School Administration
311—Science, Research and Development
315—Selling & Salesmanship
317—Sporting Goods
319—Stone Products, Etc.
323—Swimming Pools
327—Telephone & Communications
329—Textiles and Knit Goods
331—Tobacco
333—Toys, Hobbies and Novelties
335—Trailers & Accessories
337—Transportation, Traffic, Shipping & Shipping Room Supplies
339—Travel
341—Venetian Blinds/Storm Windows

343—Veterinary
345—Water Supply & Sewage Disposal
347—Welding
349—Wire & Wire Products
351—Woodworking

CONSUMER LISTS

502—Almanacs & Directories
506—Art & Antiques
508—Automotive
510—Aviation
512—Babies
514—Boating & Yachting
516—Brides
518—Business Leaders
520—Children's
520A—Collectibles
521—College & Alumni
522—Contributors (Philanthropic)
524—Crafts, Hobbies & Models
525—Credit Card Holders
528—Dogs & Pets
530—Dressmaking & Needlework
532—Education & Self Improvement
534—Entertainment
536—Epicurean & Specialty Foods
538—Ethnic
544—Fashions — Clothing
546—Fishing & Hunting
548—Fraternal, Professional Groups, Service Clubs & Associations
549—Game Buyers, Contest and Puzzle Participants
550—Gardening (Home)
551—Gay & Lesbian
552—General
553—General Merchandise Mail Order Buyers
554—Gifts — Gift Buyers
556—Health
558—Home & Family Service
559—Horses, Riding & Breeding
560—Insurance Buyers
561—Investors
562—Labor — Trade Unions
563—Land Investors
564—Literature & Book Buyers
566—Mechanics & Science
568—Men's
572—Military, Naval & Veterans
578—Music & Record Buyers
584—Occult, Astrological & Metaphysical
586—Occupant & Resident
588—Opportunity Seekers
590—Photography
592—Political & Social Topics
593—Premium & Catalog Buyers
594—Professional
596—Religious & Denominational
598—Senior Citizens
600—Society
602—Sports
604—Teenagers
606—Travel
608—Video & Home Computers
612—Women's

FARM LISTS

700—Dairy & Dairy Breeds
702—Diversified Farming & Farm Home
704—Farm Education & Vocations
710—Field Crops & Soil Management
714—Land Use & Conservation
716—Livestock & Breed
718—Poultry

Sample Mailing List Descriptions

From SRDS Listing:

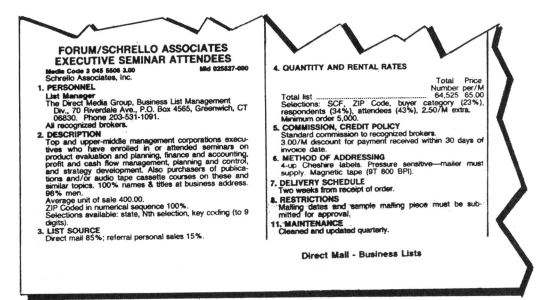

**FORUM/SCHRELLO ASSOCIATES
EXECUTIVE SEMINAR ATTENDEES**

Media Code 3 045 5506 3.00   Mid 025527-000
Schrello Associates, Inc.

1. PERSONNEL
List Manager
The Direct Media Group, Business List Management
   Div., 70 Riverdale Ave., P.O. Box 4565, Greenwich, CT
   06830. Phone 203-531-1091.
All recognized brokers.

2. DESCRIPTION
Top and upper-middle management corporations executives who have enrolled in or attended seminars on
product evaluation and planning, finance and accounting,
profit and cash flow management, planning and control,
and strategy development. Also purchasers of publications and/or audio tape cassette courses on these and
similar topics. 100% names & titles at business address.
98% men.
Average unit of sale 400.00.
ZIP Coded in numerical sequence 100%.
Selections available: state, Nth selection, key coding (to 9
digits).

3. LIST SOURCE
Direct mail 85%; referral personal sales 15%.

4. QUANTITY AND RENTAL RATES

                                            Total   Price
                                          Number per/M
Total list 64,525 65.00
Selections: SCF, ZIP Code, buyer category (23%),
respondents (34%), attendees (43%), 2.50/M extra.
Minimum order 5,000.

5. COMMISSION, CREDIT POLICY
Standard commission to recognized brokers.
3.00/M discount for payment received within 30 days of
invoice date.

6. METHOD OF ADDRESSING
4-up Cheshire labels. Pressure sensitive—mailer must
supply. Magnetic tape (9T 800 BPI).

7. DELIVERY SCHEDULE
Two weeks from receipt of order.

8. RESTRICTIONS
Mailing dates and sample mailing piece must be submitted for approval.

11. MAINTENANCE
Cleaned and updated quarterly.

Direct Mail - Business Lists

From Data Card:

FORUM/SCHRELLO EXECUTIVE SEMINAR ATTENDEES AND BUYERS	57630

```
    67,480  ATTENDEES, BUYERS & RESPONDENTS        $65.00/M*

TOP AND UPPER-MIDDLE MANAGEMENT EXECUTIVES FROM THE
NATION'S LARGEST CORPORATIONS WHO HAVE RECENTLY EN-
ROLLED IN OR ATTENDED SEMINARS SUCH AS:  "PRODUCT
EVALUATION AND PLANNING", "FINANCE & ACCOUNTING",
"PLANNING & CONTROL", "EXCEPTIONAL MANAGER", "NEW
MANAGERIAL SKILLS", "INFLUENCE MANAGEMENT", AND
EXCEPTIONAL SALES PERFORMANCE".  ALSO PURCHASERS OF
PUBLICATIONS AND/OR AUDIO TAPE CASSETTE COURSES ON
THESE AND SIMILAR TOPICS.  100% NAMES AND TITLES AT
BUSINESS ADDRESS.

SELECTIONS:  NTH SELECTION N/C; SCF, ZIP, STATE
             $2.50M; ATTENDEES (43%), BUYERS (23%)
             OR RESPONDENTS (34%) $2.50M

SOURCE: 85% DIRECT MAIL; 15% REFERRAL PERSONAL
             SALES

   UPDATED:  ONGOING
   .
   *THERE WILL BE A DISCOUNT OF $3.00M FOR PAYMENT
   WITHIN THIRTY (30) DAYS OF THE INVOICE DATE.
   .
   PAYMENT TERMS:  DIRECT MEDIA MUST RECEIVE PAYMENT
   WITHIN 45 DAYS OF THE MAIL DATE, OR MAILER WILL
   BE REQUIRED TO PAY CASH-IN-ADVANCE FOR FUTURE
   RENTAL OF ANY DMI BUSINESS MANAGED LIST.
```

```
55, DMI

****************
03   02

***UNIT-OF-SALE***
$400.00/AVERAGE

*******SEX********
98% MEN

****ADDRESSING****
4-UP CHESHIRE
MAGNETIC TAPE
9-TRACK 800 BPI
PRES. SENS. -
MAILER MUST SUPPLY

*****KEY-CODING***
NO CHARGE
UP TO 9 DIGITS

***MINIMUM-ORDER**
5,000

SAMPLE MAILING
PIECE REQUIRED
```

122 MAILING LISTS OF POSSIBLE TRAINING INTEREST

List Owner	List Name	Total Names Avail.	Price per M	How Obtained	Ave. Purchase ($)	Telephone
Adv. Technology Mktg./Learning Group	U.S. tech'l seminar attendees/inquirers	332,073	$110	D/M	$1,800	800/624–4303
Albrecht, Karl, & Associates	Book & video buyers	28,104	$85	D/M		415/381–0553
Amer. Inst. of CPA's (AICPA)	Current AICPA members	273,000	$55	D/M		212/575–3896
Amer. Management Ass'n. (AMA)	Mail order product buyers (3 years)	432,972	$80	D/M		212/685–5225
Amer. Management Ass'n. (AMA)	Seminar attendees (3 years)	235,465	$85	D/M		212/685–5225
Amer. Management Ass'n. (AMA)	Bookbuyers (3 years)	120,311	$85	D/M		212/685–5225
Amer. Management Ass'n. (AMA)	Training specifiers (3 years)	54,367	$95	D/M		212/685–5225
Amer. Management Ass'n. (AMA)	Master merged personnel managrs. file	23,423	$105	D/M		212/685–5225
Amer. Media, Inc.	A–V training product buyers	98,720	$95	85% D/M	$475	301/680–3633
Amer. Soc. for Training & Dev't.(ASTD)	Current ASTD members & attendees	83,463	$95	D/M	$120	703/683–8128
Art of Negotiating	Seminar attendees, buyers & subs	60,510	$75	90% D/M	$500	212/685–4600
Ass'n. for Ed. Comm. & Tech'y.(AECT)	Current AECT members	4,500	$100		$65	202/347–7834
Ass'n. for Quality & Partic. (AQP)	Current AQP members	7,300	$125		$75	513/381–1959
Batten, Batten, Hudson & Swab	Seminar attendees & buyers	39,526	$70	D/M		203/532–1000
Blanchard Training & Development	Buyers, attendees & inquirers	62,883	$85	D/M	$300	619/489–5005
Boardroom Reports	U.S. Book buyers (2 years)	1,114,224	$95	D/M		212/239–9000
Boardroom Reports	U.S. Multi–Buyers	367,929	$95	D/M		212/239–9000
Boardroom Reports	Active U.S. subscribers	45,931	$95	D/M		212/239–9000
Britannica Training & Dev't.	Quality/benchmarking product buyers	18,499	$90	D/M	$550	512/255–6014
Brogan Clear–Writing Seminars	Attendees & inquirers	35,358	$85	D/M	$350	415/381–0553
Career Women Ass'n.	Current members of 50 organizations	837,620	$60			914/620–0700
Careertrack	Seminar attendees	1,055,000	$90	D/M	$85	303/447–2323
Careertrack	Audio & video tape buyers	265,000	$90	D/M	$85	303/447–2323
Careertrack	Quarterly Hotline	158,000	$100	D/M	$85	303/447–2323
Center for Professional Advancement	Technical seminar attendees	32,317	$85	D/M	$850	914/277–5558
Clement Communications	U.S. training buyers & subscribers	220,443	$90	85% D/M		215/459–1700
Clemson University	Seminar & short course attendees	120,265	$90	D/M	$300	914/277–5558
Conference Board, The	U.S. Conference attendees and buyers	77,911	$100			800/526–3973
Creative Resources	Seminar attendees & subscribers	55,675	$80	D/M		913/236–6830
Crisp Publications	Book & tape buyers	39,176	$90	D/M	$37	203/532–1000
CRM Films	Product & education buyers	18,000	$90	D/M & T/M	$195	619,634–5064
Dartnell	U.S. mail–order buyers (all)	137,000	$90	D/M		800/621–5463
Dartnell	Personnel mngt. prod. buyers	22,500	$90	D/M		800/621–5463
Data Tech Institute	Computer seminar attendees	119,472	$100	D/M	$650	212/719–3850
Daytimers	Recent mail–order buyers (12 months)	1,645,761	$95	D/M	$45	203/532–1000
Dun & Bradstreet Bus. Ed. Srvcs.	Seminar attendees & buyers	1,378,685	$85	95% D/M		203/532–1000
Dun & Bradstreet Bus. Ed. Srvcs.	Quarterly Hotline	62,216	$95	95% D/M		203/532–1000
Economics Press	U.S. buyers & subscribers	184,650	$85	D/M	$85	914/925–2401
Excellence In Training Corp.	Video Inquirers & buyers	25,986	$90	75% T/M	$550	512/255–7532
Executive Enterprises	HR/personnel bookbuyers/subscribers	31,000	$100	D/M & T/M		212/645–7880
Executive Seminars In Sound	Audio cassett course buyers	12,275	$60	D/M & ads	$95	708/619–9800
Fullton Associates	Seminar attendees	54,000	$85	D/M	$65	213/878–2870
Haimes Associates	HR seminar attendees & book buyers	23,281	$70	D/M		703/978–4927
Harvard Business Review	Current paid U.S. subscribers	208,092	$100	D/M	$65	914/925–2401
HR Direct	Training product buyers	22,000	$90	D/M	$150	515/472–7188
HR Magazine (was Pers. Administrator)	Current SHRM members & paid subs.	69,044	$95		$135	914/277–5558
Human Factors Society (HFS)	Current HFS members	5,000	$100		$70	310/394–1811
Human Resource Executive Magazine	Controlled circulation recipients	45,051	$125	D/M & T/M		215/784–0860
Inc. Magazine	Current paid subscribers	601,000	$95	95% D/M	$25	800/526–3973
Inc. Magazine	Video & management report buyers	82,292	$95	95% D/M		800/526–3973
Institute for Int'l. Research	Seminar attendees (last 12 months)	227,716	$105	D/M		516/293–8550
Institute for Management	Buyers & subscribers (last 12 months)	47,629	$99	D/M	$89	201/568–0707
Institute of Management & Administration	Newsletter subscribers & expires	350,000	$95	D/M & T/M	$200	212/244–0360
Int'l. Correspondence Schools (ICS)	Buyers (12 months)	135,303	$75	Various	$685	708/550–6200
Kiplinger Washington Editors	Washington newsletter paid subscriber	311,539	$95	D/M	$58	212/819–3400
Kiplinger Washington Editors	Book buyers (4 years)	139,000	$75	Ads		212/819–3400
Lakewood Publications	Training & HRD Database	179,011	$90	Compiled	– –	800/328–4329
Lakewood Publications	Training Mag. paid subscribers	51,914	$90	D/M	$64	800/328–4329
Lakewood Publications	Newsltr, bookbuyers & conf. attends	41,936	$95	D/M	$75	800/328–4329
Lakewood Publications	Conference attendees	12,511	$95	D/M	$400	800/328–4329

List Owner	List Name	Total Names Avail.	Price per M	How Obtained	Ave. Purchase ($)	Telephone
Lant Associates, Dr. Jeffrey	Book & tape buyers & inquirers	55,234	$75	D/M	$15	203/261-5585
Learn, Incorporated	Self-study program buyers (3 years)	63,100	$70	D/M	$95	914/277-5558
Learning Annex East, The	Seminar/ course attendees (1 year)	24,614	$75	D/M & T/M	$60	516/293-8550
Learning Annex of California, The	Seminar/ course attendees (1 year)	35,392	$75	D/M & T/M	$60	516/293-8550
Learning Channel, The	Merchandise buyers	10,861	$60	TV	$30	914/273-6606
Learning Resources Network (LERN)	Members & buyers	15,000	$90	D/M		619/634-5064
Linton Publishing Co.	Top 5000 trng/quality decisionmakers	5,000	$145	Compiled	--	612/936-2288
Managing Your Money	Software buyers	599,945	$110	D/R	$90	407/393-8200
Marketing Federation	Prospects, responders & attendees	70,261	$75	Various		212/719-3850
Mensa	Society members (with high IQs)	35,730	$85		$36	201/567-3200
Naisbitt Trendletter	Newsletter subscribers & expires	6,840	$125	95% D/M		201/567-3200
Nat'l. Assoc For Female Execs. (NAFE)	Current U.S. NAFE Members	212,326	$95	D/M	$29	203/532-1000
Nat'l. Ass'n. for Self-Employed (NASE)	Current NASE members	268,018	$75	Various	$48	609/275-0050
Nat'l. Human Resources Ass'n. (NHRA)	Current NHRA members	2,000	Exchange only		$70	508/474-0750
Nat'l. Management Ass'n.	Current NMA members	99,703	$90	D/M		212/684-4800
Nat'l. Seminars	Seminar attendees & tape buyers	1,305,361	$85	D/M	$45	913/432-7755
Nat'l. Soc. for Perf. & Instr. (NSPI)	Current U.S. NSPI members	10,356	$110	D/M	$95	202/408-7969
Negotiation Institute, The	Negotiation seminar attendees	24,282	$75		$300	913/236-6830
New Yorker, The	U.S. subscribers	579,940	$100	D/R	$32	212/819-3400
Nightingale-Conant	Cassette program buyers (12 months)	507,270	$85	D/M	$75	708/619-9800
Nightingale-Conant	Quarterly Hotline	125,000	$85	D/M	$75	708/619-9800
Organization Development Netw'k (ODN)	Current national ODN members	2,600	$95		$110	503/246-0148
Organizational Consultants	3-day seminar attendees	18,331	$85	D/M	$940	415/381-0553
Padgett-Thompson	Seminar attendees	524,000	$85	D/M	$100	800/526-3973
Padgett-Thompson	Quarterly Hotline	75,000	$105	D/M	$100	800/526-3973
Performance Seminars Group	Seminar attendees (2 years)	131,369	$90	D/M	$300	914/277-5558
Personnel Department Store, The	Catalog buyers	27,406	$95	D/M		415/381-0553
Personnel Journal	Paid subscribers	22,000	$120	D/M	$55	714/751-1883
Personnel Management Ass'n.	Current members	68,634	$60		$100	914/620-0700
Peters Group, Tom	Attendees, buyers & subscribers	6,509	$120			415/381-0553
Pfeiffer & Co. (formerly University Assoc.)	Buyers & attenders	62,600	$80	D/M	$120	619/578-5900
Prime Learning Int'l..	Seminar attendees	252,246	$85	D/M	$44	913/236-6830
Pryor Seminars, Fred	Seminar attendees	1,227,448	$80	D/M	$145	913/236-6830
Pryor Seminars, Fred	Multibuyers	170,000	$100	D/M		913/236-6830
Pryor Seminars, Fred	Quarterly Hotline	74,272	$90	D/M	$145	913/236-6830
Q.E.D. Information Sciences	Seminar attendees & buyers	23,233	$80		$700	212/719-3850
Rutherford Group Int'l..	Seminar attendees & buyers	168,816	$80	D/M		913/236-6830
Sales & Marketing Management	Current paid subscribers	73,000	$125	D/M	$48	201/387-1010
Schrello Direct Marketing	Attendees, buyers & prospects	18,464	$85	70% D/M	$195	800/367-6559
Seminars Int'l.	Seminar attendees	246,491	$85	D/M	$100	913/236-6830
Seminars List Services	Training, personnel & HR managers	56,590	$65	Compiled	--	608/231-2775
Seminars List Services	Training "Hotlist"	15,332	$65	Compiled	--	608/231-2775
Sharper Image, The	Buyers & catalog requestors (22 mos.)	432,410	$100	D/M	$150	914/620-0700
SkillPath	Seminar attendees	276,332	$90	D/M	$75	212/685-5225
Soc. for Appl. Learning Tech'y (SALT)	Current SALT members	1,000	Exchange only		$45	800/457-6812
Soc. for Human Resource Mngt. (SHRM)	Current SHRM members	69,044	$95		$160	914/277-5558
Soc. of Manufacturing Engineers (SME)	Conference/seminar attendees	235,370	$60	D/M		312/271-1500
SyberVision Systems, Inc.	Catalog buyers	208,175	$95	57% D/M	$95	203/532-1000
Technology Transfer Institute	Computer seminar attendees	16,453	$130	D?M	$1,152	212/719-3850
Training Store, The	Book, cassette & video buyers	15,724	$100	D/M	$145	201/692-0018
United Training Media	Video buyers	15,830	$90	D/M	$300	301/680-3633
University Seminar Center	Seminar attendees	46,782	$90	D/M		800/526-3973
Vantage Communications	Sales training buyers & inquirers	37,951	$75	90% D/M		203/532-1000
WaldenBooks	Preferred Reader Program members	4,544,120	$70	P.O.P.	$175	212/677-6760
Wall Street Journal	Active subscribers	1,336,139	$125	D/M	$139	914/925-2401
Warren, Gorham & Lamont	HR & personnel buyers & subscribers	71,051	$110	85% D/M	$117	212/971-5000
Whole Brain Learning Institute	Seminar attendees & tape buyers	71,611	$90	D/R	$195	407/393-8200
Winthrop Seminars	1-2 week seminar attendees (2 years)	173,000	$75	D/M & ads		818/762-0036
Working Women Magazine	Subscribers	743,381	$80	D/M	$18	212/642-0310
Working Women Magazine	Monthly Hotline	29,007	$85	D/M	$18	212/642-0310
Ziff Institute for Techy & Training	Attendees & inquirers	28,993	$90	D/M	$895	212/719-3850
Zig Ziglar Corp., The	Attendees, buyers, subscribers (3 yrs)	87,475	$95	90% D/M	$70	214/985-4060

NOTES: 122 Lists containing 28,304,251 total names. Average $87 price per M.
Missing information not available at press time.

THREE-DIGIT ZIP CODE LIST

The following list includes the first three digits of each assigned group of ZIP Codes and the areas associated with these numbers. See the separate list of sectional center facilities assignments for groups of numbered areas served through each facility. Such information can be used for routing purposes. The larger post offices having their own three-digit ZIP Code and having street listings are listed in capital letters, and sectional center facilities are listed in lower case letters.

006-009 PUERTO RICO AND VIRGIN ISLANDS

006	San Juan
007	San Juan
008	San Juan (Virgin Islands)
009	SAN JUAN

010-027 MASSACHUSETTS

010	Springfield
011	SPRINGFIELD
012	Pittsfield
013	Springfield
014	Worcester
015	Worcester
016	WORCESTER
017	Worcester
018	Middlesex-Essex
019	Middlesex-Essex
020	Brockton
021	BOSTON (1)
022	BOSTON (2)
023	Brockton
024	BROCKTON
025	Buzzards Bay
026	Buzzards Bay
027	Providence, RI (Massachusetts Offices)
055	Middlesex-Essex

028-029 RHODE ISLAND

028	Providence
029	PROVIDENCE

030-038 NEW HAMPSHIRE

030	Manchester
031	MANCHESTER
032	Manchester
033	CONCORD
034	Manchester
035	White River Junction
036	White River Junction, VT (New Hampshire Offices)
037	White River Junction, VT (New Hampshire Offices)
038	Portsmouth

039-049 MAINE

039	Portsmouth, NH, (Maine Offices)
040	Portland
041	PORTLAND
042	Portland
043	Portland
044	Bangor
045	Portland
046	Bangor
047	Bangor
048	Portland
049	Portland

050-059 VERMONT

050	White River Junction
051	White River Junction
052	White River Junction
053	White River Junction
054	Burlington
056	Burlington
057	White River Junction
058	White River Junction
059	White River Junction

060-069 CONNECTICUT

060	Hartford
061	HARTFORD
062	Hartford
063	New Haven
064	New Haven
065	NEW HAVEN
066	BRIDGEPORT
067	Waterbury
068	Stamford
069	STAMFORD

070-089 NEW JERSEY

070	Newark
071	NEWARK
072	ELIZABETH
073	JERSEY CITY
074	Paterson
075	PATERSON
076	Hackensack
077	Monmouth
078	West Jersey
079	West Jersey
080	South Jersey
081	CAMDEN
082	South Jersey
083	South Jersey
084	Atlantic City
085	Trenton
086	TRENTON
087	Trenton
088	Kilmer
089	NEW BRUNSWICK

004-149 NEW YORK

004	Westchester
090-098	Military (AE)
100	NEW YORK
101	NEW YORK
102	NEW YORK
103	STATEN ISLAND
104	BRONX
105	Westchester
106	WHITE PLAINS
107	YONKERS
108	NEW ROCHELLE
109	Rockland
110	Queens
111	LONG ISLAND CITY
112	BROOKLYN
113	FLUSHING
114	JAMAICA
115	Western Nassau
116	FAR ROCKAWAY
117	Mid-Island
118	HICKSVILLE
119	Mid-Island
120	Albany (A-J)
121	Albany (K-Z)
122	ALBANY
123	SCHENECTADY
124	Mid-Hudson
125	Mid-Hudson
126	POUGHKEEPSIE
127	Mid-Hudson
128	Glens Falls
129	Plattsburgh
130	Syracuse (A-L)
131	Syracuse (M-Z)
132	SYRACUSE
133	Utica (A-L)
134	Utica (M-Z)
135	UTICA
136	Watertown
137	Binghamton (A-L)
138	Binghamton (M-Z)
139	BINGHAMTON
140	Buffalo (A-L)
141	Buffalo (M-Z)
142	BUFFALO
143	NIAGARA FALLS
144	Rochester (A-L)
145	Rochester (M-Z)
146	ROCHESTER
147	Jamestown
	Junction
148	Elmira
149	ELMIRA

150-196 PENNSYLVANIA

150	Pittsburgh (1)
151	Pittsburgh (2)
152	PITTSBURGH
153	Pittsburgh
154	Pittsburgh
155	Johnstown
156	Greensburg
157	Johnstown
158	Du Bois
159	Johnstown
160	New Castle
161	New Castle
162	New Castle
163	Oil City
164	Erie
165	ERIE
166	Altoona
167	Bradford
168	Altoona
169	Williamsport
170	Harrisburg
171	HARRISBURG
172	Harrisburg
173	Lancaster
174	YORK
175	Lancaster
176	LANCASTER
177	Williamsport
178	Harrisburg
179	Reading
180	Lehigh Valley
181	ALLENTOWN
182	Wilks-Barre
183	Lehigh Valley
184	Scranton
185	SCRANTON
186	Wilks-Barre
187	WILKS-BARRE
188	Scranton
189	Southeastern
190	Philadelphia
191	PHILADELPHIA
192	Philadelphia
193	Southeastern
194	Southeastern
195	Reading
196	READING

197-199 DELAWARE

197	Wilmington
198	WILMINGTON
199	Wilmington

200-205 DISTRICT OF COLUMBIA

200	WASHINGTON
202-205	Government

206-219 MARYLAND

206	Southern
207	Southern
208	Suburban
209	SILVER SPRING
210	Baltimore (1)
211	Baltimore (2)
212	BALTIMORE
214	ANNAPOLIS
215	Cumberland
216	Easton
217	Frederick
218	Salisbury
219	Baltimore

220-246 VIRGINIA

201	Northern VA
220	Northern VA (1)
221	Northern VA (2)
222	ARLINGTON
223	ALEXANDRIA
224	Richmond
225	Richmond
226	Winchester
227	Culpeper
228	Charlottesville
229	Charlottesville
230	Richmond (1)
231	Richmond (2)
232	RICHMOND
233	Norfolk (1)
234	Norfolk (2)
235	NORFOLK
236	NORFOLK
237	PORTSMOUTH
238	Richmond
239	Farmville
240	Roanoke (1)
241	Roanoke (2)
242	Bristol
243	Roanoke
244	Charlottesville
245	Lynchburg
246	Bluefield, WV (Virginia Offices)

247-268 WEST VIRGINIA

247	Bluefield
248	Bluefield
249	Lewisburg
250	Charleston (1)
251	Charleston (2)
252	Charleston (3)
253	CHARLESTON
254	Martinsburg
255	Huntington (1)
256	Huntington (2)
257	HUNTINGTON
258	Beckley (1)
259	Beckley (2)
260	Wheeling
261	Parkersburg
262	Clarksburg
263	Clarksburg (1)
264	Clarksburg (2)
265	Clarksburg (3)
266	Gassaway
267	Cumberland, MD (West Virginia Offices)
268	Petersburg

270-289 NORTH CAROLINA

270	Greensboro (West)
271	WINSTON-SALEM
272	Greensboro (East) (1)
273	Greensboro (East) (2)
274	GREENSBORO
275	Raleigh
276	RALEIGH
277	DURHAM
278	Rocky Mount
279	Rocky Mount
280	Charlotte (1)
281	Charlotte (2)
282	CHARLOTTE
283	Fayetteville
284	Fayetteville
285	Kinston
286	Hickory
287	Asheville
288	ASHEVILLE
289	Asheville

290-299 SOUTH CAROLINA

290	Columbia (1)
291	Columbia (2)
292	COLUMBIA
293	Greenville
294	Charleston
295	Florence
296	Greenville
297	Charlotte, NC (South Carolina Offices)
298	Augusta, GA (South Carolina Offices)
299	Savannah, GA (South Carolina Offices)

300-319 GEORGIA

300	North Metro
301	North Metro
302	North Metro
303	ATLANTA
304	Swansboro
305	North Metro
306	Athens
307	Chattanooga, TN (Georgia Offices)
308	Augusta
309	AUGUSTA
310	Macon
311	Atlanta
312	MACON
313	Savannah
314	SAVANNAH
315	Waycross
316	Valdosta
317	Albany
318	Columbus
319	COLUMBUS

320-349 FLORIDA

320	Jacksonville
321	Daytona Beach
322	JACKSONVILLE
323	Tallahassee
324	Panama City
325	Pensacola
326	Gainsville
327	Mid-Florida
328	ORLANDO
329	Orlando
330	South Florida
331	MIAMI
332	MIAMI
333	FORT LAUDERDALE
334	West Palm Beach
335	Tampa
336	TAMPA
337	SAINT PETERSBURG
338	Lakeland
339	Fort Myers
340	Military (AA)
342	Manasota
344	Gainsville
346	Tampa
347	Orlando
349	West Palm Beach

350-369 ALABAMA

350	Birmingham (A-L)
351	Birmingham (M-Z)
352	BIRMINGHAM
354	Tuscaloosa
355	Birmingham
356	Huntsville
357	Huntsville
358	HUNTSVILLE
359	Birmingham
360	Montgomery
361	MONTGOMERY
362	Anniston
363	Dothan
364	Evergreen
365	Mobile
366	MOBILE
367	Montgomery
368	Montgomery
369	Meridian, MS (Alabama Offices)

370-385 TENNESSEE

370	Nashville (A-L)
371	Nashville (M-Z)
372	NASHVILLE
373	Chattanooga
374	CHATTANOOGA
376	Johnson City
377	Knoxville (A-L)
378	Knoxville (M-Z)
379	KNOXVILLE
380	Memphis
381	MEMPHIS
382	McKenzie
383	Jackson
384	Columbia
385	Cookeville

386-397 MISSISSIPPI

386	Memphis, TN (Mississippi Offices)
387	Greenville
388	Tupelo
389	Grenada
390	Jackson (A-L)
391	Jackson (M-Z)
392	JACKSON
393	Meridian
394	Hattiesburg
395	Gulfport
396	McComb
397	Columbus

400-427 KENTUCKY

400	Louisville (East)
401	Louisville (West)
402	LOUISVILLE
403	Lexington (North)
404	Lexington (South)
405	LEXINGTON
406	FRANKFORT
407	London (West)
408	London (East)
409	London (Central)
410	Cincinnati, OH (Kentucky Offices)
411	Ashland (North)
412	Ashland (South)
413	Campton (South)
414	Campton (North)
415	Pikeville (East)
416	Pikeville (West)
417	Hazard (West)
418	Hazard (East)
420	Paducah
421	Bowling Green (East)
422	Bowling Green (West)
423	Owensboro
424	Evansville, IN (Kentucky Offices)
425	Somerset (North)
426	Somerset (South)
427	Elizabethtown

430-458 OHIO

430	Columbus (North)
431	Columbus (South)
432	COLUMBUS
433	Columbus
434	Toledo (East)
435	Toledo (West)
436	TOLEDO
437	Zanesville (South)
438	Zanesville (North)
439	Steubenville
440	Cleveland
441	CLEVELAND
442	Akron
443	AKRON
444	Youngstown
445	YOUNGSTOWN
446	Canton
447	CANTON
448	Mansfield
449	MANSFIELD
450	Cincinnati (West)
451	Cincinnati (East)
452	CINCINNATI
453	Dayton
454	DAYTON
455	SPRINGFIELD
456	Chillicothe

457 Athens
458 Lima

460-479 INDIANA

460 Indianapolis (North)
461 Indianapolis (South)
462 INDIANAPOLIS
463 Gary
464 GARY
465 South Bend
466 SOUTH BEND
467 Fort Wayne
468 FORT WAYNE
469 Kokomo
470 Cincinnati, OH (Indiana Offices)
471 Louisville, KY (Indiana Offices)
472 Columbus
473 Muncie
474 Bloomington
475 Washington
476 Evansville
477 EVANSVILLE
478 Terre Haute
479 Lafayette

480-499 MICHIGAN

480 Royal Oak
481 Detroit
482 DETROIT
483 Royal Oak
484 Flint
485 FLINT
486 Saginaw (West)
487 Saginaw (East)
488 Lansing
489 LANSING
490 Kalamazoo (1)
491 Kalamazoo (2)
492 Jackson
493 Grand Rapids (East)
494 Grand Rapids (West)
495 GRAND RAPIDS
496 Traverse City
497 Gaylord
498 Iron Mountain (East)
499 Iron Mountain (West)

500-528 IOWA

500 Des Moines(A-F)
501 Des Moines(G-M)
502 Des Moines(N-Z)
503 DES MOINES
504 Mason City
505 Fort Dodge
506 Waterloo
507 WATERLOO
508 Creston
509 Des Moines
510 Sioux City
511 SIOUX CITY
512 Sheldon
513 Spencer
514 Carroll
515 Omaha, NE (Iowa Offices)
516 Omaha, NE (Iowa Offices)
520 Dubuque
521 Decorah
522 Cedar Rapids (A-L)
523 Cedar Rapids (M-Z)
524 CEDAR RAPIDS
525 Ottumwa
526 Burlington
527 Rock Island, IL (Iowa Offices)
528 DAVENPORT

530-549 WISCONSIN

530 Milwaukee (North)
531 Milwaukee (South)
532 MILWAUKEE
534 RACINE
535 Madison
537 MADISON
538 Madison
539 Portage
540 Saint Paul, MN

(Wisconsin Offices)
541 Green Bay (West)
542 Green Bay (East)
543 GREEN BAY
544 Wausau
545 Rhinelander
546 La Crosse
547 Eau Claire
548 Spooner
549 Oshkosh

550-567 MINNESOTA

550 Saint Paul
551 SAINT PAUL
553 Minneapolis
554 MINNEAPOLIS
555 Minneapolis
556 Duluth (East)
557 Duluth (West)
558 DULUTH
559 Rochester
560 Mankato
561 Windom
562 Willmar
563 Saint Cloud
564 Brainerd
565 Detroit Lakes
566 Bemidji
567 Thief River Falls

570-577 SOUTH DAKOTA

570 Sioux Falls
571 SIOUX FALLS
572 Watertown
573 Mitchell
574 Aberdeen
575 Pierre
576 Mobridge
577 Rapid City

580-588 NORTH DAKOTA

580 Fargo
581 Fargo
582 Grand Forks
583 Devils Lake
584 Jamestown
585 Bismark
586 Dickinson
587 Minot
588 Williston

590-599 MONTANA

590 Billings
591 BILLINGS
592 Wolf Point
593 Miles City
594 Great Falls
595 Havre
596 Helena
597 Butte
598 Missoula
599 Kalispell

600-629 ILLINOIS

600 Palatine
601 Carol Stream
602 EVANSTON
603 OAK PARK
604 South Suburban (1)
605 Fox Valley
606 CHICAGO
607 Chicago
609 Kankakee
610 Rockford
611 ROCKFORD
612 Rock Island
613 La Salle
614 Galesburg
615 Peoria
616 PEORIA
617 Bloomington
618 Champaign (North)
619 Champaign (South)
620 St. Louis, MO (Illinois Offices)
622 St. Louis, MO (Illinois Offices)
623 Quincy
624 Effingham
625 Springfield (East)
626 Springfield (West)
627 SPRINGFIELD

628 Centralia
629 Carbondale

630-658 MISSOURI

630 Saint Louis
631 SAINT LOUIS
633 Saint Louis
634 Quincy
635 Quincy
636 Cape Girardeau
637 Cape Girardeau
638 Cape Girardeau
639 Cape Girardeau
640 Kansas City
641 KANSAS CITY
644 Saint Joseph
645 SAINT JOSEPH
646 Chillicothe
647 Harrisonville
648 Springfield
650 Mid-Missouri
651 JEFFERSON CITY
652 Mid-Missouri
653 Mid-Missouri
654 Springfield
655 Springfield
656 Springfield (A-L)
657 Springfield (M-Z)
658 SPRINGFIELD

660-679 KANSAS

660 Kansas City
661 KANSAS CITY
662 SHAWNEE MISSION
664 Topeka (A-L)
665 Topeka (M-Z)
666 TOPEKA
667 Fort Scott
668 Topeka
669 Salina
670 Wichita (A-L)
671 Wichita (M-Z)
672 WICHITA
673 Independence
674 Salina
675 Hutchinson
676 Hays
677 Colby
678 Dodge City
679 Liberal

680-693 NEBRASKA

680 Omaha
681 OMAHA
683 Lincoln (A-L)
684 Lincoln (M-Z)
685 LINCOLN
686 Norfolk
687 Norfolk
688 Grand Island
689 Grand Island
690 McCook
691 North Platte
692 Valentine
693 Alliance

700-714 LOUISIANA

700 New Orleans
701 NEW ORLEANS
703 Thibodaux
704 Hammond
705 Lafayette
706 Lake Charles
707 Baton Rouge
708 BATON ROUGE
710 Shreveport
711 SHREVEPORT
712 Monroe
713 Alexandria (East)
714 Alexandria (West)

716-728 ARKANSAS

716 Pine Bluff
717 Camden
718 Texarkana, TX (AR Offices)
719 Hot Springs National Park
720 Little Rock (A-L)
721 Little Rock (M-Z)
722 LITTLE ROCK
723 Memphis, TN (AR Offices)
724 Jonesboro
725 Batesville
726 Harrison
727 Fayetteville

728 Russeville
729 Fort Smith

730-749 OKLAHOMA

730 Oklahoma City
731 OKLAHOMA CITY
734 Ardmore
735 Lawton
736 Clinton
737 Enid
738 Woodward
739 Liberal, KS (Oklahoma Office)
740 Tulsa
741 TULSA
743 Tulsa
744 Muskogee
745 McAlester
746 Ponca City
747 Durant
748 Shawnee
749 Poteau

750-799 TEXAS

750 North Texas
751 Dallas
752 DALLAS (1)
753 DALLAS (2)
754 Greenville
755 Texarkana
756 Longview
757 Tyler
758 Palestine
759 Lufkin
760 Fort Worth
761 FORT WORTH
762 Fort Worth
763 Wichita Falls
764 Fort Worth
765 Waco
766 Waco
767 WACO
768 Abilene
769 Midland
770 HOUSTON
771 HOUSTON
772 HOUSTON
773 North Houston
774 North Houston
775 North Houston
776 Beaumont
777 BEAUMONT
778 Bryan
779 Victoria
780 San Antonio (West)
781 San Antonio (East)
782 SAN ANTONIO
783 Corpus Cristi
784 CORPUS CRISTI
785 McAllen
786 Austin
787 AUSTIN
788 San Antonio
789 Austin
790 Amarillo
791 AMARILLO
792 Childress
793 Lubbock
794 LUBBOCK
795 Abilene
796 ABILENE
797 Midland
798 El Paso
799 EL PASO
885 EL PASO

800-816 COLORADO

800 Denver (North)
801 Denver (South)
802 DENVER
803 BOULDER
804 DENVER
805 Longmont
806 Brighton
807 Brighton
808 Colorado Springs
809 COLORADO SPRINGS
810 Pueblo
811 Alamosa
812 Salida
813 Durango
814 Grand Junction
815 Grand Junction
816 Glenwood Springs

820-831 WYOMING

820 Cheyenne
821 YELLOWSTONE NATIONAL PARK (Montana Office)
822 Wheatland
823 Rawlins
824 Worland
825 Riverton
826 Casper
827 Gillette
828 Sheridan
829 Rock Springs (1)
830 Rock Springs (2)
831 Rock Springs (3)

832-838 IDAHO

832 Pocatello
833 Twin Falls
834 Pocatello
835 Lewiston
836 Boise
837 BOISE
838 Spokane, WA (Idaho Offices)

840-847 UTAH

840 Salt Lake City
841 SALT LAKE CITY
842 Salt Lake City
843 Salt Lake City
844 OGDEN
845 Provo
846 Provo
847 Provo

850-865 ARIZONA

850 PHOENIX
852 Phoenix (1)
853 Phoenix (2)
855 Globe
856 Tucson
857 TUCSON
859 Show Low
860 Flagstaff
863 Prescott
864 Kingman
865 Gallup, NM (Arizona Offices)

870-884 NEW MEXICO

870 Albuquerque
871 ALBUQUERQUE
872 ALBUQUERQUE
873 Gallup
874 Farmington
875 Albuquerque
877 Las Vegas
878 Socorro
879 Truth or Consequences
880 Las Cruces
881 Clovis
882 Roswell
883 Carrizozo
884 Tucumcari

889-898 NEVADA

889 LAS VEGAS
890 Las Vegas
891 LAS VEGAS
893 Ely
894 Reno
895 RENO
897 Carson City
898 Elko

900-966 CALIFORNIA

900 LOS ANGELES
901 LOS ANGELES
902 Inglewood
903 INGLEWOOD
904 SANTA MONICA
905 TORRANCE
906 Long Beach
907 Long Beach
908 LONG BEACH
910 Pasadena
911 PASADENA
912 GLENDALE
913 Van Nuys
914 VAN NUYS
915 BURBANK
916 NORTH HOLLYWOOD
917 Alhambra

918 ALHAMBRA
919 San Diego
920 San Diego
921 SAN DIEGO
922 Palm Springs
923 San Bernardino
924 SAN BERNARDINO
925 San Bernardino
926 Santa Ana
927 SANTA ANA
928 ANAHEIM
930 Oxnard
931 SANTA BARBARA
932 Bakersfield
933 BAKERSFIELD
934 Santa Barbara
935 Mojave
936 Fresno
937 FRESNO
938 Fresno
939 Salinas
940 San Francisco
941 SAN FRANCISCO
942 SACRAMENTO
943 PALO ALTO
944 SAN MATEO
945 Oakland
946 OAKLAND
947 BERKELEY
948 RICHMOND
949 North Bay
950 San Jose
951 SAN JOSE
952 Stockton (1)
953 Stockton (2)
954 North Bay
955 Eureka
956 Sacramento (1)
957 Sacramento (2)
958 SACRAMENTO
959 Marysville
960 Redding
961 Reno, Nevada (California Offices)
962-966 Military (AP)

967-968 HAWAII

967 Honolulu
968 HONOLULU

969 GUAM

969 Agana, Guam

970-979 OREGON

970 Portland (1)
971 Portland (2)
972 PORTLAND
973 Salem
974 Eugene
975 Medford
976 Klamath Falls
977 Bend
978 Pendleton
979 Boise, Idaho (Oregon Offices)

980-994 WASHINGTON

980 Seattle
981 SEATTLE
982 Everett
983 Tacoma
984 TACOMA
985 Olympia
986 Portland, OR (Washington Offices)
988 Wenatchee
989 Yakima
990 Spokane
991 Spokane
992 SPOKANE
993 Pasco
994 Lewiston, Idaho (Washington Offices)

995-999 ALASKA

995 Anchorage (1)
996 Anchorage (2)
997 Fairbanks
998 Juneau
999 Ketchikan

EVALUATE UNTRIED LISTS WITH THIS LIST EVALUATION WORKSHEET

This worksheet is a handy way to do an evaluation of mailing lists before you have any response data on them for your own offer(s). That makes it useful for paring down a large number of candidate lists to get the ones you want to test first.

1. First, Select Your Lists, and complete the left half of the worksheet using data cards or other sources of information on each list. Use a separate line for each major selection from a list (for example, Book Buyers and Attendees), since the evaluation will be different for each.

2. Next, Establish Your List Evaluation Criteria. Modify or adapt the scoring guidelines shown on the facing page as necessary to best fit your particular product and your targeted market. Notice that in this scheme, scores range from a low of zero to a high of five.

3. Now Evaluate Each List (or list selection) against the RESPONDER factor using the LIST EVALUATION CRITERIA. Evaluate all lists on this one factor before moving on to the next factor, since it's much easier to do comparative evaluations between lists this way.

When you're satisfied with your RESPONDER evaluation, then do go on to the BUYER factor, and continue in the same manner through all five List Evaluation Factors.

4. Add Up the Total Score for Each List on each of the five factors. If you used the recommended scoring of zero to five, then the range of the total will be from zero to 25.

5. Calculate the Relative Cost per Order index using this formula:

$$\frac{\text{REL. COST}}{\text{PER ORDER}} = \frac{\text{PACKAGE COST} + \text{LIST COST}}{(\text{EVALUATION SCORE})^2}$$

For example, if the package you're planning to mail, including everything but the list, costs $200/M, if the list costs $70/M and if the total evaluation score is 14, then the Relative Cost per Order Index would be:

$$\frac{200 + 70}{14 \times 14} = \frac{270}{196} = 1.378$$

6. Finally, Indicate the Rank Order of the Lists, starting with the one having the lowest Relative Cost per Order Index.

Here's what your completed worksheet might look like:

No.	List Name	Selections			Mag. Tape Config	Total Names Avail.	Price Per M	List Evaluation Factors					Total Score	Relative Cost per Order	R/O	Remarks
		A	B	ZIP Codes				Resp-onder	Buyer	Atten-dee	Inter-est	Cur-rency				
1	Schrello Dir.				N/A	18.4	$5	4	3	4	5	3	19	.71	1	
2	Mktg. Fed.	Attends				70.2	$75	3	3	5	5	3	19	.90	3	
3	ASTD	Memb.	Mgrs.			15	$95	5	4	2	3	2	16	1.34	4	
4	NSPI	Memb.			N/A	10.3	$110	4	3	2	3	3	15	1.60	6	
5	Clemson U.	Sem.& Conf.	Attends.			15	$90	5	4	5	5	2	21	.77	2	SMP req'd.
6	AMA	Trng. spec.				54.3	$95	5	0	0	3	2	10	3.45	7	
7	Lakewood	Pd. subs.				51.9	$90	5	3	0	3	4	15	1.51	5	
8	HRE	Pd or Subs.					$125	3	0		3	4	10	3.7?		

List Evaluation Criteria

1. Responder:

0	No responder indications
1-2	Responder to a "bribe" -- an attractive FREE offer
2-3	Bingo card inquiry; also society member, show attender or controlled circulation publication if no other data available
4	Mostly direct mail with some personal sales space advertisements or other sources mixed in
5	100 percent direct mail response

2. Buyer:

0	No buyer indication
1	$5 or less purchased
2	$5 - $20 purchased
3	$20 - $100 purchased; also all society members and show attenders not otherwise shown
4	$100 - $300 purchased
5	$300 - $500 or more purchased

3. Attender:

0	No one on the list is known to have attended a conference or seminar
1-2	Society members or known members of travelling profession
3	Some on the list are known to have attended a conference or seminar
5	Everyone on the list is known to have attended a conference or seminar

4. Interest:

0	No interest indication
1-2	General business interest (*WSJ, Newsweek, Business Week*, etc.)
2-3	Specific business/professional interest (trade shows, society or association membership, etc.)
4	General business or professional education interest (books, magazines, seminars, advisory services, etc.)
5	Specific training or education interest in the subject of our program (direct marketing, seminar or conference promotion, buyer of training materials on this subject, etc.)

5. Currency:

0	No list maintenance -- list several years old
1	List several years old but "cleaned" periodically
2	Quarterly updating
3	List is maintained like your house list
4	Monthly publication
5	Weekly or daily publication

List Evaluation Worksheet

No.	List Name	Selections			Mag. Tape Config	Total Names Avail.
		A	B	ZIP Codes		

Price Per M	List Evaluation Factors						Relative Cost per Order	R/O	Remarks
	Resp—onder	Buyer	Atten—dee	Inter—est	Cur—rency	Total Score			

IMPROVING RESPONSE THROUGH GEOGRAPHIC SELECTION

In renting any list, you want to select the portions that contain those most likely to buy your product/service. That's why you'll look carefully at the selection variables offered by the list owner to select only the position titles, types of business, past buying history, etc., likely to contain your best prospects.

There is another, sometimes even more powerful way to further refine your selection process -- one which you can use in addition to all of the rest. It's geographic selection: your best prospects are not distributed uniformly or even randomly. They are, instead, concentrated in certain states, cities, areas, and zip codes!

How can you find these areas of above-average response? To start with, it's not by merely looking at where your present customers are concentrated. Why? Because there are almost certainly more of them in regions of higher population and fewer of them in areas of less population, just as you'd expect.

What you are seeking are those areas where you have a higher number of customers than the population of prospects would suggest. In order to find these areas, you need two things: (1.) a list of customers (for your product or a similar product) and (2.) some model for how your prospect universe is distributed (which we call the population standard). The population standard may

be obtained from any comprehensive, reliable, available source that covers your market: government statistics, professional and trade associations -- even carefully compiled mailing lists. At the bottom of the page is a brief example of how to do it, based on a breakdown by state.

Obviously, the same logic applies to a breakdown by 3-digit SCF or 5-digit zip code. Just be sure you have enough customers and a large enough population standard for the results to be statistically significant at the finer breakdown. Generally, a minimum of 20 customers per geographic subdivision is needed.

Once you have a rank order of geographic areas for your customers in relationship to the population standard for your prospects, you can use this information to test only the best portions of any rental list. Just start with your top geographic area and go down the list only as far as necessary to get the desired test quantity. Then, based on the results you obtain, you can decide whether part or all of the remainder of the list will be worth continuing.

The graphs on the next page show how geographic selectivity can increase response rates. Notice that selectivity by SCF permits a much higher improvement in response than does state selectivity. Selectivity by 5-digit zip code improves response still more!

Sample of How State Selection Improves Response

State	No. of Customers (A)	Population Standard (B)	Market Penetration (A/B)	Rank Order
NY	100	1,500	.07	4
NJ	72	800	.09	3
MA	65	650	.10	1
TX	35	1,050	.03	6
CT	35	350	.10	2
MI	30	600	.05	5
(etc.)	(etc.)	(etc.)	(etc.)	(etc.)

Effect of SCF Selection on Improving Direct Mail Response Rates

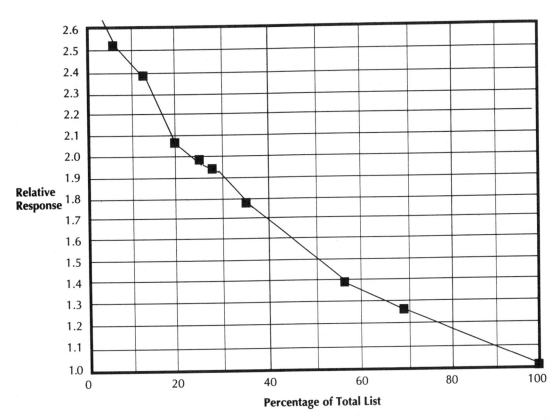

Effect of State Selection on Improving Direct Mail Response Rates

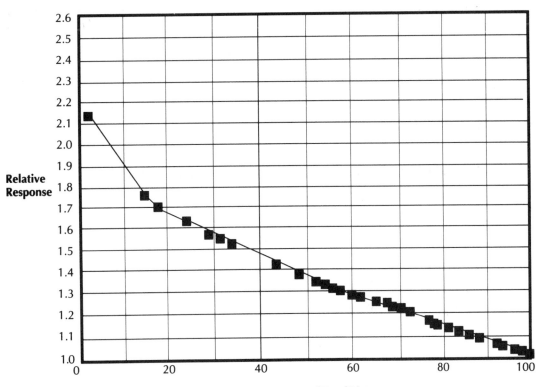

SAVE MONEY FIVE WAYS BY
MERGING AND PURGING YOUR LISTS

The benefits of merge/purge are becoming easier to obtain all the time. Five years ago, only the largest mailers could do it, using just a handful of national computer centers. Now, nearly every major city has at least one and usually several service bureaus that can do the job. And rental of lists on magnetic tape (instead of in printed form) is fast becoming the norm.

There are at least five ways you save money by MERGING your various lists into a single list in ZIP code sequence and PURGING duplicates and those not mailable from the combined list:

1. Eliminates Duplicates

This eliminates the inevitable duplication that exists both between lists *and* internally within a list. By saving wasted postage and printing costs this is (to paraphrase Ed Burnett) like picking up money on the street.

2. Saves Postage

The USPS offers sizeable postage discounts for presorting, provided you have at least 125 pieces (or 15 pounds) of bulk-rate, Third-Class mail addressed to a single ZIP code. Putting many small lists together can result in substantial postage savings.

And while you're on the computer, your lists can easily be address-updated by a USPS-approved program, get ZIP+4 codes appended, and even get barcodes printed so you qualify for the maximum possible savings. (See the extended discussion of this subject in Chapter 9.)

3. Reduces List Set-Up Charges

Most mailhouses impose set-up charges for each individual list that is to be affixed. These set-up charges are significantly reduced when one large list is used, rather than many smaller lists.

4. Permits Economical Correspondence Quality Enhancement

Expanding cryptic position title abbreviations, converting all-capital letters to mixed upper/lower case, adding gender-specific courtesy titles and similar correspondence-quality clean-up are all done cheaper and faster in the merge/purge process.

5. Avoids List Minimums

List owners all have minimum rental charges regardless of the number of names actually used. By renting names on magnetic tape, the list can be broken down into individual segments to be used (say) over a period of time. In this way, minimum charges can be virtually eliminated.

Also, large volume list renters may qualify for "net name" rental arrangements whereby the list owner agrees that the renter doesn't pay for duplicate names eliminated in the merge/purge process, up to some preset limit, usually 15%-25%.

Below are examples of Merge/Purge savings for three typical mailings.

TIP: The first few times you merge and purge, allow two to three weeks added lead time. Remember, the service bureau can't run your job until *all* your lists have been received.

An Example of Merge/Purge Savings

Mail-ing	No. Lists	Gross Names	Net Names	No. Pieces Saved	Pieces Saved @ $0.28 ea.	Number Qualifying for Presort	Postage Saving @ $0.024 ea	Set-ups Saved @ $15 / List	Total Saving	Tape Cost	Merge/ Purge Cost	Total Cost	Net Saving	Saving Per Piece
1.	6	14,356	12,951	1,405	$ 393	1,370	$ 33	$75	$ 501	$125	$171	$296	$205	$0.016
2.	5	29,388	26,983	2,405	$ 673	8,444	$203	$60	$ 936	$100	$378	$478	$458	$0.017
3.	4	64,582	59,020	5,562	$1,557	16,597	$398	$45	$2,001	$75	$511	$586	$1,415	$0.024

LIST DATABASES: WHY (AND WHY NOT) USE THEM?

What Are They?

One source of mailing lists are computer databases consisting entirely of merged and unduplicated copies of the most popular mailing lists. We call these list databases (LDBs) to distinguish them from other databases. LDBs are attractive to both List Owners and List Renters. List Owners like them because their lists can be rented more easily, especially in small quantities that would otherwise not meet the usual five-thousand name minimum. If the LDB was created by list owners who frequently rent each other's lists, they also like the simplicity and lower costs they obtain.

(The reason list renters like LDBs is detailed later in this section.)

LDBs were first created when major business publishers like Cahners, Chilton, Mc-Graw-Hill and Penton combined and unduplicated their own publication subscriber lists, sometimes including prospecting files as well. The first LDB of independently owned lists was started by Dave Florence of Direct Media in 1971. Seminar sponsors, such as the American Management Association, quickly saw the advantages of LDBs, and the practice spread.

Where to Get Them?

Today there are at least four sources of LDBs containing separately owned lists of interest for training and information products and services. More are appearing all the time:

DIRECT MEDIA GROUP
200 Pemberwick Road, Box 4565
Greenwich, CT 80303
Phone: (203) 532-1000; Fax: (203) 531-1452
Maxim C. Bartko, Executive Vice President
Ask about their Seminar Database and their Business-to-Business Database

THE LIST EMPORIUM, INC.
2000 Shawnee Mission Parkway, Suite 235
Westwood, KS 66205
Phone: (913) 236-6830; Fax: (913) 236-4842
Mark Coulter, President

LIST TECHNOLOGY SYSTEMS GROUP
1001 Avenue of the Americas
New York, NY 10018
Phone: (212) 719-3850; Fax: (212) 719-1878
Thomas A. Taylor, President

MAL DUNN ASSOCIATES (MDA)
Hardscrabble Road
Croton Falls, NY 10519
Phone: (914) 277-5558; Fax: (914) 277-8311
Stephen Dunn, President

Why Use LDBs? (The Pros)

There are at least three good reasons to use LDBs:

1. Gets More Names in a Geographic Area and accesses lists you'd never be able to use otherwise due to minimum quantity requirements. This is particularly valuable for seminars and other local event promotion.

2. Affords Better Selectability. Because more names are available, you can more tightly control the variables you get, like management level, job function, kind of business and company size; and you can even specify that names appear on two or more source lists. And demographic data may be overlaid on LDBs, even when it was not on the original source list.

3. Avoids Merge/Purge Headaches. LDBs save time and money by avoiding the complications and extra time needed to order separate lists and manage merging and purging. LDBs also save postage by letting you select only names that qualify for maximum presort, bar code or other USPS discounts.

Why Not Use LDBs? (The Cons)

You know there's no free lunch! Here are two important reasons not to use LDBs:

1. LDB Lists Are Often Stale. The best LDBs are seldom updated more than quarterly, and even annual updating is often a struggle. And if the list source used for updating is merely a copy of a "mailing list," rather than the List Owner's most up-to-the-minute customer records, the "updated" list can be "stale" to start with.

This is not a theoretical difference. Our actual, head-to-head test mailings of the same list drawn from a list database and taken from the List Owner's latest active file have shown two-to-one differences in response -- and more.

2. Your Best Lists May Not Be Available. If two lists you want aren't on the same LDB, you'll need to forego using one or mail it separately. Either way, it reduces your bene-fits. And, remember, even using LDBs, your offer must be cleared by the separate List Owners.

If you decide to use an LDB, plan on the lists being stale, and realize that responses will be reduced. Hopefully, this reduced re-sponse will be more than offset by less dupli-cation, more postal discounts and your ability to mail better-quality lists in geographic areas where list minimums would otherwise have prevented you from using them.

WHERE TO GET AND WHEN TO USE COMPILED LISTS ON DISKETTE, ON CD-ROM AND ON-LINE

Compiled lists should not usually be the first choice for marketing training and informa-tion, because their response rates are less -- often a lot less -- than responder lists. And their accuracy is usually a lot worse because they're stale.

But there are instances when compiled lists may actually be superior. Examples in-clude saturating a market (like all U.S. psy-chiatrists or all businesses in Atlanta) or tar-geting a variable (like annual sales, number of employees, type of business or management function/level/title). Complete coverage and better selectivity is where compiled lists shine. And they're often less expensive than re-sponse lists -- usually less than half the price.

This is more interesting than ever now that some of the best compiled business lists are available for your desktop PC on diskette, CD-ROM and even interactively on-line via modem. (Note that response and publication lists are almost never available this way.) The advantage is that for just a bit more than you'd pay for 1-time rental, you get unlimited use of the list. You can select, sort, and print the names you want, generate personalized correspondence with your word processor or merge the list with others.

Obviously, on-line access provides the most current data. For the other formats, ask yourself whether you'll keep the list fresh with regular telephone calls or mailings or whether the compiler will furnish regular up-dates.

Consumer and business lists are each com-piled by different supplier groups. The first U.S. consumer list was compiled right after the Civil War. Today's lists include more than 70 million families and 150 million indi-viduals, assembled and checked from drivers licenses, voter records, telephone directories, auto registrations and similar public docu-ments. Consumer lists are dominated by "The Big Three" compilers:

DONNELLEY MARKETING, INC.
70 Seaview Ave., P.O. Box 10250
Stamford, CT 06904
Phone: (800) 433-5478, (203) 353-7000

R. L. POLK & CO.
1155 Brewery Park Blvd.
Detroit, MI 48207-2697
Phone: (313) 393-0880, Fax: (313) 393-2862

METROMAIL CORPORATION
360 E. 22nd Street
Lombard, IL 60148
Phone: (708) 932-3060

Business lists address more than 10 million U.S. firms, classified into literally thousands of Standard Industrial Classifications (SICs) and graded by size, number of employees, etc. There are many business list compilers, and plenty of small, niche players. Growth has come through mergers and acquisitions, so the names always change. Here are today's six largest business list compilers:

AMERICAN BUSINESS LISTS, INC.
5711 S. 86th Circle, P.O. Box 27347
Omaha, NE 68127
Phone: (402) 593-4646; Fax: (402) 331-6287
Vin Gupta, President
On-Line Access: (402) 593-4593; Lists-on-Disk:
(402) 593-4565
*Contacts influential branch offices in major
metropolitan areas; provides local service; all
owned by American Business Information, Inc.*

COMPILERS PLUS, INC.
466 Main Street
New Rochelle, NY 10801
Phone: (914) 633-5240; Fax: (914) 633-5261
Edward Mallin, President
*Reportedly (DM News) also owned by American
Business Lists.*

DATABASE AMERICA
100 Paragon Drive
Montvale, NJ 07645
Phone: (800) 223-7777, (201) 476-2300; Fax:
(201) 476-2411
*Created by Ed Burnett, for 35 years the guru of
list compilation.*

DUN & BRADSTREET INFORMATION SER-
VICES
Three Sylvan Way
Parsippany, NJ 07054
Phone: (800) 624-5669, (201) 605-6000
*Lists derived from business credit reporting and
other services. Consult local listings for branch
offices. Acquired Market Data Retrieval (MDR),
which previously acquired National Business
Lists (NBL).*

GALE RESEARCH, INC.
P. O. Box 33477
Detroit, MI 48232-5477
Phone: (800) 877-GALE; Fax: (313) 961-6083
*Lists derived from publication of more than 400
directories on business, industry and labor, as-
sociations, The Media, government and more.*

TRW TARGET MARKETING SERVICES
P. O. Box 851918
Richardson, TX 75085
Phone: (800) 527-3933, (214) 699-1271; Fax:
(214) 437-1611
*Lists derived from credit reporting and other
business financial services.*

TIPS FOR LISTS

How to Get the Most from Your List Broker

You pay the same rental for a list whether you use a broker or not. So use one and get her/his recommendations and information on the results others have had with the list. Put another way, you waste the 20% commission the broker gets if you don't get their knowl-edge of who else is regularly using the list and for what.

If you are just starting out, work with two or three list brokers. Get their recommenda-tions and spread your test orders among them. Keep track of how their recommenda-tions compare to your actual results, and drop the low performer(s).

Demand that your broker(s) spend re-search time and effort on you, finding new re-sponder lists and other lists that evaluate high enough for you to test (see LIST EVALUA-TION earlier in this chapter).

And don't forget the List Manager (see Who's Who in the World of Lists earlier in this chapter). They also cost you nothing, but they know more about the lists they manage than anyone except (possibly) the list owners. Call them for information, but place your list orders through your broker.

Mailing a Rental List Too Often Can Reduce Its Response

Mailing to a rental list too frequently can sig-nificantly reduce its response. Generally speaking, the further away from your own customers you move, the lower the frequency tolerance. Here are some starting guidelines for the frequency of same-product mailings:

List Type	Maximum Frequency
Your customers/responders	Monthly or more
Buyers of similar products	4 times per yr.
Buyers of dissimilar products	2 times per yr.
Other prospects (e.g., magazine and association lists)	1 time per yr.

Business Title Mailings Often Work Better than Names

Position title mailings often give better results for non-personalized mailings to businesses than do mailings to specific names. This is because at least 40% of every business list changes each year, due to moves, transfers, reorganizations, layoffs, mergers, etc. The position may still be there, even if the person isn't or the organization has changed.

Consider replacing each individual name on a good-but-stale list with your best title. Or program your house database to generate a title when you don't have a name for the position you want to reach in an organization. This way, each responder automatically adds every key position in their organization to your mailing list.

When making a title mailing, be sure the title conveys function and level -- so the mail room easily knows exactly who should get it. Titles like "Research Director," "Chief Marketing Executive," "Sales Manager" or even "Christmas Gift Buyer" work well.

No Matter What, Keep Testing New Lists

Budget for regular list testing, and work hard to get new test lists that are likely to meet or exceed your criteria. The steady infusion of new lists and the customers they bring are vital to the health of every direct marketing effort. One new, winning list can be almost all added profit.

On the subject of budgets, list rental costs are only important after you know how well the list works for you. A list that costs twice as much to rent but produces twice the revenue is a real bargain (because list rental costs are only 10%-40% of the total). Never decline to test a list you think will work just because of high rental cost.

How to Keep From Mailing the Wrong List (It Happens All the Time)

The wrong list (including wrong selections from the right list) is shipped more often than you may think. Make it your practice to physically inspect all lists furnished in hard copy or to pre-process lists furnished on tape, to verify that you received what you ordered. Check zip codes included/excluded, position titles, overall quantities, etc. Be suspicious of anything that "doesn't look right." If you've used the list before, compare these items to your prior usage and look for any discrepancies. Remember, it's too late after it's affixed and mailed. CHECK, CHECK, CHECK -- AND CHECK AGAIN!

Four More Ways to Avoid Unpleasant List Surprises

1. Confirm Every List Order In Writing. Place all your list orders by phone, but work from the written order forms which you'll then send the broker as confirmation. Be certain you spell out in writing all selections you make, including any zip codes or SCF's you want/don't want.

2. Check List Counts Frequently. If you are unsure of the quantities for a list or a selected portion of a list, have the broker check the counts with the List Owner. If necessary, have them call with the exact counts after the list has been run, but before shipping. This is the only way to be sure of your printing quantities and postage requirements.

3. Allow Plenty of Time. Allow adequate lead time for your list orders. Although "overnight" delivery is possible in true emergencies, plan on two to five weeks to get your order. And follow up if you don't receive the list on the agreed-upon date; get on the phone and find out why.

4. Have a Backup List Ready. If you mail dated material, have a "backup" list, of average or better performance, that can be obtained on short notice if needed. This way, if a list you've ordered "falls through," you'll have an alternative to throwing out the printed materials or holding a seminar with too few participants.

Try This When a List Owner Turns You Down

When a broker tells you that the List Owner has refused to rent to you, tell her/him that your CEO wants to personally contact the CEO of that firm and get their reason first-hand. Often the CEOs will be able to work out a rental or exchange arrangement right at the top. Be ready to do some diplomatic education of your CEO so he/she is prepared to deal with any apprehensions or fears the other CEO may have (see also RENTING OR EXCHANGING YOUR LIST in Chapter 13).

Replace Rental Lists with a Second House List Mailing

Mailing the same piece to the same list two weeks later usually produces about 60%-70% of the response of the previous mailing. If your house list is four times better than your best rental list (it's usually much better than that), a second or even third mailing to your house list may be preferable to more rental names. Here's an example:

Mailing	Response	
First house list mailing	2.0%	
Second house list mailing	1.2%	(60% of 1st mailing)
Third house list mailing	0.7%	(60% of 2nd mailing)
First mailing to best rental list	0.5%	(1/4 of 1st house list mailing)

See Chapter 5 for more information on multiple mailings.

Personalization Requires List Clean-Up

Obviously, personalized mailings -- like direct addressing of your pieces -- requires that lists be ordered in computer-readable form, not as printed labels. But personalizing also demands added processing to make each entry of "correspondence-quality." This means expanding cryptic abbreviations (President, not PR), inserting punctuation (J. Jones, Ph.D. not J JONES PHD) and extracting salutations (like Ms., Mr., Dr., etc.). This processing adds costs and time and may reduce the available names to whatever extent there are records that can't be suitably cleaned up.

INTERNATIONAL MAILING LIST RESOURCES

Direct mail, abroad, is two to three times more costly than in the U.S. However, response rates for training and information offers are often three to four times as high, for two simple reasons: Training is more highly valued, and people get less mail. With pricing and currency differences, international programs can be much more profitable than the same program sold domestically.

Finding good international mailing lists has always been the big problem. But that's changing. Here are some U.S.-based and off-shore list resources to help you enter these new markets.

U.S.-Based International List Resources

CAHNERS DIRECT MAIL SERVICES
1350 East Touhy Avenue
Des Plains, IL 60018
Phone: (708) 390-2361; Fax: (708) 390-2779

DILLION, AGNEW & MARTON, DIV. OF COMPUTER DIRECTIONS GROUP
345 Park Avenue South
New York, NY 10010
Phone: (212) 685-4600; Fax: (212) 545-8913

MAL DUNN ASSOCIATES
Hard Scrabble Road
Croton Falls, NY 10519
Phone: (914) 277-5558; Fax: (914) 277-8311

49TH PARALLEL DIRECT MARKETING INC.
2572 Central Avenue
Baldwin, NY 11510-3633
Phone: (516) 868-1732; Fax: (516) 868-1796
(Also produces The Un-Paralleled Direct Marketer - The Newsletter of International Direct Marketing)

IBIS INTERNATIONAL DIRECT
152 Madison Avenue, Suite 803
New York, NY 10016
Phone: (212) 779-1344
Robert Howells, President

MARDEV
205 East 42nd Street, Suite 1705
New York, NY 10017
Phone: (800) 545-8517, (212) 697-3667; Fax:
(212) 667-4684

MEDIA MANAGEMENT GROUP
666 Plainsboro Road, Suite 508
Plainsboro, NJ 08538
Phone: (609) 275-0050; Fax: (609) 275-6606

PRUDENTIAL MAIL MARKETING
1500 William Floyd Parkway
Shirley, NY 11976-1817
Phone: (800) 221-0223, (516) 924-9696; Fax:
(516) 924-9129

QUALIFIED LIST CORPORATION
135 Bedford Road
Armonk, NY 10504
Phone: (914) 273-6606

ELEANOR L. STARK COMPANY
515 Madison Avenue, Suite 2300
New York, NY 10022
Phone: (212) 838-1935; Fax: (212) 751-2024

WORLD INNOVATORS, LIST MANAGEMENT
DIVISION
72 Park Street
New Canaan, CT 06840
Phone: (203) 966-0374; Fax: (203) 966-0926

WORLD PUBLICATIONS
100 Spear Street, Suite 220
San Francisco, CA 94105
Phone: (415) 777-1171; Fax: (415) 777-2371

CANADA

CORNERSTONE LIST MANAGERS, Inc.
1492 Yonge Street, Suite 304
Toronto, Ontario M4T-1Z4
Phone: (416) 969-9555; Fax: (416) 969-9566

B. J. HUNTER DIRECTORIES
5555 de Graspe, Suite 100
Montreal, Quebec H2T-2A3
Phone: (514) 273-8588; In Canada: (800) 361-
0391, (800) 361-5927

SANFORD EVANS COMMUNICATIONS Ltd.
350 Dufferin Street, Suite 103
Downsview, Ontario M3K-1N2
Phone: (416) 633-2188; Fax: (416) 633-5725

HERBERT A. WATTS LTD.
455 Horner Avenue
Toronto, Ontario M8W-4W9
Phone: (416) 252-7741; Fax: (416) 252-0037

United Kingdom/European

IBIS INFORMATION SERVICES, LTD.
Waterside, Lowbell Lane
London Colney, St. Albans
Hertfordshire AL2-1DX
Phone: (44) 727-252-09; Fax: (44) 727-264-61

RSCG COMPUTING LTD.
Media House Weston
Slough, Berkshire, SL1-4HP
Phone: (0753 571011, /516456; Fax: 0753
538164

MC CANN-ERICHSON AB
P. O. Box 5511
S-114 85 Stockholm, Sweden
Phone: (8) 665-1975; Fax: (8) 782-8049

Australia/New Zealand

DRAKE LIST MANAGEMENT
2nd Floor, 63 Exhibition Street
Melbourne, Victoria 3000 Australia
Phone: (03)650-7266; Fax: (03)650-7249

LOGOS LISTS
363 A Pitt Street
Sydney, New South Wales 2000 Australia
Phone: (02)261-5544; Fax: (02)261-1237

RESPONSE GROUP
Private Bag CPO
Auckland, New Zealand
Phone: 398-284; Fax: 777-586

ROD SPENCE, LTD.
P. O. Box 18088
Glen Innes, New Zealand
Phone: 521-4454; Fax: 521-4455

Asia

1ST DIRECT MAIL (S-PTE-LTD.)
80, Marine Parade Road, Suite 10-04
Parkway Parade, Singapore 1544
Phone: 345-5701; Telex RS 5-02-86

LISTS MEDIA ASIA PTE-LTD
190 Middle Road
No. 17-01 Fortune Center
Singapore 0718
Phone: 339-4377; Fax: 339-9409

MAILING LISTS (ASIA) LTD.
9/F Nin Lee Commercial Bldg.
45 Lyndhurst Terrace
Central Hong Kong
Phone: (852) 543-0556; Telex 7 64 17; Fax:
852-541-1124 852-850-5502

8

CREATING COMPELLING LETTERS, BROCHURES AND ADVERTISING

Marketing training, continuing education and information means advertising -- mostly in print. Even face-to-face selling and telemarketing rely heavily on pre-call or post-call literature. And, of course, the best "live" selling starts with responders -- probably responders to some form of printed advertising.

Designing advertising and writing advertising copy are art forms. They're done best by experienced professionals, at least until you've seen enough professional work to try it yourself. And if you *do* try it yourself, you need to be sure -- by thorough testing -- that your work is as good or better than the professional's.

It's my opinion that most marketers of training and information products and services will eventually end up writing all their own advertising in-house. It's too important to the long-term success of your enterprise to do otherwise. But if you're just starting, you'll need outside help. For you, this chapter will show you what you need, help you select good people to provide it, furnish guidelines to evaluate what they do -- and shorten the time until you can do it yourself. This chapter will also give you pointers that will help *all* your written communications, not just your advertising.

If you're in a large organizations chances are you already have advertising professionals in-house in the form of artists, writers, designers, etc. In your case, this chapter will help you to evaluate the work your in-house staff does and perhaps help you decide if and when resources outside the organization might be warranted.

This chapter deals only with creating the advertising: the concepts, designs, graphics, sizes, shapes and words that are used. This chapter also contains the vitally important section on testing. Chapter 9 deals with turning your ad into tangible printed form -- and getting it into the prospect's hands.

This chapter covers in turn:

- 13 key ingredients every training and information ad *must* include.

- Common direct mail formats, including observations on today's business correspondence and the role of each piece in a typical direct mail package.

- Tips for creating effective advertising, for arresting headlines, for writing persuasive advertising copy -- and for evaluating the copy written by others.

- Tips specially geared for direct mail -- organized by the type instructional materials piece: envelopes, letters, brochures, response vehicles, etc., including some examples.

- A world-class direct mail package; how it works and why it's so great.

- Ten top advertising references.

- All about testing.

- Tips for selecting and using advertising professionals.

WHAT YOUR TRAINING ADVERTISING *MUST* INCLUDE

You need to know three things to successfully market your training and information products and services: (1.) what information your prospect needs/wants in order to buy, (2.) how to fashion that information in an engaging format or package and (3.) how to write persuasive promotional copy.

This section deals with the first need. It describes the 13 subjects *every* successful ad for training and information products and services includes. The next section deals with the most common advertising formats, particularly direct mail. Later sections address writing good ads and specific tips for various parts of your advertising.

Since so much has already been published about effective advertising copy, we merely summarize the basics in this chapter. Appendix A (References and Resources) contains many *more* references to this literature, far too voluminous to be included here.

Obviously, the medium will at least partly dictate the message: You can't convey as much information on a postcard as you can in an 8-page brochure. And a page or column in a catalog falls somewhere in between. But in the available space, you must *try* to include as many of the key items described below as possible.

1. The Title: A Powerful Headline -- *and* a Benefit-Laden Subtitle

The headline of an advertisement -- or the title of a product or seminar -- is potentially the most important variable. Tests have shown that it's read by five to ten times as many people as read what follows, and it can produce up to 1,500% more response. We all know that you shouldn't judge a book by its cover (or by its title), but we all do!

Choose titles that describe the product's benefits and that promise to solve a problem the reader has. Remember that *benefits* are what you get by responding; *features* are the way you get them. Features are sometimes of interest, especially to differentiate between products that produce similar benefits, like

stereos or cars. But most people are *only* interested in -- and willing to pay for -- benefits.

Whenever possible, the title should also include reference to those who will benefit most from the product/service.

Based upon studies of persuasive words by the Yale Psychology Department, an analysis of what works best, the sixteen words that most often spell marketing success are:

Discover, Easy, Free, Guarantee, Help, Introducing, Love, Money, New, Now, Proven, Results, Save, Today, You, Win.

Don't be afraid to add a descriptive subtitle that further elaborates the benefits. There is no advantage to short headlines, short titles -- or short subtitles.

Pay attention to what you already know -- and what you receive in the mail. High-volume mailers test titles all the time: Use them as a good starting place. Choose exciting titles that have been around for decades, like *"Fundamentals of Finance for Nonfinancial Managers: Learn to Read and Understand Financial Statements Like a Pro"* or *"Introduction to Supervision for New or Prospective Supervisors."* These titles are superior to titles such as Advanced Marketing or Sales II. And avoid "cute" titles that make clever acronyms or contain multi-syllable words.

Your title and subtitle are especially important for self-mailers, where the name/title may be all that determines whether your piece is kept and read or thrown out.

2. Date(s) and Location(s) for Events

When people see a date and location in a brochure, they know it's promoting an event and not some other product or service. The reverse is also true: If you involve dates and locations in a non-event advertisement, be sure you do it in a way that doesn't confuse the reader. Also, specific hotels/facilities *should* be listed whenever possible; they're part of what's being sold.

Important questions like how many dates/locations to include are addressed in detail in Chapters 5 and 6. The most popular locations are also shown in Chapter 6.

3. Who Will Benefit And Should Respond

Start by listing the position titles and/or job responsibilities you're targeting. Then describe the kinds of problems that your product or service will solve. More positions, more responsibilities and more problems solved translate into more sales.

For highly personalized mailings, you may want to pare the list of job responsibilities to target *only* the addressee. And even in display ads, avoid claiming that *everyone* will benefit. Besides not being believable, an excessively broad claim may attract buyers who will end up disappointed. Inappropriate expectations created by ads is one of the biggest causes of product returns, money-back requests and customer ill-will.

4. *How* the Responder Will Benefit

Be clear on the actual benefits that the responder will receive: What will they be able to do (or do better, faster or cheaper) as a result of your product/service, that they can't do (or do as well) now? Be sure to include both individual *and* organizational benefits if your product/service delivers both. For example, a finance and accounting course can lead to better profit performance on the job *and* increased understanding of personal investments. Even if this is obvious, sales will increase by spelling it out clearly.

Finally, check your benefits to be sure they're believable. One calorie per glass is believable -- no calories is not. Generalities are also hard to believe. Facts, figures, examples, dates, names and places all lend credibility to your offer and increase attention and response. If your offer is true, but unbelievable, it may need to be toned down. And above all don't promise what you can't deliver.

One final note about describing benefits -- that applies to all of your copy -- *always* describe your benefits in positive terms, never in negative terms. If you find negatives, work hard to restate them as positives.

5. *What* You Get -- Including a Photo, Detailed Program, Outline or Contents

Be very clear about what the buyer gets, whether it's a product or a service. Showing photographs (*never* line drawings) are most effective for tangible products like books, tapes, videos, etc. I recommend "cornucopia" photos, with an abundance of material spilling everywhere. Show three-ring binders open to an appealing page, with more worksheets and checklists arranged in front. Always show photos of audio cassette courses so the reader can count the tapes.

Read this next sentence twice. *For seminars, avoid photographs on the cover, as line art works better.* Sounds weird, but it's true. And you can verify it by looking in your own in-basket. But *do* show a photograph of the materials a participant gets or a photo of the speaker(s), if they are well-known.

But photographs are not enough. Selling seminars, conferences, books, packaged courses -- even software -- requires that you also include a comprehensive outline, table of contents or conference agenda. I recommend very detailed, 3-level course and book outlines, showing *every* topic addressed. We've all bought a book or attended a seminar because of one or two items on the outline "hit our hot button." Intellectually, we knew that the entire book or seminar would not be devoted to our topic. Nonetheless, that topic on the outline provided a strong incentive to select *this* product or service over others that did not include it. Your product *must* win the battle of the outline!

6. *Why* Yours Is New, Unique, Different, Better, Faster or Cheaper

Although this needs to be included, it may not require a separate section. The heading, benefits or other parts of the ad may already do the job. But if there's any doubt, add a sentence or paragraph to be sure.

7. All About the Author, Speaker and/or Sponsor

We know from our *Product Evaluation and Planning Seminar* that intangible products and services -- like training and consulting -- compete heavily on the basis of who's offering them. Prospective buyers compare your organization (or you personally) to other organizations (or individuals) making similar offers. Here reputation, credits, name recognition, time in business and other credentials all contribute.

If you're selling a book, tell all about the author and her/his previous titles. If it's a film or video with a big-name star, feature the star prominently. Conference promotions can benefit from a well-known keynote or banquet speaker, industry panelists or even an award recipient.

Seminars can be different, particularly if sessions are led by different presenters. You need *not* feature the presenter unless they're well-known and their presence will attract registrants. I promoted seminars for over a decade without ever *once* identifying a single presenter. We did, however, prominently advertise our company's excellent reputation and (see below) our guarantee.

8. Glowing Testimonials from Past Buyers, Attendees or Readers

Exciting "blurbs," or testimonials, by celebrities adorn every book and every ad for them. Ditto with movies, software, and -- well, you name it. We all know that only the best testimonials are ever used. But they're used because they work!

For all training products and services, believable testimonials from satisfied customers are critical. Include each one's full name, position title, *and* organization. *Never* use anonymous quotes. They are simply not believable and hurt your credibility. Strive for a variety of genders, ethnic surnames, professions, types of organizations, position titles, etc. And seek quotations that tout the major *benefits* of your product or service, rather than its *features*.

Testimonials by recognized experts or authorities can sometimes be as good or better than customer comments. It depends on the offer and on your market. Business executives usually prefer the opinions of other executives, while individuals and consumers frequently respond better to celebrities and well-known public figures.

9. List of Satisfied Customers' or Attenders' Organizations

Include a list of past satisfied customer organizations and institutions. About 75 to 100 is enough, even if you have many more than this. If you have lots of big company clients, pick the most representative and recognizable ones for your ads. If you primarily serve small businesses, choose organizations that have their type of business in their name; for example, you know at once what the Smith Foundry or Santa Fe Importers do.

Don't be surprised if potential responders call for names and telephone numbers of people they can contact in the companies you list. We've even had prospects call those whose testimonials we used.

10. A Guarantee of Satisfaction

The public has come to expect a money-back guarantee and other protections against purchases that aren't right for them. And the courts have generally supported this practice. The result is that your customers will demand -- and probably get -- return and refund privileges from you, whether or not you explicitly offer them. So you may as well offer them and get the sales boost they provide.

Yes, there will be some inevitable abuse. But a guarantee will increase your response rate many times more, because it removes yet another possible barrier to response: the fear of being "taken."

The best way to figure out how to word your guarantee is to look at what's offered by others. Think about effect of subtle differences, for example, "14-Day Free Trial" versus "14-Day Money-Back Guarantee."

11. Advance Qualifications or Prerequisites -- If Any

Many training products and services -- particularly technical training -- require certain prerequisite courses or advance qualifications. Software requires that you have a certain type of computer. Video tapes are either VHS or Beta format. Be clear about these requirements to avoid later dissatisfaction or product returns.

Also, if Continuing Education Units (CEUs) are awarded, this fact must be shown prominently, particularly if your training is aimed at professionals seeking to meet their continuing education requirements.

12. How to Respond, Order or Enroll -- Including Price, Discounts and Methods of Payment

All successful marketing vehicles make a clear, polite -- but forceful -- "call to action" for the reader. Never be subtle or indirect. Explain clearly the steps you want them to take and how they should go about taking them. For example, if you want responders to place their order by phone, show a drawing of a phone. In magazine ads, a request for direct response is *always* improved by a coupon surrounded by a dotted line. Remarkably, this is so even when the requested method of response is via toll-free telephone. Somehow, readers equate the presence of the coupon and dotted line with a call to action. It even works on matchbook covers!

"How to order" must clearly answer the reader's remaining questions about buying. Any missing/incomplete information will delay -- and may kill -- the sale. Here's a short list of the information to have conveniently available to your reader: Price, discounts, sales tax, delivery options, shipping/handling charges, toll-free telephone number, fax number, credit cards accepted, restrictions on the method of payment, cancellation/return policies, hotel/facility information, tax deductibility status, continuing education credit.

Why is the price so hard to find in event promotions? The answer goes back to the old salesperson's rule: "Never quote the price until the customer knows what they're going to get for that price."

13. Why Act Now

Every successful direct marketing campaign has some reason for the reader to respond *now*. Sometimes this is an incentive for prompt response (the first 25 people will receive a gift of ...) or it may be a time limit (those enrolling before July 1, will receive a $100 discount). In any case, there needs to be a reason such as a discount, premium, gift, bonus or other tangible benefit for the responder to act *now*.

If you are offering a free or low-cost premium, be sure to prominently feature it. Many subscription campaigns and other offers deal almost exclusively with the premium and sell it to the exclusion of the underlying offer. An old direct marketing rule is, "If you *offer* a premium, *sell* the premium and not the product." It seems to work.

7 COMMON DIRECT MAIL FORMATS

1. Letter (and Other Things) in an Envelope

The letter is clearly best for involvement and interest, and it can achieve almost every objective. It may include a brochure and other response enhancers. You can send a letter in an envelope without a brochure -- but never, NEVER send a brochure (or anything else for that matter) in an envelope without a letter. (See the following section, "Observations on Today's Business Corre-

spondence," and the world-class example later in this chapter.)

2. Brochure/Self-Mailer

This is best for quick exposure of easily understood offers like seminars and books. This is also usually the least expensive format. Remember, the simplest self-mailer is a postcard. But with today's high postage, it doesn't make sense to mail anything that doesn't contain enough information to land the sale.

(See an example of a book self-mailer on the facing page.)

3. Catalog

The catalog is best for multiple product offers, usually five or more. That's why they are so often used by book publishers, major seminar sponsors and in-house training departments. Catalogs are retained longer than any other format, sometimes for years. They are also generally expensive to produce. Consider *mini*-catalogs for groups of related products or for special offers.

4. Postcard Deck

These are best for getting low-cost leads or inquiries and for selling inexpensive ($25 - $99) products. Never, but NEVER, use postcard decks for seminars. Responder quality is definitely lower than any other format, so be careful with any "free" offers, too. On some decks, we even make the responder furnish their own stamp, which reduces but doesn't totally eliminate prank replies. (See an example of a card deck postcard at the bottom of this page.)

5. Jumbo Broadside

This format is best where color and graphics are important, like for books, tapes, videos, films, presentation equipment, meeting facilities. It can be very expensive to design, shoot and print and is usually mailed in an envelope with a letter and reply card.

6. Promotional Audio, Video, CD or Computer Diskette

These are best where forceful communication is required or where the sights and sounds are important. Since recipient must take time to listen or watch, they are best sent ONLY to those who have already responded to some other form of direct marketing. Previews/rentals are now universally required to sell films/videos.

7. Gram (Telegram or Look-Alike)

This format is best for getting opened and read at once. It communicates a single, short, time-sensitive message, invitation or action request. But BE CAREFUL: Unless your message really IS urgent, this format is seen as a "gimmick" -- and gets people angry!

Typical Card Deck Postcard

Sample Book Self-Mailer

Observations On Today's Business Correspondence

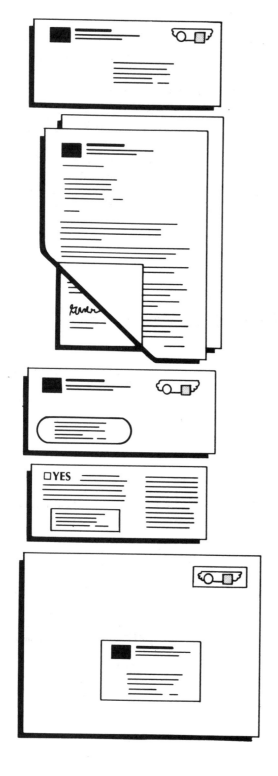

Standard:

2-color logo letterhead
Letter-quality name and address on
   both envelope and letter
Red postage-meter mark on #10 envelope
Letter text left justified only
Letter signature in blue ink

Acceptable Options:

Monarch instead of #10 envelope
Brochure enclosed
Business-reply card (BRC) enclosed
Length of letter

Not Seen:

Preprinted postage indicias
Black or blue meter marks
"Teaser" copy on envelope
Address label on envelope
Dot-matrix printing or "typeset"
   appearance in letter
Letter text justified on left and right

Trade-Offs That Usually Reduce Response and Why They Are Used:

Window envelope—Avoids cost and
   complexity of addressing
   multiple pieces

Address on BRC—Returns list source
   information with response
   vehicle

Address label on BRC—Allows use of
   lists not obtainable in computer-
   readable form

Alternate Standard:

9" x 12" envelope
3" x 5" 2-color address label matching
   sender's logo/letterhead
Red postage-meter mark on tape
Letter-quality name and address

OBSERVATIONS ON TODAY'S BUSINESS CORRESPONDENCE

Most of us don't have any trouble identifying the mail that's most important and deserves our immediate attention. And we easily spot the less important mail we can set aside until later -- or even throw out.

Take this quick test: When you've been away for a few days and have a stack of mail when you return, what is it that helps you decide what mail *not* to look at first? Chances are its things like the presence of a bulk mail indicia, "teaser" copy or a label on the outside of the envelope, a self-mailer format, a cheap appearance, etc. We all immediately recog-

nize "junk mail." So there's no excuse for using mail that looks that way unless you want to -- and unless you're using it under circumstances for which it works best.

It helps to look closely at today's truly personal business correspondence. After all, don't we want *every* piece of correspondence to be as personal as possible? On the facing page are some of the common characteristics, as well as some of the frequently seen -- and not seen -- alternatives and variations.

ROLE OF EACH PIECE IN A TYPICAL DIRECT MAIL PACKAGE

Each piece included in a direct mail package should perform a function related to the overall goal of obtaining the reader's action. Regardless of the actual number of pieces in

a package, the five steps shown below must be accomplished. Sometimes two or more steps are combined into one piece, or a single step is divided among several pieces.

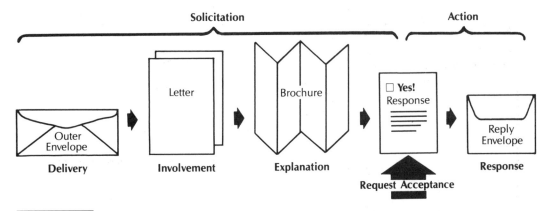

Adapted from "Mailing List and Mailing Packages" by Daniel R. Harding, Center for Direct Marketing.

TIPS FOR EFFECTIVE TRAINING ADVERTISING

The Eleven Most Important Factors For Success

The top eleven variables for marketing training, continuing education and information products and services were presented and discussed in Chapter 5. Here they are again for reference, listed in descending order of their importance:

1. List/Media
2. List/Media
3. List/Media
4. Timing (for dated material/events)
5. Location (for events)
6. Duration (for events, media-based and packaged programs)
7. Product name/title/sub-title
8. Offer (includes all other product/service elements not specified above, promotional gifts/bonuses, guarantee, refund/return privileges, etc.)
9. Price (includes discounts, method of response, method of payment, etc.)
10. Advertising package format/design
11. Advertising copy

These are also the highest priority factors to test, as described later in this chapter.

The list/media has the same importance for advertising training and information that location does for real estate: It's the *three* most important reasons for success. Put another way, a poor offer to a good list (or in a good publication) will often work -- but world's best offer to the wrong list (or in the wrong publication) will fail every time.

Test Everything

The ability to experiment and test the effectiveness of various approaches is direct marketing's underlying strength. Respected direct mail guru Ed Burnett has said, "It is the fact that direct response can be accurately measured that distinguishes it from all other marketing." By using this feature to test *every* change in your marketing *before* you make it permanent, you can always improve. The "flip side" of this is that you can start small and expand *only* when test results show that you're meeting your expectations.

By the way, don't spend lots of effort on *how* or *why* your advertising works. Test various approaches that experience has shown *do* work, and stick with those that improve your results, even if you're not sure how or why they work.

There's a whole section on testing at the end of this chapter.

It's Lifetime Customer Value that Counts

Distinguish between cost per exposure, per inquiry, per order, per sale -- and per new customer. Successful marketers are concerned mainly about the last of these, over the lifetime of the customer relationship (see how to figure this in Chapter 5). Often your best *value* will not be the *cheapest* ad.

Start a "Swipe File" of Brochures You Like

Advertising is an art form, and like any art form you learn by copying the masters. Build a file of direct marketing materials you see which advertise training and information programs like those you offer. Date each one, and put it in an envelope or box. Periodically sort through the material by subject. Look for those materials that change and for those that don't. And pay particular attention to those that are most appealing to you.

Competitor Catalogs Are Your Market Research Library

Save the catalogs from AMA, CareerTrack, Fred Pryor and the other major national training suppliers, and start a file. This provides you a database for invaluable market research across a wide range of training and information, showing increases or decreases in various areas, emergence of new programs, price changes, locations offered and other year-to-year changes.

People Want Unique Benefits

In a highly competitive market, determine how your product/service is unique/different, and make this differentiation stand out in all of your advertising. Remember your readers are seeking *better, faster, cheaper, easier* benefits for themselves. If they're convinced you can truly offer any of these, they'll buy.

Get Expert Help -- at First

Go outside for expert help on everything until you've learned how to do it well yourself. A recent article in *DM News* claimed that one-half of all the major direct marketing copy you see is written by the same handful of copywriters, because even the biggest advertisers go outside. The same article carried this valuable suggestion:

"First collect 25 to 50 direct mail pieces that you like and that have been repeated in the mail. Important: What you like personally and what works may be two different things. In fact, it probably will be. And what is working will be repeated again and again. Next, call the company for which the program was done. Ask about the writer, designer, list broker, merge/purge house, letter-shop, printer. Keep a chart. Chances are by the time you finish your round of phone calls, you will find a lot of overlapping. Many of the names will have come up again and again, because the work that is repeating over and over again is coming from a relatively small group of people."

When selecting an outside advertising resource, look for *proven* results of the type you're seeking, not evidence of agency "awards." David Ogilvy has said, "Be suspicious of awards. The pursuit of creative awards seduces creative people from the pursuit of sales. We have been unable to establish any correlation whatever between awards and sales."

There's more on finding and working with advertising professionals at the end of this chapter.

Premiums/Incentives Work

Offering a free or low-cost premium as an incentive is increasingly popular today. But it needs to be carefully conceived and tested. *Free* offers build lists but not necessarily long-term customer relationships. *Charging a nominal amount* screens out those who take every freebie but never buy. Your premium should be of real value and related to your primary product -- but not a substitute for it.

Test to find an incentive offer which correlates highly with later customer purchases and customer retention. Look beyond the initial orders to see what's *really* important: the next (and subsequent) major purchases.

TIPS FOR ARRESTING HEADLINES AND SUBTITLES

The headline's job is to stop the readers dead in their tracks and entice them into the rest of the brochure or ad. Tests show that five to ten times more people read the headline than read the ad, so these few words should receive your greatest care and attention. Sadly, many people agonize over every word of body copy and slap the headline on almost as an afterthought.

Not all training and information ads have a headline, at least not in the "newspaper headline" sense. For many training products/services (like books and seminars), the *title* is (or should be) the headline and includes the benefit and the target population as part of the product's name. (Refer to our discussion of this in the first section of this chapter). In these cases, the title and subtitle can serve the same function as the headline.

4 Tests for a Good Headline

There are some simple rules for writing good headlines. First, every good headline must pass four simple tests. It:

1. Attracts Qualified Readers and not others. Write your headline only for those you're trying to reach and no one else.

2. Appeals to the Reader's Self-Interest. The most powerful appeals to self-interest are those that tap our fears, uncertainties, doubts and desires. Politicians use this all the time.

3. Arouses the Reader's Curiosity. That's what gets them to read the rest of the ad.

4. Is Simple, Clear and Direct. Telegraph what you want to say in the simplest possible language. Readers don't stop to decipher the meaning of "cute" or obscure headlines or those containing unfamiliar words or acronyms.

Six Types of Headlines and Subtitles that Work

Here are six types of headlines, each with some examples to help you build your own:

1. The News Headline: "Announcing ...," "Finally ...," "Now you can ...," "At last ...," "New ..."

2. The Price Headline: "Reduced price," "Free offer," "Special premium."

3. The Story Headline: "How to ...," "How I ...," "Why I ...," "They laughed when I sat down at the piano, but ...," "This ...," "Advice to ..."

4. The Testimonial Headline: "Let me tell you how ...," "Let me show you why ...," "I couldn't ... until ..."

5. The Test/Quiz Headline: "Can you pass ...?" "Do you know how many ...?" "A test of your ..."

6. The Warning-to-Delay Headline: "Don't buy until you have...," "Don't decide before ..."

How Many Words Should Be in Your Headline?

In headline tests, ten words or longer sold more than short headlines. In terms of recall, headlines between eight and ten words are most effective.   In mail-order advertising, headlines between six and twelve words get the most coupon returns. On the average, long headlines sell more than short ones.

Target Your Headlines

In local advertising it pays to include the name of the city in your headline. When you advertise a product aimed at a special group, it pays to "flag" that group in your headline: "computer owners," "nonfinancial managers," "newly-appointed supervisors," etc.

TIPS FOR WRITING PERSUASIVE COPY

Follow a Plan

Follow a proven plan or outline for each type of direct marketing copy you write. For example, here is a seven-step plan for direct mail letters and copy-heavy display ads:

1. Capture the reader's interest.
2. Describe a need/want you know they have.
3. Show how your product/service can meet that need/want.
4. Establish your credibility to do what you claim.
5. Assure the reader there's no risk.
6. Request action--*now*.
7. Add a "clincher" of some kind: a bonus, premium or added reason to "ACT NOW."

Another one of the great copywriters has said, "Set up a problem the customer recognizes. Then show how your product or service can solve that problem. Then prove your solution. This technique has always been above average in sales results, and still is."

Write for Those who Already Agree with You

Write your copy for those who are *already interested* and who *already agree* with you. Gear your appeal to get them to act. For the rest, you can't change their mind or convert them, and copy that tries to do so won't be as effective for your core market.

Speak to both the *emotional* and *intellectual* needs of your reader. Like each of us, they have both components, and both play a role in their buying decision.

People Are More Interested in Other People Than They Are in Ideas

Use brief anecdotes, stories and testimonials involving people like your customer to capture and hold reader interest. Notice that *The Wall Street Journal, Reader's Digest, TV Guide* and many other respected publications start every major article this way.

Write copy that talks to your reader personally and involves them, just as you would face-to-face. Write for an *individual*, not for a group or organization. Remember, it's a personal communication you're trying to achieve.

Keep Your Copy Exciting

Use the present tense and active verbs. And use more verbs than adjectives. One direct mail consultant has said that *Time* Magazine

uses two verbs for every adjective, while most college theses use two adjectives for every verb. Which would you rather read?

Always use "you" copy; never "we" copy. For example: "You will get...," not "We will give you...". Business advertisers, in particular, are prone to make this mistake. Some have called it "the We-We syndrome."

And don't try to be funny -- EVER.

Remember *PITHY*

The dictionary defines pithy as "Precisely meaningful; cogent and terse." Put this word in large letters near where you write as a constant reminder of the objective for your copy.

Long Copy Works Better Than Short Copy

This is not a contradiction to the preceding point! Pithy refers to your writing *style* while this point refers to its *volume*.

Don't be afraid of long copy. Every test consistently shows that it produces more response than short copy. Just be sure that it really describes and explains what you're selling.

Break up copy with headlines and subheadings. The headlines themselves ought to tell your story in outline form.

Use varied type sizes, underlining, bullets, capitalization, indenting, color and other techniques to visually separate, emphasize, or distinguish different parts of your text.

TIPS FOR DIRECT MAIL PIECES

Envelopes

1. Envelope Mailings Always Pull More than Self-Mailers. But they're also more expensive. The only way to find out if the added cost and complexity pays off for you is by testing.

2. The Best All-Around Envelope Is a #10 Window, because it looks like an invoice

and over 90% of them get opened at both home *and* business addresses. A closed-face, 2-color, letterhead envelope with a typed name and address looks like a personal communication and will increase opening to nearly 100%. But it's expensive, and you'll need to test to see if the added results are worth it.

3. Be Careful How Your Postage Is Ap-

plied. Received at a business, an envelope with a real postage stamp suggests mail from an individual, possibly someone looking for a job. Mail from substantial businesses -- and from business executives -- is invariably metered with a red, Pitney-Bowes meter-mark. The only circumstances where your envelope may have a preprinted, bulk mail indicia is when you are using "teaser" copy -- and even then a meter mark works better.

4. Monarch Envelopes Sometimes Work Better. Those somewhat smaller (3-7/8" x 7-1/2") envelopes can sometimes work better for mailings to top executives than do #10 envelopes. Their smaller size may also save you money.

5. Use A 9" x 12" Manila Envelope if your material won't fit in a standard #10 envelope. Be sure to use a 3" x 5", two-color, letterhead label on which the recipient's name and address is typed. Never type directly on the envelope or use a Cheshire label! Apply postage with the red meter mark on white tape, just as it would be done on the automatic scale in any large company mailroom.

6. Colored Envelopes Don't Help. Tests have shown no correlation with color. Stick to white or off-white for your #10 envelopes and manila for your 9" x 12" envelopes.

7. Large Envelope Manufacturers, like American Envelope, with nationwide plants, offer very inexpensive envelopes with printed patterns inside that virtually eliminate see-through, even with thin paper. (This is often a better alternative than a heavier envelope.) Besides, envelope manufacturers usually offer the lowest prices.

8. Always Use Your Letterhead when corresponding with your customers. They love you, are always anxious to hear from you and will give your material high priority.

9. "Personal and Confidential" typed on the envelope (not typeset) is an inexpensive way to boost opening. But be *very* careful! If the contents really are *not* personal or confidential, your reader will get angry because you tricked them.

10. Adding a Preprinted Route Slip to your envelope, brochure, or self-mailer may improve pass-along value inside an organiza-

tion. Preprint the titles you know are most responsive and provide three lines for the recipient to write in others.

11. If You Use an Attention-Getter on the outside of the envelope (like "teaser" copy or the preprinted route slip mentioned above) save postage and send it by third-class bulk mail.

12. Deliverability Is Affected by Perceptions of postal and mail-room employees as to the value of the piece. This is heavily influenced by the appearance and size of the envelope, the identity of the mailer and assumptions *they* make about the importance of *your* message. Actual tests have shown that more important-looking mail gets delivered than does unimportant-looking mail, even though all mail of the same class is supposed to be treated alike.

Letters

1. Typewritten Letters Work Best. Always use letters that appear to have been typed on an IBM Selectric or equivalent typewriter, and always with a "ragged" right-hand margin, never typeset or right-justified. Even though today's personal computers and laser printers are capable of producing a typeset look, tests show that such letters don't work as well as the more traditional look.

2. Use Short Words, Short Sentences, Short Paragraphs. Most experts recommend a maximum of three to six lines per paragraph. And leave a blank line between each paragraph. Some even recommend indenting the start of each paragraph besides, to improve readability.

3. Stick With Pica Type. This familiar, mono-spaced, 10-characters-per-inch style is found on every typewriter. Elite (mono-spaced, 12 characters per inch) is a good second choice to conserve space. Allow ample margins all around.

4. Print Letters Only on One Side of Separate Sheets. *Never* print letters on both sides of a sheet. This *immediately* signals "junk mail." (Exception: 3-page and 4-page letters *can* be printed more economically as a 4-page, 11" x 17", 2-sided signature folded in half to 8-1/2" x 11". Response drops a little, but costs drop even more.)

5. *Long Copy Works Better than Short Copy*, although most people believe exactly the opposite is true. Millions of pieces of mail have proven this beyond reasonable doubt. For example, Learning International successfully used 8- to 10-page letters printed on one side of separate sheets for years. David Ogilvy has said, "The more you tell, the more you sell."

6. *Test Personalization*. While computer-generated personalized letters sometimes increase response, there's evidence they can also sometimes kill response. And such letters are extremely expensive. Testing is the only way to find out, but this test should be lower priority than other variables in your program. (See the section on testing at the end of this chapter.)

7. *Readers Look at Three Things First: the Opening Paragraph, the Signature, and the P.S.* Save the P.S. for your most important clincher or sales point, perhaps one that's just incomplete enough so that the rest of the letter needs to be read.

8. *Make the Signature Blue*. Even if you don't use color anywhere else in your package, spend the money for color here. Blue is best; black (like the type) is worst and should *never* be used. Green and red are *sometimes* acceptable if they match the company's logo.

9. *Be Sure Your Letter Describes the Other Pieces* (if any) in your direct mail package and clearly tells the reader what to do with them.

10. *Don't Feel You Must Use the Standard 8-1/2" x 11" Letter*. Often the smaller monarch-size letter will help differentiate it from other elements in the package and could help cut costs.

11. *Letters with Photographs* have been reported to sometimes work better than those without them. But retest this for yourself, because there's been little or no use of this for training letters.

Brochures, Self-Mailers and Catalogs

1. *If Your Brochure or Self-Mailer Is Folded*, lay it out so that the headline is readable and clear when it's folded as well as unfolded. And since you can't be sure which side will be up, *both* sides must be compelling.

2. *Don't Use Photos on the Outside of Seminar Brochures or Self-Mailers*. Tests have proven that -- contrary to intuition -- line art, *not* photographs, works best. Photos *are* O.K. for these purposes in seminar brochures: (1.) the materials participants receive (or can buy), (2.) the speaker(s) and (3.) the exciting locations where it will be held.

3. *DO Use Photos for Every Other Training and Information Product*, particularly books, tapes, videos, software -- in fact, for *any* tangible product. Photos suggest professionalism, and most people are more interested in photos than they are in copy. If you use a photo, use a headline and a caption along with it, as this gets read six to eight times *more* than copy without a photo.

4. *Catalogs Are Saved and Passed Along* to someone else when a new one is received. You can make a catalog with as few as five products -- or two products, each offered three distinct ways.

5. *Make Every Catalog Entry Complete*. Catalogs must furnish readers complete information to make their purchase decision, just as they would get in a single-product brochure, including schedules (for events) and prices. The more paging around readers must do to find the information in the catalog, the less likely it is they'll respond.

Resist the temptation to put all prices and/or event dates on one page or (perish the thought) on a separate sheet. This may be convenient for you but not for the customer -- and everyone sees that at once in today's customer-service-conscious world. Do put your toll-free phone and Fax number on each page, as well as the page number where they can turn for "how-to-order" information.

And don't even think about "updating" your old catalog by merely sending a separate sheet with the new dates, locations and prices. This is false economy. Few recipients will ever match these schedules up with the previous catalog. Better to send a complete new catalog containing everything.

6. Use Two Colors, one of which is black, and various percentage screens to expand the range those two colors can produce. Such techniques also show more professionalism. Usually three colors are too expensive, and one color -- even on a colored stock -- looks cheap. Even the so-called "El dullo" brochure benefits from a second color to yellow-high-light key words.

7. Serif Type Is Best for Body Copy. Type with *serifs* -- the horizontal lines on each letter that guide your eye (like the type on this page) -- has repeatedly proven to be more readable than *sans serif* type -- like this. Some authorities claim huge percentage differences in retention and understanding in tests conducted with both kinds of type. More importantly, look at the serious publications you receive; almost all use sans serif type *only* for short headlines and a serif type everywhere else.

8. Don't Worry if Your Brochure Is Destroyed when the coupon is removed -- you'll send them another new one when you confirm their order. However, *do* make sure that the customer will still have your name, address and telephone number after your response vehicle is removed.

9. Make Your Message Unmistakable, Even from a Distance. The outside of your brochure, self-mailer or catalog must be clear, and its message unmistakable, even from a distance. How many times have you pulled something that interested you from someone else's wastebasket? And such designs make the best use of those few seconds you have between the in-basket and the waste-basket.

10. Always Use a Preprinted Indicia on a Self-Mailer, as its purpose should be clear and obvious, and the postage mark is unimportant. If you don't have your own Third-Class bulk-rate mailing permit, use your mail house's permit. Get the particulars, number, etc., from them to print on your piece.

Response Vehicles

1. Develop Your Response Vehicle First, not last as is frequently the case. Be sure of what action you want your readers to take, and make it easy for them to take it. Remove all obstacles to action and all reasons to delay. Many direct mail authorities feel that the response vehicle is *the* most important part of the package, and often it's the most poorly done.

2. Start by Getting the Label Back. Imprint the name or affix the label to the response vehicle so it will be returned to you with the order for tracking purposes. If the response vehicle is part of a self-mailer, consider putting the label right in the response vehicle, or on the reverse side of it. Instruct responders: "Do not remove mailing label."

3. Observe Post Office Regulations regarding size, shape and paper weight for the response vehicle. For self-mailers, also observe space requirements around and below the mailing label. (See Chapter 9 for more information.)

4. Build/Maintain Reader Involvement by having them check boxes, fill in information, etc. Be sure the response vehicle starts with a reaffirmation of the benefit the customer will obtain by accepting your offer.

5. Don't Combine Response Vehicle and Reply Envelope. Use a *business reply card* (BRC) or a plain reply card and a completely separate *business reply envelope* (BRE). A "live" postage stamp on a self-addressed envelope greatly increases response over a BRE, but it costs considerably more as well.

6. "Please Keep My Name on Your Mailing List" as a box on your response vehicle stimulates those interested to respond even if they're not buying anything.

General

1. Direct Marketing Can't Change Anyone's Mind. It can only make it possible -- even easy -- for them to act to satisfy a need they *already* know they have.

2. Only Do One Thing at a Time. Get a

registration, sell a book, preview a video and request more information are the kinds of single objectives that direct mail can accomplish well. But put two or more of these together -- particularly if they pertain to different products -- and you're courting disaster.

> Usually, trying to do two things with one mailer ends up with a lower *combined* response than you'd have gotten to *either* of the offers separately!

3. Use Few Type Styles and Sizes. Today's desktop publishing allows anyone to use dozens of type fonts, sizes and shades. But this usually looks amateurish and often cuts response. Stick with a few readable styles and few sizes to engage your reader with your message -- rather than your messenger.

4. Make Each Component Different in size, shape, paper, color, etc., when folded and unfolded. However, your letter and the outer envelope should usually match.

5. Avoid Anything that Looks Like the "J" Word, such as light-weight papers or flimsy, cheap-looking envelopes. You don't like it -- and neither do your readers.

6. Check Insertability and Handling of Every Component in your mailing that's going into an envelope *before* printing. Folded inserts especially need to be checked by the mail house early in the project. Some old inserting equipment can only accept folded-side-in, and hand insertion can be costly. Get the opinion of a second mail house if you're in doubt.

And Post Office automation specifies where folds and closures of self-mailers are

required. (See Chapter 9.)

7. Be Careful Printing Where the Address Label Goes. Heavy ink coverage sometimes prevents the label from sticking and makes writing difficult on the response vehicle.

8. A Toll-Free, 800 Telephone Number Increases Response, especially for mailings aimed at individuals. And *do* advertise that you'll accept collect calls, even though very few will actually call collect. Most phone calls from those in organizations are made on their own WATS or other long-distance lines. These people often won't use your 800 number, but they'll appreciate your thoughtfulness and sophistication in having one.

9. A BRC or BRE Is Usually Not Necessary for Seminars and Conferences, because it's not a quick decision. People need to check their calendar, arrange transportation, get approvals, etc. However, business reply is important for books, materials, computer software, and the like. So, if you include a low-cost booklet offer in your seminar brochure to "capture" additional names, using business reply will improve response.

10. Use a Mailhouse or Lettershop for all but the smallest and most personalized mailings. It's easy to underestimate the work involved, and the cost of hand labor quickly exceeds most mail house charges (see Chapter 9).

11. Use "Address Correction Requested" Only on Your House List, never on a rented list (see "How to Get Your Undeliverable Mail Returned" in Chapter 9 and "Customer Address Loss: A Costly Problem and What to Do About It" in Chapter 13).

ONE WORLD-CLASS DIRECT MAIL PACKAGE

If you learn an art form like advertising by copying the masters, there's no better place to start than with one of the all-time winners, reprinted here with permission from the publisher. Although this is a subscription offer and not a training product or service, it's still extraordinarily relevant for marketing training and information. Both this offer and al-

most any training or information product is aimed at the educated professional. It presents a powerful case for the benefits of "soft" products like information (or training). And it shows how deceptively simple the final package can be: Just compelling words on paper in a form.

DIRECT response:
Never Send Out A Letter Without Testing Something

By John Caples

Shown at the right page is the complete text of the famous "Widow" letter written more than 20 years ago for Barron's Weekly by the late Les Davis.

Year after year this letter has out-pulled every letter tested against it, and it is still pulling.

What makes this letter so effective? Let's analyze it and see if we can find some of the secrets of its success.

1. The letter begins with the phrase "Dear Friend of Barron's." This is a change of pace from ordinary beginnings such as "Dear Friend" or "Dear Sir."

2. The letter looks easy to read. It is broken up into short paragraphs. For example, page one contains 11 paragraphs. *Nine of these paragraphs contain only a single sentence each.*

How often do copywriters use this simple device to attract readers? Probably not often enough.

3. Throughout the four pages of the letter, there is a liberal sprinkling of white space. This makes the pages inviting to the eye.

4. The letter begins with a story. This is one of the oldest, and still one of the best methods of conveying a message. The parables in the Bible are stories. Wall Street Journal writers frequently begin their articles with stories. The articles in Reader's Digest often start with stories.

5. Here is the beginning of the Barron's letter:

Dear Friend of Barron's:

Back in 1925, Barron's published an article suggesting how $100,000 might be well invested in securities for a widow with two small children.

The plan was based on a set of 10 rules for investors, stated in the article.

The securities (stocks and bonds), all picked in accordance with the first seven of the 10 rules, are today worth $482,663.

The stocks are worth $484,025 -- many times over their original value of $51,000.

Average annual income for the entire 49 years, has exceeded $10,988.

Latest reported income was $22,017.

This story is well chosen. It is an account of financial gain. Barron's is a financial publication.

The story is made believable by the use of specific figures. The narrative is further enhanced by the mention of a widow with two small children. The reader feels that the plan must be a safe plan. No one would be so heartless as to risk the livelihood of widows or orphans.

The letter mentions a set of 10 rules for investors. This arouses curiosity. What are these 10 rules that made the widow's investments grow.

The letter offers to send the 10 rules free to readers who subscribe to Barron's.

6. The offer is mentioned early in the letter and again in the order form. Some sales letters mention the offer only once and at the end.

The Free Offer

7. The free offer is described at length (six paragraphs). Here is the copy:

We have now reprinted these 10 rules in a little Barron's booklet, with interpretative comment on each rule.

As a piece of printed matter, the booklet is slight; takes you but a few minutes to read.

But I believe you will agree, its every word is pure gold.

You'll not only welcome the 10 rules for their immediate value. I venture to predict you'll also come back to them repeatedly in the future -- for their help on your ever-present problem of safeguarding what you have, and making it grow and produce for you.

But you can't buy this booklet. It's not for sale.

I would like you to accept it in return for a little favor I'd like to ask of you -- one that I think will interest you.

8. The last sentence of the offer tells the reader that he can have the booklet "in return for a little favor."

This arouses curiosity. The reader wants to know what the favor is. But he is not told right away. He has to read 10 paragraphs of sales copy about Barron's before he can learn what favor he has to do in order to get the booklet.

This technique of suspense has been used from time to time in sales letters, but never more effectively than in the "Widow" letter.

9. On page 3, the favor is described in these words:

Before we sink a lot of money into mailing thousands of circular letters ... we come to you as a representative prospect.

Will you do this:

Merely *try* Barron's -- and judge the information in it for scope, brevity, reader interest, and practical money value.

If Barron's does not live up to your expectations, will you send us a brief note giving us your frank and honest opinion of it?

Whether you become a Barron's enthusiast or not, we shall genuinely appreciate your part in this test.

10. A reason for quick action is given in the following paragraph:

Of course, you understand, if your participation is to be of value to us in deciding our coming mailings ... your immediate response is necessary.

11. The letter does not ask for an order in the usual manner. The last two paragraphs of the letter assume that the reader will send in the order card. Here are the paragraphs:

Will you therefore, check the accuracy of your name and address on the enclosed card and return it to us today in the accompany self-addressed envelope that requires no postage?

Thank you for your help.

12. A postscript at the end of the letter contains additional sales talk for Barron's.

Les Davis, the author of this letter, was my friend and client for 18 years. His ability as a mail order man was recognized by many admirers. It was an honor and a pleasure to serve this fine gentlemen. Les died in 1967. But his "Widow" letter lives on. The letter continues to pay dividends to his former employer, and serves as a model of great writing to all of us.

Reprinted by permission of Direct Marketing Magazine, *224 - 7th St., Garden City, New York 11530.*

The Barron's Widow Letter

BARRON'S National Business and Financial Weekly
22 Cortlandt Street, New York, New York 10007

Gilbert K. Good
Circulation Sales Manager

Dear Friend of Barron's:

Back in 1925, Barron's published an article suggesting how $100,000 might be well invested in securities for a widow with two small children.

The plan was based on a set of ten rules for investors, stated in the article.

The securities (stocks and bonds), all picked in accordance with the first seven of the ten rules, are today worth $482,663.

The stocks are worth $484,025 - many times over their original value of $51,000.

Average annual income, for the entire forty-nine years, has exceeded $10,988.

Latest reported income was $22,017.

So here you have to date how a list of securities, compiled in the third year of Calvin Coolidge's presidency, weathered the wild twenties, the woeful thirties, World War II, and the 1969-1971 market plunge - yet without benefit of the important interim supervision provided for in the last three of the original ten rules.

*   *   *

We have now reprinted these ten rules in a little Barron's booklet, with interpretative comment on each rule.

As a piece of printed matter, the booklet is slight; takes you but a few minutes to read.

But I believe you will agree, its every word is pure gold.

You'll not only welcome the ten rules for their immediate value. I venture to predict you'll also come back to them re-.

(inside, please)

- 2 -

peatedly in the future -- for their help on your ever-present problem of safeguarding what you have, and making it grow and produce for you.

But you can't buy this booklet. It's not for sale.

I would like you to accept it in return for a little favor I'd like to ask of you -- one that I think will interest you.

*   *   *

Barron's, as you probably know, is a national financial weekly -- the only one published by Dow Jones, the world's largest, fastest business news-gathering organization.

By virtue of this close connection -- this day-in, day-out working contact with Dow Jones' reporters, analysts, editors -- Barron's is an amazingly well-informed publication, continually surprising its readers with the intimacy and vital investment significance of its summaries and forecasts of industrial changes, corporate and government affairs.

Barron's own large staff of experts weighs, sifts, interprets -- to bring you each week just the information you need about business and market trends, corporation prospects, the intrinsic values of securities -- clear, concise reports based on firsthand, intimate knowledge of what's going on.

So you can readily see why Barron's (established 1921) has become the source and authority for many economists, stock-market services, investment consultants, and statisticians.

Yet the information for which you pay them high fees is just as basically available to you in Barron's weekly pages as it is to them.

I think you'll agree with me we have a honey of a story:

1. A worthwhile saving on what you must pay for financial information.

2. Thoroughly reliable data every week -- to guide you in the continuous supervision of your investment list -- in the decisions you make on investment acquisitions or sales.

- 3 -

3. Comprehensive weekly trend reports -- political, industrial, financial -- to help you plan your investment moves with greater understanding and foresight -- with fewer worries -- with added peace of mind.

But you know how "funny," how unpredictable, people are. You can never be sure of their reactions until after you have spent a great deal of money to find out. That is, unless you test first.

Which brings me to the favor I want to ask of you.

Before we sink a lot of money into mailing thousands of circular letters to the large key groups of prospective new readers we have in mind, we come to you as a representative prospect.

Will you do this:

Merely try Barron's -- and judge the information in it for scope, brevity, reader interest, and practical money value.

See what you get on stock-market trends, bonds, mutual funds -- "growth" stocks -- situations to consider for income -- securities to stay out of or sell now, because of serious weakness.

Compare Barron's with any other financial-information service, or combination of services, costing from $50 to $150 a year, or more. (Barron's costs $23 a year.)

Under this special trial arrangement, you pay ONLY OUR SHORT-TERM INTRODUCTORY PRICE, $5.75 for 13 WEEKLY ISSUES (3 months).

If Barron's does not live up to your expectations, will you send us a brief note giving us your frank and honest opinion of it?

Whether you become a Barron's enthusiast or not, we shall genuinely appreciate your part in this test.

Of course, you understand, if your participation is to be of value to us in deciding our coming mailings to the key groups, your immediate response is necessary.

Will you, therefore, check the accuracy of your name and

- 4 -

address on the enclosed card and return it to us today in the accompanying self-addressed envelope that requires no postage?

Thank you for your help.

Sincerely yours,

GKG:mk
Encs.

P. S. When Barron's arrives, be sure to examine "Stock Market at a Glance" in the back. Unique ready reference covering prices, earnings and dividends of ALL stocks traded on New York and American Stock Exchanges -- with conspicuous symbols signalling all new dividend declarations or omissions and all new earnings. Weekly range and other statistics. Also quotations on all more active stocks on the major U.S. regional exchanges, the leading Canadian exchanges, and over 1,500 Over-the-Counter quotations -- all with earnings, dividends, year's high and low. No other service like it anywhere!

THE BEST ADVERTISING REFERENCES

Here are ten advertising "classics" that will round out your perspective on writing hard-hitting copy that produces sales. Each one is by a proven master of the art, people who have made lots of money practicing what they preach. Don't bother listening to anyone else.

1. Tested Advertising Methods, by John Caples. Prentice Hall, 113 Sylvan Avenue, Englewood Cliffs, NJ 07632. Phone: (201)592-2000. 1974 (4th Edition). (318 pages, $14.95.)

For over three decades this book has been the standard guide on tested methods of getting favorable sales results from advertising. It takes the guesswork out of advertising with proven selling techniques, including what headlines attract readers; 29 formulas for writing headlines; how to write the first paragraph; how to make small ads pay big; 32 ways to get more inquiries; 20 ways to increase selling power; 17 ways to test your ads, plus much more.

2. Confessions of an Advertising Man, by David Ogilvy. Atheneum Publications, 597 Fifth Avenue, New York, NY 10017. 1988. (180 pages, $7.95.)

3. Ogilvy on Advertising, by David Ogilvy. Crown Publishers, Inc., One Park Avenue, New York, NY 10016. 1983. (224 pages, $24.95.)

Classics culled from more than 30 years of successful experience, these books tell which advertising techniques sell, which don't -- and why. They show hundreds of ads, describe Ogilvy's fabulous television commercials and provide plenty of inspiring and helpful anecdotes, analyses, philosophy and advice.

4. Positioning: The Battle for Your Mind, by Al Ries and Jack Trout. McGraw-Hill, 1221 Avenue of the Americas, New York, NY 10020. Phone: (212) 337-5945, (800) 2-MCGRAW. 1981. ($19.95.)

5. Marketing Warfare, by Al Ries and Jack Trout. McGraw-Hill, 1221 Avenue of the Americas, New York, NY 10020. Phone: (212) 337-5945, (800) 2-MCGRAW. 1985.

6. Bottom-Up Marketing, by Al Ries and Jack Trout. McGraw-Hill, 1221 Avenue of the Americas, New York, NY 10020. Phone: (212) 337-5945, (800) 2-MCGRAW. 1988.

Ries and Trout have written three extremely popular books about marketing, each widely regarded as a classic in its field. Their first, defined positioning and why the now-famous Avis "We're No. 2 and we try harder" campaign worked so well. The second likens the marketplace to -- you guessed it -- a battlefield and claims companies are in defensive, attacking, flanking or guerrilla modes. The third argues that while most people devise a grand strategy and delegate tactics to execute it, smarter ones find tactics that work and derive strategies from them.

7. The 100 Greatest Advertisements: Who Wrote Them & What They Did, by Julian L. Watkins. Dover Publications, New York, NY 1959 (2nd Edition). ($7.95.)

8. My Life in Advertising & Scientific Advertising, by Claude C. Hopkins. NTC Business Books, 4255 W. Touhy Avenue, Lincolnwood, IL 60646-1975. Phone: (708) 679-5500, (800) 323-4900; Fax: (708) 679-2494. 1993. ISBN 0-8442-3101-0. (318 pages, $11.95.)

David Ogilvy said, "Nobody should be allowed to have anything to do with advertising until he has read this book (*Scientific Advertising*) seven times. It changed the course of my life." The above edition is actually two books in one: The first, an autobiography, was written in 1927, and the second (which Ogilvy referred to) in 1923. Hopkins knew what he was talking about: He made $100,000 a year writing advertising in the 1920s!

9. Cash Copy: How to Offer Your Products and Services so Your Prospects Buy Them ... Now! by Dr. Jeffrey Lant. Jeffrey Lant Associates, Inc., 50 Follen Street, Suite 507, Cambridge, MA 02138. Phone: (617) 547-6372; Fax: (617) 547-0061. 1992. (480 pages, $38.50.)

10. Money Making Marketing: Finding the People who Need What You're Selling and Making Sure They Buy It, by Dr. Jeffrey Lant. Jeffrey Lant Associates, Inc., 50 Follen Street, Suite 507, Cambridge, MA 02138. Phone: (617) 547-6372; Fax: (617) 547-0061. (285 pages, $39.50.)

I've not seen either book. (In response to our requests for review copies, Lant keeps sending us ads!) Even if his approach to the business is sometimes unusual, his copy is always compelling and hard-hitting. And since his other books that I *have* seen are all fairly priced, practical and useful, these probably are too.

TESTING: YOUR COMPETITIVE EDGE (IF YOU USE IT!)

The ability to conduct systematic, statistically significant tests is the one aspect of direct marketing that sets it apart from all other forms of marketing. Because of this ability, direct marketers can steadily improve their promotional approach from wherever it is at the start toward the best it can possibly be.

Here are eight rules to follow for testing:

1. Know what to test and what not to test.
2. Test only one thing at a time, always against a known standard or "control."
3. Obtain enough responses for statistical significance.
4. Split your test cells in a way that doesn't bias the outcome.
5. Code everything you print or mail.
6. Aggressively track down, decode and record *every* response.
7. Don't change *anything* that testing hasn't shown to be superior.
8. Never stop testing *something*.

We'll look at some of these in the following sections.

Know What to Test -- and What Not to Test

The seven main variables to test for training, continuing education and information products and services and the extent of the improvements possible are:

1. List/media..............................up to 10:1 (900%)
2. Timing (dated events) ....up to 6:1 (500%)
3. Product name/title................ up to 5:1 (400%)
4. Offer (incl. event location & duration).....................up to 5:1 (400%)
5. Price...up to 5:1 (400%)
6. Advertising format/design...up to 2:1 (100%)
7. Advertising copy...................up to 1.5:1 (50%)

Many tests are made on inconsequential or minor variables that have little or no real impact on results. Don't waste time testing these items until/unless all the higher priority items have been settled. For instance, most format/design variables aren't worth testing until some successful lists, a good offer and the best price have been established.

When testing price, test *major* differences, not minor ones. For example, if your product is $69.95, test $79.95 and $59.95, not $70.00 and $69.50.

Test Only One Thing at a time, Always Against a Known Standard or "Control"

Ideally, everything *except* the test variable must be identical between the various test cells. This includes when and where it's mailed.

Those who understand statistics know you can test several things at once. But most novice mailers do it badly and wind up with unreliable or misleading results. You're better off sticking to *one* variable at a time and doing it right.

When testing a *new* variable, always include your proven standard to serve as a benchmark. When *everything* is new, use your best former package/list as your comparison or "control" element.

Obtain Enough Responses for Statistical Significance

The two major considerations in constructing a test are:

- How large a test sample is needed, and
- How that test sample should be selected. (This is in the next section)

The size of your test sample depends on the number of responses you'll likely get, *not* on the size of the lists, market, etc. The minimum number of responses required to evaluate each segment (or "cell") of a test is 20-30; 40 is better still.

Here's an example of a test matrix for two mailing lists with a product having a 1% average response:

House List (Control)	Test List "A"	Test List "B"
2,000 Pcs.	2,000 Pcs.	2,000 Pcs.

3 test cells x 20 traceable responses per cell
= 60 traceable responses needed.

1% response rate = 10 responses per 1,000

60 traceable responses / 10 Traceable responses per 1,000 = 6,000 pieces of mail needed.

When analyzing tests, always look at *traceable* responses. Then adjust your results to account for the untraceable responses (including those known to have originated from the advertising but not traceable to the specific test cell). This is particularly important when you have a high percentage of untraceable responses (say 20%-30%).

If the difference between the test results for two test cells is greater than the square root of their total, it is a significant difference. For example, you obtained 20 responses for "A" and 29 responses for "B": $\sqrt{(20 + 29)} = \sqrt{49} = 7$. Since the difference $(29 - 20) = 9$ is greater than 7, the difference is significant.

Although the final results of a test may take many weeks or months to complete, the first few weeks of response will generally show the trend. Jack Oldstein has cited these rules of thumb:

"If you send out a mailing First class,

DOUBLE the response you've received at the end of 2 WEEKS' TIME from the date of your first order. If you send out a mailing third class, DOUBLE the response you've received at the end of 4 WEEKS' TIME from the date of your first order. The resulting figures will be the TOTAL RESPONSE you can expect to receive by the time all responses to your mail have arrived."

(Also see the discussion of response time in Chapter 5.)

Split Your Test so You Don't Bias the Outcome

There are several common means of selecting test samples:

1. Nth name selection
2. ZIP codes or SCF's
3. States -- where neither Nth name or ZIP code/SCF can be used.

Splitting a list on every 2nd name for households is generally O.K. -- but it can be misleading for organizations. Instead, try splitting by odd and even ZIP codes, or select by ZIP codes in other ways to ensure that all pieces mailed to a given address are identical.

If you split on ZIP code, use the 4th or 5th digit, which is random but not uniform, as the following graph shows:

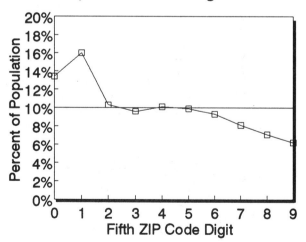

U.S. Population Distribution by 5th ZIP Code Digit

Use the table at the top of the next page to tell which ZIP codes to cluster in order to get the desired split.

Dividing a Mailing List by 5th ZIP Code Digit

5th ZIP Digit	Percent of Pop.	Halves		Thirds		
		Even	Odd	First	Second	Third
0	13.4%	13.4%		13.4%		
1	16.0%		16.0%		16.0%	
2	10.3%	10.3%				10.3%
3	9.6%		9.6%	9.6%		
4	10.1%	10.1%			10.1%	
5	9.9%		9.9%			9.9%
6	9.3%	9.3%		9.3%		
7	8.1%		8.1%		8.1%	
8	7.1%	7.1%				7.1%
9	6.2%		6.2%			6.2%
	100.0%	50.2%	49.8%	32.3%	34.2%	33.5%

Various Means of Coding Direct Mail

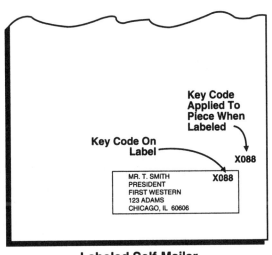

Labeled Self-Mailer

Striped Response Cards

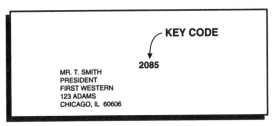

Direct Addressed Reply Card

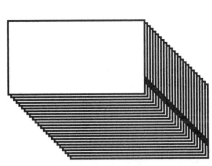

Drop-Off Numbers

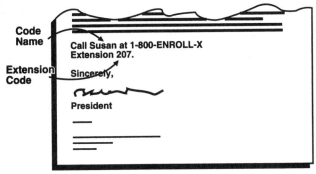

Personalized Letter

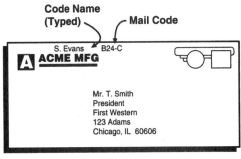

Personalized Envelope

Code Everything You Print/Mail

Set up separate codes for every variable, and keep the results for each code separate. If there's any question at all about whether or not a separate code is needed, it is.

On the previous page are some of the ways you can code your materials. You'll see other ways being used on the mail you receive, called "VIP Code," "Priority Code," or a similar name.

How much of your response will you be able to trace? It depends on how aggressive you are in politely -- but persistently -- getting the codes. It also depends on how long and in how many different ways you promote. For "1-shot" campaigns, expect 95%-98% traceability. For continuous or long-running campaigns, at least 65%-70% should be traceable.

Testing Worksheet

The purpose of the worksheet on the facing page is to help you identify and prioritize the main variables to be tested in your marketing program and to interrelate these variables in a TEST MATRIX. In some cases, you may need to construct your own test matrix in order to accommodate a wider range of variables or other circumstances, but the worksheet provided will be useful to demonstrate the procedures to be followed.

1. Identify the major VARIABLES you feel need to be tested. Think through the decisions and choices you've made in selecting your product or service, in selecting the market you are trying to reach and in your planning activities to this point. Refer to the eight rules for successful testing and the tips for testing, contained in this section, to suggest additional variables for testing.

2. Identify the ALTERNATIVES or RANGE of the variable that should be tested, in order to suitably "bracket" the variable.

3. RANK or PRIORITIZE these variables, taking account of the seven main variables shown earlier, and other factors in your marketing program. Your priorities should reflect the importance of testing these vari-

ables and the sequence in which the testing should be done.

4. Use the TEST VARIABLES MATRIX to interrelate two (or more) of the highest priority variables. The matrix provides 36 cells so that a considerable range of variables can be interrelated. Use the cells to record the number of pieces of mail or other measures of test cell size, as well as (later) the number of responses and the responses per thousand. Use the total row and column to sum up the individual cells.

Here's what a completed worksheet might look like:

Testing Worksheet

For (Product/Market): New Public Seminar

Variable to Test:	Alternative/Range:	Priority/Ranking:
Direct mail package	Envelope vs. Self-mailer	1
	Personalized vs. pre-Printed letter	2
	1-page vs. 4-page ltr.	3
	Agency vs. in-house design	4

Test Variables Matrix

Package:		June	July	Aug.	Sept.	Oct.	Nov.	Totals
Self-mailer	Agency design	26,004 / 13	13,936 / 2	12,000 / 2				51,940 / 17 / .327
	In-house design				12,706 / 15	8,715 / 6	12,849 / 9	34,270 / 30 / .875
Envelope (with brochure)	No letter	11,380 / 7						11,380 / 7 / .615
	1-Page, Pre-Printed, Agency ltr.	11,440 / 14			12,678 / 13	8,039 / 3	12,800 / 8	44,957 / 38 / .845
	1-Page, per-sonalized, Agency ltr.	11,155 / 2						11,155 / 2 / .179
	4-Page Pre-Printed In-house ltr.				12,704 / 11	6,534 / 1	12,794 / 20	32,032 / 32 / .999
Totals		59,979 / 36 / .600	13,936 / 2 / .144	12,000 / 2 / .167	38,088 / 39 / 1.024	23,288 / 10 / .429	38,443 / 37 / .962	185,734 / 126 / .678

More Tips for Testing

Never Jump from a Test Sample to the Entire List, no matter how certain or appealing it may seem. Follow up successful tests with subsequent tests of larger sizes. For example, 5,000, 10,000, 25,000, 50,000, etc., up to the complete list. This is called "pyramiding."

Testing Worksheet

For (Product/Market):_____

Variable to Test:	Alternative/Range:	Priority/ Ranking:
_____	_____	_____
_____	_____	_____
_____	_____	_____
_____	_____	_____
_____	_____	_____
_____	_____	_____
_____	_____	_____

Test Variables Matrix

Totals:							

List Continuations Usually Don't Do as Well as the Test. In spite of statistics, a given list selection rarely, if ever, does better on continuation than it did in the test. And frequently, continuations do much worse. A corollary is: Don't continue marginal lists in the hope that they'll improve. They won't.

Allow for Timing. Review your test results in light of seasonality and/or current events. Good test results during a period when most lists perform well need to be discounted for projection to other times.

When you advertise is critical for seminars, conferences and other scheduled events. You must test advertising date (or mail drop date and class of mail) in relationship to date(s) of the event you are promoting in order to determine what's right for you. Chapter 5 has lots of information on timing.

Keep looking at your own incoming mail and that received by others at your office. You'll begin to see evidence of the tests that other marketers are making.

HOW TO SELECT AND USE ADVERTISING AGENCIES AND ADVERTISING PROFESSIONALS

For compelling copy and content, the information presented in this chapter, along with your own writing skills, will probably prove most effective. This is *all* you need for classified ads and directory listings, since the typesetting and other composition issues are handled by the publisher. (See Chapter 12 for more on these kinds of print ads.)

But, for brochures, catalogs and display ads where you must provide *both* composition and graphics, by all means employ the services of an advertising professional. In my opinion, you can always see a difference between an amateur's ad and one done by a professional. However, finding and working with an advertising professional can sometimes be a problem, especially if you're not located in a major metropolitan area.

The so-called full-service ad agencies are not likely to be useful for those marketing training and information. These agencies make most of their money on commissions they earn by placing newspaper, magazine, radio and television ads. They're geared to high-volume accounts. If your annual advertising budget is less than a million dollars, you'll probably have trouble attracting the attention of any ad agency.

Occasionally, full-service agencies will be willing to work on a "fee-for-services" basis. This could be a good deal. They might be interested in this arrangement if they expect

you to become a large volume advertiser. But remember, they don't make money selling their professional services. They use their professional services to entice the placement of ads on which they can earn high commissions for comparatively little work.

Incidentally, most agencies are very naive about direct marketing, and you will need to help them with the copy and the approach. If at all possible, work only with agencies who have demonstrated success with the same kind of promotion -- and to the same market -- as yours.

A better course of action for most training and information suppliers is to find a freelance professional skilled in advertising design. You want someone who's primarily a graphic artist, not a copywriter. (Full-service ad agencies generally have "creative," "artistic," and "copywriters." You want artistic, since you are probably going to write your own copy.)

Finding this person isn't as difficult as it sounds. Start with your local college or university graphic arts or marketing department. Ask your printer or mailing house. Many times these organizations have someone on staff. If not, they certainly know the best resources in your area.

Get at least three names and interview each as you would anyone you were going to hire. Look at examples of their work and get references of those they've worked with. And discuss their rates "up-front," so there are no later surprises.

Their principal activities are going to be arranging for desktop publishing, typesetting, photography, layout and producing color separations and camera-ready artwork. Look at the ads they've created and see if they appeal to you.

This is also the time to evaluate what they'll be like to work with on a day-to-day basis. "Prima Donnas," with a "take-it or leave-it" approach, should be avoided like the plague. You want someone who will work as a member of your team, adding their graphic arts skills and talents to your knowledge of the business, to your critical examination of what others are doing and to your experience with what works or doesn't work. A creative person who is unwilling to admit there may be a better way will hurt you more than they will help.

---

10 Common Advertising Mistakes

1. Trying to do two things with one mailing or one ad.

2. Planning too tight a schedule.

3. Overestimating response.

4. Ignoring the lifetime value of a new customer.

5. Not testing.

6. Failing to integrate direct marketing with staff.

7. Maintaining a poor house list -- or none at all.

8. Not tracking down the source of *every* response.

9. Emphasizing graphics and/or copy over lists/media.

10. Paying too much for printing.

NOTES

SMARTER PRINTING AND MAILING: THE *BEST* WAY TO SAVE TIME AND MONEY

You've selected the lists and designed the mailing piece. Now your challenge is to get your mailing completed on time and within budget. This involves getting and processing the mailing lists, producing the camera-ready artwork, obtaining and evaluating printing bids, selecting and managing the printer, the service bureau, and the mailhouse, working with the Post Office on various regulations and permits and preparing to receive and process replies from the mailing. It also means managing people -- outside your organization as well as within -- who must cooperate in order to make your mailing a success.

MANAGING COSTS TO STAY WITHIN YOUR BUDGET

There are two pieces to this important topic: first, *setting* a realistic budget, and second, *managing* your activities to stay within it.

The first is easier if you've done the job before, and more difficult for new projects. This handbook, and particularly this chapter, should provide you enough solid information to reasonably project the likely costs and returns for these first-time mailings.

That brings us to the second requirement: managing activities to stay within your budget. The two most important contributors here are: (1.) selecting the right vendors and (2.) your commitment to follow good business practices. In fact, managing direct mail costs to stay within a realistic budget may be easier than you think, because everybody involved in direct mail is *very* cost-conscious.

The following guidelines and recommendations apply to purchasing almost anything but are especially relevant here, because artwork, printing and mailing typically represent one-third to one-half of your direct marketing budget.

Don't Overlook a Critical Step

The usual direct mail campaign will have some or all of the items shown below. All need close attention for the mailing to succeed. The following sections expand on those having the greatest impact on costs and schedules.

The Main Elements of a Direct Mail Campaign

- Consulting services
- Creativity (copy and design)
- Typesetting and stats
- Photos
- Production of camera-ready artwork
- Printing all elements (includes paper, bindery and delivery to mailhouse)
- List rental (includes shipping and tape charges, if any)
- Merge/purge (tape conversion, computer processing, reports, list printing)
- Mailhouse services (address, barcode, insert, sort, tie, bag, take to Post Office)
- Postage
- Bulk-rate mail fees
- Business reply mail fee
- Reply vehicle return postage
- Inbound WATS (800 number) costs (phone and/or service bureau)

Get Three Comparable Bids for Everything

Always do this for *everything* you buy -- and get three independent answers to any question you have. Check and recheck all bids and all prices. Talk to other vendors for their prices, even if you don't change from your current supplier. And make sure everyone is bidding on the same thing: same schedules, papers, colors, quantities, etc. For example, be sure sales tax (if applicable) and freight are consistently included (or excluded) in all price comparisons and cost estimates.

Pick Only Experienced Suppliers

When selecting vendors, get evidence that they've *already* done successfully what they're going to do for you. Pay special attention to whether they've (1.) successfully reached the market you're trying to reach, (2.) successfully sold a product/service like you're trying to sell and (3.) demonstrated the economics you're counting on, particularly their costs. Don't be afraid to ask for references -- and check them!

Always Buy from the Source

Go to the primary provider of what you're buying, not to middle persons who will add their mark-up or distort the information. Examples are buying envelopes from printers and mailing lists from mailhouses. It's more work to go direct -- but it pays off in the long run.

Allow Enough Time

Start planning early and expect *everything* to take longer to accomplish than you thought. Give your regular vendors early notice of what's coming and when. They'll generally try to accommodate you -- or warn you about possible schedule problems while there's still time to do something about them.

Here are some typical times to allow for various production activities:

Direct Marketing Planning Times

Activity	Figure on . . .
Selecting mailing lists	1 – 2 weeks
Obtaining mailing lists	1 – 4 weeks
Typesetting from final copy	1 day – 1 week
Preparing camera–ready art	1 day – 2 weeks
Newspaper or magazine Insertion	Depends on media schedule
Printing 1–color, 1–2 sides	3 – 5 days
Printing 2–4 colors, 1–2 sides	2 – 4 weeks
Merging/purging mailing lists	1 – 3 weeks
Obtaining envelopes from a printer	2 days – 1 week
Obtaining envelopes from an envelope manufacturer	2 – 4 weeks
Creating personalized letters or envelopes	1 – 2 weeks
Affix labels, Insert, sort, tie & bag/tray envelopes (mail house)	20 M – 50 M pieces per day
Affix labels, sort, tie & bag or tray self–mailer (mail house)	50 M pieces per day and up
Insert, label & mail (yourself)	300 – 500 pieces per day

Mock-Up Your Job in Advance

Early on, make up a complete paper dummy or mock-up of your mail package and review it with everyone involved: artists, typesetters, printers, mailhouse, Post Office, envelope supplier.

And don't forget to weigh it! If it's on the borderline between two postage rates, remember factors like humidity on the mailing day can affect what the Post Office gets when *they* weigh it. And don't fail to reweigh the final printed package as well.

Changes Will Kill You

In printing and mailing -- as in the construction trades -- changes *after* the job is let will ruin your budget. Many vendors count on such changes to rescue what would otherwise be an unprofitably low bid that got them the job in the first place. You can protect yourself from this budget-busting experience by planning so thoroughly in advance that there are few, if any, last-minute changes.

Inspect Everything Personally

Go to the printer, the mailhouse, the service bureau. Open boxes and personally look at the contents. This accomplishes two important objectives: (1.) It gives you a firsthand "feel" for how the operation is going, what your customers/vendors see, etc. And (2.) it shows your employees and vendors that you personally care.

Use a Project/Job Filing System

First, start a project file, which can be simply a big envelope or a 3-ring binder (my preference). Next, assign a project or job number containing the month, year and job sequence; for example, the first job in April, 1995, might be numbered 049501. Now make sure you do *everything* in writing, never verbally: correspondence, bid requests, quotations, purchase orders, change orders -- *everything*. Sign, date and job number each one and put a copy in the project file. Be sure the job number is on all artwork, type proofs, color keys, delivery tickets and invoices, too, and put copies of these in the project file as well. Periodically, record your costs on the envelope or on a summary sheet in the notebook.

Negotiate *Both* Payment Terms *and* Price

Always negotiate payment terms, but only *after* you've negotiated price. Both are equally important. In fact, for new/growing businesses, cash flow (hence payment terms) can be *more* important than price. But if you try to negotiate both at the same time, you'll find that your supplier won't give you the best price.

DESIGN AND ARTWORK TIPS

Successful printing begins with attention to design and to preparing artwork so your job can be printed quickly and efficiently.

Color

Two-color printing is usually the best choice; single color, even on colored paper, often looks cheap; three or more colors are usually too expensive. Besides, most printers have 2-color capability but may have to job out 3- or 4-color work or run it through their 2-color press a second time.

With a little planning, you can use a dot pattern -- or "screen" -- to make one color look like several, thereby adding polish to

your material at little or no cost. All the better mailers routinely do this, so start paying attention to the printed material you see every day. Notice that often what at first seem to be several colors is actually only several different density screens of a single color. Save examples that you like or can use.

But BEWARE! Not every color screens well. For example, many reds produce unusual and unappealing shades of pink when screened. Basic blues, greens, yellows and black usually work well.

Type

Also pay attention to the type fonts used in

your mailing materials. Always use a serif type -- bookface or equivalent -- for easy readability of body copy. The so-called "sans serif" type fonts (Helvetica being the most common) are acceptable for headlines but never for large blocks of type.

You should shop around for typesetters just as you would any other supplier. But here, convenience *may* be worth some sacrifice in cost, particularly if your artwork is being done in-house. Convenience usually means speed and delivery, as well as accuracy and availability of the type fonts you want.

In today's world of desktop publishing, using a professional typesetter may sound old-fashioned. But although desktop publishing produces great reports and informal documents, most are not yet capable of producing the professional looking type faces and letter spacing ("kerning") needed for top-notch advertising materials and for high-quality, but inexpensive, printing. This may change, so keep checking.

And avoid reverse-outs (white letters on a colored background) for copy. Art directors love it, but tests show it doesn't pull as well in direct mail. Save reverse-outs for occasional use on major headlines and that's all.

Artwork

Make sure your art is correct *before* it goes to the printer -- it's harder to change when it's done -- and printers' film charges can add up fast. Have two competent people *proofread every word* that's to be printed. One reads aloud from the original; the other reads along on the artwork, blueline or proof. Encourage them to challenge anything that "doesn't look right." Label the back of each piece with the initials of those who did the proofreading and the date.

Artwork should also be clearly marked for printing colors. Don't make the printer guess what you want. Use Pantone Matching System (PMS) color numbers for consistency. And on reruns, include a sample of a prior piece clearly marked as to changes.

Finally, be sure to promptly retrieve your artwork and photographs from the printer, and immediately inspect them for damage (for which the printer is liable). Create a secure storage area for your artwork, as replacing it is expensive. Also develop a filing system that enables you to quickly retrieve the artwork and photographs when necessary.

And get in the habit of making corrections on the artwork and reshooting negatives, rather than making changes on the negatives or flats at the printer. This ensures that your artwork is always the latest correct version, which is especially important if you decide to change printers.

HOW THE PROS BUY PRINTING AT ROCK-BOTTOM PRICES

This is the one area where its easy to spend too much money and to spend it *without* getting higher quality or better direct mail response in return.

Why do businesses pay too much for their printing? Generally because they have no idea of what a job should really cost and have no real basis on which to compare prices. Or they will fail to get three comparable bids, relying instead on the same printer they use for their business forms or reports. Here are five rules to help you cut costs and maintain (or even improve) quality.

1. Seek Out the Specialist

The first thing to know about printers is that you get the best price on a job they can run entirely in their own shop. When they must send part or all of your job out for printing, bindery work or whatever, they will be paying marked-up prices -- and so will you.

That's why there are specialists in virtually every type of printing: direct mail, books, magazines, catalogs, envelopes, postcard decks, etc. These shops have assembled all the necessary equipment under one roof. Often, the savings will justify your working with a specialist even in another part of the country. But don't rule out finding a local specialist.

Here is a short list of some high-volume printers that *could* save you money:

AMERICAN DIRECT MEDIA SERVICES (Div. of Haines & Company)
8050 Freedom Avenue, N.W.
North Canton, OH 44720
Phone: (800) 321-0448, (216) 494-9111
Fax: (216) 494-0226
Contact: Michelle Cyrill

BROWN PRINTING
U.S. Highway 14 West
Waseca, MN 56093
Phone: (800) 533-0475, (507) 835-0475;
Fax: (507) 835-0402
Contact: William Guthrie, National Sales Representative

DANNER PRESS
1250 Camden Avenue, S.W.
Canton, OH 44706
Phone: (216) 454-5692; Fax: (216) 454-4727
Contact: Tom Bolerjack, Sales

DARTMOUTH PRINTING
69 Lyme Road
Hanover, NH 03755
Phone: (603) 643-2220; Fax: (603) 643-5408
Contact: Matt Halik, Sales

DIRECT GRAPHICS
829 Vandermark Road
P.O. Box 4009
Sidney, OH 45365
Phone: (800) 848-4406, (513) 498-2194
Fax: (513) 492-1100
Contact: Tommy Mack, Sales

PACIFIC PRINTING INDUSTRIES
707 East 62nd Street
Los Angeles, CA 90001
Phone: (213) 235-4011
Contact: Gene Fouts, Sales

PENN LITHOGRAPHICS, INC.
12630 Hiddencreek Way
Cerritos, CA 90701
Phone: (310) 926-0455; Fax: (310) 926-8955
Contact: Sam Skuratofsky

PUBLISHERS PRESS
P. O. Box 37500
Louisville, KY
Phone: (800) 627-5801, (502) 955-6526
Fax: (502) 543-4700
Contact: Michael Simon

RIPLEY PRINTING CO.
4508 Bibb Blvd., Suite. B-10
Tucker, GA 30084
Phone: (404) 621-9225; Fax: (404) 621-0034
Contact: Randy Schwartz, Sales

THE JOHN ROBERTS COMPANY
9687 East River Road
Minneapolis, MN 55433
Phone: (612) 755-5500, (612) 754-4405
Fax: (612) 755-0394
Contact: Bernie Palmer, Sales

SCHMIDT PRINTING
1101 Frontage Road, N.W. Hwy. 14
Byron, MN 55920
Phone: (507) 775-6400; Fax: (507) 775-6655
Contact: Joel Skinner, Sales

TRIPLE A GRAPHICS
1740 Barcelona Circle
Placentia, CA 92670
Phone: (714) 993-1300; Fax: (714) 993-6439
Contact: Paul Aronson, President

THE WEBB COMPANY
1999 Shepard Road
St. Paul, MN 55116
Phone: (612) 690-7200

WEBCRAFT TECHNOLOGIES
Route 1 & Adams Station
N. Brunswick, NJ 08902
Phone: (908) 297-5100; Fax: (908) 821-3010
Contact: Mr. Pat Bigoss, V.P. Sales

WESTERN WEB PRINTING
4005 S. Western Avenue
Sioux Falls, SD 57117-5184
Phone: (800) 843-6805, (605) 339-2383
Fax: (605) 335-6873, (605) 339-1528
Contact: Dale Ducheneaux

WILLIAMS PRINTING CO.
1240 Spring Street, N.W.
Atlanta, GA 30309
Phone: (404) 875-6611; Fax: (404) 872-4025
Contact: Mary Lynne Reeves, Sales

2. Deal With The House

When you deal with a printer's salesperson, a broker, agent or representative, their sales commission is directly or indirectly included in your price. There's nothing wrong with sales commissions, but you need to know you're paying more as a result, and therefore you need to insist on getting the added service you're entitled to. For example, a savvy salesperson may get you a lower price, even *including* their commission, than you could get on your own. With most national printers, particularly those not in a major city, you'll probably have to deal with a regional sales rep, but hopefully a local one who will come to your office.

When I have a choice -- and they're competitive -- I prefer to deal directly with the owner or manager of a smaller shop, thereby avoiding sales commissions and *still* getting top service, especially on cost-sensitive, direct mail materials.

3. Make Sure Your Job Fits Their Equipment

The true determinant of the cost of your job to the printer -- the base from which they must mark it up in order to make a fair profit -- is the hourly cost of the press, including the equipment that is part of the press and the press operator. A 4-color press has a higher hourly cost than a 2-color press. Presses with extensive folding and bindery capabilities have higher costs than those without. Web presses are generally more expensive than sheet-fed, etc. Confer with your printers in advance to determine the type of press that is best suited for your job. Having the right press can give one printer a *very* significant cost advantage over others for a particular job.

4. Paper Is Half the Cost

This old rule of thumb is close enough for most of your printing jobs. It's affected by two variables: The *amount* of paper used and its *cost*.

The printing equipment and the amount of paper are related. Sometimes changing the finished size of your printed piece by as little as 1/8" to 1/4" can result in dramatic savings, by allowing a printer to use a lower-cost press or one with an image size that results in less wasted paper. The best printers

will work with you in this area to help you get the lowest prices. But they will *never* volunteer the information, so you need to ask: **"Is there some small change I can make in this job that will save me lots of money?"**

Regarding the cost of the paper, consider carefully the weight, color, finish, grade and availability of the paper you specify. Will a slightly lighter weight stock, lesser quality, matte or offset finish, etc., produce the same results? Your printer can often recommend alternative papers that will significantly reduce your cost. Occasionally they'll even have paper on hand from a previous job that represents a real bargain. Again, the printer will *never* volunteer the information. To find out, ask: **"Is there another paper I can use that will save me lots of money?"**

If you really want to get into printing paper, here's a good reference that may put you ahead of even your printer:

How to Choose the Right Paper at the Right Price for Any Printing Job, by Mark Beach and Ken Russon. Coast-to-Coast Books, 2934 NE Sixteenth Avenue, Portland, OR 97212. Phone: (503) 282-5891.

5. You Can *Always* Get It Printed for Less

No matter how much (or little) you're now paying for any printing job, it's certain you could get it printed for less money without sacrificing quality. And sometimes for a *lot* less money.

There are two reasons you may not want to bother: (1.) It's hard *work* bidding and screening new suppliers, taking the time and effort of some of your best and busiest people, and (2.) you may need to change a long-time supplier relationship. But stack these reasons up against the likely savings before you ignore this potent source of increased profits.

REPRESENTATIVE COSTS OF DIRECT MAIL ITEMS

You need a way to evaluate the printing prices you're quoted and for doing your preliminary planning and budgeting; for example, estimating how costs might change as you change quantity, paper, number of colors, size, etc. The tables on the next two pages provide some representative costs for the major items normally used in direct mail.

These tables are reprinted, with permission, from The *DMA Statistical Fact Book* and are the creative brainchild of Shell R. Alpert, who calls them his "BALLPARK-BUDGET COSTIMATOR. ™" He explains:

"The sole purpose of the Tables shown here is to aid marketers in the initial stages of planning cost-effective direct mail campaigns. Because of production-cost variables (labor, materials, overhead, workload, markup, etc.), these prices may be as much as 20% higher or lower than actual supplier quotations. Usually, however, mailers who seek competitive bids from different vendors -- and who allow enough turnaround time for economical production -- will be able to meet (or likely beat) these prices.

"In some cases, dramatic cost reductions can be achieved by purchasing odd-lot, rem- nant, or surplus paper stocks (paper often accounts for 40% to 60% of printing costs) -- or by scheduling out-of-season production runs (hungry suppliers may be more interested in recovering overhead expenses than making a profit). Mail marketers are well-advised to obtain quotes not only from vendors, but also printing brokers and production-oriented agencies. (They frequently know where the real 'bargains' are hiding and waiting to be exploited.)

"Table prices do not include creative costs (copy, design, layout, etc.), nor the expense of preparing camera-ready mechanical art (color separations, printing negatives, etc.) Likewise, expenditures for original illustrations and photography must also be added." Furthermore, these prices do not include state or local taxes or shipping/delivery.

For more information contact:

Mr. Shell R. Alpert
Principal
ALPERT, O'NEIL, TIGRE & CO.
114 Lancaster Avenue
Mt. Gretna, PA 17064
Phone: (717) 964-3543

TYPICAL CATALOG DEVELOPMENT COSTS

FINISHED SIZE	Pages	Colors	Cost per thousand			
			25M	50M	100M	300M
8-1/2" X 11"	32	2	$492.10	$333.45	$253.89	$199.27
8-1/2" X 11"	32	4	642.11	442.56	322.11	243.06
8-1/2" X 11"	48	2	709.44	481.75	372.55	297.80
8-1/2" X 11"	48	4	880.08	605.85	449.41	344.58
8-1/2" X 11"	64	2	911.13	618.66	475.77	375.92
8-1/2" X 11"	64	4	1101.95	757.45	566.20	437.60
8-1/2" X 11"	96	2	1252.56	817.73	663.48	534.93
8-1/2" X 11"	96	4	1475.57	1019.39	764.10	599.18
5-1/2" X 8-1/2"	32	2	292.50	199.09	148.11	110.96
5-1/2" X 8-1/2"	32	4	381.98	264.17	188.78	134.43
5-1/2" X 8-1/2"	48	2	431.00	292.54	220.54	166.30
5-1/2" X 8-1/2"	48	4	530.01	364.55	264.26	192.24
5-1/2" X 8-1/2"	64	2	609.97	415.43	314.99	238.06
5-1/2" X 8-1/2"	64	4	757.06	522.41	376.59	273.03

Printed on 60# enamel, self-cover, saddle stitched. Photography and separations not included.

Source: Alpert O'Neill Tigre, 1992.

Representative Costs of Direct Mail Items

LITHO LETTERS (NOT PERSONALIZED)

FINISHED SIZE	ITEM	LEAVES/PAGES	STOCK	COLORS/SIDES	COST PER THOUSAND			
					10M	50M	100M	300M
8-1/2" X 11"	Letter*	1/1	60# Offset	1/1	$34.15	$15.85	$12.48	$ 8.54
8-1/2" X 11"	Letter*	1/1	24# Rag Bond	1/1	41.10	19.26	15.06	10.27
8-1/2" X 11"	Letter*	1/1	60# Offset	2/1	42.85	15.20	11.92	8.54
8-1/2" X 11"	Letter*	1/1	24# Rag Bond	2/1	52.83	18.08	14.33	10.27
8-1/2" X 11"	Letter*	1/2	60# Offset	1/2	40.53	17.47	13.97	10.20
8-1/2" X 11"	Letter*	1/2	24# Rag Bond	1/2	48.39	20.96	16.71	12.61
8-1/2" X 11"	Letter*	1/2	60# Offset	2/2	67.46	18.68	14.70	10.20
8-1/2" X 11"	Letter*	1/2	24# Rag Bond	2/2	81.18	22.34	17.73	12.61
8-1/2" x 11"**	Letter*	2/4	60# Offset	1/2	65.66	27.14	23.27	18.94
8-1/2" x 11"**	Letter*	2/4	24# Rag Bond	1/2	79.35	32.56	33.31	22.76
8-1/2" x 11"**	Letter*	2/4	60# Offset	2/2	84.87	27.59	23.79	18.94
8-1/2" x 11"**	Letter*	2/4	24# Rag Bond	2/2	99.67	33.12	28.47	22.76

*Folded twice to fit #10 envelope.
**11" x 17" folded once to 8-1/2" x 11"

COMPUTERIZED LETTERS (PERSONALIZED)

MEGATYPING[a] FINISHED SIZE	ITEM	LEAVES/PAGES	STOCK	COLORS/SIDES	COST PER THOUSAND	
					50M	100M
8-1/2" x 11"*	Letter	1/1	60# Offset	1/1	$146.71	$100.92
8-1/2" x 11"*	Letter	1/1	24# Rag Bond	1/1	150.02	103.26
8-1/2" x 11"*	Letter	1/1	60# Offset	2/1	148.86	102.89
8-1/2" x 11"*	Letter	1/1	24# Rag Bond	2/1	152.21	104.55
8-1/2" x 11"*	Letter	2/2	60# Offset	1/1 ea.	202.09	197.87
8-1/2" x 11"*	Letter	2/2	24# Rag Bond	1/1 ea.	207.17	201.47
8-1/2" x 11"*	Letter	2/2	60# Offset	2/1 ea.	205.10	199.86
8-1/2" x 11"*	Letter	2/2	24# Rag Bond	2/1 ea.	209.18	203.00

XEROX 9700[b] FINISHED SIZE	ITEM	LEAVES/PAGES	STOCK	COLORS/SIDES	COST PER THOUSAND	
					50M	100M
8-1/2" x 11"*	Letter	1/1	60# Offset	1/1	$56.47	$47.92
8-1/2" x 11"*	Letter	1/1	24# Rag Bond	1/1	59.69	50.30
8-1/2" x 11"*	Letter	1/1	60# Offset	2/1	57.71	49.57
8-1/2" x 11"*	Letter	1/1	24# Rag Bond	2/1	61.31	51.76
8-1/2" x 11"*	Letter	2/2	60# Offset	1/2 ea.	96.45	89.05
8-1/2" x 11"*	Letter	2/2	24# Rag Bond	1/2 ea.	99.25	91.27
8-1/2" x 11"*	Letter	2/2	60# Offset	2/2 ea.	100.38	89.75
8-1/2" x 11"*	Letter	2/2	24# Rag Bond	2/2 ea.	103.40	92.59

*Folded to fit #10 envelope.
(a) Produced by computer driven typewriters, indistinguishable from hand-typing, superb quality.
(b) Sheetfed laser process, very clean and sharp, close to word-processing quality (but may "crack" on foldlines).
Prices for all computerized letters include litho-printed letterheads and signatures in 1 or 2 colors. Possible charges for data conversion, reformatting tapes, special programming, embedded variables, etc., are not included.

REPLY CARDS/ORDER FORMS

FINISHED SIZE	ITEM	STOCK	COLORS/SIDES	COST PER THOUSAND		
				10M	50M	100M
5-1/2" x 3-1/2"	BRC	7 pt. Hi-Bulk	1/2	$25.75	$11.15	$9.25
5-1/2" x 3-1/2"	BRC	7 pt. Hi-Bulk	2/2	39.40	14.75	12.05
8-1/2" x 5-1/2"	BRC	7 pt. Hi-Bulk	1/2	40.55	19.10	15.70
8-1/2" x 5-1/2"	BRC	7 pt. Hi-Bulk	2/2	68.40	24.25	20.65
5-1/2" x 3-1/2"	Order Form	60# Offset	1/2	23.95	10.30	8.35
5-1/2" x 3-1/2"	Order Form	60# Offset	2/2	37.30	13.70	11.10
8-1/2" x 5-1/2"	Order Form	60# Offset	1/2	38.40	17.75	14.35
8-1/2" x 5-1/2"	Order Form	60# Offset	2/2	64.50	22.60	18.80

Source: Shell Alpert, Alpert O'Neil Tigre & Co., 1992.

Representative Costs of Direct Mail Items

SELF-MAILING FORMATS

FINISHED SIZE	ITEM	LEAVES/PANELS	STOCK	COLORS/SIDES	COST PER THOUSAND		
					10M	50M	100M
3-1/2" x 6"	Double Card	2/4	65# Cover	1/2	$54.88	$20.71	$16.95
3-1/2" x 6"	Double Card	2/4	65# Cover	2/2	69.55	22.77	18.07
3-2/3" x 8-1/2"**	Self-Mailer	3/6	65# Cover	1/2	52.32	28.26	21.76
3-2/3" x 8-1/2"**	Self-Mailer	3/6	65# Cover	2/2	104.73	30.13	23.11
5-1/2" x 8-1/2"***	Self-Mailer	2/4	65# Cover	1/2	62.32	28.26	21.76
5-1/2" x 8-1/2"***	Self-Mailer	2/4	65# Cover	2/2	104.73	30.13	23.11
8-1/2" x 11"****	Self-Mailer	2/4	65# Cover	1/2	94.10	39.70	36.72
8-1/2" x 11"****	Self-Mailer	2/4	65# Cover	2/2	128.06	45.39	38.00
8-1/2" x 11"****	Self-Mailer	2/4	65# Cover	4/2	192.60	59.32	48.62

* 8-1/2" x 11" folded twice.
** 8-1/2" x 11" folded once.
*** 11" x 17" folded once.

BROCHURES, FOLDERS, ETC.

FINISHED SIZE	ITEM	LEAVES/PANELS	STOCK	COLORS/SIDES	COST PER THOUSAND			
					10M	50M	100M	300M
3-1/2" x 6"	Folder	2/4	60# Coated	1/2	$38.00	$27.50	$22.30	—
3-1/2" x 6"	Folder	2/4	60# Coated	2/2	66.75	34.50	26.05	—
5-1/2" x 8-1/2"	Brochure	2/4	60# Offset	1/2	40.10	18.93	14.90	—
5-1/2" x 8-1/2"	Brochure	2/4	60# Offset	2/2	68.35	19.87	15.65	—
5-1/2" x 8-1/2"	Brochure	2/4	60# Offset	4/2	99.40	34.40	22.15	—
8-1/2" x 11"	Brochure	2/4	60# Offset	1/2	65.85	27.85	24.25	20.72
8-1/2" x 11"	Brochure	2/4	60# Offset	2/2	83.15	28.30	24.95	21.05
8-1/2" x 11"	Brochure	2/4	60# Offset	4/2	101.50	37.40	31.25	24.25
8-1/2" x 11"	Broadside	*/8	60# Coated	2/2	154.50	86.50	72.00	57.47
8-1/2" x 11"	Broadside	*/8	60# Coated	4/2	223.20	105.40	80.10	60.10
8-1/2" x 11"	Broadside	*/8	80# Coated	2/2	171.70	98.00	79.95	64.45
8-1/2" x 11"	Broadside	*/8	80# Coated	4/2	240.25	118.20	89.35	66.80

* 22" x 17" folded twice to form eight 8-1/2" x 11" panels; same as 8-page booklet, but not trimmed & stitched.

CARRIER ENVELOPES
STOCK 24# WHITE WOVE

NO.	SIZE	STYLE	COLOR	WINDOW	COST PER THOUSAND		
					10M	50M	100M
6-1/4	3-9/16" x 6"	Diagonal Seam	1	cello	$31.10	$15.97	$13.35
6-1/4	3-9/16" x 6"	Diagonal Seam	1	open	29.90	14.81	12.26
6-1/4	3-9/16" x 6"	Diagonal Seam	2	cello	33.44	16.47	13.76
6-1/4	3-9/16" x 6"	Diagonal Seam	2	open	32.37	15.32	12.72
9	3-7/8" x 8-7/8"	Diagonal Seam	1	cello	31.70	16.91	14.84
9	3-7/8" x 8-7/8"	Diagonal Seam	1	open	30.41	15.81	13.66
9	3-7/8" x 8-7/8"	Diagonal Seam	2	cello	33.95	17.38	15.20
9	3-7/8" x 8-7/8"	Diagonal Seam	2	open	32.72	16.17	14.05
10	4-1/8" x 9-1/2"	Diagonal Seam	1	cello	34.45	17.41	15.34
10	4-1/8" x 9-1/2"	Diagonal Seam	1	open	33.40	16.14	14.28
10	4-1/8" x 9-1/2"	Diagonal Seam	2	cello	37.05	17.88	15.75
10	4-1/8" x 9-1/2"	Diagonal Seam	2	open	35.68	16.59	14.56
—	6" x 9"	Booklet, open side	1	cello	74.00	49.71	47.10
—	6" x 9"	Booklet, open side	1	open	72.63	48.44	45.85
—	6" x 9"	Booklet, open side	2	cello	76.60	50.38	47.65
—	6" x 9"	Booklet, open side	2	open	75.28	49.12	46.25

NOTE: For closed-face (no window) envelope, deduct $1.25/M from open-window price.

REPLY ENVELOPES
STYLE = DIAGONAL SEAM
STOCK = 24# WHITE WOVE

NO.	SIZE	ITEM	COLOR	COST PER THOUSAND		
				10M	50M	100M
6-1/4	3-9/16" x 6"	BRE	1	$30.02	$14.96	$12.16
6-1/4	3-9/16" x 6"	BRE	2	32.47	15.26	12.56
7-3/4	3-7/8" x 7-1/2"	BRE	1	30.69	15.12	12.43
7-3/4	3-7/8" x 7-1/2"	BRE	2	33.02	15.58	12.79
10	4-1/8" x 9-1/2"	BRE	1	33.47	16.26	14.22
10	4-1/8" x 9-1/2"	BRE	2	35.97	16.74	14.63

Source: Shell Alpert, Alpert O'Neil Tigre & Co., 1992.

MORE TIPS FOR BUYING PRINTING

Choose a Middle-Ground on Quality

Cheap-looking materials kill results, while top quality is too expensive and isn't noticed by enough people to improve results very much.

Shipping Charges Can Add Up

The most economical situation is one in which all of your suppliers are in the same location. When your suppliers (such as printers, envelope makers, computer service bureaus and mailhouse) are not in one geographic area, freight rates become an important consideration. For example, if you select suppliers in different locales because they are less expensive, you could find your savings eaten up by freight costs. By taking the time to review supplier location and freight rates, you can reduce the shipping expenses.

Always Approve Bluelines, Color Keys or Proof Sheets

Always make sure you see and approve the blueline or color key. In critical cases, have someone approve proof sheets at the printer when the job is run.

Proofread the blueline and/or color key carefully. Look for muddy halftones/ photographs, type that's shifted or lost, wrong colors, crooked placement, etc. Do *not* assume that just because your artwork was correct, the bluelines or color keys will also be correct.

Small Printers Are Sometimes Best

Don't be afraid to deal with a small printer who has the required "press power" for your job. If you're a prospective steady or large account for them, you'll get their undivided attention because your business can be counted on to pay the overhead. Besides, small shops often don't use salespersons and, therefore, have more margin in the job for negotiation.

Bindery Errors Are Common

Bindery errors (folding, die-cutting, stitching, etc.) can, and often do, completely ruin a correctly printed job. Furnishing clear instructions and unmistakable mock-ups will minimize -- but not totally eliminate -- this threat to your schedule.

Set Direct Mail Print Quantities *After* Lists Are Received

Always figure print quantities on the basis of final list counts "as received" (and after merge/purge, if you're doing it), never on the basis of the counts "as ordered." And allow for machine spoilage at the mailhouse; they'll give you guidelines on the average you should allow, which is rarely 1%.

Buy Envelopes Directly from Manufacturer

Unless your envelope quantities are small or their production is closely integrated into your other items, it's usually better to buy envelopes from an envelope manufacturer instead of from a printer or mailhouse. This offers you a chance to take advantage of trade discounts and attractive payment terms, as well as a wider choice of sizes, papers, colors, etc., *and* special help that can result in better envelopes at much lower cost.

Consider "Just-in-Time" Printing

The new Xerox DocuTech 600 dpi high-speed scanner-laser printer combination may revolutionize printing for training and information materials (but not for direct mail). It's capable of storing each page of your document in digital form where it can easily be printed, edited or replaced. This makes printing on demand, or "just-in-time" printing, a practical reality. Besides, copy quality is superb, easily matching most offset printing. Call around to your local business copying centers, and go see this hi-tech wonder for yourself.

GETTING YOUR MAILING MADE

The mailhouse (often called a *lettershop* in the trade) is your key to making successful mailings. Select a house with quality and integrity, and your problems will be few or none. Select the wrong mailhouse -- or attempt to do it yourself -- and the job can get very complicated. Here are some tips for making it easy:

Choose Your Mailhouse Carefully

Always check references on a mailhouse, and make a personal visit to see for yourself how the operation looks. This is one part of your mailing plan that can't be checked (until it's too late, if then), so reliability and integrity mean everything. Check especially for the following ten points:

1. Length of time in business
2. History of on-time mailings
3. Good prices
4. Capability to handle all your needs (including computer processing, on-line coding and fulfillment if needed)
5. Good U.S. Post Office relationships
6. Careful receiving inspection
7. Secure/insured inventory storage
8. History of accurate inventory counts
9. Minimum set-up, waste and spoilage
10. Accurate billings

Check Mailability Early and Often

Check the insertability and handling of all components in your mailing *before* printing. Give it to your mailhouse, or -- better still -- get the opinion of two or more mailhouses.

Get your Post Office to "sign-off" on the acceptability of your mail piece in advance. Start at the concept stage and get their approval on the final mock-up. In addition, get your mailhouse to check ahead with *their* Post Office on the piece's acceptability, if they'll mail from a different post office than yours.

Write Out All Mailhouse Instructions

Make sure everything about the job is clear. On the next page is a sample form that has worked well for us, both to relay instructions to the mailhouse and to record job costs and response. If necessary, visit the mailhouse in advance to explain the job.

Follow up with the mailhouse to make sure all your printing has arrived and that there's enough on hand for your mailing. Your mailhouse should conduct a receiving inspection of all shipments and notify you at once of any shortages or other discrepancies.

Here's How to "Decoy" a Cheshire List

Prepare pressure-sensitive labels with your name and address, and put them *over* a name on each rented Cheshire list in the proper ZIP code sequence. Be sure the label is key coded the same as the list itself. This will give you a sample of what was actually mailed to that list and how long it took to receive it.

Postal Advances

Make sure your postage money has been properly paid and figured correctly for the class of mail, quantities, etc. (See separate treatment of Postal Rate and Classification Decisions later this chapter.) Most mailhouses will bill you for their labor charges but require postage amounts to be paid before mailing.

With a new mailhouse, don't pay the postage advance too soon. Alternatively, make the check out to the Postmaster.

Save Old Inventory

Make sure your mailhouse does not throw away any of your materials without your approval. Even outdated items might be usable for a later mailing under emergency conditions.

Set Up a BRM Deposit Account

If your volume is sufficient, establish a deposit account at your post office so your Business Reply Mail, Address Corrections and other charges are deducted automatically. This greatly simplifies day-to-day operations and allows reduced rates on some types of return mail.

Representative Mailhouse Costs

Here are some budget and planning costs for typical mailhouse operations. They come from Shell Alpert's data (referenced earlier in this chapter) and from my own experience. All include 4-up Cheshire labeling, envelope sealing, sorting (list already in ZIP Code sequence), tying, bagging/traying and mailing via regular Third-Class bulk rate.

Item	Cost per M
Catalogs/Self-Mailers	$12 - $20/M
#10 Envelopes	
1 - 3 Prefolded items inserted	$22 - $26/M
4 - 6 Prefolded items inserted	$24 - $30/M
6" X 9" Envelopes	
1 - 3 Prefolded items inserted	$25 - $30/M
4 - 6 Prefolded items inserted	$29 - $36/M
Postal metering	Add $2/M
Machine stamp affixing	Add $5/M

Sample Mailhouse Instructions

MAILING RECORD & JOB ORDER

Job No. _____

Name of Mailing _____ Date to be Mailed _____

Source of List _____ Date of List _____

Purpose of Mailing _____ Total Number _____

Dates Mailed:
No. Mailed: Total

Items Mailed: Unit Cost(¢)   SALES:
                                          Last Name   Co.   Date

1. _____
2. _____
3. _____
4. _____
5. _____
6. _____

Outer Envelope _____

Postage (_____ class) _____

Handling (Insert, Meter, Sort, etc.) _____

Cost of List _____

Cost of Labels _____

Other Costs (Specify _____)

Total Unit Cost _____

No. Mailed x Unit Cost = _____ x _____ = Total Cost .... $ _____

Reservation Coding .... _____   No. of Sales .... _____

No. Returned Undeliverable ...... _____   Cost per Sale .... $ _____

Remarks or Special Instructions _____

WHAT YOU NEED TO KNOW ABOUT TODAY'S U.S. POSTAL SERVICE (USPS)

If you're going to market training and information, you're going to use the mail. It's that simple! So here's some of what you need to know in order to use the mail economically and well.

Controlling Costs Is What Drives Today's USPS

A postal rate increase is the kind of front-page news no one wants. That's why the USPS is "under the gun" to control their costs. But with 800,000 employees, controlling costs means controlling *labor* costs. They're doing it two ways: (1.) by automating as much as possible and as fast as possible and (2.) by incentivizing mailers to do more of the Post Offices' work *before* they mail. The result is that some high-volume mailers actually pay *lower* postage costs today than they did before the last rate increase.

Visit Your Local Section Center

To understand what's involved in automating the mail, take a tour of the facility where your mail is sorted and routed (this is probably *not* your local Post Office). Equipment is being maintained during daylight hours, so visit after 6:00 p.m. when they're processing the day's mail.

Here's what you'll see: First the day's mail is trayed so it's all facing the same way and reading from the same side. This is done by high-speed machines that locate the stamp and flip the mail over appropriately. Next, each piece is read and barcoded, either by optical character readers (OCRs) or manually for those pieces the OCRs can't read. Finally, the barcoded mail is machine-sorted to its destination delivery office and shipped.

Once the day's outgoing mail is shipped, the second half of the night's work begins. Now, incoming mail received from all over the country (and the world) is combined and sorted by sector, segment and carrier route sequence for all the post offices and letter-carriers in the service area. Since the incoming mail is already barcoded, it's sorted by the same equipment that processed the outgoing mail a few hours earlier. The final sorting is done by the letter carriers at the local Post Office before they leave to deliver the mail.

It won't take you long to see why USPS rates, discounts and surcharges revolve around: (1.) size and weight uniformity for more/better machine handling, (2.) accurate addressing *and* ZIP coding to speed the OCRs that read the address and spray on the barcodes, (3.) presorting by mailers *before* they deliver their mail to the Post Office, to save handling, and (4.) prebarcoding to save the OCR step altogether.

Why ZIP + 4 Is So Important

Currently, the first half of the letter carriers' day is spent "casing" their mail, or getting it sorted in the order they deliver mail on their route. If the mail could *already* be sorted in this order when letter carriers receive it, their in-office time could be cut in half and their delivery time correspondingly increased. That's what's behind ZIP + 4, and the new advanced 11-digit Delivery Point BarCode (DPBC), that adds the last two digits of the street address to the ZIP + 4.

How to Read the Barcode

Today's Delivery Point BarCode (DPBC) encodes the nine digits of the ZIP + 4 code, plus two additional numbers from within the address, generally the last two digits of the street address, plus a correction character (used by the barcode reader to catch reading errors) for a total of 12 digits.

The barcode itself consists of 62 bars, five bars for each of the 12 digits, plus a "frame bar" at each end. Each digit is represented by two long bars (read as 1s) and three short bars (read as 0s), much like the binary number system used by your desktop computer.

Reading and understanding the barcode is simple: The digits 0 through 9 have been assigned to these combinations of 1s and 0s:

```
1    00011
2    00101
3    00110
4    01001
5    01010
6    01100
7    10001
8    10010
9    10100
0    11000
```

Here's what each part of the barcode means:

Evolution of the Barcode

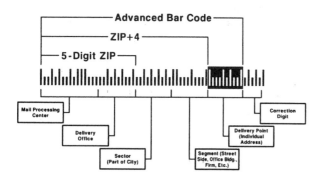

To see how it works, the bottom of this page shows a typical address and the barcode that goes with it:

The sum of the 12 digits in the barcode must always be a multiple of ten. This determines the value of the correction character used. In the example, the sum of the 11 digits of the delivery point address is 46. Using a correction character of four makes the sum of all 12 characters 50, a multiple of ten. If the sum of the digits is not multiple of ten, an error has been made and the barcode will not be used.

How the USPS Keeps Barcodes Accurate

When a letter passes through the OCR or is processed by a human operator, more than just the ZIP Code is read. In fact, both the street address line *and* the City, State and ZIP Code are read and compared against the Post Office Master File of all addresses and ZIP Codes. In this process, the barcode that's sprayed on the piece may be different than it would be by merely reading what's on the letter; for example, if a ZIP Code or street address has been changed.

That's why mailers who prebarcode their own mail must now have specially certified software, regularly updated with the latest USPS address information. It's called CASS certification, for <u>C</u>oding <u>A</u>ccuracy <u>S</u>upport <u>S</u>ystem, and a Post Office Form 3553 must be submitted with each prebarcoded mailing to show that the addressing software has a current certification.

Three Sizes of Mail

Now that we understand more about what's going on behind the scenes with the address and how it's used, let's turn to the package. For marketing training and information products/services, there are only three mailing packages of interest: cards, letters and non-letters.

Cards are rectangular in shape, at least .007" thick and not larger than 4-1/2" x 6" nor smaller than 3-1/2" x 5".

Delivery-Point BarCode (DPBC) Example

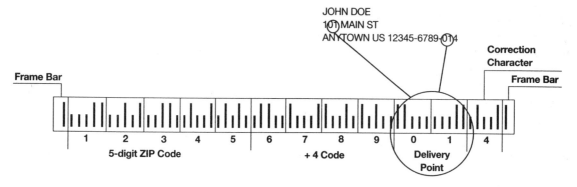

Letters can be as long as 11-1/2", as high as 6-1/8", as thick as 1/4" and as heavy as 2-1/2 oz. What the USPS calls a "letter" is *not* synonymous with "envelope," which is why many catalogs and self-mailers have been redesigned to "letter" size and shape.

Non-letters are everything else, typically "flats," parcels, etc.

Restrictions and Surcharges

Minimum Size. Pieces which are 1/4" thick or less that do not meet the following requirements are prohibited from the mails:

- At least .007" thick
- At least 3-1/2" high
- Rectangular in shape
- At least 5" long

NOTE: Pieces greater than 1/2" thick can be mailed even if they measure less than 3-1/2" x 5".

Nonstandard Mail. All First-Class mail weighing one once or less and all single-piece-rate Third-Class mail weighing one ounce or less is nonstandard and subject to a 10-cent surcharge in addition to the applicable postage and fee, if any of the following dimensions are exceeded:

- 11-1/2" long
- 6-1/8" high
- 1/4" thick
- Or if the length divided by height is less than 1.2 or greater than 2.5.

NOTE: For First-Class presort, the nonstandard surcharge is five cents, and applies to the first ounce only. Pieces subject to a surcharge are not eligible for ZIP + 4 barcoded presorted rate.

Self-Mailers, Folders, Booklets and Double Postcards. The fold must now be at the bottom. Tabs, wafer seals or spot glue must be used to keep the open side closed. Only one closure, in the center, is needed on 24-pound or heavier stock, while two are needed, one at each end, for lighter weight stock.

Barcode Area. If you prebarcode your mail, the barcode can be almost anywhere, including on the address label or in the address area. If you don't prebarcode, you must leave the bottom right corner of the mailing piece clear (4-3/4" wide by 5/8" high) so the USPS OCR machines can spray on the barcode.

First-Class Rates

Cents

Letters

First ounce	
Nonpresorted	29.0
Presorted, 3/5 digits	24.8
Presorted, carrier route	23.0
Each additional ounce (up to 11 ounces)	23.0

Machinable letters that meet postal regulations and have ZIP + 4 codes or barcodes are eligible for the following first ounce automation rates:

With ZIP + 4 code, nonpresorted	27.6
With ZIP + 4 code, presorted 3/5 digits	24.2
Prebarcoded, nonpresorted	27.0
Prebarcoded, presorted, 3 digits	23.9
Prebarcoded, presorted, 5 digits	23.3

For presorted mail weighing more than two ounces, subtract four cents per piece.

Cards	19.0
With ZIP + 4 code, nonpresorted	18.0
With ZIP + 4 code, presorted	16.4
Prebarcoded, nonpresorted	17.7
Prebarcoded, presorted, 3 digits	16.1
Prebarcoded, presorted, 5 digits	15.5

Third-Class Bulk-Rate Mail

Only mail weighing up to 2.5 ounces per piece can be paid for at the per-piece rates shown here. Mail weighing more than 2.5 ounces per piece is paid for at a piece rate plus a pound rate. Ask your Post Office for details.

	Regular (Cents)	Nonprofit (Cents)
Letters		
Basic	19.8	11.1
3/5 digit presorted	16.5	9.8
Carrier route	13.1	7.4
Saturation	12.4	7.1

Machinable letters that meet postal regulations and have ZIP + 4 codes or barcodes are eligible for automation rates as follows:

	Regular (Cents)	Nonprofit (Cents)
Basic		
With ZIP + 4 code	18.9	10.4
Prebarcoded	17.9	9.4
3/5-digit presorted		
With ZIP + 4 code	16.1	9.4
Prebarcoded, 3-digit presorted	15.4	8.8
Prebarcoded, 5-digit presorted	14.6	8.1

Non-letters (flats, parcels, etc.)

Basic	23.3
3/5 digit presorted	18.7
Carrier route	14.2
Saturation mail	12.7

Third-Class bulk mail at the per-piece rate is eligible for destination entry discounts. You can deduct 1.2 cents from each piece of the bulk-rate regular mail deposited at the destination bulk-mail center and 1.7 cents for each piece deposited at the destination sectional center. Or, if you sort your mail to the carrier route or use saturation mail, you can deduct 2.2 cents for each piece deposited at the destination delivery office.

HOW TO GET YOUR UNDELIVERABLE MAIL RETURNED

There are different techniques for First-Class and Third-Class mail.

First-Class

To begin with, remember that First-Class mail is automatically forwarded at no additional cost for up to one year, provided the USPS has a forwarding address. This gets your mail delivered but, of course, doesn't tell you the new address. If your mail cannot be delivered as addressed and is not forwardable, it will be returned to you at no charge, along with the reason for nondelivery. Your return address must be in the upper left-hand corner of the address side of the piece in order for it to be returned to you.

If you place either ADDRESS COR-RECTION REQUESTED or DO NOT FORWARD near your return address, it will not be forwarded and will be returned to you with the new address at no charge.

If you use FORWARDING AND AD-DRESS CORRECTION REQUESTED, the piece will be forwarded at no charge or, if not forwardable, returned to you at no charge. If the piece is forwardable, you'll get an address-correction form returned to you for a 30-cent charge.

Third-Class

If your Third-Class mail is undeliverable as addressed and you do not print any service endorsement (such as ADDRESS COR-RECTION REQUESTED or FORWARD-ING AND RETURN POSTAGE GUAR-ANTEED), your undeliverable mail will be thrown away. It will also be tossed out if you use DO NOT FORWARD.

If you want to have your mail either forwarded or returned or you want to get the new address, here's what you can use:

With ADDRESS CORRECTION RE-QUESTED, your mail will not be forwarded and the entire piece will be returned to you with either the new address or the reason for nondelivery. You'll pay the Third-Class, single-piece rate of 25 cents each if the piece weighs an ounce or less. If it's over one ounce but not more than two, you'll receive a form with the new address for 30 cents each.

FORWARDING AND RETURN POSTAGE GUARANTEED gets your piece forwarded at no charge. But if it's not forwardable, it will be returned to you for a charge of 62 cents for pieces weighing one ounce or less and $1.12 for pieces weighing more than one ounce but not more than two ounces.

If you use both endorsements above, the

piece will be forwarded at no charge, and a separate address-correction notice will be returned to you for a charge of 30 cents. If the piece is not forwardable, it will be returned to you and you'll be charged the appropriate fee depending on its weight.

DO NOT FORWARD means your piece will be destroyed if it's not deliverable as addressed.

DO NOT FORWARD and ADDRESS CORRECTION REQUESTED and RETURN POSTAGE GUARANTEED means your piece will not be forwarded and will be returned with the new address or the reason for nondelivery. You'll pay the single-piece rate of 25 cents if it's one ounce or less and 45 cents if it's over one ounce but under two ounces.

MAKING POSTAL RATE AND CLASSIFICATION DECISIONS

Because of technology and changes in the postal regulations, postage decisions have been somewhat simplified. There are now basically only four classes of U.S. postage of interest to those marketing training and information:

1. Express mail
2. Priority mail
3. First-Class
4. Bulk-rate Third-Class

Deciding which to use depends on the following nine factors:

1. Cost

Express Mail rates now start at $8.35 for an 8-oz. or less letter, Priority Mail starts at $2.90, and First-Class postage is 29 cents for the first ounce and 23 cents for each additional ounce. Third-Class bulk-rate postage for letters starts at 19.8 cents per piece for the first 2.5 ounces, drops to 16.5 cents for 3/5-digit presort (125 pieces or 15 lbs.) and as low as 12.4 cents for saturation mailings. More detailed information on USPS First-Class and Third-Class rates is presented in the previous section.

These costs greatly affect your mailing budget. And each class of service offers certain advantages/disadvantages you'll need to balance against these costs/savings. Read on.

2. Speed of Delivery

Here's the way delivery times for the above four classes of mail compare:

1. Express Mail: next day delivery guaranteed (!)
2. Priority Mail: usually delivered the next day.
3. First-Class: one day to one week delivery.
4. Third-Class bulk-rate: generally one week to three weeks delivery.

Express Mail is the only class of service with next day delivery "guaranteed." But I've been disappointed that a number of Express Mail packages I've sent were *not* delivered on time -- including several that were actually returned to me several days later for some technicality. Based on past performance, both Federal Express and United Parcel Service seem to offer more reliable overnight delivery than the USPS.

3. Timing Control

This is related to speed of delivery and grew out of the old direct mail practice which said that mail received on Tuesday and Wednesday did 5%-15% better than mail received any other day. It's not too important any more, particularly for mailings to businesses.

4. Perceived Importance

This refers to the perception of the recipient, their family, secretary, mailroom personnel -- even the letter-carrier. Actually, on business mail using a metermark, there's little to distinguish bulk-rate Third-Class mail from First-Class mail, except for the difference in postage and the very small "BK.RT." near the metermark.

5. Forwarding

Mail sent First-Class and higher will be forwarded for up to one year after an address change is filed. For lists which are good-but-old, mailing First-Class can pay off over Third-Class bulk-rate.

6. Package Weight

Because Third-Class bulk-rate mail permits up to 2.5 ounces for the basic rate, the difference between First- and Third-Class can be appreciable for direct mail packages weighing more than one ounce.

7. Content Uniformity

To be eligible for Third-Class bulk-rate mail, the pieces must all be identical outside and inside, with no personalization other than that necessary for mailing. This rules out Third-Class bulk-rate for billings and similar correspondence and for truly personalized mailings where each letter may be different.

8. ZIP Code Availability/ Sequencing

To be eligible for Third-Class bulk-rate mailing, each address must contain the ZIP code, and all the pieces must be presorted in ZIP-code sequence.

9. Quantity Mailed

Bulk-rate Third-Class mail requires a minimum of 200 pieces or 50 lbs. to be mailed at one time.

GETTING YOUR MAIL DELIVERED INSIDE LARGE ORGANIZATIONS

Some large organization mail rooms are not delivering Third-Class bulk-rate mail to their employees or are delivering it only when time permits. Here are a few things you can do to improve deliverability of your mail in these organizations.

First, be sure that your house list (and, if possible, lists you rent as well) contains building or department numbers, internal mail stops or other delivery-point codes for those in large organizations. Chapter 13 has tips for getting these codes and for keeping them up-to-date. Sometimes their presence on each piece is all it takes to save vital time in the mail room and get your mail delivered.

Next, if you're sending hundreds or even thousands of pieces of mail to one location, imagine how overwhelming that looks when it arrives at the mail room. "Flighting" -- breaking up one large mailing into a series of smaller ones mailed at different times over several weeks -- is one way to reduce the apparent volume hitting the mailroom "all at once." Test this for your mailings.

Finally, remember that First-Class mail *must* be delivered to the addressee by law, even in a large organization. Third-Class mail does not. This might influence your choice of postage.

SHOWCASES AND OTHER EVENTS DESIGNED PRIMARILY FOR SELLING

Showcases are free, several-hour events used to introduce prospects to a produce/service they can buy. Both parts of this definition are important.

First, showcases are just like any other event -- and obey all the rules of event promotion discussed in Chapters 5 and 6. Second, the purpose of the showcase is to sell. It's a step in the face-to-face sales process and not an end in itself. Face-to-face selling is described in Chapter 4.

What Else Are They Called?

Previews, overviews, orientations, introductions, information sessions, demonstrations and film festivals, among others.

Who Uses Showcases?

The following examples show some possibilities:

1. For years Dale Carnegie and Evelyn Wood have successfully sold courses by offering short, free, evening preview sessions at local hotels.

2. CareerTrack Seminars earn substantial income from "back-of-the-room" sales of books and other materials at their low-cost, one-day seminars.

3. A $40 million international training firm regularly schedules "orientation sessions" to acquaint potential clients with their products and services. These are conducted in their local offices, by their local staff. The sessions are run anytime they need additional sales leads. A $15 million communications training firm does the same thing.

4. A training company, just under $1 million annual sales, conducted nationwide showcases in nine metropolitan areas to develop sales leads for their 3-day management training program. They sent 55,000 invitations and obtained 325 people at the nine sessions. Two years later, as a result of these showcases, they reached $5 million in annual sales.

5. A West Coast training firm seeking to enter a new market scheduled one showcase. They mailed 1,200 invitations and got 70 attendees from the new industry, all Vice Presidents or above, at the showcase.

6. A sales trainer gives after-dinner speeches to sell his books and job aids.

In general, showcases work well for selling:

- Big-ticket training and information programs/events
- Consulting/professional services
- Investments
- Real estate/time-shares
- Books, software

When Are They Used?

They can be used as an early step in the face-to-face selling process. Think of them as an opportunity to make one sales call on 20 well-qualified prospects rather than 20 separate sales calls on one less-qualified prospect each.

Showcases give you the chance to make a presentation to those who would *never* agree to a one-on-one, face-to-face sales call in their office. By following the process outlined here you will be surprised how many top executives will attend your showcase.

When Not to Use Showcases

Rule No.1: Never hold a showcase if you can't follow up on the resulting sales leads in three to five working days (or are unable to close the sale at the showcase).

Time after time I've seen successfully run showcases fail to produce sales simply because the sponsors didn't have the time or personnel to follow up on the sales leads. One example was a consulting firm seeking to open a new territory where they had no resident salespeople. They held the showcase and got plenty of good sales leads. But the existing salespeople were all fully committed in their own territories over 450 miles away and couldn't follow up on the sales leads in the new area. These leads all "evaporated" in 45 days.

Rule No. 2: Never hold a showcase without a clear, specific product to sell.

It's a waste of time to merely acquaint people with your firm's capabilities or show *all* your products and services. This may get leads for the long-term and build customer relationships, but it's *not* a showcase.

How Well Do They Work?

Judge for yourself; Here are some typical figures:

400 - 500	Invitations sent ($4 - $5 each)
100 - 150	Positive responses received
40 - 50	Say they'll attend
25 - 30	Actually attend
5 - 10	Interested enough to get a follow-up visit the next week
3 - 5	Buy

Steps in the Showcase Process

To conceive, plan and execute a successful showcase, you need to accomplish the following nine (9) steps. We'll expand on these steps in the rest of this chapter.

1. Pinpoint your target market

   a. Who is your customer?
   b. Where are they located?
   c. Who to invite?
   d. Getting the management level you want

2. Select your best product or service

   a. Identify your "biggest WOW"
   b. Degree of participant involvement/interaction

3. Design your showcase

   a. Timing considerations: when, time of day, how long
   b. Where to hold it
   c. Room arrangement/set-up
   d. Food/beverage function(s)
   e. Participant materials
   f. Your personnel attending
   g. Should you include your satisfied customers?

4. Select your location(s)

5. Book your facility(ies)

6. Promote well in advance

   a. Obtain the best mailing list
   b. Design your invitation package
   c. Mail at the right time
   d. Handle incoming registrations professionally
   e. Follow-up several times in advance to keep attendance high

7. Hold your showcase

   a. Start on time
   b. Set up the situation
   c. Let participants experience that "big WOW"
   d. Tell how they can buy and what it costs
   e. Allow time for questions/discussion
   f. Segue to the refreshments
   g. Talk to each attendee
   h. Book sales calls/appointments with the hottest prospects before they leave

8. Follow up with prospects immediately afterward

9. Evaluate the economics: Should you do it again?

PLANNING YOUR SHOWCASE

What Should You Showcase?

I once used a presentation consultant named Paul Beall. He liked to remind those planning an important presentation about "the menu muddle." When you visit a new restaurant you have two ways to learn about it. One way is to ask for one bite of everything on the menu. You'd get about half way through the menu and you'd be stuffed or sick. No one eats this way. The second way is to ask for the one meal that's the specialty of the house. And you judge the whole restaurant on that one, well-served meal.

Most of us want to tell people about our organization by giving them one bite of everything on our menu. The result is that they get indigestion. Better to give them one well-served meal -- our specialty -- and let them judge our entire firm or personal capability by that one item.

That's a showcase. In two or three hours you serve up your one biggest "wow" -- what you know from experience produces the greatest excitement. And your participants judge your entire organization on that basis.

If you're fortunate enough to have a number of "wows," showcase the one that "gets participants' hands dirty": the one that has the greatest potential for participant involvement during the showcase.

Who Do You Invite?

Since the showcase is a step in the sales process, the answer to this question is easy. It's your best prospects.

Your best prospects come in two categories: (1.) those who are already somewhere in your sales pipeline (see Chapter 4) and (2.) those you want to do business with who have not yet shown that they're interested.

Most training and information businesses easily identify their current prospects. They're the ones you're trying to move to the next step in the sales process. If you have salespeople in the showcase territory, let them help decide which prospects to invite.

People in the second group -- those you want to do business with -- are only slightly more elusive. For big-ticket products and services, you usually know their organizations even if you don't know the specific individuals' names. A few telephone calls can usually get those names. You can also select prospects by industry, company size and/or management level using directories, which you verify by telephone.

There's a third constituency to consider including in your showcase: your current satisfied customers. At least one training company has built their business through showcases organized and promoted by satisfied customers. These customers not only hosted the showcase, they identified colleagues in other companies who should attend. Your satisfied customers also serve as important third-party references during the showcase itself.

How Many Invitations Must You Send?

The number of invitations depends on how many people you want to attend and upon the effectiveness of your invitation. The procedures described in this chapter typically get 5% - 8% who say they'll come and 4% - 6% who actually attend.

In more concrete terms, to get 20 attendees at an estimated 4% net response rate, we need:

20 participants divided by 0.04 response = 500 invitations.

This example assumes a free showcase of several hours duration, within one hour commuting time and using the invitation and pre-showcase contact practices described in this chapter.

Don't Scrimp on Your First One

Your first showcase should never be done "on the cheap." This is a strong temptation, especially for smaller organizations. But, if the showcase doesn't work as planned, you'll always have the nagging doubt that the corners you cut contributed to the failure. A better plan is to do your first one "first-class" and then carefully test less expensive alternatives later.

When to Hold Your Showcase: Timing Considerations

Timing considerations include time of year, day of week, time of day, duration and schedule frequency. Since Chapters 5 and 6 go into most of the details, we'll just summarize a few unique to showcases:

Time of Year isn't important, other than to avoid holiday periods, vacations and industry-specific events which may impact your target group. Any time is the right time for a showcase.

Day of the Week. The important consideration here is whether your showcase will be during or outside normal business hours. For showcases during normal business hours, the best days are Wednesday, Thursday and Tuesday in that order. Avoid Monday and Friday.

For showcases outside normal business hours, the best days are dictated by your target population's schedule. Generally the above days are still best, but weekend showcases work better for some groups, for example, time-billing professionals.

Time of Day. The three most popular times for showcases during normal business hours are: (1.) mid-afternoon, followed by a wine, cheese and fruit reception, (2.) late morning, followed by lunch, and (3.) the "power breakfast."

Evening functions typically begin at 7:30 or 8:00 p.m. and are over by 10:00 or 10:30 p.m. Coffee, tea and soft drinks are the usual refreshments.

This story may help you decide what time to hold your showcase: A client, whose prospects were any and all adults, promoted both afternoon and evening showcases at three locations. Attendees self-selected their best time. Most managers and employees opted for the afternoon sessions, while homemakers, individuals, entrepreneurs, salespeople and time-billing professionals preferred the evening sessions.

Duration. You can generally get the top person in an organization for a couple of hours, followed by a refreshment/food function. Anything longer than this is ineffective. The social can (and often will) go on much longer, but those pressed for time can leave early if the formal part is held to no more than two hours.

Frequency. Hold a showcase as often as you need sales leads. Two to four times a year on each topic in each location is safe. But examples of training firms using more or fewer showcases is as close as your local newspaper.

Where to Hold Your Showcase?

Hold your showcase in the center of the group you invite. About 1-hour commuting time is a practical maximum. In densely populated metropolitan areas, a 1-hour commuting radius may include too many people and the radius should be reduced. For example, a 1-hour commuting radius around New York or San Francisco may involve literally thousands of prospective invitees, whereas a 1-hour commuting radius around Phoenix or San Antonio may only involve a few hundred.

The best locations are easy to get to and "user friendly." For example, if most of the people are from downtown Los Angeles, then the airport would *not* be convenient. Conversely, if everyone was coming from out of town or is already near the airport, then downtown would not be convenient. Select a place easy to find, easy to park (if they're driving) and easy to get into and out of.

Neutral ground is better than "turf." Resist the urge to hold your showcase in your own offices. Some consultants successfully hold showcases in their sales offices, but you'll need to test and prove that before adopting it as a your standard. Traditional neutral ground is a hotel.

Pick an upscale hotel, unless you're trying to reach blue-collar workers. People have a certain "comfort zone" around hotels. For example, if you want the top people to attend your showcase, then demonstrate that by holding it at a Hyatt Regency, Westin, Marriott or similar hotel. Lower level people might be more comfortable at a Holiday Inn or Ramada Inn. For example, one of our clients reported that their seminars for Maintenance Supervisors were better attended when they switched their locations from the Marriott to the Holiday Inn and Best Western hotels.

Overall Showcase Economics

The cost of a showcase can be considerable but still very cost-effective compared to other ways to bring prospects to the same stage in the sales process. Here are some representative figures:

Direct, out-of-pocket costs for a 20-person showcase may total $4,000-$4,500. For example, 500 invitations at a total cost of $5.00 each, plus stay-in-touch costs from the time they respond through their attendance, totals a representative $3,000 for promotion. Hotel costs of $250 room rental, plus (say) $25 each for a 30-person (including your staff) wine, cheese and fruit reception adds another $1,000. Additional out-of-pocket costs might include materials furnished participants at the showcase, parking, etc.

Sound expensive? Only until you compare these costs to the cost of your getting and keeping separate appointments with all those who attend the showcase. According to the latest surveys, the average cost of a single sales call is $400 - $600, so separate sales calls for those same 20 people could total more than double the cost of the showcase.

But the showcase is even *more* valuable than separate sales calls, because the participants were interested enough to come to you, away from the interruptions in their office. And the presentation you can make at a showcase is also better than you could make in the client's office. All the evidence shows that if the process is properly applied, show-

case people are worth more than other prospects -- and they cost less to bring to a comparable stage in the selling process.

Allocate your showcase time and budget as follows: One-third to one-half for getting the participants there (including direct mail expenses, telemarketing costs, and all related promotional aspects); one-quarter to one-third for conducting the showcase (including hotel costs and the allocated time of your staff, food and/or beverage functions, etc.); and one-third for the post-showcase follow-up (including the time and expenses for the subsequent face-to-face selling that takes place).

Why You Should *Not* Charge Participants to Attend

When you pay, you expect to get something in return. Paid events attract people with different motives and desires. We want sales prospects, not those coming for personal development, educational or other reasons. Ideally, they know they're coming to learn about something they can buy. Charging for such a presentation confuses the issue.

Showcases Work Great for Marketing Training Within Your Own Organization, Too

Many successful training directors use showcases. Just follow the procedures described in this chapter, but invite the managers you want to "sell" on sending their people to your training. Obviously, when and where it's held and food/beverage arrangements may be different. But most everything else is the same -- including the need for a face-to-face follow-up meeting with each hot prospect in the three days following the showcase.

DESIGNING YOUR SHOWCASE FOR IMPACT

The typical showcase itself includes:

- Pre-event set-up.
- Registration, including capturing the names and pertinent mailing information for every attendee, as well as issuing name badges and/or handout materials.
- Introductions, including participants, your people and your organization.
- Brief presentation.
- Involvement experience, including some "hands-on" activity such as a workshop, role-play, feedback session (from a questionnaire/instruments submitted earlier), etc.
- The sales pitch.
- Closing remarks.
- Distribution of gifts, pass-out materials and/or back-of-the-room material sales.
- Refreshments and informal discussions.

These activities may sometimes be rearranged. The following sections deal with a number of these elements in more detail.

The Importance of Participant Involvement/Hands-On Activities

A showcase has an advantage over a one-on-one sales call, because it can get participants actively involved in group activities, role-plays, case studies, survey feedback, etc.

My own experience with showcases is a good example. For two years I conducted showcases on our best-selling course. The right people attended, and I got a tremendous reaction from everyone. Participants were enthusiastic. They loved every minute. Their post-showcase comments were wonderful.

But no one bought anything.

Later, Ron Smith, an expert in adult learning, pointed out what was going on. He said, "Executives appreciate what you're saying intellectually, but they're not ready to experience it internally. So it ends up being just a good lecture. The *need awareness experi-ence* has not taken place."

We changed the showcase so participants immediately got involved in a "hands-on" experience. The focus became narrower but allowed more time for participants to experience the on-the-job situations our programs were designed for. Once they "felt" the need, just as they would back on the job, there was no question about having their undivided attention. And sales soared.

You want to quickly put participants in a situation where they don't merely *hear* what you're saying, but *feel* it in their gut. For example, they actually experience the sinking feeling of knowing that if they had this tool two years ago, they could have saved their company $10 million. Then they're ready to listen and participate. It's not what you say, but what they do that causes this important transition.

Of course there's a difference between role-playing and applying the concepts to your own personal situation. For instance, we found that most training people could not role-play as first-level supervisors and get the desired reaction unless they had prior experience as a first-level supervisor. And vice-versa.

Another example may help. Our *Product Evaluation and Planning* show-cases attracted mostly product managers with problems this program could solve. But sometimes we'd get training people there to evaluate the program for a product manager. We learned quickly that the training person has no way to experience the gut-wrenching feeling of the product manager who learns that their competitor just announced a better product. What they can experience is a comparable situation in the training department. So we'd have the training people work on a training course and not let them be merely observers. We learned that when the evaluators were merely observers, they did not make as favorable a recommendation as when we got them involved in a real-world situation they could personally relate to.

Use Survey Questionnaires and Feedback

We all try to learn more about ourselves. We crave new insights about ourselves. We want to know how we compare to others. People like to look in mirrors. Anytime you can promise somebody a dimension of themselves they've never seen before, you've got them "hooked."

So offer a test or survey instrument, and promise to show participants how they compare to others in these important dimensions. It works like magic! It can be a commercial survey instrument or one you designed. One of our clients, an expert in construction company management, uses a short questionnaire his attendees complete in a few minutes. Then he compares their responses to those made by hundreds of other contractors to the same questions.

Caution! The promise of personal feedback can attract people that really have no buying interest. You can bait the trap so well that people come merely to take the bait. You do yourself a disservice with this kind of showcase; remember, the showcase is only a step in the sales process!

To avoid this problem, don't promote the feedback prominently -- or at all -- in the original invitation. Rather, tell about it in your confirming letter. This has the added advantage of reinforcing the respondents' desire to attend and giving them a greater reason not to be a no-show or to cancel.

Here's a Typical Showcase:

Participants arrive at the showcase. The staff greets each one personally, gives them their prepared name badge and introduces them to other participants. A few minutes after the appointed time, the host gets up, says a few words of welcome and positions the firm. In essence he/she says, "You know us, and if you don't know us now, you will by the time you leave. We'll attempt to answer all of your questions. We're specialists in making organizations more productive (or whatever they're specialists in). We do this in many ways, but today we want to share with you something that our clients are very excited about.

"This is what our program is all about -- we've sold it to ten thousand different customers over 25 years on eight continents. Our program takes more time than we have today, so we want to tell you about the program and then let you actually experience part of it."

At that point the host introduces the content expert or facilitator, who runs this part of the showcase. The host might say a few more words, but what you really want to do is get on with the big "wow," or experiential portion of the showcase, without delay.

The facilitator then says, "I'd like to set the stage just as it would be if you were really in our program. Over the last few days we would have done the following ... . Now we've come together to ... ." At that point the expert picks up just as though they were in a real training situation.

Introductions and getting to this point takes no more than 20 minutes. Shorter is better. The "hands on" or experiential portion runs for 45 minutes to an hour. If it's really your biggest "wow," they're going to be tired but excited by then.

Our *Product Evaluation and Planning* Seminar had one concept that was very insightful, yet 95% of the people had never seen it before. It totally "blew away" most participants. The higher in the organization the participant was, the more excited she/he became and the more powerful the concept was perceived to be. To go beyond that "wow" was always counterproductive. "Don't sell beyond the close," as my old sales manager used to say.

Returning to our typical showcase, the facilitator says, "I'm sorry we have to stop now. We could do this for another two days, but we simply don't have time." Then he/she talks the group through whatever would normally be done in the remainder of the program. This should take no more than five to ten minutes.

At that point the facilitator is finished, and turns the meeting back to the host for the sales pitch. This is fairly low-key and consists mainly of describing how this program can be purchased, delivered, installed, etc., -- including the price. I'm personally uncomfortable with a "hard sell," but I've seen many successful showcases that directly "ask for the order."

After the sales pitch, the host asks, "Are there any questions?" One or two questions may have been "planted," especially if a good customer attends and is willing to help. Usually it only takes one or two "icebreaker" questions" to start the ball rolling. If the questions don't come spontaneously, the host can always say, "I think we're ready to continue this over some refreshments."

You can pass out materials during refreshments. If you're having back-of-the-room sales, point out that during the refreshments there will be a table with materials and someone to take their payments. This also works well for a book signing.

The showcase presentation flows smoothly into the refreshments and the informal meeting. At some point you need to suggest that your salespeople can visit those who would like more information. If you have enough people, talk one-on-one to every participant. This is much more effective, because you can arrange the appointments at the showcase. If you don't have enough people present, then say something like, "Catch one of us during the wine and cheese" or "Leave your business card on the table and we'll call you tomorrow."

Use Your Best Facilitators

Showcase participants judge the competence of your firm by what they see at the showcase. That's why your very best content experts/facilitators should conduct the core of the session. There's no substitute for their skill to produce the best possible participant experience in the short time available and to demonstrate their knowledge by answering spontaneous content questions.

Similarly, your best salespeople should run the sales portion of the meeting and handle pricing and business questions. Usually a salesperson can act as master/mistress of ceremonies as well.

Have Enough of Your Own People Attend

Don't worry about out-numbering the atten-

dees. Remember, the object is to start the sales process. In an individual sales call you'd normally be one-on-one with the client. The closer you get to that ratio in the showcase, the better.

Ideally, you'd have one employee for every three to five clients. If the showcase is really hot and most attendees are worth a sales call in the next week, you'll want to schedule as many of those as possible before the showcase ends. You can't do that if you don't have enough staff on hand.

Practical Room Arrangements

The considerations for the room set-up are:

- Requirements for the presentation
- Requirements for the proper interaction of participants
- Relationship of the refreshment area to the presentation area
- The location of your people

Naturally, the facility will largely determine what your final arrangement must be, but start with a clear picture of what you want.

The best set-up is two adjacent, but separable rooms, with the showcase in one room and a moveable wall or partition to open the refreshment area, which is set up in advance. This has the advantage that during the informal discussions with refreshments, the visual aids used during the showcase are easily seen. It also keeps people from being divided between two rooms.

Chapter 6 shows a number of seating arrangements that work well. Round tables allow participants to talk to each other and are best for interaction among small groups. Seating around the outside of a U-shaped table is best where the entire group has to interact. The big advantage of this layout is that everybody can see everyone else. But the limit is about 30 - 35 participants.

Work hard to avoid "classroom seating," where all the tables point to the front of the room and participants look at the back of other peoples' heads. This really cuts down on group interaction, the key to a successful showcase.

Booking Your Showcase Facility

Chapter 6 has the information on working with hotels and meeting facilities. But a few points are worth repeating here.

Hotels generally have two kinds of rooms for small meetings. Which one you get depends partly on whose clutches you fall into at the hotel. Knowing that there are both can help you steer the best course.

The first type of room is the "ballroom," usually a large room divided by moveable walls. Sections of the ballroom have no windows or other amenities and tend to be "cold." Ballroom functions are also usually expensive, because they're geared to selling food and beverages. Ballrooms are often noisy, particularly if someone next door shows a film or plays music. Finally, events held in ballrooms tend to be unpredictable. Many times a ballroom section that was booked months in advance will suddenly be "unavailable" because of a larger, more profitable group. My advice is to avoid the ballroom altogether.

The second kind of room is a "meeting room." Most hotels have a floor -- or even several floors -- of meeting rooms, generally with solid walls, permanent doors and even windows! Meeting rooms rent for a fraction of the cost of ballroom space. For example, it is common to be able to rent two adjacent meeting rooms for less than the cost of a single segment of the ballroom. Hotels use meeting rooms to help fill sleeping rooms and only secondarily, to support food and beverage functions.

You can see your showcase is not going to be valuable business to a hotel. You're not going to use any sleeping rooms, and your food and beverage service will be minimal. (Hotels will always compare your function to what the same amount of space could bring them if sold for a major national convention.) You can partly offset this by telling them that your attendees will be top executives who book thousands of meetings for their companies every year, etc. It may or may not work.

It's even possible that your showcase food or beverage function *could* get you a discount on the room rental, if you ask for it. The rule with hotels is, *everything* is negotiable.

In deciding what to serve during the food and beverage function, resist the high-priced, fancy stuff hotels love to push. Usually the simple, common foods, beverages and hors d'oeuvres are the best choice. And this is increasingly so in today's health-conscious world. A fine wine and cheese party can be served with the hotel's house wine, chips and dip, and mixed nuts. Fruit and cheese boards are usually better than having hot hors d'oeuvres and are much less expensive. Avoid the expensive, fancy canapes the hotels will recommend. Buy your wine by the bottle, not by the glass or by the person. Tell the hotel you'll want to check the empty bottles after the party, and sign off on them. You can even arrange to take any partially opened bottles with you.

As a practical matter, the Marriott chain is very good at this kind of thing. They will give you adjacent rooms and do not charge excessively. Other hotels can be good, too. But be very careful not to spend money needlessly on the hotel.

SUCCESSFULLY PROMOTING YOUR SHOWCASE

You've already designed your showcase and made the hotel arrangements. Now all you need to do is get participants.

Building Your Invitation List

As with any direct marketing activity, the list is crucial to success. It's even more so for a showcase, because if you attract the wrong people you won't get the resulting sales.

Lists for showcases, at least to reach top management, must be *better* than for other direct mail purposes. First, your invitations will be personalized, which means the list must contain all the elements necessary for a true business-quality letter. This includes the gender prefix (Mr., Ms., Mrs., etc.) and the complete first name, middle initial and last name. It must contain an accurate position title and any internal mail code (especially in larger organizations). Finally, the list must be in computer-readable form, suitable for correspondence-quality addressing on both letters and address labels.

The three ways to obtain your mailing list are the following:

- Use your own existing prospect list.
- Research a list specifically for the showcase.
- Buy or rent one or more commercially available lists.

Your Own Prospect List. If you are an established business with a list of customers or prospects with whom you regularly correspond (e.g., via a newsletter, advertising mailings, etc.) then look here first. If you have sufficient names in a given geographic area for your showcase, this may be all you need.

Of course, if you're trying to acquire *new* customers, this may not work. So read on.

Specially Researched Lists. If you don't have a prospect list or decide to reach out to new prospects, it's often easy to build a suitable showcase list "from scratch." This is because: (1.) A small number of names are needed, usually only a few hundred; (2.) the top people in an organization are easy to identify; and (3.) the added cost of building the list doesn't add significantly to an already expensive invitation package.

Researching your own list will involve 1-time costs of about 50 cents to one dollar per name. This is mostly for the person's time to call and get the necessary information.

To research your own names, make a list of the industries and/or businesses you want at your showcase. Then use local directories, associations, newspaper listings or even the telephone book to identify the specific firms by name, address and telephone. Specially compiled listings are also available from Dun & Bradstreet, Contacts Influential and others (see Chapter 7). Many of these lists can be accessed "on-line" through your computer modem or even purchased on CD-ROM.

Armed with this starter set of lists, begin calling each organization and ask to be connected to the office of the individual in the

position you wish. For example, if you want to reach the top HRD or training decision-maker, ask the operator, "Please connect me with the office of the top Human Resources person in your firm." They will often say their name, "Oh yes, that's Dr. Smith" and connect you. When Dr. Smith's secretary answers, you say, "Hello. I'm Dale Jones from The XYZ Company. I'm preparing to mail a letter to Dr. Smith and I want to verify her mailing address. Is it ... ? Is her title ... ?" And so on. You then verify "... and Dr. Smith *is* the top HRD decision-maker at your firm, isn't she?" If the answer is yes you are almost finished. If the answer is no you need to follow up by finding out who the correct person is and ask to be transferred to them.

The final step is to ask the person you're talking to, "Please watch for our package, and be sure Dr. Smith sees it right away. It's very urgent!" Don't miss this step; it really boosts showcase response.

Through this process, a single individual on your staff can acquire about twenty good names and addresses per hour, or about 100 to 150 a day. If you have two or three people working, you can build your entire showcase list in just a day or two. Another day to enter it into your computer and you're ready to print labels and personalized letters!

Rented Lists. If your showcases are national or you don't want to bother making your own invitation list, then renting and processing commercially available mailing lists is a possibility.

Because of the high quality requirement of these lists, it may be necessary to rent several lists and merge them, purge duplicates and filter out records lacking all the elements necessary for business correspondence-quality addressing. For example, you can't personalize a letter without a first name or gender-specific salutation. Also, records with an inappropriate position title should be rejected. The packages you'll mail are simply too expensive to take chances sending them to any but the best names.

Rented lists furnished in highly abbreviated form and all capital letters need further processing. Abbreviations must be expanded, and all elements must be rendered in mixed upper- and lower-case type with correct capitalization. This processing increases the cost of a 1-time rental list to 50-75 cents per name -- about the same as the researched list.

Chapter 7 has lots more on selecting and working with rented mailing lists.

Designing Your Invitation

Let's look at the packages we know produce the desired response rates. There is surely more than one successful formula -- it's just that what's described here has been proven. If it works for you, you can then test other, possibly more economical, approaches for future showcases.

We're talking about a package that arrives on the recipient's desk in a 9" x 12" envelope with First-Class, metered postage on tape in the upper right hand corner and a 3" x 5", 2-color address label, personally addressed in letter-quality typing.

Inside are the following four (4) items:

1. Personalized, Correspondence-Quality Letter, printed on your 2-color letterhead and signed in blue ink. It can be one or several pages long, but it must be printed on only one side of your stationary. What the letter contains is detailed in a following section.

2. Brochure, hopefully one that currently exists; but if not, then one specially prepared for the showcase. Include only one brochure, because the showcase should focus on only one topic. Remember "The Menu Muddle."

3. Reply Vehicle. Generally it looks like an engraved wedding invitation reply card.

4. Reply Envelope. The front of this envelope is preaddressed to you and contains a "live," First-Class postage stamp. Tests show that if you affix a genuine stamp (and make yourself vulnerable to be ripped off), it doubles response.

These latter two items are easy to produce rapidly, because they are geared to the party circuit. There are printers in your area that do this all the time: In one day you've got the engraved cards and preaddressed envelopes.

Invitation Package Costs

To avoid "sticker shock" over what the package is going to cost, let's look at each of the pieces individually:

Letter. This letter is personalized and on a good stationary. The paper itself will be expensive, say six cents for the first page and four cents each for the second and subsequent pages. By the time you're done, the letters will cost you at least 30 cents each whether they are typed in your office on your own word processor or whether you go to a mail house that does personalization.

Brochure. These range from inexpensive to exorbitant. About $1.00 - $1.50 will be a good average for an 8- to 12-page, 2-color (or more) brochure on a decent stock. This price takes into account your limited print quantity.

Reply Card and Return Envelope. The card will probably cost about 25 cents; the reply envelope, about 15 cents; and another 29 cents (currently) for the stamp. The total is somewhere between 65 and 75 cents for these items, plus the labor to affix the stamp.

9" X 12" Outer Envelope. Probably 15 cents will cover the cost of the envelope itself. Then you have the 3" x 5" label, probably ten cents before it's typed. Add another 5 - 20 cents for personal addressing. Then add the First-Class postage on the entire package, possible another $1.50 to $1.75 depending on weight.

Labor. Folding, inserting, labeling and mailing the above will probably cost 30 cents a package if you do it yourself and a little less if you have it done at a mailhouse.

Mailing List. Whether you research the invitation list through telephone calls or rent lists and have them computer processed, the cost will be somewhere between $.50 and $1.00 per name. Naturally, if you already own the list, the cost will be substantially less.

Adding up the bill, we've got approximately $4.50 to $6.00 per package.

Typical Showcase Invitation Package

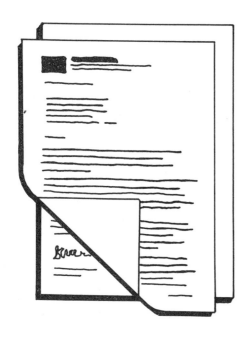

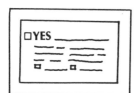

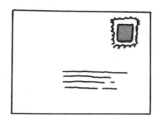

Invitation Quality Determines Who Attends

Why should the invitation be so fancy? It's easy to see how to save money on the invitation described above. And that might be appropriate if you want to get lower-level people to attend. But if you want the top decision-maker to attend personally -- and not pass it down to someone else -- our experience shows that the high-quality package is essential. It tells top executives that they'll be attending with their peers, not lower-level employees.

If you cheapen the package, the top person feels she/he can, -- even should -- pass it on to a subordinate, just like you would. The number of attendees stays the same, but their level drops.

How to Write the Invitation Letter

Writing direct mail letters is described in Chapter 8. We needn't repeat it here. Instead, we'll cover the philosophy of the show-case invitation letter, the most read part of the package, and clearly its most important element.

If you're holding a showcase on a tight budget, the last thing to cheapen or eliminate is the letter. In fact, we've seen very successful showcase promotions involving *only* a letter and a reply vehicle. And even the reply vehicle is dispensable if a toll-free telephone number is used! The letter can do everything!

The letter must steer a middle course between promising too much and building too great an incentive for attendance, on the one hand, and clearly describing the showcase as a sales pitch on the other. Remember, the showcase is part of the sales process; and if we're not careful, we may get attendees who are interested in the incentive and are not interested in buying something.

One way to handle an incentive like a book, personal feedback or the presence of a well-known authority is to announce it in the confirmation letter, *after* they've enrolled in the showcase. This practice serves as a

"hook" to further insure their participation but doesn't excessively draw those likely to be non-customers.

The letter should emphasize the important problem you know the invitees have and that your firm is the expert in solving that problem. The specifics of *how* you solve the problem isn't important. For example, one problem we all have is a stopped drain. And RotoRooter cleans stopped drains. The fact that they use 18 different tools, depending on how and where the drain is plugged, is never advertised and is of no interest. All we care about is that if we call RotoRooter, our drain will get opened fast.

Apply this to your letter. Let's suppose your specialty is conflict resolution. Conflict in the workplace is a growing problem, robbing productivity and reducing morale. The letter should contain a brief reminder of this problem. Then it should assert that you are experts in solving issues of conflict in the workplace, that you've done it for any number of past clients, have written articles and books on the subject and are nationally (even internationally) acclaimed experts in the area.

Next, the letter should tell when and where you are going to demonstrate your unique conflict-resolution techniques that have proven so effective for others. Promise an opportunity to answer all their questions. Close the letter by asking them to take a moment right now to confirm their attendance. If you're offering an incentive or giving some added reason why they absolutely must attend, put it in the P.S., which is the third most-read part of the letter. An example of an incentive in the P.S. might be that the first ten registrants will receive an autographed copy of Dr. Brown's latest book *Resolving Conflict at Work and at Home*.

The formula outlined above is very simple:

1. State the problem you know the reader has.

2. Assert that you are experts in solving the problem.

3. Establish your credibility as experts by citing the specifics on your experience, your credentials or the problems you've solved for others just like the reader.

4. Call for the action that you want.

5. Give a reason to act immediately.

You'll recognize this as the same general format for all good direct mail letters that was presented in Chapter 8.

Below is a specific example of a successful showcase invitation letter:

Sample Showcase Invitation Letter

February 24, 1994

Mr. Jon L. Smith
Vice President, Marketing, Sales and Everything
ACME INTERNATIONAL
1755 Southwest Highway
St. Paul, MN 55113

Dear Mr. Smith:

Enclosed is my personal invitation for you to be my guest at a session previewing of our HIGH PERFORMANCE MANAGEMENT SYSTEM. The session will be held at 2:00 p.m. Thursday, April 28, 1994 in the Floridian Room of the Hyatt Regency Hotel in Downtown Minneapolis. The preview will last approximately 2 hours and will be followed by a wine and cheese reception.

You probably know our founder, Terry W. Evans, is one of the foremost authorities on management. Terry's widely acclaimed Conference Board study was written up in The Wall Street Journal and several other national publications. But you may not know that thru many years of active consulting on tough management issues with hundreds of the Fortune 100 companies, our organization has developed carefully refined and proven methods to dramatically increase on-the-job productivity and attention to quality.

We have used these methods to create our new HIGH PERFORMANCE MANAGEMENT SYSTEM, which contains modules on communication, goal-setting, feedback, teamwork and other timely topics. Our preview will touch on all of these but will deal primarily with communication skills. As a special bonus, those attending the preview will, if they wish, receive a confidential evaluation of their own communications skills based on feedback from colleagues and/or subordinates of their choice.

I'm enclosing information about our firm and about our HIGH PERFORMANCE MANAGEMENT SYSTEM. In the pocket of the enclosed brochure are sheets describing the program's various modules. But since it is difficult to evaluate a program from a brochure, I hope you will join us to "taste" a small piece of our work.

Please complete and return the enclosed card, so we can plan on your attendance. We'll confirm your participation at once, and send you the materials you'll need to obtain your confidential communications skills evaluation.

Continued...

February 24, 1994
Mr. Jon L. Smith
Page 2

The group invited to this preview session are people just like yourself: Top executives who make decisions about training. For that reason, the invitation is personal and not transferable to anyone who doesn't meet that criteria.

I'm excited about being with you on April 28th and sharing how we can help your organization become even more effective.

Sincerely,

Fran E. Jones
President

Enclosures

P.S.   As an added "Thank you" for attending this preview, you will receive a personally autographed, complimentary copy of Terry's latest bestselling book, HIGH PERFORMANCE COMMUNICATION.

Addressing the Outer Envelope

With today's laser printers and PC-based word processors, the mechanics of producing personalized letters and the rest of the showcase invitation package are becoming easier than ever. But one area that still can be a problem is the label.

These 3" x 5" labels are the size most organizations use for 9" x 12" envelopes and packages. If your present label is only a single color, I urge you to consider redesigning it in two colors, which works better.

If you already have a supply of these labels, you can, of course, just roll them into the typewriter or printer. This is clearly the way to go if the whole invitation package is being assembled manually. You may also take your labels and address list to a secretarial service or to a mailhouse that will address them individually at low cost.

However, if you want to do computer addressing (either on your own printer or at a service bureau), you'll need to have continuous form labels. There are companies in your area that can quickly produce continuous form, 1-up, 2-up or 3-up, tractor-fed labels from your artwork or existing label. Most suppliers can offer rapid turnaround time, usually a couple of days.

Don't buy forms that are wider than your narrowest printer can handle, probably a maximum of 2-up. This gives you the possibility of having several printers running at once. The reason to use 2-up (rather than 1-up) format is that labels print nearly twice as fast if the printer can do two labels before it advances a line.

If you're using a laser printer, be extra careful about label stock. Alignment of the labels and the heat of the toner-fusing process both present problems. Laser printing, like other xerographic copying, may have a sixteenth to an eighth of an inch misalignment in the copies. Letters are more forgiving in this matter, because they generally have more white space around them. Before you commit to a large order of laser printer labels, get a few sheets and run them through your printer to be sure that there are no problems.

It's not important that the outer label and the inner letter have exactly the same type. As long as they're both letter-quality nobody cares if one is (say) Courier pica and the other a different pica or even Elite type. Just be sure both look like they were typed on an IBM Selectric typewriter. Even if your equipment can produce a "typeset" look, don't do it. It cuts response.

Timing Your Invitation

Event timing is covered in greater detail in Chapter 5. The important part is that your invitation *must* arrive on the individual's desk at least five to six weeks before the showcase. Since you're mailing the invitations First-Class, allow two to three days maximum delivery time, and mail them seven to eight weeks before the showcase.

Short-duration events like showcases can easily be promoted too early. Mailing invitations twelve or thirteen weeks ahead is close to the limit, and evidence suggests that mailing somewhat later will produce better results.

Deciding Whether to Do the Mailing Yourself or Farm It Out

For the size mailings we're talking about here, assuming you have three or four pairs of part-time arms and legs in your office, you can consider doing it yourself. But you need to know that mailhouses usually do these kinds of mailings cheaper, faster and with considerably less "hassle" than you can do them yourself. Of course, you must have a mailhouse you trust -- one that will treat your materials with the same care you would. Often this is found in secretarial services run by people working out of their home or in small mailhouses. Quality is paramount, so ask around.

TAKING REGISTRATIONS BY PHONE OR MAIL

Since participants are not paying to attend the showcase, their commitment is low and little things can change their plans. The key to a successful registration process is gaining and insuring the participant's commitment to attend. This is your first requirement.

The best way to gain participant commitment is to make sure they see the event as worthwhile personally and organizationally. We've already suggested some possible examples of how to do this: Receive a personal diagnosis in some area, meet with one of the foremost experts in their field, get a free autographed copy of a new book, have an opportunity to network with other executives in the area, etc. Better still, promise that they'll get to do all of them!

The registration process usually begins on the phone, because most registrations arrive this way even though you give them a stamped, self-addressed, reply envelope. The first requirement is to get all the information you need to enter this person into your marketing database. Some who call enthusiastically will never call you again. So during this first (and possibly only) conversation, you need to get all the information for any subsequent follow-up.

The second requirement is to get the person's commitment to attend. Whoever is handling registrations needs to do this in a way that's comfortable for them. But it's a classic sales situation: *you* can't tell the participant to attend -- *they've* got to make the commitment themselves.

One way to get this commitment is to tell the registrant that you are saving them a place at the showcase. For example, "We're really counting on seeing you there." Make sure the customer actually says that they will attend. If you take the time for this step, you'll often hear the person say something like, "Well, to tell you the truth, I just wanted to get my name in. Right now I have another meeting scheduled for that afternoon, but I hope I can get out of it."

That's when the telephone skills of your person can really help. Their voice drops about an octave and they say "Oh, you *really* don't want to miss this." Before the conversation ends, the prospect has agreed to do what they can to remove the conflict so they can attend the showcase. And your registrar may say, "I'm really counting on seeing you there," or "I'm going to be there, too, so I'll get to meet you," or "I'm going to send you this confidential questionnaire. It'll only take a few minutes to fill out. And if you bring it with you to the session, we'll give you that great evaluation of your skills." When the phone conversation is over you immediately send the participant a letter that reiterates, "We're delighted you are going to attend, and we're saving a place for you."

By getting the customer's commitment to attend, you stand the best chance that they'll remove any obstacles.

The third goal in the telephone conversations is to build positive expectations for the showcase. The effective registrar will reiterate the benefits described in the invitation. Technically, you're anticipating and fighting "buyer's remorse." Successful telemarketers and others reaffirm during their phone conversation that the customer has made the right decision.

Showcases offer five (5) big benefits to help generate positive expectations. First, participants will learn about a tremendous program that is making a fantastic contribution to many organizations just like theirs. Second, they're going to get an opportunity to spend one-on-one time with a leading au-

thority on the subject. Third, they're going to meet, socialize and "network" with other top executives like themselves from other, local organizations. Fourth, they'll get a personal evaluation of their own skills and abilities or learn how they stack up to others in similar positions. And fifth, they'll get wine, cheese and a free autographed book.

Finally, the registrar commits to your next action. Something like, "We've reserved your place at the showcase and I'm going to send you a confirming letter. The package will have the questionnaire which we'd like you to complete before you come. You'll be getting this in just a few days, so ask your secretary to look for it. If you haven't received it by the end of the week, please give me a call; because it's so important and you're going to find this so valuable, I want to make sure that you have it in plenty of time before the session."

The above is a rough outline of your phone confirmation process. You can write a fifteen minute training session and everyone in your organization who could possibly answer the phone can adapt it to their own style. Plan a standard reply letter that captures all these points and restates the benefits conversationally. Close by making sure that they understand that you are personally excited about having them attend the showcase and are confident they are going to find it the most valuable several hours that they'll spend this year.

For registrations received by mail, follow the above process, including the phone conversation which (in these cases) you will initiate.

You're going to have some who will call to enroll and will not know how they got the invitation. It will have been passed on to them by their boss or someone else. When they call, they're not going to know whether they got everything that was in the package. Be sure that you check on this. If they do not have the complete package (letter, brochure, etc.) then send it with their confirmation.

Pre-Showcase Follow-Up to Keep Attendance High

Roughly twice as many will reply to your

showcase invitation as actually attend. The better your pre-showcase registration process and follow-up, the higher attendance will be and the fewer cancellations or no-shows you'll have.

The key to keeping attendance up is to stay in touch with attendees (or their assistants) weekly from the time they register until the showcase occurs. The challenge here is to think of enough different reasons for repeated contact, especially for those who register early.

For example, if the invitations are mailed seven to eight weeks ahead of the event, some people are going to enroll right away. That means that you're going to need five or six reasons to contact them in order to stay in touch weekly.

The first one is easy: It's the confirmation. For those who enroll earliest, break the confirmation into two pieces, a week apart. Send the confirmation letter at once and then send the questionnaire or involvement device a week later. For those enrolling later, you could retain the two-step confirmation process or send them the confirming letter and the involvement device together.

Make subsequent contacts for reasons that are helpful to the participant but serve to remind them of their attendance commitment. Possible reasons include making sure they know the best way to the hotel, verifying information for their name badge and/or place card, confirming attendance so you can commit for the food and beverage service (especially important when sit-down meals are involved). And, of course, if the registrant alerts you to the possibility of a scheduling problem, then you have a "built-in" excuse to call again to be sure they were able to resolve the problem.

When you send something in the mail, be sure to call a week later and see if they've received it. And as a last resort, you may just have to have someone call and be friendly. "I haven't heard from you in a week."

Be aware that top-level executives are often afraid they're going to be attending a lower-level function and be surrounded by others who aren't at their same management level. If you sense this, try to reassure them during one of your contacts that "Oh, yes, everyone else is a vice-president, too."

Follow Up With Those Who Responded but Didn't Attend

Send them a note saying, "I'm sorry you couldn't attend, but here's some of the information we presented." Or, better yet, call and offer to give them a summary presentation in their office.

HOW AND WHEN TO CONTACT PROSPECTS AFTER THE SHOWCASE

Remember, the showcase is only a step in your sales process. The real challenge is to be sure the good leads at the showcase turn into sales. There are too many firms that do a successful showcase and pat themselves on the back about the fine attendance and the smooth flow of the program -- and stop there.

The rule is that you have to be in the office of the hot prospects within three to five working days following the showcase. It's a simple rule but an effective one. If you do that and then follow your normal sales process, you will maximize the benefits from the showcase.

But what about the attendees who are not hot prospects and not worth an immediate face-to-face call? Perhaps half the participants will fall in this category. How do you handle them?

This is where a quarterly newsletter or another regular "stay-in-touch program" is vital. These people took the trouble to come to the showcase and doubtless learned a lot about your firm as a result. They will later either become a customer themselves or refer other customers to you. You need to treat them that way. Enter them into your marketing database, and send them your regular communications. (If you don't have such a regular communication program, you need to institute one in order to maximize showcase returns. See Chapter 12.)

Should You Do It Again?

The ultimate economic evaluation here is the cost per sale closed. You'll need some perspective on this because of training's long sales cycle. But something like six to twelve months after the showcase, you need to carefully evaluate what kind of business closed or is still active in your sales pipeline, flowing directly from the showcase. Since we know this is going to be an issue, you need to plan your showcase to capture the relevant data. I have clients who have run a successful series of showcases; business is booming, and their natural inclination is to say, "Well it came from all of our other hard work. We think showcases are too expensive and we're not going to do them anymore." But when you dig in on an account-by-account basis, you find out that a large percentage of their recent growth of business is directly attributable to those showcases.

Certainly, if a large fraction of your business is repeat business from existing customers, then showcases will be less valuable, because they are primarily for acquiring new customer relationships. But if you're trying to grow your business and expand into to new areas or if you merely want to have in your "hip pocket" the ability to replace any major accounts you lose, then knowing how the showcase process works in your situation is absolutely vital.

TELEMARKETING: USING THE PHONE TO SELL TRAINING AND INFORMATION

A few blocks from the famous Jazz Lighthouse in Hermosa Beach, California, is the Either Or Bookstore.

It's the only business I know without a telephone. For the rest of us, the telephone is our *first* business investment. You start doing telemarketing -- using your phone to sell -- the day your phone is installed. The questions are: (1.) Can you improve what you now do? and (2.) Can you do more?

Telemarketing Is Big Business

According to Eugene B. Kordahl, pioneer developer of AT&T's Kansas City telemarketing center and president of National Telemarketing, the first printed use of the word "telemarketing" was in September, 1967, when C. Dickey Dyer, III, a Princeton management consultant, wrote an article in *Industrial Distribution News*. Since then the term has come to mean any use of the telephone for sales and marketing.

Telemarketing Magazine estimates that there are more than 4-1/2 million telemarketers and telephone sales people employed in more than 565,000 telemarketing operations in the U.S. The annual telemarketing sales volume exceeds $280 billion, which is more than the entire GNP of Sweden, Austria or the Netherlands.

Telemarketing's dollar volume is two-thirds business-to-business and only one-third consumer sales. This is because there are four times as many industrial firms using telemarketing as there are consumer businesses, and the average industrial order is more than $800 as compared to less than $50 for the average consumer order placed or taken by telephone.

Outbound and Inbound Telemarketing

There are two types of telemarketing: inbound telemarketing, and outbound telemarketing. Let's briefly look at each one.

Incoming Telemarketing occurs when the customer originates the call. The call may be prompted by direct mail, display ads, yellow pages, referral -- anything. Training and information businesses use inbound telemarketing to take both seminar registrations and product/ publication orders. Even if you never call *out* to sell something, learning more about telemarketing will pay off for these incoming calls.

Outbound Telemarketing is the proactive use of the telephone to sell something. It's sometimes called "outcalling."

Outbound telemarketing generates the annoying calls we get at dinner time. These intrusions have lead most states to pass, or threaten, privacy laws restricting telemarketing aimed at consumers at home. Fortunately, telemarketing is a normal and accepted part of business-to-business selling, and restrictions here are minimal.

Unless we specifically note otherwise, this chapter addresses outbound telemarketing.

Seminars, Packaged Training, Tapes and Books Can All Be Sold by Telephone

Few products and services *cannot* be sold by telephone. Telemarketing successes include office and copier supplies, directories, industrial equipment, tires and used machinery. Big-ticket items like real estate, stocks, bonds, diamonds, precious metals, sculptures, cruises and expensive vacation packages have all been sold successfully on the phone.

It was the late Murray Roman who introduced the telephone to political campaigning and helped elect three presidents and dozens of senators and congressmen. Roman's most notable business telemarketing campaign was 20 million phone calls to get consumers to test drive the first Ford Mustang.

Publishers and seminar firms have successfully used telemarketing for years. For example, Brentwood Publishing has relied almost exclusively on telephone sales for more than 25 years. American Management Association, American Media, Nightingale-Conant and scores of others use telemarketing.

Week-long seminars costing over $3,000 are among the highest-priced training items regularly sold by telephone, but books, audio tape programs and videos are close behind. Some of the most frequent uses of telemarketing are:

1. Taking individual registrations in seminars and conferences.

2. Selling packaged training programs, films/videos, audio tapes and software, particularly to current customers.

3. Doing market and other research with past participants.

4. Qualifying sales leads.

5. Making appointments for face-to-face sales calls.

How Telemarketing Training and Information Differs from Other Telemarketing

Telemarketing training and information differs from consumer selling and from selling other business-to-business products and services for three major reasons:

1. Training is an intangible benefit. Knowledge, skills and other benefits from training are often hard to measure -- and hard to communicate. An exception is professional courses where the CEUs are required for continued licensing or certification.

2. It's a big-ticket purchase, particularly for expensive, multi-day seminars and conferences that also involve travel and away-from-home living costs. And this usually means that the purchase has to be approved by someone else as well.

3. It takes time -- time to take the course or attend the seminar and more time to put what's learned into practice. And for events held during normal working hours, there's inevitable schedule conflicts to be resolved.

For these reasons, a Telephone Sales Representative (known universally as a TSR) needs more conceptual ability to sell seminars than almost any other product or service.

How Hard It Is Depends on Your Relationship

Whether selling by telephone is difficult or easy depends on your relationship with the person on the other end of the line. "Cold" calling a first-time buyer can be difficult, while calling a frequent customer can be as easy as calling an old friend. *The Telephone Marketing Difficulty Guide* at the top of the facing page gives a way to illustrate these various degrees of difficulty.

To use this diagram, select one item from each column and connect the square bullets for each with a straight edge. If the left-to-right slope runs *downhill* (for example, calling current or prior customers to do market research), it will be easy. On the other hand, a left-to-right *uphill* slope (for example, trying to sell an expensive product or service to a random prospect) may be difficult.

Telephone Marketing Difficulty Guide[*]

Relationship	Type Of Sale
■ Current/Prior Customer -- Same or Related Product.	■ Expensive Product/Service
	■ Inexpensive Product/Service
■ Current/Prior Customer -- Unrelated Product	■ Approval Sales
■ Inquirer Who Paid Something	■ Upgrade an Incoming Order
■ Inquirer Who Was "Bribed"	■ Make an Appointment for a Sales Call or Demo.
■ Qualified Prospect -- No Known Contact with Us Yet	■ Get Referrals (Names of Others to Contact)
■ Random Prospect	■ Market Research (Genuine -- Not as a "Trick")

Connect the Bullets with a Straight-Edge. Left-to-right Slope Shows Degree Of Difficulty: "An Uphill Battle" or "Downhill All the Way."

[*] Adapted from a diagram by Daniel E. Harding, Center for Direct Marketing

Research confirms this. AT&T has found that there's less stress in making calls to qualified leads, people who have requested information or those with whom there is an existing relationship. This can be important when getting your operation going.

Telemarketing Advantages and Disadvantages

Face-to-face selling and telephone selling are more *alike* than they are different. You can prove it to yourself: When someone cites a problem about telemarketing, ask if the same problem doesn't apply to face-to-face selling as well. Here are some advantages and disadvantages that *are* unique to telemarketing.

Telemarketing Advantages

1. Permits many more sales calls per unit of time -- and calls to smaller accounts than you could afford to call on in person.
2. Gets you a chance to talk to those who wouldn't give you the time for a face-to-face meeting.
3. Commands immediate attention and action; people almost always answer their phones.
4. People tend to be more direct and candid on the phone than they are in person.
5. You can take notes, use a script, refer to charts, etc., without the customer knowing it.
6. The customer can't see the salesperson's physical appearance, nervousness, body language, etc.

Telemarketing Disadvantages

1. Possible for the salesperson to get lots of "no's"/rejection in a short period of time.
2. Can't employ visual aids, demonstrations or group presentations as part of the sales pitch.
3. Requires better asking and listening

skills to uncover needs and to establish "fit" with your products/services.

4. Salesperson can't read the customer's body language or facial expressions.

5. Salesperson's appearance and physical characteristics aren't seen by the customer.

All-in-all, the single biggest advantage of telemarketing is its speed and flexibility. No other form of selling allows you to design, test and refine a sales approach as quickly as does telemarketing; one day (or less) to test a campaign and one week (or less) to refine it.

It's worth noting that everyone's experiences are the same: When selling intangibles or big-ticket items by telephone, you should *never* engage in a "hard sell." None of the high-pressure (or deceptive tactics) that are so offensive should ever be considered or employed in *any* form by any marketer of knowledge products. The soft-sell, providing the necessary information in a friendly, caring, and customer-oriented manner, wins every time. The power of the knowledge and information you are able to provide and the benefits you are able to furnish your prospective client will sell themselves if presented in a caring manner. This takes lots of the "pressure" out of using the telephone for selling in this area.

TELEMARKETING PRODUCTIVITY NORMS

Telemarketing follows many of the same rules as face-to-face selling: 30% of your sales will be easy. The customer was just sitting around waiting for you to call and ask them to buy something. And 30% won't buy from you under any circumstances. The 40% in the middle are the ones that separate the *real* telemarketers from the mere order takers.

This section furnishes information about the relative sales productivity you can expect from your outcalling activity. Although the figures are derived from full-time TSRs, most of the data may be easily scaled up or down for the amount of time actually worked. In fact, this matter is addressed as the first item.

Amount of Time Worked

The average "full-time" TSR does *not* spend eight hours on the telephone. Fatigue generally limits the amount of time that can effectively be spent, and in most cases telephone sales effectiveness drops markedly after about four hours of calling, even with breaks. As a result, most "full-time" TSRs have other work assigned, including paperwork, follow-up correspondence, call reports, etc., to occupy the remaining time not spent on the telephone.

Call duration has an important bearing on fatigue; shorter calls mean more fatigue and therefore less total time that can be spent calling.

Two variables dictate the average call length. The first is whether the calls are business or consumer calls. Business-to-business calls are generally longer; for example, seminar registrations average three to five minutes at the shortest to 12 - 15 minutes or more. The second determinant of call length is whether the call is incoming or outbound. Out-calls average about double the length of incoming calls.

All things considered, those telemarketing training and information products/services should plan on no more than about a 4- to 5-hour day. And this time may be even further restricted if you are calling across time zones or internationally.

Number of Calls Handled

This number sets the total volume of call activity that a single TSR can handle. Again there's an important difference between business-to-business and consumer calling. The average consumer communicator might handle between 130 and 240 calls per day, whereas the average business-to-business telemarketer will be dealing with only 80 to 120 calls per day.

These figures are based on a mixture of

incoming and outgoing calls. If the TSR is primarily outcalling, the number of calls handled will be reduced. On the other hand, if the calls are primarily incoming, the higher end of the range may be expected.

Calls Completed

About one-third to 40% of the business-to-business calls placed will be completed, assuming a reasonably fresh telephone list. This amounts to four to eight calls completed per hour, or 25 to 45 calls completed per day. Again, the more complex and involved messages are apt to result in longer calls and, therefore, fewer total completions per hour or per day.

Calls "Closed"

Before quoting these statistics we need to have a common understanding of what we mean by "closed." As used here, it means that the primary objective of the call has been met: either making an appointment, taking an order, obtaining the responses to a questionnaire, etc. Gauged over a wide range of different applications, usable figures of something like 10% of all of the calls made, or 25% of all of the calls completed, result in a "closed" sale. Translated into terms that we can use for planning, this means that a full-time TSR might be able to have somewhere between 7 and 20 "closes" per day, or two to four an hour. But, obviously, price, complexity of the sale, previous relationship to the client, etc., all have an important bearing on this figure.

Annual Sales Productivity

Telemarketing is always a risky proposition, but a target of $300,000 - $400,000 annual sales productivity should be achieved in a TSR's second year of selling training and information products. This compares with about two to three times this level for face-to-face salespersons in their third year.

The Relationship Between Face-to-Face and Telemarketing Sales Cycles

Face-to-face selling and telemarketing share many characteristics. In both cases, expected order size and whether it's a first or a follow-on order are important. In both cases, "breaking into a new account" takes more time than getting a repeat order from an existing customer.

Telemarketing has a shorter sales cycle than either direct mail or face-to-face selling. Initial orders may take from one to three months to close on the telephone, less than half of what's typical in face-to-face selling. And average initial order sizes are also restricted. As with direct mail, an initial order size much above $3,000 should not be routinely expected, although occasionally such large initial orders do occur. But repeat orders can be many times as big. I know a number of publishers and educational suppliers that take repeat orders from existing clients with average orders running into five and even six figures.

DEVELOPING AND TESTING TELEPHONE SCRIPTS

Whether you are making one call or many, working from a prepared script will improve your success. Most business people learn that working from notes they've prepared in advance of *any* telephone call produces a better-structured and shorter call and insures that all the desired points are covered in the best possible sequence. Have you ever hung up the phone and immediately realized you forgot something?

The main ingredients of any telephone script can be remembered by the four "Cs": Concise, Clear, Conversational and Convincing. Let's look at the characteristics of scripts that have these four Cs:

Keep It Short

Never plan a script longer than three to four minutes. This may vary with the type of message, and a good contact could well run longer. But the total scripted portion should be limited in length.

Ask for the Prospect by Name

Confirm that the person you called is actually on the phone. The script should provide clear questions to identify the person you're talking to and what to do if you end up with the wrong person. When you get the person's name, write it down so you can use it in the rest of your conversation.

Immediately Identify the Caller and the Caller's Company

People will simply not talk to anyone who doesn't identify herself/himself. It helps if your company name reflects the benefit you provide or if you can work that benefit into your title. Our normal telephone introduction is "I'm Jane Doe, calling for Schrello Direct Marketing. We help companies market their training and information."

Have an Opening "Hook" or Exciting Benefit to Offer *Immediately*

This is something that makes the person want to continue talking to you. The benefit may be very simple, such as referring to someone they know who asked you to call. Or it may summarize the help you've provided to others, for example, "We work with 70 of the Fortune 100 companies to improve their computer productivity." If you have name recognition, publicity or other credentials, present them here.

Get to the Point Quickly

Next, tell why you're calling. For example, "I'm calling to see if we can arrange a 10-minute meeting so I can show you what we've done for other businesses like yours." This is one area where telemarketing differs dramatically from direct mail: In direct mail, long copy has been proven superior to short copy. But in telemarketing, getting to the point quickly is much more effective than beating around the bush; people simply won't stay on the line for a long-winded, one-sided presentation.

Involve the Prospect in Conversation

Successful telemarketers find that questions get the other person talking and are more effective than monologues. This doesn't mean the phoney questions you get in those annoying dinner-time calls ("How are you today, Mrs. Smith?"). What works are honest questions that help both parties decide whether to continue the conversation. For example, "Are you involved in the decision to train people on personal computers?" If the answer is "Yes," you can then ask, "What kinds of software and systems do you generally use?" And the conversation is off and running. On the other hand, if the answer to your first question is "No," you might ask "Could you tell me who in your company *does* make those decisions?"

Ask open-ended questions that can't be answered with a simple yes or no. Ask questions that begin with who, what, when, where, why, how much, etc.

Answer All Questions

Your script should have separate pages on which the most frequently asked questions are concisely and clearly answered. As with most forms of communication, comparison is powerful. Answering questions with numbers, facts, comparisons and concrete references to other organizations using your products or services is always superior to generalities.

Use Simple, Everyday Language

Use short words, short sentences and popular, graphic phrases. Talk like real people talk, not like some textbook. Long, multi-syllable words sound pompous and artificial. Replace them with shorter words that say the same thing. Since you'll be saying your script at a much slower rate than you normally speak, the words must be clear and simple so they can communicate with the greatest power.

Be Conversational

This means both the choice of words (mentioned above) and the interaction with the prospect. The script should never, under any circumstances, be read verbatim but rather should be delivered just as you would talk to the person spontaneously. Learn the script well enough so it can be varied in measured amounts to achieve the desired results.

This also means anticipating and planning "branches" that allow you to change direction depending upon what the person says. We mentioned one already: testing for whether you're talking to the right person. Another might involve a "step-down sale" from a larger, higher-priced model that was originally pitched to a lesser, lower-priced model the customer might agree to.

Ask for the Order (Of Course...)

Every good script -- like every good sales call -- concludes by asking clearly and unmistakably for the customer to agree to whatever it is we are seeking, be it a sale or appointment.

Repeat All Order Information

In the case of telephone selling there is an-other step, which is to carefully repeat and reinforce all items agreed upon. For example, if it's a meeting, confirm the date, time, place and any advance preparation that either party is to make. You might also add that you will be sending a confirming letter, which should then be sent immediately.

Test Your Script

Telephone scripts can be tested quickly and refined or scrapped. Some telemarketing managers claim they can tell if a script is successful in less than 100 calls, often taking no more than a few hours or a few days. At the very most, 300 completed calls are enough for even the most rigorous statistical significance. This is much faster than you test and prove any other means of selling.

For the most testing validity, pick your lists carefully and be sure they are representative of your total universe. Remembering a script that works for one prospect group might need to be modified or even totally rewritten for a different prospect group. In this respect, reviewing some of the variables presented in Chapter 8 on testing may be helpful. Even though the Chapter 8 material was designed for direct mail testing, most of the principles and practices are equally applicable to telemarketing as well.

TELEMARKETING TIPS

Go Right to the Top

Starting with the decision-maker is always preferable to "working your way up the ladder." An exception is when calling others can build a referral base which adds credibility and authority to your call to the top person.

It's best to call the top person even if you only talk to their secretary. For example, if Smith's secretary says, "Smith doesn't make those decisions; Jones does," thank the secretary and ask to be transferred to Jones.

When Jones gets on the line, say "I was talking to Smith's office and they said I should talk to you about ..." Often this kind of "hand-off" is all you need to get through to the right person.

Don't Waste Time Cold-Calling

If you want to close training and information sales, your own customer/ responder list will always be better than any outside lists. Sure, you can "cold canvas" by phone cheaper and faster than you could by direct mail or face-to-face. But it usually won't pay off at the bottom line. Instead, confine your telemarketing to those who have already expressed interest in your products/services. If you run out of names, start or increase your direct mail and/or media advertisements to stimulate an additional supply of hot, qualified leads.

Call Your Past Buyers and Seminar Participants

Calling past participants to sell upcoming events like they've already attended is extremely effective. They'll enroll others themselves or direct you to those who can. Often a good script can help you to uncover the true decision-maker, who will enroll multiple people in your events every time you call.

Chapter 7 Shows You How to Find the Best Outside Lists

If you conclude that you need outside telephone lists, Chapter 7 tells you how and where to find them. You'll be interested in all the same qualities that make a good mailing list -- with the added requirement for current telephone numbers. Unfortunately, the best responder lists are usually not available for telemarketing. However, the best compiled lists, including those from American Business Lists and Dun & Bradstreet, are routinely furnished with telephone numbers and may be obtained on diskette for your unlimited use.

Every Telephone Sales Call Has These Three Parts

(1.) Preparation, (2.) the call and (3.) follow-up. It doesn't matter whether you or the prospect originates the call. So, even for primarily incoming telemarketing and/or order taking, preparation and scripts are required.

Five Ways to Be Prepared

1. Before you begin any call, review the names of those you are going to call. Make sure you know as much about them and their organization as possible.

2. Be absolutely clear about the purpose of your call. Know exactly what you want the prospect to do. Review your script to be sure you have a reason for them to talk to you and a reason for them to act.

3. Be ready to talk. Your pencil or pen and paper should always be at hand.

4. Focus your complete attention on the caller, just as you would any important visitor entering your office.

5. Beware of subtle distractions like co-workers, paperwork on your desk or trying to do something else while you're talking to someone on the phone. Do not attempt any other work or communication until the call is completed.

Your Voice Is Your Passport

Take a deep breath before you make or accept a phone call. Relax. Then put a smile in your voice. It's amazing, but you can actually "hear" a person who is talking to you on the phone and smiling.

Speak in a friendly, conversational tone, neither too fast or too slow. The telephone company and many audio tape cassette courses are available to provide basic training in the telephone skills you'll need. Take advantage of these aids yourself and for anyone in your organization who will be talking to your customers on the telephone.

Develop a Greeting for Your Organization

Your greeting should include the name of your organization and the name of the person answering the phone. For example, "Schrello Direct Marketing. This is Judy. How may I direct your call?"

Check Your Prospect's Availability

Whenever you originate a call, check the prospect's availability to talk to you right now. If you pick up clues that this is a bad time for them, make an appointment to call back at a better time.

Introduce the Caller when Transferring Calls Internally

If you need to transfer the caller to someone else in your organization, take a moment and tell the fellow employee who the caller is and the subject of the call. This is a very professional touch when the client does not have to repeat the inquiry.

Learn to Listen

Try to listen with empathy, thinking and feeling as your prospect does. Some salespeople talk about making mental contact with the prospect. These techniques all have the same effect, to encourage you to get in closer touch with what your prospect's feeling.

Use Feedback and Paraphrasing

Make sure you identify, verify and clarify any key information your prospect furnishes you or that you have about them. Make use of natural reflective phrases such as "I see," or "that's right." They'll lend an easy, conversational tone to your conversation. And also use the caller's name as often as appropriate in the conversation. This is highly personal, and some people are put off if their name is artificially used too often. However, once or twice in the conversation at an appropriate time is often all you need to communicate the real personal rapport you're trying to achieve.

Take Notes

Take notes as you're listening to the prospect, and refer to them as needed throughout the call. There's an important difference between taking notes for your later reference or call report and taking notes to help you be sure the telephone conversation meets the prospect's needs.

Handle Irate Callers with Care

Apologize for whatever problem they have, regardless of whether it's justified or not. Let the angry caller vent their anger. Do not blame anyone and do not expect the caller to respond to logic. Be empathetic and listen. Don't lose your cool!

Ask Open-Ended Questions

Questions that can't be answered with a simple yes or no are always best; for example, questions that begin with who, what, when, where, why, how much, etc.

You Have About 45 Seconds

That's the time you have to stimulate enough interest for your prospect to want to continue the conversation once they're on the line. If your opening doesn't work in that period of time, you may have to get off the line and start again with someone else.

Be Careful Putting People on "Hold"

Tests show that hold is acceptable for about 25 to 45 seconds maximum. If the hold must be longer, be specific as to how long, and let the caller have the option of holding or your returning their call.

Voice Mail Versus Answering Machines Versus Answering Services

This is a continuing issue. Today many people believe that computer voice mail is superior to *both* answering machines and answering services for business use. Reasons given are that it's more reliable (usually), projects a more modern image and "empowers" the customer by being available at all times and giving them more options. Most of this is true, but think about your own experiences with each before you just jump on the bandwagon.

If you use a machine, bear in mind that a woman's voice with a British accent is still the most acceptable to both men and women. And it would be best if the person recording the message is not one of the firm's principals, thereby suggesting more "depth" to the staff.

Call First or Write First?

It's always a question whether you should send an advance letter and then telephone -- or telephone and then send a letter. Tests show that telephoning *before* to verify the individual's name, position and address -- and to subtly alert their assistant to look for the letter you're sending -- results in higher readership of the letter. Your phone call, timed to arrive one to two days *after* they've received (and read) your letter, will then be far more effective. So the best order is call, write and call again. If you can't afford a second call, then make sure your letter is designed to elicit a direct response (see Chapter 8).

Confirm *Every* Phone Call in Writing

Follow up your phone call with a letter confirming any decisions reached, next actions and so on. A follow-up letter should be sent for *every* phone contact you make.

Coordinate Your Telemarketing with Your Other Sales Approaches

If you're selling through other means, your telemarketing needs to be carefully coordinated with these other media. And telemarketers need to be prepared to answer questions about how they relate to these other media. For example, if the customer has a salesperson from your organization calling on them, they might logically ask, "How do you relate to Mary Smith? I've been dealing with her!" A crisp businesslike reply that answers that question can be worth its weight in gold.

Organize Your Telephone Answering

Small organizations often allow telephone answering responsibilities to remain vague or undefined. Normally one person answers the phone, but if that person is busy on another call or out of the office, the phone just rings until someone gets sufficiently annoyed to answer it. This is a serious mistake and should never be allowed in any organization that wants to project a positive image.

Designate one person to answer the phone and direct calls to others who handle them. The person who answers the phone should have no other telephone responsibilities unless everyone else who can possibly take a call is busy.

You need as many people designated to handle incoming calls as you have telephone lines. It's not likely that all lines will be busy very often, but you need to be prepared when it happens .

Once you've identified the people, now designate a "pecking order" in which they'll be routed incoming calls. This should start with the designated telemarketers, their supervision, others in the sales and marketing organization -- and then other staff personnel, but always in a designated order. In my company, every secretary and staff assistant was trained to take orders; and when all of the registrars and sales people's lines were busy, the switchboard operator would direct the call to the next person on the list. And the list included my own secretary, who -- during peak times -- would be handling customer calls just like anyone else.

Try a Headset

The advantage, of course, is that it leaves your hands totally free, without having to "juggle" the telephone. Almost anyone who spend a lot of time on the phone may find these lightweight headsets are a worthwhile investment. But in the final analysis this is very much an individual choice and should be left to each TSR to personally decide.

Provide a Toll-Free (800) Telephone Number

Organizations expecting a large volume of incoming calls from small businesses or from consumers can significantly improve response with an 800 number. Tests have shown an 800 number increases response among inquirers by 20% - 30%. It's not as necessary when your customers are large corporations and/or top executives. But an 800 number conveys a sense of marketing professionalism and offers to save your customer money. And today it's not very expensive; an incoming 800 number can easily be obtained for less than $50 a month.

Make Customer Records Available to the Telemarketer

If your company maintains a central marketing database, then that information should be made available on-line to each TSR. This enables them to immediately "call up" the customer's record to verify the information and be aware of the status of the customer's current or previous orders. This not only saves time, it also allows the telemarketer to better serve the customer.

Use the Computer to Manage Calling Activity

Today's computer can assist TSRs in managing their calling activity. For example, it's common to use the customer database to prompt call-back activity or even place the calls, particularly if the next action was recorded as part of the last call. At the other end, even Lotus 1-2-3 can be a handy way to sort and display simple telephone listings and call-back prompts. And there's plenty of commercially available software between these extremes. Chapter 13 has more on this.

If you're still "allergic" to computers, set up a manual "tickler" file for call-backs. One simple way is to use 3" x 5" file cards in a box with dividers for each month of the year and 31 numbered dividers for each day of the month. Keep your notes on the cards and file them behind the divider for the next action.

STEPS FOR STARTING YOUR OWN FORMAL TELEMARKETING OPERATION

If you decide to start a formal telemarketing operation, here are the steps you'll need to take:

Steps for Starting a Telemarketing Operation

1. Select product(s)/service(s) to offer.
2. Target the market you want to reach.
3. Set realistic telephone activity and sales objectives.
4. Decide on sales staff requirements.
5. Develop compensation plan.
6. Hire telephone sales manager.
7. Hire telephone sales representatives (TSRs).
8. Train everyone.
9. Establish call and activity monitoring techniques.
10. Select and install telephone equipment.
11. Set up physical environment.
12. Develop and test scripts.
13. Design record-keeping systems and forms.
14. Test and refine everything.

Use a Telemarketing Consultant

Hire a consultant or an experienced outsider to help you set up a formal telemarketing operation. While you probably could learn to be successful by "reinventing the wheel" on your own, it's not a good use of your time or energy. Instead, let the consultant do everything the first time through and get a satisfactory telemarketing operation going for you. *Then* you can concentrate on learning how to improve it in order to better sell your product(s) to your market(s).

Like any consultant, whoever you choose must be a person who has already done successfully *exactly* what you want them to do. Get a list of references and see if they were satisfied. If possible, choose a local consultant who can deal more directly with your staff and help with the thousands of details that are sure to come up.

Characteristics of a Successful Telephone Salesperson

The overriding consideration for telemarketing success is the ability to project yourself over the telephone. Experts refer to this in different ways: The telephone personality, positive projection, telephone enthusiasm, etc. But it all amounts to the same thing: the person who is enthusiastic, intelligent, goal-oriented and *very* self-motivated. They are also, generally, people who are very well-organized in their personal as well as business lives. They keep everything "neat as a pin" and can quickly put their hands on any piece of paper they need without fumbling through a disorganized desk.

The successful TSR also has to -- obviously -- enjoy talking to people on the telephone. This is one place where a successful face-to-face salesperson and a successful TSR may differ; the former often using the phone as little as possible, preferring instead to meet face-to-face with whomever they are talking to. Experts often cite other differences between successful telephone and face-to-face sales people, but for training and related information products and services, these differences are less significant than in other fields.

One of the reasons why the successful TSR must have a strong, positive, goal-oriented personality is that it's easy to get lots of rejection in a short time on the telephone. With calls averaging only five to ten minutes in length, it's possible to get a half-dozen rejections an hour. Such a situation could be disastrous for anyone without a strong self-image or for someone who took the rejection personally.

The TSR's voice is obviously an important consideration for telemarketing success. Such qualities as tone, pitch, clarity, volume and speaking rate all combine to make some people's voices more pleasant on the telephone than others. Picking the right parents is the recommended solution, but telephone voice training is a more reliable alternative. This training is now widely available, starting with your telephone company and from many other sources. It can lead to definite improvement for virtually anyone.

It used to be said that the best telemarketers often had physical characteristics not normally associated with sales success, such as being overweight, handicapped, unattractive, etc. However, this has *not* been the experience with those who are successful selling training or other knowledge products. Gen-

erally, training TSRs are more similar to face-to-face salespeople than they are different. They think, dress and act very much the same. The only difference is that contact with the client is by phone rather than face-to-face.

Other characteristics of successful telephone salespeople are that they are very competitive, demonstrating this through their desire to play competitive sports or their evidence of wanting to "win." And always look for people with a lot of energy. Telephone selling demands a lot of self-generated energy.

Finally, look for those who manage their time effectively, using a personal organizer to keep themselves on schedule.

Where do you find good telemarketing candidates? If you're lucky, you'll find an agency in your town who has had a reasonable track record of finding such people. But more than likely you will have to advertise or work through your "network" of contacts. You might try calling others who you know use telemarketing to see if they have a source they can recommend. If you're not a direct competitor, chances are they'll be cooperative.

Overall, start with somebody who has the telephone personality and let them learn your business. This is more likely to be successful than starting with somebody who knows your business and trying to train them to sell effectively by telephone.

Compensating Telephone Sales Personnel

Like any other sales personnel, telemarketer's compensation should generally be a mixture of a base salary plus a sales incentive. But unlike face-to-face sales personnel, TSRs typically receive a far smaller percentage of their total compensation as incentive. A recent survey by the telephone marketing council of the Direct Marketing Association showed that no more than 19% of total compensation was from incentives, while 81% was base. And TSRs who typically take incoming orders have an even smaller percent of their compensation based on incentives, some as small as 6%, with the remaining 94% of their compensation being base pay.

Generally, heavier reliance on a base salary and less reliance on commissions or incentives are characteristic of businesses where customer service is important, such as the meetings business.

Many telemarketing operations also employ noncash incentives, as well as strictly financial rewards. Because telemarketers often operate in a group environment, recognition devices such as awards, travel incentives or other events, as well as merchandise, all have a role as incentives. Many telemarketing organizations have some kind of audible way to tell the whole company about a telemarketer's sale, whether it's ringing a bell, sounding a horn or some other kind of attention-getting device. Your creativity in arranging these incentives can be the key to success.

How often should incentives be paid? As with other forms of incentives, the closer the reward occurs to the rewarded behavior, the more likely it is to reinforce that behavior. That means that weekly payment of incentives is superior to bimonthly. Monthly is superior to quarterly, and they are all superior to annual rewards. The best rule of thumb is to have any cash incentives distributed in the pay period immediately following the incentivized behavior.

Training Is the Key to Telemarketing Success

Training allows telemarketers to build upon and improve whatever individual telephone characteristics they initially have. Several techniques seem to be common to all of the best telemarketer training programs.

First, the tape recorder is your most effective personal training tool, because it lets you hear how you sound to others. If your telemarketers record their side of a conversation and listen to it, they'll identify many areas in which they can improve.

A second commonly used technique is to record the telephone conversation between the TSR and a customer. Here, you'll need to be concerned with any laws and regulations that may apply (although prevailing opinion seems to be that recording such conversations for training purposes only is OK), and you'll need to add the necessary equipment to allow you to do this. But most telephone marketing managers have at least one session a week with each telemarketer, in which they go over together one or more conversations selected by the telemarketer or randomly selected by the manager. Such meetings provide an opportunity for the sales manager to "coach" the telemarketer in specific customer situations.

And do consider formal telephone training for your staff. The telephone company offers a variety of good courses, as do many local providers. All of the basic skills can usually be picked up in a 1-day course and can then be practiced and reinforced on the job.

Two other final considerations: (1.) Consider some form of voice training either as part of the normal telephone training or separately. Such training can easily help to improve the skills the telemarketer already possesses. (2.) Consider training in listening skills. Telemarketing is clearly a business in which good listening may, in the long run, be as important as good speaking.

Monitoring Telemarketing Performance

Because telephone sales activity levels (calls placed and calls completed) can be measured daily, the success and failure of a telemarketer can be determined in weeks or at most a few months. There is no doubt that daily monitoring of performance is vital. Are the calls being placed at the expected rate? Are they being completed at the expected rate? Are sales being made at rates consistent with the number of calls completed and with the telemarketers experience? Daily monitoring of these important figures and any coaching, counseling or additional training that's required in order to meet established norms are vital to success.

FINDING AND EVALUATING OUTSIDE TELEPHONE SALES ORGANIZATIONS

The decision to set up an in-house telemarketing operation rather than use an outside vendor (called a telephone service center or service bureau) is never simple. But for those selling knowledge products, it's rare for an outside organization to be the best choice. The reason is that most of what you do is far too conceptual to reliably train an outside organization. Most service bureaus, with a high personnel turnover and tight call management, are geared to simpler, higher-volume, shorter-call situations. Nonetheless, there may be circumstances in which an outside service can meet your needs.

What a Telemarketing Firm Can and Can't Do

An outside telemarketing firm can take incoming orders, sell simple products or packaged services and do well-structured telephone research. Books, software, audio cassettes and packaged programs are examples of training products that may lend themselves to a telephone service bureau. On the other hand, multi-day seminars, consulting or custom program design services can rarely, if ever, be sold reliably by an outside service bureau.

Some Representative Outside Telemarketing Service Bureaus

As with most professional service vendors, it's important to talk to others who have used the same approach and determine what they liked and didn't like about the services that they used. Look for others telemarketing products similar to yours, and respond to their telephone number. If you like the way they handle you, find out who they are and get them to propose. Here's a starter list:

AT&T AMERICAN TRANSTECH
Direct Marketing Services
8000 Baymeadows Way
Jacksonville, FL 32256
Phone: (800) 332-5290, (904) 636-1000; Fax: (904) 636-3996

ATLANTA DIRECT MARKETING
6951-J Roswell Rd.
Atlanta, GA 30328
Phone: (404) 393-0427

DIALAMERICA MARKETING
960 MacArthur Blvd.
Mahwan, NJ 07495
Phone: (800) 531-3131, (201) 327-0200; Fax: (201) 327-6821
Contact: Jim Ahearn, Director of Marketing

GLS DIRECT
2000 Market Street, Suite 1408
Philadelphia, PA 19103
Phone: (800) 232-1100, (215) 568-1100
Contact: Joan Toll, Executive Vice President

INTERSTATE TELE-MARKETING
230 S. 108th
Omaha, NE 68154
Phone: (402) 333-1900

THE MARTEL GROUP
3601 Main Street
Kansas City, MO 64111
Phone: (800) 234-3515, (816) 531-7776
Contact: Kathleen Burke

MATRIXX MARKETING (Division of Cincinnati Bell)
One Matrixx Plaza
Ogden, UT 84405
Phone (800) 543-6423, (801) 621-6423; Fax: (801) 629-6272
Contact: Opal Singleton, Corporation Accounts Director

RESPONSE MARKETING
100 W. Harrison
South Tower, 5th Floor.
Seattle, WA 98119
Phone: (206) 285-8008

TELEAMERICA, INC.
1822 Ridge Avenue, Suite 100
Evanston, IL 60201
Phone (800) 377-8353, (708) 869-9001

US SPRINT COMMUNICATIONS
5600 N. River Rd.
Rosemont, IL 60018-5156
Phone: (312) 364-4600

U.S. TELEMARKETING (UST)
5300 Oakbrook Parkway, Building 300
Norcross, GA 30093
Phone: (404) 381-0100; Fax: (404) 921-2363
Contact: Harold Benson, Vice President

WATS MARKETING OF AMERICA
2121 N. 117th Avenue
Omaha, NE 68164
Phone: (800) 351-1000, (402) 571-8866; Fax:
(402) 498-4077
Contact: Michaela S. Wright, Sales

Telemarketing organizations concentrate in places like Utah, Kansas, Oklahoma and New Jersey. The successful telephone service bureau may be virtually anywhere there's a good supply of hard-working, diligent, people. Your main concern is not *where* they are but *whether* they have already demonstrated that they can do a project like yours.

How can you tell whether an in-house operation is better than going to a service bureau? Here are the advantages of each:

Advantages of Service Bureaus

1. Lower Costs. Unless you plan to make a massive amount of calls (some say more than 100,000 calls per year), it won't be easy to match the service bureaus low prices. Most charge minimal start-up fees and have low minimum monthly charges. The cost factor can be especially important if you don't have the money to start your own operation.

2. Easier and Quicker Start-Up. Service bureaus can set up your program cheaper, faster and with fewer problems than you can, because they have personnel, telephone lines and equipment already in place.

3. Round-the-Clock-Operation. Service bureaus are the only practical way to have your lines answered 24 hours a day, 365 days a year. It is almost never economically feasible to do this yourself, unless or until call volume gets very large.

4. Ability to Handle Peaks. Service bureaus know how to staff-up to handle peak rates of incoming or outgoing calls required to match specific direct mail or broadcast campaigns.

5. Experience. Service bureaus are run by the most capable and experienced telephone marketing managers in the business. Their experience in high-volume calling allows them to avoid mistakes you will probably make on your own, and they can often project sales and calling rates with surprising accuracy.

6. Simplified Testing. A service bureau can test and develop a new program to determine whether it will work. Of course they will retain whatever scripts and other work they develop, so you cannot simply "steal" their experience in order to bring it in-house later.

Advantages of In-House Telemarketing

1. Control. The number-one advantage of doing it yourself is control. You hire the sales people, train them, write their scripts and control how and when they work.

2. Ability to Handle Complex Situations. As already mentioned, your in-house people can handle highly technical calls and customer service inquiries that no outside service bureau will even attempt. This is the reason that most seminar and conference sales programs are handled in-house.

3. Accessibility of Your Customer Database. Your telephone salespeople can have access to your on-line registration database, including previous participant transactions, organizational history, etc. This enables you to much better serve your customer than any outside service bureau ever could.

4. Employee Commitment. Your own employees are better able to project your organization's attitude and culture to customers. They have a greater knowledge of other company operations and can help the client in other matters beyond merely the current sale. This greater commitment shows.

5. Feedback. When your own employees are on the phone with the customer they will be able to pick up questions, trends or difficulties that seem to form a pattern. They will be able to bring this to your attention quickly, possibly signaling a situation that would necessitate changing the product, the service or method of advertising and promotion. Outside service bureaus will rarely identify such patterns and even less rarely communicate them back to you in a timely fashion.

Two Ways to Work with Service Bureaus

There are two common arrangements with telemarketing service bureaus. One deal is commonly called PI because payment is per inquiry (or per order), regardless of what later happens. PI is used for many radio and television spots. It's good for simple, high-volume, quick-response products but not for complex knowledge products. One common disadvantage of PI is low-quality responder information, such as missing or transposed digits, incorrect apartment or suite number,

incorrect telephone numbers or credit-card numbers.

The second arrangement with a service bureau is to pay an hourly rate based on the type of work being done, like calling, order processing, training, testing scripts, etc. Most telephone service bureaus are unwilling to enter into highly incentivized arrangements, because they must invest time and effort in order to actually do the work, and the ultimate campaign success depends on many factors outside their control. Nonetheless, even paying them a fixed hourly rate can be far more economical than attempting to do it yourself.

Of course, there are combinations of these various methods that are sometimes discussed. You will be better able to evaluate them after talking to others who have used the firm for similar types of arrangements.

SOME USEFUL REFERENCES

Here are four useful telemarketing references:

1. Encyclopedia of Telemarketing, by Richard L. Bencin and Donald J. Jonovic. Prentice Hall, 113 Sylvan Avenue, Englewood Cliffs, NJ 07632. Phone: (201) 592-2000. 1989. ISBN 0-13-275918-7. (726 pages, $69.95)

Recommended in Teleprofessional's 1993 product and service guide by Bob Van Voorhis, Jr., Editor-in-Chief. This is the definitive guide for telemarketing, with insights from 30 of the nation's top telemarketing experts. Contains chapters on how to organize and staff a telemarketing center, how computers are integral to a successful operation and how to write telemarketing scripts.

2. Newton's Telecom Dictionary, by Harry Newton. Telecom Library, Inc., 12 West 21st Street - 10th Floor, New York, NY 10010. Phone: (800) LIBRARY, (212) 691-8215; Fax: (212) 691-1190. (4th Edition). ISBN 0-936648-.

The most complete listing of telecommunications and technology terminology that is available, according to Teleprofessional's Editor-in-Chief Bob Van Voorhis, Jr. He said it provides a definition of everything imaginable ... and a few unimaginable ... in (the telemarketing) business.

3. Selling by Phone: The Salesperson's Guide to Getting New Customers and Closing Deals, by Linda Richardson. McGraw-Hill, 1221 Avenue of the Americas, New York, NY 10020. Phone: (212) 337-5945, (800) 2-MCGRAW. 1991. ISBN 0-07-052339-8. ($19.95)

4. Successful Telephone Selling in the '90's, by Martin D. Shafiroff and Robert L. Shook. HarperCollins Publishers, 10 E. 53rd Street, New York, NY 10022. Phone: (800) 242-7737, (212) 207-7000; Fax: (212) 207-7617. 1990 (Revised edition). ISBN 0-06-096491-X. (224 pages, paperback, $10.00)

Learn how to overcome every objection, develop a powerful presentation, get through the screener, close with proven techniques and project a winning telephone image.

PRINT ADVERTISING, TRADE SHOWS, NEWSLETTERS, PUBLICITY AND A VARIETY OF OTHER SALES & MARKETING METHODS

The previous chapters covered most of the essentials for marketing your training, continuing education and information products and services. But, as you know from Chapter 3, there are many other methods you can -- and sometimes should -- employ. That's what this chapter is for: To overview the sales and marketing techniques we've not addressed elsewhere, particularly:

- Advertising in newspapers, magazines and other print periodicals
- Getting the most from trade shows, expositions and conferences
- Using newsletters and other ways to stay in touch
- Customer/Client/User conferences
- Writing and publishing a book
- Writing articles and columns
- Getting and using publicity
- Directories, course listings and on-line computer databases
- Distributors, agents and sales representatives
- Radio and television -- including infomercials
- Promotional audio tapes, video cassettes and computer diskettes
- Working with associations

HOW AND WHEN TO ADVERTISE IN PERIODICALS

Four Types of Printed Periodicals

In principle, periodicals can exist in any medium, and there are examples on radio and television. But, today at least, advertising in periodicals means being in one of four basic types of print media:

Newspapers: inexpensive daily or weekly publications, published quickly and having a short life span. They're read to stay abreast of fast-breaking news.

Magazines: more polished, longer-lived vehicles, generally published weekly, monthly or quarterly. Magazines tend to be "slicker" than newspapers, with heavier paper, coated stock (rather than newsprint) and more color.

Tabloids: falling somewhere between conventional magazines and newspapers in size, appearance and publication schedule.

Directories: listings of people, products or services of interest to some group, usually published annually. Directories may appear as magazine pages, sections, special editions, supplements or separate bound volumes. Directories have the longest useful life of any print publication, frequently retained for years and even passed on when new editions appear.

How Periodicals Make Money

Print periodicals get income from three basic sources:

1.   Subscription revenues
2.   Advertising
3.   Mailing list rentals

Many publishers also find that they can make money from conferences, books and related research services, all clustered around their target market.

Subscription revenues are rarely the biggest source of income. Just look at your local newspaper; you could *never* buy that much information for the newsstand price if that were the only way the publisher made money.

Of course, subscription revenues are always welcome. They help defray distribution costs (such as delivery or postage). But you can run a very successful periodical that's free; for example, *The Penny-Saver*, the weekly advertising paper delivered door-to-door in major metropolitan areas. The business equivalent of *The Penny-Saver* is called a *controlled circulation publication*, distributed without charge to those who meet certain occupational, employment or professional qualifications. Chances are you already receive at least one controlled circulation publication.

How do such publications make money? The answer is from the other two revenue sources: *Advertising revenue* and *mailing list rentals*.

Advertising revenues are the cornerstone of almost every periodical, from the prestigious *National Geographic* and *Science* through *The Wall Street Journal* and your lo-

cal newspaper to -- you guessed it -- even the lowly *Penny-Saver*. Publishers divide their sales budget between building circulation and selling ads, but when the chips are down, selling ads wins every time. It's so vital, that publishers pay for an independent BPA (short for Business Publication Audit) to provide detailed, up-to-date circulation statistics to would-be advertisers. And many publications also offer advertisers various geographic or demographic editions to target selected groups of readers.

But don't discount mailing list revenues. Some report $5 to $10 per name per year and more! During the 1980s, some magazines were created solely to build and maintain mailing lists. In these cases, the magazine merely broke even on its subscription and advertising revenues; the *real* profit came from renting the mailing list. (See Chapter 7 for more on controlled circulation mailing lists.)

Choose From Five Kinds of Ads

The most common forms of print advertising in periodicals are the following:

Display Ads can range from a single-column wide, 1-inch high ad in a newspaper (called a column-inch) to a multi-page, four-color ad in a magazine. Display ads are designed and produced by the advertiser or the advertiser's agency, and camera-ready, color-separated artwork is delivered to the publication ready to print. Charges are based on size, color, number of times run and position.

Classified Ads are generally short listings grouped by type of product or service advertised. Classified ads are typeset by the publisher and priced by the word or line. They're big business for newspapers, and many products and services have been profitably sold for years through classified ads in *Sunset*, *Popular Mechanics* -- AND *Training*!

Inserts/Supplements are special publications bound into a periodical, inserted loose or included in its polybag or mailing envelope. Advertisers usually produce their insert and deliver it to the publisher ready to bind-in or insert. Supplements are generally produced by the publisher. Charges are based on complexity and added costs (like postage),

Directory Listings include information on an organization, its products and/or its services, typeset by the publisher from information supplied by the advertiser. Listings in business directories are often free, but extra-cost enhancements (like large or bold-face type or boxes) may be available, and many directories also accept display ads.

Calendar Listings, usually without cost, feature upcoming events, like seminars and conferences. The sheer volume of such events forces many publications to restrict these listings to (say) only the largest events or perhaps only those sponsored by nonprofit organizations.

Which of these ads will work best for your training and information product or service? There's no way to tell until you test. We can provide some guidelines and summarize the experiences of others. But ultimately you need to do your own testing.

Here's When to Use Print Advertising

Direct mail and telemarketing are the sharpshooters' mediums, while print media and broadcast are shotguns. If your targets are few, worthwhile and identified, nothing beats a rifle. But if they are hard to find, small in number or hard to identify, then you may want to use a shotgun to be sure you hit something.

Edward L. Nash, in his book *Direct Marketing*, described a reverse role of newspaper and magazine advertising this way:

"Print media extends direct mail. If subscribers to a magazine are an effective list, for instance, then an advertisement in that magazine enables you to reach not only the subscribers but also the newsstand buyers of the magazine. You'll also reach the publication's pass-along readership. According to some studies, this can be two or three times the circulation and up to six times the number of subscribers."

How do you know which publication to advertise in? This is one of the most difficult decisions you have to make. Look where your competitors or those marketing related products and services advertise regularly. One or a few ads in a publication show test-

ing, but regular ads show success. For example, if you take two editions of *Training* Magazine a year apart and compare the classified ads, you'll find some identical ad running in both editions. This shows an ad that's working! If you have a like product or service to offer, a similar ad in the same publication would likely be successful for you, too.

These same remarks apply to what the ads look like or say. Regularly repeated formats are working well. On the other hand, a format which appears briefly and is no longer seen probably didn't work well.

Be sure to evaluate *why* an ad is appearing. Display ads to get leads for a far flung sales force may be fine, provided you have a sales force. If you don't, such ads may be a total waste of money, getting you leads in places you can't easily pursue. This happened to one of our clients. They advertised in a national magazine and got leads all over the country. But they were based in the midwest. They found that the leads were scattered so far and wide that it would cost thousands of dollars to follow up on them. So although the ad worked, it was definitely *not* good for them.

You're going to have to learn what works and what doesn't work for you through testing. Here's some advice on where to start. We've had *good* success in print media with the following types of campaigns:

- Display ads for seminars held outside of normal business hours.
- Display or classified ads for inexpensive books.
- Calendar listings for seminars, meetings and other events.
- Classified ads to get leads for training and information products and services sold by telephone.
- Product announcements (Note: Sometimes these announcements are "free" to those who advertise. In some cases, the ads didn't do much but the product announcement did).

We've had *mixed* success with the following kinds of ads (mixed meaning that some have been profitable and others have not -- and we don't know *why* in either case):

- Display or classified ads for medium- and

don't know *why* in either case):

- Display or classified ads for medium- and high-priced books.
- Display ads for multi-day professional conferences.
- Directory listings.
- Display ads to get leads for big-ticket products/services sold face-to-face.

In these "mixed" cases, you really need to check carefully whether others who are selling products and services like yours are repeatedly using the media.

We've had *no* success with the following:

- Display ads for multi-day seminars.

Where to Place Your Ad

This question has two parts: What *publication* should you use, and *where* in the publication should your ad go? The first question deals with how best to reach your market. We've already discussed how to find these in general terms. Here's some specifics.

The "raw data" is provided by the industry's two "bibles":

Business Publication Rates and Data. Standard Rate and Data Service (SRDS), 2000 Clearwater Drive, Oak Brook, IL 60521. Phone: (800) 851-SRDS, (800) 851-7737; Fax: (708) 574-6565. 1-year subscription (12 issues), $497.

If your prime sales prospects read business-to-business, technical or trade publications, this book brings you the hard-to-find information you need to put together an effective marketing and media plan. It includes over 5,500 U.S. business, technical and trade publications for over 165 markets, 600 direct response listings over 8000 healthcare listings, and 514 international publications. Standardized listings include editorial profile, advertising rates, regulations, mechanical requirements, closing dates, circulation statements and more.

Newspaper Rates and Data. Standard Rate and Data Service (SRDS), 2000 Clearwater Drive, Oak Brook, IL 60521. Phone: (800) 851-SRDS, (800) 851-7737; Fax: (708) 574-6565. 1-year subscription (12 issues), $485.

This is the industry's leading sourcebook. Monthly updates show current ad costs, newspaper-distributed magazines, inserts, comics, college papers and specialized weeklies. It profiles more than 1,800 daily and weekly newspapers. It includes state, county, city and metro market data, state media/market maps and metro ranking tables. Listings allow you to locate and compare display and classified ad rates, circulation figures, mechanical requirements, contract and copy regulations, closing times and more.

(Rates are generally in agate lines, which is a standard way of expressing newspaper ad sizes. There are 14 lines to an agate inch. A 100-line ad can be 100 by 1 or 50 by 2, the second figure indicating the number of columns.)

Which daily newspaper in the U.S. boasts the largest circulation? Which Sunday newspaper enjoys the same distinction? Every six months, the Audit Bureau of Circulations -- a nonprofit organization of publishers, ad agency executives and advertisers -- compiles audited reports that are distributed to its members and serves to answer the above questions. Here's the top 10 in both groups from a recent report:

Daily	Circulation
1. *Wall Street Journal* (nat'l ed.)	1,935,866
2. *USA Today* (national edition)	1,387,233
3. *Los Angeles Times*	1,210,077
4. *New York Daily News*	1,180,139
5. *New York Times*	1,149,683
6. *Washington Post*	824,282
7. *Chicago Tribune*	740,713
8. *Newsday*	711,264
9. *Detroit Free Press*	639,767
10. *San Francisco Chronicle*	569,257

Sunday	Circulation
1. *New York Times*	1,706,013
2. *Los Angeles Times*	1,504,540
3. *New York Daily News*	1,461,316
4. *Detroit News & Free Press*	1,270,420
5. *Washington Post*	1,154,420
6. *Chicago Tribune*	1,141,455
7. *Philadelphia Inquirer*	994,539
8. *Boston Globe*	787,858
9. *Newsday*	713,779
10. *San Francisco Examiner & Chronicle*	713,172

When newspaper or display ads are not specified for a specific section, they are "*run of paper*," or ROP. Most newspaper advertising is sold ROP. Your ad can be placed anywhere. Specific classifications or sections of the paper, such as "Food," "Editorial," "Main News," "Sports," "Financial," and "Business" usually have separate and higher rates or require a placement surcharge. There are also surcharges for specific positions, such as "top of column."

Which sections of newspapers work best? In descending order: Main News, Business, Sports (males only), Life-Style/Women (females only).

Both placement (location in the publication) and position (location on the page) for display ads can and should be negotiated.

Non-cover placement and position of display ads is often tested. About half the time, the tests show that placement makes no measurable difference. The rest of the time, the following seems to be confirmed:

1. Placement near the front of a publication or section is better than placement near the back.

2. Right-hand pages are better than left-hand pages.

3. Fractional-page ads are best at lower-right-hand corner.

4. Fractional-page ads repeated for several consecutive issues are better than one full-page ad.

In buying classified ads in newspapers or magazines, be cautious about automatically placing advertisements in "appropriate" classifications. Ed Nash has said that "The education section is often not the best place for a school ad, just as the stamp and coin page would not be the best place for an ad selling coins to investors -- especially if you were seeking to bring new people into the market."

Is the Size of Your Ad Important?

The short answer to this question is an obvious yes, but the *real* question is, "What's the right size for *your* ad?" Among classified ad users, there's repeated stories of very small ads producing *more* response than larger ads -- provided the smaller ad is well-crafted and has a good headline (see the thoughts on

headlines further on in this section). Berlitz Language Schools and others have found that smaller display ads can generate as many inquiries as larger ones and, owing to their lesser cost, can make repeated advertising more attractive.

For most display ads, a third- to half-page is generally sufficient, especially if your objective is to secure direct response. If your objective is to "make a big splash," announcing some important new product or service, then a full-page ad is usually a "must."

As a general rule, trade off size in favor of frequency: Three small ads are often more productive than one large one. The same is true within a given edition -- three quarter-page ads frequently do better than one full-page ad, even if they cost a bit more.

And remember, *long copy works*! People read long copy. Readership falls off rapidly up to 50 words, but drops very little between 50 and 500 words. David Ogilvy said "The more you tell, the more you sell." It really works that way! People like Joe Sugarman and Joe Karbo demonstrated great success with "copy-heavy" ads in all sorts of publications. In fact, Joe Karbo's ad "The Lazy Man's Way to Riches" was such a long-time hit, we've included it on the next page.

When and How Often Your Ad Should Run

All the timing considerations in Chapters 5 and 6 should be reviewed. These apply to print advertising as well as other ads for training and information. What follows are timing considerations unique to print media.

Most publications schedule "theme" issues devoted to a particular topic. Examples are Industry Surveys, Annual Directories, Editions to be distributed at a trade show or an issue on one "hot" topic. Ads in theme issues sometimes cost more but are often worth it, especially if that issue has more circulation, is kept longer or is passed along more.

Publishers also offer advantageous tie-in promotions. For example, one publication offers advertisers a free product announcement in a special, high-readership section.

Sample of a Successful, Copy-Heavy, Display Ad

Too Busy Earning a Living To Make Any Money?

You think you've got problems?

Well, I remember when a bank turned me down for a $200 loan. Now I lend money to the bank — Certificates of Deposit at $100,000 a crack.

I remember the day a car dealer got a little nervous because I was a couple of months behind in my payments — and repossessed my car. Now I own a Rolls Royce. I paid $43,000 for it — cash.

I remember the day my wife phoned me, crying, because the landlord had shown up at the house, demanding his rent — and we didn't have the money to pay it.

Now we own five homes. Two are on the ocean-front in California (I use one as my office). One is a lakefront "cabin" in Washington, (that's where we spend the whole summer — loafing, fishing, swimming, and sailing.) One is a condominium on a sunny beach in Mexico. And one is snuggled right on the best beach of the best island in Hawaii — Maui.

Right now I could sell all this property, pay off the mortgages, — and — without touching any of my other investments — walk away with over $750,000 in cash. But I don't want to sell, because I don't think of my homes as "investments." I've got other real estate — and stocks, bonds, and cash in the bank — for that.

I remember when I lost my job. Because I was head over heels in debt, my lawyer told me the only thing I could do was declare bankruptcy. He was wrong. I paid off every dime.

Now, I have a million dollar line of credit; but I still don't have a job. Instead, I get up every weekday morning and decide whether I want to go to work or not. Sometimes I do — for 5 or 6 hours. But about half the time, I decide to read, go for a walk, sail my boat, swim, or ride my bike.

I know what it's like to be broke. And I know what it's like to have everything you want. And I know that you — like me — can *decide* which one it's going to be. It's really as easy as that. That's why I call it "The Lazy Man's Way to Riches."

So I'm going to ask you to send me something I don't need: money. Ten dollars to be exact. Why? Because I want you to pay attention. And I figure

PROOF!
Don't take my word for it. These are excerpts from articles in newspapers and magazines:

Time:
He only works half the year in his stunning office on California's Sunset Beach, and even when he's there he puts in short hours...In other words, Joe Karbo, 48, is the prototype for..."The Lazy Man's Way to Riches."

Seattle Times:
Is it all honest? A man who has done business with him says Karbo's reputation is excellent, and that he has managed to conduct mutually beneficial deals with him with nothing but a handshake and an oral agreement.
Want to be rich? Take my advice and follow his.

Boston Herald-American:
The book has drawn hundreds of letters from persons who have profited by it...

Los Angeles Herald-Examiner:
An unpretentious millionaire, Joe Karbo of Huntington Harbor is a vibrant, living testimonial to his intellectual, pragmatic conviction.

Forbes:
After bouncing around show biz, advertising, and real estate, he made his fortune...Last year (1972) he made $250,000.

Money Making Opportunities:
Maybe Joe Karbo has the secret. Don't you think you owe it to yourself to find out what it is all about?...I just finished it — and I'm off on a vacation myself. Get the idea?

The Boston Globe:
Jay Haws of Chico, Cal. said the pep talk...in "The Lazy Man's Way to Riches" has "changed my life," and upped his freelance graphic designer income from $2000 to $30,000 annually.
"I'm not rich yet," said Haws, "but I see the light at the end of the tunnel...It gave me the swift kick in the pants that I needed."

Long Beach Independent:
He's programmed the path to riches for the lazy man.

that if you've got $10 invested, you'll look over what I send you and decide whether to send it back...or keep it. And I don't *want* you to keep it unless you agree that it's worth at least a hundred times what you invested.

Is the material "worth" $10? No — if you think of it as paper and ink. But that's not what I'm selling. What I am selling is information. *More* information than I give when I'm paid $1000 as a guest speaker. *More* information than I give in a one-hour consultation for $300.

But you're really not risking *anything*. Because I won't cash your check or money order for 31 days *after* I've sent you my material. That's the deal. Return it in 31 days — and I'll send back your check or money order — uncashed.

How do you know I'll do it? Well, if you really want to be on the safe side, post-date your check for a month from today — *plus 2 additional weeks*. That'll give you plenty of time to receive it, look it over, try it out.

I know what you're thinking: "He got rich telling people how to get rich." The truth is — and this is very important — the year before I shared "The Lazy Man's Way to Riches," my net income was $216,646. And what I'll send you tells just how I made that kind of money...working a few hours a day...about 8 months out of the year.

It doesn't require "education." I'm a high school graduate.

It doesn't require "capital." Remember I was up to my neck in debt when I started.

It doesn't require "luck." I've had more than my share. But I'm not promising you that you'll make as much money as I have. And you may do better. I personally know one man who used these principles, worked hard, and made 11 million dollars in 8 years. But money isn't everything.

It doesn't require "talent." Just enough brains to know what to look for. And I'll tell you that.

It doesn't require "youth." One woman I worked with is over 70. She's travelled the world over, making all the money she needs, doing only what I taught her.

It doesn't require "experience." A widow in Chicago has been averaging $25,000 a year for the past 5 years, using my methods.

What does it require? Belief. Enough to take a chance. Enough to absorb what I'll send you. Enough to put the principles into *action*. If you do just that — nothing more, nothing less — the results will be hard to believe. Remember — I guarantee it.

You don't have to give up your job. But you may soon be making so much money that you'll be able to. Once again — I guarantee it.

I know you're skeptical. Well, here are some comments from other people. (Initials have been used to protect the writer's privacy. The originals are in my files.) I'm sure that, like you, these people didn't believe me either when they clipped the coupon. Guess they figured that, since I wasn't going to deposit their check for at least 31 days, they had nothing to lose.

They were right.

And here's what they gained:

'Wow, it does work!'
"Oddly enough, I purchased Lazy Man's Way to Riches some six months ago, or so, read it..and really did nothing about it. Then, about three weeks ago, when I was really getting desperate about my financial situation, I remembered it, re-read it, studied it, and this time, put it to work and WOW, it does work! Doesn't take much time, either...I guess some of us just have to be at a severe point of desperation before we overcome the ultimate laziness, procrastination."
Mr. J.K., Anaheim, CA

'Made $50,000 just fooling around'
"In February 1974 you sent me (for ten bucks) your Lazy Man's Way to Riches. Since then I have made approximately 50 grand ($50,000) just fooling around on the basis of your advice. You see, I really

am lazy — otherwise I could have made 50 million! Thank you!"
Mr. R. McK., Atlanta, GA

'$24,000 in 45 days'
"...received $24,000.00 in the mail the last 45 days. Thanks again."
Mr. E.G.N., Matewan, W.VA

Made $70,000
"A $70,000 thanks to you for writing The Lazy Man's Way to Riches. That's how much I've made...

"I use this extra income for all of the good things in life, exotic vacations, classic automobiles, etc. Soon I hope to make enough to quit my regular job and devote full time to making money the easy way..."
Mr. D.R., Newport Beach, CA

$260,000 in eleven months
"Two years ago, I mailed you ten dollars in sheer desperation for a better life...One year ago, just out of the blue sky, a man called and offered me a partnership...I grossed over $260,000 cash business in eleven months. You are a God sent miracle to me."
B.F., Pascagoula, Miss.

'There's no stopping me'
"Since I've got your (Lazy Man's Way to Riches) in July, I've started 4 companies...there's no stopping me and I'm so high I need chains to keep me on the ground."
M.T. Portland, OR

What I'm saying is probably contrary to what you've heard from your friends, your family, your teachers, and maybe everyone else you know.

I can only ask you one question.

How many of them are millionaires?

So it's up to you.

A month from today, you can be nothing more than 30 days older — or you can be on your way to getting rich. You decide.

The wisest man I ever knew told me something I never forgot: "Most people are too busy earning a living to make any money."

Don't take as long as I did to find out he was right.

I'll prove it to you, if you'll send in the coupon now. I'm not asking you to "believe" me. Just try it. If I'm wrong, all you've lost is a couple of minutes and a postage stamp. But what if I'm right?

©Joe Karbo - 1979, 17105 South Pacific, Sunset Beach, Calif. 90742

Sworn Statement:
"On the basis of my professional relationship as his accountant, I certify that Mr. Karbo's net worth is more than one million dollars."
Stuart A. Cogan

Bank Reference:
Home Bank
17010 Magnolia Avenue
Fountain Valley,
CA 92708

- -
Joe Karbo
17105 South Pacific, Dept. 206-A
Sunset Beach, California 90742

Joe, you may be full of beans, but what have I got to lose? Send me the Lazy Man's Way to Riches. *But don't deposit my check or money order for at least 31 days after it's in the mail.*

If I return your material — for *any* reason — within that time, return my *uncashed* check or money order to me. On that basis, here's my ten dollars.

Name _____
        (Please Print Clearly)
Address _____

City _____

State _____ Zip _____
SORRY — NO COD'S

Since product announcements usually receive greater response than display ads, a good strategy is to take a minimum display ad merely to qualify for the product listing.

How often should your ad run? The short answer is, as often as it's profitable. Get in the habit of repeating your winners. Scores of great advertisements have been discarded before they have begun to really pay off. Readership can actually *increase* with repetition, some authorities saying up to five repetitions, but evidence seems to suggest that the limit -- if one exists -- may be higher still.

Finally, if your ad supports other parts of your marketing campaign, such as direct mail, a news conference, seminar or workshop, then time the ad in relation to these other marketing events.

Spend Half Your Writing Time on the Headline

On the average, five times as many people read the headline of an ad as read the body copy. If follows that if you don't sell your product or service in the headline, you've wasted 80% of your money. And headlines that promise a benefit sell more than those that don't. That's why most successful headlines include the product or service *and* the promise. Chapter 8 has a section on creating arresting headlines. Read it!

Ogilvy and Mather claim that time after time, they've found it pays to inject genuine news into headlines. Everyone is always on the lookout for *new* products or *new* improvements to an old product or *new* ways to use an old product.

When schools and seminar sponsors advertise in newspapers to build enrollments, course location and starting date should be prominently featured, as in "Long Beach Classes Start October 1st." This makes the ad a news item in itself, with its own elements of localness, immediacy and newness.

Include a Photograph

Every test shows that photographs invariably work better than drawings. They attract more readers, are more believable, are better remembered, pull more responses and sell more books. The one exception seems to be for seminars, where tests have shown that line art -- or no art -- is superior to photos. But even here, photos must still be used to show what materials, books or job-aids participants receive at the seminar.

Use captions under every photograph. On the average, twice as many people read the captions under photographs as read the body copy. It follows that you should *never use a photograph without putting a caption under it*; and each caption should be a miniature advertisement for the product -- complete with the name and benefits promised.

The question is always whether adding a photo will boost the ad's effectiveness enough to cover the higher costs and complexity. Usually it will, but if the benefits are uncertain, then devise a test to be sure.

Some experts claim notable results with photographs which suggest a story. The reader glances at the photograph and asks, "What goes on here?" Then he or she reads the copy to find out. Harold Rudolph called this magic element "story appeal." The more of it you put into your photograph, the more people look at your ad. However, it's easier said than done.

More Tips for Using Print Advertising:

Ads that Look Like Editorial Material Often Do Better than Those that Look Like Ads. Editorial layouts get higher readership than conventional ads. One way to use this involves "reader notice" advertising, 50- to 100-line ads designed to resemble other newspaper articles. Successful "reader notice" ads included many self-improvement subjects, in areas such as memory, vocabulary and conversation.

An 800 Number Increases Response. An ad promoting a 24-hour, 7-day toll-free (800) telephone number can generate up to 30% *more* responses by including the redundant phrase, "Including Sunday" when the ad appears on a Sunday. The easier an 800 number is to see in an ad, the greater the response. And always use a drawing of a telephone next to the number.

Alert Your Best Customers Before Your Display Ad Runs. To increase effectiveness of your advertising in trade publications, try mailing a pre-print of your ad to your active customers/responders so they get it two weeks *before* the publication date, along with a letter telling them when and where to look. Giving advance "insider" information this way can increase response and readership with other groups as well.

"Image" Ads Are a Waste Of Money -- for two reasons: (1.) They don't work and (2.) you can't measure their results. Even scientific surveys of advertising's impact on "share of mind" -- conducted by and for those who earn their livelihood from print advertising -- are mixed. *Always* advertise to sell something, and ask for the order in the ad. Market share (sales) beats mind share (image) every time.

Always Include a Coupon. Even if your primary response will be by phone, including a coupon increases that response. Coupons should *always* be surrounded by a dashed line to show they're to be cut out. Include in the coupon all the information you want the reader to furnish you (or to have available when they respond by phone). Coupons *call* for action -- and *get* action -- more than any other device.

It also provides you a direct means to gage the effectiveness of your ad. For instance, if you include the same or similar coupon in a number of different ads, the relative response you obtain from each of them can be easily measured. (See Chapter 8 for how to distinctively code each coupon.)

Color Works. Virtually every test shows that color improves response over black and white. But 2-color is usually all that is required. The tests show that in direct response ads, 2-color is about four times as effective as single color, but 3- and 4-color ads begin to diminish in their increased effectiveness while costing substantially more.

Which colors work best? Every test I've seen shows that black printing on a yellow background is the most readable and the most memorable. Our own tests have borne this out. The second favorite colors seem to be blue and red; the latter primarily for accent and emphasis. The added premium for the

second color in print-media is generally always worth it.

Reader Service ("Bingo") Cards Are Often Counterproductive. Many magazines feature this easy way for readers to get more information. They assign each ad a reader service number and include in small print at the bottom of the ad "For more information circle #32 on the enclosed Reader Service Card."

This vehicle greatly increases the number of responses you get, but (sadly) diminishes their quality even more. Besides, in most cases, by the time your literature does reach the responder, they've forgotten why they asked for it. I advise my clients to insist they *not* be included on the Reader's Service Card, thereby requiring that interested readers contact them directly, using the ad's coupon or other response method described in the ad. "Bingo" Cards are great for the magazine, giving them a steady flow of new names for their mail list and impressive statistics for the unwary advertiser. But you want *only* the response from those who read your ad and were moved to act upon it.

Take Advantage of All Free Calendar Listings for your seminars, conferences and other events. This is a proven, effective way to promote them. Be sure to send publications with *free* calendar sections regular calendar releases on all your events. Treat *paid* calendar sections as you would any other classified ad: Test with an ad in three consecutive issues, carefully measure the response and then decide whether it's cost effective to continue.

Don't Count Too Much on Directories. Take advantage of any and all free listings of your products/services in directories, bibliographies or the like. There are any number of such listings which you can find in the section on this subject further back in this Chapter. Don't expect significant response from such listings, but don't overlook them either!

The Rate Card Is Negotiable. The cost to place your ad in a print publication -- called the publication's *rate card* -- has always been negotiable, and today more than ever. Sometimes you can get reduced rates for testing or for orders placed close to the closing date, particularly if there's remaining space in the issue or if the salesperson is below quota. Whatever the reason, you need to start with the idea that you won't have to pay rate-card prices.

There Must Be a Reason Why There Are so Few Training Magazines. In the Training and HRD fields there are only five or six magazines, each containing little advertising. By comparison, the same-size computer industry has 300 publications in which $1.26 billion is spent annually on advertising. If display advertising worked, do you really think there'd be so few training magazines? Remember this before committing much of your budget to magazine advertising.

GETTING THE MOST FROM PARTICIPATING IN CONFERENCES, TRADE SHOWS, EXPOSITIONS AND OTHER MEETINGS

In this section we'll use the word "show" to refer to a wide variety of events, including trade shows, conventions, conferences, expositions, congresses, meetings, symposia, etc. These are all events with multiple speakers and including some form of booths and/or vendor displays, called "Expos." Shows bring together a group of like-minded people for a single purpose.

Shows are the key marketing ingredient for some industries like toys, electronics and housewares. They provide instant exposure and credibility, especially with those in your sales and distribution channels. Unfortunately, for training and information products and services, shows rarely provide any direct business but, rather, support your other sales and marketing efforts.

Participation in a show must always be viewed as *part* of a marketing plan and *not* as an end in itself. There are other marketing efforts which must take place *before* the show, *during* the show and *after* the show if your participation is to be effective. Failure to look at shows in this way frequently leads to unrealistic expectations and is a common cause of much dissatisfaction with shows.

Conducting shows has become a multi-billion dollar industry throughout the world. Many organizations exist solely to promote and arrange trade shows. Show sponsors make money from registration fees, by renting exhibit space and by selling advertising in the show program. Sponsors also make money from paid workshops before or after the show. Finally, many show sponsors sell or rent the attenders mailing list after the show.

To learn about the major shows, conventions and expositions held anywhere in the world, see Appendix A. Here's a sample:

The Directory of Conventions. Successful Meetings Division, - Bill Communications, Inc., 633 Third Avenue, New York, NY 10017.

This annual publication, which is also available at many libraries, lists over 23,000 meetings and conventions scheduled by organizations in the United States and Canada. It is arranged chronologically and cross-indexed by industry and profession.

Six Ways to Participate in Shows

There are many ways to participate in shows, but six (6) are especially valuable for our industry:

1. Be on the program.
2. Conduct a pre-/post-conference workshop.
3. Exhibit.
4. Host a hospitality suite.
5. Hold a press conference.
6. Work the crowd.

We'll discuss each of these in the following sections.

1. Be on the Program means being a speaker, a presenter or a panelist or conducting one of the growing number of "cracker barrel" or non-traditional sessions. All of these enable you to make direct contact with participants most interested in you or your training programs. In order to be on the program, you need to have your presentation *accepted*, you need to *prepare early* and you need to *use the opportunity* for maximum marketing advantage.

Get Accepted. Otherwise it's impossible to be on the program. This is obvious, and yet many routinely overlook show announcements and miss proposal submittal deadlines.

Start early. Identify the conferences you want to participate in, get the sponsor's Request for Session Proposals and go out of your way to learn what's wanted at *this* particular conference. Then write a complete proposal that addresses all elements the sponsor asked for. Write and rewrite your proposal for the maximum amount of action and enthusiasm (see Chapter 8 on Direct Marketing Copy). Above all, make sure your proposal shows that you care -- and intend to furnish good value to the participants in your session.

Prepare Early. Since your proposal may be nearly a year before the conference, it's easy to ignore your preparation until the last minute. Don't make that mistake.

Pay particular attention to your pass-out materials. Even for hundreds of participants, it's *still* a good idea to provide a pass out of your major visuals, with your name, address and phone number prominently displayed, with ample room for participant notes. Take advantage of the show sponsor's offer to reproduce your handout. But even if the sponsor doesn't print them, you should. And print enough *additional* copies so you can send them to your best customers and prospects after the show.

Make a checklist of supplies to take with you. Include business cards, sales brochures, samples of your books or courses, tape, pens, blank transparencies and other presentation supplies, so you can succeed even if these items aren't available at the meeting. Plan to code everything you distribute (see Chapter 8), especially your sales brochures. These have amazing pass-along value, and you'll be surprised to find them turn up months later -- with an order on them!

Finally, make arrangements to have your presentation tape recorded. Many show sponsors make money selling session tapes. These can be valuable for you, too, giving you a record of your talk, which you can have transcribed as the text for a subsequent article. Don't worry about surrendering the rights for your taped presentation; you'll probably get more benefit from the tape than you'll lose.

Use Your Opportunity. Deliver genuine value in your presentation. Don't hold back! Many speakers are afraid to give specific numbers and recommendations from the platform. They mistakenly believe that giving away such "free" advice will lose them clients.

My experience is exactly the opposite. Giving your best information generates the most appeal to buy your product or services. And the more practical and usable your recommendations, the more your audience will feel your other products and services can help them, too.

The other side of this is: Don't "sell" from the platform. Most show sponsors are adamantly opposed to this practice, and your audience will resent it. However, by reporting success stories you've had with customers similar to your audience, you *indirectly* sell even more effectively.

At the conclusion of your presentation, ask those who want more information to leave their business card.

2. Conduct a Pre-/Post-Conference Workshop. Many show sponsors have discovered they can enter the seminar business with paid single and multi-day events before and after a show. Since people are investing time and travel expenses to attend the show, extending the trip a couple of days for a seminar or workshop entails only a small added cost. Sometimes it works that way, but in some cases these workshops are even attended by people who wouldn't otherwise attend the conference.

Pre-/post-conference workshops are more valuable than just presenting a paper. It affords you more time with participants. And, since you'll generally be paid, these workshops can also make money for you.

If this is your first time on the program, merely getting your workshop accepted may be enough. But if your workshop is already a proven performer, don't be bashful about negotiating per-person payments and/or speaking fees, reimbursement for travel, materials and even your promotional expenses. While the larger shows have fairly rigid policies in all of these areas, smaller shows have more flexibility, and your request may be all that's needed to improve your deal substantially.

3. *Exhibit* at the show to demonstrate your market presence and get sales leads for later follow-up and closing. It is unrealistic to expect to close business at the show, unless that's the way this show (or market) works. Some shows even prohibit selling, but others encourage it, and you could sell enough books or courses to cover expenses.

Is exhibiting right for you? Only if you need to establish your presence as a player in the market. One reason would be to support your face-to-face sales force, especially if your competitors exhibit. For many training and information firms, this is the most compelling reason.

Exhibiting is the most costly part of show participation. Besides renting booth space and paying for utilities and services, you need to create your display, ship it to and from the show (including any products you intend to exhibit) and arrange to have enough people at the show to staff the booth and any other functions connected with it. It's easy to spend $5,000 to $10,000 on even a small show, and the bill can run many times more if you're not careful.

As a result, you need to set an overall policy and budget for exhibiting at shows. Then you need to allocate that budget *only* to events that give you the best exposure in the markets you want to reach. Usually there are one or two national shows and a few local or regional shows that will merit your consideration. If you've never been in a show before, start with one and carefully evaluate the results before committing further. Fortunately, and unlike the long lead-times required to get on the program, exhibiting usually can be arranged within a few months of the show, affording you quite a bit more planning flexibility.

To maximize your benefits from exhibiting, there are activities before, during and after the show.

Before the Show

1. Decide extent of participation:
   - Booth(s)
   - Hospitality suite(s)
   - Papers/Speakers
   - Press conference/Announcements
   - Meet the author/Autograph sessions
   - Other
2. Design, build (or arrange for) booth.
3. Submit papers for acceptance (see above sections).
4. Make staff assignments.
5. Reserve booth space.
6. Make travel arrangements and hotel reservations.
7. Make pre-meeting mailings/advertisements.
8. Prepare, collect, package and ship materials to the exhibit site.
9. Invite guests to booths and hospitality suites.

Most show sponsors furnish exhibitors a pre-conference registration list to promote their booth. Usually the list is furnished on pressure sensitive labels. Since labels on an envelope are a sure sign of "junk mail," it's probably more effective and economical to use a self-mailer. As we noted in Chapter 8, the simplest self-mailer is a post card -- which is often all that's required to invite participants to stop by your booth or hospitality suite.

During the Show

1. Set up and staff the booth(s).
2. Set up and staff hospitality suite(s).
3. Present papers/participate in meeting.
4. Hold press conference/media event.
5. Collect names of all contacts.
6. Gather marketing and competitive information.

Be careful about violating union work rules when setting up your booth at major hotels and convention centers. As a rule, you won't be allowed to touch *any* of your materials until they are delivered to your display area. In some places you aren't even allowed to plug in your own electric light; an electrician must do it for you. Occasionally, efforts by your own staff to uncrate and set up your display can trigger a work stoppage. Best to check with the show manager in advance of any such activity.

You'll often see booth "gimmicks" used to collect business cards and identify those who "stopped by the booth." These include hourly drawings and give-a-ways, contests, "free offers," etc. As with all marketing, the greater the "bribe" you pay to acquire a name, the less that name is likely to be worth. Resist expensive give-a-ways designed solely to attract booth traffic. What you *really* want are those who are truly interested in your products and services and who seek you out.

Besides, the show sponsor will *give* you a post-show mailing list with the correct name and mailing address of *all* attendees. This list will be for your unlimited use, so you can even add the names to your mailing list. This is a far more reliable and comprehensive way to acquire the names of those attending than gimmicks at the booth.

Remember that exhibiting at the show isn't an end in itself, but rather a step in your sales and marketing process. The important activities that should be accomplished after the show include:

After the Show

1. Prepare, collect, package and ship materials home from the exhibit site.
2. Add contact names to your mailing list.
3. Follow up show contacts with personalized letters and/or face-to-face sales calls.
4. Use complete registration list furnished by the show manager for post-show promotional mailings.
5. Issue a post-show news release.
6. Mail copies of any new materials prepared for the show to your clients and best prospects.

4. Host a Hospitality Suite.

This is an effective show marketing device, especially in combination with other means of participating.

Book your hospitality suite early. All shows have a "headquarters hotel" and that's where your hospitality suite should be. This is where all the action is, and being there shows your marketing sophistication. Book a good floor with a good view. If you're a frequent traveler and belong to the hotel's "club," use all the clout you can to get the best room. Be careful of "concierge floors," which require

special elevator keys and can pose an awkward deterrent for your guests. Book a multi-room suite, so you have private space for telephone calls and meetings. Ask about suites in conjunction with your sleeping room to further reduce your costs.

Contact the show sponsor for a copy of their pre-show registration list. Mail *only* to those whose position, title and/or organization you want to do business with. This is likely only a small percentage of the total list. Also, as always, send a personal invitation to your customers and best prospects.

Be sure you have the staff to handle your hospitality suite. You'd like nothing better than to have your best customers use your suite as their "headquarters." But to do that you'll need to have someone there all the time. And since you'll have many other demands on your time during the conference, you may need to have at least one, and possibly several, assistants for this purpose.

Be sure whoever is on duty in your hospitality suite challenges anyone they don't know. You need to do this diplomatically but forcefully. There are plenty of "freeloaders" who look for every opportunity to get something for nothing. You don't want to offend a genuine prospect whom you've never met, but you also want to restrict your hospitality to those *you* want to do business with. And you certainly don't want your competitors learning about your latest products and meeting your clients, especially if *you're* furnishing the food and drink!

On this subject of refreshments, you should refer to the section of Chapter 6, "Win-Win Relationships with Hotels and Meeting Facilities." In your own sleeping room, you can generally furnish your own liquor and beverages, but you may find it more convenient during busy periods to hire a hotel bartender. As always, steer a middle course between the very expensive -- and unnecessary -- and the austere. Dried nuts and cocktail mix, popcorn and perhaps at most one hot hors d'oeuvre is more than adequate for the normal hospitality suite during mid-afternoon to early evening hours. Of course, if you schedule a formal reception, you'll need to provide more.

5. Hold a Press Conference in Connection With a Show. Shows often attract national and local media coverage. And even if they don't, your holding a press conference in conjunction with a show gives the reporter two reasons to attend and can boost their participation and their subsequent articles about you.

See the section "Getting and Using Publicity" later in this chapter for tips.

6. Work the Crowd. This old circus expression describes the lowest-cost way to participate in a show. The best investment you'll make at shows is an ample supply of business cards and any simple but graphic job-aid that represents your business. Invite prospects to have a drink at the bar or join you for lunch or dinner.

Three More Ways to Use Shows and Conferences

There are at least three other ways you can use conferences and trade shows, even those you don't actually attend: (1.) Use the conference mailing list, (2.) use the conference programs and printed materials to do market research and (3.) use the exhibitor programs and conference programs to do competitor analysis.

The Power of Post-Conference Mailing Lists. We've already discussed using the post-conference attenders list for those conferences you attend or participate in. You'll get it free if you're an exhibitor, and may be able to negotiate obtaining it free if you're on the program. But even if you have to pay for it, this list can be one of the best obtainable.

I had a personal experience that confirmed this. I mailed to a list of attendees two and a half years *after* the conference, as part of a test along with eight other mailing lists. The list had never been updated after the conference and was quite difficult to obtain because it was considered "out of date." How do you think that list compared to the other eight lists? Well, it had the second best response, right behind our own house list! Conference attender lists are unusually "hot," especially for promoting other events.

So, start right now to look for conferences

from which you'd like to have a list of attenders, and contact the conference sponsor to try and arrange it. If you do not currently have a direct mail program, see if you can obtain the list for use in telemarketing or for direct contact. Generally these lists are not expensive. (It's like selling ice on a hot day: It won't be useful to very many people for very long.) If you're successful in getting the list, cull through it to identify those prospects whose title and/or organization make them most appealing. Then treat them just like any other prospect.

Do Market Research. Even at conferences you don't attend, try to get someone to give you the final conference program, the conference exhibitors list and any other conference pass-out material.

Look carefully at what's being presented and who's presenting it. If the exhibitors list contains a description of the product or service being offered, see if there are any "surprises." Be on the lookout for new trends and/or changes. You may need to read the descriptions of the various sessions in order to detect this. Spending an hour with the conference programs is usually a good investment, especially for conferences you *don't* attend.

Competitor Analysis. Use materials picked up at booths (by a colleague if you don't attend yourself) to see whether there are any new products or services being offered that compete with yours. Shows are a good time to do price shopping, too, since many salespeople are more open with their pricing than they would be at any other time. I've even found a competitor's price list sitting unattended (they later wondered where it went).

And don't miss the opportunity to add your name to a competitor's mailing list. This is an effective way to see their mail campaigns and learn about their marketing program.

Evaluating Show Participation

Now that we've identified how you can participate in shows and conferences, or use them for your marketing advantage, the question is, "*Should* you?"!

Of course people participate in shows for a variety of reasons. Opportunity for travel, camaraderie and even force of habit compete with logical, systematic reasons why the show should be attended. The following sections try and describe some of these more tangible considerations.

Choose Your Shows Carefully. There are already a large number of candidate shows for your participation, and more appear all the time. It's safe to assume there will be more shows than you can *ever* afford to participate in. The challenge is to limit your participation *only* to those that are going to be most effective for you.

If you've never participated in a show before, plan ahead far enough to actually attend the show the year before you want to be there (now *that's* long-range planning!). Look at the show from top to bottom, especially those who are participating the same way you intend to (as an exhibitor, on the program, hospitality suite, etc.). Talk to them frankly. Tell them you're thinking about participating, and ask them if they feel that it's worthwhile. Listen carefully to what they have to say. Are they happy? How long have they participated? Are they able to trace benefits from their participation? And -- most importantly -- will they be back next year?

And if the show *does* look productive, before you "plunk down your money," find out about next year's show. If it's a show that moves around the country, will it be in an undesirable or unproductive location? Is the show sponsor changing the format for the show? Will next year's show be significantly different from this year's? How?

As a general rule shun any new or untested shows, including significantly different formats or new locations for established shows.

Realistically Estimate All Show Costs. As you can see from the foregoing sections, there are many costs connected with participation in shows other than the registration fees, travel and away-from-home living expenses. It's important for you to make an itemized listing of all these costs as part of your economic analysis. A short list that can represent the starting point for your own itemized costs is shown below:

Representative Non-Travel Costs for Participating in Shows and Expositions

Professional time
- Planning participation
- Writing session proposals
- Doing research for papers/presentations
- Writing papers
- Travelling to/from show
- Making presentations
- Other time at show

Other costs of presentations
- Outside research costs
- Outside typing costs
- Slide preparation
- Printing session handouts
- Printing workshop materials
- Shipping materials

Administrative/ clerical time
- Typing forms and proposals
- Typing papers
- Coordinating production of session materials
- Packaging and shipping time
- Making hotel and travel arrangements

Salesperson(s) time
- Planning participation
- Travelling to/from show
- Time in the booth/ hospitality suite
- Other time at show
- Post-show follow-up activities

Sales and Marketing costs
- Printing brochures and sales literature
- Pre- and Post-show mailings
- Entertainment at show
- Long distance telephone/FAX

Hospitality suite costs
- Suite rental
- Food and beverages
- Bartenders
- Other service personnel

Booth costs
- Space rental
- Design
- Construction
- Shipping
- Set-up/tear-down
- Handling

Identify the Benefits. As with costs, it's clear that there are some significant benefits possible from participating in shows. Make a list of what you expect these benefits to be.

We found one of our clients obtained no sales whatsoever from participating in 1-day or less events at trade shows and conferences. But we found a 1-in-5 conversion of $40,000 average sales from his participation in 2-day or longer events. Clearly this company's best way to use trade shows was to participate in multi-day, pre-/post-conference workshops. Participation as a speaker or panelist was unproductive.

Carefully track sales leads obtained from shows and look at how many have closed a year later. Such comparisons can sometimes be subjective, especially when there are many opportunities for contact, and it's not clear whether subsequent sales derived *solely* from participation in the show. But you must try to measure the sales results from your show participation any way you can.

USING YOUR OWN NEWSLETTER AND OTHER MEANS TO STAY-IN-TOUCH WITH YOUR CUSTOMERS AND PROSPECTS

Throughout this handbook we've emphasized the importance of staying close to your customers and attendees. They're your best source of additional business, and marketing to them frequently will always pay off.

In this section, we look at other means of staying in touch with this important group -- methods that do *not* directly ask for business, but rather inform, entertain or merely say "we care about you."

The table at the bottom of this page shows some of the many reasons you have to be in touch with your customers and prospects. It's divided into activities of theirs or yours and spans both business and non-business reasons.

Newsletters Really Work

Most of the reasons for being in touch with your customers and prospects can be achieved by a newsletter. Newsletters can also do much more.

Those who already have a newsletter swear by it. At the start they're a lot of work, but the rewards far exceed the investment of time, effort and money.

Reasons to be in Touch with Your Customers and Prospects

	In Their Life	In Your Life
Business	• Confirm dates/arrangements. • Say "thank you" (after meeting or engagement). • Send clippings or other information they can use. • Request permission to use their testimonials. • Solicit referrals.	• Transmit information through speeches articles (by/about you), newsletters, etc. • Let them know about awards, new products/job aids, new publications, internal events, moving (new address), conferences and trade shows (see Chapter 12), showcases (see Chapter 13). • Say "thank you" (after meeting, engagement, payment). • Conduct a client conference. • Conduct research/surveys.
Nonbusiness	• Contact about promotions, mergers, moving/relocation. • Inform them that they are in the news. • Send cards/remembrances on holidays. • Acknowledge birthdays, weddings, anniversaries, deaths in the family.	• Invite them to participate in golf, tennis, hunting, fishing, bridge, aerobics, skiing, etc. • Invite them to attend sporting events with you (as spectators). • Entertain them at lunch, dinner, the theater, etc. • Send them gifts.

The personal computer revolution, particularly desktop publishing, has spawned a revolution in newsletters. We're all getting more of them. And there's no reason to believe that this trend will reverse anytime soon. But you don't need a high-tech newsletter. It's the *information* that counts.

The first newsletter in North America was *The Boston News Letter* in 1704 by John Campbell to report ship arrivals and other commercial information. He didn't need a PC. Today, newsletters produced on old mechanical typewriters are still distributed -- and eagerly awaited and read.

Send Your Newsletter to Everyone

Everyone, that is, with whom you want to stay in touch. This includes your current and past customers and your best prospects, employees, suppliers, investors -- to name just some. When in doubt about whether or not someone should get a newsletter, they should. After a while you'll evaluate whether circulation should be increased or decreased based on results.

Newsletters are an ideal way to use and update your customer/prospect database (see Chapter 13). These regular mailings allow address corrections. People are more likely to forward a newsletter than a piece of advertising. And using the newsletter to get address corrections helps defray some of the newsletter costs against the costs of maintaining your marketing database.

Inform -- Don't Sell -- with Your Newsletter

Almost every topic in the above table can be addressed in your newsletter. Newsletters provide an ideal way to mix a variety of topics and agendas in one concise and entertaining format.

Newsletters provide a way to include *your internal news* and still keep it in perspective. It is also an easy way to capture and distribute *client success stories*, especially those reported by third-parties. And your newsletter provides a handy way to include a *calendar of events* in your business or profession, including some of your own paid seminars and workshops.

But be careful! If your newsletter is ever perceived as a sales vehicle, it will kill its value. Avoid including sales pitches and obviously self-promoting articles. Do *not* include response vehicles or other ways to order your goods or services. *Do* include a way for recipients to correct their names and addresses on your mailing list or recommend others who should get the newsletter. But save your sales pitches and your requests for direct response to other, dedicated sales vehicles.

Resist the urge to include other advertising material *with* your newsletter. While some have successfully included promotional literature with their newsletter, this should be deferred until the value of your newsletter as a "contribution" to your customers has been established. Then -- and only then -- you may wish to carefully test the inclusion of advertising materials with your newsletter. My own recommendation is: Don't do it, ever!

Tips for Planning Your Newsletter

There are a number of other issues and decisions that will need to be made in launching your own newsletter. Some of the more important of these are covered in the following sections.

Start with Four Pages. I've seen successful newsletters printed on one or two sides of 8-1/2" x 11" stapled sheets. But today's standard is four pages printed on two sides of an 11" x 17" sheet and folded in half to 8-1/2" x 11". This 4-page signature is either (1.) mailed flat, (2.) folded once and mailed as a self-mailer or (3.) folded twice to fit into a #10 envelope.

Adopt a Standard Layout. Desktop publishing using a PC and a laser printer provides plenty of possibilities. But you don't need this technology to do a professional job.

A standard 4-page, 11" x 17" letter is shown below. Page 1 contains the name of the newsletter and any headlines. The page 4 contains the mailing label, preprinted bulk mail indicia and your return address. The inner two pages are reserved entirely for copy with the lower left-hand corner of page 2 for

Typical Newsletter Layout

OUTSIDE

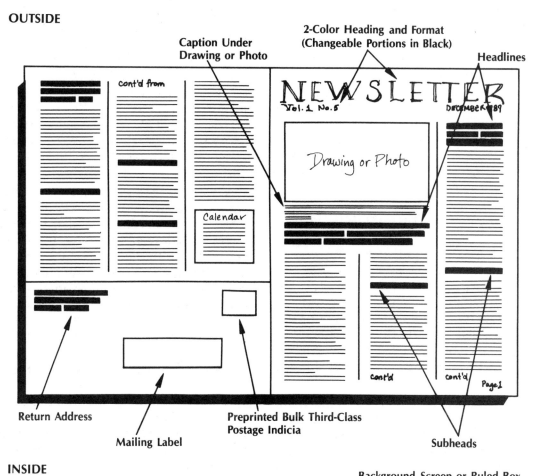

Caption Under Drawing or Photo

2-Color Heading and Format (Changeable Portions in Black)

Headlines

Return Address

Mailing Label

Preprinted Bulk Third-Class Postage Indicia

Subheads

INSIDE

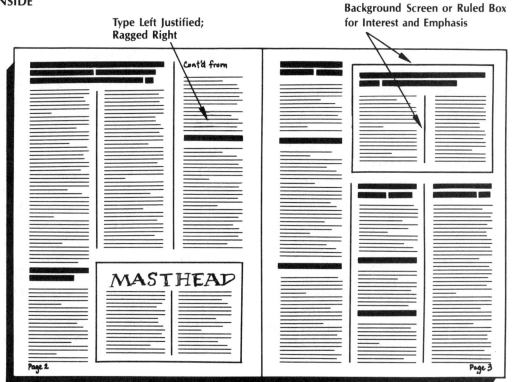

Type Left Justified; Ragged Right

Background Screen or Ruled Box for Interest and Emphasis

the masthead (the information on the publisher, editor, etc.) and any internal organizational news.

Today's standard for newsletters is the three-column format. Occasionally two columns are acceptable. It actually takes less space for the same copy using three columns, and readability is improved.

Newsletter text may be left-justified only, leaving "ragged" right margins, which tests confirm are more readable than text justified on both sides. Since newspapers and magazines retain the right *and* left justified format, if you can produce copy justified on both sides, it will give your newsletter a more polished appearance.

If you use more than four pages, you'll need a way to attach the extra pages for mailing. This may be by "saddle stitching" (stapling) on the spine like a very thin magazine or by sealing "tabs" on the edge. Your printer will suggest the most economical method. Of course, if you mail your newsletter in an envelope, this problem vanishes.

Publish Four Editions a Year. The quarterly format fits most business cycles and represents a natural choice. Publish it frequently enough that people haven't forgotten the last edition by the time the new edition hits their desk. But not everyone agrees. Bob Mager publishes his *Update* newsletter "when the spirit moves," and it's eagerly awaited by all.

Don't Charge. Although some organizations charge a subscription fee for their house organ, its purpose is to stay in touch with your customers and good prospects. Remember, your objective is to "make a deposit before you make a withdrawal." You want your newsletter to be seen as high-value, yet cost nothing but the time required to read it.

Have Two or Three Editions Before You Start. Many newsletters begin with a bang and end with a whimper. Don't let this happen to you. Have enough editorial copy for at least two or three editions *before* you start. Try to keep working two editions ahead so you always have ample time and material.

A newsletter represents a long-term commitment because it is only after the third or fourth edition that readership increases and

people begin to "look for it."

Don't Be Cheap. Your costs consist of printing and mailing and the opportunity cost of the writing and editing time. A representative figure for a 4-page newsletter might be $.50 to $.75 each in the recipient's hand. Longer newsletters will be more expensive.

But remember that the purpose of your newsletter is to stay in touch with your customers and best prospects. Don't cut corners on anything that will look cheap or second-rate to your readers. As always, negotiate hard for the lowest prices and best terms -- but insist on top quality in every detail.

Find a Good Editor. The secret to publishing your newsletter is to designate one individual who's responsible not only for preparing the copy, but for getting it all pulled together, composed and printed. If they have writing or editing skills, so much the better, but their main job is to "manage the process."

In short, the key to getting it all done is to find the right editor.

Your editor will also have their eyes open for correspondence, documents and announcements that are newsletter candidates. They'll remind others on your staff to write articles or furnish interviews to include. And they'll look for articles in other publications that can be reprinted (with permission) in your newsletter.

Keep Your Artwork Simple. Except for the nameplate and masthead, the rest of your newsletter can be merely typed. Many newsletters are made with typewriter copy, cut and pasted onto preprinted forms. Look at *The Kiplinger Newsletter* as an example. Do *not* feel you need to have desktop publishing for your newsletter.

If you don't use photographs, the artwork can be easy. The trick is establishing a standard format and sticking with it. This also increases your newsletter's recognition *and* makes your editor's job easier.

Stress Printing Quality over Cost. Printing your newsletter places a greater emphasis on quality and timeliness than it does on price. This is a good place where your local quick copy printer may be the best choice. Generally such small, business-oriented printers concentrate on good quality and quick turnaround time, albeit at higher prices.

Here's how to get a 2-color newsletter at the lowest cost. Use the second color in the parts that won't change, like the nameplate, masthead, mailing area or feature boxes. Get sheets with just this color printed economically in large quantity. Then use your office copying machine or local "quick copy" printer to put each issue's black copy on these pre-printed, colored forms. This technique is among the least expensive and most flexible you'll find.

Your printer should deliver the newsletter to you folded for labeling and mailing.

Since buying printing is always a serious task, review the tips in Chapter 9.

Here's a Valuable Resource. There's a lot of helpful resources for newsletters. One of the best is:

Editing Your Newsletter: How to Produce an Effective Publication Using Traditional Tools and Computers (Third Edition), by Mark Beach. Published by Coast To Coast Books, 2934 N.E. Sixteenth Ave., Portland, OR 97212. (503)283-5891. ISBN 0-943381-01-0. 1988. ($18.50 plus shipping.)

Other Ways to Stay in Touch

We now move our attention to the upper right-hand corner of the table on Page 12 - 15, focusing especially on other reasons for staying in touch with your customers and prospects. Of particular interest are the books and articles you publish, the speeches you deliver, the new products you announce, the awards or other recognition that you receive and internal events in your company.

Your Articles and Speeches. Get in the habit of distributing copies of speeches or reprints of the articles to all appropriate customers and prospects. Almost nothing else you routinely do can be as directly beneficial. Transmit each one with a short note or cover letter highlighting the circumstances of the speech or article and the key points you want to emphasize. Add hand-written notes that further connect the article with each individual client.

I also send out the handouts from my recent workshops and seminars, providing they are not already purchasable products. I work hard to design pass-outs that will have this added use after my presentation. (See the section in this Chapter "Getting the Most from Participating in Conferences, Trade Shows, Expositions and Other Meetings.")

To facilitate this mailing, we code each record in our marketing database with the product(s) they're interested in. This enables us to select only those who are likely to be interested in the particular speech, article or workshop pass-out we're mailing.

And I also include a paragraph in every cover letter that specifically asks the recipient to call me if they have any questions about the applicability of the article to their business. About one out of every seven recipients do.

Your New Book, Booklet or Other Publication. Every new publication should be announced to all of your customers and prospects. The announcement itself, even via direct mail advertising, serves a minor stay-in-touch function. But what *additional* use can you make of this new publication? For example, should you send complimentary copies? Should you offer them an opportunity to purchase it at a discount? What is the best way to use this opportunity for your very best contacts?

I believe you should *give* your very best long-time customers a free autographed copy of your book or booklet. There's room for some judgement about what constitutes "long-time," but generally the choice will be clear.

Send others on your marketing database an announcement and offer them an opportunity to purchase the book at a highly discounted price or to return a card to receive their complementary copy. This has the advantage of causing them to do something in order to "pay" for the book. You might also invite them to a book-signing or other event celebrating the book's publication.

New Products/Job-Aids. Treat production of a new product (audio or video tape course, computer software, etc.) or job-aid (laminated card, checklist, process diagram, etc.) just like a new book or booklet. Make sure each customer/prospect gets a notification of the product and furnish a small, select group their own complimentary copy.

Some firms use their best customers to "beta test" their new products, putting them into daily use and following up to learn the benefits -- or problems -- they found. This can have three benefits: (1.) an excuse to stay-in-touch with your customers, (2.) a source of valuable product testing information and (3.) a way to get great testimonials to use in your advertising.

Awards or Other Recognition You Receive. Let your customers/prospects know anytime you receive an award or are mentioned favorably in articles and speeches. Treat these events *about* you the same as the articles and speeches *by* you described earlier in this section.

Remember the power of the third-party referral: It's much more believable and persuasive than anything you could possibly say about yourself. It also reaffirms your customer's wisdom in doing business with you.

And the same applies to major new contracts you get. If a prestigious firm makes a big purchase or retains your services (and will let you talk about it), an announcement of this can be very powerful for your existing customers and for prospects who are "on the fence." That's one of the reasons firms specializing in mergers and acquisitions place ads in *The Wall Street Journal* when one of their deals closes.

Other Events in Your Organization. Virtually anything you do in your organization is a reason to notify your customers. Here are a few:

- Move to new offices -- maybe even an office warming party.

- A new telephone system, facsimile line or a telex.

- New-hires, including a short biography, a brief description of their duties and an encouragement for recipients to welcome them to the firm.

- The company picnic.

WHEN AND HOW TO USE CUSTOMER, CLIENT AND USER CONFERENCES

A client conference is a meeting or gathering of your clients and prospects, usually annually. It may have a variety of purposes and outcomes, and all of them are valuable.

Eight Benefits of Client/User Conferences

Client/user conferences have at least eight major benefits to you and your organization:

Renew Customer Commitment and Enthusiasm. Customers renew their commitment by attending. And the conference program provides still more reinforcement and commitment, which translates into more of everything you want from your customers.

Provide the Latest Training/Retraining. This is a fast way to communicate new developments, particularly those that need a bit of explanation.

Let Users Share Their Experiences. Customers who attend are always glad to tell others how well your product worked for them. Occasionally they'll tell about what didn't work, but usually with a positive "spin." This produces that continuous improvement we all want, in the best possible atmosphere.

Close Business in Your Sales Pipeline. Client conferences are often "the closer" for prospects, and for repurchases by existing clients. You won't actually write orders at the conference, but you'll probably do more than enough business immediately afterward to pay the entire cost of the conference and more.

Cross-Sell Your Other Products and Services. When your customers who bought two different products meet at your conference, each will sell the other on the benefits of the one they're using. This surprised us at our first client conference, but we've since seen it happen every time. With a little thought, your conference program can help stimulate this cross-selling by systematically exposing attendees to all your products/services.

Launch New Products. Launching a new product at a client/users conference gives your best customers an "inside track" to buy before anyone else. They'll appreciate that. And you can use your client conference as an opportunity to "beta test" a new product before making a production commitment. This gives you the benefit of cooperative clients giving you the best information on how the product actually works -- and can produce some great testimonials, too.

Conduct Product/Market Research. Client conferences are ideal opportunities to ask your customers what new products and services, or changes to your current products and services, they want. We've made many changes in our products as a direct result of suggestions received at our client conferences. And focus groups conducted in conjunction with these conferences can be fertile sources of new product ideas.

Let Your Staff Meet Your Customers in Person. Besides the marketing and sales benefits you get from client conferences, you derive some internal benefits as well. Not the least of these is the opportunity for your clients/users and your staff to meet face-to-face. This exposure is especially valuable for telemarketers and others who deal with customers on the phone. You'll notice a definite change in their conversation after the conference, with more frequent and spontaneous references to "our" clients and to their success with "our" products and services. This internal benefit alone could justify the client conference in many organizations.

Seven Tips for Your Client/User Conference

Client/user conferences obey all the same rules for event marketing that we've described in Chapter 6. Pay particular attention to lead-times, covered in Chapter 5. Here are some special tips and recommendations unique to these events:

Invite Current Customers, Past Customers and Your Hottest Prospects. Get your sales force involved in deciding who should (and should not) be invited. And don't forget your own staff.

Expect High Response Rates. You're inviting your very best customers and prospects, so response rates could be astronomical. But, like any campaign seeking the most registrations from a group of fixed size, plan on making three or four mailings.

Hold the Conference Near Your Headquarters. Your conference can be held at your own offices, in a nearby hotel, or at an off-site resort. The number invited, attendee perceptions and costs will dictate the choice. Holding the conference so participants can visit your offices has important team-building values that shouldn't be overlooked. If you select a remote location, consider scheduling a pre- or post-conference visit to your offices to try and get the best of both worlds.

Schedule the Conference When Your Customers Can Come. No one time of year seems better suited to client/user conferences than others. The two general rules are: (1.) Pick a time when your clients are most likely attend to and (2.) pick a time when your staff can devote time to the conference without taking it away from the rest of your business.

2-3 Days Seem to Be About Right. Because travel is generally expected for client conferences, two to three days seem about the right duration. If your customers are all in one place, you may be able to get many of the benefits in a 1-day or shorter event. But if attendees have to travel and stay overnight, then multiple days will yield better results.

Don't Charge a Registration Fee. This is an important financial consideration, especially if you have big-name speakers or lavish entertainment. My bias is that client/user conferences should have NO registration fee, but participants should pay their *own* travel and away-from-home living expenses. Keep in mind that not charging a registration fee increases the likelihood of last-minute cancellations and no-shows.

Registration fees may be required when government employees are included. In this case, set the lowest possible fee that would be acceptable to your government attendees.

Offer a Variety of Reasons to Attend. The most effective client/user conferences offer a mix of motivations to attend, as well as a variety of useful sessions. This means combining big-name speakers, presentations by your key staff, opportunities for participation in "hands-on" sessions, new product presentations, "sharing" of experiences, training, research results, etc.

For example, our client conferences afforded participants opportunities to sharpen their training skills, to clinic their own presentations and to get real-time "feedback" on their classroom style and delivery. It gave them a chance to discuss their difficult situations with others who solved similar problems. We were told that the practical solutions participants obtained from just these sessions more than justified the cost of the entire conference.

THE MAGIC OF WRITING AND PUBLISHING A BOOK

As a trainer, you're in the knowledge and information business. And being seen as the expert, at least in your field, counts a lot.

How do you get to be the expert?

To answer that question, think with me for a moment: Who do *you* think is the expert on future trends? On excellence? On managing your money? On selling? On virtually any subject you wish to name? If you're like me, the name that comes to mind is probably the author of a book on the subject, maybe even a book you haven't read, but one which has been widely quoted.

It's no accident that the words *author* and *authority* have the same root. Because of our educational system, our culture -- or for reasons we may *never* know -- our society is quick to bestow "expert" status on just about anyone who's written a book.

Although today's technology permits "publishing" in many forms, don't be fooled. The enduring, accepted standard form of publishing is *still* the hardcover book, just as it was over 400 years ago.

Writing a book gives you more than credibility. It gives you a profitable back-of-the-room item to sell at your seminars. Your book can spin off articles, newsletters, speeches and opportunities for publicity, all described in other sections of this chapter.

One important point before proceeding: Writing and publishing books is growing more complex and sophisticated by the minute. To be successful you'll need to take advantage of the many resources in this section, and -- if you choose to self-publish -- the marketing techniques described throughout this handbook.

Credible (and Non-Credible) Forms of Publishing

"Publishing" today can take many forms, both in print and via electronic media. There are also a variety of what we might call "live" publication forms, such as seminars, lectures, audio tapes and video tapes.

Today, the accepted, credible forms of publishing are, in declining order:

- Hardcover books.
- Soft-cover books and booklets.
- Newspaper and magazine articles.
- Video Cassettes.
- Audio tapes.

Experience shows the non-credible forms of publishing are:

- Seminars and workshops.
- Packaged training programs.
- Computer software.
- Everything else.

Deciding Whether to Self-Publish or to Find a Publisher

R. R. Bowker Company, who manages The International Standard Book Numbering

(ISBN) System, and publishes the authoritative *Books In Print*, identifies 300 new publishers each month in the U.S. Many are individuals self-publishing their own first book.

Anyone can do it. Start with your manuscript and *you* arrange for editing, typesetting, graphics, printing, binding, promotion and sale of your book. The alternative, working through a publisher, takes the *same* manuscript and hands it to them for editing, typesetting, graphics, printing, binding, promotion and distribution. There are collections of resources listed later in this section to help you do it either way. In either case, heavy author involvement in the introduction and early promotion is essential, both for the success of the book *and* to harvest the fallout to your training or information business (which, after all, is why you wrote the book in the first place).

Often, a book from a publisher will languish in the warehouse and on bookstore shelves until the author jumps in personally to aggressively promote it. One author wrote what is now regarded as a landmark sales training book. But this book was ignored by the publisher for six months before the author loaded the trunk of his car with copies (which he had to *buy* from the publisher at half the list price!) and went around the country on a radio talk show and bookstore selling spree that catapulted his book to fame.

To understand how this happens, realize that publishers release more new books each year than they can afford to promote. New releases from proven, successful authors get the lion's share of their promotion budget. For the rest, the publisher relies on the process of natural (market) selection to show which titles are most popular and, therefore, most worthy of added promotion.

Well, if you're going to have to work hard promoting your book anyway, why use a publisher? There are two main reasons: One is that the publisher takes care of all the details to get your book into print, steps you may be unwilling or unable to take yourself. The second reason is that a publisher can provide access to sales and distribution channels that would be difficult or even impossible for you to enter as a first-time self-publisher.

But publishers provide their services at a cost, both an economic cost and a cost in lost control. Either or both of these costs may be inconsequential or serious, depending on your reasons for publishing.

Notice that "prestige" is *not* a factor in selecting a publisher. Few business books are bought on the basis of the publisher's name, and there's been such a whirlwind of mergers, acquisitions and new names (called "imprints") only the experts can keep them straight. Of course, if it's for your own personal (read "ego") reasons that you want your book published by McGraw-Hill or Simon and Schuster, that's another matter.

So the four major factors that dictate whether working through a publisher or self-publishing is right for you are:

1. Financial considerations
2. Getting-it-all-done headaches
3. Control (or loss thereof)
4. Market access

Let's look at each of these.

1. Financial Considerations. There are three important aspects of book publishing finances:

- Income: How much you get and when you get it.
- Investment: How much you'll have to shell out.
- Unit Cost: For the books you'll use yourself.

Your income from a publisher is usually a royalty on books sold, paid (say) every six months. Royalties may be figured as a fixed sum per copy or a percentage of list price, wholesale price, net revenues over some period of time or some other formula. The bottom line is that the publisher agrees to pay based upon *actual* sales of your book. How much they'll pay depends upon their costs to publish and promote your book and their expectations of how many they'll sell at what price over two or three years. A business or professional book that sells 8,000-10,000 copies over three to five years is considered successful.

Royalties range from 5% of net price through 20% of retail price. Higher royalties go to better-known authors, popular titles or those who will provide assured sales. Lower royalties go to new authors, business/professional works or those who will do little to sell their book.

The self-publisher, on the other hand, has to bear all the costs of publishing and promoting the book. This requires up-front costs in the thousands of dollars and the investment of time to do things the publisher would do, thereby incurring an opportunity cost, if not an actual cost. As a result, a self-publisher's profits are low at the start but grow rapidly once the up-front costs are recovered. I expect 30% to 50% profit on sales for self-published books in their second or third year, perhaps sooner if the initial sales are high or the initial costs are low.

Now let's look at unit cost. This is vitally important if you want to use your book in your seminars and training programs. Here, your perspective and the publisher's are diametrically opposed. Whereas you think in terms of how much the book cost to produce, the publisher thinks only in terms of discounts from retail price, just as they would for distributing through bookstores. For example, a book that costs $5 to produce might be priced at $39 retail. If the publisher offers you copies at a the customary 45% discount, that's a staggering $21 each! Instead, offer to buy books at (say) $1 over the publisher's cost, or offer to print your copies at the same time they print theirs, thereby increasing the size of the print run and lowering unit costs for *both* you and the publisher. However you do it, you must acquire the copies of your book you use in your training at closer to their production cost than to their retail price.

Financial return for self-publishing might be three to six times higher than the return from working with a publisher, provided you're able and willing to handle all the details.

2. Getting-It-All-Done Headaches. If you self-publish, you'll need to do everything to convert your manuscript into print *and* everything to fulfill orders. This may involve at least the following:

- Editing the manuscript
- Having rough illustrations drawn in final form
- Specifying the type style and size

- Proofreading typed galleys
- Preparing final manuscript artwork
- Designing the dust jacket/cover
- Getting the book printed and bound
- Obtaining and warehousing the book
- Obtaining shipping materials and supplies
- Advertising and promoting the book
- Preparing and sending press releases
- Lining up distribution agreements
- Taking orders
- Installing an (800) telephone number
- Accepting credit-card payments
- Checking credit
- Shipping ordered books
- Accepting, inspecting and restocking returned books
- Refunding customer monies for returned books
- Billings and collections

And even this list is probably not complete. Of course, you can buy many of these services. For example, there are fulfillment houses catering to small publishers. These organizations accept orders either directly from customers or the publisher, maintain inventory, ship, accept returns, inspect them for reusability and restock them, all for a fairly nominal fee. (Resources for finding these are in the next section.)

It's also possible to arrange the same services at a local mail house specializing in high-quality and/or small-quantity operations. Sometimes even a printer who also has mailing operations will take on these fulfillment activities.

If you already have an office staff and someone who can spend a few hours a week in this process, then the order fulfillment and processing responsibilities may be easy to absorb.

At the front end of the process, today's PC-based desktop publishing makes it more convenient and economical to get the book printed. Whereas desktop publishing systems may not be adequate to prepare advertising artwork, virtually all are suitable for your books, booklets or other publications. And most major metropolitan areas have one or more printers who specialize in short press runs of hardcover and/or soft-cover books.

3. Control (or Loss Thereof). A publisher will make *all* the major decisions about format, size, design, availability and even content of the book. You'll have a chance for input, of course, but they'll decide. For example, I wanted my *Complete Marketing Handbook for Consultants* to be a trade hard-cover book priced at $79. In spite of my arguments, the publisher made it a boxed 2-volume, 3-ring binder, priced at $145. This seriously hurt sales for both of us, but there was nothing I could do.

The publisher will also decide when and whether to reprint the book, and if they let it go "out of print," your supply is gone too.

The publisher will also decide what distribution channels and markets the book will be in, including overseas. This may or may not fit your needs.

All-in-all, if you need to be in control of your own destiny, linking up with a publisher is probably a mistake.

4. Market Access. Publishers can get your book into distribution channels that are all but closed to the first-time self-publisher. An example is retail distribution through bookstores (called "The Book Trade"): It's nearly impossible for a new publisher to crack this market given the literally tens of thousand of new titles published each month. Crown, B. Dalton, Waldenbooks and the other biggies rely on well-established, specialized, distribution channels even the pros have difficulty working successfully.

International distribution may also be difficult for the self-publisher. If this is your interest, by all means seek out an experienced publisher with proven international outlets.

Learn What's Worked Well for Others

Avail yourself of all the information in your local library. Or use the following references and resources, which are divided into two groups: the first group for self-publishing and the second group for those seeking a publisher.

Self-Publishing:

1. The Self-Publishing Manual, by Dan Poynter. Para Publishing Co., P. O. Box 4232-R, Santa Barbara, CA 93140-4232. Phone: (800) PARAPUB, (805) 968-7277;

Fax: (805) 968-1379. 1989.

Informative and complete step-by-step, how-to-do-it text by the principal of one of the most successful small publishing firms in the country. I found it the easiest to read and (for my style) the most practical of the three most popular "How to self-publish" books. One of his competitors said, "If you can afford to buy only one book on publishing, buy this one."

2. The Complete Guide to Self-Publishing. Everything You Need to Know to Write, Publish, Promote, and Sell Your Own Book, by Marilyn A. Ross and Tom M. Ross. Writer's Digest Books, 1507 Dana Avenue, Cincinnati, OH 45207-1005. Phone: (800) 759-0963, (513) 531-2222. 1989 (2nd Edition). ISBN 0-89879-354-8. (420 pages, $18.95.)

A wonderful overview and introduction to the marvels of self-publishing, including choosing a marketable subject, operating procedures, design and production, manufacturing, advertising, publicity and promotion, attracting a trade publisher and more. It's full of practical, how-to advice and plenty of references and resources.

3. Book Publishing Resource Guide, by John Kremer. Ad-Lib Publications, P. O. Box 205, Fairfield, IA 52556-0205. Phone: (800) 669-0773, (515) 472-6130; Fax: (515) 472-3186. 1990.

Comprehensive listings for book marketing contacts and resources. Contains a vast bibliography and references to other resource guides.

4. 1001 Ways to Market Your Books -- For Publishers and Authors, by John Kremer. Ad-Lib Publications, P. O. Box 205, Fairfield, IA 52556-0205. Phone: (515) 472-6130; Fax: (515) 472-3186. 1989. ($19.95.)

A new, revised edition of his widely-acclaimed *101 Ways*. A great source of down-to-earth, sensible, innovative and sometimes inspiring advice on producing the most marketable book possible and then marketing it effectively.

5. PMA Newsletter: The International Newsletter of the Publishers Marketing Association, Jan Nathan, Editor. Publishers

Marketing Association, 2401 Pacific Coast Highway, Suite 102, Hermosa Beach, CA 90254. Phone: (310) 372-2732; Fax: (310) 374-3342.

Loaded with good information, event calendars and ads for vendor services, this is a free newsletter no self-publisher should miss. While strictly available only to members, they'll send it to nonmembers as supplies permit.

6. Signature: A Newsletter for the Publishing Industry, Ernest L. Weckbaugh, Editor. Griffin Printing & Lithograph, Co., Inc., 544 West Colorado St., Glendale, CA 91204-1102. Phone: (800) 826-4849, (800) 423-5789, (818) 244-2128. (Published quarterly.)

An informative, free newsletter for the self-publisher. Features articles and reprints of all the experts, plus handy calendars and more. An exceptionally useful compilation of great ideas on publishing and promoting your own books.

Finding and Working with a Publisher:

1. The Insider's Guide to Book Editors, Publishers and Literary Agents, by Jeffrey H. Herman. Prima Publishing, P.O. Box 1260HER, Rocklin, CA 95677. Phone: (916) 786-0426. 1993-94 (3rd Edition). ISBN 1-55958-231-6. (452 pages, $19.95.)

This new, expanded edition proved to be a truly useful reference compared to other works claiming the same coverage (*Writer's Market*, for one). *Insider's Guide* contained more of the publishers we sought and provided better up-to-date information. And the 18 short articles in Part Three are "must" reading for every new or prospective author.

2. 1993 Writer's Market, Mark Kissling, Editor. Writer's Digest Books, 1507 Dana Avenue, Cincinnati, OH 45207-1005. Phone: (800) 759-0963, (513) 531-2222. 1992 (Annually). ISBN 0-89879-498-6. (1,008 pages, $26.95, hardcover.)

This comprehensive directory offers instant access to 4,000 buyers of free-lance materials. Lists U.S., Canadian and International book publishers, consumer magazines, trade, technical and professional journals, scriptwriting and more. Besides listing the buyer's name and address, writer's will also find additional information which is just as vital to get their work published.

3. Literary Market Place. Richard D. Lanam, III, Managing Editor. Reed Reference Publishing Co., P.O. Box 31, 121 Chanlon Road, New Providence, NJ 07974. Phone: (800) 521-8110; Fax: (908) 665-6699. 1993 (53rd Annual Edition). ISBN 0-8352-3237-9. (1,800 pages, $148.)

With 15,599 total entries and 3,686 publishers, *LMP* (as it is universally known) is one of the most comprehensive directories available. From R. R. Bowker, publishers of *Books In Print*. In addition to publishers, key sections include editorial services and agents, advertising, marketing and publicity, book manufacturing, sales and distribution, services and suppliers, publishing associations and events and more. Yellow pages list organizations and individuals alphabetically for quick reference.

4. Writer's Digest Magazine, P.O. Box 2123, Harlan, IA 51593, Phone: (800) 333-0133. (Published monthly.)

One of the best all-around sources for information on becoming a published author, it's full of information on all aspects of the book business. It contains how-to articles on both the creative process *and* marketing. *Writer's Digest* is also one of the best sources for books on how to succeed as a writer. Write or call for complete book catalog.

5. ISBN, International Standard Book Number Agency, c/o R. R. Bowker Company, 245 W. 17th Street, New York, NY 10011. Phone: (212) 337-7071.

If you elect to self-publish, by all means secure an International Standard Book Number from the ISBN Agency, R. R. Bowker Company. Call or write to the above for the necessary forms and instructions. The main advantage is that your publications will then appear in Bowker's regular publication of *Books In Print*, which is one of the standard ways libraries and others use to identify their book purchases.

Whether or Not to Use an Agent

A literary agent represents the author to the publisher. The more effective agents know how to get your work published, can find and influence the right publishers and can help you negotiate the best possible deal. Since agents generally get compensated on a percentage of author income, they *only* make money when they sell books in volume. The average professional-turned-author is not likely to find an agent anxious to invest the time and effort to promote their work unless it is viewed as a likely "best seller."

Some say that today's book publishing marketplace is so competitive that an agent is your only hope. Not everyone agrees, but for the best description of the process I've seen, look at Part Three of Jeff Herman's *Insider's Guide* listed above.

The best way to locate an agent that's familiar with your field is from other authors. Most authors are quite willing to talk about the writing process and are happy to share the name of the agent who's worked for them. If authors in your field generally have not used agents, that may signal that you will have to do it yourself. Furthermore, many smaller publishers are unwilling to deal with agents because they prefer a less formal arrangement with their author. In cases where both of the parties are honorable people, this may be a better arrangement. Long, formal author agreements may be required by the larger publishers but may be unnecessary or even undesirable for the smaller ones.

How to Find the Right Publisher

If you decide to seek a publisher, allow time to do your homework and to negotiate the best possible deal.

You already know the publishers who specialize in your field. Their names are on the books on your bookshelf. Even so, you'll notice that some are more prominent than others. Make a list of the publishers you believe would be the most desirable for you, that will give you maximum exposure to your field. Then find out the names of their acquisition editors and anything you can learn about how they do business. In addition to the great resources above, most public libraries have a rich selection of books devoted to new or prospective authors. And librarians *love* to help aspiring authors.

The usual drill is to prepare a query let-

ter/package, which may be followed by a comprehensive outline and one sample chapter to use if your query letter generates interest. As with the rest of the publishing business, it's a "numbers game," so be prepared for lots of rejection. Try your wings first with the publishers you're least interested in, saving your later, more experienced efforts for the publisher(s) you most want to work with. Again Jeff Herman's reference above is a "must."

Of course, if you're already well-known in your field, the best approach might be an informal chat with a publisher at some event where you and they meet casually. The advantage of this informal contact is that it allows them to suggest the orientation or "slant" they'd like to have on your subject -- the one that would be most marketable to them or would best fit their acquisition plans.

Having It Both Ways

The best strategy for some will be to *both* self-publish *and* turn the book over to a publisher. This apparent contradiction occurs because *first* you self-publish it, concentrating your marketing/promotion so the book is a big, early hit. *Then*, after having proven the book's market potential, you start the process of seeking a publisher. This sequence was followed by lots of the training industry's biggest successes, including *The One Minute Manager, Zapp! The Lightening of Empowerment* and *Managing from the Heart*.

What You Need to Promote Your Book

Whether you elect to self-publish or use an established publisher, promoting your book is the most important thing you do. *You* must take the initiative. The purpose of this section is to help identify what you need. Those working with a publisher may be able to obtain some of these items at low- or no-cost through them.

Promoting your own book needs to be a carefully orchestrated and timed activity. It's important that all the activities take place in a sufficiently short time to build the "momentum" of the new publication. As we used to say, the Saturn V Rocket that sent our astronauts to the moon burned 85 railroad tank cars full of fuel. If it burned them in two minutes you would get to the moon. If it burned them in ten minutes all you got was a big fire. Timing and coordination is everything.

Your "media kit" consists of the following six (6) ingredients:

1. 1- to 2-page press release
2. Glossy black-and-white photo(s) of the book *and* author
3. "Blurbs" (favorable testimonials)
4. A favorable, 1- to 3-page book review
5. Complimentary review copies
6. 1-page personalized cover letter

You don't usually send all six items to every contact, just what's appropriate for them. Here's what each entails:

1. Press Release. Since the media are only interested in "news," you *must* convey a sense of immediacy and nowness. Merely publishing a book is occasionally news, especially if the subject is newsworthy (like the biography of a famous person or the detailed treatment of some well-known event). But with so many books published daily, just publishing one is *not* likely to be news. If you want your press release to be newsworthy, try describing your book as a research report or emphasize the "new findings" it contains. The media are *always* interested in new information, especially those that might be controversial, surprising or even outrageous. Just *one* unexpected result or number taken from your book can be the reason your entire press release gets published.

2. Glossy Black-and-White Photo(s) of the book *and* the author. Look for low-cost photo labs that can print these for under $1.00 each.

If you can't find a satisfactory, local source, try:

DUPLICATE PHOTO LABORATORIES, INC.
1522 North Highland Avenue, P.O. Box 2670
Hollywood, CA 90028
Phone: (213) 466-7544

3. "Blurbs" are favorable quotes and testimonials that appear on the book jacket, in your advertising and maybe even in your bi-ography. They're essential! Get them by circulating advance copies of your book to key opinion-setters and decision-makers in your market.

It's O.K. to ask reviewers directly for a favorable testimonial and to rewrite someone's verbal testimonial so it says what you wish they would have said. In either case, *never* use a blurb without the person's express written consent.

4. Prepared Reviews give smaller publications and newsletters something they can print directly without having to read the book. Many association newsletters and other publications are done "on a shoestring" with a volunteer staff. Such publications are simply unable to write all the copy they need, and they may use your press release and book review almost verbatim. For this reason, it's important that these items be as free of unnecessary "hype" as possible. The more biased and unbelievable these are, the less likely they'll be used.

5. Complimentary Review Copies are the accepted means of getting coverage for your new book. Unfortunately, it's also a frequently-abused part of the publishing business.

Some believe that a minimum of 200 to 500 review copies of a low-priced book is required to adequately cover the review market. That's about the same number of press releases you'll distribute.

Send a review copy to every major publication book-review editor you seriously want to "plug" your book. The "second tier" might be offered a chance to request a review copy with a business reply card or call to your 800 number. This will save you money but will also lose you some reviews.

This is clearly an economic issue for self-publishers: the cost of the review copies, including shipping and handling, versus the likely sales you'll get from reviews. If you're working with a publisher, the costs to you may be less, especially if you negotiated a liberal number of review copies in your contract.

If the actual cost of your book is high (for example, a looseleaf manual) consider sending review copies "on loan," furnishing a return label and/or return postage.

Expect review copy requests from people you've never heard of. There's a surprising number of those who have "a publication" they use mainly to get freebie books, software and other considerations extended to "real" publishers. Some routinely write or call for *every* new book, claiming they're doing an article and would like to review your book. Evaluate such requests carefully. If you've never heard of the publication, ask for their BPA, which gives statistics on their circulation. If they don't have a BPA, ask questions about their number and type of readership. And always request a recent edition of the publication to see for yourself. If you're not satisfied they reach your market, respectfully decline.

6. Your Personalized Cover Letter starts with a "hook" or "gee whiz" opener geared personally to the individual (and publication) you're writing to. See Chapter 8 for help writing compelling letters.

Where to Promote Your Book

Once your media kit is ready (and while you're thinking of drafting the letter that goes with it) you need to consider who will get it. There are basically six (6) groups:

1. Trade Press in Your Field -- both major publications (magazines and newspapers) and minor publications (like newsletters), as well as any archive journals that have a news or book-review section.

2. General Business Press, including major business publications such as the *Wall Street Journal, Fortune, Business Week, Forbes*, etc. It's unlikely any of these publications will pick up your press release, but it could stimulate your inclusion in a "round-up" article or could provoke research leading to an article on the subject, in which you and your book might be included.

3. Local Media and Publications, including all the daily, weekly and less frequently published magazines and papers in your area. You're more likely to be news to them. And don't forget your local broadcast media as well: the AM/FM and TV stations which have talk shows or other local programing. This goes for cable television, too,

which is rapidly moving to serve business interests.

4. Associations that Serve Your Field, especially those you belong to or your customers belong to. And don't forget your college or university alumni association.

5. Your Existing Customers, Clients and Prospects. These people love you and are always pleased to learn what you're doing. If you're planning to distribute complimentary copies of your book to them, then save money on this step and merely include your press release with the copy of the book. Or, to get the benefit of "two hits," send the press release, followed in two to four weeks by their complimentary copy of the book.

6. Significant Others. Don't forget your investors, bankers, organizations you may wish to acquire or merge with or just friends who would like to know about your book without a lot of technical mumbo-jumbo.

Whom to Send It to

O.K. So your letter is personally addressed. But personally addressed to whom? Probably the editor, feature editor for the subject of your book, book reviewer or all three. In your local publications it will probably be the business editor or the local news editor or both. For the major national media, look for the editor who covers your subject. When in doubt, send it to several people within the same publication.

The best way to get these individual names is with a trip to your local library to look at a number of the publications there. Start with the first three self-publishing resources listed earlier in this section, which have chapters devoted to just this search. Also use the three resources listed in the section on publicity, later in this chapter.

Finally, three other publications that list feature editors of newspapers and magazines are:

Ayer Directory of Publications, Ayer Press, One Bala Avenue, Bala Cynwyd, PA 19004. Phone: (215) 664-6205.

Working Press of the Nation, National Research Bureau, 310 S. Michigan Avenue,

Suite 1150, Chicago, IL 60604. Phone: (312) 663-5580.

Advertisers Guide to Scholarly Periodicals, American University Press Services, Inc., One Park Avenue, New York, NY 10016. Phone: (212) 889-3510.

Follow up by looking at the masthead of any of the publications you know that you would like to include. Start this research with the magazines you have in your own office.

Here's What Works Best to Sell Your Book

Averaged over a number of different book promotions in the training and information field, we've had success with the following, listed in order of increasing selling cost:

1. News releases
2. Book reviews
3. Postcard decks
4. Catalogs
5. Direct mail advertising
   - Envelope mailings to customers & prospects
   - Self-mailers to customers & prospects
   - Envelope mailings to rented lists of similar book buyers
   - Self-mailers to rented lists of similar book buyers
   - Envelope mailings to other rented lists
   - Self-mailers to other rented lists
6. Back-of-the-room sales at seminars, conferences and speeches
7. Distribution agreements with associations and other organizations (see below)
8. Libraries and book-buying services (see below)
9. Sales at trade shows, expositions and other booth-type functions
10. Author promotion/interviews on talk radio/TV
11. Author book signings
12. Bowker's *Books In Print*
13. Display ads
14. Classified ads

In terms of selling cost as a percentage of revenues, the above sources range from a low 5% for the news releases to a high of about 50% for the poorest acceptable campaign. Overall average direct mail selling costs in the range of 20% to 30% are common for book promotion.

Distribution Agreements with Associations and Others. One avenue of selling the books you self-publish, or that you buy from a major publisher at an attractive wholesale price, is through resale or distribution agreements with others. The most common of these are distribution agreements with associations who handle books of interest to their members.

Most of the larger associations have a members' bookshelf function. Some deal only with their own publications, but most also handle appropriate books from others. If you self-publish or if your major publisher is not interested in pursuing these avenues, then you should negotiate arrangements with any and all associations that will have you. Generally these associations buy their books at a discount, but considerably less of a discount than in the normal book trade. They are primarily interested in serving their members -- and only defraying their added costs, not making lots of money.

Additional distributor leads are presented in the section "Distributors, Agents, Speakers Bureaus and Sales Representatives" later in this Chapter.

Libraries and Book Buying Services. Essentially every library in the country gets its books through one of two jobbers:

QUALITY BOOKS
918 Sherwood Drive
Lake Bluff, IL 60044-2204
Phone: (312) 295-2010

BAKER & TAYLOR
50 Kirby Avenue
Somerville, NJ 08876
Phone: (201) 722-8000

Your key to these services is getting your books before them. Plan on a separate letter, book review, news release and, of course, the obligatory review copies. If one or both of these organizations pick up your book, they access literally thousands of libraries.

Having your publication in libraries has some interesting multiplying effects, over and above the book sales it represents. I've sold many copies of my books to people who saw it in their local library and wanted their own copy. Of course, your book is more likely to be picked up by a library if it has reference value -- hence another reason to position your book as a research report, if that is possible.

How Your Book's Price Affects Returns

Pricing is a big issue, as discussed in Chapter 2. For books in particular, two other important elements are closely related to price: (1.) whether or not to offer a free trial and (2.) how to handle product returns and their attendant requests for refunds. There is absolutely no doubt that a "14-day free trial," or its less powerful but functional equivalent "14-day money back guarantee," is expected for books today. Either offer will certainly increase the number of books you sell. These increased sales come at a price, of course, and that price is the need to actually handle returns and refunds. As a rule, about half of the returned books will be reusable; the remainder will not.

What rate of product returns can you expect? The answer depends upon two variables: the perceived *quality* of the product in relation to it's *price*. High-priced products usually generate more returns than low-priced ones. And high-priced products that do not have a correspondingly high perceived value generate extraordinarily high returns.

The following table illustrates several examples from our files.

PRODUCT	PRICE	RETURNS
Get Rich Quick Book	$ 10.00	Effectively none
Market Research Report	$ 69.95	Under 5%
How To Market Training Handbook	$169.95	Under 7%
(Overpriced) Management Video Tape Program	$695.00	Over 50%

As this illustrates, the higher the price the more likely are returns.

The reason given for most product returns is that the product was just "not suitable" or "not what I expected." You will really need to dig hard in order to uncover the *real* reason, especially if that reason is low quality in relation to the price. Plan to look at the percentage of returns along with sales, as you design your price testing program.

WRITING ARTICLES AND COLUMNS

Articles and columns in periodicals help individual authors, speakers and consultants more than it helps organizations. It's just not practical for an organization to write a column.

Articles can help build your individual credibility, but less than a book. A regular column keeps you visible to your market and produces inquiries/leads.

If your column excerpts your book, report, newsletter, etc., offer to send/sell the complete work to those who write/call.

Reprints of your articles mailed to your customers/prospects are good stay-in-touch vehicles. Reprints also make good leave-behinds for face-to-face sales calls.

The best publications for your articles are those whose mailing lists work best for you -- and vice versa. If you don't mail, then pick those that best cover your target market.

To get accepted, learn what's expected of authors generally: the publication's guidelines for submittals and what the editor wants. *Writers Market*, referenced in the previous section, is a great starting point.

GETTING AND USING PUBLICITY

Publicity is any third-party mention of you, your firm, your products or your services. Typical examples include being quoted in print, mentioned or interviewed on radio or TV, reviews of your books, articles on your accomplishments, etc.

Whoever said, "There's no such thing as bad publicity" and, "I don't care what you say about me, as long as you spell my name right," understood publicity. Even an unfavorable reference can produce business; look at how many criminals later make money by writing a book on their crime.

Publicity implies endorsement. If you say something nice about yourself, it's self-serving. If your customer says something nice about you, it's expected -- everyone publishes testimonials. But a favorable third-party mention in the media carries much more weight. Think about your own reaction.

Publicity doesn't *replace* other marketing and sales approaches -- it *multiplies* their effectiveness.

Understanding the Media

Most of the publicity you're seeking will appear in print periodicals or on the air, collectively referred to as "the media." Print media include newspapers, magazines and newsletters. Broadcast media are radio and television, including cable TV.

The media live and breathe "news": the current, the controversial, the different. Remember, "If man bites dog, that's news." This mentality means that the ordinary things you do are *not* newsworthy and never will be -- unless you put a fresh "spin" on them.

The media also have a *very* short attention span, measured by the time to their next deadline. Media timetables are measured in minutes or hours rather than days or weeks.

Sure, there are feature stories that are researched over a long time. But it's usually some "news" that triggered the story, and the people who made the news are usually included in the feature. If you make enough news, over a long enough time, you may rate a feature article or a program on radio or TV

devoted entirely to you.

The media have a long and fierce tradition of independence. That's why they've been called "the fourth estate." Media journalists value this independence and resist any efforts to manipulate them or use them for personal gain. *Remember this in all your dealings with the media.* They *know* that the reason you're contacting them is to promote yourself. And that's O.K. as long as what you have to say or what you've done is *truly* newsworthy. Otherwise it's a waste of time for both of you.

One final point: Writing for the media requires a special mindset. Although opinions differ, writing for somewhere between the fifth- and tenth-grade level is considered a requirement. This is not because the audience may only have that level of education. It's because writing geared to that level is easier to understand and easier to work with. As we've noted in earlier chapters dealing with writing, that means short sentences, short paragraphs and simple words. It also generally means getting your most important points out first and then supporting them with examples and other information that can be cut to fit the available space.

You're Already News

Although the routine and ordinary things you do don't qualify as "news," chances are that many of your accomplishments *are* genuinely newsworthy. Most of us don't recognize this and fail to do what's necessary to have these newsworthy occurrences reported in media that will benefit us.

Take insurance sales people, for example. They generally work in a small geographic area. And most insurance sales manuals have chapters on getting and using local publicity. You'll often see your insurance salesperson's name in print. They belong to Rotary, help the YMCA, raise funds for the hospital, organize little league, etc. These organizations are newsworthy, so the salesperson's name is usually included in any stories. This has always been a staple of insurance promotion.

Until recently, attorneys and accountants

couldn't advertise. But they'd use their participation in civic events, golf tournaments or even the school board to secure favorable "exposure" in local media.

As a trainer or consultant, you may have even more genuinely newsworthy accomplishments. Here are some activities which might be "news":

- Publishing a book
- Writing an article
- Conducting a new seminar
- Giving a speech, especially to a well-known group or at a prestigious location
- Receipt of an award or recognition
- Winning a big contract, especially from a well-known customer
- Hiring a key employee
- Completing a research project, especially if some surprising findings can be disclosed
- Moving into new offices
- Being quoted on or interviewed by a major national media (especially newsworthy for your local media)

The list goes on and on. But most of these truly newsworthy events will not be "picked up" by the media without some help from you.

You need to develop a systematic procedure for, first, *recognizing* your newsworthy accomplishments and, second, *getting them before the media* (print or broadcast) most likely to use them. You can do this yourself (using some of the references and techniques in this section) or you can hire a professional publicist to assist you (more on that later).

The main ingredients of a good publicity campaign are always the same: A continual program spread over years is better than a "1-shot" approach. You'll need a list of the media of most interest to you and the individuals in those publications or stations you want to know about your accomplishments. And you'll need a simple, standard format for communicating with them -- one that fits their normal and customary way of receiving information.

There are some great references on how to create and distribute your own press releases at the end of this section.

Print Media

The three main kinds of print media of inter-est here are: *Newspapers*, generally published on a daily or weekly basis; *magazines*, generally published on a weekly, monthly or quarterly basis; and *newsletters*, which can be published on any frequency but are generally characterized by a much shorter, less formal, format.

Newspapers generally have two types of articles: news stories and feature articles. Feature articles are written over a longer period of time and take more research. They are often written by different people than the news. Magazines generally have the same division, but more of their content is devoted to feature articles. Although newsletters have the word "news" in their title, there's little uniformity in their content. Associations and other organizations often emphasize "news," but industrial newsletters usually have more "features."

When you send your press release to any publication, send it to the editor by name. If you don't know the right person's name, call to find out. The editor's job is to distribute incoming information to the specialized editor or writer responsible for the area. Larger publications will have separate editors for each department or section. For example, your newspaper probably has an editorial page editor, a business editor, a local news editor, an education editor, etc. As you develop your own list of the publications you want to be in, read them thoroughly and understand which editors or sections are likely to be of greatest interest. A publication's masthead lists all of these people. If your particular announcement applies to several areas, be sure to send duplicate copies to each editor.

Your news releases will be handled differently by large and small publications. Large publications will be much more selective, using your release only if it's newsworthy. Small publications often have more difficulty filling their space and are more likely to use your announcement. The very smallest publications -- for example, society newsletters -- may be handled entirely by unpaid, part-time editors and will often use whatever you submit verbatim, provided it is written well and is free of obviously self-serving "hype."

Sometimes your news release will be routed to a reporter who's already working on a feature story connected with the subject of your release. Indeed, your news release could actually trigger a feature article. In these cases expect the reporter to call you for a telephone interview.

Broadcast Media

Broadcast media includes AM and FM radio, broadcast television and cable television. Although in a state of flux, cable television offers many local opportunities for exposure under less structured conditions than any of the others. This is especially useful for those serving primarily a local market.

It's virtually impossible to have anything broadcast that's not genuinely newsworthy. Whereas newspapers and magazines have remnant space where they can tuck a headline and a few sentences about something you've done, this is unheard of in broadcasting. Generally they have to devote a half minute or more to your item. That is *only* going to happen when it's really newsworthy.

The large and growing number of "talk shows" offer many opportunities for interviews on a variety of program formats. If your press release suggests that what you know or what you've just uncovered might be of interest to their viewers or listeners, there's at least a possibility that you'll be invited to participate in a interview or on a talk show. Increasingly, this participation will be done from your home or office either with a camera crew coming to you or with a radio interview using your telephone.

Finding and Using Publicity Agents

Virtually all non-news articles you read or programs you see are today the result of efforts by someone to get the exposure. Occasionally, you can do it yourself, but often you'll need professional help. That's the job of the professional publicist, publicity agent or "flack," as they used to be called.

There are plenty of individuals and organizations around who claim to be professional publicists. These range from advertising agencies to specialized firms for whom this is their sole activity. Unfortunately, most of these will be of absolutely no interest or value to trainers or training suppliers.

Only consider hiring a publicist who has demonstrated knowledge/experience about the markets you're trying to reach or the publications/media in which you'd like to appear. One way to find them is to ask those whose names are appearing frequently to tell you who they use for their publicity. If you are not competing with them, chances are they'll tell you who they use and what they like or dislike about them. Try calling your local newspaper or radio station, and talk to the business editor. Ask who *they* think would be helpful to you locally. Although they're not likely to do it on "the record," most editors or program directors work closely with the best publicists, who are probably of similar professional interests. This could be an excellent source. Also, try your local college or university, especially if there's an advertising or journalism department with a specialty for public relations. And the university's own public relations department might be another good source of full- or part-time talent.

The principal contribution your publicist makes is knowing the ropes! Publicists who are not on a first-name basis with the media you wish to reach are of little value. That's why it's so important to find a publicist who already does for others what you want them to do for you.

Some publicists will work on the basis of a regular monthly fee (plus expenses) for which they'll "guarantee" a certain number of articles published or program slots filled. Some will even "guarantee" the type of publication in which the exposure will occur. Be prepared for at least $300 - $500 a month if you go this route.

Publicity agents also insist that you be available as required. For example, if they've worked hard to get you on a radio talk show, you can bet they want you to make time available for it. A publicist I used for several years became very upset with me because I got busy and wasn't able to devote enough time to the PR activities he scheduled.

And this suggests another characteristic of publicity. It's the *individual* who gets the publicity, not the organization. People are more interested in other people than they are in ideas or institutions. That's why it's Albert Einstein who got the publicity, not his theory of relativity. It also means that your public relations starts with your willingness to see and be seen and to actively participate. If you're fundamentally a private person who shuns exposure, then you should seek other means of marketing. Publicity probably isn't for you!

Publicists can't always control what is said about you or your firm. They can provide the opportunity and the exposure. They can even help to shape the direction. But they cannot control what the media do or say unless the article or program is done entirely by you. This is especially true when you grant interviews or when your publications are excerpted for inclusion in an article. Your publicist can help identify the statements most likely to be picked up and repeated by the media. They can also help to give you the fundamental dos and don'ts, musts and must nots, so you'll come across in the most favorable possible way.

Making the Most of the Publicity You Get

Getting exposure in publications or on the air is not the end of your publicity efforts, just the beginning. If your article or appearance was successful, you want to immediately use that success with others you've been working on and see if that will encourage them to give you similar coverage. No media likes to be "left behind," especially with someone who's truly newsworthy or is becoming so.

In this regard, be careful with your publication of articles. Major national publications seek "exclusives," which means that if they agree to print your article, they don't want to see it in another publication. This is altogether understandable, but you need to decide whether you can live with this.

The only professional way around an exclusive is to rewrite the article for other publications. If the article can be given a "slant," then writing it with a different "slant" may be all that's required to allow its publication elsewhere. And since it's usually only the largest media that insist on exclusives, you may find it's not a serious problem.

And when an article *does* appear in a magazine or newspaper, be sure to reprint it (always with written permission from the publisher) and send the reprints, along with a cover note or letter, to your customers and clients.

Three Very Practical References

There's a lot written about publicity, and most of it will probably help you do a better job. But when time and resources are short (as usual), it's nice to know a few "don't miss" references. In my opinion, these are:

1. The Unabashed Self-Promoter's Guide: What Every Man, Woman, Child and Organization in America Needs to Know about Getting Ahead by Exploiting the Media, by Dr. Jeffrey L. Lant. Jeffrey Lant Associates, Inc., 50 Follen Street, Suite 507, Cambridge, MA, 02138. Phone: (617) 547-6372; Fax: (617) 547-0061. 1992 (2nd Edition). ISBN 0-940374-18-8. (365 pages, 8-1/2" x 11" format, $39.50 postpaid.)

An outstanding collection of advice and step-by-step procedures on how to make best use of the media to increase your exposure. It now claims over 20,000 in print, making this a "best-seller" for this type of book. In distinction to Lant's hard-hitting and pithy advertising copy, the book is occasionally wordy and hard to read. But it's contents are definitely worth it!

2. Lesly's Handbook of Public Relations and Communications, edited by Philip Lesly. AMACOM Publishing Co., P.O. Box 1026, Saranac Lake, NY 12983-1026. Phone: (518) 891-5510; Fax: (518) 891-3653. 1991 (4th Edition). ISBN 0-8144-0108-2. (874 pages, $79.95, hardcover.)

The most widely used, standard desk reference for the field, this new edition's 48 chapters and five appendixes include contributions from 44 other experts, besides many chapters written or co-written by Lesly. There's plenty of help here to understand the media, including its use for advertising as well as for publicity. The lists of sources, contacts and public relations organizations are also useful.

3. Bacon's Publicity Checker. Bacon's

Publishing Company, 332 S. Michigan Avenue, Chicago, IL 60604. Phone: (800) 621-0561, (312) 922-8419, (312) 922-2400; Fax: (312) 922-3127. ($110.)

Published annually; a standard public relations directory of magazines and major newspapers. It shows you what to send to every publication in various market classifications and the types of publicity materials used.

DIRECTORIES, COURSE LISTINGS, ON-LINE COMPUTER DATABASES AND LOCATOR SERVICES

We've recommended that you take advantage of all free, and even some paid, course calendars and product listings in newsletters and magazines that reach your targeted market. We know this time and money is well-spent.

But what about broader, generic directories and on-line computer databases of organizations, consultants, products and training programs? Does anyone besides researchers and mailing list compilers ever use them? Will sales result for you?

The answer used to be a clear "no." And in my opinion, it still is. But that could be changing for several reasons:

1. *Greater Demand*. Our information-age society is increasingly seeking quick, convenient sources for alternatives and for decision-making information. The rise of shopping malls, merchandise catalogs and even TV's Home Shopping Network points the way. People buying training products and services want the same wider range of choices and information.

2. *More and Better Sources*. When I wrote *The Seminar Market* in 1980, there were practically no published data on the training field, save the landmark *Directory Of Management Education Programs*, published by AMA in 1977, and the membership directories of a few societies. Today, there are several dozen organizations compiling printed and on-line computer listings. On the whole, they're not very good yet. But it's a start. (More on these shortly.)

3. *Where Technology Is Headed*. Sure, lots of people *still* can't program their VCR. But that's apparently not stopping the headlong rush to high definition TV and the emerging mind-meld of telephone, television, fiberoptics and computers to deliver information and entertainment. If Interactive TV takes off -- and it's still an "if" -- do you seriously think it won't affect where and how people shop for training?

We really have three separate kinds of products and services, each having a different change cycle which affects how successfully they can be included in a directory or on-line service:

1. *Organizations, Institutions and Individual Product/Service Providers* (like consultants, training companies, universities, etc. -- see Chapter 1 for a more comprehensive review). These change most slowly of all, and good directories exist.

2. *Print- and Media-Based Training Programs and Products* (like books, audio tapes, films/videos, CBT, interactive programs, software, etc.). These change over time, but directories are available, and more are appearing all the time.

3. *Training Events* (like seminars, workshops, conferences and courses). These change most rapidly of all. Printed course lists are clearly obsolete by the time they go to press -- but, surprisingly, today's on-line computer databases are not the answer either. Maybe that's why a number of firms have emerged who do custom searches to find training events to meet client needs.

Lets look at what's available in each of these three areas.

Organizations, Institutions and Individual Providers

There are any number of directories, buyer's guides and other print resources focussing primarily on the organizations supplying training and information products/services. Nine of them are listed below. Be sure your firm is listed in all the free ones, and monitor the others to see how your competitors are using them.

1. ASTD Buyers Guide and Consultant Directory. American Society for Training and Development, 1640 King Street, P. O. Box 1443, Alexandria, VA 22313-2043. Phone: (703) 683-8100; Fax: (703) 683-8103.

Published annually and distributed free to members, this contains paid listings of more than 500 organizations offering training products and services. It includes subject and geographical indexes.

2. Dun's Consultants Directory. Dun's Marketing Services, Inc., Three Sylvan Way, Parsippany, NJ 07054. Phone: (800) 526-0651. (Published annually.) ISBN 1-56203-122-8.

Compiled from D&B's comprehensive business files, this directory includes hard-to-find data on the size of the various organizations it lists. Listings are free.

3. Consultants and Consulting Organizations Directory: A Reference Guide to Concerns and Individuals Engaged in Consultation for Business and Industry, Janice McLean, Editor. Gale Research Inc., 835 Penobscot Bldg., Detroit, MI 48226-4094. Phone: (800) 877-GALE, (313) 961-2242; Fax: (313) 961-6083, (313) 961-6815. 1993 (13th Edition). ISBN 0-8103-7608-3. (Two-volume set; 2,804 pages.)

This lists more than 18,000 firms and individuals worldwide, including 1,500 new listings. It is indexed in 14 major and hundreds of minor subject classifications, as well as geographical, by organization's and individual consultant's name. Listings are free. (Also available on-line through the Human Resource Information Network (HRIN).)

4. Training and Development Organizations Directory, Janice McLean, Editor. Gale Research Inc., 835 Penobscot Bldg., Detroit, MI 48226-4094. Phone: (800) 877-GALE, (313) 961-2242; Fax: (313) 961-6083, (313) 961-6815. 1991 (5th Edition). ISBN 0-8103-4349-5. (677 pages, $270.)

This lists more than 2,300 companies offering more than 11,500 public, in-house and custom-designed workshops, seminars and other training programs. Organizations are classified in more than 575 subject areas, including computer, education, executive development, HRD, management, manufacturing, marketing and sales and university-based training programs. Listings are free.

5. The Directory of Management Consultants, James H. Kennedy, Editor. Kennedy Publications, Templeton Road, Fitzwilliam, NH 03447. Phone: (605) 585-6544; Fax: (604) 585-9555. 1993 (6th Edition). ISBN 0-916654-73-7. (843 pages, $106.95, hardcover; $96.95 to newsletter subscribers; $130., international price.)

This profiles 1,500 firms, classified and indexed by 95 services offered, by 70 industries served, by 5,400 principal names and geographically. Entries furnish data on both staff size and revenues. The introduction contains handy guidelines for using consultants and a comprehensive directory of consultants' organizations. Listings are free.

6. The Linton Trainer's Resource Directory. Linton Publishing Company, 1011 First Street South, Hopkins, MN 55343-9823. Phone: (612) 936-2288; Fax: (612) 936-9623. 1992 (2nd Edition). (2,000 pages, hardcover, $395.)

This lists training suppliers, vendors and consultants; videos; off-the-shelf programs; seminars and workshops; software; industry books; conference/training sites and other topics. Listings are free.

7. NSPI Performance Improvement Resources Directory. National Society for Performance and Instruction., 1126 16th Street, N.W., Washington, DC 20036. Phone: (202) 861-0777. 1990. (120 pages, spiral-bound.)

This lists more than 110 NSPI member organizations who paid to be included. Each entry provides address, telephone/fax numbers, services offered and contact. It is also cross-referenced by type of service.

8. The Global Connector. PASport Publishing International, 20 Libertyship Way, Suite 190A, Sausalito, CA 94965. Phone: (415) 331-2606; Fax: (415) 331-3903. (Published annually, 310 pages, $295.)

PASport is a subsidiary of Persona, Inc., a

Sausalito, CA, international training company headed by Jon Gornstein. Directory lists 239 companies, 125 associations and 97 conference centers in 25 countries on 3 continents (Asia/Pacific, Europe, the Americas). Despite omission of major international training firms like ARC, DDI, Learning Group, Pfeiffer, Tack and others, this is still a valuable compendium of otherwise hard-to-find information. Listings are free.

9. Computer Training and Support Buyer's Guide. Ziff Institute, 25 First Street, Cambridge, MA 02141. Phone: (617) 252-5000; Fax: (617) 252-5113.

This lists more than 430 organizations providing computer training products and services in the U.S., classified both by topic and by state. This is the latest edition of the useful annual directories published by Weingarten, following their acquisition by Ziff. Listings are free.

Print- and Media-Based Training Programs and Products

More directories, on-line sources and CD-ROMs are appearing here than in any other area. This is partly because so much information and entertainment is being released on video, on CD-ROM, on software -- even on the decades-old audio tape -- that new catalogs and directories are rushing to keep up. Rather than try to list all the possible sources, here's the reference I've found most useful:

The Training and Development Yearbook 1992/1993, Richard E. Frantzreb, J.D., MBA, Editor. Prentice Hall, 113 Sylvan Avenue, Englewood Cliffs, NJ 07632. Phone: (201) 592-2000. 1992 (3rd Edition, published annually). ISBN 0-13-921891-2. (624 pages, hardcover, $79.95.)

Although more than three-quarters of this book is devoted to reprints of articles, it's the directories at the back that offer a wealth of hard-to-find-in-one-place information for anyone marketing training. You'll find countless opportunities among 48 membership organizations, 100 conferences (most held annually), 45 directories / references and 53 newsletters and periodicals. The 287 train-the-trainer programs and ten non-membership organizations are also interesting.

To get the latest information, try contacting the editor directly. He's done the best job I've seen of pulling together the most comprehensive list of sources:

Richard E. Frantzreb, J.D., MBA
President and Editor
ADVANCED PERSONNEL SYSTEMS
P.O. Box 1438
Roseville, CA 95661
Phone: (916) 781-2900; Fax: (916) 781-2901

Once you've identified those directories where your program or product should be listed, send them a complete information package. Most will list your product at no charge.

Seminars, Workshops, Conferences and Courses

Because open registration training events are constantly changing, print directories must be periodicals, or they can only cover the most stable, longest-running programs and those offered only in-house or on-site "on-demand." That's why this is such a logical application area for on-line computer databases and for services that will find training programs to match customer needs. We'll look at both kinds of resources, because you'll want to have your program available as many ways as possible.

Print Directories. There are more than the six sources listed below (for example, the directory of trade shows and expositions described earlier in this chapter), but these are representative. Chances are your program will only be appropriate for one or two of these.

1. SIS Workbook. Seminar Information Service, 17752 Skypark Circle, Suite 210, Irvine, CA, 92714. Phone: (714) 261-9104; Fax: (714) 261-1963. (Published annually, in September; updated monthly; nearly 500 pages, looseleaf notebook, $295. per year.)

This contains over 5,200 seminar titles offered over 50,000 times a year by nearly 500 seminar sponsors. Subscriptions go to more than 2,000 Fortune 500 training and personnel directors. Information is sponsor-furnished and listings are free. It is arranged alphabetically by topic and cross-referenced by calendar and by sponsor. (This database is also available on-line through the *Human Resource Information Network (HRIN)*, described in the next section. SIS also takes seminar registrations -- see the discussion in a later section of this chapter.)

2. Seminars Directory, Julie E. Towell, Sr. Editor. Gale Research Inc., 835 Penobscot Bldg., Detroit, MI 48226-4094. Phone: (800) 877-GALE, (313) 961-2242; Fax: (313) 961-6083, (313) 961-6815. 1991 (2nd Edition). ISBN 0-8103-5049-1. (1,079 pages, $130.)

Compiled from Seminar Clearinghouse International's proprietary database, and previously only available to subscribers or on-line through the *Human Resource Information Network (HRIN)*, this publication provides detailed descriptions of 8,000 U.S. public seminars and workshops in more than 2,000 subject areas, including data processing, engineering, finance, health and medicine, human resources, law, manufacturing and marketing. No third edition is currently planned.

3. Bricker's International Directory of University-Based Executive Programs. Peterson's Guides, 202 Carnegie Center, P.O. Box 2123, Princeton, NJ 08543-2123. Phone: (609) 243-9111, (800) 338-3282; Fax: (609) 243-9150. 1993 (24th Edition, published annually). In 2 volumes: Vol. 1, (ISBN 1-56079-213-2), 593 pages, $135, covers long-term programs; Vol. 2, (ISBN 1-56079-214-0), 231 pages, $95, covers short-term programs.

Originally compiled by George W. Bricker, the latest edition lists more than 600 non-degree, upper-management programs in 11 subject categories, including general management, leadership, humanities, marketing and human resources. Programs are indexed by subject, location and duration. Executive MBA and industry-specific programs are also identified.

4. The Corporate University Guide to Management Seminars, Douglas A. Mackey and Lawrence Gilius, Senior Editors. The Corporate University, Inc., P. O. Box 2080, Fairfield, IA 52556. Phone: (515) 472-7720; Fax: (515) 472-7105. Published each year in October. (796 pages, soft-cover, $69.95.)

Listing more than 750 U.S. and Canadian management development programs, this edition includes 150 new programs. It includes

private providers as well as university sources and is indexed by topic, institution and program name.

5. Physicians' Travel & Meeting Guide. Cahners Publishing Company, 249 West 17th Street, New York, NY 10011. Phone: (212) 463-6403, (212) 463-6412; Fax: (212) 463-6404. (Published monthly as a controlled circulation publication; $70/year to non-qualified recipients.)

Aimed only at physicians (and *not* other healthcare professionals), the magazine presents travel and other articles of continuing medical education interest. A calendar of upcoming meetings and travel opportunities is classified by date and cross-referenced by location and by one of 26 specialties from allergy through urology. Each issue covers the latest information in a 4- to 5-month "window" after publication, plus additional meetings at the locations or on the topics featured in the issue. Ongoing/weekly and late-breaking listings are also included. How complete is the *Guide*? Well, not even one meeting from the extensive calendar for psychiatrists offered by CME, Inc. of Irvine, CA -- the one sponsor I looked for -- was included!

6. Medical Meetings: The International Guide for Healthcare Meeting Planners. The Laux Company, Inc., 63 Great Road, Maynard, MA 01754. Phone: (508) 897-5552; Fax: (508) 897-6824. (Published bimonthly, with extra editions in Spring and Fall, $48/year.)

This caters primarily to healthcare meeting planners and meeting facilities in the U.S., Canada and international destinations for U.S. organizations. It covers all of healthcare, not just meetings for physicians, and contains an annual directory of medical associations and meetings lists by location, by healthcare category and by meeting date. Some well-respected university- and privately-sponsored programs are missing (e.g., Harvard, USC, CME, Inc., etc.)

On-Line Databases and Locator Services. These go hand-in-hand; those compiling a database of courses are in the best position to search that database for programs to meet user-specified criteria. Besides, once you start using these on-line resources, it's easy to decide you'd like someone else to do it for you. Finally, this field is changing so fast that its final configuration may not be known for some time.

On-line course databases have been around for more than a decade; I've personally been using them for at least eight years. In spite of their enormous potential, they've been a disappointment to me during this whole time -- and still are. I can't imagine *anyone* who would use one of these as their main source of training program information for two reasons:

1. *They're incomplete.* No on-line database yet has all -- or even most -- of the courses on a given subject, in a given location or at a given time. Compare the three or four independent databases for a particular subject and you'll find little overlap. Why? Because, all current databases depend upon the *sponsor's* initiative to get their courses listed and to keep them current. (Marketers: Note this well!)

2. *They're hard to use.* I've used a number of different computers, modems and communications software packages to access on-line databases from various U.S. cities. None of them has been problem-free. Search protocols are primitive and often slow, noisy phone lines insert unwanted characters and connections get broken at exactly the wrong time.

Sooner or later (hopefully sooner) someone will compile a single source that contains most training programs. Until then, the locator *services* will continue to grow.

Since there's no cost to include your program in these, do it and track the resulting sales. (The two services that offer commission sales of live training programs are noted here and discussed again in the later section in this chapter on agents and sales representatives.)

1. TRAINET. American Society for Training and Development, 1640 King Street, P. O. Box 1443, Alexandria, VA 22313-2043. Phone: (703) 683-8100; Fax: (703) 683-8103.

This is a version of Timeplace's *EdVENT* database available to ASTD members and others on a subscription basis. ASTD will also do custom searches and compile lists of possible sources for members and nonmem-

bers, presumably using *TRAINET* as well as other sources.

2. Business Education/Seminar Training Database (BEST). This is on-line access to the SIS database described in the previous section. It is available through the *Human Resource Information Network* (HRIN), described below.

3. EdVENT PLUS. Timeplace, Inc., 460 Totten Pond Road, Waltham, MA 02154. Phone: (800) 544-4023, (617) 890-INFO; Fax: (617) 890-7274.

Founded in 1983, Timeplace provides public and contract on-line training information services. *EdVENT* is a public database of training programs Timeplace compiles and maintains themselves (as distinguished from HRIN that brokers databases created and maintained by others). *EdVENT* contains information on over 125,000 scheduled seminars, conferences and workshops from more than 6,000 sponsors in the United States and Canada. The database also includes information on meeting/conference facilities, consultants, speakers, audio tapes, films/videos and CBT. Major Timeplace contract database clients include ASTD (*Trainet*, available to member-subscribers) and various governmental bodies (available to employees) like the states of New Jersey and New York, and the U.S. Army, Navy and Air Force.

4. First Seminar. 600 Suffolk Street, Lowell, MA 01854. Phone: (800) 321-1990, (508) 452-0766.

First Seminar is one of only two national seminar brokers and it's the only one to actually take seminar registrations, bill and collect money from attendees and pay the seminar sponsor a discounted "wholesale" price. The other organization is Seminar Information Service, SIS, of Irvine, CA. Both are described more fully in the next section.

5. The Human Resource Information Network (HRIN). ETSI (Formerly Executive Telecom System, Inc.), 1200 Quince Orchard Blvd., Gaithersburg, MD 20878. Phone: (800) 638-8094, (301) 590-2300; Fax: (301) 990-8378.

Established in July, 1981 and for more than ten years in Indianapolis, IN, as subsidiary of the Bureau of National Affairs, Inc.

(BNA), the service was sold in the spring of 1993 to a Washington, DC, area firm. HRIN links subscribers with databases, bulletin boards, E-mail and business services in eight areas: administration, systems and planning, affirmative action, benefits and compensation, employment and recruiting, labor/legal, labor/management relations, safety and health, and training and development. In addition to access to the various third-party databases described in this section, HRIN offers some services of its own to those marketing training programs, such as the "Human Resources Events Calendar." For more information, contact Victor Garaycochea, President.

6. *Seminar Clearinghouse International*, Inc., P. O. Box 1757, St. Paul, MN 55101-0757. Phone: (612) 293-1044; Fax: (612) 293-0493.

Originally founded by the late Elmer R. John as MANTREAD Seminar Registry, Seminar Clearinghouse provides custom searches, evaluations and other training decision-making information to subscribers who pay $400 - $2,200 per year based on size and usage. The database includes about 60,000 open enrollment presentations of about 16,000 titles from 1,500 sponsors, as well as a growing library of books, films, videos and interactive media. Printed indexes are published in subject areas such as leadership, TQM, employee empowerment, service quality and others. The database is available on-line through the *Human Resource Information Network (HRIN)* and has been published as the *Seminars Directory* by Gale Research, most recently in 1991. No future edition of this print version is currently planned. Custom searches are conducted to meet subscriber needs. SCI does not take registrations, merely puts subscribers in touch with the appropriate training firm(s). For more information, contact David L. Shores, Ph.D., President.

7. *TR/ED*. Linton Publishing Company, 1011 First Street South, Hopkins, MN 55343-9823. Phone: (612) 936-2288; Fax: (612) 936-9623.

The name is an acronym for TRaining and EDucation, a custom research and resource service which links buyers of training-related products and services with appropriate suppliers and providers. Suppliers, vendors, consultants and their products are listed at no cost, but members pay for the service.

DISTRIBUTORS, AGENTS, SPEAKERS BUREAUS AND SALES REPRESENTATIVES

Most trainers, consultants and other professionals enter the training field with little or no appreciation for the huge amount of sales and marketing sophistication needed for success. Once they see what's involved, many would love to find someone who could "represent" them, selling their products and services on commission, so they can spend their time doing what they do best: consulting or training.

On the other hand, those experienced in marketing and selling training know very well that training *products* are abundant and cheap; it's the *sales and marketing* that's scarce and expensive -- and that represents the *real* value added.

You'd think these mutually supportive needs would have converged naturally to a network of training "representatives," "distributors" or "brokers." That's typical in so many other industries like manufacturing, housewares, food, mailing lists -- even works of art.

Well, it hasn't worked out that way, at least not for all training and information products and services. There are a number of areas where sales organizations *have* emerged -- others where there are a few trying -- and still other areas where nothing has worked very well. The following sections present a brief summary:

Distributors Work Well For Books, Tapes and Packaged Programs

A number of organizations routinely market other people's packaged training programs. Some have been around for years, so the process *must* work. The model is the publisher's distribution agreement, although there are lots of variations.

A cross-section of those most visible are listed below. Contact their CEO or acquisitions editor to see if there's a fit with your product.

But don't expect too much. If the distributor thinks there's a match and you agree on terms, they'll put your product in their catalog and see what happens. Any added sales are "found money" to you, but the distributor may drop your product if sales are below their expectations or returns are excessive.

AMERICAN MEDIA INCORPORATED
1454 30th Street W., Suite 105
West Des Moines, IA 50265-1311
Phone: (800) 262-2557; Fax: (515) 224-0256
Contact: Mr. Arthur R. Bauer, President

AMERICAN SOCIETY FOR TRAINING AND DEVELOPMENT
1640 King Street, Box 1443
Alexandria, VA 22313
Phone: (703) 683-8100; Fax: (703) 683-8103
Contact: Ms. Nancy Olson, Vice President, Publications

BLANCHARD TRAINING & DEVELOPMENT INC.
125 State Place
Escondido, CA 92029
Phone: (800) 728-6000; Fax: (619) 489-8407
Contact: Dr. Kenneth H. Blanchard, Co-Founder

HUMAN RESOURCES DEVELOPMENT PRESS
22 Amherst Road
Amherst, MA 01002
Phone: (800) 822-2801, (413) 253-3488; Fax: (413) 253-3490
Contact: Mr. Robert Carkhuff, President

LAKEWOOD PUBLICATIONS
50 South Ninth Street
Minneapolis, MN 55402
Phone: (800) 328-4329, (612) 333-0471; Fax: (612) 333-6526
Contact: Ms. Linda Klemstein, Vice President

LEARNING RESOURCES NETWORK
1554 Hayes Drive, P. O. Box 1448
Manhattan, KS 66502
Phone: (913) 539-5376; Fax: (913) 539-7766
Contact: Mr. Bill Draves, President

NIGHTINGALE-CONANT CORP.
7300 N. Lehigh Avenue
Chicago, IL 60648-4075
Phone: (800) 323-5552; Fax: (708) 647-7145
Contact: Mr. Vic Conant, President

PFEIFFER & COMPANY
8517 Production Avenue
San Diego, CA 92121-2280
Phone: (619) 578-5900; Fax: (619) 578-2042
Contact: Dr. J. William Pfeiffer, President

TRAINING HOUSE, INC.
P. O. Box 3090
Princeton, NJ 08543-3090
Phone: (609) 452-1505; Fax: (609) 243-9368
Contact: Dr. Scott B. Parry, Chief Executive Officer

Distributors are also the key to open many overseas markets. See Chapter 1 for a starter list of those to contact.

Agents and Speakers Bureaus May Work for "Talent"

If you're a stand-up trainer, a platform speaker, a writer or other "talent," an agent may work for you. You know all about the love/hate relationship people have with their agent from watching old movies on TV. It's usually true! Here's what Alan Weiss had to say in his great book *Million Dollar Consulting*: "Speakers' bureaus generally only help when you don't need them; that is, they disdain speakers without a national reputation and embrace those who are already well-known. They are often demanding and unreasonable in their working relationships, and some of the most unethical stories I've heard in our profession emanate from relationships with speakers' bureaus." Yet some very reputable people -- like Tony Alessandra, Joe Batten, Ken Blanchard, Herb Cohen, Gerard Nierenberg, Denis Waitley, Zig Ziglar and others -- use agents.

For most writers, a literary agent is required to gain access to a major publisher, if the author decides not to self-publish. (See the discussion of this subject in the section on writing a book, earlier in this chapter.)

If you're interested in speakers bureaus and other resources for speaking, here is a short list of some of the more prominent:

CAPITAL SPEAKERS, INC
655 National Press Building
Washington, DC 20045
Phone: (202) 393-0772
A consultancy that advises organizations on which speakers will best meet their needs and helps them contact appropriate agents.

THE INTERNATIONAL GROUP OF AGENTS AND BUREAUS
18825 Hicrest Road
Glendora, CA 91740
Phone: (800) 438-1242
An association of speakers bureaus and agents.

KEPPLER ASSOCIATION
4350 N. Fairfax Drive
Arlington, VA 22203
Phone: (703) 516-4000; Fax: (703) 516-4819
Speakers bureau. Contact: Jim Keppler.

JACK MORTON PRODUCTIONS
1850 K street, N.W., Suite 370
Washington, DC 20008
Phone: (202) 296-1860
Speakers bureau contact: Theresa Brown.

NATIONAL SPEAKERS ASSOCIATION
4747 N. 7th Street, Suite 310
Phoenix, AZ 85014
Phone: (602) 265-1001
Contact: Douglas Kerr, CAE, Executive Vice President.
This is an association of speakers and trainers whose subjects cover a wide range of topics. Contact them for a copy of their annual membership directory, Who's Who in Professional Speaking, *sent to about 8,000 meeting planners. (NSA is not a speakers bureau and doesn't recommend specific speakers.) NSA also publishes a monthly magazine,* Speak Out. *Membership: $250/year.*

NATIONAL SPEAKERS BUREAU
222 Wisconsin Ave.
Lake Forest, IL 60045-1777
Phone: (800) 323-9442, (708) 295-1122; Fax: (708) 295-5292
Contact: John Palmer.

NATIONAL SPEAKER'S FORUM
5028 Wisconsin Ave., N.W., Suite 301
Washington, DC 20016
Phone: (202) 244-1789.

NIGHTINGALE-CONANT SPEAKERS AND TRAINING BUREAU
7300 North Lehigh Avenue
Chicago, IL 60648
Phone: (800) 323-5552, (312) 647-0300
Speakers bureau representing Tony Alessandra, Joe Batten, Ken Blanchard, Charles Hobbs, Gerard Nierenberg, Frank "Buck" Rodgers and others.

TOASTMASTERS INTERNATIONAL
2200 N. Grand, P.O. Box 10400
Santa Ana, CA 92711
Phone: (714) 542-6793
Contact: Terrence J. McCann, Exec. Dir.
This is not a speakers bureau, but a self-help way to basic platform speaking skills. If you're just getting started in speaking, attend a trial meeting of your local group and consider joining.

THE HARRY WALKER AGENCY
One Penn Plaza, Suite 2400
New York, NY 10119
Phone: (212) 563-0700.
One of the most prestigious speakers bureaus representing people like George Bush, Dick Cheny, Marlin Fitzwater and Lynn Martin, among others.

WALTERS' INTERNATIONAL SPEAKERS BUREAU
P. O. Box 1120
Glendora, CA 91740
Phone: (818) 335-8069, (818) 335-1855; Fax: (818) 355-6127
Contact: Lillet Walters.

WASHINGTON SPEAKERS BUREAU, INC.
310 S. Henry Street
Alexandria, VA 22314
Phone: (703) 684-0555; Fax: (703) 684-9378
Contact: Bernie Swain.
Speakers bureau representing Dan Quayle, Jack Kemp, Norman Schwarzkopf, John Sununu and Paul Tsongas among others.

A variation on the agent theme could be interesting for some individual stand-up trainers. The large national and international public seminar providers need lots of contract trainers, i.e., organizations like:

AMERICAN MANAGEMENT ASSOCIATION (AMA)
135 West 50th Street
New York, NY 10020-1201
Phone (212) 586-8100; Fax (212) 903-8168
Contact: Mr. David Fagiano, Chief Executive Officer & President

CAREERTRACK, INC.
3085 Center Green Drive
Boulder, CO 80301-5408
Phone: (800) 325-5854; Fax: (303) 447-1696
Contact: Mr. James C. Calano, President

NATIONAL SEMINARS GROUP
6901 W. 63rd Street, P. O. Box 2949
Shawnee, Mission, KS 66201-1349
Phone: (800) 258-7246; Fax: (913) 432-0824
Contact: Mr. Mark R. Truitt, President

PADGETT-THOMPSON, INC.
P. O. Box 8297
Overland Park, KS 66208
Phone: (800) 255-4141
Contact: Mr. Bernie Erdman, President

FRED PRYOR SEMINARS
2000 Shawnee Mission Parkway
Shawnee Mission, KS 66205
Phone: (800) 255-6139; Fax: (913) 384-1802
Contact: Mr. Philip R. Love, President

SKILLPATH, INC.
P. O. Box 2768, 6900 Squibb Road
Mission, KS 66201-2768
Phone: (800) 873-7545; Fax: (913) 362-4241
Contact: Mr. Jerry E. Brown, President

And there are many others. While what you present may be dictated by them, if you're good you'll get plenty of work and possibly consulting, authoring or other opportunities that fall out from the seminars and from the relationship. There's also the possibility you could sell your course idea to them.

Sales Representatives -- Supplement but Don't Replace Your Own Marketing for Seminars

If you already have your own seminar, you know that there's no consistent alternative to marketing it yourself. However, there *are* two primarily customer-oriented services that will take registrations for your seminar at reasonable commissions. If you're holding the seminar anyway, those added enrollments can be very profitable. These services can also help sell in-house/on-site presentations.

The two services are on opposite coasts:

FIRST SEMINAR
600 Suffolk Street
Lowell, MA 01854-3685
Phone: (800) 321-1990, (508) 452-0766; Fax: (508) 441-2755
Contact: John G. Tumminello, President

First Seminar was founded in 1985. It's the only one of the two to actually take seminar registrations, bill and collect money from attendees, and pay the seminar sponsor a discounted "wholesale" price. First Seminar actively sells to organizations that consume training by promising to save them time and money by presenting more and better training options to meet specific training needs and by furnishing program evaluations, literature and other decision-making information. Their clients include large corporations like Chevron, B.F. Goodrich, Hewlett-Packard, Mercedes Benz, NEC, Philip Morris, United Technologies and others, totalling more than 500,000 employees.

On the seminar supplier side, Tumminello says they have a proprietary database of 100,000 seminars from providers (who receive payment from First Seminar according to the suppliers expected terms -- including payment in advance -- less a 30% commission). Suppliers include AMA, CareerTrack, The Center for Professional Advancement, Communispond, Dun & Bradstreet, Fred Pryor and Technology Transfer Institute.

Seminar subject areas include data processing, engineering and technology, finance, general management, human resource management, legal, manufacturing, medical, personnel development and sales and marketing.

SEMINAR INFORMATION SERVICE (SIS)
17752 Skypark Circle, Suite 210
Irvine, CA 92714
Phone: (714) 261-9104: Fax: (714) 261-1963
Contact: Ms. Catherine P. Bellizzi, President

Seminar Information Service has been around for over ten years and is best-known for its *SIS Workbook* containing over 5,200 seminar titles from nearly 500 seminar sponsors and received by more than 2,000 Fortune 500 training and personnel directors. Taking registrations is a fairly recent addition, for which SIS charges a 10% commission. SIS turns registrations over to participating sponsors, who follow their normal confirmation and billing practices and remit the SIS commission after the seminar.

SIS follows the pattern developed in the 1970s by Richard Brostrom's Comcor/Seminar Locator of Madison, WI, and refined by successor Howard Nelson of Seminars. We used this service to help sell our seminars just as soon as it became available. We obtained at best a trickle of registrations.

Other similar services have come and gone over the years with similar results.

RADIO AND TELEVISION, BROADCAST AND CABLE -- INCLUDING INFOMERCIALS

Major Broadcast Media

AM and FM radio, broadcast television and cable television are the four main forms of broadcasting today. But the phone companies are rewiring with fiberoptics and acquiring programing, so they may enter the field. And direct broadcast from a satellite to the home could also become a reality.

Cable TV allows easy access to highly segmented markets because residential areas cluster by economic level. Installation of "smart" decoders needed for pay-for-view TV, may even make it possible to precisely target individual homes. This so-called "narrowcasting" could mature into a viable medium for marketing training as well as delivering it.

Like the print media described earlier, broadcasters make money by selling advertising. With cable TV, subscriber service charges help defray installation and maintenance costs, but advertising revenues are still a dominate source of income.

Three Types of Broadcast Ads

Cash Buys. Paid ads, or "cash buys," constitute most ads you see on broadcast TV and listen to on radio. They may be read by the announcer from your script or prepared by your agency and furnished "ready to run," just like a display ad is furnished to a magazine. Local stations will often help make your ad for you or arrange it through outside professionals.

Per Inquiry. If you're going after response, try placing your ad on a "per inquiry" (or "PI") basis if possible. In this case, the station supplies the order-takers, the toll-free (800) telephone numbers and any other services necessary. You're *not* charged for the ad, but you are charged for each response the ad produces. Some stations will even help you prepare the ad.

PIs minimize your up-front expenses. The station will only run a PI if they think it will make money. They'll run it when they see fit, which might be 3 a.m. Happily, your motives and the station's coincide, so you can expect them to do the best job they can. Once your ad becomes a "winner," they'll air it more often and move it to better time-slots trying to find the greatest pay-out.

Be aware that PI responses often contain many errors, leading to a high rate of undeliverable products and returns. Because the station gets paid for each *response* and not by whether the product is accepted and paid for, accuracy sometimes suffers. PI may be worth testing if you have a product with broad appeal or if the media targets exactly the group you're trying to reach.

Infomercials. These are *program-format ads* that closely resemble regular station programming. They've been successful for sales training programs, self-improvement videos and the like. These half-hour programs also resemble a seminar with periodic "commercials" for the products and services described in the seminar. Such ads may run on a cash buy *or* PI and -- judging from how often they run -- apparently are profitable. (More on infomercials below.)

When Broadcast Advertising *Might* Work

Over the years any number of large firms have tested broadcast media for seminars in high-density markets like New York, Chicago, San Francisco or Los Angeles. None have continued the practice on a regular basis, suggesting that it hasn't been as successful as other advertising means.

Broadcast media has been effective for the author/expert on talk shows or interviews. While it's rare that orders or enrollments are obtained directly from such exposure, there's no doubt that it stimulates sales if the product or service is mentioned and a phone number or city is given.

One final thought: If you are considering testing these media, by all means use an experienced outside professional resource. Even where we will readily accept the amateur in publishing, we apparently have been trained by years of TV-watching to accept only the most professional broadcast presentations. Test after test has shown very low, if any, tolerance for anything but the most professional video. And the problem is getting worse. So demand and get professional production of *any* broadcast ads you employ.

Infomercials

The infomercial industry began in 1984, when the Federal Communication Commission (FCC) deregulated broadcast TV stations, allowing them to air half-hour TV commercial programs. Before then a broadcast station could only air up to 16 minutes of commercial time per clock hour.

At first, stations sold "remnants," the unprofitable, late night slots. Then, in 1987, American Telecast Corp. produced *Where There's a Will There's an A*, that has sold more than a million audio and video cassettes at $60 to $90 each. Since then, the infomercial business has exploded.

Most infomercial and direct marketing companies are privately held so the statistics are hard to come by. However, billions of dollars in sales revenues will be generated from infomercials this year alone. How far will it go? "Entertainment Tonight" recently reported that by the end of this decade, over 50% of all television revenues would be generated from half-hour infomercials. It has become a legitimate form of advertising. Many Fortune 500 companies are testing this "results oriented and highly measurable" form of marketing. Ross Perot even uses it for his political campaign.

The long-form, direct-response TV commercial has been called by various names. "Info-tainment," "info-commercials," "informercials" and "showmercials" were all used before the now standard infomercials.

An infomercial is an extension of direct response television (DRTV) advertising. One definition is: a long-form commercial program that is informative, educational, newsworthy and entertaining, targeted to a specific audience. Its primary purpose is to sell, sell, sell, via a direct call to action using an 800 (or 900) number. They are usually 28-1/2 minutes in length. The primary advantage of the infomercial over the DRTV commercial is that the half-hour commercial controls the program environment in which direct response TV spots are placed.

From a selling point of view, the infomercial is a well-thought-out, in-depth, one-to-one sales presentation that consistently delivers the same vital key selling messages every time it airs. (The following 15 were adapted from an article by Rodney H. Buchser, president of Financial Marketing Services (FMS), 1437 7th Street, Suite 204, Santa Monica, California, (310) 451-3883. He has created and produced over one thousand direct response TV commercials and about 220 half-hour infomercials, generating over one billion dollars in sales revenues for clients. Rodney was also the creator and co-founder of the Financial News Network (FNN).)

1. Repeatedly Identifies the Benefits of the product or service. Its Unique Selling Proposition (USP) *always* relates to the consumer whose needs are being fulfilled.

2. Overcomes Skepticism, doubt and objections (like credibility, price and quality) and instills confidence in the buyer.

3. Provides Both a Promise and a Guarantee -- and doesn't promise what it can't back up.

4. Constantly Asks for the Order, using compelling sales copy, both verbal and visual.

5. Provides Bonuses or Free Gifts for Ordering Now ("but wait there's more"); gives people more than they expect.

6. Selling Messages are Pinpointed to the primary target audience and does not try to reach everyone. It focuses benefits and selling messages *only* on the prospects' needs.

7. Has Sincere and Credible Host(s) with integrity (people buy from people).

8. Shows a Magical Transformation (demonstration of product or before and after).

9. Provides Many Genuine, Sincere and Credible Testimonials of "real people" who have already purchased and benefited from the product or service. The most effective infomercials that have been produced are clearly testimonial driven.

10. Celebrity Endorsements if possible -- these can produce up to 25% more sales.

11. Defines a Common (or Uncommon) Problem the prospect has and offers the product or service as the answer to that problem.

12. Motivates the Viewer to Act, using the two primary motivators: fear or desire and sometimes guilt or shame.

13. Good Price-to-Value ($100 value for only $29.95). Compare low price to huge savings derived or profits gained. (Retail price should be five to eight times the cost of the product).

14. Offers Risk-Free Trial of the product or service, because of the strong money-back guarantee; when appropriate, indicates there's no cost or obligation.

15. Instills a Sense of Urgency in its call to action; for example, a limited time offer or limited product availability.

In addition to a high-quality production and an excellent product or service that is constantly being sold to the viewer, the above key elements are usually found in all successful infomercials. Most of these elements must be clearly expressed, featured or re-vealed several times every seven to ten minutes. In fact , experts say a good infomercial should be able to sell the product within ten minutes. So, each ten minute segment must repeatedly deliver or provide the selling elements.

Here are four more infomercial tips:

First and most important, the finished product should have plenty of "click stop" appeal. That is to say, it should hit with its best marketing punch during the few seconds between regular TV program segments. That way, as the consumer "shops" channels to avoid boring commercials, you are airing your most seductive images and information. There's a science to the way in which this seamless sort of sales "looping" should be done. And it's worth the money it takes to involve experts who know the basic laws of that science.

Second, and a corollary to the first, work with experienced professionals who have a positive track record in creating, developing and executing successful direct marketing campaigns, Anyone can create a video -- that's not enough anymore, with as few as one in ten infomercials being a success.

The Wall Street Journal reported that infomercials are now dominated by just three major companies: American Telecast, whose annual revenue is estimated at $150 million, and National Media Corp. and Regal Communications, each estimated at $100 million annually.

Third, have a great up-sell product -- this additional up-sell revenue can make the difference between a success or failure.

Finally, direct marketing guru Joe Sugarman says that if the potential product-user audience is 20 million or less, it isn't big enough for an infomercial.

PROMOTIONAL AUDIO TAPES, VIDEO CASSETTES AND COMPUTER DISKETTES

With a large and growing "installed base" of play-back equipment, it was inevitable that these media would also be used for advertis-ing. After attracting attention due to their novelty, each of these media has attracted its own group of followers.

Promotional Audio Tapes

Today nearly everyone has at least one, and often several, audio cassette players. The number of books-on-tape is exploding, and 20% - 40% of the titles are on self-improvement or training and information topics. This represents a fertile environment for promotional audio tapes.

Most of us have received at least one promotional audio cassette, often promoting tape editing/duplicating services or books-on-tape. In theory, any message could be tested, but the ones likely to work for training and information products are those in which the sound can make a difference -- like the voice of a well-known or inspirational speaker or one of the industry's "Gurus."

Costs for duplicated and labeled tapes are now below $1.00, so other costs are actually more important in figuring campaign economics. And production/duplication capabilities are now so widespread that your best resources may be found in your own telephone yellow pages.

Promotional Video Cassettes

By the latest counts, 80% of U.S. homes have at least one video cassette recorder, up from 65% in 1990. And many businesses -- particularly those interested in training and information -- have VCRs on the job.

Promotional videos have been around for years. They've been given away as premiums, used to sell cars and used for political and fund raising appeals. Video previews and rentals are a staple of the training video marketplace, and no serious provider can survive without these means of "trying before you buy."

The added time commitment and the need to stop what you're doing to watch a promotional video makes it vital they *not* be sent "cold" to anyone who hasn't requested it. Still, even those who toss out fancy direct mail brochures without a second thought are hesitant to throw away a video cassette, often passing it on to others. This phenomenon accounts for some surprisingly high response rates for this approach.

According to *The Wall Street Journal*,
videos can now be copied, packaged and mailed for under $2.00 each, thanks to cheaper, lighter-weight cases and better taping technology. That's half the price of only two years ago. Even adding in production costs at $1,000 to $5,000 a finished minute, video mailings can be in the same ballpark as print mailings using a glossy brochure. And most experts now agree that promotional videos shouldn't be longer than seven to nine minutes.

Every test has confirmed that our experience as television viewers has made all of us very *in*tolerant of anything less than commercial broadcast quality. If you have cable TV, notice how easy it is to spot the locally produced ads by their low production values. That means your promotional videos should *only* be produced by experienced professionals capable of the highest quality work. Don't economize here.

Since video production is now everywhere, your best resources here may also be found in your telephone yellow pages. If these aren't satisfactory, call those whose promotion videos you receive or see advertised, and find out who they used for production.

One final thought: If video-on-demand becomes a reality in the next few years, through interactive TV, as many expect, the costs of duplication, packaging and shipping will vanish, making promotional videos *less* expensive than other media. This could trigger an explosion in advertising videos that could leave behind the unprepared.

Promotional Computer Disks

According to the Census Bureau, one-third of all Americans use personal computers at home or at work, and more than half of all households earning over $75,000 a year own a PC. The number is growing by 15% - 20% annually. That "installed base" of players means that computer diskettes can be a useful marketing medium -- under the right circumstances.

One reason that diskettes don't always work is that reading text on a computer screen is S-L-O-W -- it takes too long and you can't easily scan the document. Better to use the computer for tasks like searching/finding things, integrating text/graphics/motion/sound and for user interactivity. It's unequalled for these uses.

Diskettes are the accepted medium to demonstrate software like CBT and/or authoring systems. But they've been used to help sell everything from ad agencies and automobiles, through banks and computer chips.

Costs for creating a disk are dropping all the time, and now range from $5,000 to $85,000 depending on the graphics, animation, sound and user interaction desired. Reproduction and labeling is about $1.00 per diskette. Packaging adds $1.00 to $1.25 each. And First-Class postage adds $.50 - $.75 more.

Four Tips:

1. See if diskettes are already working in your market. Is someone using them repeatedly for sales?

2. Use experienced production professionals who have done it before. Doing-it-yourself will look that way.

3. Send diskettes only to responders -- those who've asked for it because of some other promo.

4. Track conversions/sales to see if diskettes are working enough to pay for their costs.

Ad agencies are adding computer diskette capabilities, and new firms are entering the field all the time. Check the "Computers" heading in your telephone yellow pages for the subheadings "Software and Services," "Graphics" and "Consultants" for the latest resources. Here are some starting-point resources:

CREATIVE DISC
1370 Dell Avenue, Suite B
Campbell, CA 95008
Phone: (800) 526-9153, (408) 376-2700; Fax: (408) 376-2712
Contact: Mr. Jim Moreton, Marketing Director

E.A.S.I.
530 W. 23rd Street, Suite 232
New York, NY 10011
Phone: (212) 627-0970
Contact: J.G. Sandom

INMAR GROUP, INC.
4242 E. Piedras Drive
San Antonio, TX 78228
Phone: (210) 733-8999

THE SOFTAD GROUP
311 North Street
Sausalito, CA 94965
Phone: (415) 332-4704
Contact: Ms. Paula L. George

SYSTEMAX COMPUTER GRAPHICS
201 E. 87th Street
New York, NY 10128
Phone: (212) 348-8756
Contact: Mr. Tom Hudock, President

MARKETING THROUGH PROFESSIONAL SOCIETIES AND TRADE ASSOCIATIONS

There are more than 200,000 associations in the U.S. (20,000 with a full-time executive director), almost all of which have education, professional development and/or training as a primary objective. Strategic alliances between associations and training firms make sense for both.

How to Find Associations of Interest

Chances are you already know the associa-

tions most likely to be interested in your products/services and whose members are likely to be your customers. The executive director and key staff in these associations should already be on your mailing list. You'll want to distinguish between the association's full-time paid staff and the elected/volunteer members. The latter are your customers or prospects, whereas the former are part of your sales and marketing system. Distinguish these roles carefully; mixing them up can be disastrous.

If you don't know which associations serve your market, here are two of the most comprehensive references, which may be available at your library:

1. Encyclopedia of Associations. Gale Research Inc., 835 Penobscot Bldg., Detroit, MI 48226-4094. Phone: (800) 877-GALE, (313) 961-2242; Fax: (313) 961-6083, (313) 961-6815.

Published annually, a recent edition contained 3,395 pages in three volumes and described over 22,000 trade and professional associations, labor unions, fraternal and patriotic organizations, religious, sports, hobby groups and more. It includes descriptions and addresses, plus phone, toll-free and fax numbers. Entries are divided into 18 broad subject categories and indexed by names and key words.

2. National Trade and Professional Associations of the United States. Columbia Books, Inc., 1212 New York Avenue, N.W., Suite 330, Washington, DC 20005. Phone: (202) 898-0662; Fax: (202) 898-0775.

Also published annually, a recent edition had 609 pages and described nearly 7,000 national trade associations, labor unions, professional, scientific or technical societies and other organizations. It is indexed by subject, budget, geographically, chief executive and acronym. There's also a handy directory of association management firms, showing which associations they manage.

Appendix A, "References and Resources," contains a number of other directories that may be available at your library.

Five Ways Associations Can Help Your Marketing

There are at least five distinct ways associations can help your sales and marketing effort (apart from renting their mailing list, participating in their conference or advertising in their publication):

1. Providing more speaking opportunities
2. Publishing articles and publicizing your business
3. Sponsoring your seminars and workshops
4. Selling and distributing your books and packaged training programs

5. Affording opportunities for research projects and favorable exposure to your marketplace

The following sections touch upon each of these.

1. Providing Speaking Opportunities. Professional and trade associations hold many national, regional and local meetings, besides their annual conferences. Most of these meetings have speakers and are opportunities to meet and talk with possible customers. Most of what's presented elsewhere in this chapter on using trade association shows and expos applies here.

2. Publishing Your Writings. The second most common marketing vehicle professional and trade associations present are their regular periodicals. These may be magazines or newsletters and may go to the entire membership or be devoted only to a special working group or committee. If you are known in the association's profession or industry, your works will probably get published, including articles, research reports, news releases and even letters to the editor.

Exposure in association publications can be more valuable than comparable exposure elsewhere. And many association publications are always "hurting" for good content. So your thoughtful submittals are even *more* likely to get published.

3. Sponsoring/Promoting Your Seminars/Workshops. This is a good match if your education or training program serves an important association function or if it's been designed expressly to meet their members' requirements. Proposed financial arrangements can range from nothing to very lucrative. You need to understand lifetime value economics (see Chapter 5) to know if you're getting a good deal. If not, negotiate. The result can be worth it: A number of consultants I know have discontinued their own seminars, because they're getting all the exposure they need through seminars sponsored by associations.

4. Selling and Distributing Your Books and Packaged Training Programs. This ranges all the way from publication announcements and book reviews in the association's magazines to a "bookstore" of publications for sale to members. The advantages of this last arrangement are obvious: If your publications help the association's members, they are going to buy them in much greater volume. Moreover, the association's marketing costs are small compared to yours or to most other means of distribution. The result is that you will sell a lot more publications and could offer the association a small discount to cement the relationship.

5. Other Ways Associations Can Help. Many associations fund research studies of interest to their members. If you or your firm are experts, your participation in such a study could be valuable. If you have important research ideas or have done similar studies in other industries or associations, you may be able to persuade the society to repeat the study for their members. If the association cannot afford to pay you, ask them to feature your name prominently in the final report or allow you to sell the report to nonmembers.

Association task forces are another opportunity. While many of their activities are routine and will not help your marketing, others deal with issues likely to dominate the society's future. Participation in such groups could be seen as evidence of your forward thinking.

Some associations have a resource list of products and services their members can use. This listing is maintained as a service to members, and your inclusion on the list could produce business. At the very least, try to get your product or service endorsed by the association, even if you have to market it yourself.

Don't Seek Elective Office

Association office requires lots of voluntary, uncompensated participation. You may wish to do this in associations that serve *your* business or profession, but it's unwise to get involved in your *customer's* associations. Generally it won't produce any business, and your participation may be considered suspect.

Some professional areas have had more success with this than others. The American Society for Training and Development (ASTD), for example, has a very high percentage of members who are consultants. The ideal client for most consultant members is a nonconsultant member: a training director or professional in a large organization that hires consultants. This is a case where organizational participation could well result in ideal exposure to prospective clients. But test this carefully in your market before committing.

NOTES

CREATING AND MAINTAINING YOUR MARKETING DATABASE

There's no doubt that your own client and prospect list will quickly become -- if it isn't already -- your most important asset. Even if you now use primarily face-to-face selling, you can easily imagine any number of good reasons to contact those who have previously attended your events or bought your products. Examples include new product announcements, old product updates, client/user conferences, newsletters and organization address changes, to name just a few.

And, of course, a house mailing list (one frequent use of a marketing database) is central to your direct marketing.

The three activities vital for a healthy, growing database are (1.) capturing plenty of new names, *and* the pertinent information on each, (2.) storing the information in a convenient, usable manner and (3.) keeping the information current and correct.

This chapter deals with all three activities, as well as with other marketing database considerations, such as security, renting or exchanging your mailing list with others and establishing its value.

HOW TO ESTABLISH YOUR OWN MARKETING DATABASE

What Is a Marketing Database?

A marketing database is the central source for all pertinent information on those individuals and organizations you now do business with or want to do business with and others important to your sales and marketing efforts. Your database contains your customers, prospects, responders, referrers, key staff, investors and even your friends.

These different types of individuals and organizations coexist in one database, but you can select and separate them depending on your needs. For example, a current *customer* who's also a *reference* and who may be a *prospect* for some new product would only appear in your database once, with all of their information that shows they play all three roles.

Is a marketing database really a mailing list by a different name? No! A mailing list is only *one* application of a marketing database -- although clearly a very important one, especially for businesses that use direct marketing.

What Can a Marketing Database Do for You?

A flexible customer database can do the following:

- Instantly find any customer by number, by first or last name, by company or by specifying characters from their names, address, ZIP code and/or telephone number.

- Allow you to enter or change any and all customer information, including their name, address, phone numbers, source, full history of all current and previous transactions, etc.

- Select, sort, count and/or print demographic reports about those in the database, including what products have been purchased, when and from what source.

- Compile, sort and print mailing lists in a variety of label formats, as well as on floppy disks or tape for processing at a mailing house or computer service bureau.

- Print personalized, letter-quality correspondence to one or more customers, selected according to criteria you specify.

- Prepare event attendance rosters, sales reports or other reports and counts of the database by any customer variable or combination of variables.

- Automatically track direct mail response by source code as a function of time since the mailing occurred.

The Process for Establishing Your Own Marketing Database

There are ten steps in the process of deciding upon, selecting, and implementing your own marketing database:

1. Forecast intended use(s).
2. Determine information required.
3. Select information "capture" mechanism(s).
4. Estimate database size and growth.
5. Set maintenance/updating schedule and procedures.
6. Set the budget.
7. Select the system/hardware.
8. Decide whether to "make" or "buy" the software.
9. Plan the implementation/conversion.
10. Provide user documentation/training.

The following sections discuss each of these steps.

1. Forecast Intended Use(s). Think through your business and determine how you want to use the database. For example, will it be used for tracking sales in your sales and marketing pipeline? Will it be used to mail promotions, newsletters, meeting announcements, etc.? Will your database be part of your financial system, including invoicing, accounts receivable, sales reports and/or inventory? Will your database be employed for market research and analysis, helping you spot the geographic or demographic characteristics of your best customers?

Your answers to these questions -- and others like them -- will point toward the system that will be best for you. A well-developed database can actually do all of the above and much more.

2. Determine Information Required. Generally, three types of information are needed: (1.) for *contact* purposes (by mail, fax or phone or in person), (2.) *source* information on how they were obtained (vital for market analysis) and (3.) complete information on each *transaction* which they initiate with your firm.

On the facing page is an example of information you might want to collect in each of these categories. The information preceded by an a bullet is considered the minimum acceptable. Other information is optional, depending upon the uses you determined in Step 1.

Take care selecting the information to be recorded; too much can be an unnecessary burden, while adding additional information later can be costly or even impossible. Besides, the information you need for the database will determine what information is collected, and some information may not be available if you later change you mind.

Client/Prospect Information

Contact Information

- Customer number/I.D.
- Title (Mr., Ms., Dr., Capt., etc.)
- First name, middle initial
- Surname/family name
- Suffix (Jr., III, Ph.D., etc.)
-- Nickname
- Position title
-- Organization I.D. number
- Organization name
- Division/unit name
- Street address and/or P.O. Box
- Internal mail code/stop
- City
- State/Province
-- Country
- ZIP/Postal code (including ZIP +4)
- Telephone number (include area code and extension)
-- Alternate telephone No. (organization switchboard, toll-free number or residence phone)
- Facsimile phone number
-- Bill-to address information
-- Ship-to address information
-- Personal data (gender, birthday, height, weight, size, income, spouse, etc.)
-- Social Security or Taxpayer I.D. Number
-- Type of business (SIC codes or equivalent)
-- Organization size (annual sales revenues, number employees, etc.)
-- Status (active, inactive, delete, do not mail, bad credit, etc.)
-- Secretary's or assistant's name

- ■ *Denotes minimum acceptable information*

-- Account assigned to (salesperson/territory)
-- Remarks on contact

Source Information

- How name was first acquired (source or key code for media/advertisement responded to, mail list used, referral, etc.)
- Date of acquisition
-- Date entered
-- Type of initial contact if any (mail, telephone, store, salesperson, etc.)
-- Remarks on source (How did this person learn about you?)

Transaction Information (for Each Transaction)

- Source or key code for transaction (the specific ad, mailer, etc., or even if it's unknown)
-- Type of transaction (inquiry, purchase, address change, etc.)
- Date received
-- Action(s) taken (merchandise ship date/means, sent catalog/date, telephoned, assigned to salesperson, changed address, etc.)
-- Financial information on the transaction (credit-card information, how paid, when paid, invoice number, check number, whether or not merchandise was returned, date of return, how account was credited, etc.)
-- Other remarks pertinent to this transaction

3. Select Information "Capture" Mechanism(s). This determines the places, times and methods you'll use in acquiring the information that goes into your database. If the database is truly central to your whole business, then you'll be capturing customer information daily with every transaction. What we're really concerned with is establishing the means you'll use to "capture" new customer records and to help identify the information

you need for each of them in order to determine whether they're already in your database (in which case you can merely update their record) or whether a new record must be created.

Our recommendation is to ask for *all* the information you want during the initial contact. It's helpful to design a standard form so that the customer/prospect can furnish you the information easily and with enough room so that the information can be complete.

We also recommend that you use both paper records *and* the computer for small operations that don't create a mirror-image backup in real time. This facilitates reconstructing the day's transactions if something "crashes."

4. *Estimate File Size and Growth*. This step is important for determining the ultimate scale of your database. A very small business, with only a few meetings, may effectively use systems that would be unsuitable for larger businesses. Admittedly, this determination was far more significant in the days before widespread use of personal computers. Then the size of your file would often dictate whether it could be maintained in-house or had to be done externally.

5. *Set Maintenance/Updating Schedule and Procedures*. If your need for a database is basically "one-shot," connected with some important promotion and/or kickoff of an activity, then you will never need to maintain or update it. Similarly, if you only use your database annually (say, in connection with an annual conference or other event), then it may be possible for you to essentially recreate your entire database for each application.

But if your needs are for more frequent updating -- including updating your database continuously as part of your ongoing business -- then this dictates the type of database you'll need and the appropriate means of interacting with it. The section Maintaining Your Marketing Database, later in this chapter, contains more information on this topic.

6. *Set the Budget*. To accomplish this step you'll need to identify a number of candidate approaches to creating and maintaining your database and develop a list of the major costs. The later section on choosing the right system will help with this.

7. *Select the System/Hardware*. Although there are still a wide range of possible systems, today's choice invariably involves some application of an IBM PC or compatible personal computer. And even within the PC world, there are still a great many hardware

and software choices. The good news is that costs have been steadily declining. This means that your selection is probably not going to be made primarily on cost considerations, but on its ultimate utility to your business -- and on its ability to grow with you into the future. (We've made specific hardware recommendations in the next section.)

8. *Decide Whether to "Make" or "Buy" the Software*. This refers to whether your software is to be custom designed for you or whether you'll be able to use or adapt commercially available software.

This is where the really big costs of a marketing database lie. That's why we'll have lots more on this in the next sections.

9. *Plan the Implementation/Conversion*. If you're just starting out, this is less of a problem than if you already have registrations, attendees or buyers in another form -- or in many different forms. Then, how and when you convert these existing records into the new system can have a major impact on your ongoing business.

As with all other types of planning, you need to follow a systematic set of steps and procedures, including setting objectives, programing, scheduling, assigning responsibilities, budgeting, setting performance standards and conducting a risk analysis to determine what can prevent the successful accomplishment of your plan. (See Chapter 5 for help with your planning process.)

10. *Provide Documentation and Training to All Personnel*. It's easy to forget these tasks, but their omission leads to continuing costs and inefficiencies that last for years. For example, several years ago we worked with a client to upgrade their marketing database. In the process we discovered that many of their desired capabilities had been there all along, but no one knew it. Those who developed the system never documented the capabilities or trained anyone how to use them. Standard documentation should include a hard-copy manual at each work station plus suitable on-screen interactive help.

HOW TO CHOOSE THE RIGHT DATABASE HARDWARE AND SOFTWARE

Don't even think about creating a marketing database on anything but a personal computer or a network of PCs. Even organizations that used mainframe computers are switching to PCs in droves. Why? Because they're cheap, fast and far more flexible than their predecessors ever were. But *which* hardware and software you use depends on availability, personnel, cost and other factors.

What PC Hardware Should You Use?

There are still plenty of hardware choices to make even after you settle on a personal computer platform. There are four main types of hardware to be selected:

- Computers
- Printers
- Local Area Networks (LANS)
- Tape Drives

We'll look at each of these in the following sections, which furnish pertinent information on how to contact the major source(s). Because specific prices, model numbers and availability are changing so fast, you'll need to call and get the latest information when you're ready to buy.

Computers. The IBM PC and compatibles marketplace is still shaking itself out. Everyday prices plummet, speed and capabilities increase, manufacturers fold and the survivors rush to set up direct distribution, bypassing local dealers and value-added resellers (VARs).

In this environment, it makes no sense to build your marketing database on anything except the most reliable, best warranted, top-of-the-line hardware from the strongest companies who will be around if and when you need them. This means basically IBM, Compaq and (maybe) Dell. Because of aggressive pricing, you can often buy the biggest name brands at *lower* prices than an equivalently configured "Brand-X" machine. Today, $3,000 is considered a lot to spend.

Get the largest hard-disk drive and fastest operating speed you can afford. At least 4 MB of Random Access Memory (RAM) is standard, but more is better. A math co-processor almost always improves performance, if one is not already built in (as it is on Intel 486 DX and Pentium computer chips). Finally, make sure your system has -- or provides enough expansion room for you to later add -- five important accessories: (1.) backup tape drive (or equivalent removable mass storage medium), (2.) CD-ROM drive, (3.) telephone modem, (4.) network adapter/connecter card and (5) 1/2", 9-track, reel-to-reel tape drive. If you're on a network, then each machine only needs its network card, and the other resources can be shared wherever they are attached.

And what about Apple Computers? While the Macintosh has become the desktop publishing standard, it does not yet have the best capability for moving data to/from other machines in the IBM-dominated world of direct marketing. That's why the Apples are not addressed here.

Here is the direct sales information on PC's big three:

1. COMPAQ COMPUTER CORPORATION
P.O. Box 692000
Houston, TX 77269-2000
Phone: (800) 888-5858, (713) 370-0670; Fax: (800) 888-5329

2. DELL COMPUTER CORPORATION
Direct Sales
9505 Arboretum Blvd.
Austin, TX 78759-7299
Phone: (800) 695-5059

3. IBM - PC Direct
3039 Cornwallis Road, Bldg. 203, Dept. WMD
Research Triangle Park, NC 27709
Phone: (800) 426-2968

Printers. Your marketing database will print reports, mailing lists in various formats and correspondence-quality letters and envelopes. As a result, you need two kinds of printers: a wide-carriage, tractor-fed, heavy-duty, dot-matrix printer for labels and reports *and* a laser or ink jet printer capable of handling stationery and envelopes in volume.

Most manufacturers now divide their printer lines by the volume they'll handle, so the higher duty-cycle machines are more apt to be trouble-free than those designed for less frequent use. For example, we have a top-of-the-line Toshiba that's been reliably printing 4-up Cheshire labels since 1984!

The following are the major printer manufacturers. Get their latest model specifications, then shop price locally or via mail-order. Most will be under $1,000 at "street prices."

1. EPSON AMERICA, INC.
   20770 Madrona Avenue, P.O. Box 2842
   Torrance, CA 90509-2842
   Phone: (800) 922-8911, (310) 782-0770;
   Fax: (310) 782-5220

2. HEWLETT-PACKARD
   19310 Prunridge Avenue
   Cupertino, CA 95014
   Phone: (800) 752-0900; Fax: (208) 344-4809
   Hewlett-Packard dominates the laser printer and ink jet markets with a wide range of powerful and low-cost models.

3. PANASONIC COMMUNICATIONS AND SYSTEMS
   2 Panasonic Way
   Sacaucus, NJ 07094
   Phone: (800) 742-8086; Fax: (201) 348-7000

4. PRINTRONIX, INC.
   17500 Cartwright Road
   Irvine, CA 92714
   Phone: (800) 826-3874; Fax: (714) 660-8682
   Long-time maker of "industrial strength" line printers for mainframes and mini computers now offers PC models.

Local Area Networks (LANs). You can have an excellent single-user marketing database, with all the input and output resources hooked up to a single computer. If you're a small organization, this is the way to start.

But if your marketing efforts pay off, you'll soon need to have more than one person access the database at the same time. That's when you'll connect two (or more) computers in a Local Area Network, or LAN. The LAN also lets each computer share printers, modems, tape drives and other resources hooked up to other computers on the network.

You need at least four items to create a LAN:

1. An adapter card in each computer, to which the wires linking the computers are connected.

2. The wires or cabling, possibly including a junction box.

3. A Network Operating System, or NOS, that manages the flow of information between and among the computers.

4. The Network/Multi-User version of any software to be accessed simultaneously by two or more users.

Unless you're very "techie" or you have only a few computers to connect, a local supplier/or network consultant may be helpful. For example, your wiring may require electricians or other tradespeople, landlord approval, fire code inspections, etc. Also, if something doesn't work or you start getting interference, it can be comforting to call someone to fix the problem.

There are three common types of LAN wiring: (1.) shielded coaxial cable, like your cable TV's, (2.) 10BaseT, basically telephone wires with modular, telephone-style connectors, and (3.) shielded, multi-conductor cable with 9- or 25-pin connectors. Coax is the standard, and some computers now come equipped with an Ethernet coaxial cable port. 10BaseT wiring is already in many new buildings; its easier to install and less obtrusive. But 10BaseT lacks integral shielding, so your network could interfere with other equipment and/or receive interference.

Any NOS can operate with just about any wiring, so these choices can be independent. One exception is a starter version of LANtastic (see below) that has its own shielded, multi-conductor cable and adapter cards. If you start with this, then future additions to your LAN will need to have the same connections.

The biggest difference between LANs is whether they require a central "dedicated file server" or whether any computer can access any other computer, called "peer-to-peer." The first LANs used dedicated file servers, as does today's best-selling Novell Netware. But the latest, top-of-the-line, LANtastic offers virtually all the same capabilities with the simpler "peer-to-peer" system. In fact, LAN-tastic is as close to a "plug-and-play" network as I've seen.

1. *LANtastic*
   ARTISOFT, INC.
   691 E. River Road
   Tucson, AZ 85775-0439
   Phone: (800) 846-9726, (602) 293-6363; Fax: (602) 293-8065
   This is a "peer-to-peer" network that does not require a dedicated file server or network administrator. It can handle over 100 computers but is ideal for fewer.

2. *Netware*
   NOVELL, INC.
   122 East 1700 South
   Provo, UT 84606-6194
   Phone: (800) 526-5463
   The defacto network software standard and capable of virtually unlimited growth. Uses a dedicated file server; complex enough to require special training for a network administrator.

Tape Drives. Ideally, you need two tape drives connected to your single-user computer or available on your LAN. The first, which every business computer system must have, is a backup tape drive or similar removable mass storage medium for daily system backups. We've discussed this component previously and will revisit it again in the section on security measures, later in this chapter.

The second tape drive is the 1/2", 9-track reel-to-reel format that's become the mailing list standard, used for renting/exchanging lists, merging/purging and for preparing lists going to direct mail letter shops for printing. For around $5,000, any of the following manufacturers can give your PC mainframe-like tape capability:

1. DIGI-DATA CORPORATION
   8580 Dorsey Run Road
   Jessup, MD 20794-9990
   Phone: (800) 782-6395; Fax: (301) 498-0771

2. OVERLAND DATA, INC.
   5600 Kearny Mesa Road
   San Diego, CA 92111
   Phone: (800) 729-8725, (619) 571-5555; Fax: (619) 571-0982

3. QUALSTAR
   9621 Irondale Avenue
   Chatsworth, CA 91311
   Phone: (818) 882-5822

4. TDX PERIPHERALS
   80 Davids Drive
   Hauppauge, NY 11788-2003
   Phone: (800) 842-0708, (516) 273-5900; Fax: (516) 273-6476

What Software Should You Use?

The answer to this question comes down to matters of money and time, both of which depend on what you want your marketing database to do and how customized to your operation you want it to be. But we're getting ahead of the story.

Databases are fundamentally different from word processors, spread sheets, calendars, project managers -- and other kinds of PC software. These more popular programs provide you both a structure *and* various standard operations; all you do is furnish your own information.

Databases are more complicated for several reasons. First, you must provide *both* the structure *and* the data. You determine the structure by deciding what kinds of information (*fields*) you'll use for each individual *record* in your database (like their name, address, telephone, product purchased, price paid, etc.). You also need to specify how this information will be entered, related, indexed, sorted and displayed. What's more, every marketing database is used by many people in the organization and for many different purposes, from analyzing buying patterns and reporting sales to printing mailing lists and tracking response.

This added complexity is why you can't just go buy a marketing database "off-the-shelf." Every organization's needs become so specialized that even if a software package was successful, it would sell only a few thousand copies, rather than the millions of copies which the popular programs often sell.

Well, what *can* you buy? On one extreme, you can buy a database "engine," with names you may know like dBASE, Paradox and Access. Each of these is basically a hollow shell and tool kit which you can use to build your marketing database. They're relatively inexpensive: from $100 to about $1,000. But, of course, that's just the start. As *The Wall Street Journal* put it, "Thousands of people got their $99 copy of Paradox or Access home and realized they were far too complex to use ... because they often require professional programmers to set up, these databases cost $99 to buy and $10,000 to deploy."

And even *that's* a gross underestimate for a marketing database. David M. Raab, a direct mail marketing consultant, writing in *DM News* said, "Database marketing software is expensive -- very expensive. Even a rudimentary system costs well over $100,000 to develop. In a world where powerful PC/Macintosh software usually runs well under $1,000, this seems just plain crazy. Hasn't anyone created a software package for a marketing database?"

As a matter of fact, they have. Dozens of them. The problem is these packages were built for salespeople, telemarketers, mail-order product businesses and other specialized users, each of whom has their own unique requirements. They may give you part -- but not all -- of what you need.

If you can live with that, you're getting a bargain. If not, and you hire a programmer at $50 to $100 an hour to add the missing pieces and tailor the software to fit your specific business, you could end up spending as much as if you started from scratch with just a database "engine." And you *still* won't have a really customized system!

Why Is a Marketing Database So Expensive?

To get some feel for why marketing database costs soar into the hundreds of thousands of dollars, here are some of the tasks that must be accomplished to bring your database "online."

As you read this, think not only about programming cost, but also about how much time all the others in your organization will have to spend in order to get it right:

1. Designing Input Screens. What fields, where do they go on screen, how many characters, to what extent is information tested/"masked" to verify or standardize it, how are errors "trapped," does each screen look the way the users want?

2. Creating Reference Lists of products, product codes, prices, part numbers, source codes, standard abbreviations, SICs, correspondence requirements and similar files unique to your business. Often this is a 1-time activity, followed by routine updates.

3. Designing Indexes, cross-references, "B-Trees," auxiliary screens, files and other internal architecture.

4. Converting Data from its current form, or keyboard inputting of data that can't be converted. Either way, the converted files must be checked and verified, and any glitches "cleaned up."

5. Designing Output Reports. What gets printed, and where? It's rare that any two people or organizations are content to use the same report. Just look at the supposed "standard" financial statement; every one is just enough different from every other one, that this is an important part of every accounting program.

6. Designing Computer Links to other databases/software, like inventories, accounts receivable, general ledger, etc.

7. Testing the System. Working with system users to determine their needs in daily use, and changing anything that doesn't work properly or comfortably.

8. Preparing and Distributing Documentation specific to your organization, and building in suitable on-screen help.

9. Training users in how the system works.

The Best Commercially Available Software

To help make your decision, we've collected here a cross-section of the best tools and software packages from which you can build your database. We're going to look at five kinds of software:
- Relational database "engines"
- Contact Manager software
- Mail-order product software
- Mailing list software
- Postal coding or sequencing software

This diagram shows how these packages relate to each other.

Commercial Software Relationships

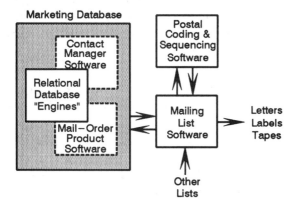

In the following section we'll describe the integrated marketing database we know best -- our own -- which integrates many of these functions into one package specifically designed for a seminar and training and information business.

Relational Database "Engines." To create your own custom database, start with one of the available relational database "engines." Designed expressly for storing, retrieving and manipulating data, they come with programming, screen building, data importing, report writing and other programming tools, so they can be tailored for specific applications.

A *relational database* is one in which the contents of one file may refer to and use the contents of additional files. For example, individuals in a large company would not need to have the company name and address entered in every record, because that information can be found in the company file. Similarly, a customer's purchase might use information on product name, price, stock number, shipping weight, and other data maintained in a separate product file. Relational databases afford much more flexibility to change and grow with your business.

These powerful database "engines" are often the core of specialized commercial programs; for example, the popular *TeleMagic* Contact Manager was written using *Clipper* (described below).

Most are available in single-user or network versions. And don't even think about using anything simpler -- the so-called "flat

files" that lack relational ability. You'll spend nearly as much time programming and get only a fraction of the functionality.

The best relational database "engines" are:

1. *Clipper*
COMPUTER ASSOCIATES, INC.
One Computer Associates Plaza
Islandia, NY 11788-7000
Phone: (800) 255-5224
A compiled version of dBASE, with much faster performance and more utilities and tools; originally developed by Nantucket, and purchased by Computer Associates in 1992.

2. *dBASE*
BORLAND INTERNATIONAL
1800 Green Hill Road, P.O. Box 660001
Scotts Valley, CA 95066-0001
Phone: (800) 331-0877; Fax: (408) 439-9103
The most widely used database, with the most third-party add-ons and the largest number of available programmers. Originally by Ashton-Tate, the company was bought by Borland in 1990.

3. *Foxpro*
MICROSOFT CORPORATION
One Microsoft Way
Redmond, WA 98052-6399
Phone: (800) 426-9400; Fax: (206) 883-8101, (206) 936-7329
Purchased by Microsoft in 1992, Foxpro (along with Advanced Revelation below) are considered the fastest and most powerful of the breed.

4. *Paradox*
BORLAND INTERNATIONAL
1800 Green Hill Road, P.O. Box 660001
Scotts Valley, CA 95066-0001
Phone: (800) 331-0877; Fax: (408) 439-9103
A well-regarded product that has attracted a small but loyal following.

5. *Pick*
1691 Browning
Irvine, CA 92714
Phone: (714) 261-7425; Fax: (714) 250-8187
Originally developed for minicomputers, this powerful system is now available on PCs.

6. *Revelation*
REVELATION TECHNOLOGIES
181 Harbor Drive
Stamford, CT 06902
Phone: (800) 262-4747, (203) 973-1000; Fax: (203) 975-8755
Based originally on Pick architecture (see above), Revelation is powerful, fast and runs well on earliest PCs as well as on the latest.

Mail-Order Product Software. This is software geared specifically to a mail-order product business. Training and information product examples include books, audio and video tapes, packaged training programs and software. Since, today, customer service is paramount, these packages help provide instantaneous access to the information needed to take and process a telephone order. For example: finding existing customers, identifying inventory on hand (including low stock/back-order items), identifying cross-sell/substitute products, applying customer type/quantity discounts, figuring state and local sales taxes (based on ZIP Code), figuring shipping charges, authorizing and processing credit-card transactions (via modem) and handling separate bill-to and ship-to addresses.

In addition, these packages can help keep track of internal matters like stock numbers, source/key codes, preparing UPS manifests and "pick" lists, product serial numbers, automatically reordering vendor products -- even managing telemarketing callback dates, salesperson ID and call notes. Some even furnish sales reports by campaign or catalog, including predicting sales at completion!

Here are some popular alternatives:

1. *Mail Order Wizard*
   HAVEN CORPORATION
   1227 Dodge Avenue
   Evanston, IL 60202-1008
   Phone: (800) 676-0098
   $495 to $1,895 for a single user, depending on features; $6,995 for unlimited users.

2. *Mail Order Manager (MOM)*
   DYNACOMP DEVELOPMENT CORPORATION
   150 River Road, Suite N 1
   Montville, NJ 07045
   Phone: (800) 858-3666
   $1,195 to $1,900 for a single user, depending on features; additional users $595 each up to 12, $95 each over 12.

3. *Response*
   COLINEAR SYSTEMS, INC.
   1000 Johnson Ferry Road, Suite F-130
   Marietta, GA 30068
   Phone: (404) 578-0000, (404) 433-3217
   $795 to $5,995 for a single user, depending on features; $500 each for additional user.

4. *Mail Order Management Expert (MOMe)*
   INTERNATIONAL SOFTWARE TECHNOLOGIES
   1112 7th Avenue
   Monroe, WI 53566
   Phone: (800) 356-0022
   $1,995 for a single user; $2,995 for unlimited users.

Sales Contact Manager Software. These were the earliest PC applications specifically developed for keeping track of telephone and face-to-face sales situations -- sort of an electronic Rolodex and tickler file rolled into one. The best have evolved to be much more than this, offering ability to store and select on a wider range of information than would be needed for contact management alone. Some are in use by Fortune 500 companies and have attracted a large following, making support widely available.

But these are not complete marketing databases. They lack the flexibility to record, index, retrieve and make available a detailed customer transaction history and to select specific records based on that data. They are not geared to seminar registrations or to mail-order product sales. To get those capabilities you'd need to do custom programming or buy additional software packages and link them together. But if contact management is your problem, here are some of the most popular:

1. *ACT!*
   CONTACT SOFTWARE INTERNATIONAL
   1840 Hutton Drive, Suite 200
   Carrollton, TX 75006
   Phone: (800) 370-8997, (214) 919-9500;
   Fax: (214) 919-9760
   $395 for a single user.

2. *Activity Manager*
   BROCK CONTROL SYSTEMS
   2859 Paces Ferry Road, Suite 100
   Atlanta, GA 30339
   Phone: (800) 221-0775, (404) 431-1200;
   Fax: (404) 431-1201
   $2,000 to $4,000 per user, depending on modules purchased/capabilities desired; introduced in 1985.

3. *EMIS II*
   EMIS SOFTWARE, INC.
   901 N.E. Loop 410, Suite 526
   San Antonio, TX 78209
   Phone: (512) 822-8499
   $2,500 for 3-users; offers flexible sorting and selecting capabilities.

4. *Maximizer*
RICHMOND TECHNOLOGIES & SOFT-
WARE, INC.
6400 Roberts Street, Suite 420
Burnaby, BC V5G 4C9 Canada
Phone: (604) 299-2121
$249 for a single user, $899 multiuser.

5. *TeleMagic*
REMOTE CONTROL INTERNATIONAL
5928 Pascal Court, Suite 150
Carlsbad, CA 92008
Phone: (800) 992-9952
*$1,995 for a 25-user network version. In-
troduced in 1985; one of the most widely
available, with more than 270 third-party add-
on programs, products and services.*

Mailing List Software. Geared mainly to
maintaining and processing mailing lists, this
class of software handles data import (from
other databases or list sources), merg-
ing/purging (including match code design and
duplicate identification/separation), record
processing (such as upper- lower-case conversion, gender identification, abbreviation expansion, etc.), data export (in the form of
various format labels, letters and magnetic
tapes and including barcoding where necessary) and preparing Post Office paperwork
(bag and tray labels, bundle counts, bundle
separators, forms, reports, etc.). Most also
offer data entry capability, indexing to facilitate sorting and selecting, basic word processing for merge letters and the like and report generation. Here are some of the most
popular:

1. *Arclist*
GROUP 1 SOFTWARE, INC.
6404 Ivy Lane, Suite 500
Greenbelt, MD 20770-1400
Phone: (800) 368-5806, (301) 982-2000
*Best-known of this type of software; $995 for
24-user Novell-only network version.*

2. *Mail Manager 2000*
BUSINESS COMPUTER CENTER
39 Saginaw Drive, Suite 16
Rochester, NY 14623-3131
Phone: (800) 453-3130
*$995 - $1,795 for 1-year, single-user system,
plus $300 annual maintenance fee.*

3. *PostWare 4.0*
POSTALSOFT, INC.
4439 Mormon Coulee Road
LaCrosse, WI 54601-8220
Phone: (800) 831-6245, (608) 788-8700

4. *Professional Mail*
ARC TANGENT, INC.
121 Gray Avenue, Suite 203
Santa Barbara, CA 93101-1831
Phone: (805) 965-7277

***Postal Coding and Sequencing Software
(ZIP + 4).*** This software works in conjunction with your mailing list/database software
to standardize addresses, correct ZIP codes
and add ZIP +4 coding and carrier route
coding. To do this, the packages all use quarterly-updated, CD-ROM databases of all
valid U.S. addresses, CASS-certified by the
USPS (CASS stands for Coding Accuracy
Support System). The result is that your
mailings can take maximum advantage of
postal First-, Second- and Third-Class presort
discounts and even discounts for pre-barcod-
ing. (See Chapter 9 for more on Post Office
automation discounts.)

Tests of these systems show they successfully code about 60%-70% of a typical business file and about 85%-99% of a typical consumer file, the difference being the increased
complexity of business addresses, which include building names, internal mail stops,
P.O. boxes, etc.

1. *AccuMail*
GROUP 1 SOFTWARE, INC.
6404 Ivy Lane, Suite 500
Greenbelt, MD 20770-1440
Phone: (800) 368-5806, (301) 982-2000
*$780/year including quarterly updates; this is
the same as Arc Tangent's ZIP++4 listed
below.*

2. *Micro FINALIST*
PITNEY BOWES, INC.
40 Lindeman Drive
Trumbull, CT 06611-4785
Phone: (800) 672-6937
*$2,295 plus $995/year for quarterly updates;
package developed by List Processing
Company (LPC) of Lisle, IL but sold only
through Pitney Bowes.*

3. *PostWare*
POSTALSOFT, INC.
4439 Mormon Coulee Road
LaCrosse, WI 54601-8220
Phone: (800) 831-6245, (608) 788-8700
*$4,000 plus $1,500/year for quarterly up-
dates.*

4. *ZCR 2000*
   BUSINESS COMPUTER CENTER
   39 Saginaw Drive, Suite 16
   Rochester, NY 14623-3131
   Phone: (800) 453-3130
   $995/year including quarterly updates.

5. *ZIP++*
   ARC TANGENT, INC.
   121 Gray Avenue, Suite 203
   Santa Barbara, CA 93101-1831
   Phone: (805) 965-7277
   $1,000/year including quarterly updates; this package is also sold by Group 1 Software under the name AccuMail, listed above.

The Schrello Direct Marketing Database

This proprietary software has been developed and refined for over 20 years at a cost of more than $500,000. It represents one of the most powerful tools available to organize and manage the marketing and customer communications of any training, information, consulting or publishing business.

We started in 1972 with what was then the best database hardware, a minicomputer produced by Microdata (since bought by McDonnell Douglas, and still doing nicely), and the best relational database "engine," The Pick System (see previous section).

In the 1980s, when Cosmos (now Revelation Technologies) introduced a version of the Pick database for IBM PCs (again see the previous section), we switched to *Revelation* and downloaded all the minicomputer software and files to a PC. And the PC version is faster and even MORE powerful than the minicomputer version.

What follows are samples of some of our system's menus and screens which we use on our day-to-day operations. Although we occasionally need a bit of outside programming help, 98% of what's needed is done by our office staff, right off these "point-and-shoot" menus.

Sample Menus. The easiest way for most of us to use a computer is by selecting items from a menu. Below is the TOP MENU in our system.

```
┌─────────────────────────────────────────────────┐
│  SCHRELLO MARKETING DATABASE  -- MAIN MENU       │
│                                                   │
│   1. Enter or Change CUSTOMER RECORDS             │
│   2. Enter or Change SOURCE CODES                 │
│   3. "SCAN" Customer File for Existing Records    │
│   4. Enter or Change COMPANY CODES                │
│   5. CORRESPONDENCE and INVOICING                 │
│   6. ROSTERS, SEMINAR, MAILING and SALES Routines │
│   7. List or Change MISCELLANEOUS REFERENCE FILES │
│   8. HOUSEKEEPING Routines                        │
│   9. Set PRINTER Characteristics                  │
│  10. Run OPEN INVOICE and AGED RECEIVABLES Reports│
│  11. UTILITY Routines                             │
│  12. LOGTO SYSPROG Account                        │
│  13. LOGOFF MARKETING DATABASE                    │
└─────────────────────────────────────────────────┘
```

In some cases, another menu will appear, enabling you to select from further options. For example, if you select CORRESPONDENCE, the menu shown below appears.

```
┌─────────────────────────────────────────────────┐
│           CORRESPONDENCE  MENU                    │
│                                                   │
│   1. Prepare INQUIRY, BOOK or CUSTOM Letters Merge Data │
│   2. Prepare Seminar CONFIRMATION Letters Merge Data   │
│   3. Prepare COLLECTION Letters Merge Data         │
│   4. Prepare Seminar CANCELLATION Letters Merge Data│
│   5. Prepare PERMISSION TO QUOTE Letters Merge Data │
│   6. Prepare "BY THE WAY" Referral Letters Merge Data│
│   7. Prepare Seminar TRANSFER Letters Merge Data   │
│   8. Prepare General LETTER QUALITY Merge Data     │
│   9. Print INVOICES                                │
│  10. Access WORD PROCESSOR to Print or Edit Letters│
└─────────────────────────────────────────────────┘
```

This menu prepares Merge Data files for use by your favorite word processor, so the letters can be easily customized to meet changing needs. Data extracted from individual database records can also be used in many other ways.

Entering and Maintaining Information. There are three activities involved in any database: (1.) *inputting* new records or new information to update existing records; (2.) selecting, sorting, counting and other forms of *analyzing or manipulating* the stored information; and (3.) *outputting* of results, reports, correspondence, etc., either on the screen or in printed form. Normal activities in each of these three categories are performed by menu choices. New, special or infrequent sorts and selections use English language query commands, for example:

:LIST RECORDS WITH PRODUCT "SDM" AND PRICE GREATER THAN $500 AND DATE PAID AFTER "10-10-93"

Remember GIGO; "Garbage In -- Garbage Out." The integrity of any marketing database rests solely on the quality of the data entry -- it's one of the most time-consuming activities but also the most important. Data entry has two distinct phases: entering *new* records and changing or updating *existing* records.

Determining if the Person Is Already Entered. Before entering a new record, it's *vital* that you determine if the person's record is already on file. If it is, then the existing record should merely be updated with the latest information, and a new record should *not* be created.

Internal duplication exists on every database. It can never be totally eliminated, because people and organizations are constantly changing their names, addresses, telephone numbers, etc., thereby making it difficult to tell whether two similar records are, in fact, the same person. (See also Customer Address Loss later in this chapter). But internal duplication can -- and MUST -- be kept to a minimum.

In many files, using a surname cross-reference is a convenient way to quickly determine if the person already has a record on file. Our database matches full first and surname for this purpose. But names can and do change, so we also use a proprietary method we call "SCAN" to catch possible duplicates. It's a unique cross-reference system designed to cast as broad a net as possible. It works by taking three characters from the following five fields: Company Name, Street Address, ZIP Code, Telephone and Surname. The program then finds and displays all records that match various combinations of *pairs* of the field characters (e.g.: company-ZIP, company-surname, ZIP-surname, etc.). The record with the most correct matches is listed first. (By the way, the number of characters used *and* the pairing of fields are both critical to the success of this approach.) Here's a sample of "SCAN":

Because of how the files are maintained, records are found and displayed instantaneously regardless of how many records are in the Database.

Once you've determined whether a new or changed record is needed, selecting the entry screen produces the following:

The information displayed, field lengths, etc., are evident. Each transaction occupies two lines, one for the transaction data and a second line for remarks pertinent to that transaction. You can have as many transactions as you want.

Every new record is given a unique customer number, or "key." If you try to use a customer number that's already been assigned, the system tells you so and displays the record with that number. Otherwise, it displays the message, "You are creating a new record" and allows you to proceed.

Since the database employs variable *word* length, *field* length and *record* length, essentially any amount of information can be entered in any field of any record. If the display length for that field is set to -- say -- five characters, that's all you'll see on the screen. But the rest of the information is still there and can be used for sorting, etc. This hidden information may be viewed anytime by changing the number of characters displayed for that field.

Using Related Files. A relational database makes common information stored in auxiliary files automatically available to save time and avoid data entry errors. Such files include prefixes and suffixes, titles, position abbreviations, source codes, state abbreviations and literally dozens of others.

Two auxiliary files deserve special mention: the company file and the product file.

The company file allows standard information on a company to be accessed through a unique company number. Company numbers serve the same purpose as customer numbers: We use them to quickly find all those from a single organization and to instantly change that organization's name or other data everywhere it appears. This is an especially valuable feature if you deal with large organizations.

```
F.COMPANY.ENT          F.COMPANY FILE ENTRY               (1-1)

01 Company Code      ASTD
                                        09 ISA      MEM
02 Company/Sort Name  AMERICAN SOCIETY FOR TRAINING |  10 Business A
03 Print/Label Name   AMER SOC FOR TRNG & DEVEL     |  11 Form     A
04 Letter Qual. Name  AMERICAN SOCIETY FOR TRAINING AND DEVELOPMENT

    05 Source   06 Date   07 M#ales  08 Size Notes
01> NTPA.92    12-31-92   $5+M    110 EMPL
02> GALE.91    12-31-90           100 EMPL

12 Remarks  F:1944:

---------------13 Customers:  14 Total Record(s)------------
06> 23011  MC QUARRIE, PAUL
07> 27495  BONNER, PETER C        VICE PRESIDENT-MARKETING/SALES
08> 27524  PLOTT, CURTIS E        EV
09> 27622  SOBRINO, LIZ           SALES REPRESENTATIVE
10> 30402  OLSON, NANCY           VP/PUBLICATIONS

VIEW ONLY! ENTER "F" OR "B" TO SCROLL THRU RECORDS (1 to 14)?
```

Product files allow you to set standardized product names, product codes/numbers, prices, invoicing information and inventory data, to name just a few. One special product file is for seminars and identifies each event by its product, date and location.

It's a good idea to adopt a standardized list of products (names, abbreviations or numbers) which the system can then use to compare with any proposed entry in order to be sure its a legitimate product. This is especially necessary if you're using your system for

any accounting-related functions. Our product list is shown below.

```
PAGE  1                                  06:19:07  20 SEP 1993
PRODUCT...  PRODUCT TYPE.........  DESCRIPTION.............  Unit
CODE                                                         Price

ALL     1 PUBLIC SEMINAR       INQUIRY ON ALL PRODUCTS
PEP     1 PUBLIC SEMINAR       PRODUCT EVALUATION & PLANNING
SDM     1 PUBLIC SEMINAR       HOW TO MARKET TRAINING        545.00
                               PROGRAMS
MTYO/IC 2 IN-COMPANY SEMINAR   MKTG TRNG W/IN YOUR OWN ORG  3600.00
PEP/IC  2 IN-COMPANY SEMINAR   PRODUCT EVALUATION & PLANNING 8500.00
SDM/IC  2 IN-COMPANY SEMINAR   HOW TO MARKET TRAINING       6000.00
                               PROGRAMS
SDW/IC  2 IN-COMPANY SEMINAR   STRATEGY DEVELOPMENT WORKSHOP 8000.00
HTMT/TK 3 TALKS AND PRESENTATI HOW TO MARKET TRAINING
MTYO/TK 3 TALKS AND PRESENTATI MKTG TRNG W/IN YOUR OWN ORG
TALK    3 TALKS AND PRESENTATI SPECIAL TALK OR PRESENTATION
ADV     4 CONSULTING           ADVANCE RETAINER
CON     4 CONSULTING           CONSULTING
EXP     4 CONSULTING           EXPENSES
CMH     6 BOOK                 CONSULTANTS MARKETING HANDBOOK 149.00
CPB     6 BOOK                 COMPETITIVE POSITION BOOKLET    4.95
FTF     6 BOOK                 SELLING TRAINING PROGRAMS      17.95
                               FACE-TO-FACE
MIHT    6 BOOK                 MARKETING IN-HOUSE TRAINING     5.95
                               PROGRAMS
MIHT/SDM 6 BOOK                MARKETING IN-HOUSE TRAINING     5.95
                               PROGRAMS - SDM MAILING
MMM     6 BOOK                 MONEY-MAKING MEETINGS          19.95
MTP     6 BOOK                 HOW TO MARKET TRAINING        139.95
                               PROGRAMS
NB      6 BOOK                 SDM COURSE NOTEBOOK           169.95
```

Outputs and Housekeeping. Standard outputs from the system are available on the menu shown below.

```
              MAILING LISTS OUTPUT MENU

 1. Print MASTER SEMINAR File Report
 2. Print ROSTERS and GUMMED LABELS
 3. Print selected CUSTOMER RECORDS
 4. Print The SEMINAR Mailing Report
 5. Print The BOOK Mailing Reports
 6. Print INDIVIDUAL P.O. SALES SHEETS (Changes Only)
 7. Get Mailing List COUNTS On Screen
 8. Print Mailing List COUNT REPORT
 9. Print 1-Up to 4-Up MAILING LABELS
10. Run 5-DIGIT PRESORT Processes
11. Set Up Mailing Labels on FLOPPY DISK(S)
12. Print Publications SALES REPORT
13. Check Date/Time of Current "Exploded" SALES File
```

Marketing Database Tips

Forget About Windows and other "bells and whistles." Most of what you'll do with a marketing database won't benefit from the graphical user interface, and many of the same "point-and-shoot" features are available with DOS programs.

Get an On-Site Service Policy. When your marketing database has a problem, it can bring your business to a standstill. So, in addition to everything else, contract for reliable, on-site service. This is no place for false economy.

You Need Local Help. Your marketing database is not static. It will constantly change as your business changes. That's why you need someone "techie" enough to create special reports, add/change capabilities and solve problems as they occur. Ideally this is someone in your company -- but it can be a local consultant. Find the right person *first* and they can help you decide on the software to use.

Be Sure Third-Party Hardware Doesn't Void Your Warranty. Since your system will be assembled from components built by different companies, it's easy for one manufacturer or dealer to blame "the other guy" when things go wrong. This is not likely to be a problem under an on-site service policy provided by a local specialist, but can present difficulties with manufacturer's warranties. Get any agreements in writing before you buy.

Be Prudently Slow Buying New Hardware and Software. Invest in new hardware and software *only* when you need them, rather than constantly trying to "have the latest available." In fact, our own database software is still running very nicely on some of the earliest IBM PCs and XTs. And because of its design, this software can do everything our clients require even on these early-technology machines.

Three More Money-Saving Resources. Here are three unique and valuable resources for anyone who uses their computer for marketing training and information products and services:

1. MELISSA DATA CORPORATION
   32122 Paseo Adelanto, No. 8A
   San Juan Capistrano, CA 92675-3600
   Phone: (800) 443-8834, (714) 661-5885; Fax: (714) 661-5002
   Contact: Ray Melissa
   The Melissa Mailer's Software catalog is a cornucopia of direct mail hardware and software for PC marketing databases. Includes many of the software packages in this chapter, plus CD-ROM and data diskettes for news releases, assigning gender to 100,000 first names, 9.5 million business telephones, atlases, street maps and more.

2. PC CONNECTION
   6 Mill Street
   Marlow, NH 03456
   Phone: (800) 800-5555, (603) 446-5555; Fax: (603) 446-7791
   Incredibly fast, careful delivery, low, competitive prices and consistently top-rated customer service and reliability. Check with them before buying anything for your computer.

3. TOPITZES AND ASSOCIATES
   6401 Odana Road
   Madison, WI 53719
   Phone (800) 233-9767, (608) 273-4300; Fax: (608) 273-8804
   Contact: Nick Topitzes, CMP
   Their Meeting Planner's Computer Catalog rounds up lots of hard-to-find meeting-related computer software and supplies for printing name tags, badges, place-card tents, banners, registration envelopes, labels, ribbons, signs and more.

MAINTAINING YOUR MARKETING DATABASE

How to Acquire a Steady Stream of New Names

Once you have a marketing database, you're going to want to be constantly alert for high-quality names you can add. Obviously this includes anybody who responds or inquires. But it also includes other sources you may not have considered.

For example, if you mail to a rented list, capture the address corrections people send you, as well as any orders or responders. The person who writes to correct their address was favorably impressed by your offer, or they wouldn't bother.

And don't forget to ask your current customers for the names of their friends and associates they'd like to know about you. Your satisfied customers will gladly help you find other prospects with tastes and needs like theirs -- if you just ask them.

When asking clients for referrals, provide a separate sheet with space for three names. Tests have shown that the fourth and subsequent names furnished are not better than cold canvassing. These tests also show that asking for only one name frequently removes the possibility of getting more (good) contacts. And *always* ask for permission to use the name of the person making the referral. Using their name in your subsequent contact will increase response two to five times.

If you conduct training programs or seminars, provide a sheet for your attendees to recommend others. Allow time for this and you'll be rewarded with some very good prospects.

Below is a form that we've used to secure referral names both through the mail and at seminars.

Also, have your sales people collect business cards of new prospects they call upon. On a weekly basis, ask them to put the cards face-down on a copying machine (10 - 12 at a time) and to give the copy to whoever adds names to your database. This practice benefits the salesperson, too, because the new prospect begins getting your regular mailings as reminders. But most importantly, it adds fresh names, of those who already know your organization, to your database.

Sample Form to Solicit Referral Names

. . . AND BY THE WAY

Do you know of someone who you feel would profit from our *How To Market Training Programs* seminar? If you do, please use the space below to jot down their name and whatever else you know of their address. We will be happy to furnish them information on the program --- and they will likely appreciate your thoughtfulness in suggesting it.

Name _____ Title _____

Company _____ Phone _____

Street address _____

City _____ State _____ ZIP _____

Remarks _____

Name _____ Title _____

Company _____ Phone _____

Street address _____

City _____ State _____ ZIP _____

Remarks _____

Name _____ Title _____

Company _____ Phone _____

Street address _____

City _____ State _____ ZIP _____

Remarks _____

Suggested by _____

Tips for Maintaining Your Database

Through the years we've evolved eight (8) key points that are helpful in thinking about the ongoing maintenance of your database. These are:

Maintain ONE Customer/Prospect File with complete transaction and demographic information, *not* a separate "mailing list." This ensures that every new transaction automatically updates the file, and when a list *is* run for any purpose it's always the freshest possible.

Maintain Your List In-House, using your own employees. No outside service will ever have the same high regard for your clients, customers and prospects that you and your staff do.

Capture and Record Information, NOT Judgments, classifications, arbitrary action codes, etc. For example, entering the number of employees is preferable to storing a code for the organization's size. If your code system changed, you'd need to re-code your entire file.

Never Enter a Directory into Your Database nor buy a mailing list for repeated use, unless you'll mail often enough (three to four times a year) to keep it fresh -- or unless the list source will provide regular updates. It's almost always a bad idea.

Hire People who Care About Their Work, and train them on your record-keeping procedures. Encourage them to suggest improvements you can make to do a better job of staying in touch with your customers/responders. There is no doubt that the *people* are far and away the most important ingredient here.

Look for Ways to Improve the accuracy of the information input to your system and to verify that information by cross-checks or independent research, etc. Small discrepancies, duplications, omissions and the like frequently signal a more serious underlying problem that should be corrected.

Stay Current with your database maintenance, and don't "get behind." If you do get behind, hire more staff or work overtime to get caught up as soon as possible.

Never, Under any Circumstances, Delete a Client or Responder. If they become unmailable for any reason, encode the record so it won't be used to print labels or for other solicitations. But a surprising number of those "lost" customers reappear (especially if they were satisfied), allowing you to update their addresses, remove the non-print designator and proceed. Besides, this is a key difference between a marketing database and merely a mailing list. And this policy also applies to "phonies" or prank responders. They'll show up over and over again, and it saves time when you can easily find them in the database.

CUSTOMER ADDRESS LOSS: A COSTLY PROBLEM -- AND WHAT TO DO ABOUT IT

Fully 20% - 50% of the records in your files will require change or updating every year, not counting buying transactions.

For individuals at home addresses (similar to consumer lists), roughly 20% - 25% will move each year. Fortunately, 75% - 85% of those will have a forwarding address which you can inexpensively obtain using the Post Office address correction services described in Chapter 9. The remaining 15% - 25% are

moves made without leaving a forwarding address, but most of those can also be found using the techniques outlined in this section.

The problem is more serious for individuals at business addresses. Each year, between 25% and 50% of these will have some change in one or more fields, such as job title, telephone number, extension, internal mail code, street address, organization or division name, etc. These changes result from normal business activities, like acquisitions, mergers, re-organizations, bankruptcies and plant openings/closings, not to mention all the individual's moves, job changes and promotions.

Only about 20% - 25% of these changes will be obtainable with the Post Office's address correction service (more if they're smaller organizations). Another 10% - 20% will be businesses that have been dissolved or terminated (again, more if they're smaller organizations). This mail will be returned by the Post Office marked with the reason the address isn't available. The remaining 55% - 70% are individual moves for whom their new address must be obtained using the techniques outlined below.

Lost Customers Cost You Plenty

If you're not convinced of the seriousness of customer address losses from the statistics just described, consider the economic implications. Referring to Chapter 5 on how much a new customer/responder name is worth, the lifetime value of each name could well be hundreds or even thousands of dollars. Put differently, *each lost name that you could otherwise recover actually costs you the amount of all future sales you'd derive from that name.* That figure can easily be $50-$100 per name per year. So every lost address that you recover is like finding another $50-$100 of income *every year!*

How to Recover Lost Customer Addresses

At least three times a year, use the Post Office's "Address Correction Requested" service on mailings made to your house list (exception: When several mailings are being made in quick succession, only one mailing need use ACR). This will prevent those address losses that *are* preventable.

Remember that if your customer is at a large organization, chances are the organization is still there -- it's only your customer who's gone, so this method works best with small organizations.

If the Post Office's "Address Correction Requested" with your Third-Class bulk mailings doesn't produce a new address for a lost

customer, send a First-Class letter to them at their last known address. Put "Address Correction Requested: Use Form 3547" on the envelope. Explain in the letter that the Post Office has reported his/her address had changed, and ask them to furnish you their new address and phone number to update your files. Supply a form *and* self-addressed, stamped envelope or business reply envelope.

What to Do With Large Organizations on Your Database

Large organizations present a special problem for your database. Many Fortune 500 mail rooms are swamped with Third-Class bulk mail that arrives (literally) by the truck load. The problem has become so acute, that General Motors and others are throwing out bulk Third-Class mail without delivery. (Only First-Class mail *must* be delivered internally.) Issues -- like whether this violates anybody's rights -- quickly becomes academic if it's *your* mail that's being thrown out.

If you have lots of names at any one facility, work with their mail room supervisor to make sure your mail gets through. Write or call and ask if they'll furnish you the proper internal mail codes on a listing you'll provide. Chances are you'll get address and title changes, too (if your listing includes these), and you *may* establish a relationship that will be helpful in the future as well.

Sometimes a customer will insist that you remove from your mailing list the names of *everyone* in their organization *but* them. Such requests show someone trying to get control over a group's buying by controlling their information about what's available. Like most censorship in a free society, chances are it won't last long. Still, you don't want to alienate the requester (who's probably a good customer). So here's what to do:

Explain that their people's names also appear on other lists you rent; they've joined associations, subscribed to magazines, attended meetings, bought products, etc. It's practically impossible to keep them from receiving your mailings. Chances are the requester hadn't thought of that and will quickly agree.

In tough cases, and when you genuinely want to avoid mailing to a particular customer, you'll need to do it as part of your merge/purge process. Start a "negatives" file for all such organizations and individuals, as well as for your bad debts and phonies. Ask the service bureau to suppress/delete all names on your negatives file before printing labels.

Post Office Address Correction Services

Besides the usual address correction/forwarding services available for what you mail (see "How To Get Your Undeliverable Mail Returned" in Chapter 9), the USPS offers help for mass corrections and updating, too:

1. Free One-Time Cleaning of Manually Maintained Address Files. Send your typewritten or other machine-printed mailing list of up to 300 addresses and USPS will clean it up, correcting street and city names, state abbreviations, ZIP Codes, and adding ZIP + 4 codes, all in the strictest confidence and at no cost.

2. Free, One-Time Cleaning of Files on Computer Diskette. Mailers who have their address lists maintained on diskettes can have them converted at no charge by the Postal Service. Diskette lists may not be smaller than 300 or larger than 50,000 addresses. USPS will convert your records to ZIP + 4 codes. Corrections will also be made to any incorrect 5-digit ZIP Code, misspelled street/city name and incorrect state abbreviation. The coding service can process 3-1/2", 5-1/4" and 8" diskettes in most formats. To apply for this service, ask your local Postmaster or Customer Service Representative for Form 5601, ZIP + 4 Address List Coding Order Form or Form 5603, Diskette Conversion Order Form.

3. Free ZIP + 4 Directory Tapes. Mailers who have a 1/2", 9-track tape drive can obtain at no charge the Postal Service's National or State ZIP + 4 Directory tapes covering 109 million delivery addresses. These non-returnable magnetic tapes contain ZIP + 4 codes for all delivery points. To order the tapes, ask you Postmaster or Customer Service Representative for Form 5600, Request Form for ZIP + 4 National/State Directory Computer Tapes. A set of technical notes

and instructions for developing the matching software accompanies the tapes.

4. Free Telephone Help with Addresses. When you phone one of the over 100 ZIP Code information units and request a ZIP Code, a computer operator keys in the address. In seconds, the system finds a matching address from among 109 million addresses on the laser disc and displays it along with the corresponding ZIP + 4 code on the computer screen. The operator can also tell you of mistakes in abbreviations, spelling, street names and suite numbers.

5. Low-Cost Address Corrections Through NCOA Licensees. NCOA stands for National Change Of Address. The way it works is that all change-of-address data from the entire country is telecommunicated *daily* to the USPS National Address Information Center (NAIC) in Memphis, TN, where it is then transmitted biweekly to the private companies licensed by the USPS. These private firms perform ZIP + 4 conversions, provide matching software for customers wishing to do their own conversions and provide other related assistance to mailers for a fee. Some firms also can provide a ZIP + 4 file on microfiche and/or microfilm, again for a fee. The Postal Service, on a non-endorsement basis, has compiled a free directory of these firms. Ask for Publication 148, Directory of ZIP + 4 Coding Services. You can also call (800) 262-9541, ext. 80 from 7 a.m. - 6 p.m. C.S.T. In Tennessee, (800) 233-0453.

Before you spend too much with an NCOA vendor, check out the quarterly-updated postal coding and sequencing software (and CD-ROM) packages described earlier in this chapter. It may be more economical to acquire the capability on your own computer.

More Tips for Recovering Lost Customer Addresses

Call the Last-Known Telephone Number you have for the lost record. Often this will be unchanged (even though the address has), or the phone company will automatically give you the new phone number. If not, call information (either the phone company's directory assistance or one of the new lower-cost directory services), giving only the person's or organization's name and the city. When the operator gives you a phone number, write it down and *then* ask what the address is. These services will generally not look up addresses but *will* furnish them to help you confirm the phone number.

When the Organization Is Still There but the Person Isn't, send a First-Class letter to the Personnel Director (by title if you don't know the name), requesting the forwarding address and other information on the person. Ask them to put it right on your letter (provide space for this purpose) and to return it to you in the self-addressed, stamped (or business reply) envelope you provided. Education and training suppliers, especially, will find that this approach will get a very high percentage response, although not always the desired address, because of organizational policies and/or privacy concerns.

Ask Sales to Help. Your telemarketing staff and/or field sales force can often help locate lost direct mail customers. (Presumably they keep track of their own customers who move.) If necessary, pay them a small commission for each name recovered. If you know the present value of your future customer relationship, you'll have no difficulty figuring a fair payment.

Use Computer Overlays/Enhancements -- services that will match the name with their files and furnish the missing/updated information. This works best for individuals and small companies. These databases are described in Chapter 7.

Periodically "Clean" Your List by sending a First-Class letter asking for current information from customers/responders who have been inactive for a while. *Don't make this communication part of any other solicitation;* limit it strictly to updating your file. A similar effect is obtained by publishers including a postcard in their controlled circulation publications, which must be completed and returned in order to continue receiving the magazine.

Use Your Newsletter. If you publish a newsletter, include a regular column of lost names. Ask your readers to help you re-establish contact with them.

DATABASE SECURITY

Once your marketing database is "up and running," it will become a vital ingredient in your entire business. That means that it needs to be treated with respect and attention to its security. As used here, security refers to two aspects: security from improper use and security from physical harm.

Protecting Your List from Improper Use

Most improper use of a marketing database or mailing list is by employees and suppliers having routine access to the system. So, even if you never intend to rent or exchange your mailing list with others, you need to think about its security right from the start.

Protect your database from the beginning by including dummy or decoy names, who will return to you, unopened (and with the date received), all mail received by them. Select family and friends in as many locations as possible, as most list thieves routinely drop the ZIP codes around the organization's headquarters. Have the dummy names and/or addresses set up in such a way that they won't be used anywhere else, but that do look like any other record. Remember, the object is to have each dummy name survive merge/purge and/or reformatting and *still* be recognized as having come from your list.

Let everyone know your list is protected; the deterrence value is much more important -- and easier -- than trying to recover damages if the list is improperly used.

Use *both* real *and* fictional decoys to avoid their detection with credit bureau checks and/or telephone lookup. Make sure your decoys are sorted and listed in the proper ZIP sequence, not all at the beginning or end of the list.

Supplement the decoys that you create using people you know with purchased decoys. The References and Resources listing in Appendix A shows several such sources. The most frequently employed is:

U.S. MONITOR SERVICE
86 Maple Avenue
New City, NY 10956-9988
Phone: (914) 634-1331

These decoys can be provided in dozens of U.S. cities. You will be furnished with a surname and address to use in your database. The surname can be used at the designated address in any context you wish. For example, it can be used as part of the company name, it can be combined with various first names, middle initials, and/or position titles. All mail received to that name at that address will be promptly date stamped and returned to you. U.S. Monitor Service will furnish you with a monthly bill for the nominal charges involved, plus an annual fee. Purchased decoys are an "absolute must" if you intend to rent or exchange your mailing list.

Physical Security Measures

Physical security of your list means protecting it from loss or damage due to water, fire, earthquake, etc. If you have active modems allowing telephone access to your system, then you need to provide security from "hackers" as well. And don't overlook computer viruses, either.

The most likely threat is data loss due to hardware "crashes." Institute a regular daily back-up routine that ensures you'll be able to reconstruct any lost or damaged computer files with minimum effort. A simple, effective system uses a high density backup medium such as magnetic tape, removable hard disk or Bernoulli Box, (not floppy disks, which take too much time and hassle). Acquire one set of backup media for each day of the week, and three or four extra for archive purposes. Label each media with their day of the week (e.g., Monday, Tuesday, etc.).

When you use the medium for a given day's backup, write the date on the label. This way the label shows the history of backups and ensures that at least five consecutive workdays of backup are always available. Periodically run an extra backup, or print an extra hard copy of your list, and store this in a different, secure location, such as a bank vault or your home.

Experienced computer operations personnel can recommend additional simple but effective backup procedures that are right for your system. They'll also help with conventional computer security measures geared to "hackers" and computer viruses. These matters are too involved to repeat here.

And today, with more and more corporate assets being tied up in electronic media, the insurance companies are beginning to recognize and provide for coverage of this vital element. After all, the cost of recreating data can be expensive: According to a report by the National Computer Security Association, it costs on average $17,000 to recreate 20MB of sales and marketing data and $19,000 to rebuild the same amount of accounting data. Check with your insurance agent to be sure that your policy properly includes not only payment for the media itself, but also appropriate costs to reconstruct your database (see the last section in this chapter on valuing your database as a capital asset).

RENTING OR EXCHANGING YOUR LIST

Once you have a list of unique clients/ prospects, or a list of 5,000 or more mail-order customers, renting it to others can be an excellent source of added income, at very high profit margins. Rental of your list can be done with safety and efficiency by securing the service of a list manager, or you can do it yourself. This section provides information to help you evaluate this profitable option and gives you some pointers on how to do it.

Deciding Whether or Not to Use a List Manager

Before deciding how best to proceed with rental or exchange of your list, review the pertinent sections of Chapter 7, particularly the various roles in the world of mailing lists.

As list *owner*, you may be able to secure the services of a list *manager* who will promote your list to *brokers* and others in the mailing list community. If your list is small or specialized, don't expect a list manager to spend much time or energy -- it simply won't generate enough revenue for them. The same is true for mailing list brokers, who always give their greatest attention to large lists that generate significant commissions.

But if your mailing list is at least 5,000 to 10,000 direct mail responders, you'll probably find a list manager who will be interested in your business.

How do you find them? For starters, who's managing the lists you now rent? These managers already understand your market. And you've sampled their professionalism, service, accuracy, billing errors, etc., as a renter.

There's also a list of good candidates in Chapter 7.

Select a list manager who will commit to actively promoting your list and working hard to arrange competitor exchanges. They will also help you set the proper rental price for your list, extra charges for selections, etc.

If you're ever dissatisfied with your list manager, let them know about it in positive but specific terms. Allow a reasonable period for them to respond, but don't hesitate to get a new list manager if you're still not satisfied.

Remember, list managers typically get paid 20% of any rentals that they generate. If you already have list rental business without a manager, don't fail to exclude from their commissions any continued rentals by the people you now serve. Most managers are willing to do this, betting that they will significantly increase your rental revenues from among those you don't now serve.

Should Your List Be Included on a List Database?

You'll recall list databases from Chapter 7, those composites of many popular mailing lists, combined, unduplicated and available for rental. List databases allow great geographic selection and are popular with seminar promoters and other training and information suppliers.

Including your list on a list database has two benefits to offset the control you surrender. First, you'll get the other lists on the database for your own use quickly, easily, at low cost and already merged and purged with your house list. If you're already using those lists for your direct mail, that's going to save you money and time. Second, you'll generate mailing list rental income, paid to you by the list database owner, based on how many of your names were rented and whether they were on other lists in the database.

Overall, putting your list on the list database(s) that serves your primary market is probably a good idea. Just be sure you take pains to keep the copy of your list that's on the database as fresh as possible.

Pricing and Promoting Your Own List

Promoting your own list is simpler than you think, because the more specialized your list, the fewer people who are likely to be interested in it -- *and* the more likely it is that you know exactly who they are.

Of course, there are a number of standard techniques that will help gain exposure for your list. First, advertise in the Standard Rate and Data Service (SRDS) directory *Direct Mail Rates and Data*. Particulars on this service are in Chapter 7.

Next, prepare your own "mailing list data card" describing your list and providing pertinent counts, demographics, costs, etc. Keep this information current and be prepared to send it to those inquiring about your list. Chapter 7 provides guidance and a sample of a list data card.

For pricing, again Chapter 7 offers data. But your best guide will be the going rates for other lists like yours, perhaps the rates you now pay for lists you rent.

Make two or three promotional mailings a year to your mailing list renters, exchangers and prospects. Reasons for these mailings can include updated counts, new selections available and new users of your list (always mentioned only with their permission).

Most importantly, be alert to other mailing list promotions you see, especially those in businesses like yours. The presence of other mailing lists demonstrates a viable market for lists, a market you can probably serve. In fact, the absence of other mailing lists like yours can suggest that the market doesn't now exist (maybe you will be able to create it!).

Mailing List Rental Income Can Be *Very* Interesting

Rental revenues of $1.00-$5.00 per year per name can be achieved in your second or third year of active list rental promotion. Some in the training and information business do even better! If you approach renting your list aggressively you will be rewarded with some really exciting revenues.

To estimate the economics of list rental, consider that your costs will be at most 40% (20% to the list broker and 20% to the list manager, if you've hired one). Add to that another 5% to cover printing, promotion, internal labor and handling (shipping costs are normally paid by the renter). That leaves a tidy 55% profit contribution from list rentals. For many companies these revenues more than cover the cost of maintaining their list and provide supplemental revenue they can use to further develop their marketing database system.

Tips for Renting Your List

Over years of renting our own mailing list and working with clients who rent theirs, here are some tips:

Use a List Rental Agreement that clearly spells out what can and cannot be done with your list (see sample on next page). Insist that it be completely executed and returned to you *before* your list is shipped.

Demand Advance Payment for first or-

ders from new renters whose prior payment history can't be verified to your satisfaction or whose current payment isn't guaranteed by the broker.

Require a Sample Mail Piece for each proposed use of your list, and examine it carefully. When you receive only agency draft copy and cannot satisfactorily evaluate the offer, ask for a comprehensive mock-up or even the final mail piece. Remember, it's too late after it's mailed!

Rip-Offs Are Rare. No thinking mailer will jeopardize their access to a profitable list by deliberate unauthorized and/or unethical use. But after a while, even the most fastidious can get careless, and this is when problems occur, generally in three areas: (1.) mailing a legitimate offer but not the one cleared, (2.) mailing on a different date than agreed and (3.) stretching out payment.

Don't Allow Low-Cost/Free Offers which can pull a significant percentage of responder names off your list. These names then become the renter's property and can be added to their own list. This is especially important when renting or exchanging your list with a close competitor.

Demand Prompt and Complete Payment for your list, according to the list rental agreement. Late payment is the most widespread problem, but you can relieve most of this by aggressive collection actions. And it goes without saying that you *never* ship a new list order to/for *any* renter whose payment for a previous rental is delinquent.

Exchanging Lists with Your Competitors

Your closest competitor will probably not rent you their list. But they *may* exchange with you on a name-for-name basis. Where the lists are unequal in size or the two organizations' mailing programs are different, a rental fee is paid on the difference in counts, or a "reciprocal" rental agreement can be reached.

Most list owners who don't already rent or exchange lists start out dead-set against *ever* releasing their list for any reason, let alone to a competitor. Yet, the most effective lists for both parties are *always* obtained by exchange. So don't hesitate to pursue an exchange; it will benefit both organizations. Just be prepared to spend time on education and diplomacy, and always be willing to pay a broker's fee if you think they can be more successful negotiating an exchange than you will be.

One way to rent or exchange lists with complete security is to ship the renter's *mail pieces* to the list owner's mail house, for label affixing, processing and mailing entirely under the list owner's control. This may be a good "icebreaker" -- a way to overcome the last objections to closing a deal.

In all exchanges and reciprocal rentals, be sure the lists are equivalently maintained and offer comparable selections for both parties. For example, can both lists offer selection by ZIP code, date of most recent purchase, product, etc.? But remember, all you really care about are *results*.

Sample List Rental Agreement

This document represents a voluntary agreement between **SCHRELLO DIRECT MARKETING**, the **LIST OWNER**, whose principal office address is P.O. Box 1610, Long Beach, CA 90801, and the **LIST RENTER** named below.

1. **SCHRELLO DIRECT MARKETING** agrees to furnish a specified list to the **LIST RENTER**, for a specified one-time use on a specified date. Neither the **LIST RENTER**, or his agents, employees, or contractors shall reuse, copy, duplicate, reproduce, retain, electronically process, transfer, sell or disclose to any other party in any form whatsoever any portion of this list.

2. The one-time use of the list shall be limited solely and exclusively to that named below and described by the sample mailing piece and/or the list rental order and/or the solicitation plan, and approved in writing by **SCHRELLO DIRECT MARKETING** in advance. Any change in the intended use, or change in the date of use, shall be reapproved in writing by **SCHRELLO DIRECT MARKETING** in advance.

3. The list, and all portions of it, are hereby acknowledged to be the copyrighted property of **SCHRELLO DIRECT MARKETING**, and to be of considerable proprietary value and, further, that unauthorized use or disclosure of this list or any portion thereof is acknowledged to be a serious matter entitling the **LIST OWNER** to monetary damages and penalties, as well as injunctive relief. If the **LIST RENTER** or his agents, employees, contractors or anyone else who shall be given access to the list by the **LIST RENTER** uses the list contrary to the provisions of this agreement, the **LIST RENTER** agrees to pay said monetary damages and penalties to **SCHRELLO DIRECT MARKETING** including all costs and reasonable attorney's fees related to its collection. The **LIST RENTER** also consents to the entry of an order enjoining any use of the list in violation of this agreement to prevent further and continuing damages.

4. It is understood and agreed that the rented list is protected, and will be monitored to prevent unauthorized use of the list, by a combination of one or more methods of computer control and/or planted "decoy" names and addresses and/or arrangements with legitimate persons on the list whose records are created in a way that enables them to identify contacts originating from the list. As a practical matter, it will be impossible to remove all, or even most of these protection devices, and the **LIST RENTER** consents and agrees to such protective measures.

5. The rented list will be selected according to the specifications supplied by the **LIST RENTER**. The list should be carefully checked by the **LIST RENTER** before use for any apparent discrepancies. No adjustments will be made after the list has been used by the **LIST RENTER**. **SCHRELLO DIRECT MARKETING** hereby disclaims any guarantees expressed or implied regarding said list. Under no circumstance shall **SCHRELLO DIRECT MARKETING** be liable for loss of profits or for special, consequential, or exemplary damages resulting from use of this list. Receipt of the list by the **LIST RENTER**'s designee shall be deemed receipt by the **LIST RENTER**.

6. **SCHRELLO DIRECT MARKETING** makes no warranty or representation of any nature as to the accuracy of the list, of the addresses on the list, nor is any warranty or representation made with respect to the results to be obtained or to the number of mailing pieces which are undeliverable.

7. Rental rates are those in effect at the time of order, and are subject to change without notice. Advance payment is required for new renters. Terms of payment for all others are thirty (30) days from receipt of list by **LIST RENTER**. **LIST RENTER** agrees to pay a one and one-half percent (1-1/2%) per month charge on all past due amounts.

By their signatures below, **SCHRELLO DIRECT MARKETING** and the **LIST RENTER** expressly agree to be bound by the foregoing for a period of two (2) years from the below date, or two (2) years after the last authorized use of the list, whichever shall be longer.

LIST RENTER:

Organization:_____

Address:_____

City, State, ZIP:_____ Phone:_____

Nature of one-time use:_____ Date of use:_____

Authorized signature:_____ Date:_____

Name (type or print):_____ Title:_____

SCHRELLO DIRECT MARKETING:

Authorized ture:_____ Date:_____ Signature:

Name:_____ Title:_____

VALUING YOUR MAILING LIST

Valuing a mailing list, like any business asset, can be based on many different approaches and viewpoints. If the valuation is for legal or tax reasons, the counsel of a licensed appraiser or other professional should be retained. The following is presented primarily for your internal planning use:

The three most common ways to value a mailing list are (1.) based on its future income-producing potential, (2.) based on its replacement cost and (3.) compared to the price paid for other, similar mailing lists bought and sold in "arms length" transactions.

Future Income Production

When using *future income production*, value is usually based on a multiple of the list's annual net revenue-producing capacity. This is defined as the revenue obtained from mailing the list at its maximum frequency, less the costs of those mailings and, of course, including mailing list rental income. Typical multiples range from two to five, with 2-1/2 times a common figure.

Replacement Cost

Replacement costs are best estimated from your detailed records of the actual time and efforts expended in originally creating the list, including any costs involved. For example, were low-priced promotions that lost money made primarily to build the list? If so, some or all of these costs might need to be incurred again to replace it.

Sales of Comparable Lists

Use your mailing list broker to help get *comparable values* for lists similar to your own that have been bought or sold recently. Similarity should reflect at least three variables:

How closely do the individuals on the comparison lists fit your market? (Highest if they're buyers of products like yours; lowest if it's a compiled list.)

How recent is the comparison list? (Highest is current or less than one year old; lowest is three years old or more.)

How large is the comparison list? (Smaller lists generally command a higher valuation per name.)

Be prepared for some wide variations between the various methods, perhaps by a factor of 100 or more. For example, one Chicago mail-order house estimates that each name on its list is worth $350, while in another actual company sale, an active mailing list brought an estimated $6 per name.

Your Mailing List Can Be Your Biggest Asset

If you sell your business, your mailing list could command an even higher premium. In 1993 the U.S. Supreme Court ruled that businesses can assign value to intangible assets such as customer lists, thus creating a tax deduction for companies that acquire them.

The five to four decision involved the Newark, NJ, *Star Ledger's* subscribers list. Justice Harry Blackmun, writing the majority opinion, said businesses can now assign values for tax purposes to subscriber lists, mailing lists, client files, insurance renewal files, drugstore prescription files and "any other identifiable assets the value of which depends on the continued and voluntary patronage of customers."

Although the ruling only applies to lists from a company that is being acquired, and not to routinely used house lists, it's still significant. Robert Levering, senior vice president of DMA told *DM News* that now, in the event a direct marketing company is sold, 70%-80% of the purchase value, generally, could be assigned to the house list and then depreciated by the buyer. Since such a file is most valuable for only three to five years, he explained, the ruling presents "an envious tax advantage" for direct marketers.

NOTES

A

REFERENCES AND RESOURCES FOR MARKETING TRAINING AND INFORMATION

If the rest of this manual has done its job, you're only reading this appendix to fine tune your sales or marketing, or just to see what else is available. That's because it's been our goal in this edition to put just as much essential help as possible right in each chapter, where it's easy to find and use when you need it -- things like key references and directories, lists of suppliers and contacts, and addresses, telephones and fax numbers.

But there's still more sales and marketing information you might need or want. For example, identifying the best general sales and marketing books, finding the classics on selling and selling skills, and accessing the growing number of business information publications, directories, listings and databases.

We've reorganized this appendix from earlier editions to follow the book's sequence of chapters and subjects. Experience suggests that this is the most common way these pages are used. Note, however, that although the section and chapter numbers match, the section titles sometimes differ, particularly if we've included references on related topics.

Chapters 1 and 6 receive special treatment because there's a wealth of literature in these areas that hasn't been summarized anywhere else. Here we wanted to create a somewhat more complete bibliography, if only for others -- like us -- who feel a bit compulsive about these matters.

Overall, the number of references in this Appendix has remained at just over 300 ... 311 to be exact. But now most are related *only* to sales and marketing of training and information. We can now concentrate on these issues because some *very* complete bibliographies of the training and information fields have appeared. These works include references on core competencies, professional practices, available products and services periodicals, software and more. A number of these fine handbooks are included among the Chapter 1 resources that follow.

A last -- and welcome note: Except for some real classics, most of the entries in this Appendix carry publication dates within the last seven years. That's becoming more important as the pace of change accelerates. But don't scoff at a reference just because of it's age; The basic truths don't seem to change over time.

Note: Remarks followed by initials are attributable to these sources:

DMA   *Direct Marketing Association*
DMN   *DM News*
HCI   *Hoke Communications*
INC   *Inc. Magazine*
TM   *Target Marketing*
WSJ   *Wall Street Journal*
ZTM   *ZIP Target Marketing*

1. - THE TRAINING INDUSTRY AND MARKETPLACE

1. Bard, Ray, Bell, Chip R. et al. *The Trainer's Professional Development Handbook.* Jossey-Bass, Inc. Publishers, 350 Sansome Street, San Francisco, CA 94104. Phone: (415) 433-1767; Fax: (415) 433-0499. 1987. ISBN 1-55542-067-2. (346 pages, $39.95)

    This is another great reference book. The last half of the book, "A Catalog of Learning Resources," presents directories of books, professional journals/periodicals, conferences, associations, on-line databases and software. Although some references are a bit old, they are truly classics. And if they publish a new edition, get it!

2. Black, Gilbert J. *The Management Development and Education Market: 1977-1982.* Knowledge Industry Publications, Inc., 701 Westchester Avenue, White Plains, NY 10604. Phone: (800) 800-5474, (914) 328-9157; Fax: (914) 328-9093. 1977. ($450.00)

    At the time this was published, there was little known about the training industry. This landmark report is included here largely for historical completeness, as it includes profiles of 17 management development companies and materials suppliers.

3. Carnevale, Anthony Patrick. *America and the New Economy: How New Competitive Standards are Radically Changing American Workplace.* Jossey-Bass, Inc. Publishers, 350 Sansome Street, San Francisco, CA 94104. Phone: (415) 433-1767; Fax: (415) 433-0499. 1991. ISBN 0-318-22200-0. (291 pages, $30.95)

    The final report on a 5-year R&D project conducted jointly by the U.S. Department of Labor and ASTD.

4. Craig, Robert L., Editor. *The Training and Development Handbook: A Guide to Human Resource Development.* McGraw-Hill, 1221 Avenue of the Americas, New York, NY 10020. Phone: (212) 337-5945, (800) 2-MCGRAW. 1987 (3rd Edition). (864 pages, hardcover, $67.50)

5. *Directory of Management Education Programs.* American Management Association, 135 W. 50th Street, New York, NY 10020. Phone: (212) 586-8100; Fax: (212) 903-8168. 1978 (2nd Edition).

    Listing of training programs offered throughout the U.S. in the late 1970's. Compiled by AMA the document covered both academic and non-academic contributors. Although the volume is no longer in print, and there are no plans to republish it, the reference is included for historical completeness.

6. *Employee Training in the Federal Service.* U.S. Office of Personnel Management, 1900 E Street N.W., Washington, DC 20415. Phone: (202) 632-5491. 1982.

    Presents statistics and information on training done for civilian employees of the major Federal agencies. Included here for historical completeness; there is evidence this report will not be published again.

7. Frantzreb, Richard E., J.D., MBA, Editor. *The Training And Development Yearbook 1992/1993.* Prentice Hall, 113 Sylvan Avenue, Englewood Cliffs, NJ 07632. Phone: (201) 592-2000. 1992 (3rd Edition). ISBN 0-13-921891-2. (624 pages, $79.95)

    Although more than three-quarters devoted to reprints of articles, it's the directories that offer a wealth of hard-to-find-in-one-place information for anyone marketing training. You'll find countless opportunities among 48 membership organizations, 100 conferences (most held annually), 45 directories / references and 53 newsletters and periodicals. The 287 train-the-trainer programs and 10 non-membership organizations are also interesting.

8. Gery, Gloria J. *Electronic Performance Support Systems: How and Why to Remake the Workplace Through the Strategic Application of Technology.* Ziff Institute, 25 First Street, Cambridge, MA 02141. Phone: (617) 252-5000; Fax: (617) 252-5113. 1991. ISBN 0-9617968-1-2. (291 pages, paperback, $29.95)

    Elliott Masie, President of Ziff Institute, said that this book was the first to concretely show how currently available technology can dramatically increase workplace productivity in any organization. Since such "just-in-time" performance support will change in how and when training is used, this is an important subject for every trainer.

9. Goad, PH.D.., Tom W. *The Handbook of HRD Technology.* 1992. ISBN 0-685-57056-8. (350 pages, paperback, $39.95)

    Covers technology and the HRD practitioner, computer training, management and support by computer, artificial intelligence and expert systems, video, teleconferencing, audiovisuals other than computers and video, simulations, games and other technology. Also includes material on accelerated learning, creativity, and "just in time" training.

10. Haywood, Peter G., Editor. *A Bibliography of Adult Education: A Source Book.* National Technical Information Services, U.S. Department of Commerce., 5285 Port Royal Road, Springfield, VA 22161. Phone: (703) 487-4650; Fax: (703) 321-8547. 1983. ISBN 0-902031-68-6. ($29.00)

11. *Hope Reports: Training Business Directory.* Hope Reports, Inc., 58 Carverdale Drive, Rochester, NY 14618-4004. Phone: (716) 442-1310; Fax: (716) 442-1725. 1984.. (Volumes 1 and 2, $60.00)

No longer available; Listed for historical interest only.

12. Instructional Systems Association (ISA)., P.O. Box 1196, Sunset Beach, CA 90742. Phone: (714) 846-6012; Fax: (714) 846-3987.

The Instructional Systems Association is a group of those providing packaged training programs of all types. The purpose of ISA is fourfold: 1) To expand primary demand, 2) To gather and disseminate industry statistics, 3) To provide members with business education, and 4) To establish common positions on significant issues. The ISA holds two national meetings a year. Terry Broomfield, Exec. Dir.

13. Klein, Bernard T. *Guide to American Educational Directories.* B. Klein Publications, P.O. Box 8503, Coral Springs, FL 33065. Phone: (305) 752-1708; Fax: (305) 752-2547. 1993. ISBN 0-915344-29-7. (350 pages, $75.00)

"This book places at the reader's fingertips the best and most up-to-date sources of information in all fields of commerce, industry, science and education. It's an invaluable aid to those in advertising, marketing, public relations, educational and general research." - DMA

14. Lusterman, Seymour. *Education in Industry.* The Conference Board, Inc., 845 Third Avenue, New York, NY 10022. Phone: (212) 759-0900; Fax: (212) 980-7014. 1977. (97 pages, $15.00)

A study of the aim, scope and character of employee education and training activities among corporations with 500 or more employees. Most of its data are projected from responses by 610 companies to a lengthy Conference Board questionnaire. It describes industry's use of outside resources for employee development, its own after-hours programs, and the internal programs provided during working hours. Several case illustrations provide a glimpse of the full range of education and training activities in individual companies. Special prices on group orders for classroom use are available. Contact the Information Service Division at the above address.

15. Merriam, Sharan B. and Cunningham, Phyllis

M. *Handbook of Adult and Continuing Education.* Jossey-Bass, Inc. Publishers, 350 Sansome Street, San Francisco, CA 94104. Phone: (415) 433-1767; Fax: (415) 433-0499. 1989. ISBN 1-55542-161-X. (750 pages, $52.00)

16. Nadler, Leonard and Nadler, Zeace, Editors. *The Handbook of Human Resource Development.* John Wiley and Sons, Inc., 605 Third Avenue, New York, NY 10158. Phone: (800) 225-5945, (212) 850-6000; Fax: (212) 850-6088. 1990 (2nd Edition). (813 pages, hardcover, $90.00)

Divided into four main sections: The field, programs, international perspectives and related areas (such as HR management and career development).

17. Ostendorf, Virginia A. *Teletraining & Distance Education Directory.* Virginia A. Ostendorf, Inc., P. O. Box 2896, Littleton, CO 80161-2896. Phone: (303) 797-3131; Fax: (303) 797-3524. 1992 (4th Edition). (394 Pages, $100)

"This directory lists 130 vendors who offer products and services for those who teach at a distance. Also included are hundreds of user organizations -- associations, corporations, hospitals, colleges/universities, and public schools that teach at a distance." (Training & Development Yearbook)

18. Schrello, Don M. *The Seminar Market.* Schrello Enterprises, P.O. Box 1610, Long Beach, CA 90801-1610. Phone: (800) EN-ROLL-X, (310) 493-0200; Fax: (310) 493-0962. 1980. ISBN 0-935823-01-8. (125 pages, 17 illustrations and tables, 42 references, $19.95 softcover.)

This book is now out of print, but is included for historical completeness. It presented market research findings and analyses of the multibillion dollar business of open-to-the-public short courses and business seminars in North America as they were seen in 1980. Integrates prior published reports with the author's own original research to estimate the industry's size, growth rate and factors needed for success. The book also included an appendix listing more than 1,200 firms known to be supplying open seminars at the time.

19. *Stern's SourceFinder™: Human Resource Management.* Michael Daniels Publishers, P. O. Box 3233, Culver City, CA 90231-3233. Phone: (310) 838-4437; Fax: (310) 838-2344. 1991. (512, $169.95)

2,700 entries including books, directories, journals, databases, information services, associations and other resources. Indexes by subject, author, title (among others) are provided.

20. Stolovitch, Harold D. and Keeps, Erica J., Editors. *The Handbook of Human Performance Technology: A Comprehensive Guide for Analyzing and Solving Performance Problems in Organizations.* Jossey-Bass, Inc. Publishers, 350 Sansome Street, San Francisco, CA 94104. Phone: (415) 433-1767; Fax: (415) 433-0499. 1992. ISBN 1-55542-385-X. (863 pages, hardcover, $75.00)

Sponsored by The National Society for Performance and Instruction (NSPI), the book contains 44 original chapters on HUMAN PERFORMANCE TECHNOLOGY theory and practice by some of the leading professionals in the field.

21. Thomson, Frances Coombs, Editor. *New York Times Guide to Continuing Education in America.* Quadrangle Books, Inc., 330 Madison Avenue, New York, NY 10017. 1972.

The first book to describe the opportunities available to adults at accredited educational institutions in the U.S. Recommended by the College Entrance Exam Board, along with the New York Times. Included here for historical completeness.

22. Tracey, William R. *The Human Resources Glossary: A Complete Desk Reference for HR Professionals.* AMACOM Publishing Co., P.O. Box 1026, Saranac Lake, NY 12983-1026. Phone: (800) 262-9699, (518) 891-5510; Fax: (518) 891-3653. 1991. ISBN 0-8144-5011-3. (416 pages, $49.95)

Contains more than 3,000 sometimes lengthy and very complete definitions, acronyms and abbreviations that apply to HR.

23. Training Media Association (TMA)., 198 Thomas Johnson Drive, Suite 206, Frederick, MD 21702. Phone: (301) 662-4268; Fax: (301) 695-7627.

A trade association of producers and distributors of training media concerned with copyright protection. The association offers meetings and educational seminars to member organizations and opportunities to showcase member products. The annual meeting is held in conjunction with the American Society for Training and Development's yearly conference and exposition. Robert A. Gehrke, Exec. Officer.

24. *Training: The Human Side of Business.* Lakewood Publications, 50 South Ninth, Minneapolis, MN 55402. Phone: (800) 328-4329, (612) 333-0471; Fax: (612) 333-6526. (Published monthly). ($36/year.)

Information on all aspects of human resource development, mainly in large organizations. The October issue is devoted to a status report and overview of the U.S. Training industry, based on a comprehensive survey conducted each year by Lakewood Research. It's one of the "don't miss" resources in the field.

25. Willis, Barry. *Distance Education: A Practical Guide. 1993.*

A how-to book aimed at those responsible for distance education programs, primarily in academic settings. Includes chapters on significant research findings, how to prepare or use faculty, materials, media and instructional strategies, and what the future might hold. (Adapted from a review by Leslie Moller in Performance & Instruction, May/June 1993)

26. Woodbury, Marda. *A Guide to Sources of Educational Information.* Information Resources Press, 2100 M Street, N.W., Washington, DC 20036. 1976.

2. - SELECTING AND EVALUATING PRODUCTS AND MARKETS

1. *The 1992 Directory of Business Information Resources.* Grey House Publishing, Pocketknife Square, Lakeville, CT 06039. Phone: (203) 435-0868; Fax: (203) 435-0867. 1992 (1st Edition). ISBN 0-939300-15-X. (674 pages, $135 Hardcover, $125 Softcover.)

2. Boston Consulting Group. *Perspectives on Experience.* Boston Consulting Group, Exchange Place, Boston, MA 02109. Phone: (617) 973-1200; Fax: (617) 973-1399. 1968. ISBN 0-7837-0000-8. ($29.50)

The original exposition of the Boston Consulting Group's now familiar observations on the relationships between price, cost and volume. It's clearly stated and well-documented with data on a number of industries. University Microfilms, Intl., P.O. Box 1467, Ann Arbor, MI 48106 will furnish copies of the book for $27.30. Contact them at 313/761-4700; the order number is #AU0039.

3. Breen, George and Blankenship, A. B. *Do-It-Yourself Marketing Research.* McGraw-Hill, 1221 Avenue of the Americas, New York, NY

10020. Phone: (212) 337-5945, (800) 2-MC-GRAW. 1991 (3rd Edition). ISBN 0-07-007451-8. (272 pages, paperback, $39.95)

A guide detailing market research methods and tactics, including how to collect and tabulate data, determine your market's size and income level, and what pitfalls to avoid.

4. *Encyclopedia of Business Information Sources.* Gale Research Inc., 835 Penobscot Bldg., Detroit, MI 48226-4094. Phone: (800) 877-GALE, (313) 961-2242; Fax: (313) 961-6083, (313) 961-6815. 1992 (9th Edition). ($245.00)

Provides sources of the latest facts and figures on over 1,000 information sources on more than 1,000 business-oriented topics. For each it provides the important live, print and electronic information sources like directories, periodicals, organizations, handbooks, on-line data bases, bibliographies, etc.

5. Ferber, Robert, Editor. *Handbook of Marketing Research.* McGraw-Hill, 1221 Avenue of the Americas, New York, NY 10020. Phone: (212) 337-5945, (800) 2-MCGRAW. 1974. ISBN 0-07-020462-4. (1,344 pages, $94.50)

"The only book of its kind with contributions by dozens of top authorities in every aspect of marketing research. Invaluable for marketing and management executives in business or government ... an ideal reference source for current methods of marketing research as applied to a wide variety of problem areas." - HCI

6. Findex staff. *FINDEX 1991: The Worldwide Directory of Market Research Reports, Studies and Surveys.* Cambridge Information Group, 7200 Wisconsin Avenue, Bethesda, MD 20814. Phone: (800) 843-7751, (301) 961-6700; Fax: (301) 961-6720. 1991 (6th Edition). ISBN 0-942189-03-5. (Over 900 pages, 8-1/4"x10-3/4" softcover, $325.00)

A directory of over 13,500 market research reports, studies and surveys in over 2,000 topics. Each listing gives the official title and a 50-100 word summary of the research. Includes a mid-year supplement, and unlimited toll-free call-in Subscriber Hotline service.

7. Levitt, Theodore. *"Marketing Myopia II."* Harvard Business Review, P 26-39. Harvard Business School Publications, Boston, MA 02163. Phone: (800) 545-7685, (617) 495-6192; Fax: (617) 495-6985. September-October, 1975.

This generally acknowledged "classic" was first printed in the Harvard Business Review July-August, 1960 issue. Here it's reprinted with the author's comments 15 years later. There is little doubt that the business reader will find the article as valuable today as it was 34 years ago.

8. Porter, Michael E. *Competitive Strategy: Techniques For Analyzing Industries and Competitors.* The Free Press, 866 Third Avenue, New York, NY 10022. Phone: (212) 605-9364. 1980. ISBN 0-02-925360-8. ($32.95)

Provides step-by-step techniques for analyzing industries and competitors. Enables managers to anticipate and prepare for -- rather than simply react to -- sudden competitor moves, new entries into their business, and shifts in industry structure, as well as to take forceful positive action to improve a company's position through tested competitive strategies.

9. Robert, Michel. *The Strategist CEO.* Greenwood Publications Group, Inc., 88 Post Road West - P.O. Box 5007, Westport, CT 06881. Phone: (800) 225-5800, (203) 226-3571; Fax: (203) 222-1502. 1988. ISBN 0-89930-268-8. (140 Pages)

"Is your company product-driven or customer-driven? Your answer, Robert believes, should determine how you make strategies and allocate resources."-INC.

10. Schrello, Don M. *Improving Your Competitive Position.* Schrello Direct Marketing, P.O. Box 1610, Long Beach, CA 90801-1610. Phone: (800) ENROLL-X, (310) 493-0200; Fax: (310) 493-0962. 1976. ($4.95)

Even though you may know who your competitors are, you probably don't fully analyze what you already know about them and their products. Such analysis can frequently reveal how your customers really make their buying decisions. This booklet's checklists, worksheets, and step-by-step instructions show you how to compare yourself to the competition, spot your competitive strengths and weaknesses, and develop a wining product/market strategy.

11. Schrello, Don M. *Product Evaluation and Planning Seminar.* Schrello Direct Marketing, P.O. Box 1610, Long Beach, CA 90801-1610. Phone: (800) ENROLL-X, (310) 493-0200; Fax: (310) 493-0962. ($895/three day seminar.)

Don Schrello's unique process for making top-notch product and marketing decisions is as much of a "winner" today as it was when it was developed over 25 years ago. The basic questions of "Is It Real?", "Can We Win?", and "Is It Worth It?", teamed with a powerful step-by-step way to get the best information and objectively evaluate it, have made this program the way decisions are made in thousands of the world's best-managed companies.

12. *The Sourcebook of Demographics and Buying Power for Every ZIP Code in the U.S.A.* CACI, 1815 N. Fort Myer Drive, Arlington, VA 22209. Phone: (800) 336-6600. 1984.

($795.00)

1984 and 1989 forecasts of key demographic characteristics, including distributions of family and household income, age, race, population and *household counts, buying power indexes for major consumer products and services, business statistics by ZIP Codes, 1980 and 1970 key census characteristics, and rankings of national indexes by key variables.*

3. - SALES AND MARKETING

1. Buell, Victor P. *Handbook of Modern Marketing.* McGraw-Hill, 1221 Avenue of the Americas, New York, NY 10020. Phone: (212) 337-5945, (800) 2-MCGRAW. 1986 (2nd Edition). ISBN 0-07-008854-3. (1,296 pages, $89.95)

An ideal reference guide on marketing. Contains extensive bibliographies and practical descriptions on every facet of the field.

2. Chase, Cochrane and Barasch, Kenneth L. *Marketing Problem Solver.* Chilton Book Company, 201 King of Prussia Road, Radnor, PA 19089. Phone: (800) 695-1214, (215) 964-4000; Fax: (215) 964-4745. 1988 (3rd Edition). (512 pages)

"For virtually any marketing, advertising and public relations task, this book directs you through each state of development on a step-by-step basis. It outlines responsibilities, schedules, and methods of measuring results, complete with procedures, checklists, reference sources, fill-in forms, facts, and examples. A very practical book, it also covers pricing, research, trade shows, inquiry handling and more." - DMA

3. *Dartnell's 27th Sales Force Compensation Survey.* Dartnell Corporation, 4660 N. Ravenswood Avenue, Chicago, IL 60640. Phone: (312) 561-4000, (800) 621-5463; Fax: (312) 561-3801. (300 pages, 8-1/2" x 11" 3-ring binder, $199.00)

4. Hopkins, Claude C. *My Life In Advertising & Scientific Advertising.* NTC Business Books, 4255 W. Touhy Avenue, Lincolnwood, IL 60646-1975. Phone: (708) 679-5500, (800) 323-4900; Fax: (708) 679-2494. 1993. ISBN 0-8442-3101-0. (318 Pages, $11.95)

(See Chapter 8)

5. Kotler, Philip. *Marketing Management: Analysis, Planning, Implementation and Control.* Prentice Hall, 113 Sylvan Avenue, Englewood Cliffs, NJ 07632. Phone: (201) 592-2000. 1990 (7th Edition). ISBN 0-13-552480-6. (784 pages, $52.00)

"A textbook on the elements of marketing and how to incorporate them into strategic planning.

Reference Software International's Emery, who also teaches marketing at San Francisco State University, says it's the best of the 50 books on the topic he's read."-INC.

6. Lant, Dr. Jeffrey L. *Money Making Marketing: Finding The People Who Need What You're Selling And Making Sure They Buy It.* Jeffrey Lant Associates, Inc., 50 Follen Street - Suite 507, Cambridge, MA 02138. Phone: (617) 547-6372; Fax: (617) 547-0061. (2nd, Revised edition). ISBN 0-940374-19-6. (285 Pages, $35.00)

(See Chapter 8)

7. *Marketing Times.* Sales and Marketing Executives International, 330 W. 42nd Street, New York, NY 10036. Phone: (212) 239-1919. (Published bimonthly). ($10/year.)

Covers management, marketing research, product development, pricing, distribution, promotion and advertising.

8. Moynahan, John K. Editor. *The Sales Compensation Handbook.* AMACOM Publishing Co., P.O. Box 1026, Saranac Lake, NY 12983-1026. Phone: (800) 262-9699, (518) 891-5510; Fax: (518) 891-3653. ($69.95)

A compendium of practical works from 14 Towers-Perrin compensation experts. Provides guidance, examples and insights on all the basics including goal setting, cash and non-cash incentives, base salaries, designing a compensation plan and tying incentives to customer service.

9. Ogilvy, David. *Confessions Of An Advertising Man.* Atheneum Publications, 866 Third Avenue, New York, NY 10022. Phone: (212) 702-2000; Fax: (212) 605-3099. 1989. ISBN 0-689-70800-9. (180 pages, paperback, $9.95)

(See Chapter 8)

10. Ogilvy, David. *Ogilvy on Advertising.* Crown Publishing Group, 201 East 50th Street, New York, NY 10022. Phone: (212) 572-6117; Fax: (212) 572-6192. 1983. (224 pages, $24.95)

(See Chapter 8)

11. *Portfolio of Sales and Marketing Plans.* Bill

Communications, Inc., 355 Park Avenue South, New York, NY 10010. Phone: (212) 592-6400; Fax: (212) 592-6409. (Published annually). ($9.95)

Tactics in the management of your sales force, time and territory, sales training and recruiting, market research, advertising and the computer in marketing.

12. Posch, Robert J., Jr. *What Every Manager Needs to Know About Marketing and the Law.* McGraw-Hill, 1221 Avenue of the Americas, New York, NY 10020. Phone: (212) 337-5945, (800) 2-MCGRAW. 1984. ($16.95)

A guide to marketing laws to help you avoid the dollar loss of fines and adverse publicity, save enormous amounts of time in research and legal consultation, establish a profit center, and forecast the regulatory environment.

13. Ries, Al and Trout, Jack. *Bottom-Up Marketing.* McGraw-Hill, 1221 Avenue of the Americas, New York, NY 10020. Phone: (212) 337-5945, (800) 2-MCGRAW. 1989. ISBN 0-07-052733-4. (240 pages, $22.95)

(See Chapter 8)

14. Ries, Al and Trout, Jack. *Marketing Warfare.* McGraw-Hill, 1221 Avenue of the Americas, New York, NY 10020. Phone: (212) 337-5945, (800) 2-MCGRAW. 1986. ISBN 0-07-052730-X. (224 pages, $23.95)

(See Chapter 8)

15. Ries, Al and Trout, Jack. *Positioning: The Battle for Your Mind.* McGraw-Hill, 1221 Avenue of the Americas, New York, NY 10020. Phone: (212) 337-5945, (800) 2-MCGRAW. 1989. ISBN 0-07-065265-1. ($23.95)

(See Chapter 8)

16. *Sales and Marketing Management.* Bill Communications, Inc., 355 Park Avenue South, New York, NY 10010. Phone: (212) 592-6400; Fax: (212) 592-6409. (Published 16 times a year). ($38/year.)

17. Sales Executive Club of New York. *Sales Forecasting: Timesaving and Profit-Making Strategies That Work.* Scott Foresman & Company, 1900 East Lake Avenue, Glenview, IL 60025. Phone: (800) 782-2665, (708) 729-3000; Fax: (708) 657-3999. 1984. (192 pages, $24.95)

Designed to be a working manual for every sales and marketing manager, this non-technical book makes accurate forecasting easy. It clearly describes the most popular sales forecasting techniques.

18. Schlom, Charles C. *The Complete Guide to Sales Territory Planning & Management.* Dartnell Corporation, 4660 N. Ravenswood Avenue, Chicago, IL 60640. Phone: (312) 561-4000, (800) 621-5463; Fax: (312) 561-3801. (214 pages, 8-1/2" x 11" 3-ring binder, $91.50)

19. Shornberger, Richard J. *Building a Chain of Customers.* The Free Press, 866 Third Avenue, New York, NY 10022. Phone: (212) 605-9364. 1990. ISBN 0-02-927991-7. ($32.95)

"Outlining the relationship between suppliers and vendors, the book describes how everyone in an organization can be part of customer service, by redefining who in fact, customers are."-INC

20. *Survey of Selling Costs.* Bill Communications, Inc., 355 Park Avenue South, New York, NY 10010. Phone: (212) 592-6400; Fax: (212) 592-6409. (Published annually). ($35.00)

Compilation of useful selling facts, including a "selling cost index" and "cost per sales call" estimates for the leading markets in the United States. Highlights those markets with the highest and lowest selling costs and outlines the process for creating a sales cost budget.

4. - PERSONAL SELLING SKILLS

1. ASTD Information Center. *Sales Training Resources in Print.* American Society for Training and Development, 1640 King Street - P. O. Box 1443, Alexandria, VA 22313-2043. Phone: (703) 683-8129, (703) 683-8100; Fax: (703) 683-8103. 1993. ($12.00 plus shipping.)

A bibliography covering 90 topics pertaining directly to sales training, some even for specific industries. Most entries have a brief description and how-to-order information, in addition to the usual bibliographic data. All references have been published since 1986.

2. Allesandra, Anthony J. *Non-Manipultive Selling.* Prentice Hall, 113 Sylvan Avenue, Englewood Cliffs, NJ 07632. Phone: (201) 592-2000. 1987 (2nd Edition). ISBN 0-13-623307-4. (Paperback, $12.95)

3. Bodi, Madeline, Dawson, Keith and McInerney, Lori. *The Dictionary of Sales and Marketing Technology and Terms.* Telecom Library, Inc., 12 West 21st Street - 10th Floor, New

York, NY 10010. Phone: (800) LIBRARY, (212) 691-8215; Fax: (212) 691-1190. 1992. (116 pages, softcover, $15.95)

4. Boyan, Lee. *Successful Cold Call Selling.* AMACOM Publishing Co., P.O. Box 1026, Saranac Lake, NY 12983-1026. Phone: (800) 262-9699, (518) 891-5510; Fax: (518) 891-3653. 1989 (2nd Edition). ISBN 0-8144-7718-6. (225 pages, paperback, $15.95)

5. Carlsen, Robert D. *Handbook and Portfolio of Successful Sales Proposals.* Prentice Hall, 113 Sylvan Avenue, Englewood Cliffs, NJ 07632. Phone: (201) 592-2000.

6. Carnegie, Dale. *How To Win Friends & Influence People.* Simon & Schuster, 1230 Avenue of the Americas, New York, NY 10020. Phone: (800) 223-2336, (212) 698-7000; Fax: (212) 698-7007. 1964.

Originally published in 1936, this valuable classic is now said to have sold more than 15 million copies. A "must" for every successful business person. Try ordering ISBN 0-671-42517-X, if you can't find a copy of the original in a used book store.

7. Fisher, Roger and Ury, William L. *Getting to Yes: Negotiating Agreement Without Giving In.* Viking Penguin Books, 375 Hudson Street, New York, NY 10014-3657. Phone: (800) 331-4624, (212) 366-2000. 1991. ISBN 0-14-015735-2. (208 pages, Paperback, $10.00)

A clear, common sense method of negotiating, based on a few powerful guidelines. Readers learn to "say yes" no matter what the other side says or does.

8. Girard, Joe and Brown, Stanley H. *How to Sell Anything to Anybody.* Warner Books, Inc., 1271 Avenue of the Americas, New York, NY 10020. Phone: (212) 522-7200; Fax: (212) 522-7991. 1986. ISBN 0-446-38532-8. (240 pages, $8.95)

9. Girard, Joe. *How to Sell Yourself.* Warner Books, Inc., 1271 Avenue of the Americas, New York, NY 10020. Phone: (212) 522-7200; Fax: (212) 522-7991. 1988. ISBN 0-446-38501-8. ($11.99)

10. Hanan, Mack, Cribbin, James and Donis, Jack. *Systems Selling Strategies: How to Justify Premium Prices for Commodity Products.* AMACOM Publishing Co., P.O. Box 1026, Saranac Lake, NY 12983-1026. Phone: (800) 262-9699, (518) 891-5510; Fax: (518) 891-3653. 1978. ISBN 0-317-10206-0. ($14.95)

This book introduces strategies for selling products that are price sensitive by connecting the product to systems of products and services, therefore creating a new customer benefit. It is not only valuable to salespeople, but will also

help anyone who is selling an idea rather than a product. This is a book on how to sell to customer needs.

11. Hanan, Mack. *Consultative Selling: The Hanan Formula for High-Margin Sales at High Levels.* AMACOM Publishing Co., P.O. Box 1026, Saranac Lake, NY 12983-1026. Phone: (800) 262-9699, (518) 891-5510; Fax: (518) 891-3653. 1985 (4th Edition). ISBN 0-317-26906-2. ($22.95)

12. Hanan, Mack. *Key Accounts Selling.* AMACOM Publishing Co., P.O. Box 1026, Saranac Lake, NY 12983-1026. Phone: (800) 262-9699, (518) 891-5510; Fax: (518) 891-3653. 1989 (2nd Edition). ISBN 0-8144-5985-4. (226 pages, $18.95)

Includes guidance on how to target customers with the highest growth potential, getting in at the top, working with them as a partner, using databases to find high-margin opportunities, devising account plans and more.

13. Healy, James T. *Winning the High Technology Sales Game.* Reston Publishing Company, Englewood Cliffs, NJ 1985. ISBN 0-8359-8700-0. ($33.95)

The high-tech selling game is one of strategy, maneuvers and patterns. When you sell, you must be able to discern the business and political patterns of customers and the strategic and tactical patterns of competitors -- then control the selling situation.

14. Jandt, Fred E. *Win-Win Negotiating: Turning Conflict Into Agreement.* John Wiley and Sons, Inc., 605 Third Avenue, New York, NY 10158. Phone: (800) 225-5945, (212) 850-6000; Fax: (212) 850-6088. 1987. ISBN 0-471-85877-3. (300 pages, $14.95)

A professional negotiator and mediator sets out to demonstrate how positive results can emerge from a conflict successfully resolved.

15. Johnson, Spencer and Wilson, Larry. *The One Minute Salesperson.* William Morrow and Company, 1350 Avenue of the Americas, New York, NY 10019. Phone: (800) 843-9389, (212) 261-6500; Fax: (212) 261-6595. 1984. ISBN 0-688-03946-4. (112 pages, $16.95)

16. Karrass, Gary. *Negotiate to Close: How to Make More Successful Deals.* Simon & Schuster, 1230 Avenue of the Americas, New York, NY 10020. Phone: (800) 223-2336, (212) 698-7000; Fax: (212) 698-7007. 1985. ISBN 0-671-55483-2. ($16.95 (including tape).)

17. Kuswa, Webster. *The Sales Rep's Letter Book.* AMACOM Publishing Co., P.O. Box 1026, Saranac Lake, NY 12983-1026. Phone: (800)

262-9699, (518) 891-5510; Fax: (518) 891-3653. 1984.   ISBN 0-8144-7618-X.   (224 pages, $12.95)

18. LeRoux, Paul. *Selling To A Group: Presentation Strategies*. HarperCollins Publishers, 10 E. 53rd Street, New York, NY 10022.   Phone: (800) 242-7737, (212) 207-7000; Fax: (212) 207-7617. 1984. ISBN 0-06-463598-8. (176 pages, $10.00)

Selling to a group involves a different set of problems and opportunities from giving speeches. This book presents solid techniques in convincing, persuading, selling your ideas, products, services or point of view to a group.

19. Mandino, Og. *The Greatest Salesman in the World*. Bantam Books, 666 Fifth Avenue, New York, NY 10103. Phone: (800) 223-6834, (212) 765-6500; Fax: (212) 765-3869. 1985. (112 pages, $6.95)

20. Miller, Robert B. and Heiman, Stephen E. *Conceptual Selling*. Warner Books, Inc., 1271 Avenue of the Americas, New York, NY 10020. Phone: (212) 522-7200; Fax: (212) 522-7991. 1989. ISBN 0-446-38906-4. (320 pages, paperback, $12.95)

(See Chapter 4)

21. Miller, Robert B., Heiman, Stephen E. with Tad Tuleja. *Strategic Selling: The Unique Sales System Proven Successful by America's Best Companies*. William Morrow and Company, 1350 Avenue of the Americas, New York, NY 10019. Phone: (800) 843-9389, (212) 261-6500; Fax: (212) 261-6595. 1985. ISBN 0-688-04313-5. (352 pages, $19.95)

(See Chapter 4)

22. Moine, Donald J. and Herd, John H. Modern *Persuasion Strategies: The Hidden Advantage in Selling*. Prentice Hall, 113 Sylvan Avenue, Englewood Cliffs, NJ 07632. Phone: (201) 592-2000. 1990. ISBN 0-13-594185-7. (204 pages, paperback, $12.95)

These dynamic, customer-focused selling strategies enable you to actually "read" the emotional and mental makeup of a sales prospect -- then build a customized sales presentation the prospect will find totally irresistible.

23. Molloy, John T. *John T. Molloy's New Dress for Success*. Warner Books, Inc., 1271 Avenue of the Americas, New York, NY 10020. Phone: (212) 522-7200; Fax: (212) 522-7991. 1988. ISBN 0-446-38552-2. (Paperback, $10.95)

24. Nierenberg, Gerard I. *Fundamentals of Negoti-* *ating*.   HarperCollins Publishers, 10 E. 53rd Street, New York, NY 10022.   Phone: (800) 242-7737, (212) 207-7000; Fax: (212) 207-7617. 1987. ISBN 0-06-097120-7. (320 pages, paperback, $10.00)

25. Patton, Forrest H. *The Psychology of Closing Sales*. Prentice Hall, 113 Sylvan Avenue, Englewood Cliffs, NJ 07632. Phone: (201) 592-2000. 1990. ISBN 0-13-735663-3. (192 pages, paperback, $8.95)

26. Rackham, Neil. *S.P.I.N. Selling*. McGraw-Hill, 1221 Avenue of the Americas, New York, NY 10020. Phone: (212) 337-5945, (800) 2-MC-GRAW. 1988. ISBN 0-07-051113-6. (224 pages, $22.95)

(See Chapter 4)

27. Rackham, Neil. *Major Account Sales Strategy*. McGraw-Hill, 1221 Avenue of the Americas, New York, NY 10020. Phone: (212) 337-5945, (800) 2-MCGRAW. 1989. ISBN 0-07-051114-4. ($22.95)

(See Chapter 4)

28. Rackham, Neil.   *Managing Major Sales*. HarperCollins Publishers, 10 E. 53rd Street, New York, NY 10022. Phone: (800) 242-7737, (212) 207-7000; Fax: (212) 207-7617. 1991. ($27.95)

(See Chapter 4)

29. Wilson, Larry and Wilson, Hersch. *Changing The Game: The New Way To Sell*. Simon & Schuster, 1230 Avenue of the Americas, New York, NY 10020. Phone: (800) 223-2336, (212) 698-7000; Fax: (212) 698-7007. 1988. ISBN 0-671-67135-9. (286 pages, paperback, $9.95)

(See Chapter 4)

30. Zunin, Leonard MD with Zunin, Natalie. *Contact: The First Four Minutes*. Ballantine Books, 201 E. 50th Street, New York, NY 10022. Phone: (800) 638-6460, (212) 751-2600; Fax: (212) 572-4912. 1986. ISBN 0-345-33692-5. (Paperback, $4.95)

What two people communicate during their first four minutes of contact is so crucial that it will determine whether strangers will remain strangers or become acquaintances, friends, etc. How those first few minutes turn out hinge on how each person evaluates themselves and how they evaluate the other person; on the assumptions and preconceptions each person brings to the first minutes of contact; and on the circumstances under which the people meet.

5. - SALES AND MARKETING PLANNING

1. Schrello, Don M. *The Complete Marketing Handbook for Consultants.* Schrello Direct Marketing, P.O. Box 1610, Long Beach, CA 90801-1610. Phone: (800) ENROLL-X, (310) 493-0200; Fax: (310) 493-0962. 1990. ISBN 0-88390-247-8. (590 pages, boxed, two-volume, looseleaf binding, $149.00)

   Furnishes consultants and other time-billing professionals everything they need in order to select, plan and successfully execute the right marketing program for them. Its 16 chapters and 3 appendices contain 140 tables, graphs, checklists and charts, and cover topics such as choosing the right sales and marketing strategy, personal selling, managing the sales activities of others, getting the most from seminars, conferences and trade shows, promoting and conducting "showcases," staying in touch with your clients and prospects, writing and promoting your own book and much more. (Note: This was originally

   published by University Associates, but is now distributed by the author.)

2. Schrello, Don M. *How To Market Training Programs, Seminars and Instructional Materials.* Schrello Direct Marketing, P.O. Box 1610, Long Beach, CA 90801-1610. Phone: (800) ENROLL-X, (310) 493-0200; Fax: (310) 493-0962. 1990 (3rd Edition). ISBN 0-935823-06-9. (3-ring binder, 15 sections, 364 pages, 38 illustrations, 45 tables, 18 worksheets, 350 references, $169.95)

   Contains hundreds of "insider" tips on selecting marketable training products and services, choosing the right sales method, developing a winning marketing plan, estimating realistic costs and schedules, getting the best mailing lists, creating compelling advertising, conducting open seminars, taking and processing orders, starting and maintaining your own customer database, testing, and much more.

6. - SEMINARS, WORKSHOPS, CONFERENCES AND OTHER EVENTS

1. *ACT National Registry Service.* American College Testing Program, P.O. Box 1008, Iowa City, IA 52243. Phone: (319) 337-1353.

   Provides record maintenance services for associations and technical societies as required by the "Council on the CEU. (The maintenance of permanent records of CEU awarded is the responsibility of the institution or organization sponsoring the program. If you wish to purchase this service, contact the firm above.)

2. Brodsky, Bart and Geis, Janet. *The Teaching Marketplace: Make Money with Free-lance Teaching, Corporate Training and on the Lecture Circuit.* Community Resource Institute, P.O. Box 7880, Berkeley, CA 94709. Phone: (510) 526-7190. 1991. ISBN 0-9628454-0-6. (176 pages, paperback, $14.95)

3. *The Continuing Education Unit Criteria and Guidelines.* Council on the Continuing Education Unit (CCEU)., 1101 Connecticut Avenue N.W., Suite 700, Washington, DC 20036. Phone: (202) 857-1122. 1979. ($5.00)

   The CEU has been designed as a uniform unit of measurement to facilitate the accumulation and exchange of information for individual participation in noncredit continuing education. This

   publication outlines procedures for determining the number of CEU to be awarded for each activity, for establishing and maintaining the required permanent records for CEU awarded, and for the development and implementation of evaluation methods for noncredit continuing education activities. Orders for copies of this publication should be sent to the above address. Price breaks are available for copies of this publication ordered in quantity.

4. Dobmeyer, Edward. *Producing Successful Practical Conferences.* The Learning Resources Network (LERN), P.O. Box 1448, 1550 Hayes Drive, Manhattan, KS 66502. Phone: (800) 678-LERN, (913) 539-5376; Fax: (913) 539-7766. ($19.95)

   Deals with the how-to's of managing the details of conferences, based on the author's experience planning and managing conferences. Contains checklists, sample letters and forms.

5. Dodson, Dorian. *How to Put on a Great Conference: A Straightforward, Friendly and Practical Guide.* Adolfo Street Publications, P.O. Box 490, Santa Fe, NM 87054. Phone: (505) 473-4433. 1992. ISBN 0-9632445-0-7. (120 pages, paperback, $10.95)

Designed for the community-minded volunteer or staff person who has been given the job of designing and putting on a conference or workshop on a limited or nonexistent budget. Written in a humorous style.

6. Elliot, Ralph D. *Marketing In-House Seminars.* The Learning Resources Network (LERN), P.O. Box 1448, 1550 Hayes Drive, Manhattan, KS 66502. Phone: (800) 678-LERN, (913) 539-5376; Fax: (913) 539-7766. ISBN 0-914951-17-3. (131 pages, $39.95)

Covers selling techniques, different in-house positioning strategies, the best selling technique to use and how to generate inquiries and leads.

7. Finkel, Coleman Lee. *The Total Immersion Learning Environment: Its Critical Impact On Meeting Success.* Conference Center Development Corporation, 205 E. 59th Street - Suite 6-F, New York, NY 10128. Phone: (212) 722-6005. 1982. (120 pages, hardcover, $23.95)

(See Chapter 6)

8. Finkel, Coleman. *How to Plan Meetings Like a Professional.* Bill Communications, Inc., 355 Park Avenue South, New York, NY 10010. Phone: (212) 592-6400; Fax: (212) 592-6409. 1983. ($12.95)

(See Chapter 6)

9. Gilley, Jerry W. and Eggland, Steven A. *Marketing HRD Within Organizations: Enhancing the Visibility, Effectiveness, and Credibility of Programs.* Jossey-Bass, Inc. Publishers, 350 Sansome Street, San Francisco, CA 94104. Phone: (415) 433-1767; Fax: (415) 433-0499. 1992. ISBN 1-55542-402-3. (262 pages, $32.95)

10. Hart, Lois B. and Schleicher, Gordon. *A Conference & Workshop Planner's Manual.* AMACOM Publishing Co., P.O. Box 1026, Saranac Lake, NY 12983-1026. Phone: (800) 262-9699, (518) 891-5510; Fax: (518) 891-3653. 1979. ISBN 0-911777-12-1. (150 pages, paperback, $25.95)

Identifies the tasks involved in planning both large and small meetings with suggestions for forms, charts and checklists to use while coordinating the events.

11. Heenan, Cathy and Cooper, Susan. *Preparing, Designing and Leading Workshops: A Humanistic Approach.* Von Nostrand Reinhold Company, 135 W. 50th Street, New York, NY 10020. 1979.

12. Holtz, Herman R. *Marketing with Seminars and Newsletters.* Greenwood Publications Group, Inc., 88 Post Road West - P.O. Box 5007, Westport, CT 06881. Phone: (800) 225-5800, (203) 226-3571; Fax: (203) 222-1502. 1986. ISBN 0-89930-099-5. (243 pages, $55.00)

13. International Association of Convention and Visitors Bureaus (IACVB), Bloomington Road, P.O. Box 758, Champaign, IL 61824-0758. Phone: (217) 359-8881; Fax: (217) 359-0965.

In most locations, the IACVB can put you in touch with a member bureau. They, in turn, can be a valuable source of information for both seminar and conference sponsors and participants, and can also be a source of temporary personnel in the area.

14. Karasik, Paul. *How To Make It Big In The Seminar Business.* McGraw-Hill, 1221 Avenue of the Americas, New York, NY 10020. Phone: (212) 337-5945, (800) 2-MCGRAW. 1992. ISBN 0-07-033185-5. (256 Pages, $19.95)

(See Chapter 6)

15. Kemp, Jerrold. *The Instructional Design Process.* HarperCollins Publishers, 10 E. 53rd Street, New York, NY 10022. Phone: (800) 242-7737, (212) 207-7000; Fax: (212) 207-7617. 1990. ISBN 0-06-043589-5. (310 pages, paperback, $21.00)

16. Kidd, J.R. *How Adults Learn.* Association Press, 291 Broadway, New York, NY 10017. 1988. ISBN 0-8428-2211-9. (324 pages)

17. LERN staff. *Pricing Seminars and Conferences.* The Learning Resources Network (LERN), P.O. Box 1448, 1550 Hayes Drive, Manhattan, KS 66502. Phone: (800) 678-LERN, (913) 539-5376; Fax: (913) 539-7766. ($19.95)

18. Lant, Dr. Jeffrey L. *Money Talks: The Complete Guide to Creating a Profitable Workshop or Seminar in Any Field.* Jeffrey Lant Associates, Inc., 50 Follen Street - Suite 507, Cambridge, MA 02138. Phone: (617) 547-6372; Fax: (617) 547-0061. 1992 (2nd Edition). (308 pages, 8-1/2" x 11" format, $35.00)

(See Chapter 6)

19. Levant, J. and Cleeton, D. *Marketing the Training Function.* GP Publishing, Inc., 5727 S. Lewis Avenue - No. 727, Tulsa, OK 74105-7148. Phone: (918) 749-8642. 1993. ISBN 0-7494-0934-7. (144 pages, paperback, $14.95)

20. Marketing Federation, 109 58th Avenue, St. Petersburg, FL 33706. Phone: (813) 367-5629; Fax: (813) 367-6545.

Conducts various courses on the marketing of seminars and conferences. Holds an annual conference, usually in June, featuring several leading authorities on direct marketing, promo-

tional strategies, list maintenance and computer applications, advertising means, etc. Home base for Anver S. Suleiman, who is well-known in the meeting planning and continuing education communities as a frequent writer and speaker on the subject of promoting conferences and seminars.

21. Materka, Pat R. *Workshops and Seminars: Planning, Promoting, Producing, Profiting.* Prentice Hall, 113 Sylvan Avenue, Englewood Cliffs, NJ 07632. Phone: (201) 592-2000. 1986. ISBN 0-13-967787-9. (224, 10.95)

22. *Medical Meetings: The International Guide For Healthcare Meeting Planners.* The Laux Company, Inc., 63 Great Road, Maynard, MA 01754. Phone: (508) 897-5552; Fax: (508) 897-6824. (Published bimonthly, with extra editions in Spring and Fall). ($48/year.)

(See Chapter 12)

23. *Meeting News.* Gralla Publications, 1515 Broadway, New York, NY 10036. Phone: (212) 869-1300. (Published monthly). ($36/year, controlled circulation also available.)

Reports the news, trends, ideas, methods and specific locations that affect the work of the meeting planner.

24. *Meetings and Conventions.* Ziff-Davis Publishing Co., Inc., One Park Avenue, New York, NY 10016. Phone: (212) 725-3737. (Published monthly). ($15/year.)

Covers the techniques involved in planning and executing meetings, incentive travel and conventions, including editorial material. Also publishes Gavel Annual International Directory which provides hotel, conference bureaus and resort information. Gavel is published annually and is included in the subscription, or can be purchased separately.

25. Mulligan, Allan. *The Complete Guide to Developing and Marketing Your Own Seminar.* Independence House Publishing Co., 15100 Birmingham Drive, Burtonsville, MD 20866. Phone: (301) 490-0112. 1984. ISBN 0-912551-00-3. (164 pages, paperback, $14.95)

26. Munson, Lawrence S. *How To Conduct Training Seminars: A Complete Reference Guide For Training Managers & Professionals.* McGraw-Hill, 1221 Avenue of the Americas, New York, NY 10020. Phone: (212) 337-5945, (800) 2-MCGRAW. 1992 (2nd Edition). ISBN 0-07-044201-0. (245 pages, $34.95)

(See Chapter 6)

27. Murray, Sheila L. *How to Organize and Manage a Seminar: What to Do and When to Do It.* Prentice Hall, 113 Sylvan Avenue, Englewood Cliffs, NJ 07632. Phone: (201) 592-2000. 1983. (204 pages)

(See Chapter 6)

28. Nadler, Leonard and Nadler, Zeace, Editors. *The Comprehensive Guide to Successful Conferences and Meetings: Detailed Instructions and Step-by-Step Checklists.* Jossey-Bass, Inc. Publishers, 350 Sansome Street, San Francisco, CA 94104. Phone: (415) 433-1767; Fax: (415) 433-0499. 1987. ISBN 1-55542-051-6. (466 pages, $44.00)

29. *National Registry for Training Programs.* American Council on Education, One Dupont Circle, Washington, DC 20036. Phone: (202) 939-9380; Fax: (202) 833-4760.

Provides record maintenance services for non-collegiate organizations and nonprofit agencies as required by the Council on the CEU. (The maintenance of permanent records of CEU awarded is the responsibility of the institution sponsoring the program. If you wish to purchase this service, contact the firm above.)

30. *Official Meeting Facilities Guide.* Ziff-Davis Publishing Co., Inc., One Park Avenue, New York, NY 10016. Phone: (212) 725-3737. (Published semiannually). ($60/year.)

Lists the primary international meeting facilities and services available. Includes key personnel, location and transportation information, room rates and principal meeting space for each property.

31. *Physicians' Travel & Meeting Guide.* Cahners Publishing Company, 249 West 17th Street, New York, NY 10011. Phone: (212) 463-6403, (212) 463-6412; Fax: (212) 463-6404. (Published monthly). (Controlled circulation publication; $70/year to non-qualified recipients.)

(See Chapter 12)

32. Piskurich, George M., Editor in Chief. *The ASTD Handbook of Instructional Technology.* McGraw-Hill, 1221 Avenue of the Americas, New York, NY 10020. Phone: (212) 337-5945, (800) 2-MCGRAW. 1992. (650 pages, $60.00)

33. Price, Catherine H. *The AMA Guide for Meeting and Event Planners.* AMACOM Publishing Co., P.O. Box 1026, Saranac Lake, NY 12983-1026. Phone: (800) 262-9699, (518) 891-5510; Fax: (518) 891-3653. 1989. ISBN 0-8144-5928-5. (400 pages, $75.00)

34. Public Management Institute Staff. *Successful Seminars, Conferences and Workshops.* Public Management Institute, 358 Brannan Street, San Francisco, CA 94107. Phone: (415) 896-

1900; Fax: (415) 896-0321. 1980. ISBN 0-916664-19-8. (400 pages, 3-ring binder, $59.00)

35. Schrello, Don M. *Marketing In-House Training Programs*. Schrello Direct Marketing, P.O. Box 1610, Long Beach, CA 90801-1610. Phone: (800) ENROLL-X, (310) 493-0200; Fax: (310) 493-0962. 1984. ISBN 0-935823-02-6. (44 pages, 7 Illustrations, $5.95)

This informative booklet shows you how to apply proven marketing principles to promote training programs within your organization. It outlines the 9 steps to effective in-house training and details 8 keys to successful in-house promotions. It contains handy worksheets, checklists and step-by-step instructions. And it reveals dozens upon dozens of specific actions that others have shown really work in selling in-house training programs.

36. Shea, Gordon F. *Managing A Difficult or Hostile Audience*. Prentice Hall, 113 Sylvan Avenue, Englewood Cliffs, NJ 07632. Phone: (201) 592-2000. 1984. (252 pages, $16.95)

Designed as a practitioner's handbook, this book offers plenty of advice on how to plan, organize and run successful meetings. It also shows how to work productively with groups when hostility, fear, apathy, boredom or defeatism shadow the proceedings.

37. Shenson, Howard L. *How to Create and Market a Successful Seminar or Workshop*. Bermont Books, Box 309, Gleneg, MD 21737. 1987 (Revised Edition). ISBN 0-930686-30-6. (102 pages, paperback, $29.00)

(See Chapter 6)

38. Shenson, Howard L. *How to Develop and Promote Successful Seminars and Workshops: A Definitive Guide to Creating and Marketing Seminars, Workshops, Classes and Conferences*. John Wiley and Sons, Inc., 605 Third Avenue, New York, NY 10158. Phone: (800) 225-5945, (212) 850-6000; Fax: (212) 850-6088. 1990. ISBN 0-471-52709-2. (Paperback, $19.95)

39. Simerly, Robert G. & Associates. *Handbook of Marketing for Continuing Education*. Jossey-Bass, Inc. Publishers, 350 Sansome Street, San Francisco, CA 94104. Phone: (415) 433-1767; Fax: (415) 433-0499. 1989. ISBN 1-55542-142-3. (560 pages, $59.95)

40. Sipos, J. (Business Handbooks Service). *How to Develop and Conduct Successful Seminars: A Practical Guide for Entrepreneurs and Managers*. International Business and Management Institute, P.O. Box 3271, Tustin, CA 92681-3271.

1991. ISBN 0-935402-38-1. (Paperback, $29.00)

41. *Successful Meetings*. Bill Communications, Inc., 355 Park Avenue South, New York, NY 10010. Phone: (212) 592-6400; Fax: (212) 592-6409. (Published monthly). ($41/year.)

Provides tips and ideas on convention and meeting planning, incentive travel and training seminars. Two annual publications are available as part of the subscription, or they can be purchased separately: Facilities Directory ($35) gives specific information on meeting facilities, and the Destinations Guide ($35) provides specific information and background on various cities to consider as meeting destinations.

42. Talbot, Randy. *Meeting Management: Practical Advice for Both New and Experienced Managers Based on an Expert's Twenty Years in the "Wonderful Wacky World" of Meeting Planning*. EPM Publications, 1003 Turkey Run Road, McLean, VA 22101. Phone: (800) 289-2339, (703) 442-7810. 1990. ISBN 0-939009-44-7. (175 pages, paperback, $11.95)

43. Universal *Training Systems Company Staff. How to Develop and Conduct Successful In-Company Training Programs*. Dartnell Corporation, 4660 N. Ravenswood Avenue, Chicago, IL 60640. Phone: (312) 561-4000, (800) 621-5463; Fax: (312) 561-3801. 1974. ISBN 0-85013-037-9. ($57.95)

A basic guide to help you train your employees. Partial contents include areas where training is valuable, analyzing performance to identify the training needs, planning the training, and evaluating and reporting the results of training. The publisher claims that by following its procedures, you can reduce training time, costs and grievances, and improve employee morale and production. Contains checklists, forms and charts.

44. Williams, William G. *Money-Making Meetings: Ninety-Seven Keys to Marketing Your Knowledge in the Multi-Million Dollar Workshop and Seminar Industry*. Share Publishing Co., P.O. Box 3453, Annapolis, MD 21403. 1982. ISBN 0-933344-02-3. (153 pages, $11.95)

45. Wrobleski, Toni and De la Concha, Hector. *Secrets to Successful Conferences: A Step by Step Guide*. Quantum Publications, Heritage Station, P.O. Box 3756, Schenectady, NY 12303. Phone: (518) 356-2471. 1991. ISBN 0-9631146-0-3. (168 pages, paperback, $21.95)

7. - MAILING LISTS

1. Burnett, Ed. *The Complete Direct Mail List Handbook: Everything You Need to Know About Lists & How to Use Them for Greater Profit.* Prentice Hall, 113 Sylvan Avenue, Englewood Cliffs, NJ 07632. Phone: (201) 592-2000. 1988. ISBN 0-13-159278-5. (736 pages, $59.95)

   Ed Burnett is one of the thoughtful, analytical experts in general direct mail, and his wisdom is easily available in this 744 page work. Unfortunately, there's practically nothing on marketing training products/services, but the book is so practical and valid, it is "must" reading for everyone doing direct mail.

2. *Direct Mail List Rates and Data.* Standard Rate and Data Service, 2000 Clearwater Drive, Oakbrook, IL 60521. Phone: (800) 851-SRDS, (708) 574-6000; Fax: (708) 574-6541. (Published every other month). ($345/year.)

   A catalog of over 10,000 mailing lists and sources, each presented in a brief, standardized format that includes list descriptions, counts, selections, sources, rates, restrictions, commissions and more. Business lists, consumer lists and package insert programs are included. "The Bullet" update bulletin is published on alternate months. A current edition of this publication is a "must" for every direct marketer.

3. *The Handbook of International Direct Marketing.* European Direct Mail Association (EDMA), 36 rue du Gouvernement Provisoire, Brussels, Belgium B-1000, Phone: (322) 217-6985. 1992. (300 pages, $40.00 plus postage and packing.)

   Written by leading professionals from 14 countries, this handbook presents vital country-by-country data for the world's top 40 direct mail markets from Belgium to Brazil. Includes local information on what's legal and what isn't, how to find the best lists, postal services and rates and where to find local research.

4. Harper, Rose. *Mailing List Strategies, A Guide to Direct Mail Success.* McGraw-Hill, 1221 Avenue of the Americas, New York, NY 10020. Phone: (212) 337-5945, (800) 2-MCGRAW. 1987. ISBN 0-07-026675-1. (224 pages, 52 illustrations, $29.95)

   The author, President of the Kleid Co., has written an introductory text that even experts can learn from. Includes chapters on all of the basics, and summarizes the industry's problems and promises.

5. Klein, Barry T. *Directory of Mailing List Companies.* B. Klein Publications, P.O. Box 8503, Coral Springs, FL 33065. Phone: (305) 752-1708; Fax: (305) 752-2547. 1991 (11th Edition). ISBN 0-915344-18-1. (150 pages, $55.00)

   "A dependable reference book of mailing list companies which specialize in the lists you need to plan a more effective and more profitable direct mail program. Approximately 2,000 list houses, brokers, compilers, list managers and list owners who rent their lists are included." - DMA

6. Miles, Steven A., Editor. *The National Directory of Addresses and Telephone Numbers.* Omnigraphics, Inc., Penobscot Bldg., Detroit, MI 48226. Phone: (800) 234-1340; Fax: (800) 875-1340. 1993. ISBN 1-558888-141-7. (1,632 pages, $89.95 Hardcover, $79.95 Softcover.)

   Contains more than 115,000 verified entries with names, addresses, telephone, fax and toll-free "800" numbers for frequently called organizations and individuals. Includes top corporations in nearly 500 industries, every four-year college and university, city, state and federal government listings, U.S. Senators and Representatives, foreign embassies and consulates, major sports teams, media and more. Has 30,000 changes from last year, and 5,000 all-new listings.

7. *The National Directory of Mailing Lists.* Oxbridge Communications, Inc., 150 Fifth Avenue - Suite 302, New York, NY 10011. Phone: (800) 955-0231, (212) 741-0231; Fax: (212) 633-2938. 1993 (3rd Edition). ISBN 0-917460-43-X. (1,420 pages, $345)

   This annual newcomer claims 20,000 lists, or twice as many as venerable SRDS. But our comparisons showed fewer lists of training interest, because their focus is on publications lists and not on responders/attenders. The directory is also available on computer diskettes, with quarterly updates.

8. *Rand McNally ZIP Code Finder.* Rand McNally and Co., P.O. Box 7600, Chicago, IL 60680-9913. Phone: (800) 284-6565, (708) 329-8100. 1993. ISBN 0-528-20508-0. (634 pages, $6.95)

   Geographic selection has become vital for improving list performance. This publication is the essential reference for that task. In addition to detailed state and major city ZIP Code maps, there are useful tables and an interesting discussion of the philosophy behind ZIP Coding and how they can be used in marketing (primarily consumer).

9. Russell, John J., Managing editor. *National*

Trade and Professional Associations of the United States. Columbia Books, Inc., 1212 New York Avenue, N.W. - Suite 330, Washington, DC 20005. Phone: (202) 898-0662; Fax: (202) 898-0775. 1992 (27th Annual Edition). ISBN 0-910416-94-X. (609 pages, $65)

Provides listings and descriptions of nearly 7,000 national trade associations, labor unions, professional, scientific or technical societies, and other organizations. Indexed by subject, budget, geographically, chief executive and acronym. There's also a handy directory of association management firms, showing which associations they manage. Mailing lists are also available.

10. Zapenski, David, Business Reference Editor. *1992 Commercial Atlas & Marketing Guide.* Rand McNally and Co., P.O. Box 7600, Chicago, IL 60680-9913. Phone: (800) 284-6565, (708) 329-8100. 1992 (Annually). ISBN 0-528-20066-6. (567 pages)

Measuring a huge 15" x 21" x 1-1/2" thick, this isn't just a coffee table book ... it's the whole coffee table! But the wealth of detailed population data, economic data maps, statistics, indexes, transportation and communication data here almost defies description, and will be a regular reference for database marketing or careful list segmentation projects.

8. - DIRECT MAIL ADVERTISING

1. Benson, Richard. *Secrets of Successful Direct Mail.* NTC Business Books, 4255 W. Touhy Avenue, Lincolnwood, IL 60646-1975. Phone: (708) 679-5500, (800) 323-4900; Fax: (708) 679-2494. 1991. ISBN 0-8442-3294-7. (Paperback, $16.95)

2. Bird, Drayton. *Commonsense Direct Marketing.* NTC Business Books, 4255 W. Touhy Avenue, Lincolnwood, IL 60646-1975. Phone: (708) 679-5500, (800) 323-4900; Fax: (708) 679-2494. 1990 (2nd Edition). ISBN 0-8442-3182-7. (348 pages, $29.95)

3. Burstiner, Irving. *Mail Order Selling: How to Market Almost Anything by Mail.* Prentice Hall, 113 Sylvan Avenue, Englewood Cliffs, NJ 07632. Phone: (201) 592-2000. 1989. ISBN 0-13-546045-X. (272 pages, $17.95)

"This straightforward, nontechnical book shows how to earn an excellent livelihood selling almost anything by mail -- whether you're launching your own business or just want to supplement your income. Covers preliminary critical steps needed before starting a mail business, plus proper operation and management of finances when money starts coming in. Covers building mail lists, direct mail, print and broadcast." - HCI

4. Canadian Direct Marketing Association (CDMA), 201 Consumers Road, Willowdale, ON M2J 4G8. Phone: (416) 494-8585.

"Holds seminars, conferences and education courses and acts as an information center and government liaison. Operation Integrity program is a complaint-handling system. Mail Preference Service helps consumers who wish to have their names removed from, or added to, mailing lists." - ZTM

5. Caples, John. *Tested Advertising Methods.* Prentice Hall, 113 Sylvan Avenue, Englewood Cliffs, NJ 07632. Phone: (201) 592-2000. 1986 (4th Edition). ISBN 0-13-906891-0. (318 pages, $9.95)

(See Chapter 8)

6. Cohen, William A. *Building a Mail Order Business: A Complete Manual for Success.* John Wiley and Sons, Inc., 605 Third Avenue, New York, NY 10158. Phone: (800) 225-5945, (212) 850-6000; Fax: (212) 850-6088. 1991 (3rd Edition). ISBN 0-471-52082-9. (608 pages, $34.95)

"Here is a detailed volume for everything from financing and start-up to the most sophisticated techniques, including how to use testing, copy that sells, where the big money is in direct mail, developing a complete marketing plan, how to find hot products to sell using little known source. This is a key volume loaded with financial and creative material for all direct marketers." - DMA

7. *DM News.* Mill Hollow Corp., 19 W. 21st Street, New York, NY 10010. Phone: (212) 741-2095. (Published monthly, controlled circulation).

Services the direct marketing industry with articles and reports concerning developments, legislation, etc.

8. The Direct Marketing Association, Inc., 11 West 42nd Street, New York, NY 10036-8096. Phone: (212) 768-7277; Fax: (212) 599-1268.

"The oldest and largest, with over 3,000 member companies, trade association serving the direct marketing field since 1917. The association provides educational opportunities through seminars and courses and information exchange through

numerous conferences and forums, as well as the activities of 11 special interest councils. DMA has active government affairs and public relation/communications programs that work to advance direct marketing. DMA also publishes Direct Marketing Journal and Direct Line." - ZTM

9. Direct Marketing Computer Association, 60 E. 42nd Street, Room 718, New York, NY 10165. Phone: (212) 867-2290.

"A nonprofit, professional association comprised of suppliers and users of data processing services and procedures as they relate to direct marketing. DMCA was formed to foster better communications and understanding between different elements of the direct response community. The association maintains its national headquarters in New York City, with Chicago and Fort Worth chapters." - ZTM

10. *Direct Marketing Magazine.* Hoke Communications, Inc., 224 7th Street, Garden City, NY 11530. Phone: (516) 746-6700. (Published monthly). ($36/year.)

One of the most widely read direct marketing monthlies. Contains news, a directory of services, product reviews, feature articles on how-to-do-it, latest developments, new technology, and how it all impacts direct marketing.

11. Elliot, Ralph D. *Direct Mail.* The Learning Resources Network (LERN), P.O. Box 1448, 1550 Hayes Drive, Manhattan, KS 66502. Phone: (800) 678-LERN, (913) 539-5376; Fax: (913) 539-7766. (Three book set, $29.95)

The three books in this set aimed at continuing educators are How to Create a More Responsive In-House Mailing List, Outside Lists *and* Multiple Mailing Strategies. *Includes procedures for building names, for organizing and maintaining names and for increasing returns.*

12. Rene Gnam Consultation Corporation, One Response Road, Tarpon Springs, FL 34689. Phone: (813) 938-1555; Fax: (813) 934-0416.

Mr. Gnam is a well-known lecturer and direct marketing personality, having been selected as the individual to do a multi-part PBS course on the subject. He is also involved in presenting various seminars relating to direct marketing and direct response.

13. Gottlieb, Richard, Editor. *Directory of Mail Order Catalogs IV.* Grey House Publishing, Pocketknife Square, Lakeville, CT 06039. Phone: (203) 435-0868; Fax: (203) 435-0867. 1989 (4th Edition). ISBN 0-939300-47-8. (400 pages, $135.00)

Lists and describes over 4,000 mail order companies and their key personnel, with the size of catalogs and frequency of mailings, availability of

mailing lists and the kind of products sold by each company.

14. Gross, Martin. *The Direct Marketer's Idea Book.* AMACOM Publishing Co., P.O. Box 1026, Saranac Lake, NY 12983-1026. Phone: (800) 262-9699, (518) 891-5510; Fax: (518) 891-3653. 1989. ISBN 0-8144-5947-1. (256 pages, $19.95)

A witty and readable idea book that covers direct mail, radio, TV, print advertising and telemarketing, with emphasis on creativity, strategy and planning.

15. Harper, C. Rose. *Seasonality Study.* The Kleid Company, Inc., 530 Fifth Avenue, New York, NY 10036-5101. Phone: (212) 819-3400; Fax: (212) 719-9727. 1992 (Annually). (13 pages, Free upon request.)

For nearly two decades now, The Kleid Company has conducted an annual survey of when mailers mail. Categorized by the various markets served (e.g., Educational/Technical/Professional, Business/Finance, Self-Improvement, etc, the study shows what percentage of direct mail advertising is dropped in each month of the year., and a five-year moving average. Very authoritative, and virtually the only source for this information.

16. Hatch, Denison. *Million Dollar Mailing$.* Regnery Gateway, Inc., 1130 17 Street N.W. - Suite 600, Washington, DC 20036. Phone: (800) 462-6420, (202) 457-0978; Fax: (202) 457-0774. 1993. ISBN 0-89526-509-5.

A collection of what's worked best from the creator of Who's Mailing What.

17. Hoge, Cecil C., Sr. *Mail Order Moonlighting.* Ten Speed Press, P.O. Box 7123, Berkeley, CA 94707. Phone: (415) 845-8414; Fax: (510) 524-1052. 1988 (2nd Edition). ISBN 0-89815-222-4. (416 pages, $9.95)

"Shows beginners how to start a mail order business in weeks, from home, in spare time, at own pace and with little or no risk, while maintaining present job. Hoge's method is simple and fundamental, and eliminates much of one of the greatest threats to any starting business." - HCI

18. JS&A Direct Marketing Seminar, One JS&A Plaza, Northbrook, IL 60062. Phone: (800) 323-6400.

After establishing himself as a leading authority in direct response through copy-heavy ads for high-tech products in the Wall Street Journal and elsewhere, Joe Sugarman (the JS in JS&A) decided to share his secrets. This executive seminar/retreat is the result.

19. Katzenstein, Herbert and Sachs, William S. *Di-*

rect Marketing. MacMillan Publishing Company, 866 Third Avenue, New York, NY 10022. Phone: (212) 702-2000; Fax: (212) 605-3099. 1992 (2nd Edition). ISBN 0-02-362425-6. (528 pages)

Written from the viewpoint of the marketing manager, this book furnishes basic principles and fundamentals, tips and techniques for successful direct marketing. Divided into four parts: The overall framework for DM, the planning process, implementation and contemporary and future issues.

20. Klein, Bernard. *Mail Order Business Directory.* B. Klein Publications, P.O. Box 8503, Coral Springs, FL 33065. Phone: (305) 752-1708; Fax: (305) 752-2547. 1992. ISBN 0-685-46356-7. (375 pages, $85.00)

"Contains information on more than 7,000 mail order firms in the U.S. This unique reference can be a powerful sales tool to open new distribution accounts for your products or services." - DMA

21. Kobs, Jim. *Profitable Direct Marketing.* NTC Business Books, 4255 W. Touhy Avenue, Lincolnwood, IL 60646-1975. Phone: (708) 679-5500, (800) 323-4900; Fax: (708) 679-2494. 1992 (2nd Edition). ISBN 0-8442-30294-4. (396 pages, $47.95)

"How to start, improve or expand any direct marketing operation. Includes 11 detailed case studies of prominent direct marketing companies. Planned and structured to have something for everyone. For the newcomer, it covers the basic questions to consider in launching a new program, selecting a product or service, creating an effective offer, testing, and developing multimedia plans. For the experienced practitioner, it deals with improving already successful programs and shows how to boost results with advanced ideas for creative effectiveness, management, marketing, and fulfillment." - HCI

22. Kremer, John. *Mail Order Selling Made Easier: How to Plan, Organize and Carry Out a Successful Direct Mail Promotion.* Open Horizons Publishing Co., P. O. Box 205, Fairfield, IA 52556-0205. Phone: (515) 472-6130; Fax: (515) 472-3186. 1990. ISBN 0-912411-29-5. (288 pages, $19.95)

23. Lant, Dr. Jeffrey L. *Cash Copy: How To Offer Your Products And Services So Your Prospects Buy Them ... Now!.* Jeffrey Lant Associates, Inc., 50 Follen Street - Suite 507, Cambridge, MA 02138. Phone: (617) 547-6372; Fax: (617) 547-0061. 1992 (2nd Edition). ISBN 0-940374-20-X. (480 Pages, $30.00)

(See Chapter 8)

24. Lewis, Herschell Gordon. *Direct Mail Copy That Sells.* Prentice Hall, 113 Sylvan Avenue, Englewood Cliffs, NJ 07632. Phone: (201) 592-2000. 1986. ISBN 0-13-214750-5. ($12.95)

25. Lewis, Herschell Gordon. *How to Make Your Advertising Twice as Effective at Half the Cost.* Prentice-Hall, 111 N. Canal Street, Chicago, IL 60606. Phone: (312) 930-9446. 1986. ISBN 0-13-417882-3. (273 pages, $27.95)

Aimed at small and medium-sized businesses, this book discusses the ad world and techniques for creating advertising on a small budget. Covers broadcast and print media.

26. Lewis, Herschell Gordon. *More Than You Ever Wanted to Know About Mail Order Advertising.* Prentice Hall, 113 Sylvan Avenue, Englewood Cliffs, NJ 07632. Phone: (201) 592-2000. 1986. ISBN 0-13-601039-3. (330 pages, $10.95)

"Must reading if you're looking for down-to-earth, practical, workable advise. Reveals a new wealth of advertising methods to boost bottom-line results. Offers high impact ideas on copy, testing lists, media, timing, post-sale plus new developments." - HCI

27. Ljungren, Roy G. *The Business-To-Business Direct Marketing Handbook.* AMACOM Publishing Co., P.O. Box 1026, Saranac Lake, NY 12983-1026. Phone: (800) 262-9699, (518) 891-5510; Fax: (518) 891-3653. 1989. ISBN 0-81445834-3. (456 pages, $75)

28. Maas, Jane. *Better Brochures, Catalogs and Mailing Pieces.* St. Martin's Press, 175 Fifth Avenue, New York, NY 10010. Phone: (800) 221-7945, (212) 674-5151; Fax: (212) 420-9314. 1984. ISBN 0-312-07731-9. (128 pages, $6.95)

29. Mail Advertising Service Association, International, 7315 Wisconsin Avenue, Bethesda, MD 20814. Phone: (301) 654-6272.

"The only trade association designed for companies that process mail, i.e.: lettershops and mailing services. Association membership is also available to suppliers to the industry as well as to in-plant mailing operations. Services to members include postal representation, a confidential newsletter, a dozen meetings, seminars and conferences throughout the year, ranging from technical seminars with hands-on training for machine operators to the annual conference." - ZTM MASA offers a booklet listing all members by their geographic location and services available, called Who's Who in Mailing Services, and What MASA Means, an explanation of the organization, its members and other available publications.

30. Mailing List Users and Suppliers Association, Inc., 322 Eighth Avenue, 12th Floor, New York, NY 10001. Phone: (212) 206-8301.

"To advocate and further the recognition and respectability of the mailing list industry. Conducts industry seminars on mailing list direct mail topics and publishes a member newsletter apprising members of events, including postal regulations pertinent to the mailing list industry. Has established, for members only, CISP, the industry's first credit information sharing program." - ZTM

31. Mayer, Edward N. and Ljungren, Roy G. *The Handbook of Business Direct Mail Advertising.* The Direct Marketing Association, Inc., 11 West 42nd Street, New York, NY 10036-8096. Phone: (212) 768-7277; Fax: (212) 599-1268. 1977.

"A precise, thorough, easy-to-read handbook especially for industrial direct marketers. You'll find simple ways to unravel complexities of selling; how to integrate direct mail into the marketing and advertising mix, what lists to use, how to get, handle, screen and follow-up inquiries." - DMA

32. Nash, Edward L. *Direct Marketing: Strategy, Planning, Execution.* McGraw-Hill, 1221 Avenue of the Americas, New York, NY 10020. Phone: (212) 337-5945, (800) 2-MCGRAW. 1985 (2nd Edition). ISBN 0-07-046024-8. (464 pages, $44.95)

"Here's the practical, step-by-step book bringing you the strategies and techniques, the complete science and art, from planning and positioning to implementation and follow-through. How to create faster-action ads in direct mail, newspapers, magazines, TV, radio, and telephone marketing -- and produce a higher rate of response in mail orders, sales leads, subscriptions, memberships, contributions and enrollments." - DMA

33. Nash, Edward L., Editor. *The Handbook of Direct Marketing.* McGraw-Hill, 1221 Avenue of the Americas, New York, NY 10020. Phone: (212) 337-5945, (800) 2-MCGRAW. 1991. ISBN 0-07-046027-2. (832 pages, $49.95)

A reference book on the methods of direct marketing, divided into 60 chapters contributed to by 50 direct response authorities. Despite its value for general direct marketing, its one chapter on Marketing Education and Services is of limited practical value to those marketing training today.

34. National Register Publishing Company Staff. *The Direct Marketing Market Place, 1992: The Directory of the Direct Marketing Industry.* National Register Publishing Co., 121 Chanlon Road, New Providence, NJ 07974. Phone: (800) 521-8110, (908) 464-6800. 1992. ISBN 0-87217-326-7. (Two volumes (ISBN for vol 2: 0-87217-327-5), $157.00)

35. Posch, Robert J., Jr. *The Complete Guide to Marketing and the Law.* Prentice Hall, 113 Syl-

van Avenue, Englewood Cliffs, NJ 07632. Phone: (201) 592-2000. 1988. ISBN 0-13-160904-1. (848 pages, $79.95)

Covers all major federal rules involving direct marketing and how to comply with them.

36. The Shell Alpert Direct Marketing War College, 444 Lakeview Court, Dept. No. 3,, Langhorne, PA 19047. Phone: (215) 752-3433.

A one or two-day War College gives participants the opportunity to interact with and learn from one of direct marketing's top "field generals."

37. Simon, Julian L. *How to Start and Operate a Mail-Order Business.* McGraw-Hill, 1221 Avenue of the Americas, New York, NY 10020. Phone: (212) 337-5945, (800) 2-MCGRAW. 1987 (4th Edition). ISBN 0-07-057531-2. (576 pages, $44.95)

Includes chapters by top advertising professionals and a listing of 500 of the most profitable products. Discusses the least expensive ways to promote the product you select and how to define its market, and create effective mail order copy for selling it.

38. Stearn, Edward, Editor. *The Direct Marketing Marketplace.* Hilary House Publishers, Inc., 980 North Federal Highway, Suite 206, Boca Raton, FL 33432. Phone: (407) 393-5656; Fax: (407) 368-5115. 1985 (6th Edition). ($67.00)

"This outstanding directory contains 15,800 major direct marketing companies, suppliers, prominent individuals, agencies, consultants, media buyers -- involved in the direct marketing industry. It details company names, addresses, phone numbers, products, services, chief executives, sales and advertising volume, and more. An extremely valuable reference tool." - DMA

39. Stone, Bob. *Successful Direct Marketing Methods.* NTC Business Books, 4255 W. Touhy Avenue, Lincolnwood, IL 60646-1975. Phone: (708) 679-5500, (800) 323-4900; Fax: (708) 679-2494. 1990 (4th Edition). ISBN 0-8442-3180-0. (528 pages, $34.95)

Provides information on starting a direct mail operation, choosing the media for marketing, considering mail lists and telephone marketing, creating and producing direct market materials and managing the business itself. A comprehensive reference; includes case studies.

40. *Target Marketing.* North American Publishing Co., 401 N. Broad Street, Philadelphia, PA 19108. Phone: (800) 627-2689, (215) 238-5300, (215) 574-9600; Fax: (215) 238-5457. (Published monthly). ($65/year.)

Features "how-to" articles on marketing, adver-

Features "how-to" articles on marketing, advertising, list selection and testing, creation and monitoring of mailing packages, mailing procedures, regulations, circulation and fulfillment. The December issue includes the Who's Who in Direct Marketing, one of the most comprehensive directories assembled on the industry.

41. *Who's Mailing What!.* Who's Mailing What, P.O. Box 8180, Stamford, CT 06905. Phone: (203) 329-1996. (Published monthly). ($99/year.)

A newsletter, analysis and record of the direct mail industry.

42. *Wiland's Webster: A Dictionary of Direct Marketing, Data Processing and Business Terminology.* Wiland Services, Inc., 6707 Winchester Circle, Boulder, CO 80301. Phone: (303) 530-0606; Fax: (303) 530-7495. ($10.00)

The newest version is divided into four sections: direct marketing terminology, including fulfillment; postal/lettershop terminology; data-processing/computer-programming symbols and systems; and market analysis, statistical and segmentation definitions.

9. - ARTWORK, PRINTING AND MAILING

1. *1992-93 DMA Statistical Fact Book.* The Direct Marketing Association, Inc., 11 West 42nd Street, New York, NY 10036-8096. Phone: (212) 768-7277; Fax: (212) 599-1268. 1992 (Yearly). ISBN 0-933641-39-7. (319 pages, $89.95 for members, $119.95 for non-members.)

Provides updated statistics for estimated direct response advertising expenditures, sales volume and various research and testing studies. Useful for program planning, analysis, sales presentations, speeches and in-depth studies.

2. Bruno, Michael H., Editor. *Pocket Pal.* International Paper Co., 2 Manhattanville Road, Purchase, NY 10577. Phone: (800) 223-1268, (914) 397-1500; Fax: (914) 397-1567. 1983 (13th Edition). ($4.00)

A handbook/introduction to the graphic arts, including printing processes and the use of computers and electronics, along with a glossary of terms. This little gem is a "must" for anyone involved in printing.

3. *Domestic Mail Manual.* Superintendent of Documents, P.O. Box 371954, Pittsburgh, PA 15250-7954. (Quarterly). ($36/year.)

"The DMM is the bible of the industry. It's very complete and very difficult to understand, but it does have all the information on all classes of mail."-DMN

4. Lem, Dean, Editor. *Graphics Master IV.* Dean Lem Associates, Inc., 1526 Pontius Avenue, Los Angeles, CA 90025. Phone: (310) 478-0092. 1988 (4th Edition). ISBN 0-914218-07-7. ($69.50)

"The revised edition of the graphic arts workbook that has been acclaimed the most complete, comprehensive, easy-to-use reference source for print production and technical information." - HCI

5. *Memo to Mailers.* Public and Employee Communications Department, U.S. Postal Service, 475 L'Enfant Plaza SW, Washington, DC 20260-3112. (Published monthly). (Free of charge to customers originating significant quantities of mail.)

Includes news and updates on the U.S. Postal Service and on bulk mailing practices. One of the most useful "freebies" available to the direct mailer.

6. *The National Five Digit ZIP Code and Post Office Directory.* National Information Data Center, P.O. Box 2977, Washington, DC 20013. (Published annually). ($24.95)

Includes two volumes and a map. Lists all U.S. ZIP Codes by names and numbered streets and all U.S. post offices. If you mail anything, you need this!

7. *National ZIP Code Post Office Directory.* National Address Information Center, U.S. Postal Service., 6060 Primacy Parkway, Ste. 101, Memphis, TN 38188-0001. (Annual). ($15)

"This guide features information on the 28,000 post offices, 400,000 streets and 43,000 ZIP codes, plus other useful information. Each postal region also publishes a Regional Reference Booklet with all the names, addresses and telephone numbers of all the offices and divisions of that region. There are five regions; the Northeast, for example has 14 divisions. You can get these booklets from your postal service account representative or your local post office."-DMN

8. Stevenson, George A., Edited by William A. Pakan. *Graphic Arts Encyclopedia.* TAB

1128, (717) 794-2191; Fax: (717) 794-5344. 1992 (3rd edition). ISBN 0-8306-2530-5. (624 pages, $57.50)

A reference source about everything you'd need to

know about the products and tools needed in graphic arts to create reproducible artwork and mailing pieces. The latest machinery, processes and techniques are discussed.

10. - SHOWCASES AND SALES EVENTS

(The references and resources for this chapter are contained throughout this manual.)

11. - TELEMARKETING

1. Bencin, Richard L. and Jonovic, Donald J. *Encyclopedia of Telemarketing.* Prentice Hall, 113 Sylvan Avenue, Englewood Cliffs, NJ 07632. Phone: (201) 592-2000. 1989. ISBN 0-13-275918-7. (726 pages, $69.95)

   (See Chapter 11)

2. Fisher, Peg. *Successful Telemarketing: A Step-by-Step Guide to Increased Sales at Lower Cost.* Dartnell Corporation, 4660 N. Ravenswood Avenue, Chicago, IL 60640. Phone: (312) 561-4000, (800) 621-5463; Fax: (312) 561-3801. (370 pages, 8-1/2" x 11" 3-ring binder, $91.50)

3. Goodman, Gary S. *Reach Out and Sell Someone: Phone Your Way to Success Through the Goodman System of Telemarketing.* Prentice Hall, 113 Sylvan Avenue, Englewood Cliffs, NJ 07632. Phone: (201) 592-2000. 1983. ISBN 0-13-753624-0. (141 pages, $8.95)

   Techniques for effective telemarketing. Includes the 60 'golden rules' for selling over the telephone: what you should know, have at hand, and what not to do when using the telephone.

4. Idelman, Steven A. and Dobbs, Grady L. *How to Manage Growth and Maximize Profits in Outbound Telemarketing.* Prentice Hall, 113 Sylvan Avenue, Englewood Cliffs, NJ 07632. Phone: (201) 592-2000. 1990. ISBN 0-685-33211-X. (336 pages, $49.95)

5. Mahfood, Phillip E. *Teleselling, High Performance Business-to-Business Phone Selling Technique.* Probus Publishing Co., Inc., 1925 North Clybourn, Chicago, IL 60614. Phone: (800) 776-2871, (312) 868-1100. 1990. ISBN 1-55738-167-4. ($22.95)

6. Newton, Harry. *Newton's Telecom Dictionary.* Telecom Library, Inc., 12 West 21st Street - 10th Floor, New York, NY 10010. Phone: (800) LIBRARY, (212) 691-8215; Fax: (212) 691-1190. (4th Edition). ISBN 0-936648-.

   (See Chapter 11)

7. Richardson, Linda. *Selling by Phone: The Salesperson's Guide to Getting New Customers and Closing Deals.* McGraw-Hill, 1221 Avenue of the Americas, New York, NY 10020. Phone: (212) 337-5945, (800) 2-MCGRAW. 1991. ISBN 0-07-052339-8. ($19.95)

8. Roman, Murray. *Telemarketing Campaigns That Work!* McGraw-Hill, 1221 Avenue of the Americas, New York, NY 10020. Phone: (212) 337-5945, (800) 2-MCGRAW. 1983. ISBN 0-07-053598-1. (320 pages, $39.95)

   "A timely, authoritative book that describes in detail 18 classic telemarketing campaigns that worked. Shows the strategies behind each campaign, the methods used in day-to-day implementation, and the results. In fields ranging from banking to consumer retailing, service companies, industrial products, and executive seminars, the reader will see just what makes up a successful telemarketing campaign, and how to turn this information to advantage."-HCI

9. Roman, Murray. *Telephone Marketing: How to Build Your Business by Telephone.* McGraw-Hill, 1221 Avenue of the Americas, New York, NY 10020. Phone: (212) 337-5945, (800) 2-MCGRAW. 1976 (New edition). ISBN 0-07-053595-7. ($59.95)

   This guide was one of the first references in the field on how to create professional telephone selling campaigns. It answers every question you're likely to have, cites costs, shows how to plan and install a complete telephone selling operation, how to recruit and train operators and supervisors, recommended controls, facilities and accountability procedures. One of the "classics."

10. Shafiroff, Martin D. and Shook, Robert L.

Successful Telephone Selling in the '90's. HarperCollins Publishers, 10 E. 53rd Street, New York, NY 10022. Phone: (800) 242-7737, (212) 207-7000; Fax: (212) 207-7617. 1990 (Revised edition). ISBN 0-06-096491-X. (224 pages, paperback, $10.00)

(See Chapter 11)

11. *Telemarketing Magazine.* Technology Marketing Corp., One Technology Plaza, Norwalk, CT 06854. Phone: (800) 852-6002, (203) 846-2029. (Published bimonthly). ($49/year.)

12. - PRINT ADVERTISING, TRADE SHOWS, WRITING BOOKS OR NEWSLETTERS, PUBLICITY AND OTHER SALES AND MARKETING METHODS

Advertising

1. *Ayer Directory of Publications.* IMS Press Co., One Bala Avenue, Bala Cynwood, PA 19004. Phone: (800) 523-5824. (Published annually)). ($99.00)

Lists over 21,000 nationally published newspapers and magazines, including feature editors. Covers all trade publications, foreign language, fraternal, religious, and agricultural college publications.

2. *Business Publication Rates and Data.* Standard Rate and Data Service, 2000 Clearwater Drive, Oakbrook, IL 60521. Phone: (800) 851-SRDS, (708) 574-6000; Fax: (708) 574-6541. (Published monthly). ($497/year.)

(See Chapter 12)

3. *Canadian Advertising Rates and Data/The Media Authority.* MacLean-Hunter Ltd. and Standard Rate and Data Service, Inc., 481 University Avenue, Toronto, ON M5W 1A7. Phone: (416) 596-5000. (Published monthly). ($127/year.)

Provides rates and data listings for advertising agencies in Canada and the U.S. on all Canadian media-based publications, including consumer magazines, daily newspapers, radio stations, television, etc.

4. *Consumer Magazine and Agri-Media Rates and Data.* Standard Rate and Data Service, 2000 Clearwater Drive, Oakbrook, IL 60521. Phone: (800) 851-SRDS, (708) 574-6000; Fax: (708) 574-6541. (Published monthly). ($485/year.)

Alphabetical listings across 70 editorial classifications/markets. Includes over 2,275 magazines and card decks, 275 farm magazines and 130 international publications. Presents Area of Dominance Influence (ADI), Designated Market Area (DMA) and Metro Statistical Area (MSA) rankings. Listings feature buying information, editorial policy, ad rates/discounts, mechanical requirements, copy regulations, issue/closing dates, audited circulation and more rankings

5. Eicoff, Alvin. *Eicoff on Broadcast Direct Marketing.* NTC Business Books, 4255 W. Touhy Avenue, Lincolnwood, IL 60646-1975. Phone: (708) 679-5500, (800) 323-4900; Fax: (708) 679-2494. 1987. ISBN 0-8442-3144-4. (256 pages, $29.95)

6. Eicoff, Alvin. *Or Your Money Back.* Crown Publishing Group, 201 East 50th Street, New York, NY 10022. Phone: (212) 572-6117; Fax: (212) 572-6192. 1982. ($14.95)

"Considered an 'original' in broadcast advertising, Alvin Eicoff has written an informative book on the subject, citing his own experience and how he overcame low-budgeting obstacles to achieve millions of dollars in sales." - HCI

7. *Folio: The Magazine for Magazine Management.* Folio Magazine Publishing Corporation, 125 Elm Street, P.O. Box 697, New Canaan, CT 06840. Phone: (203) 972-0761. (Published monthly). ($42/year.)

Devoted to the management, editing, circulation, production and sales of consumer business, technical and trade magazines.

8. *Gale Directory of Publications and Broadcast Media.* Gale Research Inc., 835 Penobscot Bldg., Detroit, MI 48226-4094. Phone: (800) 877-GALE, (313) 961-2242; Fax: (313) 961-6083, (313) 961-6815. 1994 (126th Edition). ISBN 0-8103-8059-5. ($305.00)

Covers approximately 25,000 U.S. and Canadian newspapers, magazines, journals and periodicals, and 11,000 radio, television and cable stations or systems. Includes publisher index, arranged alphabetically, that includes address, telephone, fax and a list of publications.

9. Gebbie, Amalia, Editor. *All-In-One-Directory.* Gebbie Press, P.O. Box 1000, New Paltz, NY 12561. 1984. ($58.00)

"Includes basic information about daily newspapers, weekly newspapers, radio stations, television stations, general consumer magazines, professional business publications, trade magazines, farm publications, Black press and news syndicates." - JL

10. *Newsletters in Print.* Gale Research Inc., 835 Penobscot Bldg., Detroit, MI 48226-4094. Phone: (800) 877-GALE, (313) 961-2242; Fax: (313) 961-6083, (313) 961-6815. 1992 (6th Edition). ISBN 0-8103-7520-6. (1,483 pages, $185.00)

Describes 11,000 subscription, membership and free newsletters, bulletins, digests and similar serial publications covering 4,000 subjects available in the U.S. and Canada. Also available online through HRIN.

11. *Newspaper Rates and Data.* Standard Rate and Data Service, 2000 Clearwater Drive, Oakbrook, IL 60521. Phone: (800) 851-SRDS, (708) 574-6000; Fax: (708) 574-6541. (Published monthly). ($485/year.)

(See Chapter 12)

12. Oxbridge Communications staff. *The National Directory of Advertising -- Print Media.* Oxbridge Communications, Inc., 150 Fifth Avenue - Suite 302, New York, NY 10011. Phone: (800) 955-0231, (212) 741-0231; Fax: (212) 633-2938. 1992. ($295.00)

Lists over 27,000 media sources in the U.S. and Canada including magazines, journals, newspapers, newsletters, directories and even catalogs. Claimed to be over twice as many listings as the competition.

13. Stansfield, Richard H., Editor. *Advertising Manager's Handbook.* Dartnell Corporation, 4660 N. Ravenswood Avenue, Chicago, IL 60640. Phone: (312) 561-4000, (800) 621-5463; Fax: (312) 561-3801. 1982 (3rd Edition). ISBN 0-85013-128-6. ($49.95)

Presents all the skills involved in advertising: how to choose an agency; how to buy art and photography; how to write copy that demands attention; media selection methods that work ... plus much, much more. Brings you over 2,600 separate subjects.

14. Watkins, Julian L. *The 100 Greatest Advertisements: Who Wrote Them & What They Did.* Dover Publications, Inc., 31 Second Street, Mineola, NY 11501. Phone: (800) 223-3130, (516) 294-7000; Fax: (516) 742-6953, (516) 742-5049. 1959 (2nd Edition). ISBN 0-486-20540-1. (Paperback, $10.95)

Conferences, Trade Shows and Expositions

1. *Directory of Conventions.* Bill Communications, Inc., 355 Park Avenue South, New York, NY 10010. Phone: (212) 592-6400; Fax: (212) 592-6409. (Published annually). ($85.00)

(See Chapter 12)

2. *Public Holidays in 154 Independent* Countries. Executive Handbooks, 98 Riverside Drive, New York, NY 10024. 1984. ($5.00)

A useful reference for anyone scheduling meetings or conferences. Helps avoid unfortunate conflicts.

3. *Trade Shows Worldwide.* Gale Research Inc., 835 Penobscot Bldg., Detroit, MI 48226-4094. Phone: (800) 877-GALE, (313) 961-2242; Fax: (313) 961-6083, (313) 961-6815. 1993 (8th Edition). ISBN 0-8103-8079-X. (1,600 pages, $205.00)

Profiles more than 6,000 trade shows and more than 5,000 trade show organizers and sponsors worldwide. Also includes listings of 800 convention centers and 650 exhibit builders, transportation firms, consultants published resources and other industry suppliers. Indexed by date, location, subject as well as a master index.

4. *Tradeshows & Exhibits Schedule.* Bill Communications, Inc., 355 Park Avenue South, New York, NY 10010. Phone: (212) 592-6400; Fax: (212) 592-6409. (Published annually). (Includes a mid-year supplement, $185.00)

A listing of over 9,500 U.S. and 1,500 Canadian trade shows and exhibits worldwide, covering 82 business, professional and special-interest market classifications. Shows when and where scheduled, expected attendance, show managers with phone and fax numbers, industry served and more. Indexed by industry or profession, chronologically, geographically and alphabetically. A useful guide for those interested in entering the trade show market.

5. *World Convention Dates.* Hendrickson Publishing Co., Inc., 79 Washington Street, Hempstead, NY 11550. Phone: (516) 483-6881. (Published monthly). ($50/year.)

Newsletter listing 11,400 future events on a geographical basis. Use this to be sure your meeting doesn't conflict with another. It's also a way to learn of the events with which you may want to cooperate. Will list your program free of charge if contacted at least 3 months prior to the event. Hendrickson Publishing also offers an annual Event Planner's Guide, providing information on site selection, speakers and trainers.

Writing and Publishing Books and Newsletters

1. Beach, Mark. *Editing Your Newsletter: How to Produce an Effective Publication Using Traditional Tools and Computers.* Coast to Coast Books, 2934 NE Sixteenth Avenue, Portland, OR 97212. Phone: (503) 282-5891. 1988 (3rd Edition). ISBN 0-943381-01-0. (168 pages, softcover, $18.50)

   There are lots of references on this subject but few, if any, come more highly recommended than this one. Covers everything you need from budgeting and choosing topics, through headlines and formats to the mechanics of layout, printing and distribution.

2. Herman, Jeffrey H. *The Insider's Guide to Book Editors, Publishers and Literary Agents.* Prima Publishing, P.O. Box 1260HER, Rocklin, CA 95677. Phone: (916) 786-0426; Fax: (916) 786-0488. 1993-94 (3rd Edition). ISBN 1-55958-231-6. (452 pages, $19.95)

   (See Chapter 12)

3. Kiefer, Marie. *Book Publishing Resource Guide.* Open Horizons Publishing Co., P. O. Box 205, Fairfield, IA 52556-0205. Phone: (515) 472-6130; Fax: (515) 472-3186. 1993 (4th Edition). ISBN 0-912411-38-4. (320 pages, softcover, $25.00)

   Includes more than 8,000 book marketing contacts from book clubs and chain stores to mail order catalogs and media contacts. Also lists other marketing services such as list suppliers, 800 answering services, book publishing associations and more.

4. Kissling, Mark, Editor. *1993 Writer's Market.* Writer's Digest Books, 1507 Dana Avenue, Cincinnati, OH 45207-1005. Phone: (800) 289-0963, (513) 531-2222; Fax: (513) 531-4744. 1992 (Annually). ISBN 0-89879-498-6. (1,008 pages, $26.95 Hardcover.)

   (See Chapter 12)

5. Kremer, John. *One Thousand & One Ways to Market Your Books.* Open Horizons Publishing Co., P. O. Box 205, Fairfield, IA 52556-0205. Phone: (515) 472-6130; Fax: (515) 472-3186. 1990 (3rd Rev. Edition). ISBN 0-912411-33-3. (448 pages, 19.95)

   (See Chapter 12)

6. Lanam, Richard D., III, Managing Editor. *Literary Market Place.* Reed Reference Publishing Co., P.O. Box 31, 121 Chanlon Road, New Providence, NJ 07974. Phone: (800) 521-8110; Fax: (908) 665-6699. 1993 (53rd Annual Edition). ISBN 0-8352-3237-9. (1,800 pages,

$148)

(See Chapter 12)

7. Nathan, Jan, Editor. *PMA Newsletter: The International Newsletter of the Publishers Marketing Association.* Publishers Marketing Association., 2401 Pacific Coast Highway - Suite 102, Hermosa Beach, CA 90254. Phone: (310) 372-2732; Fax: (310) 374-3342.

   (See Chapter 12)

8. Poynter, Dan. *Book Reviews.* Para Publishing Co., P. O. Box 4232-R, Santa Barbara, CA 93140-4232. Phone: (800) PARAPUB, (805) 968-7277; Fax: (805) 968-1379. 1992. ISBN 0-915516-56-X. (53 pages, $19.95)

   Book reviews shows how to take advantage of the free publicity available to books. Book reviews are the least expensive and most effective form of book promotion. This handy report covers pre-publication reviews, early reviews, retail reviews and continuing reviews, with examples of the packages to use for each. It even tells what to do with the reviews after you receive them.

9. Poynter, Dan. *Direct Mail for Book Publishers.* Para Publishing Co., P. O. Box 4232-R, Santa Barbara, CA 93140-4232. Phone: (800) PARAPUB, (805) 968-7277; Fax: (805) 968-1379. 1992 (3rd edition). ISBN 0-915516-59-4. (55 pages, $19.95.)

10. Poynter, Dan. *The Self-Publishing Manual: How to Write, Print and Sell Your Own Book.* Para Publishing Co., P. O. Box 4232-R, Santa Barbara, CA 93140-4232. Phone: (800) PARAPUB, (805) 968-7277; Fax: (805) 968-1379. 1993 (7th Edition, completely revised). ISBN 0-915516-90-X. (416 pages, softcover, $19.95)

    (See Chapter 12)

11. *Publishers Directory: 1993.* Gale Research Inc., 835 Penobscot Bldg., Detroit, MI 48226-4094. Phone: (800) 877-GALE, (313) 961-2242; Fax: (313) 961-6083, (313) 961-6815. 1993 (13th Edition). ISBN 0-8103-8154-0. (1,992 pages, $255.00)

    Provides information on 18,000 currently active U.S. and Canadian book publishers and 600 distributors, wholesalers and jobbers.

12. Ross, Marilyn A. and Ross, Tom M. *Complete Guide to Self-Publishing: Everything you need to know to write, publish, promote, and sell your own book.* Writer's Digest Books, 1507 Dana Avenue, Cincinnati, OH 45207-1005. Phone: (800) 289-0963, (513) 531-2222; Fax: (513) 531-4744. 1989 (2nd Edition). ISBN 0-89879-354-8. (420 pages, $18.95)

(See Chapter 12)

13. Ross, Marilyn and Ross, Tom. *Book Promotion and Marketing: Success Strategies To Increase Your Sales.* About Books, Inc., P.O. Box 1500-B, 425 Cedar Street, Buena Vista, CO 81211-1500. Phone: (800) 548-1876, (719) 395-2459; Fax: (719) 395-8374. 1987. (6 hour audio tape cassette program, $72.95 postpaid.)

14. Weckbaugh, Ernest L., Editor. *Signature: A Newsletter For The Publishing Industry.* Griffin Printing & Lithograph, Co., Inc., 544 West Colorado St., Glendale, CA 91204-1102. Phone: (800) 826-4849, (800) 423-5789; Fax: (818) 242-1172. (Published quarterly).

(See Chapter 12)

Getting and Using Publicity

1. *Bacon's Publicity Checker.* Bacon's Publishing Company, 332 S. Michigan Avenue, Chicago, IL 60604. Phone: (800) 621-0561, (312) 922-8419, (312) 922-2400; Fax: (312) 922-3127. ($110.00)

(See Chapter 12)

2. Darrow, Richard W., Forrestal, Dan J. and Cookman, Aubrey O. *The Dartnell Public Relations Handbook.* Dartnell Corporation, 4660 N. Ravenswood Avenue, Chicago, IL 60640. Phone: (312) 561-4000, (800) 621-5463; Fax: (312) 561-3801. 1979 (2nd Edition).

3. Graham, Scott Bl., Editor. *News Media Yellow Book (Of Washington And New York.).* Monitor Publishing Co., 104 Fifth Avenue, New York, NY 10011. Phone: (212) 627-4140; Fax: (212) 645-0931. 1993 (7th Edition, Vol. IV, No. 1). ISBN 1043-2620. (939 pages, $165 First Subscription, $115 each Additional Subscription.)

4. Lant, Dr. Jeffrey L. *The Unabashed Self-Promoter's Guide: What Every Man, Woman, Child and Organization in America Needs to Know About Getting Ahead by Exploiting the Media.* Jeffrey Lant Associates, Inc., 50 Follen Street - Suite 507, Cambridge, MA 02138. Phone: (617) 547-6372; Fax: (617) 547-0061. 1992 (2nd Edition). ISBN 0-940374-18-8. (365 pages, 8-1/2" x 11" format, $39.50 postpaid.)

(See Chapter 12)

5. Lesly, Philip, Editor. *Lesly's Handbook of Public Relations and Communications.* AMACOM Publishing Co., P.O. Box 1026, Saranac Lake, NY 12983-1026. Phone: (800) 262-9699, (518) 891-5510; Fax: (518) 891-3653. 1991 (4th Edition). ISBN 0-8144-0108-2. (874 pages, $79.95 Hardcover)

(See Chapter 12)

6. Weiner, Richard. *Professional's Guide to Public Relations Services.* AMACOM Publishing Co., P.O. Box 1026, Saranac Lake, NY 12983-1026. Phone: (800) 262-9699, (518) 891-5510; Fax: (518) 891-3653. 1988 (6th Edition). ISBN 0-8144-5932-3. (516 pages, $95.00)

Directories, Course Listings, On-Line Services and More

1. *The 1992 Global Connector.* PASport Publishing International, 20 Libertyship Way, Suite 190A, Sausalito, CA 94965. Phone: (415) 331-2606; Fax: (415) 331-3903. 1992 (Published annually). (310 pages, $295.00)

(See Chapter 12)

2. *ASTD Buyers Guide and Consultant Directory.* American Society for Training and Development, 1640 King Street - P. O. Box 1443, Alexandria, VA 22313-2043. Phone: (703) 683-8129, (703) 683-8100; Fax: (703) 683-8103. (Published annually). (236 pages, soft-cover, Free to members; $55.00 nonmembers.)

(See Chapter 12)

3. *Bricker's International Directory of University-Based Executive Programs.* Peterson's Guides, 202 Carnegie Center, P.O. Box 2123, Princeton, NJ 08543-2123. Phone: (609) 243-9111, (800) 338-3282; Fax: (609) 243-9150. 1993 (24th Edition, Published annually). ISBN 1-56079-213-2. (In 2 volumes; Vol. 1, 593 pages, covers long-term programs; Vol. 2, (ISBN 1-56079-214-0), 231 pages, covers short-term programs, Vol 1: $135; Vol 2: $95.)

(See Chapter 12)

4. *Computer Training and Support Buyer's Guide.* Ziff Institute, 25 First Street, Cambridge, MA 02141. Phone: (617) 252-5000; Fax: (617) 252-5113. 1993. (120 pages, soft-cover)

(See Chapter 12)

5. *EdVENT PLUS.* Timeplace, Inc., 460 Totten Pond Road, Waltham, MA 02154. Phone: (800) 544-4023, (617) 890-INFO; Fax: (617) 890-7274.

(See Chapter 12)

6. *The Human Resource Information Network (HRIN).* ETSI (Formerly Executive Telecom System, Inc.), 1200 Quince Orchard Blvd., Gaithersburg, MD 20878. Phone: (800) 638-8094, (301) 590-2300; Fax: (301) 990-8378. ($890 per year plus connect charges.)

(See Chapter 12)

7. *The Linton Trainer's Resource Directory.* Linton Publishing Company, 1011 First Street South, Hopkins, MN 55343-9823. Phone: (612) 936-2288; Fax: (612) 936-9623. 1992 (2nd Edition). (2,000 pages, hard-cover, $395.00)

(See Chapter 12)

8. Mackey, Douglas A. and Gilius, Lawrence, Senior Editors. *The Corporate University Guide To Management Seminars.* The Corporate University, Inc., P. O. Box 2080, Fairfield, IA 52556. Phone: (515) 472-7720; Fax: (515) 472-7105. 1993. (796 pages, soft-cover, $69.95)

(See Chapter 12)

9. McLean, Janice, Editor. *Training And Development Organizations Directory.* Gale Research Inc., 835 Penobscot Bldg., Detroit, MI 48226-4094. Phone: (800) 877-GALE, (313) 961-2242; Fax: (313) 961-6083, (313) 961-6815. 1991 (5th Edition). ISBN 0-8103-4349-5. (677 pages, $310.00)

(See Chapter 12)

10. *NSPI Performance Improvement Resources Directory.* National Society for Performance and Instruction., 1126 16th Street N.W., Washington, DC 20036. Phone: (202) 861-0777; Fax: (202) 408-7972. 1990. (120 pages, spiral-bound)

(See Chapter 12)

11. *SIS Workbook.* Seminar Information Service, 17752 Skypark Circle, Suite 210, Irvine, CA 92714. Phone: (714) 261-9104; Fax: (714) 261-1963. (Published annually, in September; Updated monthly). (Nearly 500 page, looseleaf notebook, $295.00 per year.)

(See Chapter 12)

12. *Seminar Management System (SMS).* First Seminar, 600 Suffolk Street, Lowell, MA 01854-3685. Phone: (800) 321-1990, (508) 452-0766; Fax: (508) 441-2755.

(See Chapter 12)

13. *Seminar Searches And Evaluations.* Seminar Clearinghouse International, Inc., P. O. Box 1757, St. Paul, MN 55101-0757. Phone: (612) 293-1044; Fax: (612) 293-0493. ($400 - $2,200 per year based on number of employees and usage.)

(See Chapter 12)

14. Shores, David, Editor. *Seminars Directory.* Gale Research Inc., 835 Penobscot Bldg., Detroit, MI 48226-4094. Phone: (800) 877-GALE, (313) 961-2242; Fax: (313) 961-6083, (313) 961-6815. 1993 (4th Edition). ISBN 0-8103-8011-0. (1,079 pages, $130.00)

(See Chapter 12)

15. *TR/ED.* Linton Publishing Company, 1011 First Street South, Hopkins, MN 55343-9823. Phone: (612) 936-2288; Fax: (612) 936-9623.

(See Chapter 12)

16. *TRAINET.* American Society for Training and Development, 1640 King Street - P. O. Box 1443, Alexandria, VA 22313-2043. Phone: (703) 683-8129, (703) 683-8100; Fax: (703) 683-8103.

(See Chapter 12)

17. *Who's Who in Training and Development: The Official Membership Directory.* American Society for Training and Development, 1640 King Street - P. O. Box 1443, Alexandria, VA 22313-2043. Phone: (703) 683-8129, (703) 683-8100; Fax: (703) 683-8103. (Published annually).

A telephone directory of ASTD members, the Board of Directors, the Board of Governors, ASTD management and staff, committee leaders, chapter presidents, etc. Also contains advertising for training products.

Written and Spoken Communication

1. Barnet, Sylvan and Stubbs, Marcia. *Practical Guide to Writing.* Scott Foresman & Company, 1900 East Lake Avenue, Glenview, IL 60025. Phone: (800) 782-2665, (708) 729-3000; Fax: (708) 657-3999. 1989 (6th Edition). ISBN 0-673-39878-1.

2. Brusaw, Charles T.; Alfred, Gerald J.; and Oliu, Walter E. *The Business Writer's Handbook.* St. Martin's Press, 175 Fifth Avenue, New York, NY 10010. Phone: (800) 221-7945, (212) 674-5151; Fax: (212) 420-9314. 1987 (3rd Edition). ISBN 0-312-10958-X. (832 pages, $21.35)

3. Capp, Glen R. and Capp, Richard G. *Basic Oral Communication.* Prentice Hall, 113 Sylvan Avenue, Englewood Cliffs, NJ 07632. Phone: (201) 592-2000. 1990 (3rd Edition). ISBN 0-13-065996-7. (360 pages, paperback)

A practical approach to interpersonal communication, small group dialogue and public communication. The authors give steps in finding, organizing, analyzing and recording materials in order to transmit ideas.

4. Carnegie, Dale. *Quick and Easy Ways to Effective Speaking.* Pocket Books, 1230 Avenue of the Americas, New York, NY 10020. Phone: (800) 223-2336, (212) 698-7000. 1990. ISBN 0-671-72400-2. (Paperback, $5.50)

Carnegie discusses practical tips in gaining self-confidence and the art of winning any size audience.

5. Communispond, 300 Park Avenue, New York, NY 10022. Phone: (212) 486-2300; Fax: (213) 486-2680.

    The largest and most comprehensive communications consultants in the world have many regional offices and a wide range of courses for written and oral communications of all kinds. They also offer courses geared to salespeople ("Socratic Selling") and one-on-one coaching for important presentations.

6. Dumaine, Deborah. *Write to the Top: Writing for Corporate Success.* Random House, 201 E. 50th Street, New York, NY 10022. Phone: (800) 726-0600, (212) 751-2600; Fax: (212) 872-8026. 1989 (Revised Edition). ISBN 0-679-72346-3. (169 pages, $9.95)

    At less than 170 pages, this book is exceptionally useful for everyone who has to write. It breaks writing down into bite-sized tasks, and provides several step-by-step ways to accomplish each task. One of the best "how-to-do-it" writing books ever.

7. Feierman, Joanne. *Action Grammar: Fast Answers on Grammar, Usage and Punctuation.* Hastings Press, Hastings-on-Hudson, NY 1990. (58 pages, $5.95)

    Unless you're surrounded by expert writers, the questions quickly and clearly answered in this tiny book keep occurring over and over again. It almost makes sense to have one at every keyboard. Call the author at Seminars in Communication, (212) 427-7395, to get copies.

8. Flesch, Rudolf. *The Art of Clear Thinking.* HarperCollins Publishers, 10 E. 53rd Street, New York, NY 10022. Phone: (800) 242-7737, (212) 207-7000; Fax: (212) 207-7617. 1973. (212 pages)

9. Flesch, Rudolf. *The Art of Plain Talk.* MacMillan Publishing Company, 866 Third Avenue, New York, NY 10022. Phone: (212) 702-2000; Fax: (212) 605-3099. 1962.

    One of the real classics of communications; must reading for everyone in training, advertising or selling, along with S.I. Hayakawa's Language in Thought and Action.

10. Flesch, Rudolf. *The Art of Readable Writing.* MacMillan Publishing Company, 866 Third Avenue, New York, NY 10022. Phone: (212) 702-2000; Fax: (212) 605-3099. 1986 (Revised Edition). ISBN 0-02-046470-3. ($4.95)

11. Hayakawa, S.I. *Language in Thought and Action.* Harcourt Brace Jovanovich, Inc., 6277 Sea Harbor Drive, Orlando, FL 32887. Phone: (800) 225-5425, (407) 345-2000; Fax: (407) 345-9354. 1991 (5th Edition). ISBN 0-15-648240-1. (224 pages, $8.95)

    Along with Rudolph Flesch's The Art of Plain Talk, this classic is a "must" for anyone who makes a living with words.

12. Leech, Thomas. *How to Prepare, Stage, and Deliver Winning Presentations.* AMACOM Publishing Co., P.O. Box 1026, Saranac Lake, NY 12983-1026. Phone: (800) 262-9699, (518) 891-5510; Fax: (518) 891-3653. 1985. ISBN 0-8144-7630-9. (416 pages, $19.95)

    This book will show you how to make your presentations more effective, speed up the frequently tedious and costly process of putting together a presentation and make the giving of the presentation a much more enjoyable experience for you and your audience.

13. Mambert, W.A. *Effective Presentation: A Short Course for Professionals.* John Wiley and Sons, Inc., 605 Third Avenue, New York, NY 10158. Phone: (800) 225-5945, (212) 850-6000; Fax: (212) 850-6088. 1985 (2nd Edition). ISBN 0-471-80358-8. (324 pages, $64.95)

14. Mandel, Steve, edited by Crisp, Michael G. *Effective Presentation Skills.* Crisp Publications, Inc., 95 First Street, Los Altos, CA 94022. Phone: (800) 442-7477, (415) 949-4888; Fax: (415) 323-5800. 1987. ISBN 0-931961-24-6. (80 pages, softcover, $8.95)

15. National Speakers Association (NSA), 3877 N. 7th Street, Suite 350, Phoenix, AZ 85014. Phone: (602) 265-1001; Fax: (602) 265-7403. ($250/year.)

    (See Chapter 12)

16. Poe, Roy W. *The McGraw-Hill Handbook of Business Letters.* McGraw-Hill, 1221 Avenue of the Americas, New York, NY 10020. Phone: (212) 337-5945, (800) 2-MCGRAW. 1988 (2nd Edition). ISBN 0-07-050369-9. (320 pages, $49.95)

    Focusing on the need of letter writers in all kinds of businesses, this book examines more than 160 different letter writing situations, and provides model letters to demonstrate how each of these diverse situations can be handled effectively.

17. Qubein, Nido. *Communicate Like a Pro.* Prentice Hall, 113 Sylvan Avenue, Englewood Cliffs, NJ 07632. Phone: (201) 592-2000. 1986.

    By a past president of the National Speakers Association. Also available directly from the author at: Creative Services. Inc., P. O. Box 6008, High point, NC 27262, Phone: (919) 889-3010.

18. Roman, Kenneth, and Raphaelson, Joel. *Writing That Works.* HarperCollins Publishers, 10 E. 53rd Street, New York, NY 10022. Phone: (800) 242-7737, (212) 207-7000; Fax: (212) 207-7617. 1992 (Revised and enlarged edition). ISBN 0-06-273144-0. (144 pages, paperback, $9.00)

19. Strunk, William, Jr. and White, E. B. *The Elements of Style.* MacMillan Publishing Company, 866 Third Avenue, New York, NY 10022. Phone: (212) 702-2000; Fax: (212) 605-3099. 1979 (3rd Edition). ISBN 0-02-418190-0.

This is the classic reference text every writer is supposed to have at their elbow.

20. *Stylebook for Writers and Editors.* U.S. News & World Report., 2400 N Street, N.W., Washington, DC 20037-1196. 1993 (6th Edition). ($9.95 plus $2.45 shipping and handling.)

Arranged alphabetically for quick access, this book shows when to use punctuation marks, when to capitalize or when and how to abbreviate. It also addresses the fine points of grammar and words and phrases that are frequently misused. Available only by mail from the publisher.

21. Sweetnam, Sherry. *The Executive Memo: A Guide to Persuasive Business Communications.* John Wiley and Sons, Inc., 605 Third Avenue, New York, NY 10158. Phone: (800) 225-5945, (212) 850-6000; Fax: (212) 850-6088. 1986. ISBN 0-471-81826-7. (248 pages, $19.95)

A how-to book with over 40 practical exercises and self-instructional quizzes, including one at the start so you can focus on the skills you need.

22. Toastmasters International (TI), 2200 N. Grand, P.O. Box 10400, Santa Ana, CA 92711. Phone: (714) 542-6793.

(See Chapter 12)

23. Walters, Dottie and Walters, Lillett. *Speak And Grow Rich.* Prentice Hall, 113 Sylvan Avenue, Englewood Cliffs, NJ 07632. Phone: (201) 592-2000. 1989. ISBN 0-13-825803-1. (276 pages, paperback, $12.95)

The legendary Earl Nightingale wrote in his Foreword to this book, "This is a first-class book for budding speakers. It is also a first-class book for professional speakers who want to know more about the industry, and to see if they're on track when it comes to fees and such." I agree. The Walters (mother and daughter) have written a truly valuable book, particularly since about half the trainers I know have serious platform entertainer credentials too.

24. Wohlmuth, Ed. *The Overnight Guide to Public Speaking.* Running Press Book Publishers, 125 S. 22nd Street, Philadelphia, PA 19103. Phone: (800) 345-5359, (215) 567-5080; Fax: (800) 453-2884, (215) 568-2919. 1990 (2nd Edition). ISBN 0-89471-744-8. (160 pages, paperback, $9.95)

"Mercifully short, because this task cannot be learned from a book, this book addresses not only the basics, but also the sophisticated points of overcoming this unusually feared management task. There is more useful information in this short volume than can be found in works ten times its length on the same subject." - WSJ

13. - MARKETING DATABASE AND COMPUTERS

1. Holtz, Herman R. *Database Marketing.* John Wiley and Sons, Inc., 605 Third Avenue, New York, NY 10158. Phone: (800) 225-5945, (212) 850-6000; Fax: (212) 850-6088. 1992. ISBN 0-471-55187-2. ($34.95)

2. Nash, Edward L. *Database Marketing: The Ultimate Marketing Tool.* McGraw-Hill, 1221 Avenue of the Americas, New York, NY 10020. Phone: (212) 337-5945, (800) 2-MCGRAW. 1993.

3. U.S. Monitor Service, 86 Maple Avenue, New City, NY 10956. Phone: (914) 634-1331.

(See Chapter 13)

SOME HANDY DIRECTORIES AND REFERENCES

1. *Acronyms, Initialisms & Abbreviations Dictionary.* Gale Research Inc., 835 Penobscot Bldg., Detroit, MI 48226-4094. Phone: (800) 877-GALE, (313) 961-2242; Fax: (313) 961-6083, (313) 961-6815. 1994 (18th Edition). ISBN 0-8103-8203-2. (3,800 pages in 3 parts, $245.00)

A compilation of 520,000 acronyms and abbre-

viations, including those used in all aspects of business, advertising, banking, finance, trade, economics, statistics and more.

2. *Business Organizations, Agencies and Publications Directory.* Gale Research Inc., 835 Penobscot Bldg., Detroit, MI 48226-4094. Phone: (800) 877-GALE, (313) 961-2242; Fax: (313) 961-6083, (313) 961-6815. 1993 (7th Edition). ISBN 0-8103-8355-1. (1,415 pages, $345.00)

   A comprehensive guide to 26,000 organizations and agencies which provides information on 39 special fields. Includes trade fairs, business publishers, commercially available data banks, commodity and stock exchanges, labor unions, franchise companies, etc. Also available on-line through EPIC and FIRST-SEARCH.

3. *Directories in Print.* Gale Research Inc., 835 Penobscot Bldg., Detroit, MI 48226-4094. Phone: (800) 877-GALE, (313) 961-2242; Fax: (313) 961-6083, (313) 961-6815. 1994 (11th Edition). ISBN 0-8103-8197-4. (2,200 pages in 2 volumes, $285.00)

   An annotated guide of nearly 14,000 U.S. national and international directories covering 26 different subject areas. In addition to traditional formats, directories on CD-ROM, microfiche, mailing lists and other non-traditional formats are included.

4. *Directory of Special Libraries and Information Centers.* Gale Research Inc., 835 Penobscot Bldg., Detroit, MI 48226-4094. Phone: (800) 877-GALE, (313) 961-2242; Fax: (313) 961-6083, (313) 961-6815. 1993 (17th Edition). ISBN 0-8103-8017-X. (In 3 volumes, $430.00 (Vol. 1))

   Covers 21,000 special libraries in the U.S., Canada and elsewhere. Furnishes information on the facilities, holdings, availability and staff. Volume 2 covers geographic and personnel indexes. Volume 3 presents new special libraries.

5. *Encyclopedia of Associations.* Gale Research Inc., 835 Penobscot Bldg., Detroit, MI 48226-4094. Phone: (800) 877-GALE, (313) 961-2242; Fax: (313) 961-6083, (313) 961-6815. 1993 (28th Edition, published annually). ISBN 0-8103-8314-4. (3,395 pages in 3 volumes, $355.00)

   This is said to be Gale's best-known product. The basic title contains information on over 23,500 American associations of national scope, arranged by subject in 18 topics, and indexed by name and keyword. Separate geographic and executive indexes and supplements are available at additional cost. In addition there is a separate directory of 12,000 multinational, binational and foreign associations (2 volumes), and 53,000 U.S. state and local associations are also avail-

able (5 volumes). Needless to say all this is also available on diskette, on CD-ROM, on line through Dialog ... and Gale also offers a dial-in version!.

6. *Johnson's World-Wide Chambers of Commerce Directory.* Johnson Publishers, P.O. Box 455, Loveland, CO 80537. Phone: (303) 667-0652. (Published annually).

7. Kennedy, James H., Editor. *The Directory of Executive Recruiters.* Kennedy Publications, Templeton Road, Fitzwilliam, NH 03447. Phone: (800) 531-0007, (605) 585-6544; Fax: (604) 585-9555. 1992. ISBN 0-916654-82-6. (800 pages, 5-1/2" x 8-1/2" paperback; Corporate Edition also 800 pages but 8-1/2" x 11" and hardcover, $39.95; Corporate Edition: $79.00.)

   (See Chapter 4)

8. Library of Congress, Washington, DC 20540. Phone: (202) 287-5639.

   Maintains a division of the reference section known as "Technical Research for Free or a Fee," which offers both free and fee-based reference and bibliographic services.

9. National Referral Center, Library of Congress, Washington, DC 20540. Phone: (202) 287-5670.

   Will locate the organization you need to provide free information in your area of interest.

10. *The North America On-Line Directory* (formerly known as Information Industry Marketplace). R.R. Bowker Co., 1180 Avenue of the Americas, New York, NY 10036. Phone: (212) 916-1600; Fax: (212) 463-6890. (Published annually). ($75.00)

    Provides a listing of over 2,000 firms and individuals who produce information products or who service the information industry.

11. Schwartz. *Small Business Sourcebook.* Gale Research Inc., 835 Penobscot Bldg., Detroit, MI 48226-4094. Phone: (800) 877-GALE, (313) 961-2242; Fax: (313) 961-6083, (313) 961-6815. 1992 (6th Edition). ISBN 0-8103-8076-5. (2 volumes, $210.00)

    Profiles 100 small businesses and covers the information sources where applicable, including associations, educational programs, reference works, statistics sources, trade periodicals, shows and conventions, consultants, franchises, and sources of supply. Also contains a compilation of nearly 1,000 books and periodicals particularly useful for small businesses.

12. Thomsett, Michael C. *The Little Black Book of Business Words.* AMACOM Publishing Co., P.O. Box 1026, Saranac Lake, NY 12983-1026.

Phone: (800) 262-9699, (518) 891-5510; Fax: (518) 891-3653. 1991. (161 pages, softcover, $14.95)

13. *Ward's Business Directory of U.S. Private and Public Companies.* Gale Research Inc., 835 Penobscot Bldg., Detroit, MI 48226-4094. Phone: (800) 877-GALE, (313) 961-2242; Fax: (313) 961-6083, (313) 961-6815. 1993. ISBN 0-8103-7566-4. (5 volumes, $1,210.00)

Presents current, verified data on 135,000 U.S. companies, 94% of which are privately held. Includes address, phone and fax, SICs, financial and employment information, year founded, and up to eight company officers may also be listed. Volume 4 provides state-by-state listings with contact data, while volume 5 ranks companies by sales volume within SIC classifications. This information is available on magnetic tape and diskette, and as part of a larger, Companies International database on CD-ROM.*

A FEW CURRENT "CLASSICS"

1. Bennis, Warren. *On Becoming a Leader.* Addison-Wesley Publishing Co., Inc., One Jacob Way, Reading, MA 01867. Phone: (800) 447-2226, (617) 944-3700; Fax: (617) 944-9338. 1990. ISBN 0-201-55087-3. (Paperback, $10.53)

"Bennis has written a number of books on leadership, but this synthesis of interviews with notables from Betty Friedan to John Sculley is a favorite. 'Especially good,' says Jimmy Calano of Career-Track, a professional training company in Boulder, Colo., 'is the last chapter, 'Forging the Future.' It tells how to shift from being a manager to being a leader; it's a synthesis of the book. I think you can learn vicariously, which is why I like to see how high-profile people work.' Also recommended: Bennis's Leaders, written with Burt Nanus (Harper & Row, 1985), which looks at artistic, political and corporate leaders and finds a common trait in their ability to retain original and compellingly articulated points of view."-INC.

2. Covey, Stephen R. *Seven Habits of Highly Effective People.* Simon & Schuster, 1230 Avenue of the Americas, New York, NY 10020. Phone: (800) 223-2336, (212) 698-7000; Fax: (212) 698-7007. 1990. ISBN 0-671-70863-5. ($10.00)

3. Drucker, Peter F. *Adventures of a Bystander: Memoirs of People and Places.* HarperCollins Publishers, 10 E. 53rd Street, New York, NY 10022. Phone: (800) 242-7737, (212) 207-7000; Fax: (212) 207-7617. 1991. ISBN 0-06-016565-0. (352 pages, $25.00)

Drucker's freewheeling self-portrait, with entertaining and insightful observations about business and political figures and lively anecdotes about his life and work as a management consultant.

4. Gardner, John W. *On Leadership.* The Free Press, 866 Third Avenue, New York, NY 10022. Phone: (212) 605-9364. 1989. ISBN 0-02-911311-3. ($19.95)

Jack Zenger said, "Gardner's books for me are an incredible combination of profound thoughts expressed with great eloquence. He quotes from history, literature and his years of service in the government. The combination makes for delicious reading. The other thing is that he doesn't rush to publish; he takes his time and writes good books."

5. Harragan, Betty L. *Games Mother Never Taught You: Corporate Gamesmanship for Women.* Warner Books, Inc., 1271 Avenue of the Americas, New York, NY 10020. Phone: (212) 522-7200; Fax: (212) 522-7991. 1989 (Revised edition). ISBN 0-446-35703-0. (400 pages, $5.95)

"This book started out as a women's primer for management. It has since been recognized as one of the best books written on organizational dynamics." - WSJ

6. Kouzes, James M. and Posner, Barry M. *The Leadership Challenge: How to Get Extraordinary Things Done in Organizations.* Jossey-Bass, Inc. Publishers, 350 Sansome Street, San Francisco, CA 94104. Phone: (415) 433-1767; Fax: (415) 433-0499. 1990. ISBN 1-55542-211-X. (394 pages, paperback, $15.95)

7. Naisbitt, John and Aburdene, Patricia. *Megatrends 2000: Ten New Directions for the 1990's.* Avon Books, 1350 Avenue of the Americas, New York, NY 10019. Phone: (800) 238-0658, (212) 261-6800; Fax: (212) 261-6895. 1991. ISBN 0-380-70437-4. (448 pages, paperback, $5.95)

8. Senge, Peter M. *The Fifth Discipline: Mastering the Five Practices of the Learning Organization.* Doubleday, 666 Fifth Avenue, New York, NY 10103. Phone: (800) 223-6834, (212) 765-6500; Fax: (212) 492-9700. 1990. ISBN 0-385-26094-

6. (425 pages, $25.00)

"An organization's relative ability to learn is becoming the only sustainable source of competitive advantage," says the author. His five ways to do this: Building shared vision, personal mastery, mental models, team learning and systems thinking. This top-selling and somewhat unconventional work draws together science, spiritual wisdom, psychology and management theory.

9. Walton, Mary. *Deming Management at Work.* Putnam Publishing Group., 200 Madison Avenue, New York, NY 10016. Phone: (800) 631-8571, (212) 951-8400; Fax: (212) 213-6706. 1991. ISBN 0-399-51685-9. (256 pages, paperback, $10.95)

"W. Edwards Deming's theories on quality and management in Japanese and U.S. companies are well regarded; unfortunately, most executives say Deming's own writing is too turgid and dense to wade through. Mary Walton's book is a middle ground: a 14-page summary of Deming's doctrine, coupled with case histories of six companies that use his revolutionary techniques."- INC.

A VOCABULARY OF COMMON TERMS FOR MARKETING TRAINING AND INFORMATION

This VOCABULARY contains 300 words and phrases frequently used in the sales and marketing of training, continuing education and information products and services. It is intended as a starting point for building your own larger working vocabulary in this dynamic and fast-moving field:

A/B SPLIT - The process of dividing a mailing list, or other marketing material, into two equal parts differing only in some desired test variable. Mail lists are often split (or "feathered") into two equal parts by sorting alternate names into each list.

ADDRESS CORRECTION REQUESTED - An endorsement which, when printed in the upper left-hand corner of the address portion of the mailing piece (below the return address), authorizes the Postal Service, for a fee, to provide the new address of a person no longer at the address on the mailing piece.

AFFIX - To attach stamps and/or labels to mailing pieces, usually by machine.

ASSIGNED MAILING DATE - The date(s) on which the list user has the obligation to mail a specific list, based on prior agreement between the list owner and the renter. No other date is acceptable without specific approval of the list owner.

ATTENDEE - One who enrolls in a course or program and is actually present on a given occasion or at a given place.

ATTRITION CURVE - A graphic representation of the rate at which human relationships are ended. In direct marketing, it refers to the rate of loss of customer relationships, once they are obtained, and depends, among other things, on the type of product/service being sold.

AUDIO-VISUAL - Instructional materials that make use of both sight and sound. Often abbreviated A-V.

AUDIT - To attend a course or program without working for, or expecting to receive, formal credit. Usually, those auditing expect to do so at a reduced price.

A-V - (See Audio-Visual.)

BACK-END - A direct marketing expression for the sales and/or profits derived from a responder after the initial transaction or acquisition. The back-end revenues can often match or exceed those obtained on the front-end (acquisition), and the knowledge of the relative importance of these two parts is essential to evaluating the marketing economics of a product, service or list.

BACK-OF-THE-ROOM SALES - Sales of publications, products -- and sometimes even services -- in conjunction with an event such as a seminar or conference.

BANQUETS - (See Catering.)

BATCH MODE - The method of updating a file at periodic intervals. (Compare with On-Line Entry and Real Time.)

BINDERY - A place where books are bound or other operations are performed relating to the printing process, such as punching, folding, trimming, collating, stitching, round-cornering, die-cutting, etc.

BINGO CARD - A promotional means whereby a periodical has numbered each advertisement in an issue and compiled the numbers on a business reply postcard bound into the magazine. The responder then indicates interest in receiving further information by marking the appropriate number on the card and returning it by mail, usually to the publisher of the magazine.

BIT - Contraction of Binary Digit. A basic unit of computer information in the binary number system. Most information in a computer is stored as a series of bits, represented by a magnetized spot on the recording surface of a storage device.

BLEED - An extra amount of printed image which extends beyond the trim edge of a page.

BLUE LINE - A trial sheet of printed material (made by creating a positive print of the negative from which the printing plate will be made), used for approval and/or correction before the actual printing is done. (Often the print appears in a blue color.)

BPA - Business Publication Audit, an independent audit of a publication's circulation and readership, conducted by BPA International, 270 Madison Avenue, New York, NY 10016-0699. Phone: (212) 779-3200.

BPI - An abbreviation for Bits Per Inch. The spacing of bits on a magnetic medium which is measured in the direction of motion of the magnetic material.

BRC - An abbreviation for Business Reply Card.

BRE - An abbreviation for Business Reply Envelope.

BREAK-OUT ROOM - A separate room or area used to accommodate small groups at various times during an organized function.

BRIEFING - A short meeting, often for executives, dealing with a single topic or a group of closely related topics.

BROADCAST MEDIA - Direct response sources which involve radio, television and/or cable television.

BROCHURE - A pamphlet folded and/or bound in booklet form. Often accompanied by a letter when used to advertise a product or service.

BROWN LINE - (See Blue Line.)

BUDGET - An allocation of resources (capital, land, materials, human efforts, etc.) to accomplish specified objectives. Budgeting is one of the steps in planning.

BULK MAIL - (See Third-Class Bulk Mail.)

BUSINESS - A broad market classification referring to organizational, institutional and/or professional purchases of goods and services. (Compare with Consumer.)

BUSINESS REPLY - The postal classification which enables mail pieces to be returned to the sender at no charge to the recipient. Business Reply cards and envelopes are often abbreviated BRC and BRE, respectively.

BUYER - One who purchases a product or service and has paid for it. The buyer may not be the attendee at a training program or conference.

BUYING HISTORY - A record of the previous purchases made by a customer or prospect, including at least the following for each purchase: date, type of purchase, dollar amount, how paid and source of the order.

BYTE - A sequence of 8 adjacent binary digits (bits) that a computer will process as a unit and defines a single character.

CAMERA-READY ARTWORK - Artwork complete and ready for printing.

CARRIER ROUTE SORT - Refers to mail pieces that are sorted and bundled by the mailer in a manner specified by the Post Office to facilitate delivery by a postal carrier, in the exact order in which he/she actually delivers mail on his/her route. A permit is required to mail by this classification.

CASSETTE - A magnetic tape medium encased in a protective plastic shell, used for audio, video and computer data storage and transfer. Also TAPE CASSETTE.

CATALOG - A pamphlet or book that systematically lists items or programs with descriptive details. When used for advertising, information on how to order the products or services is also included. Small catalogs with offerings limited to selected items are called Mini-Catalogs.

CATERING - A hotel department responsible for supplying food and beverages to a group function. Also called the Banquets Department, or Food and Beverage.

CBT - An abbreviation for Computer-Based Training.

CD-ROM - The common abbreviation for Compact Disk Read-Only Memory, a high-density computer memory medium like that used for recorded music.

CEU - An abbreviation for Continuing Education Unit, a standard measure of the duration of a course or program. One CEU is approximately ten contact hours of supervised instruction.

CHECK DIGIT - A digit added to a match code by the computer in order to verify the accuracy of the match code.

CHESHIRE - Denotes various aspects of the process wherein names and addresses printed on specially prepared tractor-fed paper are cut, glued and mechanically affixed to an envelope or mailing piece one at a time. The process, named for the company that developed it and markets the affixing equipment, accommodates various label formats and types of paper.

CLASS - A group of students meeting to study the same subject, usually at an educational institution.

CLASSIFIED ADVERTISEMENT - A systematic arrangement of advertising by the type of service or product available, usually in periodicals.

CLEAN LIST - A list that has been updated or corrected and is current. Can refer to mailing and/or telephone lists. (See also List Cleaning.)

CLUSTER SELECTION - A selection routine based upon taking a group of names in series, skipping a group, taking another group, etc. For example, a cluster selection on an Nth name basis might be the first ten out of every 100 or the first 125 out of 175. A cluster selection using limited ZIP codes might be the first 200 names in each of the specified ZIP codes. (See also Nth Name.)

COLOR KEY - A set of transparencies in each of the colors to be used for printing. By placing various colors on top of one another, the exact color a piece will be after printing can be seen.

COLOR LAP - Refers to the amount of overlap of one or more colors to avoid a white line or gap between two areas, cuts,

colors or separations.

COMPILED LIST - A list of names and other pertinent information derived from sources other than direct response, such as from directories, resource books, computer data bases, etc., which identify groups of organizations or individuals with something in common.

CONFERENCE - Any meeting for consultation or discussion, but particularly a multi-day gathering for a program delivered by many presenters. Often involves food/beverage functions, exhibitors and/or entertainment.

CONFERENCE CENTER - A self-contained facility specifically designed to accommodate training or business meetings, often in a scenic and/or remote locale.

CONFIRMATION - The written verification of something; for example, an individual's order, reservation, etc.

CONSORTIUM - A group of cooperating organizations or individuals. Consortium training takes place when two or more organizations act to sponsor a course or program for their mutual benefit.

CONTINUATION - The second or subsequent group of names used from a test list, usually selected in such a manner as to ensure that none of the names supplied in earlier usage(s) are included.

CONTINUOUS TONE - A photograph before it is re-photographed and broken down into small dots for printing, after which it is called a half-tone.

CONTROL - A standard or benchmark used in testing. In direct marketing, the current list, package or promotional approach against which changes are measured.

CONTROLLED CIRCULATION - The distribution of a publication, usually at no charge, to individuals or companies on the basis of their titles or industries or that meet certain criteria set by the publisher. (Compare with Paid Subscriber.)

CONVENTION - An assembly or meeting of members, representatives or delegates of a group. (See also conference.)

CONVENTION SERVICES - A hotel department responsible for setting up meeting rooms, organizing the audio-visual requirements, and managing the function at the actual time it's taking place. Most larger hotels utilize a Convention Services Department; at smaller hotels, meetings are usually handled by the Catering Department.

CONVENTION AND VISITOR BUREAU - An organization created to stimulate and facilitate tourism and meetings in a community. For more information, contact the International Association of Convention and Visitor Bureaus, P.O. Box 6690, Champaign, IL 61824-6690. Phone: (217) 359-8881, Fax: (217) 359-0965.

CONVERTER - One who makes up envelopes, starting with paper and performing the necessary die-cutting, folding and gluing operations.

CO-OP MAILING - A mailing in which two or more offers are included in the same envelope or other carrier and share mailing costs according to some predetermined formula.

COPY - Any material that is to be used in the production of printing, but most commonly refers to the text.

CORPORATE RATE - A sleeping room rate extended by hotels to frequent individual business travelers who are not attending group meetings. This rate is typically 10 percent lower than the published rate. (Contrast with Rack Rate.)

CROSS SECTION - A group of names and addresses selected from a mailing list in such a way as to be representative of the entire list.

CUSTOMER - Literally, one who purchases, or has purchased, a product. More broadly, customer refers to everyone who participates in a buying decision up to and including the end user.

DATABASE - A collection of related information, organized for rapid analysis, selection, retrieval and/or reporting, usually by computer. For example, a marketing database would contain complete information on each customer or prospective customer showing how they were acquired, what they've bought or inquired about, how to contact them and demographic or other information about their interests and/or preferences. (See List Database.)

DATA CAPTURE - Any method or medium used to acquire information for data entry. Media may include order forms, bingo cards or log sheets from telephone communications, etc.

DATA CARD - A 5" x 8" card which provides specific information about a particular list, such as how the list was obtained and maintained, the broker involved, number of names and the rental cost.

DATA ENTRY - The process by which data are input to update a file, usually on a computer.

DECOY NAMES - A means of controlling the security of a mailing list by inserting unique names into the list, or by using known recipients to monitor mail from a given list. Also called "seeds." The process of adding decoy names is often called salting the list.

DEMOGRAPHICS - The study of the measurable externals of a market segment or individual, such as sex, age, education, occupation, income level, marital status, family size, home value, etc. (See also Psychographics.)

DEMONSTRATION - A showing of the merits of a product or service to a prospective buyer, often at no charge. (Sometimes shortened to "demo.")

DIFFERENTIATION - The real or imagined differences in a product's design, performance and/or features which permit customers to distinguish between and identify the products of various producers.

DIRECT MAIL - Any promotional effort using the Postal Service or any other mail delivery service for distribution of the advertising message directly to a specified individual.

DIRECT MARKETING - Any communication which is intended to produce an order or other specific action without a face-to-face meeting.

DIRECT RESPONSE - Refers to the active interest in a product or service that has been generated by advertising through any means (such as mail, television or telephone) and evidenced by the customer's communication or other action.

DISKETTE - A small magnetic medium used for the storage and transfer of computer information. The most common sizes for personal computers are 3.5 and 5.25 inches.

DISPLAY AD - That part of a periodical devoted specifically to the advertising of a product or service. Display ads are priced according to their size, color, placement in the publication and/or the number of times the ad is committed to run.

DISTRIBUTION CHANNEL - The collection of steps through which a product passes from the producer to the end user.

DMMA - An abbreviation for Direct Mail Marketing Association, a large international trade association representing users, creators, and suppliers of direct mail advertising and other direct marketing techniques.

DMMA MAIL PREFERENCE SERVICE (MPS) - A service provided by DMMA that enables individuals to have their names and addresses removed from or added to mailing lists. These names are available to both members and non-members.

DOT MATRIX - A type of printing created by a computer in which each character is formed by separate dots of ink. (See also Impact Printer.) A dot is also the individual element of a half-tone.

DPBC - Delivery-Point BarCode, the U.S.P.S. barcode employing 12 digits consisting of the 9-digit ZIP+4 code, plus two additional digits to code the exact delivery point (usually the last two digits in the street address) plus a check digit.

DROP DATE - The date on which a mailing is entered at the Post Office for delivery.

DROP OUT - Refers to the portions of camera-ready artwork not meant to be reproduced, often represented by a mask. Also refers to a printing defect where something is too light or missing entirely.

DRY TEST - Advertising a product or service that doesn't exist at the time the advertisement is placed, or isn't available for delivery within the 30-day period permitted by the Federal Trade Commission. The opposite of a wet test. (See also Testing.)

DUBBING - The process of adding sound to an existing film, record or tape.

DUMMY - A preliminary layout of the piece to be reproduced, showing positions of the text and illustrations, as they are to appear in the final rendition. Also called a mock-up. Can also apply to how a piece will fold, called a folding dummy.

DUMMY NAMES - (See Decoy Names.)

DUOTONE - A term for a two-color half-tone reproduction from a one-tone photograph.

DUPLICATES - Names that appear two or more times on one list (internal duplicates), or on several lists (duplicates between lists). The latter are sometimes referred to as multibuyers when they occur on responder lists. Duplicate elimination (part of the purging operation) is the process of deleting all but one of the duplicates.

EDITING RULES - Specific rules used in preparing name and address records in order to treat all elements the same way at all times. Although most companies use some editing rules in common, few conform in all respects. Therefore, knowledge of specific editing rules for each list is important to the user.

ENHANCE - To add information to a file or record during computer processing. (See also Overlay.)

ENVELOPE - A flat, usually paper container completely enclosing a letter or other piece of mail. Standard sized envelopes are frequently denoted by number; for example, a #10 business envelope is 9 1/2" x 4 1/8".

EXPIRE - A subscriber who has let the subscription run out without renewing. (See also Paid Subscriber and Controlled Circulation.)

EXPOSITION - A structured opportunity for organizations to display their goods or services to conference attendees or others, usually at rented "booths" in an exhibit hall. Commonly referred to as an Expo or Show.

FACILITATOR - One who conducts a meeting and facilitates information exchange, learning or skill-building processes for participants.

FACILITY - A term typically used in reference to a meeting site, such as a hotel or conference center, where sleeping rooms, meeting space and meal service are available.

FACE-TO-FACE SELLING - A sales technique in which one or more personal meetings and/or contacts is crucial for success. The most common fact-to-face selling takes place in retail stores. Older business-to-business sales literature often used "direct sales" to mean face-to-face selling, but this terminology is ambiguous with today's widespread use of mail, print advertising, TV and other direct response methods that employ no face-to-face contact.

FACING PAGES - Refers to pages such as two and three, four and five, six and seven; also known as "reader's spreads".

FEDEX - An abbreviation for Federal Express, the company that pioneered overnight delivery of letters and small packages. Often used generically for any next-day delivery service such as offered by Airborne Express, DHL, Federal Express, United Parcel Service, U.S. Post Office, and others.

FEATURE - A characteristic or property of a product which allows it to be distinguished from other similar products. Features may be found in the hardware, software or service that comprise the product. (Contrast with Benefit.)

FIELD (DATA) - A subdivision or elemental portion of a computer record, one or more characters (bytes) representing a unit of information.

FIELD (SALES) - A means of selling which uses live salespersons making face-to-face sales calls. The prospect universe is usually divided into territories based on geography or some other customer characteristic, as the basis for salesperson responsibility assignments.

FILE - A group of records, each of which contain a name, address or other data. Files are maintained on paper in boxes or file cabinets, on cards or plates, in a computer's memory or on magnetic tapes or disks. Files are used to produce lists.

FILM FESTIVAL - An organized opportunity for prospective buyers to see many related films or videos, often from a number of producers.

FLAT - The assembled composite of negatives from which a printing plate is made.

FOUR-COLOR PROCESS - (See Process Printing.)

FOUR-PAGE - A form of printing in which a sheet of paper, printed on both sides, is folded to produce a booklet of four pages consisting of a front cover, two inside pages and a back cover. Most booklets, catalogs, etc., involve four-page multiples.

FOUR-UP - Any arrangement in which four items, images or impressions are placed together; for example, a sheet of mailing labels which are placed in linear rows of four labels, or a press sheet in which four images are printed simultaneously.

FREQUENCY - Refers to the number of times to which an individual or list is mailed. The term can also refer to the number of times an individual has ordered within a specific period of time. (See also RFM).

GALLEY - A shallow metal tray into which each line of type is deposited as it comes from the typesetting machine. A galley holds about three book pages worth of type.

GALLEY PROOF - An intermediate step in printing where paper, printed from galleys and without page breaks, is used for proofreading and final page composition. In modern photographic typesetting, the term refers to any proof of the correct width, but without page breaks.

GRAM - A form of correspondence that looks like a telegram and dramatically boosts opening and reading (98 percent reported by Opinion Research in one test).

GRAPHICS - Relating to or involving the art of design, printing and reproduction.

GROUP SALES - A hotel department responsible for renting meeting space and associated blocks of sleeping rooms for group functions. Usually, after the initial booking has been made through the salesperson, the function is then handled by the Catering or Convention Services Departments.

HALF-TONE - A printed picture that has been broken down into a pattern of dots. Half-tones are used to create shadings of tone between black and white. (See also Continuous Tone and Duotone.)

HARD COPY - Information in printed form.

HOTLINE LIST - The most recent names available on a specific list, but no older than three months. In any event, use of the term "hotline" should be further modified by weekly, monthly, etc.

HOTEL - An establishment that provides lodging, meals and meeting space to the public.

HOUSE LIST - A list of an organization's customers, clients, donors or other names acquired as a result of inquiry, or buyer action of that company's products or services.

IMPACT PRINTER - Any printing means in which the image is made by striking through an inked medium, such as a ribbon. Impact printers generally use keys, balls, wheels, etc., with preformed characters in specific styles, or a collection of small wires which extend to form the characters out of a pattern of dots (dot matrix printers).

INDICIA - The postal markings imprinted on mail or on labels to be affixed to mail pieces.

IN-HOUSE - Relating to a training session or program restricted entirely to members of one group or organization. Also known as an on-site program.

INK JET - A computerized printing means in

which the ink is sprayed onto the paper without a mechanical impact.

INQUIRER - One who inquires about a product or service without actually purchasing. For most direct marketing programs, inquirers have a high rate of conversion to customers and should be accorded the same treatment as customers.

INSERTER - A mechanical device which places printed pieces into an envelope in a certain sequence for mailing. Requirements for insertion must be taken into account early in the design of any mail piece. Sometimes called Phillipsburgs.

INSTITUTE - A short, intensive workshop or seminar, usually on a single subject.

I/O - An abbreviation for Input/Output, usually in connection with data processing and computers.

JOB-AID - Any chart, table, diagram, placard or device that provides assistance for performing some task or operation by presenting a concise summary of the steps, sequences, rules, guidelines, etc. needed.

KEY CODE - A group of digits or other markings imprinted on a label or mail piece to identify a particular mail list and/or test package.

LABEL - The portion of a mail piece identifying the recipient and containing address and/or coding information.

LAN - An abbreviation for Local Area Network, a means of connecting personal computers so that they can share information and connected devices such as printers.

LASER PRINTER - The class of printers based on xerography, in which the image on the light sensitive drum is written by a computer-controlled laser beam rather than by optical imaging (as used in the common copier). The process subjects the printed material to substantial heating (to fuse the toner/ink) which can limit its applications.

LEADING - A term used to refer to the distance between typeset lines, measured in points.

LETTER SHOP - (See Mailhouse.)

LICENSING - Granting permission to an individual or organization to use something, usually for payment of a licensing fee. Training programs are an example of something that may be licensed.

LIFETIME VALUE - The total economic contribution made to an enterprise by a single direct responder during the period from acquisition to loss of the relationship. The principal determining factors are acquisition cost, length of the relationship, present value of all future purchases made or influenced by the responder, and cost of obtaining those future sales. (See also Attrition Curve.)

LINE ART - In the graphic arts usage, refers to any negative, print, copy or printing plate which is composed of solid image areas without half-tone patterns. Line art is usually type.

LINE PRINTER - A high-speed, computerized printing device that prints each line as a unit rather than character by character, usually based on impact printing.

LIST BROKER - A specialist who makes all necessary arrangements for one company to make use of the list of another company. A broker often recommends, selects and evaluates a particular list. The broker is usually paid a commission of 20 percent, based on the total rental cost, by the list owner. Well-informed list brokers serve as important sources of information on the results obtained by other renters, which can be valuable in evaluating lists.

LIST CLEANING - The process of correcting and/or removing a name and address from a mailing list because it is no longer correct. Addresses may be corrected as a result of Address Correction Requested and/or Return Postage Guaranteed, or by the individual.

LIST COMPILER - One who assembles a list on which all entries have one or more common attributes or demographic features (e.g., income, type of business or profession, organizational level, etc.) Compilers usually work from existing sources and maintain their lists in computerized form. (See also Data Base.)

LIST DATABASE - One or more mailing lists with a common connection, merged into a master list with duplicates eliminated in the process. List databases may be enhanced or overlaid with additional information from other databases or sources. (See also Overlay.)

LIST ENHANCEMENT - The process of matching a house list against a master file/data base, and for each "hit," or match, transferring to the house list some or all of the data contained on the master file for that record.

LIST EXCHANGE - A barter arrangement between two companies for the use of a mailing list(s). May be list for list, list for space or list for something else of comparable value other than money.

LIST MANAGER - The organization hired by a mailing list owner to promote rental of their list. Managers typically receive a 20% commission on list rentals they produce. Most lists are "self-managed" by the List Owner.

LIST OWNER - One who, by promotional activity or compilation, has developed a list of names having something in common, or one who has purchased such a list from the developer. (Contrast with List Rental.)

LIST PROTECTION - All of the means taken to ensure against unauthorized use of a list and to enable detection of unauthorized use if it occurs. The principal means employed is the use of dummy names, also called seeds. (See also Dummy Names.)

LIST RENTAL - An arrangement in which a list owner furnishes names on his/her list to a mailer for one-time use, in exchange for payment at a pre-specified rate.

LIST SELECTIONS - The variables specified to define a portion of a larger list. Because of restrictions imposed by the manner in which the list is maintained, not all types of selections are available on every list, hence those available become important for determining whether or not a list will be appropriate for any given offer.

M - The Roman numeral meaning a thousand.

MAIL CLASSIFICATION - Refers to the regulations, specifications, mode of payment for postage and the type of service associated with categories of mail established by the USPS.

MAILHOUSE - A facility which handles printed material to be mailed. A mailhouse is typically responsible for affixing labels; inserting material into envelopes; sorting, tying, bundling and bagging or traying the material to postal regulations; and delivering mail to the Post Office for acceptance and distribution. (Also called Letter Shop.)

MAIL ORDER BUYER - One who orders and pays for a product or service through the mail.

MAILGRAM - A combination letter and telegram which is designed to provide overnight delivery service. A mailgram is or-dered through a Western Union office.

MAILING LIST - A compilation of names and addresses, usually including titles and organizations. Mailing lists may be furnished on plates, in printed form for affixing, or on magnetic tape for computer processing. Labels may be printed on perforated, gummed stock to be moistened and affixed, on pressure-sensitive stock which adheres itself, or on plain paper which is cut, glue-applied and affixed by the Cheshire or similar process.

MAINFRAME - A major and central computer which is capable of processing large amounts of data. A mainframe is usually the largest of available computers.

MAINTENANCE (LIST) - Any manual or mechanical system for keeping names and addresses, phone numbers and other information current. One measure of the degree of list maintenance is the frequency with which the list is updated. (See also List Cleaning.)

MARKETING - The job of identifying the needs/wants of selected customer groups, arranging for the appropriate goods/services to fulfill these needs/wants, and providing timely, relevant information on which these customers can make enlightened, voluntary buying decisions.

MASK - An opaque film material used on selected areas of the artboard while shooting the negative in offset printing.

MASTER FILE - The central or main list, or data base, with records listed in customer number or match code order.

MASTER TAPE - The final copy of an audio or video tape, from which other tapes or records will be made, or to which additional information will be added. The process of creating the master tape is referred to as "mastering."

MATCH CODE - A type of "account number" for each name or record in a file, usually composed of elements from the surname and/or the organization name, part of the address, the ZIP code and/or other characters drawn from the record.

MECHANICAL - A page or layout prepared as an original for photographic reproduction. This can be a single card with all elements of the finished page in place, ready for single shot photography. Hinged overlays are sometimes put over the solid type to allow multiple shots to be made off of the base art or mechanical.

MEDIA - Channels of communication which carry advertising, usually divided between print and electronic media.

MEDIA-BASED PROGRAMS - Those packaged training programs and instructional systems that rely primarily on audio, video, film, CD or a combination of these, even though workbooks, job-aids and/or other materials are used, and even though a live facilitator or administrator is employed. Computer-based training (CBT) is one type of media-based program, but usually is treated separately.

MEETING - Any coming together or assembly. The most general term encompassing seminars, conferences, conventions and other, similar specific descriptions.

MEETING ROOM - The space used for a group function, such as a training program, conference or seminar, usually including the seats, tables, desks or other furniture. In hotels or other commercial facilities, the meeting room is usually rented for the length of the meeting.

MEMORY DEVICE - The part of a computer used to store information, generally in the form of bits. A memory device may be a tape, hard disk, floppy disk, an integrated circuit (IC), or a CD-ROM "chip."

MERGE/PURGE - Any system used to remove duplicate names (or outdated material) from among two or more source files and to produce a single resultant unduplicated file in some desired sequence. When done on modern computers, the source lists are usually furnished on magnetic tape, and the results are either returned to a tape or printed, along with a detailed report.

METER - To print postal indicia on a mailing piece by means of a postage meter.

METER MARK - The printed mark which indicates postage on an envelope. Used instead of a postage stamp.

MICROCOMPUTER - A small, relatively inexpensive, general purpose desk-top computer, often for small business or personal use. Also called a personal computer or "PC."

MINICOMPUTER - A self-contained, general purpose, free-standing computer, usually larger in size than a microcomputer, but smaller than a mainframe.

MONETARY VALUE - The average value of purchases made by a buyer or a list. (See also RFM.)

MONITOR - To regulate or control a mailing list in terms of its responsiveness.

MONITORING RESULTS - The step in planning that provides information on progress against the plan and identifies appropriate action(s) to restore activities to the desired standards.

MULTIBUYERS - Individuals who have purchased more than once during a given period of time. Multibuyers can be on a single list or can be revealed as the result of merge/purge operations between several lists.

NEGATIVE - Film containing an image in which the light and dark areas are reversed. In printing, the negative is used to create the plate from which a piece is printed. Sometimes referred to as a neg.

NEGATIVE OPTION - A buying plan in which a customer or club member agrees to accept and pay for products or services announced in advance at regular intervals, unless the individual notifies the company within reasonable time after each announcement.

NEG(S) - (See Negative.)

NET NAME ARRANGEMENT - An agreement between list owner and list renter, at the time of ordering or before, in which the list owner agrees to accept adjusted payment for less than the total names shipped. Such agreements can be for a percentage of names shipped or names actually mailed, whichever is greater, or for only those names actually mailed.

NEWS RELEASE - An item circulated to various media and news services informing them of an individual or public event or occurrence of interest to those they serve. News releases are an important step in publicizing a product or service. (See also Publicity.)

NDG - An abbreviation for National Distribution Guide, Canada's equivalent of the U.S. Carrier Route and Zip Code combined. A list for mailing Third Class in Canada must be obtained in "NDG Sort" order.

NFA - An abbreviation for No Forwarding Address. This term is used on mail that has been returned to the sender due to an obsolete address.

NIXIES - Pieces of mail that are undeliverable for any reason. Nixies are only automatically returned to the sender by the USPS for First-Class mail, but similar services may be obtained for other classes of mail by payment of certain charges.

NON-PROFIT - An organization created, chartered, incorporated or declared to be for philanthropic, charitable or other allowable not-for-profit purposes. Non-profit organizations are entitled to mail at low, preferred postal rates, and thereby have an economic advantage over their for-profit competitors.

NO-SHOW - A registrant who failed to show up at the event.

NTH NAME - A fractional unit that is repeated in sampling a mailing list. For instance, in an "every tenth" sample, the first, eleventh, twenty-first, etc., records would be selected. (See also Cluster Selection.)

OCR - An abbreviation for Optical Character Recognition. The term is used to refer to machine identification of printed characters through the use of light-sensitive devices. The United States Postal Service is installing OCRs in most mail processing facilities to improve the distribution of the nation's mail volume.

OFFSET - A printing process in which an inked impression from a plate is first made on a rubber-blanketed cylinder and then transferred to the paper being printed. Offset printing is often used to print from typewritten copy in order to avoid the cost of typesetting. Also called planographic or lithographic printing.

ON-LINE CODE - An operation in which the mail piece and/or label is coded at the time of affixing or insertion, and is therefore "on-line" at a mail house. On-line codes may be used to distinguish between various test packages or between labels which do not have key coding.

ON-LINE ENTRY - A method of data entry in which the operator calls up the customer data base to make corrections or additions directly to the file. (See also Real Time.)

ONE-UP LABELS - A sheet of mailing labels which are placed vertically on the page in a single row.

OPEN ENROLLMENT PROGRAM - (See Public Session.)

OVER-PRINT - Solid type printing over a background halftone or another area.

OVERLAY - A transparent covering over the copy to be printed on which corrections, color breaks and printing instructions are marked.

Also used in computer list processing to refer to adding information from one file to another, using merge/purge or other match code techniques to ensure a proper correspondence between individual records.

OVERVIEW - A broad, comprehensive survey or perspective. Often a brief, simplified summary of a longer, more comprehensive topic or course.

PACKAGE - The collection of materials received by the addressee; for example, a "letter, brochure and labeled business reply card in a No. 10 window envelope sent by Third-Class bulk mail" or a "4-page self-mailer."

PAID SUBSCRIBER - One who has committed by purchase for the regular delivery of a publication or goods within a specific time period. (Compare with Controlled Circulation.)

PANTONE MATCHING SYSTEM (PMS) - An industry-standard means of referring to reproducible colors. In the system, Pantone has numbered various colors, thereby allowing a consistent means for referring to the shades available for reproduction.

PARTICIPANT - (See Attendee.)

PASS-OUTS - The collection of material furnished to participants at a seminar, workshop or conference, including notebooks, booklets, job-aids, tapes, etc.

PERFECTER - A type of web press that prints both sides of the paper on a single pass through the press.

PERMIT - Consent purchased on a regular basis from the United States Postal Service allowing mail to be sent by a certain classification.

PHILLIPSBURG - A common type of inserter manufactured by Bell & Howell. Sometimes used generically to refer to any inserting machine.

PHONEY - An order or inquiry received from a nonexistent person or organization and/or a nonexistent address and telephone. Some fraction of all direct responses will be in this category; they can often be identified by experienced and alert order-entry persons or computer comparison with directories and/or other sources.

PHOTOSTAT - The photographic process of copying, enlarging or reducing the size of type or artwork.

P.I. - An abbreviation for Per Inquiry, a method of purchasing advertising in which payment is based on the number of responses, orders or inquiries received.

PICA - A unit of 1/6th inch used in measuring typeset material. (See also Point.)

PLATE (ADDRESSING) - A mechanical means of maintaining a mail list, in which the information is stored as raised letters on a metal or plastic plate, or cut in a stencil. The plates may be sorted and then placed in a machine which imprints the mail piece, envelope or address label.

PLATE (PRINTING) - A flat or curved sheet of metal used in printing.

PMS - (See Pantone Matching System.)

POINT - A unit of about 1/72nd inch, used to measure the dimension of printing type. Leading is also measured in points. (See also Pica.)

POSITIVE - Film with a clear background where the image is black. A positive form from which to print. (Contrast with Negative.)

POSTCARD DECK - Advertising done on a postcard-size reply card, groups of which are packaged and mailed to individuals who share a common interest. Postcard decks are usually published by a mailing list owner or direct marketer on a regular schedule. Advertisers furnish camera-ready artboards for their postcards, using their own business reply mail for response. Charges are usually based on the numbers of cards and colors used.

PRESENTER - One who makes a presentation or imparts information. While the term is most appropriate for those presenting information, it is also used to describe any speaker or meeting leader. (See also Facilitator.)

PRESSURE SENSITIVE LABEL - A label which may be peeled from its backing and affixed. This process may be used to affix the label for the outgoing mailing (usually done manually), or the label and its backing may be affixed to the outgoing mail, so the responder can peel off and affix the same label to the response vehicle.

PRINTED MATTER - Material printed by any of various processes that is eligible for mailing at a special rate.

PRINTING PAIRS - Refers to pages such as the front and back cover. In a 16-page book, the printing pair would be pages 1 and 16, or 2 and 15. A way to check facing pages is to add the two numbers together and they should equal one page more than the number of total pages in the book. (See also Facing Pages.)

PROCESS COLOR - One of the primary colors used in printing: magenta (red), yellow, cyan (blue), and black. Any intermediate color can be produced by combining these three process colors, along with black.

PROCESS PRINTING - A method of printing in which the three primary process colors (red, yellow and blue) are superimposed on one another, along with black, to form varying shades of all colors. The full-color, continuous tone original is "separated" by optical scanning equipment, producing four separate printing plates. A printed image on one side is then obtained by four passes through a one-color press, or two passes through a two-color press, or one pass through a four-color press, each pass and/or press station adding one of the required colors.

PROMOTION - The active furthering of sales through advertising, publicity, offering of sales incentives and other means aimed at the end consumer or at the trade.

PROOFS - A duplication of what you plan to print from. Proofs run the range from a 4-color reproduction to a black-and-white image on a piece of paper. A proof is used to show trim, bleed, size, copy and color reproduction.

PROPERTY - (See Facility.)

PROSPECT - An individual who has one or more characteristics suggesting their receptivity to a particular offer, but who has not yet purchased.

PSYCHOGRAPHICS - The study of the history and patterns of how people live, work, play and buy. These patterns can be employed to use past purchases/actions in order to more reliably predict their future purchases/actions. (See also Demographics.)

PUBLIC SESSION - Commonly used to indicate a training program which is accessible to anyone wishing to enroll, subject to space availability.

PUBLICITY - The dissemination of information or promotional material designed to attract public interest. (See also News Release.)

PURGING - The process of eliminating duplicates and other undesirable records from a file, usually done on a computer.

RACK RATE - A term used in the hotel industry to indicate the hotel's published range of sleeping room rates. Rack rates generally reflect the highest rates since they are exclusive of any group discount, etc.

REAL TIME - Updating a file as data are received, as contrasted with batch mode.

REAM - Commonly used to refer to a package containing 500 sheets of paper.

RECENCY - The latest purchase or other activity for an individual recorded on a specific mailing list. (See also RFM.)

RECORD - The information on an organization or individual, including the name, address, telephone number and any transactions. Each piece of information is stored in a field. A group of records constitutes a file.

REGISTRAR - An individual in an educational institution or firm who is responsible for enrolling students, corresponding with applicants and maintaining the records associated with their participation in training programs.

REGRESSION ANALYSIS - A mathematical procedure in which the effects of a number of variables on an end result may be analyzed, their contributions separated and the variables ranked in terms of their relative importance in producing the end result.

RENTAL AGREEMENT - The contract to obtain possession and use of a product or service in accordance with certain limits and/or restrictions, at a fixed rate paid to the owner.

REPLY CARD - The response vehicle, usually mailed as part of the promotional material, which the recipient can return to the sender to indicate interest in the product or service being offered. Reply cards often use business reply permits so that the responder need not affix postage.

RESPONDER - One who makes an answer, usually favorable, to a direct marketing solicitation or offer.

RESPONSE VEHICLE - The portion of a direct marketing ad or mail piece that asks for the desired action and facilitates the responder doing so. It may be viewed as creating the circumstances whereby the responder accepts the offer and, as such, it is vitally important.

RESPONSIVE - A term referring to the degree of response activity previously generated by a mail list.

RETURN POSTAGE GUARANTEED - An endorsement often printed on mailing pieces to ensure that the merchandise or other material, should it be undeliverable, will be returned to the sender at the sender's expense.

RFM - An abbreviation for Recency/Frequency/Monetary value. RFM applies to the data indicating the date of the last purchase by a customer, the number of orders in a given period of time and total or average price paid for the goods ordered. RFM is often used with other data for list segmentation.

ROLL OUT - The period following testing, in which successful elements are increased and unsuccessful elements are dropped or retested at reduced scale.

ROOMING LIST - A list of attendees who have requested sleeping rooms during an organized function. This list is mailed to the hotel prior to the meeting and outlines arrival and departure dates and any other pertinent information relating to the attendee's stay.

SADDLESTITCH - A bindery operation in which books are assembled by spreading the pages over a "saddle," then either stapling or stitching the pages together. To complete the trim on a book, it is then run through a knife trimmer.

SCANNING - A method of computer data entry in which the information is automatically read from printed material by optical character recognition or bar-code reader equipment. (See also OCR.)

SCF - An abbreviation for Sectional Center Factor, a Postal Service distribution unit comprised of Post Offices whose ZIP codes start with the same first three digits. Generally, the SCF will indicate a specific mailing region.

SCREEN (PRINTING) - A term used to refer to the density of dots constituting printing. The separation of these dots determines the shades of color produced.

SEEDS - (See Decoy Names.)

SELF-MAILER - A folder, usually of promotional nature, which can be sent by mail without enclosure in an envelope.

SEMINAR - A scheduled meeting of a small group to exchange and discuss ideas in a subject area under the guidance of an expert leader.

SEPARATION (COLOR) - A photographic process which isolates each color in negative or positive form. (See also Process Printing.)

SEQUENCE (LIST) - The order in which names appear in a list. While most lists are in ZIP-code sequence, some are alphabetical by name within the ZIP code, or are in carrier sequence, or may even be arranged alphabetically by state (or city within the state). There are many variations of list sequence.

SERVICE BUREAU - An organization paid by the list owner to maintain their list(s) on a computer, process lists for merge/purge, enhancement, create magnetic tapes or printed copies of lists, etc.

SHEET-FED - Refers to a printing process done on paper cut in sheet form rather than on a continuous roll of paper. (Contrast with Web Press.)

SHOW - (See Exposition.)

SHOWCASE - A meeting to describe or demonstrate a product or service to prospective purchasers. Often an early, introductory step in a face-to-face (or occasionally telemarketing) sales process.

SIC - (See Standard Industrial Classification.)

SLEEPING ROOM - A term commonly used by hoteliers to refer to the bedded rooms available for use by the public on a nightly basis (as contrasted to meeting room or other public space).

SOFTWARE - The entire set of programs, procedures and related documentation associated with a computer system. Also documented information in any form supplied as part of a product.

SORT (LIST) - The process of putting a list in a specific sequence.

SORT-TIE-BAG - The process a mailhouse uses in handling printed material to be mailed. In sorting, the mail is separated as required by applicable postal regulations; in tying, the mail is bundled by mail classification codes; in bagging, the mail is placed into mail bags (or trays) that indicate the ZIP code to which it will be mailed. In common usage, this phrase refers to all of the mailhouse operations after inserting, sealing and/or metering.

SOURCE CODE - An alphabetical or numerical identification of the original source of a record on a file, or the source of a later transaction. (See also Key Code.)

SPLIT - A method of using two or more names from the same mailing list to test the effectiveness of the list. (See also A/B Split.)

SRDS - (See Standard Rate and Data Service.)

STAMP (POSTAGE) - A small, decorative, adhesive-backed paper affixed on mail as evidence of prepayment of postage.

STANDARD INDUSTRIAL CLASSIFICATION (SIC) - A method defined by the United States Department of Commerce for classifying all businesses. An SIC can be applied to a list in order to specify the types of businesses represented on the list and to facilitate selection.

STANDARD RATE AND DATA SERVICE (SRDS) - Publishers of regularly-printed directories which list available mailing lists, magazines, newspapers, brokers, broadcast stations, etc., with rates and other information of importance to advertisers.

STAT - A contraction of photostat.

STRIPPING (PRINTING) - The positioning of negatives on a flat prior to plate-making.

SURNAME - An individual's family name, less any prefixes or suffixes. Surnames may be compound or two words. Whenever possible, the surname should be stored in a separate field of a computer record.

SUSPECT - Those who, you believe, have a need for and can possibly buy your services or products.

SYMPOSIUM - A meeting or conference to discuss some topic, usually involving several presenters or discussion leaders.

TAPE FORMAT - A simple "map" of the data fields included in each record and their specific locations on the tape.

TELECONFERENCE - A meeting involving real-time participation by those at remote sites. The simplest teleconference is a one-way voice link, so remote-site participants can hear the presentation/discussion at the primary site. The most sophisticated teleconference permits two-way, real-time voice, large-screen picture and computer-assisted imagery. If the communication linkage employs satellite transmission, it is often described as Satellite Teleconferencing.

TELEMARKETING - The method of selling products or services using the telephone. Telemarketing may be divided into inbound, where the call is originated by the customer, usually in response to some other form of direct marketing, or outbound, where the salesperson originates the call.

TESTING - The process of determining the contribution of any variable in producing an end result. In direct marketing, testing refers to the process of systematically altering various aspects of a campaign while holding all others constant, in order to measure the effects of the changes on response. (See also Regression Analysis.)

THIRD-CLASS, BULK-RATE MAIL - The least expensive class of U.S. mail. To be eligible, mail must meet certain requirements (for example, no personal letters or bills are permitted), have a minimum number of identical pieces, be entirely in ZIP-code sequence and be sorted, prepared, tied and bagged by the mailer in accordance with Post Office regulations.

TIME-SHARING - Simultaneous computer access by two or more users.

TINT - The percentage (between ten and 90) of dots which provide even coverage in printing. (See also Screen.)

TRADE SHOW - A meeting, conference or convention devoted to an industry or topic, usually including exhibits and social functions for customers and suppliers.

TRAINING - Any product or service that develops human skills/abilities, conveys information/knowledge or changes an individual's attitudes/perceptions, and is not part of an elementary, secondary or degree program.

TSR - An abbreviation for Telephone Sales Representative.

TUTORIAL - A computer-based training program, often dealing with skills needed to operate a particular software program on a personal computer.

TWO-COLOR - Printed matter consisting of only two colors, different shades of which may be created by the use of screens.

TYPESET - The process of creating, mechanically or photographically, characters in a specific size and style ready for reproduction.

UPDATE - The process by which new data on recent transactions, or new and changed names, are added to a file to reflect the current status of each record on the list. (See also List Cleaning.)

UNIVERSE - The total number of individual prospects in a market or market segment.

UPS - An abbreviation for United Parcel Service.

USERS CONFERENCE - A conference of buyers and/or users of a particular product or service, often including the users and/or suppliers of related products/services.

USPS - An abbreviation for the United States Postal Service, the quasi-government agency that handles and delivers the mail.

VAR - An abbreviation for Value-Added-Reseller, typically an individual or organization which provides additional services or support to buyers of hardware and/or software.

VIDEO DISK - An optical recording medium used for storage and retrieval of data, pictures and sound, either single frames (up to 56,000 can be stored on a single laser disk), full-motion video or even computer programs.

WAITING LIST - A list of those wanting to attend a seminar or other event, usually created when enrollments exceed meeting-space constraints. When a registration is cancelled, the next wait-listed individual is allowed to attend.

WEB PRESS - A method of printing done on a roll of paper which is cut to the desired size after printing. (Contrast with Sheet-Fed.)

WET TEST - The opposite of a dry test.

WINDOW ENVELOPE - A type of envelope with a portion cut out through which the name and address can be seen. The window may be open or covered with transparent material affixed to the inside. Although window envelopes are most economical when they are of standard size and window placement, virtually any window location can be obtained.

WORKSHOP - A group of people who meet regularly for a seminar, usually producing some tangible output or result.

ZIP CODE - An abbreviation for Zone Improvement Plan. A group of five digits assigned by the USPS to designate each postal delivery area in the United States.

ZIP PLUS FOUR - Four digits added to a ZIP code in the early 1980s, to more precisely pinpoint the address within the ZIP-code region. Separated from the first five digits by a dash.

INDEX

HOW TO ORDER SCHRELLO DIRECT MARKETING PUBLICATIONS AND SOFTWARE

Schrello Direct Marketing, Inc. offers a variety of publications, software products, training programs and consulting services to help those who market training, continuing education or information in just about any form. Our clients include some of the world's largest publishers, management, sales and technical training firms, professional associations and manufacturers, as well as smaller businesses and individuals.

Here are some of the groups who have found our products and services of value:

1. Seminar, workshop and conference sponsors ... including those who use meetings to sell other products and services.

2. Producers, publishers and distributors of books, audio tapes, films, videos, multimedia programs, computer software, games, simulations, tests, instruments, job-aids, CD-ROMs and other instructional and informational materials.

3. Associations and association management firms ... for whom publications, conferences, workshops, videos and information products and services are key to success.

4. Schools, colleges and universities continuing education departments, executive development programs and extension schools.

5. Human resource, training and personnel organizations in government and **business** -- particularly those who see training of employees, suppliers and customers as a vital part of their future strategy.

6. Individual training professionals, custom training program developers, facilitators, speakers ... and others whose livelihood depends on delivering knowledge, information or training.

7. Hotels, conference centers, convention centers, visitors bureaus, travel agents and others involved in the travel, meetings and hospitality industries.

8. Organizations whose products or services support the training and information industries such as teleconferencing firms, advertising agencies, mailing list brokers, printers, TV direct response and audio-visual companies, to name just a few.

See Order Form On The Next Page

The following page is an order form for our most popular publications and software, several of which are described in this book. Copy the page and mail or Fax it to us with your order. For faster service on credit card orders -- or if you have questions about our publications, software, seminars or other services -- call us TOLL-FREE at 1-800-EN-ROLL-X (that's 1-800-367-6559).

SDM **ORDER FORM**

We offer a complete line of products and services for marketing training and information. A few of them are listed below. To order, complete this form and mail it to the address shown at the right:

> **Schrello Direct Marketing, Inc.**
> **Post Office Box 1610**
> **Long Beach, California 90801−1610**
> **Phone: (310) 493−0200**

Item	Price Each	Qty.	Total
How To Market Training & Information (This Book)	$ 69.95		
The Complete Marketing Handbook For Consultants (Boxed, 2−volume looseleaf notebook set, 590 pages)	$ 79.95		
Event Attendance Forecaster Spreadsheet Kit (See Chapter 6 for a more complete description)	$ 995.00		
A Directory of References and Resources for Marketing Training and Information (Appendix A in booklet form)	$ 14.95		
A Vocabulary of Common Terms for Marketing Training and Information (Appendix B in booklet form)	$ 8.95		
Marketing In−House Training Programs Booklet	$ 5.95		
Improving Your Competitive Position Booklet	$ 4.95		

Shipping & Handling

Based on order subtotal, add:
Under $50.00................$ 5.00
$ 50.01−$ 75.00..........$ 8.00
$ 75.01−$100.00..........$10.00
$100.01−$150.00..........$13.00
$150.01 and over..........$15.00
All orders shipped UPS Ground.
Call for rates on overnight &
international delivery.

Subtotal: _____

California Residents add 8.25% Sales Tax: _____

Shipping and Handling (See Box at Left): _____

All funds in U.S. dollars.   **Total:** _____

Name_____Position/Title _____
Company_____Division _____
Address_____Mail Stop _____
City _____State_____ ZIP/Postal Code _____
Phone (_____)_____Extension _____
Fax (_____)_____ (800) _____
Type Of Business_____

Method of Payment: ☐ Check Enclosed
                     ☐ Charge My Credit Card: ☐ MC ☐ Visa ☐ Amex
                     Card Number: _____Expires: _____

Signature: _____Date: _____

For faster service on credit card orders...
1. Call Toll−Free: 1−800−ENROLL−X
or
2. Fax this form to: (310) 493−0962.